ISBN 978-1-330-17214-8
PIBN 10044000

English
Français
Deutsche
Italiano
Español
Português

www.forgottenbooks.com

Mythology Photography **Fiction**
Fishing Christianity **Art** Cooking
Essays Buddhism Freemasonry
Medicine **Biology** Music **Ancient
Egypt** Evolution Carpentry Physics
Dance Geology **Mathematics** Fitness
Shakespeare **Folklore** Yoga Marketing
Confidence Immortality Biographies
Poetry **Psychology** Witchcraft
Electronics Chemistry History **Law**
Accounting **Philosophy** Anthropology
Alchemy Drama Quantum Mechanics
Atheism Sexual Health **Ancient History**
Entrepreneurship Languages Sport
Paleontology Needlework Islam
Metaphysics Investment Archaeology
Parenting Statistics Criminology
Motivational

A TREATISE

ON THE

LAW OF STOCK-BROKERS

AND

STOCK-EXCHANGES

BY

JOHN R. DOS PASSOS

OF THE NEW YORK BAR

Author of " Interstate Commerce Act," " Commercial Trusts,"
" The Anglo-Saxon Century," etc.

SECOND EDITION
In two volumes

Vol. I.

THE BANKS LAW PUBLISHING CO.
21 MURRAY STREET, NEW YORK
1905

T
D 7407 s
1905

PREFACE.

According to a computation made in a financial journal of New York, the sales of shares, alone, of corporations, in the year 1904, upon the New York Stock Exchange, reached the enormous total of about one hundred and eighty millions (180,000,000), representing in cash, at one hundred dollars per share, the sum of eighteen billions of dollars ($18,000,000,000).

When the aggregate transactions for the same period of the London Stock Exchange, the Paris Bourse, and the other well-known bourses of the Continent are added to those of the New York Stock Exchange, it will be appreciated that the capital involved, yearly, in the business of dealing in shares and other securities, reaches figures which are almost too vast for human comprehension. If one wishes to profitably study the financial and commercial history of this country, let him put in juxtaposition the lists of the New York Stock Exchange of 1882 and 1904—the period intervening between the publication of the first and second editions of this work. They are worth volumes of general history. In view of these facts, the occupation of the Stock-broker, and the dealings on the Stock Exchanges, have become subjects of the profoundest concern and of a public interest which increases every year. No matter how true it may formerly have been that the opera-

iii

tions on the Stock Exchange were of interest merely to the professional speculator, to-day the dealings of these bodies are of national and absorbing importance. Shares and bonds of commercial corporations now constitute permanent investments in all countries; and real estate, at one time the sole source of investment, has, in this respect, fallen into a secondary rank. The securities of railroad and other commercial companies not only offer attractive and regular returns to capital, but the shares may be carried about by their owners wherever they may go, with more safety than money, defying alike the depredations of criminals, the ravages of time, or the destruction of the elements.

Brief allusion to some striking features of Stock Exchanges is pertinent in this connection.

All securities which have been admitted to their lists can, as a general rule, be readily converted into cash. Irrespective of the demands of regular investors, and of the professional operators outside of the exchanges (factors of the greatest magnitude in these dealings), there is a trading element inside of those bodies—represented in the London Exchange by the "Jobber," and in the New York Exchange by the "Scalper" or "Trader"—which is ready at a moment's notice to deal in, and pay for, any number of shares that may be offered for sale; and which, in times of exciting panics, constitutes a breakwater against great financial disasters. It is universally conceded that without the existence of great public marts, like the New York and London Stock Exchanges, the marvelous development and progress of this country would not have been attained. And this general truth was recognized by Bramwell, L. J.,

Preface to the Second Edition.

in a leading case in England, in which the transactions of the London Stock Exchange had been violently assailed as mere gambling devices and in hostility to the true interests of the country,[1] and who in sustaining those operations said: "I am not sure that it is a disadvantage that there should be a market where speculation may go on, for it is owing to a market of that kind that we now have so many railways and other useful undertakings."

No one will claim that Stock Exchanges are institutions of unqualified good and benefit to the community. They have their evil side. But it is beyond the scope of this work to discuss that branch of the subject.

In May, 1877, a commission[2] was appointed in England by royal decree to inquire into the origin, object, present constitution, customs, usages, and mode of transacting business on the London Stock Exchange, which reported, in July, 1878, after a careful study of the subject, among others, the following suggestions to Parliament, then in session:

"The main object of the association appears to be the easy and expeditious transaction of business, and the enforcement among themselves of fair dealing.

"Our opinion is that, in the main, the existence of such an association, and the coercive action of the rules which it enforces upon the transaction of business, and upon the conduct of its members, have been salutary to the interest of the public.

"We recognize a great public advantage in the fact that those who buy or sell for the public in a market of such enormous magnitude in point of value should be bound in their dealings by rules for the enforcement of fair dealing and the repression of fraud, capable of afford-

[1] Thacker v. Hardy, L. R. 4 Q. B. Div. 685, 693. And a kindred remark was made by Baker, J., in N. Y. & Chicago Stock Exchange v. Chicago Board of Trade, 127 Illinois, 153.

[2] See post, p. 969.

ing relief and exercising restraint far more prompt, and often more satisfactory, than any within the reach of the courts of law."

The commission closes its report as follows:

" It is recommended by us, not because we have any reason to think that the present association has at all, in the main, fallen short of its duties in the past, but rather for the purpose of strengthening its hands and increasing its efficiency in the future, that the London Stock Exchange be incorporated either by royal charter or an act of Parliament; and if, preserving the element of self-government, additional weight could be given to the institution, and additional consideration and reliance be bestowed upon its members, by investing the existing association with a public character in the form of a charter of incorporation, we are of opinion that it would be a sensible gain to the public."

At various times within the last century and a half, the legislatures of different Countries and States, acting under a spasmodic public sentiment, have sought to prevent speculation in securities and stocks by enacting stringent and severe laws against such practices, generally known as " Stock-jobbing Acts." But, as will be seen in the fifth chapter of this work, such laws have been vain and futile; they have been openly and persistently defied, and at length, so far as regards England, and the States of New York and Pennsylvania, they have been repealed.[1] In face of this experience, it is not too much to affirm that, at this day, when it is almost impossible to distinguish legitimate investment operations from pernicious speculations, the subject is beyond legislative prevention. The evil of excessive speculation carries its own corrective; the blow falls upon its own authors rather than on the general community; and, although prices or quotations may be affected or diverted by these gambling transactions, to the temporary inconvenience of the legitimate investor, the

[1] See Chap. V, p. 487 et seq.

inevitable laws of true value will assert themselves, and the tide again flow on in its regular channel.

Yet it may well be that occasions may occur when it will become the duty of the General or State Governments to intervene in Stock Exchange transactions. When, and under what circumstances, such interventions may be necessary, it is quite useless to speculate. The latent legal power exists, if events should occur which may unhappily require its exercise.

A Stock Exchange fulfils another highly important mission in forming a barrier between the public and many enterprises and schemes which are constantly springing up in our midst, some of which are manifestly corrupt, and others visionary and extravagant; but all being calculated, by alluring or deceitful representations, to induce the public to invest in them. For the prevention of such schemes each of the Stock Exchanges has established rules against the listing of securities without a previous rigid examination by committees appointed for this purpose, consisting of well-trained and experienced Brokers; and while at times, as must be expected from a variety of causes, these rules are eluded and defeated, yet, in the main, the character of securities which are enrolled on the list represent fair business enterprises, and, although not always fulfilling the hopes and expectations of their promoters, are nevertheless the fit subjects of speculation or investment.

To a discussion of the legal nature and character of Stock Exchanges, to a history of the various transactions made in such places, and to a consideration of the reciprocal legal rights and duties which are evolved from the relation of Broker and Client, as well as to the nature and kind of securities dealt in on the Exchanges, I have devoted this work. In 1875, discovering that there was no legal treatise covering the whole subject, I began the collection of materials, which, after great labor and expenditure of time, were shaped into the first edition of this work published in 1882.

The ground covered in the present work, when the first edition was issued, was entirely new, and hence I did not hesitate to discuss the various questions with freedom; but, as I trust, without dogmatism. I take some pride in the fact that, so far as I have ascertained, the statement of principles by me, as applicable to different questions embraced in the treatise during a period of twenty-two years, has never been questioned by the courts before which they have come for determination.

The new edition contains about 4,692 cases. The old edition contained only 2,277. So that there have been added 2,415 cases, an enormous increase of litigation in twenty-two years, making nearly 200 cases more than were decided during the previous two hundred years.

In the preparation of the second and third chapters of this edition I beg to acknowledge the great services rendered by my partner, Edmund Francis Harding, Esq., who, unfortunately, was prevented from continuing his work by exacting professional labors, and in the whole work I have had the co-operation of P. J. Power, Esq., without whose care and continuous labor this edition would not yet have seen the light of day.

John R. Dos Passos.

January 2, 1905.

CONTENTS.

ix

Contents.

CHAPTER III.

ANALYSIS OF TRANSACTION BETWEEN BROKER AND CLIENT UPON PURCHASE OR SALE OF STOCKS IN THE UNITED STATES.

CHAPTER IV.

USAGES OF STOCK-BROKERS.

Contents.

CHAPTER VIII.

MEASURE OF DAMAGES.

CHAPTER IX.

STOCK-BROKERS IN ENGLAND.

CHAPTER X.

ANALYSIS OF TRANSACTION BETWEEN BROKER AND CLIENT UPON PURCHASE OR SALE OF STOCKS ON LONDON STOCK EXCHANGE.

CHAPTER XI.

THE PARIS BOURSE.

Contents.

TABLE OF CASES.

[The references are to pages.]

(xvii)

Table of Cases.

Table of Cases. xxxiii

Table of Cases.

LAW OF STOCK-BROKERS

AND

STOCK EXCHANGES.

CHAPTER I.

INTRODUCTION.

Origin of Stock-brokers and Stock Exchanges.

THERE is a great diversity of opinion respecting the origin of the word " Broker," some of the authorities maintaining that it was originally applied to those who broke up goods into small pieces—retailers ; while others contend that the term is derived from the Saxon word *broc*, misfortune, and that the name " Broker " comes from one who was a broken trader by misfortune, which is often the true reason for a man's breaking, and that none but that class of persons were formerly admitted to that employment in London.[1] But the

---

[1] Jacob's Law Dict., tit. " Brokers." "The etymology of the term Broker has been variously given. By some it has been derived from the Saxon *broc*, misfortune, as denoting a broken trader; the occupation being formerly confined, it is said, to unfortunate persons of that description (Tomlins). According to others, it was formed from the French *broteur*, a grinder or breaker into small pieces; a Broker being one who *beats* or draws a bargain into particulars (Termes de la Ley, Cowell). The law Latin from *obrocator*, however, seems to point distinctly to the Saxon *abræcan* (to break), as the true root, which in the old word *abbrochment* (q. v.) or abroachment, had the sense of *breaking up goods*, or selling at retail. A Broker, therefore, would seem to have originally been a *retailer*, and hence we find the old word *auctionarius* (q. v.) used in both these

statutes passed in the reigns of Edward the First and James
the First, hereafter referred to, would seem to indicate that
the latter view can hardly be correct.   In England the term
" Broker " occurs in an act of Parliament as early as the year
1285.[1]   It recites, in substance, that whereas divers persons
do resort unto the city (London) from parts beyond the sea,
fugitives from their own lands, and of these some become
" Brokers," ostlers, and innkeepers, etc., and they do wear
fine clothing, and do eat costly meat and food, etc. ; it therefore enacts that " there shall be no Broker in the city except
those who are admitted and sworn before the warden, mayor,
or aldermen."   It is evident, from a perusal of this statute,
that the occupation of Brokers in those days was subverted
by persons who used the name as a cover to transact a species of disreputable pawnbroker's business ; and hence the
severe penalties of the second section of the act, which provided that "if any other innkeeper or Broker be found
within the city, or any other of whom there is evil suspicion, he shall be arrested by the warden, or mayor, or the
sheriffs, or the alderman of the ward, and punished ; viz.,

senses " (Burrill's Law Dict., tit.
" Broker "). Wharton gives, as
the derivation of the word, the
French *broceur*, and the Latin
tritor, a person who breaks into
small pieces (Whar., Law Dict.,
tit. " Broker "). Webster gives as
its derivation, the old English *brocour*, Norman French *broggour*,
French *brocanteur*. Under the
word "broke," to deal in second-
hand goods, to be a Broker, Webster says it is probably derived
from the word *brock*. Worcester
derives it from the Anglo-Saxon
brucan, to discharge an office ; *bro-*
cian, to oppress; and the French
broyer, to grind. See " Broke "
and " Broker." The word " Broker " seems first to occur in litera-
ture in Piers Ploughman, " Among
burgeises have I be Dwellyng at
London. And gart Backbiting be
a brocour. To blame men's ware."
It clearly means here a *fault-finder*,
as in Provençal *brac* is refuse. The
Broker was originally one who in-
spected goods and rejected what
was below the standard (Wedge-
wood).

[1] 13 Ed. I., Stat. Civ. London,
1285.

innkeepers and Brokers shall be incapable of their freedom
and adjudged to prison, and the others shall be punished by
imprisonment or otherwise."[1]

The next statute, passed in the reign of James the First,
more than three hundred years after that just recited,[2] regu-
lates the calling of Brokers with greater detail than the first
act, and clearly shows, by the use of the words "merchandise and wares," that down to this period the Broker in
money, stock, and funds had no recognized legal existence.
The preamble to the statute also indicates that the regular
calling was and had been a favored one : " Forasmuch as of
long and ancient time by divers hundreds years there have
been used within the City of London and Liberties thereof,
certain Freemen of the city to be selected out of the Companies and Mysteries whereof they are free and Members,
and the same persons to be presented at least by six approved
and known honest persons of the same Mystery to the Lord
Mayor of London for the time being, and to the Aldermen
his Brethren, and to be recommended by such Presentors
to be persons for their known approved Honesty, Integrity,
and Faithfulness, Persons meet for to be Broker or Brokers."
It was not until the latter part of the seventeenth century,
when the East India Company came prominently before the

[1] See also 2 Crabb's Dig. of Stat.,
tit. "Brokers," 261. There were
a class of persons known to the
Romans, who were deemed public
officers, and who united the functions of bankers, exchangers, Brokers, commissioners, and notaries
all in one, under the description of
proxenetæ. (Whar., Law Dict., tit.
"Brokers;" Story on Ag. 9th ed.
S. 30, Dig. Lib. 50, tit. 14, ch. 3.)
Spelman, cited in Gibbons vs. Rule,

12 Moo. 539, 543. There is very
high authority, however, for asserting that the term *proxenetæ*
does not occur in any Latin author
before the first century after Christ.
See Freund's Latin Dictionary, revised by Lewis and Short, where
proxenetæ is thus given: "negotiator, factor, broker, agent, Sen.
Ep. 119; Mart. 10, 3, 4; Dig. 50,
14, 3."

[2] 1 Jac. I. c. 21, 1604.

public,[1] that trading or speculating in stock became an established business in England; and the term "Broker," which had then a well-understood meaning, was promptly transferred to those persons who were employed to buy or sell stock or shares, and who thenceforth became known as "Stock-brokers." In 1692, William the Third having adopted, for the first time in England, the system of raising funds[2] for governmental purposes by creating a national debt, speculations in the "funds" and the shares of the East India Company at once became general;[3] and in 1697 the Brokers and Stock-jobbers, to borrow from the language of the statute passed in that year, had been guilty of such "unjust practices and designs" in selling and discounting tallies, bank stock, bank bills, shares and interest in joint stock, that it became necessary to pass a stringent act, by which no persons except regularly sworn appointees were permitted to act as Brokers; and the latter were compelled to keep a register in which all contracts were to be entered within three days after they were made, and their compensation was fixed at ten shillings per centum.[4] And Best, C. J., in commenting upon this statute, says: "The statute 8 and 9 William III., ch. 20, by which the first government loan was raised, speaks of a new description of 'Brokers'— persons employed in buying and selling tallies, the government securities of those days: these have since been called *Stock-*

---

[1] This company was incorporated by Queen Elizabeth in 1600.

[2] The system of obtaining money for government purposes by loans is said to have originated in the fifteenth century in Venice. It was next adopted by Holland, and was introduced into England shortly after the Revolution of 1688 (Tit. "Funds," Cyclopedia of Com. [Waterston]).

[3] Francis's Chronicles and Characters of the Stock Exchange, 24.

[4] 8 & 9 Wm. III. c. 32, 1697, continued by 11 and 12 Wm. III. c. 13.

brokers."[1] Several other similar statutes were passed in the subsequent reigns of Anne and George.[2]

An early legal author (writing about the year 1813) gives the following account of Stock-brokers, which is interesting in this connection : "Stock-brokers are persons who confine their transactions to the buying and selling of property in the public funds and other securities for money, and they are employed by the proprietors or holders of the said securities. Of late years, owing to the prodigious increase of the funded debt of the nation, commonly called the stock, they are become a very numerous and considerable body, and have built, by subscription, a room near the Bank, wherein they meet to transact business with their principals, and with each other ; and to prepare and settle their proceedings before they go to the transfer-offices at the Bank, the South Sea, and India houses, thereby preventing a great deal of confusion at the public offices, where the concourse of people is so great, during the hours of transferring stock, that if the business was not prepared beforehand, it would be impossible to transact it within the given time."[3] The whole business of stock-jobbing being contrary to law, except as the persons acting as Brokers were licensed, under the act of 6 Anne, ch. 16 ; and as many other persons, irrespective of the requirements of the statute, acted as Stock-brokers without having received a license as such, a *silver medal* was given to each licensed Broker, having the king's arms on one side, and the arms of the city of London on the reverse, with the Broker's name, which he was ordered to pro-

---

[1] Gibbons vs. Rule, 1827, 12 Moo. 539 ; 4 Bing. 301.

[2] 6 Anne, c. 16, 1707 ; 10 ibid. c. 19, 1711; 12 ibid. Stat. 2, c. 16 ; 6

Geo. I. c. 18, 1719 ; 3 Geo. II. c. 31, 1730 ; 7 Geo. II. c. 8, 1734.

[3] Beaw. Lex. Mer. 3rd ed. 620.

duce upon every occasion when he should be required to
show his qualification ; and, to give further publicity to the
names of the regular Brokers, a list of the licensed Brokers
was annually printed by the order of the Lord Mayor and
Court of Aldermen, which was hung up in the walks of
the Royal Exchange and in Guildhall, and at most of the
reputable coffee-houses near the Exchange. In 1708, the
year after this act was passed, the Court of Mayor and Aldermen of the city of London, who, by the act were permitted
to license brokers, made rules and regulations for the government of Brokers, and by virtue of which every person, previously to his being admitted a Broker, was required to enter
into a bond, conditioned for the proper performance of his
employment, to the Mayor, Commonalty and citizens of
London, and also to take an oath to faithfully execute and
perform the office and employment of a Broker without fraud
or collusion.   The form of the bond and oath may be found
in the report of a case arising in 1816, when these rules were
still in force.[1]   The Brokers had some years previously (about
the year 1698, vide c. IX.) left the Royal Exchange and located their business in Change Alley.[2]   By an act passed in
1870,[3] called the " London Broker's Relief Act," the re-

[1] Ex parte Dyster, 1 Mer. 155;
Clarke vs. Powell, 4 B. & Ad. 846.
   [2] " Jonathan's " Coffee-house, in
Change Alley, the general mart for
Stock-jobbers, was the precursor of
the present Stock Exchange in
Capel Court.—Addison in Sir R.
De Coverley. Among the relics of
these earlier days, collected by a
Stock Exchange antiquarian, is
an illustrated card or advertisement plate, whereon a shield is
suspended from a tree with the
inscription, " Morgan   Vaughan,
Hatter, Hosier, and Stock-broker,
No. 7 Finch Lane, Cornhill, London," from which it would appear
that Stock-brokers and jobbers
could combine their callings with
other forms of business. Galig-
nani's Messenger, Jan. 1, 1891.
   [3] 33 & 34 Vict. c. 60. In the
year 1884 the last remnant of the
city's authority was swept away.
47 Vict. c. 3. Vide c. IX.

strictions and guards which were formerly placed upon
Stock-brokers were removed, and the jurisdiction of the
Court of Aldermen over Brokers ceased. The effect of this
act is practically to enable any person to exercise the calling of Broker in London, outside of the Stock Exchange ;
and this result seems to be justly deplored in the Report of
the Royal Stock Exchange Commission presented to Parliament in 1878.[1]

The advantage of employing Brokers as intermediaries, in
the purchase and sale of property, seems to have been early
recognized among the merchants ; and a very old writer on
the law merchant says, " It is an old proverb, and very true,
that between *what will you buy?* and *what will you sell?* there
is twenty in the hundred differing in the price, which is the
cause that all the nations do more effect to sell their commodities with reputation by means of Brokers than we do ; for
that which seems to be gotten thereby is more than double
lost another way. Besides, that by that course many differences are prevented which arise between man and man in
their bargains or verbal contracts ; for the testimony of a
sworn Broker and his book together is sufficient to end the
same." [2]

The Venetians, says Malynes, had an office called *Mes-
sacaria* (Messageria?), consisting only of Brokers who dealt
between man and man ; " and in Spain they are of such esti-
mation that they ride on horseback, upon their foot-cloths ;
and, having the invoices of merchants' goods, they will deal
for great matters at a time, against the lading of the fleet
from Nova Espagna, and the islands of the West Indies, to
be paid partly ready money and partly at the return of the

---

[1] See post, p. 947.   [2] Mal. Lex Mer. 143 (1622).

said fleet; and these afterwards let you understand their merchant." [1]

The origin of stock-certificates—dealings in which, at the present date, constitute the main business of Stock-brokers—cannot in England be satisfactorily traced beyond the middle of the seventeenth century. Such species of property was altogether unknown to the law in ancient times, nor, indeed, was it in usage and practice until a short period antecedent to the passage of the Bubble Act in the reign of George the First. [2]

Although it is fully established that mercantile or commercial corporations existed among the Romans, [3] and though

[1] Mal. Lex. Mer. 143.

[2] Garrard vs. Hardey, 5 Man. & G. 471, 483.

[3] Ang. & Ames on Corps. (11th ed.) § 46: "A Collegium Mercatorum existed at Rome 493 B. C. ; but the modern bourse, from the Latin bursa, a purse, originated about the fifteenth century. Bourges and Amsterdam contend for the honor of having erected the first bourse. The Paris Bourse was erected in 1808" (Johnson's New Univ. Cyclop. tit. "Bourse"). "À Rome, malgré que le commerce n'y fût pas en grande considération, nous trouvons ce même usage publiquement pratiqué. Tite Live nous apprend, en effet, qu'en l'an 259 de sa fondation, sous le consulat d'Appius Claudius et de Publius Servilius, on construisit un vaste édifice, dont les vestiges portent encore le nom de Loggia, et qui, sous la dénomination de Collegium Mercatorum, avait une destination analogue à celle de nos bourses actuelles " (Droit Commercial, " Bourses de Commerce," par Bédarride). But, according to Livy (ii. 27), the Collegium Mercatorum does not belong to this period. Livy says that when the consuls were disputing which of them should have the honor of dedicating a temple to Mercury, the question was referred to the people; and the Senate decreed that whichsoever of the consuls should be chosen should also form a " Collegium Mercatorum," or association of corn-dealers, to help him and the priest in religious and mercantile matters related to the temple. But the plan fell through, and it does not appear that the " Collegium " was ever formed; nor that it would have had, if formed, anything but a religious significance. Accordingly, the above citations seem to be unfounded. The nearest approach to a Stock Exchange membership in ancient times was the right of ownership in a " gild "

much light has been thrown upon the character and mode of conducting these bodies,[1] there is an utter dearth of information respecting the form and manner by which ownership in the corporate property was attested and established. The Roman law required three persons to organize a corporation ;[2] and as each body had at least that number of members, if not more, it would seem but natural that a certificate, or some other substantial muniment of title, should have been issued by the corporation to its respective members, in which the proportion of interest of each in the capital or corporate property of the association appeared. But whether a certificate was, in fact, issued, and, if so, was regarded as property capable of sale or other negotiation, and of vesting in the representatives of the owner, on his decease, or whether the corporations were all of the nature of guilds conferring upon the members mere *personal* rights—all of these questions seem now to be incapable of solution ; and the Roman law, which sheds such floods of light upon commercial subjects, apparently leaves the above matters in total darkness.

In England stock-certificates were not introduced into the courts of law for many years after they had become es-

---

or "guild." A person's "*gilda*" that is his right as a member of the gild is treated as an object of ownership. With the consent of the Court (evolved out of the fraternity) a man might give or sell it. If he be dispossessed of it then it will descend to his heir. History of English Law (Pollock & Maitland), vol. 1 (2d ed.), p. 668.

[1] Brown's Lect. Civ. Law (2d ed.), 111.

[2] *Tres faciunt* collegium, Ang. & Ames on Corps. (11th ed.); Ortolan's Hist. Roman Law, 603.

Though in Rome, it seems, corporations did not require charters from the State, the latter, by virtue of its police power, suppressed those which appeared to be dangerous, mostly those of a political character. In order to determine whether such a corporation existed, the words *tres faciunt collegium* were used. But that a corporation could exist with only one member left is well settled (l. 7, 2, D. 3, 4,). Gaudsmit Pandects, l. 71, 1; Windscheidt, I. 60, 3; Arndts, 44, 2.

tablished in the mercantile community ; for Lord Mansfield, in 1770,[1] in a case wherein it was contended that such certificates were *money*, in deciding against that view, said : " This is a *new* species of property *arisen within the compass of a few years*. It is not money." [2]   The Bubble Act [3] having been repealed,[4] it was held [5] that the formation of a company, the stock in which should be transferable, was not an offence at common-law.   And this doctrine was subsequently affirmed.[6]

A Stock Exchange or Bourse, in the sense in which it is considered in this work, is also a creation of modern times.

An Exchange was erected in Cornhill, London, in 1571, but it was used exclusively by dealers and Brokers in merchandise.   This structure was destroyed in the great fire of 1666 ; [7] but it was not until several years after, when it was rebuilt, that the Brokers in funds and stock were assigned a portion of the building for the transaction of their business.

In 1698 the Stock-jobbers, annoyed by the objections made to their remaining in the Royal Exchange, and finding their numbers seriously increased, removed to Change Alley, a large and unoccupied space, where extensive operations might be carried on.[8]

In the United States there seems to be no trace of a Stock Exchange until about the beginning of the present century,

[1] Nightingale vs. Devisme, 5 Burr. 2589.

[2] To same effect, Jones vs. Brinley, 1 East. 1.

[3] 6 Geo. I. c. 18.

[4] 6 Geo. IV. c. 91.

[5] Garrard vs. Hardey, 5 Man. and G. 471.

[6] Harrison vs. Heathorn, 6 Man. and G. 81; 1 Pars. Con. (6th ed.) 144.

[7] Johnson's New Univ. Cyclop. tit. " Stock Exchange."

[8] Francis's Chronicles and Characters of Stock Exchange, 24. The " cannibals of Change Alley " is a name Lord Chatham once applied to the Stock-jobbers. Calignani's Messenger, Jan. 1, 1891. See also Report of Royal Stock Exchange Commission, July, 1878, and post, p. 971.

at which time there existed in Philadelphia a Board of Stock-brokers, possessing a formal organization and regular constitution, which the Brokers in New York, in 1817, used as a model in framing the rules of their own Exchange.[1]

Although there is in the archives of the New York Stock Exchange a document bearing date May 17, 1792, signed by a number of Brokers, in which it is, *inter alia*, stated that "We, the subscribers, Brokers for the purchase and sale of public stock, agree to do business at not less than one fourth of one per cent.," no organization appears to have been formed in the city of New York until the year 1817, when a constitution was adopted, which is no longer in existence, it having been destroyed in the great fire of 1835.[2]

It appears that in the beginning, the dealings of the Stock-brokers in this country were confined to speculations in Con-

[1] Medbery's Men and Mysteries of Wall Street, 286.

[2] "The earliest annals of the New York Stock Exchange are meagre, the fire of 1835 having destroyed the record of the constitution adopted in 1817, the date of its first regular organization. A tablet in the wall of the present room recites that the Exchange was founded in 1792, but the evidence of that exists only in a document still preserved among its archives" (Johnson's New Univ. Cyclop. tit. "Stock Exchange," by Strong Wadsworth).

The following account is from Medbery's Men and Mysteries of Wall Street, 286: ". . . when Washington was President, and Continental money was worth a trifle more as currency than as waste paper, some twenty New York dealers in public stock met together in a Broker's office, and signed their names, in the bold, strong hand of their generation, to an agreement of the nature of a protective league. The date of this curious paper is May 17, 1792. The volume of business of all these primitive New York brokers could not have been much above that of even the poorest first-class Wall Street house in our time. The Revolutionary 'shinplasters,' is the irreverent already styled them, were spread over the land in such plenty that there were a hundred dollars to each inhabitant. Something was to be made, therefore, from the fluctuations to which they were liable. Indeed, one of the greatest Broker firms of subsequent years derived its capital from the lucky speculations of its senior

tinental money ; but when, in 1812, the United States government issued Treasury notes and negotiated loans to the
amount of many millions of dollars, the dealings embraced
all these securities, beside operations in the stocks of banks,
which were being rapidly formed in all parts of the country.
From the year 1820, when the real history of the New York
Stock Exchange may be said to have commenced, it has
gone on steadily increasing in its members, power and influence, until to-day it can be safely affirmed to be the most
powerful organization of the kind in the world ; and by
forming a mart where all kinds of securities can be promptly
converted into cash, it has largely contributed to the development and wealth of the country by encouraging and sustaining our great railroad systems, which have brought all
parts of the Republic into a closer relation to each other, and
firmly strengthened the union and prosperity of the States.

member in this currency. "The
war of 1812 gave the first genuine
impulse to speculation. The government issued sixteen millions in
Treasury notes, and put loans
amounting to one hundred and
nine millions on the market.
There were endless fluctuations,
and the easy-going capitalists of
the time managed to gain or lose
handsome fortunes. Bank stock
was also a favorite investment.
An illustration of one of the
sources of money-making to
Brokers at this period is found in
the fact that United States 6's of
1814 were at 50 in specie and 70 in
New York bank currency.

"In 1816 one could count up
two hundred and eight banks with
a capital of $82,000,000. . . . "One
day in 1817, the New York stock-
dealers met in the room of an associate, and voted to send a delegate over on the stage line to investigate the system adopted in the
rival city. The visit was successful; and the draft of a constitution
and by-laws, framed from that of
the Philadelphia Board, received
the final approbation of a sufficient
number of the brokers to enable
the New York Stock Exchange to
become a definite fact. Three
years after, on the 21st of February, 1820, this preliminary code
of rules received a thorough revision, and the organization was
strengthened by the accession of
some of the heaviest capitalists in
the city. Indeed, with 1820, the
real history of the Exchange may
properly be said to commence."

Chapter II.

LEGAL NATURE OF STOCK EXCHANGES ; CHARACTER AND INCIDENTS OF MEMBERSHIP THEREIN ; AND RULES AND REGULATIONS THEREOF.

I. Organization of Stock and other Exchanges.

The New York Stock Exchange is an unincorporated association of more than one thousand members and exists under a written constitution.[1]

The constitution vests the whole government of the Exchange in forty members, elected in classes, to serve one, two, three, and four years, together with the president and treasurer, making in all forty-two persons, called the "Governing Committee."

All applications for membership are publicly announced by the presiding officer, with the names of the proposer and seconder. Every applicant[2] must be twenty-one years of age ; and any wilful misstatement by any applicant for admission, upon a material point, shall, in certain cases, subject the offending party to loss of membership. It is now a prerequisite to admission that an applicant shall be a citizen of the United States.

The Constitution of the New York Stock Exchange states (Art I.) its object thus : "Its object shall be to furnish exchange rooms and other facilities for the convenient transaction of their business by its members, as Brokers ; to maintain high standards of commercial honor and integrity among its members ; and to promote and inculcate just and equitable principles of trade and business."[3]

---

[1] People ex rel. Lemmon vs. Feitner, 167 N. Y. 1-4; Commercial Telegram Co. vs. Smith, 47 Hun, 494–497; Matter of Renville, 46 A. D. (N. Y.) 37–42.

[2] Art. XIII., § 1, Const. N. Y. Stock Exchange.

[3] The following extract from the opinion of Bartlett, J., in the recent case of People ex rel. Lemmon vs. Feitner, 167 N. Y. 4, may be quoted: "The principal purposes and objects of the association (the New York Stock Exchange) are the affording to members facilities for the transaction of business as Brokers in stocks, bonds and other securities, the providing for a convenient

The constitution of the New York Stock Exchange sets forth the manner in which the business shall be conducted, the rates of commission to be charged, and the acts or omissions which constitute a ground for dismissing a member. Such of these provisions as are important, and which have been made the subject of legal adjudication, will be particularly noticed hereafter.[1]

The Philadelphia and San Francisco Stock Exchanges (the latter known as the Stock and Exchange Board) are unincorporated associations organized in the same manner as the New York Stock Exchange.[2]

The Company of Associated Stockbrokers (of San Francisco) is a corporation without capital stock composed of the members of the unincorporated association (the San Francisco Stock and Exchange Board) and was formed for the purpose of purchasing land and building thereon a Stock Exchange out of funds contributed by the Stock and Exchange Board.[3]

The Chicago Stock Exchange was formed as a voluntary unincorporated association in the year 1882 and its constitution is modelled on those of the New York, Philadelphia and San Francisco Stock Exchanges.[1]

The other Stock Exchanges in the United States and Canada are those which have been organized as unincorporated associations or corporations in the following cities,

exchange or salesroom for the transaction of such business, and the maintenance of rectitude and honorable dealings between its members in their business transactions." See also Bernheim v. Keppler, 34 Misc. 321.

[1] Full copies of the Rules and Regulations of the New York and London Stock Exchanges will be found in the Appendix.

[2] Vide Leech vs. Harris, 2 Brew. (Pa.) 575, 576; Hyde vs. Woods, 2 Sawy. 655, aff'd 94 U. S. (4 Otto) 523.

[3] Clute vs. Loveland, 68 Cal. 254.

[4] Clews vs. Jamieson, 182 U. S. 462.

viz.: Boston,[1] St. Louis, Baltimore, Pittsburg, Cleveland, Cincinnati, Denver, Detroit, Kansas City, New Orleans, Providence, Los Angeles, Indianapolis, Richmond, Washington, Montreal and Toronto.

The Chicago Board of Trade[2] was unincorporated prior to its incorporation by special act on February 18, 1859.[2] Although the Board is incorporated, it is, in effect, but a voluntary association, not maintained for the transaction of business, or for pecuniary gain.[3]

The New York Produce Exchange was incorporated by special statutes (L. 1862, c. 359; L. 1867, c. 30), its former name having been the "New York Commercial Association."[4] The use of the word " Produce " in its present corporate name does not restrict its dealings to agricultural produce.[5]

The New York Cotton Exchange is also a corporation formed under Laws of 1871, c. 365.[6]

A considerable number of other exchanges and mercantile associations have also been organized either as corporations or unincorporated associations and transact their business in the city of New York, such as the New York Mercantile Exchange, the Consolidated Stock and Petroleum Exchange, the Coffee Exchange, the Consolidated Milk Exchange, the Clearing House of the New York Stock Exchange, the Consolidated Clearing House of New York, the Merchants Credit Exchange, the Metropolitan

---

[1] The Boston Stock Exchange is an unincorporated association. Currier vs. Studley, 159 Mass. 17.

[2] New York, etc., Stock Exchange vs. Board of Trade, 127 Ill. 153; Priv. Laws, Ill. 1859, p. 13.

[3] People ex rel. Rice vs. Board of Trade, 80 Ill. 134; Board of Trade vs. Nelson, 162 Ill. 431.

[4] In re Haebler vs. New York Produce Exchange, 149 N. Y. 419.

[5] In re Haebler vs. N. Y. Produce Exchange, supra.

[6] People ex rel. Khron vs. Miller, 39 Hun, 557.

Mining Exchange, the International Mining Exchange, the Chamber of Commerce, the Harlem Board of Commerce, the Italian Chamber of Commerce in New York, the New York Dry Goods Exchange, American Horse Exchange, the Board of Real Estate Brokers, the Real Estate Salesroom, the Builders Brokers Exchange, the Building Material Exchange, the Choir Exchange, Crockery Board of Trade, Cut Flower Exchange, Hay Exchange, the Lager Beer Brewers Board of Trade, Leaf Tobacco Board of Trade, Maritime Exchange, Mechanics and Traders Exchange, National Railway Exchange, Fruit Exchange, Furniture Board of Trade, Furniture Exchange, Metal Exchange, Retail Coal Exchange, Southern California Fruit Exchange, and the U. S. Export Association, and numerous similar associations and corporations have been organized in the other chief cities of the Union.

A corporation was created by chapter 279, New York Laws of 1868, called the " Public Exchange," the name being subsequently changed to the Mutual Trust Company, having power to establish and conduct in the City of New York an Exchange for the daily meeting of merchants, bankers and tradesmen and for the convenient delivery and interchange of stocks and bonds and other securities between the dealers therein, and for other purposes. The corporation was judicially dissolved in 1884.[1]

By Laws of New York of 1886, c. 333, corporations or associations may be organized to foster trade and commerce. This statute was held not void as against public policy.[2]

[1] People vs. Mutual Trust Co., 96 N. Y. 11. As to nature of seats in the Exchange (American Mining Stock Exchange) organized under this charter, see Brown vs. Mutual Trust Co., 22 W. D. 395.

[2] Reynolds vs. Plumbers' Assn., 63 N. Y. S. 303.

2

Under the " Membership Corporations Law " of New York,
Art. XI., there may be formed as corporations, boards of
trade or exchanges, " for the purpose of fostering trade and
commerce, or the interests of those having a common trade,
business, financial or professional interest, to reform abuses
relative thereto, to secure freedom from unjust or unlawful
exactions, to diffuse accurate and reliable information as to
the standing of merchants and other matters, to procure
uniformity and certainty in the customs and usages of
trade and commerce, and of those having a common trade,
business, financial or professional interest, to settle differences between its members and to promote a more enlarged
and friendly intercourse between business men." [1]

A Stock Exchange by the name of " The New Jersey
Stock Exchange " was incorporated by an act of the Legislature of that state, approved March 16, 1875 (N. J. L. 1875,
ch. 130). The act does not show where the Exchange was
to be located, and no public organization seems to have
been effected under it. Provision is now made by ch. 138,
Laws of New Jersey, 1890, for the incorporation of boards
of trade or chambers of commerce, and similar associations.
See also Stat. Indiana (1875, ch. 5, §§ 1, 2 and 3), providing
for the organization of boards of trade, commercial or real

[1] Although such a corporation,
having a capital stock, and distributing profits amongst its members, might come within the definition of a Stock Corporation (Gen.
Corp. Law of N. Y. § 2) and be
therefore required at first sight to
organize under the Business Corporations Law, it is submitted that
the reference to such a corporation
in sec. 1 of the Gen. Corp. Law, as a
membership or mixed corporation,
and the provisions of sec. 33 of the
latter law, as to conflicting laws,
would render its organization under
the Membership Corporations Law
sufficient; although such a corporation organized under a law repealed
by the Membership Corporations
Law is not governed by the latter.
§ 131.

estate exchanges, chambers of commerce, or other commercial organizations.

Corporations may be formed for a like purpose in California (§ 591, Pomeroy's Civ. Code), and the statutes of Pennsylvania (P. L. June 10, 1893, 417) and of Wisconsin and Kansas also provide for the organization of boards of trade and business exchanges. The Pittsburgh Stock Exchange was held entitled to a charter of incorporation under the Corporation Law of 1874, enabling corporations to organize for "trade or commerce." [1] Some of the States however prohibit such organizations. In Louisiana corporations for mercantile, or commission brokerage, stock-jobbing, or exchange business are prohibited, and in Connecticut, corporations for dealing in bonds, notes or other evidences of debts, cannot be organized.

The Company of Associated Stock-Brokers (San Francisco) is a corporation composed solely of the voluntary association, *supra*.[2]

Nearly all of the Stock Exchanges organized in the United States are unincorporated associations, whilst, on the other hand, the majority of the Produce Exchanges have been formed as corporations.

Although we have, in this subdivision, given a reference to the principal Produce Exchanges, this chapter will chiefly treat of the legal nature, character and incidents, and the rules and regulations of unincorporated Stock Exchanges. For a more extended consideration of the nature and incidents of Produce Exchanges, the reader is referred to Messrs. Bisbee and Simonds' "Law of the Produce Ex-

[1] Re Pittsburgh Stock Exchange, 26 Pitts. L. J. N. S. 308.

[2] Clute vs. Loveland, 68 Cal. 254.

change," and to the American and English Enc. of Law
(2d ed.), and the Cyc. of Law and Procedure.

II. General Legal Nature of Unincorporated Stock Exchanges.

A voluntary association of persons, like the New York
Stock Exchange, by which each individual Broker is enabled
to carry on his separate business, under regulations made
alike for the protection of himself and his Client or principal, has no technical name or place in the law.

Mr. Justice Daly, in describing an association formerly
known as "The Open Board of Stock-brokers,"[1] an organization almost similar to the Stock Exchange, said that it was[2]
"an association of persons engaged in the same kind of business, who have organized together for the purpose of establishing certain rules, by which each agrees to be governed
in the conduct and management of his separate transactions
or business." And the New York Stock Exchange has been
judicially described as "a voluntary association of individuals united, without a charter, in an organization for the purpose of offering to the members thereof certain facilities in
the transaction of their business."[3]

It is purely a voluntary association.[4]

---

[1] This body, on the 8th of May, 1869, consolidated with the N. Y. Stock Exchange.

[2] White vs. Brownell, 4 Ab. Pr. (n. s.) 162; s. c. 2 Daly, 329.

[3] Belton vs. Hatch, 109 N. Y. 593; People ex rel. Lemmon vs. Feit-ner, 167 N. Y. 1, at page 4. See also Bernheim vs. Keppler, 34 Misc. 321; 69 N. Y. S. 803.

[4] Commercial Tel. Co. vs. Smith,

47 Hun, 505; Wilson vs. Telegram Co., 18 N. Y. St. Rep. 78; Matter of Renville, 46 App. Div. 37.

In reference to Produce Ex-changes it was held in Chicago Open Board of Trade vs. French, 61 Ill. App. 349, that the Chicago Open Board of Trade being a pri-vate corporation might discrimi-nate as to persons, not being mem-bers, it may admit to its floors or

So, in describing a similar board in a sister city,[1] the court said : " The Philadelphia Board of Brokers is not a corporation. It is not a joint-stock company, in the sense in which such companies are regarded by the English law, although it has a large amount of property which belongs to it in its joint or aggregate capacity. Such private associations are said not to be partnerships as between themselves, whatever may be their relation to third persons." [2] " The Board of Brokers is a voluntary association of persons who, for convenience in the transaction of business with each other, have associated themselves to provide a common place for the transaction of their individual business, agreeing among themselves to pay the expenses incident to the support of the objects of the association, in which each for himself, at stated hours of the day, and for his individual profit, may prosecute his own business, and enter into separate engagements with his fellow-members. The association does not share in the losses of the individual associates ; each member takes his own gains, and individually sustains the losses incident to his engagements." [3] The Exchange itself transacts no business as such in the buying and selling of stocks. The business therein transacted is that of the individual members.[4]

gallery, and it might therefore exclude a member's women customers. Quære: Whether a corporation can be admitted to membership in such a corporation? Live Stock Commission Co. vs. Live Stock Exchange, 143 Ill. 228. Although the business of such a corporation has become of great volume, the courts are not empowered to declare their markets public. Ib. As to when a Live Stock Exchange is not engaged in interstate commerce in violation of the Anti-Trust Act, see Hopkins vs. United States, 171 U. S. 578.

[1] Leech vs. Harris, 2 Brews. (Pa.) 571.

[2] The court cited White vs. Brownell, 3 Ab. Pr. (n. s.) 318; Thomas vs. Ellmaker, 1 Pars. Cas. (Pa.) 98.

[3] Leech vs. Harris, supra; White vs. Brownell, 3 Ab. Pr. (n. s.) 318.

[4] People ex rel. Lemmon vs. Feitner, 167 N. Y. 1.

These associations have some elements in common with corporations, joint-stock companies, and partnerships.[1]

An institution like the Stock Exchange is an anomaly in the law. It is amphibious in its nature ; for, without being either a corporation or a partnership, it possesses some of the characteristics of both. Like a corporation, it has perpetual being ; and .in this respect it has an advantage over bodies politic, for the charters of the latter generally limit their existence to some definite period ; whereas the New York Stock Exchange can preserve its organization (as it has since 1817) until it voluntarily dissolves itself.[2]

Is the Stock Exchange in any legal sense a public institution, charged with public duties ?   The question has arisen principally in respect to the right of such exchanges to control the publication of the quotations or prices reached in dealings on its floors.   In Illinois the Supreme Court,[3] relying on the doctrine of the United States Supreme Court in Munn vs. Illinois,[4] that when private property has been devoted to a public use and has become affected with a public interest it ceases to be *juris privati* only, and is subject to public regulation, held that the Chicago Board of Trade, an incorporated organization, having so conducted its affairs for many years, as to create a standard market for agricultural products, and acting in combination with tele-

---

[1] Leech vs. Harris, supra, 575, 576; Belton vs. Hatch, 109 N. Y. 593.   See also Hyde vs. Woods, 2 Sawy. 655, aff'd 94 U. S. (4 Otto) 523.

[2] See also Thompson vs. Adams, 93 Pa. St. 55.

[3] New York and Chicago Grain & Stock Exchange vs. Chicago Board of Trade, 127 Ill. 153, rev'g 27 Ill.

App. 93.   See also Public Grain & Stock Exchange vs. Western Union Tel. Co., Circuit Court of Cook County, May, 1883, 17 Fed. Rep. 830, note; Murphy vs. Chicago Board of Trade, 20 Chic. L. N. 59; Wiley vs. Board of Trade, 14 Nat. Corp. Rep. 181, and note to 17 Fed. Rep. 828.

[4] 94 U. S. 113.

graph companies, built up a system for the instantaneous and continuous indication of the fluctuations of that market, until the public and all persons dealing in such products had conformed to such system, and thus such market quotations had become necessary to the safe conduct of business, this system had become affected with a public interest, and the Board could not make any unjust discrimination, in furnishing the quotations, between persons willing to pay therefor and to conform to all reasonable rules. This decision was expressly limited to the facts above stated, and it was admitted that the Board could at any time, at its own pleasure, cease the collecting and publication of the quotations entirely. In so far as they rule to the contrary, either expressly or by implication, the decisions of the United States Circuit Court mentioned in the footnote[1] must, in view of the prior decision of the Supreme Court of the United States in Munn vs. Illinois, *supra*, and of the State Supreme Court decision just cited, be considered as overruled.

But the Chicago Board of Trade will not be compelled to supply its quotations to a " bucket shop."[2]

[1] Metropolitan Grain Exchange vs. Chicago Board of Trade, 15 Fed. Rep. 847; Bryant vs. Western Union Telegraph Co. (U. S. Cir. Ct.), 17 Fed. Rep. 825; Marine Grain and Stock Exchange vs. Western Union Tel. Co. (U. S. Cir. Ct.), 22 Fed. Rep. 23; Board of Trade v. Christie, 116 Fed. Rep. 944. See also valuable note appended to Bryant vs. Co., 17 Fed. Rep. 825–828.

[2] Christie St. Commission Co. vs. Board of Trade, 94 Ill. App. 229; Central Stock and Grain Exchange vs. Board of Trade, 198 Ill. 396.

The Board of Trade and telegraph companies may require that persons, to whom quotations are supplied, should sign an agreement not to keep a bucket shop. Sullivan vs. Postal Tel. Co., 123 Fed. Rep. 411. Such an agreement is not in restraint of commerce. Board vs. Christie, 121 Fed. 608. It has been recently held, however, that as over 90 per cent of the transactions on the Chicago Board

And it was held in Board of Trade of the City of Chicago vs. Thomson Commission Co.,[1] that the Board had only the common-law property right in the quotations, viz., till their first publication, and it could guard against subsequent publications only through the statutory copyright. In that case as it was doubtful whether the defendants had interfered with plaintiff's common-law right of first publication, a preliminary injunction restraining defendants from using the quotations was denied pending the taking of the proofs.

And it was held in Cleveland Telegraph Co. vs. Stone,[2] that the Board may assign this property right (viz., the right of property in the quotations till the same are made over to the public) to a third person who may restrain the unauthorized distribution of such quotations before publication.

In New York, with particular reference to the Stock Exchange, the decisions have been uniformly opposed to the Illinois case of New York, &c., Exchange vs. Board of Trade, supra, and have answered the reasons of the Illinois court. In the principal case,[3] the plaintiff was engaged in the business of collecting upon the floor of the New York Stock Exchange quotations of dealings in stock and distributing such quotations to its customers. The Stock Exchange threatening to oust the plaintiff from the Exchange, an injunction was sought to restrain such action, upon the ground that the Stock Exchange being a body created for the bene-

of Trade are gambling ones, the board cannot restrain the use of its quotations. Board vs. Donovan Co., 121 Fed. 1012. To same effect Board vs. O'Dell Co., 115 Fed. 574; Christie Co. vs. Board of Trade, 125 Fed. 161, rev'g s. c. 116 Fed. 944; Board vs. Kinsey, 125 Fed. 72.

[1] Board of Trade vs. Thomson Co., 103 Fed. 902. See also Board vs. Ex., 121 Fed. 433.

[2] 105 Fed. 794.

[3] Commercial Telegram Co. vs. Smith, 47 Hun, 494.

fit of the public, it was against public policy, irrespective of contract, to refuse to permit the plaintiff to enter the Exchange for the purposes above mentioned. But the court refused to entertain that view, saying : "The claim that the Stock Exchange has no right to exclude the Commercial Telegram Company from its floor upon the ground of public policy evidently proceeds upon an entirely erroneous theory. The Exchange is a private association; it has the right to admit to its floor whom it pleases; it obtained nothing from the State except that protection which the law affords to every citizen; it has sought no special privilege and obtained no special powers. It is, therefore, just as much the master of its own business and of the method of conducting the same as any private individual within the State. It may make public the transactions that occur within its walls, or it may refuse all information in respect thereto. No matter which course is pursued, so long as it violates no law, it has a right to continue its business as it pleases.[1] It

[1] Matter of Renville, 46 App. Div. 37; Wilson vs. Telegram Co., 18 N. Y. St. R. 78.

A related question to that discussed in the text is the duty of a telegraph company, as a public servant, like a common carrier, to furnish the quotations collected by it to all who comply with its conditions, without discrimination. As to this, quære in Matter of Renville, supra. The relations which telegraph Companies bear towards the public may be such as to prevent any such discrimination. Bryant vs. Western Union Tel. Co., supra. But it is said: "It is no part of the duty of the telegraph company to transmit such information." Met- ropolitan Grain and Stock Exchange vs. Board of Trade, supra. The business of collecting and furnishing commercial news is distinct from its business as a common carrier, and in engaging in it, the company is in the same position as a private person would be who buys and sells goods, selling to one and refusing to sell to another. Bradley vs. Western Union Tel. Co., Cincinnati Commercial Gazette, April 8, 1887, 17 Fed. Rep. 834, note. See, however, State ex rel. Telegraph Co. vs. Bell Telephone Co., 36 Ohio St. 296, where it was held that under the statute of that state, a telephone company was a public servant and possessed no

may give its quotations to one man and deny them to another."

But the fact that the business at a particular market, owned or conducted by a private corporation or a voluntary association, has become so great as to influence the commerce of a large section of the country, or more or less largely of the whole country, does not permit the courts to declare such markets public and impressed with a public use, or to apply to it any rules of public policy peculiar to that class of market. Markets overt, such as exist in England are unknown here. If the magnitude of a particular business is such, and the persons affected by it are so numerous, that the interests of society demand that the rules and principles applicable to public employments should be applied to it, this would have to be done by the Legislature.[1] The court distinguishes the Case of New York and Chicago Grain and Stock Exchange vs. Board of Trade, *supra*.[2]

Although the last cited case decided that a public interest attached when the quotations were given out, which entitled the applicants to receive them without unjust discrimination, it nevertheless held that the Board possessed a property right in the quotations before publication and it was

right to discriminate as to whom it would provide with instruments. A telegraph company will not be compelled to furnish quotations to a "bucket shop." Bryant vs. Western Union Tel. Co., supra; Wiley vs. Board of Trade, 14 Nat. Corp. Rep. 181. See also National Tel. News Co. vs. Western Union, 119 Fed. 294; Illinois Commission Co. vs. Cleveland Tel. Co., 129 Fed. 301; Smith vs. Co., 84 Ky. 664.

[1] American Live Stock Co. vs.

Chicago Live Stock Exchange, 143 Ill. 210.

In Russell vs. N. Y. Produce Exchange, 58 N. Y. Supp. 842, the claim was made that the business done on the New York Produce Exchange was so affected by a public use that it was subject to judicial regulation at the instance of an outsider, but no evidence to substantiate the claim was produced.

[2] 127 Ill. 153. See also Kiernan vs. Co., 50 How. Pr. 194.

subsequently held [1] that the furnishing of the quotations to a customer either through a ticker or by means of a blackboard in the customers' office, not being a universal publication, was not a publication thereof, and therefore when defendants obtained such quotations from a firm who purloined them from the customers' office before they were given out to the press, they were enjoined from taking and using the reports so derived, without authority. And reasonable regulations may be made by the Board, and therefore when defendant declined to comply with a requirement of the Board that the quotations should not be used in the conduct of a bucket shop, it will be enjoined from recovering or surreptitiously acquiring them, and the defendant cannot argue that the complainant Board violated the "bucket shop" statutes without very clear proof that gambling transactions were carried on in pursuance of, and not in violation of, its rules.[2]

The recent case of Board of Trade vs. Christie, *supra*, decided that courts cannot by their decree assume the initiative in declaring private property to be impressed with a public use. There should exist first the condition of expansion of a private business justifying the assertion of a public interest therein, followed by legislative recognition of such condition. When such a condition arises, the measure of the public control is limited by the extent of the public interest, and the making of regulations pertaining thereto is of legislative, not judicial, cognizance. See also State vs. Associated Press,[3] where it was held that

---

[1] Board of Trade of Chicago vs. Hadden-Krull Co., 121 Fed. 1017. See also Board vs. Ellis, 122 Fed. 319; Ex. vs. Gregory (1896), 1 Q. B. 147.

[2] Board of Trade vs. Christie, 116 Fed. 944.

[3] 159 Mo. 410 at p. 421.

to bring the property or business of a person under governmental control there must be an exercise of the police power. The conclusions reached in Munn's Case, *supra*, are very ably criticised in this case.

III. Stock Exchange not a Partnership.

But the Stock Exchange does not come within the legal definition of a partnership. The general rule undoubtedly is that "no partnership or *quasi* partnership subsists between persons who do not share either profit or loss and who do not hold themselves out as partners. Societies and clubs, the object of which is not to share profits, are not partnerships, nor are their members, as such, liable for each other's acts." [1]

The Stock Exchange exists under an agreement between its members to pay the expenses incident to the support of a "Mart," in which each for himself, at stated hours of the day, and for his individual profit, may prosecute his own business, and enter into separate engagements with his fellow-members. The association does not share in the losses of the individual associates; each member takes his own gains, and individually sustains the losses incident to his engagements. The organization of this board grew out of a necessity for new and greater facilities for exchange and negotiation, incident to the rapidly developing interests of the country and the increasing number and value of its commercial securities. [2]

---

[1] Lindley on Part. (3d ed.) 57. See also edition of 1893; Belton vs. Hatch, 109 N. Y. 593; Lafond vs. Deems, 81 N. Y. 507–514.

[2] White vs. Brownell, 3 Ab. Pr. (n. s.) 318. The views expressed in the text are confirmed by the Court of Appeals in the case of Belton vs. Hatch, 109 N. Y. 593, where the court, through Associate Judge Gray, said:

"It (The New York Stock Exchange) cannot be said to be strictly a copartnership, for its objects do

Although it may possess property derived from the payment of dues or fines, such property is a mere incident, and not the main purpose or object of the association. A member has no severable proprietary interest in it, or a right to any proportionable part of it upon withdrawing.[1]

There are no profits earned to be divided among its members, nor are there any losses to be borne arising out of the acts of the joint body.[2] If a partnership, the death of one of its members would, *ipso facto*, dissolve it.[3]

In the case of Caldicott vs. Griffiths[4] it was held that a society called " The Midland Counties Guardian Society for

---

not come within the definition of one. A copartnership results from a contract between the parties by which they agree to combine their property or labor, or both, in some common enterprise and for a common profit, to be shared in the proportion stated in their agreement. The objects of a voluntary association of brokers do not, however, involve any such combination, or any communion of profits from the business transacted by the members. Like a business club, its principal object is the promotion of the convenience of its members by furnishing facilities which aid them in doing their business, and are, therefore, of benefit to them."

To same effect, People ex rel. Lemmon vs. Feitner, 167 N. Y. 1.

An incidental purpose, but of great importance to the business and investing community, is the maintenance of a high standard of commercial integrity among the members and protection, so far as

may be, against financial irresponsibility. Bernheim vs. Keppler, 34 Misc. 321.

[1] Daly, P. J., in White vs. Brownell, 4 Ab. Pr. (n. s.) 191. This subject is fully treated, post, p. 33.

[2] Belton vs. Hatch, 109 N. Y. 593; Bernheim vs. Keppler, 34 Misc. 321.

[3] White vs. Brownell, 3 Ab. Pr. (n. s.) 325; 1 Lindley on Part. (3d ed.) 57. See also discussion as to the nature of unincorporated associations, People ex rel. Platt vs. Wemple, 117 N. Y. 136; People ex rel. Winchester vs. Coleman, 133 N. Y. 281; Sandford vs. Supervisors of New York, 15 How. Pr. 172; Waterbury vs. Merchants' Union Exp. Co., 50 Barb. 160; Thomas vs. Ellmaker, 1 Pars. Cas. (Pa.) 98; Flemyng vs. Hector, 2 M. & W. 172; Regina vs. Whitmarsh, 15 Q. B. 600; Bear vs. Bromley, 18 id. 271. See also case of Ash vs. Guie, 11 Pitts. L. J. (Pa.) n. s. 449; s. c. Alb. L. J. July 30, 1881, 83.

[4] 8 Ex. 898.

the Protection of Trade," the professed object of which was
to "watch the progress of any measure in Parliament affecting the trade interests, and to protect its members from the
practices of the fraudulent and dishonest," and which was
organized with a president, vice-president, treasurer, secretary, and committee—to which committee was given the
general management of the affairs of the society, and which
society was organized under a series of rules adopted for the
management of the same—was not a partnership; and that,
therefore, one of the members of the society who had furnished certain printing to the committee might sue the committee; and that the principle that one partner cannot sue
the partnership did not apply.

In the argument the defendants referred to a case [1] which
held that the promoters of a railroad company constituted
a partnership, as showing that a partnership existed in the
case before the court.   The court, in reaching its conclusion,
said: "The question is, whether, by entering into this
scheme, the subscribers form a partnership or a *quasi*-
partnership; or whether the case is similar to that of a
number of persons subscribing to a hospital or to an ordinary club.   The solution of that question is not to be arrived
at by examining cases which have reference to the liability
of committee-men or shareholders in projected railway companies, and in other undertakings of that description, but
by consulting the rules themselves."

Yet unincorporated associations are, in law, often regarded
as mere partnerships. [2]

[1] Holmes vs. Higgins, 1 B. & C.   Co. vs. Fry, 4 Phil. (Pa.) 129; Green-
74.   wood's Case, 23 Eng. L. & Eq. 422;
[2] Robbins vs. Butler, 24 Ill. 397;   Wells vs. Gates, 18 Barb. (N. Y.)
Bullard vs. Kinney, 10 Cal. 60; Coal   557; Butterfield vs. Beardsley, 28

And although a voluntary unincorporated association like the New York Stock Exchange is not a partnership, the rights of the associates do not differ from a partnership, so far as their rights in the property of the association are concerned. When therefore a member violates the contractual relation between him and the association, by being guilty of reckless dealing, or doing business with improper parties, and he is thereupon deprived of his membership and declared ineligible for readmission, he, or his assignee, forfeits all right to the proceeds of his seat, and the same may be disposed of as the association may direct.[1]

IV. Nor is the Stock Exchange a Corporation or Incorporated Joint-stock Association.

It does not exist by virtue of a charter or legislative grant. It has neither franchises, special privileges nor special powers. It obtains nothing from the state save that protection afforded to every citizen.[2]

The obligations and rights of its members are not determined by any statutory provision.[3] There is no contribution of capital by its members for the prosecution of any kind of business by the association. It issues no stock,

Mich. 412; Moore vs. Brink, 4 Hun (N. Y.), 402; Koehler vs. Brown, 2 Daly (N. Y.), 78.

[1] Belton vs. Hatch, 109 N. Y. 593.
[2] Commercial Tel. Co. vs. Smith, 47 Hun, 505; Wilson vs. Telegram Co., 18 N. Y St. Rep. 78; Matter of Renville, 46 App. Div. 37. For statutes under which exchanges may be incorporated see ante, p. 17.

[3] A voluntary unincorporated joint-stock company is, however, liable to be taxed on its capital, as a corporation, under the laws of New York. Sandford vs. Supervisors of N. Y., 15 How. Pr. (N. Y.) 172; People ex rel. Platt vs. Wemple, 117 N. Y. 136. Compare People ex rel. Winchester vs. Coleman, 133 N. Y. 281.

nor can the individual members claim any rights of property in it as stockholders.[1]

Unlike an incorporated commercial joint-stock company, the privilege of membership in such a voluntary association may be conferred or withheld, at its pleasure, and the law cannot compel the admission of an individual into the society against its wish.[2]

The above are some of the general elements which distinguish stock exchanges from corporations, incorporated joint-stock associations, or partnerships, and these distinctions will be further developed in the ensuing subdivisions of this chapter.

V. Rights of Members in Property Held by Non-incorporated Stock Exchanges.

In respect to the property which the Stock Exchange may, from time to time own, interesting questions are involved in which the distinction between this body and corporations and partnerships will further appear.

As has been shown, the Exchange is in no wise interested in the pecuniary gains or profits of its members; and the sole source of its revenue is derivable from such dues, fines, assessments, or contributions as it may, from time to time, collect or receive from its members, together with any increase of its present accumulations.

At common-law, the legal title of the personal property of the Exchange, it being unincorporated, is vested in all

---

[1] White vs. Brownell, 3 Ab. Pr. (n. s.) 318.

[2] Id. 4 Ab. Pr. (n. s.) 162; Commercial Tel. Co. vs. Smith, 47 Hun, 505; Wilson vs. Telegram Co., 18 N. Y. St. Rep. 78; Matter of Renville, 46 App. Div. 37; Live Stock Commission Co. vs. Live Stock Exchange, 143 Ill. 210.

of its members, in like manner as the title to partnership property is vested in all the partners. But, unlike the relation of partners, a member of the Exchange, or his legal representatives, has no right to call for an account of the property and a division of the same. The interest of each member in the property of the association is equal, but is subject to the constitution and by-laws. They express the contract by which each member has consented to be bound, and which measure his duties, rights and privileges as such.[1]

A member has no several proprietary interest in it, or a right to any proportionable part of it, upon withdrawing. He has merely the enjoyment and use of it while he is a member; but the property remains with, and belongs to, the body while it continues to exist, like a pew, the ultimate and dominant property in which is in the congregation, and not in the pewholder; and when the body ceases to exist, those who may then be members become entitled to their proportionate share of its assets.[2]

This principle arises mainly from the fact that organizations of this character are not constituted for *gain*, but for the *convenience* of their members, and the possession of property by them is a mere incident, and not the main purpose or object of the association.[3]

When a person is elected a member of the Exchange, he becomes entitled to what is commonly called a "seat," and such a proportionate interest in the property of the association as he would be entitled to if he should happen to be a mem-

[1] Belton vs. Hatch, 109 N. Y. Pr. (n. s.) 162–191; Fassett vs. First 593. Parish in Boyleston, 19 Pick. 361;
[2] St. James's Club, 13 Eng. L. & Caldicott vs. Griffith, 8 Ex. 898. Eq. 592; White vs. Brownell, 4 Ab. [3] White vs. Brownell, supra.

ber at the time of its dissolution; and that interest would be found by dividing the amount of property by the number of "seats" then existing after deducting debts and liabilities. These "seats," under the 15th Article of the Constitution of the New York Stock Exchange, are transferable, but the transferee must be approved by two thirds of the Committee on Admissions. The transfer, sale or assignment of the interest of a partner would work a dissolution of the partnership.[1]   In the present instance, however, the transferor, by such an act, does not disturb or affect the general organization; he simply ceases to be a member and to have any legal interest or concern in the Exchange, and the transferee becomes invested with all of the privileges, duties, and attributes of membership.   When a member dies, his membership may be disposed of by the Committee on Admissions; and, after satisfying claims of the members, the balance remaining is paid to the legal representatives of the deceased.   If the Committee on Admissions should, for even arbitrary reasons, refuse to approve a person to whom a member has bargained to sell his seat, it follows that the latter is forced to continue his membership.   By signing the Consitution each member agrees to the same, and to all the by-laws, rules, or regulations which may be adopted (provided they are legal, as we shall hereafter see); and thus a contract is expressly established, by which the ordinary principles that govern the relations of partnerships and corporations are avoided.[2]

---

[1] Pars. on Part. (5th ed.) 433, 434; 1 Lindley on Part. (4th ed.) 698, 6th ed. p. 575, 577.

[2] In the case of exchanges which by their rules expressly permit a member to dispose of his seat, subject, however, to the condition that before the purchaser can participate in the proceedings of the board he must be elected a member, then there can be no doubt that if a member should sell his seat to one

As to any real estate which the Exchange may acquire, the questions which would ordinarily arise in relation thereto are more difficult and numerous. Their property being, as we have seen, technically held by them as partners, it follows that the persons who are members, when they acquire lands are vested with equal interests therein; and that the Stock Exchange at common law, being an unincorporated body, could confer no title upon a purchaser unless all of its members joined in the conveyance; or, if any of them were deceased, the heirs of such of them as were members at the time the real estate vested in the Exchange.

To avoid the many questions of the above nature which doubtless would have arisen if real estate were held by the Exchange, a company was incorporated under the laws of the State of New York,[1] duly empowered to hold real estate,

who should not be elected a member of the board, such purchaser would take, subject to any rules imposed by the association, the interest of his vendor in the property of the association, and this was so held in the case of Clute vs. Loveland, 68 Cal. 254.

Article XV. of the constitution of the New York Stock Exchange, differs, however, from the rules of Exchanges permitting, as above shown, a "disposal" of the membership, before the approval of the purchaser by the Exchange, by denying the right of transfer of his seat to a member until his transferee has been approved by two thirds of the committee on admissions.

A seat in the Philadelphia Produce Exchange, having no money value attached, is a personal privilege, and a bill will not lie for an injunction to restrain the Exchange from issuing new certificates of membership to four members whose seats plaintiff had purchased. Under the rules plaintiff could not be "approved" as a member more than once. If he were injured, he had his remedy at law. Shoemaker vs. Exchange, 15 Phila. R. 103; 39 Leg. Int. 373. As to retransfer of a seat by an employee of a member in whose name the seat was held, see Sproul vs. Morris, 31 Pitts. L. J. (n. s.) 310. See also Allien vs. Wotherspoon, 50 N. Y. Super. Ct. 417.

[1] Incorp. Jan. 30, 1863.

the stock of the company being exclusively owned and held by the Stock Exchange.[1]

In the year 1867 there was enacted in the State of New York a general law authorizing any joint-stock company or association to purchase, hold, and convey real estate: 1st, To an extent necessary for its immediate accommodation in the convenient transaction of its business; 2d, Such as shall be mortgaged to it in good faith, to secure loans made by or moneys due to it; or, 3d, Such as it shall purchase at sales under judgments, decrees, or mortgages held by it; but in no other case, nor for any other purpose.

Conveyances shall be made to the president of the association, as such, and he and his successors may sell, assign, and convey, free from any claim of shareholders, or any person claiming under them.[2]

This act may be construed as a restraint upon the right of joint-stock associations to purchase and hold real estate not needed for immediate use. Such seems to have been the construction given to it in Rainey vs. Laing.[3] But if the statute is violated in this respect, no one can question the title but the State.[4]

---

[1] The ownership of the building in which the London Stock Exchange is situated is also in a distinct body. Melsheimer & Lawrence Stock Ex. 3d ed. 4; Brodhurst's Law and Practice of the Stock Ex. p. 32. The real estate of the San Francisco Stock and Exchange Board, a voluntary association, is held by a corporation composed exclusively of the members of the board. Clute vs. Loveland, 68 Cal. 255.

[2] L. of N. Y. 1867, vol. i, ch. 289, 576.

[3] 58 Barb. 489.

[4] Id.; Howell vs. Earp, 21 Hun (N. Y.), 393. Aside from the statute just quoted, it is a question whether, in view of the fact that the members of the Exchange are partners, in some aspects, a grant to the Stock Exchange would be valid. It has been held that a community or society, not incorporated, cannot purchase land and take in succession. Co. Litt. 3 a, 10 Co. 266; Com. Dig. tit. Capacity, B 1; Goesely vs. Bimeler, 55 U. S. 589; German Land

The question is not, however, now of moment as this statute was repealed by the Joint Stock Association Law,[1] and as the second section of the latter law restricts its

Association vs. Scholler, 10 Minn. 331; Liggett vs. Ladd, 17 Cr. 89; Douthitt vs. Stimson, 73 Mo. 199; Jackson vs. Cory, 8 Johns. (N. Y.) Reps. 385; Hornbeck vs. Westbrook 9 id. 73; same vs. Sleight, 12 id. 198. In this last case it is said: "The inhabitants of Rochester were not a body corporate, so as to be competent to take an estate in fee. And if a grant to them in a deed would be void, a reservation to them in a deed, in fee, to a third person would be equally void. Nor would it be valid as a covenant to stand seized. The inhabitants of Rochester were strangers to the deed. The present inhabitants, at all events, must be so considered. For they not being a body corporate so as to perpetuate the rights granted to the patent, these rights must be restricted to the then inhabitants." Although if a voluntary association is subsequently incorporated, the title to land held by its officers by adverse possession, passes to the corporation. Ref. Ch. of Gallupville vs. Schoolcraft, 65 N. Y. 134. But see Ticknor's Est., Sup. Ct. Mich. 4 Am. Law Reg. (n. s.) 269 note; Hamblett vs. Bennett, 88 Mass. 140; East Haddam Bapt. Ch. vs. East Haddam Bapt. Soc., 44 Conn. 259. A grant to a voluntary unincorporated association, whose members are ascertainable may be construed as a grant to such members

as tenants in common. Byam vs. Bickford, 140 Mass. 31. A voluntary association unincorporated is incapable of taking a legacy. A legacy bequeathed to such an association is invalid, and the property so bequeathed vests in the testator's next of kin if not otherwise disposed of. Shipman vs. Rollins, 19 N. Y. Weekly Dig. 370; Supm. Ct. Gen'l Term, 1st Depart., and cases there cited. So a voluntary unincorporated association for charitable purposes cannot take property by devise in the State of New York. White vs. Howard, 46 N. Y. 144, aff'g 52 Barb. 294; Sherwood vs. American Bible Society, 1 Keyes (N. Y.), 561, 567; Owens vs. Missionary Society, 14 N. Y. 380; Downing vs. Marshall, 23 N. Y. 366; McKeon vs. Kearney, 57 How. Pr. (N. Y.) 350; Contra, Hornbeck vs. Am. Bible Soc., 2 Sandf. Ch. 133. Nor can such an association take a bequest, although subsequently to the death of the testator it becomes incorporated. Baptists' Association vs. Hart's Executors, 4 Wh. (U. S.) 1; 3 Pet. 497; see also 2 Redf. on Wills, ch. i, § 7. That a bequest to such an association may be valid or be made to take effect indirectly, see Preacher's Aid Society vs. Rich, 45 Me. 552; Cahill vs. Bigger, 8 B. Monr. (Ky.) 211; Smith vs Nelson, 18 Vt. 511, 516; Peabody vs. Eastern Methodist Soc., 87 Mass. 540;

---

[1] L. 1891, c. 235, ch. 45, of the Gen. Laws.

operation to unincorporated joint-stock associations, companies, or enterprises, having written articles of association, and capital stock divided into shares, qualifications not possessed by the New York Stock Exchange, that body could scarcely be held entitled to the benefit of its sixth section which substantially reënacts the provisions of the prior statute,[1] except as to alienation of the land by the president.

VI. Liability of Members for Debts, etc.

Another question which arises, in considering the nature of an unincorporated association like the Stock Exchange, is as to the individual liability of the members thereof, *ex contractu* or *ex delicto*, for the acts of its officers, committees, representatives, or of their fellow-members.

The general rule is, that members of unincorporated companies are regarded as partners and are subject to the whole law of partnerships.[2] But the application of this principle to a body like the Stock Exchange is very re-

---

Gibson vs. McCall, 1 Rich. (S. C.) Rep. 174. But now by L. 1893, c. 701, conveyances, devises, gifts or bequests to charitable, etc., uses which shall be in other respects valid, shall not be deemed invalid by reason of the indefiniteness of the beneficiaries. The Real Property Law, L. 1896, c. 547, § 93, contains a similar provision as to real estate. Under these statutes a devise of real estate for permanent charitable purposes has been held valid although the testator did not direct the formation of a corpora-tion. Allen vs. Stevens, 161 N. Y. 122. Also a bequest of personal property, Matter of J. Fitzsimmons, 29 Misc. 204, and a bequest to an unincorporated charitable association is valid. Matter of B. Fitzsimmons, 29 Misc. 731. See also Dammert vs. Osborne, 140 N. Y. 30; People vs. Powers, 147 N. Y. 104.

[1] L. 1867, c. 289.

[2] Pars. on Part. (4th ed.) § 431; Wordsworth on Joint-stock Companies, 21, 220.

stricted. One case seems to have occurred which is impliedly decisive of the personal liability of members of a Stock Exchange ;[1] but there are very many instances in the books in which members of clubs and other associations have been sought to be charged as individuals, for acts of committees, etc., and which would doubtless control a case of the former character, if it ever should arise. For the acts of its officers or servants, directly authorized by the constitution, laws, or regulations of the Stock Exchange, its members would be individually liable under the general principle above cited.[2]

But the great contention has arisen in those cases where the officers or servants have contracted obligations or incurred liability, without any direct or express authorization from the association. This question seems to have been determined, in the modern cases, by the law of principal and agent rather than that of partnership. Mr. (now Lord) Lindley says on this subject: "If liabilities are to be fastened on any of their members, it must be by reason of the acts of those members themselves, or by reason of the acts of their agents; and the agency must be made out by the person who relies on it, for none is implied by the mere fact of association." [3]

This question is, at present, entirely speculative, and there can be no practical use in discussing it at any length,

[1] Kronfield vs. Haines, 20 Misc. 102.

[2] In McGrew vs. City Produce Exchange, 85 Tenn. 572, it was held that the incorporators of an incorporated exchange were individually liable for sums received by the exchange managers in wagering contracts, it being the intention of all the incorporators to engage in such unlawful contracts, and the incorporation being a mere device to escape their otherwise individual liability.

[3] 1 Lindley on Part. and Company Law (4th ed.), 57. The liability of partners is now regulated in England by the Partnership Act, 1890. See Lindley on Partnership (6th ed.), p. 133 et seq.

but a collection of modern authorities upon the general subject will be found below.[1]

VII. Suits by and against the Stock Exchange.

At common law, carrying out the analogy between unincorporated bodies and partnerships, in a suit by or against the former, it was necessary that all persons composing the same should be made parties.[2]

But the Legislature of the State of New York, by the act of 1849, ch. 258, has provided that any joint-stock company or association, consisting of seven or more stockholders or associates, may sue and be sued in the name of the president or treasurer, for the time being, of such joint-stock company or association.[3]

[1] 2 Lindley on Part. 57, note (d) and cases cited. See also Lindley on Partnership (6th ed.), p. 133 et seq. See, also, Wordsworth on Joint-Stock Companies, ch. viii. and cases cited; Pars. on Part. (3d ed.) 45 note (b); (4th ed.) § 60, and note 2; Ebbinghousen vs. Worth Club, 4 Ab. New Cas. (N. Y.) 300, and note, where a full discussion of this subject is made; Park vs. Simmons, 10 Hun (N. Y.), 128, which seems to be contrary to the majority of the cases on this subject, and is expressly repudiated by Ebbinghousen vs. Worth Club (supra); Lafond vs. Deems, 1 Ab. New Cas. 318; 81 N. Y. 507. As to the question of liability of members of a club for negligence in the management of their property, see English vs. Brenan, 60 N. Y. 609; 2 Hilliard on Torts, 230.

[2] Ang. & Ames on Corp. (10th ed.) §§ 591, 599; Williams vs. Bank of Michigan, 7 Wend. 542; Wells vs. Gates, 18 Barb. (N. Y.) 554; Dicey on Parties, 170, 172 (Truman's notes); East Haddam Bapt. Ch. vs. East Haddam Bapt. Soc., 44 Conn. 259; Haskins vs. Alcott, 13 Ohio St. 216. But in equity in certain circumstances suit may be maintained by the trustees of a voluntary association on behalf of themselves and their associates. Birmingham vs. Gallagher, 112 Mass. 190; or against the board of directors, Greer vs. Stoller, 77 Fed. 1.

[3] This act and its amendments (L. 1851, ch. 455, and L. 1853, ch. 153) were repealed by L. 1880, ch. 245, and their provisions have been re-enacted in the Code Civ. Pro. §§ 1919–1924. The amendment of 1854 (L. 1854, ch. 245) was repealed by and re-enacted in the Joint-Stock Association Law (L. 1894,

This provision, not being deemed broad enough, was extended by the Laws of 1851, ch. 455, to any company or association composed of not less than seven persons who are owners of, or have an interest in, any property, right of action or demand, jointly or in common, or who may be liable to any action on account of such ownership or interest.[1]

The New York statute provides that where an association consists of more than seven members,[2] the action may be brought in the name of the president,[3] and this

ch. 235). Whether this act extends to private voluntary copartnerships or associations, which are not organized in pursuance of some statute, was questioned in Austin vs. Searing, 16 N. Y. 112; and in Rorke vs. Russell, 2 Lans. Rep. (N. Y.) 244; see also Ebbinghousen vs. Worth Club, 4 Ab. New Cas. 300. But this question is put at rest by § 1919, Code Civ. Pro., which specifically includes partnerships and unincorporated associations.

It has been held that such a state statute, authorizing one or more members of an unincorporated association to represent the others in the courts, will be followed by a Federal court of equity, and the members conclusively presumed to have the same citizenship as such officers. 1 Foster's Fed. Pr. (2d ed.) § 45, p. 118, and cases cited in note 27.

[1] By the laws of Pennsylvania, in the case of joint-stock companies, unincorporated, process may be served upon any officer, agent, etc. Pepper & Lewis's Dig. vol. 4, p. 1361. By the Rev. Stat. of Ohio, § 5011, a partnership formed for the purpose of carrying on a trade or business in that State, or holding property therein, may sue or be sued by the usual or ordinary name which it has assumed, or by which it is known; and, in such case, it shall not be necessary to allege or prove the names of the individual members thereof. The above statute only applies to companies doing business within the State. Haskins vs. Alcott, 13 Ohio St. 216..

In England several acts have been passed allowing certain specified unincorporated associations to sue and be sued in the name of their officers for the time being. 1 Chitty's Pl. 16 (16th Amer. ed.).

[2] The allegation that the association consists of seven or more members is material and issuable. Tiffany vs. Williams, 10 Abb. P. R. 204.

[3] Or treasurer. 3 N. Y. Rev. Stat. (6th ed.) 762; Code Civ. Pro. § 1919. But the action cannot be brought against both president and treasurer. Schmidt vs. Gunther, 5 Daly, 452. The action cannot be brought against the association as such, and service on the secretary is

provision has been held to extend the remedy to all associations.[1]

The statute applies to the remedy, and the *lex fori*

insufficient. Hanke vs. Cigar Makers' Union, 58 Supp. 412. If the association has no president, the action may be brought by some of the members on behalf of themselves and the other members, and such action may be so brought whether there is a president or not, § 1919 of the Code not limiting the effect of § 446 and § 448. Bloete vs. Simon, 12 Civ. Pro. Rep. 114.

[1] Bridenbecker vs. Hoard, 32 How Pr. (N. Y.) 289; Tibbetts vs. Blood, 21 Barb. 650; Corning vs. Greene, 23 id. 33; De Witt vs. Chandler, 11 Ab. Pr. (N. Y.) 459, 470; National Bank vs. Lasher, 1 T. & C. (N. Y.) 313; Waller vs. Thomas, 42 How. Pr. (N. Y.) 346; Ebbinghousen vs. Worth Club. 4 Ab. New Cas. 300; Allen vs. Clark, 65 Barb. 563; National Bank vs. Van Derwerker, 74 N. Y. 234; and see 4 Duer, 362; 18 Ab. Pr. 191; 55 Barb. 487. § 1919, N. Y. Code Civ. Pro., extends the remedy to all associations having a president or treasurer. So an action may be brought in the name of the president, to recover calls from shareholders. Bray vs. Farwell, 3 Lans. (N. Y.) Rep. 495. So a member of a joint-stock association may maintain an action against such association. It is not an action against himself. Westcott vs. Fargo, 61 N. Y. 542; Saltsman vs. Shults, 14 Hun (N. Y.), 256. See McMahon vs. Rauhr, 47 N. Y. 67; Sander vs. Eidlen, 13 Daly, 238; Snow vs. Wheeler, 113 Mass. 179. But see Bullard vs. Kinney, 10 Cal. 60; Coal Company vs. Fry, 4 Phil. (Pa.) 129; Wilson vs. Curzon, 15 M. & W. 532; Perring vs. Hone, 4 Bing. 28; Holmes vs. Higgins, 1 B. & C. 74. As to when the agent of a Lloyd's Assn. may be sued, see New York vs. Whipple, 36 App. Div. 49.

The officer sued in his representative capacity is a party to the action and as such may be examined before trial. Woods vs. De Figaniere, 1 Rob. 607; McGuffin vs. Dinsmore, 4 Abb. N. C. 241; Brooks vs. Hoey, 18 Civ. Pro. (N. Y.) 98; Whitman vs. Hubhill, 30 Fed. Rep. 81. Contra Duncan vs. Jones, 32 Hun, 12, where, however, it was said that, in a proper case, he may be examined before trial as a witness.

No power is given to the designated officers to sue where the members themselves could not have sued. Corning vs. Green, 23 id. 33.

And it is immaterial whether the officer sued is an infant or not. The action is against the officer as such, not against him as an individual. Nicoll vs. Munn (N. Y. Sup. Chambers), N. Y. Law Journal, p. 432, Nov. 16, 1894.

The statute, of course only applies to the remedy in the State, and members of such an association, may be sued in other states as partners. Boston & Alb. R. Co. vs. Pearson, 128 Mass. 445.

In France the syndic who is at the

governs. It is not confined to associations of the State of New York, but applies to all associations which come into court under it. Where the statute provides a remedy, it extends to all persons who use it, unless the act, by its terms, expressly limits its application.[1]

In the case of Rorke vs. Russell[2] it was held that the above-cited statutes were passed for the purpose of facilitating a certain class or kind of legal actions, relating to, or by which a remedy is sought as regards, the " joint property and effects " of the company or association; and that where, in an action against the president of the New York

head of the syndical board as governing committee, is the legal representative (mandataire) both of the committee and of the association and brings action on their behalf in his own name.

In the case of Thomas, a member of the Lyons Exchange or company of *agents de change,* the Court of Cassation decided in 1885 that it is the "syndic qui lui-même représente légalement la chambre et toute la corporation; qu'il en résulte qu'au cas de nécessité d'agir contre un débiteur de la caisse, c'est le syndic qui a seul qualité pour intenter l'action; et qu'il exerce en son nom propre en vertu de son titre de mandataire légal; et à défaut du syndic, au liquidateur que la justice aura désigné pour en remplir les fonctions." (Sirey, 1886, 1, 456). In a note on the same page the functions of the syndic and syndical chamber are thus defined: "Les agents de change de chaque place doivent se réunir et nommer, à la majorité absolue, un syndic et six

adjoints, pour exercer une police intérieure, rechercher les contraventions auxlais et réglements et les faire connaître à l'autorité publique. Comme toutes les corporations analogues instituées par la loi, telles que celles de notaires, avoués, avocats, et du sein desquelles est tirée une représentation chargée de régler les questions de discipline intérieure et de faire valoir leur intérêts au dehors, la corporation des agents de change a été par cette disposition pourvue d'un corps représentatif, la chambre syndical ayant à sa tête le syndic, chargé de personnifier et de représenter la corporation dans toutes les circonstances où ce serait nécessaire."

[1] See also N. Y. Code of Civil Proc. § 448, allowing one to be sued, where a large number of persons are interested. See Diepenbrock vs. Produce Exchange, N. Y. L. J., July 11, 1901.

[2] 2 Lans. (N. Y.) 245.

Mining Stock Board, the only relief asked for was that the president of the board, its officers and members, should be restrained from enforcing the vote or resolution of the board, suspending the plaintiff from his membership for a certain number of days, it was held that the action was not within either of these statutes; that plaintiff could not bring a suit against the president alone; that such a suit could not be regarded as a suit against the company or board; that no member of the latter would be regarded as a party to it; and that, accordingly, an injunction could not be regularly issued against any one else than the president.

This construction seems too narrow, and it was dissented from by one of the justices; but, although the decision does not appear to have been expressly overruled, subsequent cases would seem to show that it has not been followed as a precedent.[1]

And in the later case of National Bank vs. Van Derwerker,[2] where the defence was, that to bring a case within the statute in question it was necessary to show the existence of a company having stock divided into shares, and shareholders holding the same, the court held that the stat-

---

[1] Since the above was written the case in question has been expressly overruled by Mervin, J. (Spec. Term, Sup. Ct.), who held in Fritz vs. Muck, 62 How. Pr. 69, that an action may be maintained against the president of a voluntary association, by an expelled member, to compel his restoration. The object of the plaintiff is to place himself in a position where he can reach the joint property; and so the action is in regard to the joint rights and property of the association and within the purpose designed to be accomplished by the acts of 1849 and 1851. See also McKane vs. Dem. Gen. Comm., 21 Abb. N. C. 89. White vs. Brownell, 2 Daly, 329, and Hutchinson vs. Lawrence, 67 How. Pr. 38, are cases of the same nature, brought against the president, where, however, the point in question was not raised.

[2] 74 N. Y. 234; § 1919, Code Civ. Pro., expressly includes any partnership having a president or treasurer.

ute required no greater formalities in that respect for the formation of such associations than for the formation of ordinary partnerships. In that case it appeared that an association existed which had adopted for its title the *Old Saratoga Union Store Association*. It had more than fifty members, but there were no written articles signed by the members, nor any articles of incorporation, except a constitution and by-laws. There were also a president and board of directors. The president of the association, under authority of the body, made certain promissory notes. In an action on these notes the court held that the suit was properly brought against the association, in the name of the president; and that judgment in such an action, and execution thereon, bound the joint property of the association, and not the individual property of the president.

In the cases cited in the notes suits were instituted against the Stock Exchange in the name of its president,[1] and in the State of New York, under the statutes in question, there appears to be no legal impediment to the bringing of a suit against the Stock Exchange in the name of the president, treasurer, or other officer named in the act.[2]

[1] Heath vs. Prest. Gold Exchange, 7 Ab. Pr. (n. s.) 251; s. c. 38 How. Pr. 168; White vs. Brownell, 3 Ab. Pr. 318; 4 id. 162; Sewell vs. Ives, 61 How. Pr. 54; Rorke vs. Russell, 2 Lans. (N. Y.) 215; Commercial Tel. Co. vs. Smith, 47 Hun, 494; Weston vs. Ives, 97 N. Y. 222; Kuhnmundt vs. Smith, 2 N. Y. Supp. 625; Belton vs. Hatch, 109 N. Y. 593; Haight vs. Dickerman, 18 N. Y. Supp. 559. As to the New York Consolidated Stock and Petroleum Exchange, see 50 Hun, 166, aff'd 121 N.Y. 284. Suit may be brought by the latter Exchange in the name of its president. Wilson vs. Commercial Tel. Co., 3 N. Y. Supp. 633. And a local assembly (an unincorporated body) of the Knights of Labor, may sue in the name of its treasurer (Code Civ. Pro. § 1919). Wicks vs. Monihan, 54 Hun, 616.

[2] In the case of Sewell vs. Ives, 61 How. Pr. 54, the question was directly raised, and the form of the action against the President of the Stock Exchange sustained, under

In the case of Rorke vs. Russell, above referred to,[1] it was held, by Mr. Justice Ingraham, that where an injunction was issued and served on the defendant, in an action against the president of an association which purported to restrain him "as president" of the association, "its officers and members," the associates to whom the service was made known, and the summons, complaint, and order were read, at a meeting of the association, by its officers acting thereat, were amenable for contempt in taking proceedings contrary to the prohibitions of the injunction.

The New York statute further provides that after judgment shall be obtained against any joint-stock company or association, and execution thereon shall be returned unsatisfied in whole or in part, suits may be brought against any or all of the shareholders or associates, individually ; but no more than one suit shall be brought or maintained against

the aforementioned act. See also Olery vs. Brown, 51 How. Pr. (N. Y.) 92. It is immaterial by what name the chief executive officer is called, whether president, or chairman or otherwise. Hathaway vs. Am. Min. St. Ex., 31 Hun, 575. For cases interpreting § 1919, N. Y. Code Civ. Pro., see cases cited in the notes to that section, 2 Bliss's 5th ed. Code Civ. Pro. Also Stover's, 6th ed., and the cases cited in Birdseye's Rev. Statutes, Codes and Gen. Laws of N. Y., vol. 2, pp. 1953, 1954. For other cases, interpreting the statutes of 1849 and 1851, see Schmidt vs. Gunther, 5 Daly, 452. Also cases cited in note to Ebbinghousen vs. Worth Club, 4 Ab. New Cas. 311; Tibbetts vs. Blood, 21 Barb. 650; De Witt vs. Chandler, 11 Ab. Pr. 459; Bridenbecker vs. Hoard, 23 How. Pr. (N. Y.) 289; Austin vs. Searing, 16 N. Y. 112; Masterson vs. Botts, 4 Ab. Pr. Rep. 130; N. Y. Marbled Iron Works vs. Smith, 4 Duer (N. Y.), 362; East River Bank vs. Judah, 10 How. Pr. 135; Leonardville Bank vs. Willard, 25 N. Y. 574; People vs. Olmsted, 45 Barb. 644, 647. In providing by sec. 1919 of the Code that actions and proceedings may be brought by or against such associations, it would be a forced construction to hold that legal process of every kind (such as mandamus) available against public or private individuals and corporations may be levelled against unincorporated associations. Weidenfeld v. Keppler, 84 A. D. 235; aff'd 68 N. E. 1125.

[1] 2 Lans. (N. Y.) Rep. 245.

said shareholders at any one time, nor until the same shall have been determined, and execution issued and returned unsatisfied, in whole or in part.[1]

The effect of these statutes permitting an unincorporated association to sue and to be sued in the name of one or more of its officers, has been to remove another great objection to such organizations, and to make them equal in dignity and efficacy to corporations.

In Pennsylvania the first case which seems to have arisen, involving a question between the Philadelphia Stock Exchange and its members, was that of Leech vs. Harris.[2] There a bill was filed to prevent the plaintiff from being suspended as a member of the Exchange. In that case a committee of the Exchange was appointed by the president to investigate a certain claim against the plaintiff. Apprehending that the committee would suspend him, the plaintiff asked for an injunction. The action was brought against the members of the committee as a "Committee and Members of the Board of Brokers," and no objection seems to have been taken to this form of the action, the injunction being granted preventing the plaintiff's expulsion.

In another case[3] the action was brought against the "Treasurer of the Board of Brokers and the Philadelphia Board of Brokers;" and in a previous case, Leech vs. Leech,[4] "the Board of Brokers" were made garnishees.

---

[1] Laws, 1849, ch. 258, § 4, as amended, L. 1853, ch. 153, and since the text was written embodied in §§ 1922, 1923, N. Y. Code Civ. Pro. See Humbert vs. Abeel, 7 Civ. Proc. R. 417.

[2] 2 Brews.(Pa.) 571.

[3] Singerly vs. Johnson, 3 Weekly Notes Cas. (Pa.) 541, 542, and see Leech vs. Leech, id. 512, where a suit was brought against "The Board of Brokers," garnishees. Also Evans vs. Wister, infra.

[4] Id. 542, note.

So in the case of Moxey's Appeal, decided by the Supreme Court of Pennsylvania in January, 1881,[1] where the action was, in equity, to restrain defendants, *inter alia*, from interfering with plaintiff's right and privilege of using his seat in the board, the bill was filed against " The Philadelphia Stock Exchange, A. B., president thereof." [2]

In view of these authorities, there would seem to be no difficulty, in the State of Pennsylvania, in maintaining an action against the Exchange as a body, without joining the individual members.[3]

[1] 9 Weekly Notes Cas. 441, aff'g 37 Legal Int. 82.

[2] See also Evans vs. Wister, 1 Weekly Notes Cas. 181. In Pancoast vs. Gowen, 93 Pa. 66, an attachment execution was sought against Henry Gowen and others trading as the Philadelphia Stock Exchange, garnishees, and no objection was made to the form of the proceeding. In Cochran vs. Adams, 180 Pa. St. 489, certain officers of the Philadelphia Stock Exchange were sued without objection being raised as copartners trading as the Philadelphia Stock Exchange. The action, however, was not to charge them as partners but to reach a particular fund in their official custody. See also Sheppard vs. Barrett, 17 Phil. 145. In Liederkranz Singing Society vs. Turn-Verein, 163 Pa. St. 265, followed in Powell vs. Dunn, 7 Pa. Dist. R. 275, it was held that in the case of unincorporated associations whose membership is large, suit may be brought by some of the members on behalf of all, but if the action is brought in the name of the association by certain of its members, the plaintiff cannot be nonsuited for want of parties, when there is no plea in abatement, and the plaintiffs are responsible for costs. This case was also followed in Sparks vs. Husted, 5 Pa. D. R. 189; Virtue vs. Ioka, id. 634. But an action at law is not maintainable against an unincorporated beneficial society. McDonnell vs. Trustees, 24 Pa. C. C. 40. And it is still the law in Pennsylvania that an unincorporated association cannot be sued as such. McConnell vs. Apollo, 146 Pa. St. 79.

[3] See ante. p. 41, n. 1, for statutes of Pennsylvania relating to suits against unincorporated joint-stock associations. By P. L. 1890, p. 353, service on unincorporated associations for business purposes may be made on any officer. And by P. L. 1901, p. 614, service on limited partnerships, etc., may be made on any officer or agent. See Camden vs. Guarantors, 35 A. 796. In the case of Kurz vs. Eggert (9 Weekly Notes Cas. 126), the plaintiff brought an action of assumpsit against the

There seems to be no statute in Massachusetts providing for the bringing of actions by or against voluntary associations, in the name of their officers or otherwise. Nor are there any laws declaring the status or regulating the management of such bodies. But such associations have been recognized as legal, and suits have been brought against, and in the name of, their trustees. But the actions were brought in respect to contracts made with trustees, by name, and their successors, of such associations.[1]

Under the General Statutes of Connecticut actions and suits may be brought by and against voluntary associations as such, and judgment may be had and execution issued against them.[2] It has been held that such an association may compromise a suit brought against it.[3] Formerly it could not be sued by a member.[4] But, by section 588

---

president, a trustee, and the treasurer of The Augusta Teutonia Lodge, No. 34 Deutsche Order of Hamgari, an unincorporated beneficial association, to recover the amount to be paid during the sickness of plaintiff. The defendant demurred, on the ground that plaintiff could not maintain an action at law against the officers of the association. The court held that, notwithstanding the act of April 28, 1876 (P. L. 53, Purd. Dig. 1981), declaring that such benefits shall be paid from the treasury only, such associations still continue to be partnerships, and that the action was improperly brought. See also Rivers vs. Fame, 11 C. C. 241; Manning vs. Klein, 11 C. C. 525.

[1] Merrill vs. McIntyre, 13 Gray, 157; Baxter vs. McIntyre, 13 Gray, 168; Delano vs. Wild, 6 Allen, 1.

See also Edwards vs. Warren, 168 Mass. 564. In a case in California (Rorke vs. San Francisco Stock Exchange Board, 99 Cal. 196) the plaintiff sought by mandamus to compel his restoration to membership in the defendant, an unincorporated voluntary association. No objection appears to have been made to the form of remedy. But in a prior case in that State it was held that the Exchange could not be sued by its common name under the Code Civ. Proc. § 388, as it was not engaged in any business. Swifts vs. S. F. S. & E. Board, 67 Cal. 567.

[2] Gen. Stat. Conn. Rev. of 1902, § 588.

[3] Ancient Order of Foresters vs. Court Abraham Lincoln, 40 A. 606.

[4] Huth vs. Humboldt, 61 Conn. 227, contra McCabe vs. Goodfellow, 61 Hun, 619.

of the General Statutes (Revision of 1902), a member may sue the association, which may also sue a member.

It is optional with a creditor of such an association to sue the association as such, in which case he can only levy on its property ; or to sue the members, in which case the members are individually liable.[1] Under section 573 of the General Statutes, service of process in actions against voluntary associations may be made upon the presiding officer, secretary or treasurer.

In Colorado two or more persons associated in business under a common name may be sued by such name.[2] An unincorporated association may, under this section, be sued by the name under which it did business.[3]

And a similar statute has been enacted in Minnesota.[4]

In Kentucky an association consisting of over 3,000 members will, under the Constitution and statutory enactment, be treated as a corporation for the purpose of process.[5]

In Texas suit may brought by an unincorporated society by its name, if the petition describes it as a voluntary association composed of certain named persons as plaintiffs, and there is no allegation of incorporation.[6]

In Ohio a few individuals may sue or be sued as representatives of a class.[7]

In Illinois a voluntary association may be sued in equity

[1] Davison vs. Holden, 55 Conn. 103.

[2] Code, § 14.

[3] Endowment Rank (Knights of Pythias), 53 P. (Col.) 285.

[4] Gen. St. 1878, ch. 66, § 42; Gale vs. Townsend, 45 Minn. 357. See as to this subject generally, American Digest (Century ed.), vol. 4, p. 2536 et seq., and Annuals.

[5] Adams Express Co. vs. Schofield, 64 S. W. (Ky.) 903. But see 48 S. W. (Ky.) 1091.

[6] Ackerman vs. Ackerman, 60 S. W. (Tex.) 366.

[7] American Steel & Wire Co. vs. Wire Drawer's Unions, 90 Fed. 598.

as such if it is a *de facto* corporation, viz., if it has an organization consisting of directors, president, secretary and other officers, if its name implies a corporation, and if it exercises corporate powers. When its members are numerous, service of process upon a part, who act for other members as well as themselves, is sufficient. If the members are scattered all over the United States and Canada, service on the secretary will suffice,[1] but in a common-law action all the members, however numerous, must join.[2]

In Missouri a judgment cannot be rendered in favor of or against an unincorporated association as such.[3]

A statute similar to the New York statute was enacted in Michigan in 1897 (Comp. L. § § 10,025-6). But the statute does not take away the right to sue the members individually.[4] This statute is constitutional.[5]

In Georgia an objection that all the beneficiaries of a voluntary association should be parties to a suit against it, must be taken by special, and not by general, demurrer.[6]

There is another class of cases which should be referred to in this connection, viz., where instruments are given to unincorporated associations whereby money is secured and made payable to some officer of the company and his "*successors in office.*" A number of the English cases hold that effect cannot be given to such an instrument, it being an attempt to provide for payment to official successors ; that it is in law constituting the officer a corporation sole, which

[1] Fitzpatrick vs. Rutter, 160 Ill. 282.

[2] O'Connell vs. Lamb, 63 Ill. App. 652.

[3] Hajek vs. Bohemian Society, 66 Mo. App. 568.

[4] Jenkinson vs. Wysner, 83 N. W. 1012.

[5] United States Co. vs. Union, 88 N. W. (Mich.) 889.

[6] Plant vs. Dickerson, 45 S. E. (Ga.) 483.

cannot be done by agreement, but must be done by the crown.[1]

In such a case it would seem that the right of action at common law (unless affected by statute) on a contract made with several persons jointly passes on the death of each to the survivors, and, on the death of the last, to his representatives.[2]

In the United States, however, the law, in some of the States, is different; and it is held that the right to sue exists in the subsequent incumbent of the office; at all events, where the engagement or undertaking is for the benefit of some public or *quasi*-public body.[3]

There have been some decisions, as to the effect of the recovery of a judgment against these non-incorporated associations, which it may not be amiss to refer to in this connection.

Where a judgment is recovered against the president of an association for a debt owing by the latter, it does not preclude individual members, when sued for the same debt, from contesting their liability for the debts of the association.

A suit against the president is necessary, in the first instance, by the express terms of the statute, before an action against the members can be maintained; but the judgment therein is only so far effective as to reach the property

[1] Dance vs. Girdler, 4 B. & P. 40; Strange vs. Lee, 3 East, 484; Graves vs. Colby, per Lord Denman, 9 Ad. & E. 356; Metcalf vs. Bruin, 12 East, 400; also, 2 Camp. 422; Pigott vs. Thompson, 3 B. & P. 147; but see this latter case explained in Bowen vs. Morris, 2 Taunt. 381; Hybart vs. Parker, 4 C. B. (n. s.) 209; Gray vs. Pearson, 5 L. R. C. P. 568; Evans vs. Hooper, L. R. 1 Q. B. D. 45; Howley vs. Knight, 14 Q. B. 240.

[2] Dicey on Parties, 128.

[3] Fishe vs. Ellis, 20 Mass. 532; Kean vs. Franklin, 5 Serg. & R. 154; Commonw. vs. Shurman's Adm., 18 Pa. St. (6 Har.) 347.

owned by the association ; when it fails to secure satisfaction of the debt, then an action against the associates
directly to enforce the payment of the debt out of their
own individual property is proper.[1]

At most, a judgment against the president can be no more
than *prima facie* evidence in the plaintiff's favor in a subsequent action against the associates. It will not sustain
his right to recover, where the evidence shows that the
judgment so recovered exceeds the amount for which the
association or its members were liable in the action.[2]

The statutes of New York also provide that whenever the
property of a joint-stock association is represented by shares
of stock, such association may provide, by articles of association, that the death of any stockholder, or assignment of
his stock, shall not work a dissolution of the association ;
nor shall said company be dissolved, except by judgment of
a court, for fraud in its management, or other good cause to
such court shown, or in pursuance of its articles of association.[3]

Under this section it has been decided, in the State of
New York, that a dissolution of a joint-stock company is to
be conducted mainly according to the methods employed in

[1] This is changed by § 1923, N. Y.
Code Civ. Pro., and an action may
be maintained in the first instance
against all the members. Schwartz
vs. Wechler, 29 Abb. N. C. 332;
Hudson vs. Spalding, 6 N. Y. Supp.
877; Humbert vs. Abeel, 7 N. Y.
Civ. Pro. Rep. 417, opposing Flagg
vs. Swift, 25 Hun, 623, and distinguishing Witherhead vs. Allen, 4
Abb. Ct. App. 628. See also April
vs. Baird, 52 Supp. 973.

[2] Allen vs. Clark, 65 Barb. 563;
Witherhead vs. Allen, 4 Ab. (N. Y.),
App. 628, reversing 28 Barb. 661;
Kingsland vs. Braisted, 2 Lans. 17;
Robbins vs. Wells, 1 Robt. (N. Y.)
666. If the treasurer of a volun-
tary association gives a note as such,
he is not personally liable, but he
thereby binds all the members
Kierstead vs. Bennett, 93 Me. 328.

[3] Laws, 1854, ch. 245.

the case of insolvent corporations, and not according to those derived from the law of simple partnerships.[1]

The causes for which the courts will dissolve such bodies are either those for which a dissolution is specifically provided in the constitution, or, where that instrument is silent upon the subject, a dissolution will be decreed in the same cases as a corporation.[2]

This statute (Laws, 1854, ch. 245) was repealed by the Joint Stock Association Law (Laws of 1894, ch. 235), section 2 of which provides that the articles of a joint-stock association may (1) provide that the death of a stockholder, or the transfer of his shares, shall not work a dissolution of the association; (2) prescribe the number of its directors, not less than three, to have the sole management of its affairs; (3) contain any other provision for the management of its affairs not inconsistent with law. Section 5 provides that a joint-stock association shall not be dissolved except in pursuance of its articles of association, or by consent of all its stockholders, or by judgment of a court for fraud in its management, or for good cause shown.

It can scarcely be contended that the Joint-Stock Association Law would include unincorporated associations like

[1] Waterbury vs. Mer. Union Ex. Co., 50 Barb. 157, s. c., 3 Ab. Pr. (n. s.) 163.

[2] There are some reported cases where the courts have been asked to dissolve these unincorporated associations, and it might not be unprofitable to refer to a few of them in this connection.

Thus it has been held that in case of violent dissensions and irreconcilable differences between the members of a voluntary association judgment will be rendered at the suit of one or more members against all the others dissolving the society; but they should not be dissolved for slight causes, and, if at all, only when it is entirely apparent that the organization has ceased to answer the ends of its existence and no other mode of relief is attainable. Lafond vs. Deems, 1 Ab. New Cas. (N. Y.) 318; 81 N. Y. 507; Fischer vs. Raab, C. P., Sp. T., 51 How. Pr. 57.

the New York Stock Exchange within its purview, inasmuch as the definition of joint-stock associations could not, as has been already stated (*ante*, p. 37), be held to apply thereto, and as there are substantial changes made in the statute as re-enacted, the provision of the Statutory Construction Law, section 32, continuing a statute so re-enacted, would be scarcely applicable.[1] Besides, the seventh section of the Joint-Stock Association Law contains provisions as to increase or reduction of capital stock, etc., which clearly indicate the legislative intent to confine its operation to joint-stock associations, as such associations are usually understood, and not to unincorporated stock exchanges without capital stock, directors, articles of association, or terminable existence.

There is no provision in the constitution or by-laws of the New York Stock Exchange relative to its dissolution; and were the period to arrive when its dissolution should be asked for, the question would probably be determined either by a court of equity in an equitable action to compel its dissolution or, if they could be held applicable, by the statutes above referred to, together with such cases as have been decided under them.[2]

---

[1] McLoughlin vs. Erdlitz, 50 A. D. 518.

[2] Where the interests of the stockholders of an unincorporated business Exchange are so discordant as to prevent effective management, and a large majority of both trustees and members wish to wind up its affairs, dissolution and distribution of the assets among the stockholders will be beneficial to the interests of the stockholders, within section 2429, Code of Civil Procedure, providing that where a majority of the trustees favor dissolution, and it appears that a dissolution will be beneficial to the interests of the stockholders, . . . the court must make a final order dissolving the corporation. Under such circumstances it is better for all that a dissolution should be ordered, so that a majority may reincorporate upon some more practical basis, if they so desire, and the majority may no longer be

Under the present laws of the Stock Exchange of New
York, there would appear to be little difficulty in dividing
its property if a dissolution were to take place.   By dividing
the property by the number of seats, the result would clearly
appear.   But as there has arisen considerable dispute upon
the dissolution of voluntary societies, a number of cases are
collected in the notes which show upon what principle and
by what methods the court directs a distribution in those instances where the regulations or laws of the associations
have left the matter unsettled or in doubt.[1]

forced to keep up a feeble and useless organization, in which they
take no interest, and from which
they derive no benefit.   In re Importers & Grocers' Exchange of
New York, 132 N. Y. 212; 8 N. Y.
Supp. 319, affirmed.

[1] In Brown vs. Dale, 27 W. R.
149, in the chancery division of the
English Court, the Master of the
Rolls held that where a voluntary
society has a fund—in this case
arising on the sale of some of their
real property—there being no rule of
the society nor any express obligation to the contrary, the members,
at a given time, were entitled to
divide the fund among themselves;
hence, that new members coming in
after such a determination, though
before actual division, could not
share, nor insist that the fund be
invested and only income divided.

A minority have the right to enjoin the majority from distributing
the funds among the members in a
manner different from that provided
by the constitution without a vote,
according to the constitution, to
make the necessary alteration.   So

held in the case of a benefit society,
although for fifty years there had
never been a call for relief upon the
society pursuant to its articles, and
the fund was the accumulation of
voluntary assessments, all made
more than forty years before the
suit.   Torrey vs. Baker, 83 Mass.
120.

Where a sale and distribution of
the property in a certain period is
positively provided for by private
articles of association, any of the
shareholders have a right to insist
upon the sale and distribution according to the articles, though it
may not be for the interests of the
concern, or may be against the will
of the majority.   Mann vs. Bulter, 2
Barb. Ch. 362.

A club formed for the purpose of
relieving its members from draft,
provided that the sum of $300
should be paid to every member
who should volunteer or put in a
substitute.   The funds of the association were paid by its treasurer to
the defendants, who were not members, upon the agreement that they
would fill the quota of the whole

VIII. Rules and Regulations of Stock Exchanges.

(a) *General Power to Make Rules, etc.*

By the 13th Article of the constitution of the New York

township. The plaintiff, a member of the club, was drafted, and put in a substitute. Held that the fund passed to the defendants, covered with a trust to pay it according to the terms of the subscription; that they stood in the position of the club; and that the plaintiff was entitled to his share of the fund. Foley vs. Tovey, 54 Pa. St. 190. And where the majority of the members of a lodge withdraw and form a new lodge under the old name, the minority who remain are entitled to the property of the old lodge. Altman vs. Benz, 27 N. J. Eq. 331.

Divers persons subscribed various sums to assist an unincorporated musical association to erect a building for their use as a band. Held that these subscriptions were absolute gifts to the members of the association, and that the building erected by means of them and of funds otherwise obtained was owned by the members as tenants in common. Higgins vs. Riddell, 12 Wis. 587.

An agreement under seal that "we, the owners in the R farm, hereby agree to any division of the remaining portion of said farm unsold, which a majority of interest in said property shall decide upon as fair and equitable," held to refer to the mode of division, and not to authorize the majority in interest to set off to any owner a certain portion of land without his assent.

Harkness vs. Remington, 7 R. I. 154.

An association was formed for the purpose of obtaining gold in California. By the articles each agreed to pay $25 to furnish an outfit for, and to pay the expenses of, eight of their number, to be elected by the members to go to California and labor for the association in procuring gold; and that from the products of their labor their expenses should be first paid, and of the residue one half should be divided among the eight and the remainder among all the members. The eight, on arriving in California, sold their outfits, divided the proceeds, and each one took his own way. One of the eight returned to Ohio, and a bill was filed to compel him to account. Held that the eight members of the associations stood in relation thereto in the character of employés, and that their acts, on arriving in California, did not discharge them from any of their obligations to it. Eagle vs. Bucher, 6 Ohio St. 295.

B was a member of the "Cheshire Company," and A and B advanced $500 each, which was paid by B as his contribution thereto, with the agreement that they should share in certain proportions the profits of the enterprise, and that the directors of the company might retain A's share as his attorneys. B sold his interest therein at an advance of $1,000 before the company

Stock Exchange,[1] every person elected to membership, is required, before he shall be admitted to the privileges thereof, to sign the constitution and by-laws, and by such signature pledge himself to abide by the same, and all amendments thereto.

The general effect of a rule like the above will be first considered, and afterwards reference will be made to such particular rules as are important, or have been made the subject of legal interpretation.

realized any profits to the other members. Held that A was entitled to receive his stipulated portion of that advance as profits. Richardson vs. Dickinson, 26 N. H. (6 Fost.) 217.

A, the owner of a share of the outfit of a California gold company, sold to B "one half of his interest in the company;" but the writing provided that B should not be a partner in the company, but only "purchaser of A's interest in the metals and ores" that might be obtained. Held that B acquired no interest in the outfit. Phillips vs. Jones, 20 Mo. 67.

The defendants, owners of mineral lands, entered into a written agreement with the plaintiff, reciting their intention either to sell the lands or to form a joint-stock company for the working of the mines thereon; and promising, in consideration of services rendered and to be rendered by the plaintiff, to pay to him a certain sum out of the proceeds of the sale of the lands, if the same should be sold, or, if they should not be sold, and a company should be formed for working the mines, then to convey to him stock to that amount; and the plaintiff, on his part, agreed, in consideration of the foregoing agreements, to remain in their service as long as they might require, not exceeding one year, for a fixed salary and a house and land free of rent. Held that the defendants were not bound to sell the land, nor to form a joint-stock company, until by using reasonable efforts it should be for the mutual interest of all the parties concerned; and where, without negligence on their part, they had failed to do so, although more than seven years had elapsed, that the plaintiff has no claim upon them in equity, except for the stipulated salary. Pinch vs. Anthony, 10 Allen (Mass.) 470. Where the members unanimously agree to incorporate, the association is thereby dissolved, and the members' rights transferred to the corporation. Red Polled Club vs. Red Polled Club, 78 N. W. (Iowa) 803. The consent must be unanimous. Schiller vs. Jaennichen, 74 N. W. (Mich.) 458; Associate vs. Seminary, 49 Supp. 745. See also American Digest, vol. 4, p. 2541, and Annuals.

[1] As amended to April, 1903

It is well settled that before a member of an unincorporated association is bound by the constitution and by-laws of a society, it must appear that he personally assented to the same.[1] This assent, however, need not necessarily be based upon an actual signing of the by-laws or rules, but it may be inferred or presumed from the circumstances of each case, and especially from the fact of admission and acting as a member.[2] And it seems that where an association, through a committee or otherwise, seeks to suspend or expel a member for acts not provided for in the by-laws or constitution, or by an *ex post facto* resolution, the courts will interfere by injunction to prevent the same.[3] So a member of a Stock Exchange is bound by a by-law passed while he is a member, whether he votes for it or not.[4]

As to the limit and extent of the rules which such an organization can adopt, it appears to be established that its members possess the right to make such regulations for the government of the body as they may deem proper, providing that they contain nothing unreasonable[5] or against

[1] Austin vs. Searing, 16 N. Y. 112; Heath vs. Prest. Gold Exchange, 7 Ab. Pr. (n. s.) 251. By-laws are of equal obligation with the constitution. Jackson vs. South Omaha Live Stock Exchange, 49 Neb. 687.

[2] Innes vs. Wylie, 1 Car. & K. 262; Brancker vs. Roberts, 7 Jur. (n. s.) 1185; Hopkinson vs. Marquis of Exeter, 5 L. R. Eq. 63; Inhabitants of Palmyra vs. Morton, 25 Mo. 593; White vs. Brownell, 4 Ab. Pr. (n. s.) 162, 193.

[3] Per Ingraham, J., Rorke vs. Russell, 2 Lans. (N. Y.) Rep. 244, 248. And courts will not be bound by a determination of an Exchange ultra their rules, or where the latter conflict with the established principles of law. Commercial Telegram Co. vs. Smith, 47 Hun, 494–505.

[4] MacDowell vs. Ackley, 8 Week. Notes Cas. 464.

[5] No member is bound by a by-law which is unreasonable and which he does not consent to. Hibernia Fire Eng. Co. vs. The Commonw., 8 Week. Notes Cas. (Pa.) 320; id., April 21, 1880, 521; Dunham vs. Trustees of Rachael, 5 Cow. 462; People vs. Med. Soc. of Erie, 24 Barb. 570. By-laws must be reasonable. Albers vs. Mer-

the law of the land, which, of course, includes anything immoral or against public policy ; and that, with these necessary limitations, their rules will be obligatory upon each member assenting thereto.[1]

"It follows, from the very nature of such an organization," says the court, in White vs. Brownell, "with such objects, intents, and purposes, that there must be rules and regulations for the good order of the association ; and such rules should be held to be conclusive as to the mode of transacting

chants' Exchange, 138 Mo. 140; American Live Stock Co. vs. Chicago Live Stock Exchange, 143 Ill. 210. A rule of the Chicago Board of Trade subjecting to expulsion a member who shall knowingly execute an order for firms or organizations dealing in differences, is not unreasonable or against public policy. Board of Trade vs. Riordan, 94 Ill. App. 298. The principle stated in the text applies to all voluntary associations whether incorporated or not. American Live Stock Co. vs. Chicago Live Stock Exchange, 143 Ill. 210, supra.

[1] White vs. Brownell, 4 Ab. Pr. (n. s.) 162, 193; Haight vs. Dickerman, 18 N.Y. Supp. 559; Belton vs. Hatch, 109 N. Y. 593; Weston vs. Ives, 97 N. Y. 222; Lewis vs. Wilson, 121 N. Y. 284; People ex rel. Johnson vs. N. Y. Produce Exchange, 149 N.Y. 401; In re Haebler vs. N. Y. Produce Exchange, 149 N. Y. 414; Goddard vs. Merchants' Exchange, 9 Mo. App. 290, aff'd 78 Mo. 609; Albers vs. Merchants' Exchange, 138 Mo. App. 161; People ex rel. McIlhany vs. Chicago Live Stock Exchange, 170 Ill. 556; American Live Stock Com-

mission Co. vs. Chicago Live Stock Exchange, 143 Ill. 210; Green vs. Board of Trade, 174 Ill. 585; Farmer vs. Board of Trade, 78 Mo. App. 557; Lehman vs. Feld, 97 Fed. 852; Com. Tel. Co. vs. Smith, 47 Hun, 494, 505; Hyde vs. Woods, 2 Sawy. 665, per Sawyer, J.; affirmed, 94 U. S. Rep. 528; Leech vs. Harris, 2 Brews. (Pa.) 571; Singerly vs. Johnson, 3 Week. Notes Cas. (Pa.) 541; Leech vs. Leech, id. 542, note; Evans vs. Wister, 1 Week. Notes Cas. 181; Thompson vs. Adams, 7 id. 281; Ang. & Ames on Corp. (10th ed.) § 332-335; Moxey's Appeal, 9 Week. Notes Cas. 441, aff'g 37 Leg. Int. 82; Hibernia Fire Eng. Co. vs. The Commonw., 8 Week. Notes Cas. 320; id. April 21, 1880, 521; People vs. Board of Trade, 80 Ill. 134; but see this case questioned by the Supreme Ct. of Wisconsin in State ex rel. Cuppel vs. Milwaukee Chamber of Comm., 47 Wis. 670. See also Baxter vs. Board of Trade of Chicago, 83 Ill. 146; Sturges vs. Board of Trade, 86 Ill. 441; Commw. vs. St. Patrick's Benev. Soc., 2 Binn. (Pa.) 442; The Butchers' Beneficial Assoc., 35 Pa. St. (11 Casey) 151.

business between the members, and as to the privilege of admission to and continued enjoyment of membership." [1]

The provisions of the constitution and by-laws of the association are obligatory upon the members as a contract.[2] They express the contract by which each member has consented to be bound, and measure his duties, rights, and obligations as such. Whatever are the rights acquired by a member and created by his admission to membership, the rules by which the membership is created or dissolved and which control the affairs of the organization and the relations of members, entered into those rights when created and remained a part of them. This condition is self-imposed.[3]

No person can insist upon remaining a member and at the same time refuse compliance with its rules.[4]

But, in passing upon questions involving the propriety

[1] Per Van Vorst, J., White vs. Brownell, 3 Ab. Pr. (n. s.) 318, 326. In Dillard vs. Paton, 19 Fed. Rep. 619, at p. 624, the court said: "It cannot be denied that merchants may voluntarily associate together, and prescribe for themselves regulations to establish, define and control the usages or customs that shall prevail in their dealings with each other. These are useful institutions, and the courts recognize their value and enforce their rules whenever parties deal under them, in which case the regulations become undoubtedly a part of the contract." See 20 Am. L. Rev. (1886), p. 17, where the validity of by-laws in relation to option dealings is discussed.

[2] Weston vs. Ives, 97 N. Y. 222; In re Haebler vs. N. Y. Produce Exchange, 149 N. Y. 414; Russell vs. N. Y. Produce Exchange, 58 N. Y. Supp. 842. When the members make a contract subject to the rules of the Exchange (in this case the Union Merchants' Exchange of St. Louis) the rules become part of the contract. Bassett vs. Irons, 8 Mo. App. 127. But not if a rule of the Exchange (the Memphis Cotton Exc.) is habitually violated by the contracting members. Dillard vs. Paton, 19 Fed. 619. If a rule of the Board of Trade is changed before the completion of the contract, the latter is nevertheless governed by the rule as it existed when the contract was made. Hess vs. Warren, 15 Ill. App. 596.

[3] Belton vs. Hatch, 109 N. Y. 593; Haight vs. Dickerman, 18 N. Y. Supp. 559.

[4] Lewis vs. Wilson, 121 N. Y. 284.

and legality of their rules, where there is the slightest property interest involved,[1] the courts will apply the same rule which is used in the case of corporate bodies.

In Leech vs. Harris[2] the court said : " I have very little doubt, therefore, that the same rules of law and equity, so far as regards the control of them, and the adjudication of their reserved and inherent powers to regulate the conduct and to expel their members, apply to them as to corporations and joint-stock companies."

In the case of The People ex rel. Page vs. The Board of Trade of Chicago[3] the charter conferred upon the defendants the right to admit or expel such persons as they might see fit, in manner to be prescribed by the rules, regulations, or by-laws thereof ; but the court held that this language only conferred upon the defendants the power to admit or expel for some just or reasonable cause. This must now be regarded as the settled law of Illinois, the cases in that State[4] indicating a contrary doctrine, the reasoning of which was criticized in the first edition of this work[5] having been, after some contrariety of opinion, distinguished and in effect overruled in the case of Ryan vs. Cudahy,[6] where the court said : "Expressions may be found

---

[1] See, as to distinction between unincorporated associations possessing property, and those instituted for mere social enjoyment or benefit, State vs. Ga. Med. Soc., 38 Ga. 608; People vs. Med. Soc. of Erie, 24 Barb. 577. See Board of Trade vs. Riordan, 94 Ill. App. 298.

[2] 2 Brews. (Pa.) 571–576.

[3] 45 Ill. 112.

[4] People ex rel. Rice vs. Board of Trade of Chicago, 80 Ill. 134; Fisher vs. Board of Trade of Chicago, 80 Ill. 85; Sturges vs. Same, 86 Ill. 441; Baxter vs. Same, 83 Ill. 146; Wright vs. Same, 15 Chic. L. News, 239; Pitcher vs. Same, 121 Ill. 412. See also Ryan vs. Lamson, 44 Ill. App. 204.

[5] pp. 35–38.

[6] 157 Ill. Rep. 108. See also Board of Trade vs. Nelson, 162 Ill. 431; Green vs. Board of Trade, 174 Ill. 585; State ex rel. Cuppel vs. Milwaukee Chamber of Commerce, 47 Wisc. 670; 3 N. W. 713; 21 Alb. L.

in the opinion of the court (referring to People ex rel.
Rice vs. Board of Trade),[1] which may bear the construction
that a court would not interfere in any case, with the action
of an organization like the Board of Trade, but those expressions were not necessary to a decision of the case, and cannot
be regarded as authority."[2] The court also said:[3] "Language may have been used in some of the cases cited, which
might, without a close examination of the questions involved
in the cases, lead to the conclusion reached by counsel
(viz., that a court of equity had no jurisdiction to interfere
with the action of the board of trade). But upon a careful consideration of the questions involved and decided in
each case, it will be found that the question presented by
this record did not arise in those cases, and was not before
the court." And the plaintiff was held entitled to an injunction restraining the Board of Trade from indorsing
its certificates of deposit made by plaintiff, to a contractor
of plaintiffs, on the ground that at a hearing before a committee, appointed by defendant, under one of its rules,
plaintiff was not allowed to produce evidence that the
market value of produce sold by him was no higher on the
day of delivery than when it was sold.

J. 23; Albers vs. Merchants Ex. of
St. Louis, 39 Mo. App. 583.

[1] 80 Ill. 134.

[2] 157 Ill. Rep. at p. 123. The
court had previously indicated its
adoption of the correct doctrine in
Live Stock Commission Co. vs.
Live Stock Exchange, 143 Ill. 210.
(See post, p. 64.) Here the objection that the rules were illegal was
urged by a non-member and the
court refused to interfere, because of
the non-membership of the complainant, saying, however, "If the
association, or a majority of its
members, pass by-laws which are
unreasonable, or contrary to law or
public policy and attempt to enforce them as against a dissenting or
controlling minority, such minority
may doubtless, in proper cases, appeal to the courts for relief against
their enforcement."

[3] At p. 123.

. The general rule now seems to be that the courts will in all cases interfere, by appropriate legal remedy, to prevent the expulsion or interference with a member's rights in an unincorporated association where the latter is acting under a by-law, rule, or regulation which is illegal, unreasonable, or contrary to public policy.[1]

In the case of Dawkins vs. Antrobus,[2] where the plaintiff sought to have the court review a resolution expelling him from a club, James, L. J., after referring to the observations of the Lords Commissioners in another case[3]—to the effect that shareholders, assembled at a meeting duly convened, were the judges of what was a reasonable cause for removing their directors ; and that although the court might inquire whether the meeting was regularly held, and in cases of fraud, clearly proved, might interfere with the acts done, still there was no jurisdiction, where no case of direct fraud was proved, to determine whether the decision

---

[1] White vs. Brownell, 4 Ab. Pr. (n. s.) 162, 193; People vs. Union, 118 N. Y. 100; Wachtel vs. Society, 84 N. Y. 28; Austin vs. Searing, 16 N. Y. 124; People vs. Society, 32 N. Y. 196; Belton vs. Hatch, 109 N. Y. 593; Haebler vs. Exchange, 149 N. Y. 421; Lonbat vs. Le Roy, 40 Hun, 549; Lewis vs. Wilson, 121 N. Y. 284; Fisher vs. Keane, L. R. 11 Ch. Div. 362; Sperry's Appeal, 116 Pa. St. 391; Savannah &c. Ex. vs. State, 54 Ga. 668; Connelly vs. Assn., 58 Conn. 552; Otto vs. Union, 75 Cal. 314; Huston vs. Ruethinger, 91 Ky. 333; Medical Society vs. Weatherly, 75 Ala. 252; Burlington vs. White, 41 Neb. 547; Zabriskie vs. Railroad, 18 N. J. Eq. 183; Hoeffner vs. Lodge, 41 Mo. App. 349; Glardon vs. Supreme Lodge, Knights of Pythias, 50 Mo. App. 45; Lysaght vs. Assn., 55 Mo. App. 547; Albers vs. Exchange, 138 Mo. 165; Ellerbe vs. Faust, 119 Mo. 653; Mulroy vs. Lodge, 28 Mo. App. 463; Ludowiski vs. Society, 29 Mo. App. 337; Am. L. Stock Co. vs. Exchange, 143 Ill. 210; Croak vs. High Court, 162 Ill. 298; Board of Trade vs. Nelson, 162 Ill. 438; State vs. Williams, 75 N. C. 135; Lawson vs. Hewell, 118 Cal. 618; Karcher vs. Lodge, 137 Mass. 371; Vaughn vs. Herndon, 91 Tenn. 68; Farmer vs. Board of Trade, 78 Mo. App. 557.

[2] L. R. 17 Ch. Div. 615.

[3] Inderwick vs. Snell, 2 Mac. & G. 221.

of the meeting had, or had not, been unduly influenced by
unfounded statements made by persons taking an active
part in the proceedings—said that he agreed with every
word of these observations, which were equally applicable
to the case of a club. . . . " *Unless it could be said that their
decision* was so grossly unfair and unreasonable, that it
could not have been arrived at unless from some malicious
motives, this court had no power to interfere." [1]

In State ex rel. Cuppel vs. Milwaukee Chamber of Commerce [2] the visitatorial power of courts over corporations was
examined. The relator had been suspended from membership of the defendant for refusing to pay a fine imposed by
its directors for violation of one of its rules. The rule in
question prohibited its members from " gathering in any public place in the vicinity of the Exchange room," and " forming a market " for the purpose of making any trade or contract for the future delivery of grain or provisions, before
the time fixed for opening the Exchange room for general
trading, or after the time fixed for closing the same, daily.
The charter authorized the corporation to make reasonable
rules for the regulation of its members. The rule in question was held to be reasonable, and not an unlawful restraint
upon trade, nor void for uncertainty ; and the relator having been fairly tried, upon due notice, and in accordance
with the rules of the corporation, and there being abundant
proof against him tending to show that he had committed
the offence charged, it was decided that he could not be
restored by mandamus.[3]

---

[1] See also, in this connection, Labouchere vs. Earl of Wharncliffe,
L. R. 13 Ch. Div. 346.

[2] 47 Wis. 670; 3 N. W. 760 (bottom paging); 21 Alb. L. J. 23.

[3] As to when a rule may be reasonable or unreasonable under circumstances, see Chicago vs. Tilton,
87 Ill. 517.

A non-member may not enjoin the operation of a by-law, or the posting of a notice prohibiting members from doing business for or with him on the ground that such by-law or notice violated public policy, as in restraint of trade.[1]

If it be admitted that such by-laws are so far in restraint of trade as to be invalid for that reason, still the position of the complainant is in no respect improved. By-laws or contracts in restraint of trade are illegal only in the sense that the law will not enforce them. They are simply void. The law does not prohibit the making of contracts in restraint of trade ; it merely declines, after they have been made, to recognize their validity.[2] A party to such contract is not bound to perform it, but he may perform it if he sees fit, and his doing so exposes him to no legal animadversion. If the by-laws in question are invalid because of being in improper restraint of trade, they are merely void, and the members of the Exchange, being under no obligation to obey them, may, perhaps, be entitled, at their own instance, to protection against such disciplinary consequences as the Exchange may see fit to impose in case of disobedience. But such protection cannot be invoked in their behalf by a stranger, nor can they be required to disobey such rules except at their own volition.[3]

---

[1] American Live Stock Commission Co. vs. Chicago Live Stock Exchange, 143 Ill. 210; Russell vs. New York Produce Exchange, 58 N. Y. Supp. 842.

[2] Mogul Steamboat Co. vs. McGregor, L. R. 23 Q. B. D. 598.

[3] In this connection the following quotation from Williams' Forensic Facts and Fallicies (Lond. 1885), 106, is interesting. "The rules of the Stock Exchange being the rules of a domestic forum, cannot affect persons who are neither members, nor the clients of members. Thus they cannot affect the rights of the general creditors of a defaulting member. A defaulting member, therefore, cannot voluntarily pay money to the official assignee to be distributed exclusively amongst those creditors whose claims arise

But the courts will issue a writ of *quo warranto*, to inquire into the enforcement of an illegal by-law of a corporation. Thus, in People ex rel. McIlhany vs. Chicago Live Stock Exchange,[1] it was said: "When a corporation is created there goes with it the power to enact by-laws for its government and guidance, as well as for the guidance and government of its members. . . . But (such) by-laws must be reasonable and for a corporate purpose. . . . They must not infringe the policy of the state nor be hostile to public welfare." Thus, men engaged in trade and commerce may advertise, employ solicitors, and offer rewards and inducements to secure trade without violating the law. A by-law, therefore, prohibiting such means, is unlawful, as hostile to public welfare, and in restraint of trade and commerce.[2]

And the courts, at the instance of the attorney general, will annul the charters of incorporated " Exchanges " organized by dealers in particular products, such as coal, milk and meat, where the purpose of the incorporation, and the effect and intent of the by-laws, is to control the prices of such products.[3] Indeed the members of such an " Exchange " may be indicted and convicted of the offence of criminal conspiracy to do an act injurious to trade or commerce.[4]

---

out of Stock Exchange transactions. And if it be urged that this is the rule of the Stock Exchange, the answer, as Lord Justice James said, is that the Stock Exchange is not an Alsatia; the Queen's laws are paramount there, and the Queen's writ runs even into the sacred precincts of Capel Court."

[1] 170 Ill. 556

[2] Cf. Matthews vs. Associated Press, 136 N. Y. 333; People ex rel. Pinckney vs. Fire Underwriters, 7 Hun, 248; Jackson vs. South Omaha Live Stock Exchange, 49 Neb. 687.

[3] People vs. Milk Exchange, 145 N. Y. 267; Ford vs. Chicago Milk Shippers' Assn., 27 L. R. A. 298.

[4] People vs. Sheldon, 139 N. Y. 251.

And when the constitution and by-laws of a corporation regulated the credit to be allowed to members; discriminated (in the price to be paid for produce) against non-members; controlled the delivery of goods; and provided a penalty by fine and suspension against offending and defaulting members, it was held, that such an organization was in restraint of trade, and a member who was suspended for violating such by-law might maintain an action for damages against the corporation and its members for the subsequent boycotting of his business.[1]

The visitorial or superintending power of the State over corporations created by the Legislature will alway be exercised in proper cases, through the medium of the courts of the State, to keep those corporations within the limits of their lawful powers, and to correct and punish abuses of their franchises. The power extends to the investigation of their proceedings for the purpose of protecting the rights of members against usurpation of the governing body to their prejudice.[2] To this end the courts will issue writs of *quo warranto*,[3] mandamus,[4] or injunction,[5] as the exigencies of the particular case may require; will inquire into the grievance complained of, and, if the same is found to exist,

[1] Ertz vs. Produce Exchange, 51 L. R. A. 825.

[2] People ex rel. Johnson vs. Produce Exchange, 149 N. Y. 401.

[3] Or permit the filing of an information in the nature of quo warranto.   People ex rel. McIlhany vs. Chicago Live Stock Exchange, 170 Ill. 556.   In New York an action by the attorney general for the annulment of the charter of the corporation may be maintained.   Code Civ. Pro. § 1798; People vs. Milk Exchange, 145 N. Y. 267, the writ of quo warranto and proceedings by information in the nature of quo warranto have been abolished.   Code Civ. Pro. § 1983.   See also Hopkins vs. U. S., 171 U. S. 578; Anderson vs. U. S., id. 604.

[4] People ex rel. Johnson vs. N. Y. Produce Exchange, 149 N. Y. 401; In re Haebler vs. N. Y. Produce Exchange, 149 N. Y. 414.

[5] Ryan vs. Cudahy, 157 Ill. 108.

will apply such remedy as the law prescribes. Every corporation of the State, whether public or private, civil or municipal, is subject to this superintending control, although, in its exercise, different rules may be applied to different classes of corporations.

Although, as we have shown, a Stock Exchange is not a corporation, yet it practically exercises the functions of one; and there seems to be no good reason why the courts should not be guided by the same principles, in interpreting their by-laws, as they apply in the case of corporations,[1] keeping in view, of course, the different objects and ends for which the incorporated and non-incorporated bodies may have been instituted. To confer upon an unincorporated association an unlimited power to make by-laws would be not

[1] This is the view expressed in Leech vs. Harris, 2 Brews. (Pa.) 571, by Mr. Justice Pierce, who said: "I have very little doubt, therefore, that the rules of law and equity, so far as regards the control of them, and the adjudication of their reserved and inherent powers to regulate the conduct and to expel the members, apply to them as to corporations and joint-stock companies." See also Otto vs. Journeymen Tailors' Protective Union, 75 Cal. 308; American Live Stock Co. vs. Chicago Live Stock Exchange, 143 Ill. 210; Waterbury vs. Mer. Union Exp. Co., 50 Barb. 160; Sandford vs. Supervisors of New York, 15 How. Pr. (N. Y.) 172; People ex rel. Platt vs. Wemple, 117 N. Y. 136; cf. People ex rel. Winchester vs. Coleman, 133 N. Y. 281. See note on judicial interposition in the affairs of a voluntary association. Loubat vs. Le Roy, 15 Abb. N. C. 44. In White vs. Brownell, however (4 Ab. Pr. [n. s.] 162), the court said: "*A member of a body of this description* (a Stock Exchange) *has, as such, undoubtedly rights which the law will protect;* but they do not rest upon the same ground, and are by no means coextensive with the franchise enjoyed by a member of a corporation. They depend upon the nature of the organization, upon the object for which it was formed, and upon the rules, regulations, constitution, or by-laws which are explanatory of its purpose, and which the body has adopted for its government." But the learned judge who delivered the opinion in that case expressly admitted that the rules of these voluntary associations must have "*nothing in them in conflict with the law of the land.*"

only to raise it above corporations which are supposed to have special franchises, but to endow it with legislative authority.[1]

The courts will never be bound by a determination of an Exchange, *ultra* its rules or by a determination in accordance with rules, which conflict with established principles of law.[2]

The utmost that these associations can claim, therefore, is the power to make rules and regulations for their internal government, which the courts will not pronounce oppressive or unreasonable; and, when their rules are brought into a court of justice, for construction, they must also submit to the test which is applied to the by-laws of incorporated bodies, and submit to have them declared as void, when they violate the Constitution or laws of the United States, or of the individual States where the associations exist, or the common law as it is generally accepted.[3]

And in the exercise of any reserved or inherent power to

---

[1] See Ang. & Ames on Corp. (11th ed.) § 591, note 5; Lindley on Part. (4th ed.) 5. See also ed. of 1893. In People ex rel. Platt vs. Wemple, 117 N. Y. at p. 144, it is pointed out (with numerous citations) that such associations, when formed without authority of parliament, were declared in England to be illegal and void and to be deemed a public nuisance (6 Geo. I. chap. 18, § 18), the statute in this respect, it is said, following the common law, and enforcing its rules by the imposition of penalties.

[2] Weston vs. Ives, 97 N. Y. 222, where it was held that no appropriation of the proceeds of a sale of a member's seat could be made, other than that which was provided by the rules and to which he has assented.

[3] Ang. & Ames on Corp. (11th ed.) § 332. But a by-law establishing a rule of contract differing from the common-law rule is not void, unless some principle or policy of the common law is violated. Goddard vs. Merchants Exchange, 9 Mo. App. 290, aff'd on opinion below, 78 Mo. 609. A rule requiring compulsory submission of property rights is illegal. Bank of Montreal vs. Wonte, 105 Ill. App. 373; Alton Co. vs. Norton, id. 385.

amend, alter, or repeal the by-laws they will be governed by the same general principles.

This is so with corporations. No private corporation may repeal a by-law so as to impair rights which have been given and are vested thereby.[1] Nor so as to destroy the contract rights of the members.[2] Subject to these limitations, the power to amend a by-law is inherent.[3] In the interpretation of by-laws the words are given their ordinary and popular meaning, *uti loquitur vulgus*, being made and enforced by men unlearned in the law.[4]

And the strict rules of criminal pleadings are not applicable to the proceedings of a Board of Trade for expulsion of a member for violation of one of its by-laws.[5]

By-laws must possess reasonable certainty in terms.[6]

---

[1] Kent vs. Quicksilver Mining Co., 78 N. Y. 159.

[2] Weston vs. Ives, 97 N. Y. 222; Parish vs. N. Y. Produce Exchange, 169 N. Y. 34. As to when an amendment of a by-law as to a gratuity fund does not impair the contract right, see McDowell vs. Ackley, 93 Pa. St. 277. See also Greer vs. Stoller, 77 Fed. Rep. 1.

[3] Parish vs. N. Y. Produce Exchange, 169 N. Y. 34. The adoption, by an unincorporated society, of a new constitution is illegal, and of no force where it has not been carried in accordance with the provisions of the existing constitution of the society. Hochreiter's App., 8 Week. Notes Cas. 461.

[4] Nelson vs. Board of Trade, 58 Ill. App. 399, rev'd on other grounds 162 Ill. 431.

[5] Board of Trade vs. Nelson, 162 Ill. 431.

[6] People ex rel. Johnson vs. N. Y. Produce Exchange, 149 N. Y. 401.

The following is an apt and amusing case illustrative of the rule that an association cannot pass any rule or by-law which is in violation of the principles of law. It was an indictment for assault and battery, the defendants justifying under a rule of a voluntary unincorporated society. The defendants and the prosecutrix were members of a benevolent society known as the "Good Samaritans," which society had certain rules and ceremonies known as the ceremonies of initiation and expulsion. The prosecutrix having been remiss in some of her obligations, and, when called upon to explain, having become violent, the defendant, with others, proceeded to perform the ceremony of expulsion, which consisted in suspending her

When a Commercial Exchange is empowered by its charter to regulate its members in the conduct of their business, a rule that members who were warehousemen should execute a bond to secure to shippers or members the proceeds of the sales of their property is valid, and such a bond is binding.[1]

(b) Power of Suspension and Expulsion.

One of the most important functions of an association or company, whether incorporated or unincorporated, is the power of suspension and expulsion from membership. As several of the Stock and Produce Exchanges in the United States have become incorporated, whilst others, like the New York Stock Exchange, remain unincorporated bodies, it is desirable to point out the distinction which exists between rights in a corporation and rights in an unincorporated association. In the former case, the member is in the enjoyment of a *franchise*, the right to which is not derived from the body, but is created by statute, or exists by prescription, and cannot be taken away by the act of the corporation, except authorized by its charter, or for the three

from the wall by means of a cord fastened around her waist.

This ceremony had been inflicted upon others, theretofore, in the presence of the prosecutrix. She resisted to the extent of her ability. The court, on appeal, held:

"When the prosecutrix refused to submit to the ceremony of expulsion established by this benevolent Society, it could not be lawfully inflicted. Rules of discipline for this and all voluntary associations must conform to the laws. If the act of tying this woman would have been a battery, had the parties concerned not been members of the "Society of Good Samaritans," it is not the less a battery because they were all members of that humane institution. The punishment inflicted upon the person of the prosecutrix was wilful, violent, and against her consent, and thus contained all the elements of a wanton breach of the peace." State vs. Williams, 75 N. C. 134.

[1] Warren vs. Louisville Exchange, 55 S. W. (Ky.) 912.

causes mentioned *supra* (pp. 74 and 75). But in the latter case the member has no rights of a higher dignity than those springing out of a voluntary contract between himself and his fellow members. Such contracts are upheld when they are not unreasonable or contrary to law or public policy, and the member may thereby voluntarily subject himself to summary expulsion for causes and in modes which would not be justified in the case of a chartered corporation.[1]

It seems to be reasonably well settled that, as unincorporated societies have the right to prescribe rules for the conduct of their business, they have the correlative power to enforce them ; and that for a violation of such rules, after a hearing in accordance with the methods prescribed in the constitution or rules, any offending member may be either suspended or expelled from membership, as the nature of act justifies.[2]

---

[1] Thompson's Commentaries on Corporations, § 846, and cases cited in footnotes. Some of the authorities seem to hold that in the case of moneyed corporations a member cannot be expelled unless the right has been conferred by statute, even for the three causes mentioned in the text. Angell & A. on Corp. (11th ed.) 410; Thompson's Com. on Corp. § 846, and cases cited in note 1. But the soundness of this doctrine may be questioned, as a member might, by continuous violation of his duty as an incorporator, ensure the destruction of the corporation, and the latter be powerless to prevent its enforced dissolution by his expulsion. But that he would be entitled to the amount of his stock and could recover it in an action against the corporation seems undoubted. Angell & Ames on Corp. §§ 410, 411, and cases cited.

For cases arising between corporations and their members as to the power to suspend or expel, see Ang. & Ames on Corps. (11th ed.) § 408 et seq.; Potter on Corps. § 721; Morawetz on Corp. (2d ed.) §§ 277, 493; Beach on Corp. §§ 97, 595; Speeling on Corp. § 523 et seq.; Thompson on Corp. § 799 et seq.; Cook on Corporations (4th ed.), §§ 11, 561, 710; American & English Ency. of Law (2d ed.), tits. "Amotion" and " Disfranchisement."

[2] Leech vs. Harris, 2 Brews. (Pa.) 571; White vs. Brownell, 4 Ab. Pr. (n. s.) 162, aff'g 3 id. 318; Belton vs. Hatch, 109 N. Y. 593; Lewis vs. Wilson, 121 N. Y. 284; Kuehne-

And unincorporated bodies have not only the right to
expel a member for a violation of their express rules, where
such a penalty is attached to the act, but such associations
equally with corporations have the inherent power to expel
their members, in the following cases, for certain acts,
although they may not be specifically mentioned in their
by-laws :

1. When an offence is committed, which has no immediate
relation to a member's corporate duty, but is of so infamous
a nature as to render him unfit for the society of honest men.
Such as the offences of perjury, forgery, etc.   But before an
expulsion is made for a cause of this kind, it is necessary
that there should be a previous conviction by a jury according to the law of the land.

2. When the offence is against his duty as a corporator ;
and, in that case, he may be expelled, on trial and conviction,
by the corporation.

3. When the offence is of a mixed nature, against the
member's duty as a corporator, and also indictable by the
law of the land.[1]

Upon this question of disfranchisement there is a well-
defined distinction between those bodies, corporated or unincorporated, where the members exercise a personal and
active supervision or duty, and in those commercial organ-

mundt vs. Smith, 2 N. Y. Supp.
625. In California it has been held
that a member may be also expelled
for conduct clearly violating the
fundamental objects of the association. Otto vs. Tailor's Union, 75
Cal. 308. When by the rules the
offense is punishable by fine only,
the association cannot expel the
member. Id.

[1] Leech vs. Harris, 2 Brews. (Pa.)
571; People ex rel. Thacher vs. N.
Y. Commercial Assn., 18 Abb. Pr.
271.   Expulsion is justified by
guilt of any act, which though not
expressly prohibited by the by-
laws, yet violates the fundamental
objects of the association.   Otto vs.
Tailors' Union, 75 Cal. 308.

izations instituted mainly for gain, where the members do
not actively participate in the management, but merely
hold certificates of stock, which are transferable by assignment and delivery, and which entitle each holder to a
proportionate share of the assets, profits, and earnings of
the company. In the former class the personal character
and conduct of the member may be of great importance,
and the rules stated above, respecting the power of expulsion, will rigidly apply ; but in the latter class the personal
character of the stockholder is of no particular concern ;
and, consequently, it seems to be settled, both by reason
and precedent, that, generally, a member cannot be dis-
franchised, and deprived of his rights in the corporate
property, for acts of misconduct disconnected with the corporate business.[1]

The rule that seems to be applied to all cases is that when a
member disqualifies himself from assisting in promoting the
object and purpose of the corporation, he forfeits his corporate franchise, and may thus justify a vote of expulsion ; but
even then, it seems, in a commercial joint-stock company,
the member would be entitled to the amount of his stock,
and could recover it in an action against the corporation.[2]

With this statement of the general rule, reference will now
specially be made to the cases which have arisen between
Stock and Produce Exchanges and their members relating
to the power of expulsion ; and, as the subject is comparatively a new one, we deem it better to set them out fully,

[1] Ang. & Ames on Corp. (11th law in 27 Albany L. J. 326; article
ed.) § 410; White vs. Brownell, 4 on conclusiveness of decisions of
Ab. Pr. (n. s.) 162-169. See also tribunals of associations or corpora-
Loubat vs. Le Roy, 15 Abb. N. C. tions, 49 L. R. A. 353; Neukirch
1, and valuable note appended vs. Keppler, 66 N. E. (N. Y.) 1112.
thereto at p. 44, and article on club [2] Ang. & Ames, §§ 410, 411.

that the views of the court may be thoroughly appreciated.

In the case of White vs. Brownell [1] a claim and matter of difference arose between the plaintiff, a member of the Open Board of Brokers, an unincorporated association, and C. M. & Co., also members, growing out of their rights and obligations under a contract for the purchase of certain railroad stock, agreed to be sold and delivered by plaintiff to said C. M. & Co. The contract was made at the board, and as members thereof. A dispute subsequently arose, and, after notice to plaintiff, C. M. &. Co. purchased a certain amount of the stock under the rules, but plaintiff refused to recognize the transaction or pay for the stock; and, in consequence thereof, C. M. & Co. made a claim against him for a large sum of money, being the amount of the difference in their favor. C. M. & Co. subsequently presented their claim to the Arbitration Committee, which, under the constitution of the board, had cognizance of all claims and matters of difference between members of the board, and its decision was declared binding. Under the constitution, an appeal would lie from the Arbitration Committee to the Board of Appeals. It was also provided in the by-laws that, as a means of mutual protection, it should be the duty of any member to report to the board all cases of defalcation of contracts of other members, and all cases of refusal or inability to pay differences, whereupon the president should declare the member so reported suspended. From such suspension the reported member might appeal, and demand a hearing before the Executive Committee. After the claim of C. M. & Co. had been pre-

[1] 3 Ab. Pr. (n. s.) 318.

sented to the Arbitration Committee, a day for hearing was appointed, and plaintiff duly summoned to appear and answer. The plaintiff declined to appear before the committee, whereupon the latter heard and determined the matter upon the statements of C. M. & Co., and rendered judgment to the Board of Appeals; and, after the time for appeal had elapsed, C. M. & Co. brought the matter to the notice of the Committee on Membership, which, after investigation, reported to the board that plaintiff was in default under his contract, whereupon the president, in accordance with his duty, declared the plaintiff suspended. The plaintiff thereupon appealed to the Executive Committee; but before that body had convened he brought an action praying that the president and board should be restrained and enjoined from interfering with him in the full exercise of his rights, etc., as a member of the board, alleging that the action of the respective committees was unjust, and insisting that his original contract with C. M. & Co. was still in force. The court refused to give the plaintiff any relief, and dissolved the preliminary injunction which had been granted, on the ground that, as all the proceedings had been conducted in accordance with the by-laws, which plaintiff had submitted to upon becoming a member, a court would not interfere where there was no claim that the terms of the constitution were hard and unconscionable. The court said: "The very existence of this body depends upon the faithful observance of its organic law by all its members. The court must regard the constitution and laws of this board as the contract by which all the members are bound. The court cannot make any other contract for the parties than they have solemnly made for themselves. It is not the province of courts of law to make contracts for parties. It may explain, interpret, enforce, and in some instances, where contracts are hard and unconscionable, relieve from them. But there is no claim in this suit that the terms of this constitution adopted by the plaintiff are hard and unconscionable. The plaintiff does not ask to be relieved from his membership, he rather demands that he may be allowed to remain in the association, under the constitution; he does not wish to be suspended, or have his connection determined and ended. In an organization of the character of the Open Board of Brokers, with its several hundred members, the business transacted at its rooms being daily large in amount, and the stocks and securities dealt in being ever fluctuating in value, it was not unreasonable to apprehend that there would be constantly occurring differences between members acting as agents for others, in regard to the terms of contracts and as to the obligations and duties of contracting parties, under agreements often hastily made. The temptation to avoid a contract in a rapidly rising or falling market, as the pecuniary interest of a party might prompt, rendered it imperative that some tribunal in the body of the association should be appointed, and agreed upon, to take cognizance of, and exercise jurisdiction over, all claims and matters of difference which might arise between members of the board. This appears the more important, as confidence in each other and in the engagements which they might make one with the other, and in the fairness, openness, and uprightness of their transactions, and in the certainty that their engagements would be fulfilled, are announced as the causes which led to the organization. To be effective, their decisions should be prompt. As these engagements would be constantly maturing, it was eminently proper that a tribunal should be near to render speedy and exact justice.

Confidence in the real life of such engagements; hence the appointment of a Committee of Arbitration is a prominent feature in the constitution of this board ; and, by the express assent of each member, jurisdiction is awarded to this committee *in advance* of all claims and matters of difference which might arise between the members. . . . The plaintiff agreed, when he became a member, that the Arbitration Committee should take notice of all claims and differences between members, and that he would be bound by its decision. He refused either to acknowledge its conclusive force in a case in which he was interested, or to appeal from its decision. The constitution must be taken as a whole. The contracting part is an entirety. All its obligations are to be assumed and discharged ; all its benefits are to be enjoyed. The enjoyment of the latter depends upon the performance of the former. Were it otherwise, the association would be of no real advantage to its members. It clearly appears that good faith in the observance of the constitutional obligations of the members was intended to furnish a test for the right of continued membership."

" There was some discussion on the argument of this motion as to the right of the plaintiff to revoke his consent to the jurisdiction of the Arbitration Committee over the claim and difference in question. In an action in a court of law to enforce the award, such question might be raised. For the purposes of this action, under the facts of the case, it can give him no relief. If the plaintiff would revoke the part of his agreement with his associates, which imposes duties and obligations upon him, he cannot insist, in a court of equity, that he shall be protected in the enjoyment of rights and privileges created by the same contracts. He that would have equity must do equity."

This cause was subsequently appealed,[1] and the judgment of the lower courts was affirmed. It will be observed that in neither of the two elaborate opinions delivered in the cause did the court consider the legal aspect of the issue between the plaintiff and M. C. & Co., but the same was deliberately avoided, it being held that, under any circumstances, the plaintiff was first bound to exhaust his remedy—an appeal to the executive committee, in the manner pointed out in the constitution and by-laws of the board—before any resort to the courts could be had.

But *it seems* that where an unincorporated association, through a committee or otherwise, seeks to suspend or expel a member for acts not provided for in the constitution or by-laws, or by an *ex post facto* resolution, the courts will interfere by injunction to prevent the same.[2]

The case of Sewell vs. Ives, President, etc., New York Stock Exchange[3] is an interesting case, illustrating this question of the right of suspension and expulsion. The plaintiff was a

[1] 4 Ab. Pr. (n. s.) 162; s. c., 2 Daly, 318.

[2] Per Ingraham, J., Rorke vs. Russell, 2 Lans. (N. Y.) 244, 248. As to the power of an unincorporated association to suspend or expel a member, where there is no specific provision in the constitution or by-laws to that effect, see Leech vs. Harris, 2 Brews. 571. If a member of an incorporated association directly violates its charter or by-laws, he may be expelled. People ex rel. Thacher vs. N. Y. Commercial Assn., 18 Abb. Pr. 271. In that case the corporation was organized (inter alia) "to inculcate just and equitable principles of trade" and it was held that the obtaining by the relator of goods under false pretences was a breach of his duty to the association. Id. But a member of the New York Cotton Exchange (incorporated) cannot be expelled for contesting his title to a seat, there being no provision in the charter or by-laws relative thereto. People ex rel. Elliott vs. New York Cotton Exchange, 8 Hun, 216. The presumption should be against the power to expel except for the causes recognized by the adjudged cases, citing White vs. Brownell, supra. Id.

[3] N. Y. Supreme Ct., Sp. T., reported in N. Y. *Daily Reg.* Feb. 11, 1879.

member of the firm of J. B. & Co., which failed. An investigation of the affairs of the firm showed that it had re-hypothecated securities upon which it had loaned money to Brokers; and the members of the firm, consisting of B. and the plaintiff, were arraigned before a sub-committee of the Governing Committee of the Stock Exchange, which reported in favor of their expulsion, on the ground that they had been guilty of obvious fraud under Article XX. (now Art. XVII., sec. 2, in amended form) of the Constitution of the Exchange, as follows: "Should any member be guilty of obvious fraud, of which the Governing Committee shall be the judge, he shall, upon conviction thereof, by a vote of two thirds of the members of the said committee present, be expelled, and his membership shall escheat to the Exchange; subject, however, to the provisions of Article XIV. of the constitution as regard the claims of members of the Exchange who are creditors of such persons."

The resolution of expulsion was approved of by the Governing Committee. There was a unanimous vote on B.'s guilt; but only a majority subscribed to the finding in plaintiff's case, though there was a two-third vote in favor of the latter's expulsion.

The plaintiff applied for an interlocutory injunction, restraining the president and other officers of the Exchange from interfering with his entering the Exchange and carrying on business there, alleging that his expulsion was unjust, and that it deprived him of his interest in the property of the Exchange and all of the rights and incidents pertaining to a membership therein. The Court held that, although the plaintiff's expulsion had been technically irregular, yet, as it was an admitted fact that the firm of which he was a member was insolvent, he could not justly complain of being sus-

6

pended from membership ; as under Article XIV. (now article XVI.) of the Constitution of the Stock Exchange, all members becoming insolvent shall be suspended until they have settled with their creditors.[1]

This decision may be open to question, upon the ground that the effect of the difference between a " suspended " and an "expelled" member does not seem to have been fully regarded ; inasmuch as a "suspended" member is one who under the rules of the Exchange can be restored to membership, whereas an "expelled" member forever loses his prop-

[1] The full decision of Mr. Justice Sedgwick is given in this connection:

"It seems clear to me that Article XX. of the Constitution of the defendant means that before a member can be expelled he must be found guilty by a vote of two thirds of the members of the committee present, and that the attempted expulsion was void. This, of itself, does not give a cause of action. The illegal act must have some relation to a right which the law can protect. It must appear that an injunction to prevent the defendant acting upon the illegal expulsion will permit the plaintiff to enjoy some substantial right, capable of present or future actual enjoyment. The complaint charges that the defendant, under the pretence of the void expulsion, deprived said plaintiff of the power to enter said building, or mart, to carry on such business as he may have to carry on, and has unlawfully deprived him of his seat, which cost him $2,000; has wrongfully and unlawfully deprived him of the interest in such property as the association may own; and has wrongfully and unlawfully deprived him of all the rights and privileges incident to such membership, which are very valuable to plaintiff, and absolutely essential to the discharge of plaintiff's business as Broker.

"The testimony showed that the defendant did exclude the plaintiff from the enjoyment of any and every privilege of a member, of a kind that would actually accrue to a member in his lifetime, and did claim that he was properly expelled. One of the defences was that before the expulsion, and, by reason of the plaintiff becoming insolvent, he became, by force of certain articles of the constitution, a suspended member, or suspended from membership, and had so ever remained. The effect of this suspension was that it legally deprived him of every present and future advantage of membership, and until he should settle with his creditors and should apply for readmission to membership. His readmission would then depend upon the vote of the committee or committees to which ap-

erty and privileges.[1] If the basis of proceeding against a member is under one particular rule, and the action of the Exchange held to be unauthorized and illegal, it seems rather anomalous to uphold the decision in ousting a member upon another rule merely justifying suspension, and to which no reference was made to the proceedings before the Exchange.[2] And this view seems to have finally prevailed in the case.

The most recent New York case illustrative of the power of the Stock Exchange over its members is Young vs.

plication must be made. The testimony was that he had not applied for readmission, and that he had not made a settlement with his creditors. There was no proof that he had the means of making one. Therefore, there is no present right recognized by the constitution to apply for readmission or to be readmitted. A mere lapse of time will not bring him to such a right. An injunction against using the void expulsion would not enable him to enjoy or go into possession of any advantages. While present facts exist there is no possibility of any right accruing to him; and whether there will be a possibility hereafter is incapable of determination, if a mere possibility as distinguished from a contingent right to the subject of adjudication. If there be a doubt as to the correctness of this, it rests upon—first, that a suspended member had a right to go into what the witness called the "long room;" second, that after the attempted expulsion, and before a year had passed, there was a sale of the plaintiff's right of membership. The first refers to a

right that of itself is not in the nature of property, has no pecuniary value, and an unlawful exclusion from it could be adequately compensated by damages. The second was not an injury to the plaintiff; as, from the nature of membership, he could be fully reinstated without setting the sale aside, and any claim of right to a resale would be repugnant to the foundation of this action."

"For the reason that the plaintiff has no substantial right that would be protected by injunction, the complaint must be dismissed."—N. Y. *Daily Reg.* Feb. 11, 1879.

[1] As to recognition by the courts of the difference between suspension and expulsion under the by-laws of a Masonic lodge, see Palmetto Lodge vs. Hubbell, 2 Strob. Law (S. Car.), 457.

[2] And see this case again reported at p. 126 of this chapter, where in an action against the Stock Exchange for a conversion of his "seat" the plaintiff recovered damages on the ground that it had been illegally disposed of by the Stock Exchange.

Eames.[1] In that case the plaintiff, who had been expelled
for fraud, brought an action against the Exchange demanding judgment that it be decreed that he was a member
in good standing, and that the Exchange be restrained
from preventing him transacting business upon the Exchange, thereby compelling the defendant to prove the
validity of the expulsion, and it was held that the Exchange
was only bound to prove the preparation of charges, notice of the hearing, the calling of witnesses and the decision
reached, and that the committee had followed the procedure required by the constitution, and that it was not
incumbent on them to produce all the evidence taken before them. A presumption arose that the decision was
valid, and it rested upon the plaintiff to show in what respect it was void. It was also held that the plaintiff was
rightly expelled for fraud, although under another rule he
might have been only suspended for making a fictitious
sale, when the sale, besides being fictitious, was also
fraudulent, and of which the Committee was to be the
judge.

The case of Powell vs. Abbott[2] illustrates a case in which
the courts will interfere. That was a bill in equity to restrain the defendants, members of the Philadelphia Mining
and Stock Exchange, an unincorporated association, from
carrying into effect the suspension of the plaintiff from

[1] 78 A. D. 229. See also Board
vs. Weare, 105 Ill. App. 289.

[2] 9 Week. Notes Cas. 231, Nov.
1880. When a member of the New
York Coffee Exchange, an incorporated association, was suspended
from membership for refusing to
pay for alleged adulterated coffee,
it was held that he was entitled to

mandamus compelling his reinstatement on the ground that the committee should have investigated the
question of adulteration, as he could
not be compelled to do an illegal
act (L. 1893, c. 661, § 41) without
such investigation. Matter of Lurman, 149 N. Y. 588.

membership in the association, and from disposing of certain stock belonging to him and deposited as security.

The bill set forth that the plaintiff had made a time contract with A., one of the defendants, for the sale of certain mining stock, and deposited with another member of the Exchange certain shares of other stock as security; that, the stock having advanced in price, A. demanded a further security, which plaintiff declined to make, on the ground that the sales at the advanced price were fictitious; that the question was then referred to the Arbitration Committee of the Exchange, whose duty it was to investigate and decide all claims and matters of difference arising between members of the Exchange, and also to adjudicate such claims as may be preferred against members by non-members, when non-members agree in writing to abide by its decision. The decision of the committee shall be final, except in cases involving a difference of one hundred dollars or over, when either party may appeal, within three days, to the Exchange for final adjudication. The committee decided that the plaintiff must make the additional deposit called for by A., from which decision plaintiff forthwith notified the acting chairman of the Exchange that he appealed; but before any further action could be taken on said appeal, at the request of said A. the acting chairman of said Exchange appointed a committee of three members, who called upon plaintiff, and inquired of him why he had not complied with the report of the Arbitration Committee. Plaintiff replied to them that he had appealed from its decision. The said committee thereupon reported back to the acting chairman of the Exchange that the following section of the by-laws be enforced:

"Section XI. Any member who fails to comply with his contracts, or who becomes insolvent, shall immediately inform the chairman of the Exchange of the fact, whose duty it shall be to give notice forthwith, from the chair, of the failure of such member; and in case of the refusal or neglect of such delinquent to make such report to the chairman, it shall be the duty of any member, having a knowledge of the fact, to report the same forthwith to the Governing Committee or the chairman, who shall thereupon appoint a committee of three members to inquire into the facts, and report thereon, without delay; and if said committee report the charge to be true, and the Exchange confirm the report, said member shall be suspended; and it shall, furthermore, be the duty of the Governing Committee, upon receiving information thereof, or having, directly or indirectly, any knowledge of such failure on the part of any member to comply with his engagements, as above stated, to report the same, without delay, to the chairman, and· ask for the appointment of a committee as before provided. And, in case of the insolvency of any member, he shall within three days make good, to the full amount thereof, all friendly loans of cash or stock from members, or any overdraft on any bank; but seven days shall be allowed him in which to settle stock contracts."

A meeting of the members who were present at the Exchange in the afternoon of the same day was called, without any preliminary notice, to take action on the report of the committee. Plaintiff protested, at the time, that he had appealed from the decision of the Arbitration Committee, and asked that his appeal should be heard before any further action was taken in the matter. His objection and request were overruled, and his right of appeal denied him; and a

motion was made to suspend him, which was thereupon put
and carried.

The court, after commenting upon the nature of the association and its rules, and holding that where there was a conflict between the constitution of the association and by-laws
the former must prevail, said:

"But whether this be so or not, the right of the plaintiff
to the protection of a court of chancery rests upon the denial
to him of his right of appeal from the decision of the Arbitration Committee, and the consequent threatened sacrifice
of his rights as a member of the association, and the selling and disposing of the stock deposited as security for
his contracts before his rights have been adjudicated, in
the manner prescribed by the constitution of the association.

"It has been alleged by the learned counsel for the defendants that the plaintiff has a legal remedy by mandamus for
restoration of his rights as a member if he has been improperly suspended, and that consequently he cannot invoke
the equitable powers of this court.

"A writ of mandamus would not secure to the plaintiff the
protection which he seeks. The object of that writ would be
to restore him to his rights as a member if he had been improperly suspended. In the meanwhile there might be the
threatened sacrifice of his property, as complained by him.
And as this court has equitable jurisdiction for the supervision
and control of these associations, and to prevent threatened
mischief, upon the well-settled principle that where a court of
equity has jurisdiction for any purpose it will draw to itself
jurisdiction of all questions incident to the subject-matter of
inquiry, to make a final determination of the rights of the
parties, and to prevent multiplicity of actions, I think the

jurisdiction can be maintained." The special injunction was accordingly continued.

Incorporated Exchanges have in more than one instance made it an express recital of their charters or certificates of incorporation, that, the purpose, or one of the purposes, in organizing, was to " inculcate just and equitable principles of trade." And a similar purpose is readily discernible in the constitution and rules of the New York Stock Exchange.[1]

A by-law punishing infractions of just and equitable principles of trade is to be liberally construed in aid of its purpose and " extends to conduct in respect to a contract either in its inception or execution, or the failure to execute it, which is inconsistent with just and fair dealing, although it may fall short of actionable fraud, and although it is not of that specific and definite character of which the law in an action between the parties will take notice. The law does not undertake to enforce mere moral obligations. Their observance, however, by parties to contracts is required by the principles of commercial honor and integrity, and it would seem to be the policy as well as the duty of an association, organized to inculcate just and equitable principles of trade, to discourage by disciplinary action any disregard of business rectitude on the part of its members in their business transactions." [2]

A person, it is pointed out, " may perform the very letter of his contract and respond to the full extent of the law and

[1] Bernheim vs. Keppler, 34 Misc. 321.

[2] Per Andrews, C. J., People ex rel. Johnson vs. New York Produce Exchange, 149 N. Y. 411. See also In re Haebler vs. New York Produce Exchange, 149 N. Y. 428; Hurst vs. New York Produce Exchange, 1 Cent. Rep. 260; People ex rel. Thacher vs. New York Commercial Assn., 18 Abb. Pr. 279.

yet be guilty of proceedings inconsistent with the just and equitable principles of trade. He may exact no more than the pound of flesh precisely nominated in the letter of his bond and yet be guilty of unfair dealing and gross misconduct." And, therefore, the fact that the matter is also under judicial investigation, does not oust the jurisdiction of the Exchange.[1]

It seems, however, that the simple non-performance by a member of a contract is not within the by-law. For that there is usually another provision of the by-laws.[2]

Such a by-law will reach and punish a member for offenses committed outside of the Exchange, and even if not committed against a fellow-member.[3]

A member is not acting in antagonism to the corporate power of establishing just and equitable principles of trade, in refusing to submit to an adverse report by a committee upon his title to his seat in the Exchange, there being no express or implied power in the body to determine the ownership of a disputed seat.[4]

In a recent case in Wisconsin a temporary injunction was granted against the Milwaukee City Chamber of Commerce, enjoining it from suspending or expelling plaintiff from the Chamber for an alleged violation of a rule as to

---

[1] Hurst vs. N. Y. P. Ex., 1 Cent. Rep. 260, and other cases cited in preceding note. A by-law of a body having among its corporate objects the inculcation of just and equitable principles of trade, may prescribe suspension for the breach of a contract, even though the contract violated be void under the statute of frauds. Dickenson vs. Chamber of Commerce, 29 Wis. 45.

[2] People ex rel. Johnson vs. New York Produce Exchange, 149 N. Y. 410.

[3] In Matter of Haebler vs. New York Produce Exchange and People ex rel. Thacher vs. New York Commercial Assn., supra; Dickenson vs. Chamber of Commerce, 29 Wis. 45.

[4] People ex rel. Elliott vs. Cotton Ex., 8 Hun, 216.

contracts, it appearing that a certain contract which plaintiffs declined to fulfil, was made by their clerk without
their authority, with a person having knowledge of the
clerk's scope of employment.[1]

The case of Leech vs. Harris was another Stock Exchange
case,[2] and it was there held that where a charter of a
society provides for an offense, directs the mode of proceeding, and authorizes the society, on conviction of a member,
to expel him, this expulsion, if the proceedings are not
irregular, is conclusive, and cannot be inquired into collater-
ally by mandamus, action, or any other mode.

It is like an award made by a tribunal of the party's own
choosing, for he became a member under and subject to the
articles and conditions of the charter, and, of course, to the
provisions on this subject as well as others. The society
acts judicially, and its sentence is conclusive, like that of
any other judicial tribunal.[3] The courts entertain a jurisdiction to preserve these tribunals in the line of order, and
to correct abuses; but they do not inquire into the merits
of what has passed *in rem judicatam* in a regular course of
proceedings.[4]

But it seems, in view of the generally summary character of

[1] Bartlett vs. Bartlett, 93 N. W.
(Wis.) 473.

[2] 2 Brews. 571. The court cited the
following authorities: Commonw.
vs. Pike Benev. Soc., 8 W. & S. 247;
The White and Black Smiths' Soc.
vs. Van Dyke, 2 Whart. 309; The
Soc. for the Visitation of the Sick vs.
The Commonw., 2 P. F. Smith
(Pa.), 125

[3] Otto vs. Tailor's Union, 75 Cal.
309; Albers vs. Merchants' Exchange, 138 Mo. 164; Farmer vs.

Board of Trade, 78 Mo. App. 557;
Ryan vs. Cudahy, 157 Ill. 108; Nelson vs. Board of Trade, 58 Ill. App.
399.

[4] Hutchinson vs Lawrence, 67
How. Pr. 39; Solomon vs. McKay, 49
N. Y. Super. Ct. 138; People ex rel.
Johnson vs. N. Y. Produce Ex-
change, 149 N. Y. 401; Lewis vs.
Wilson, 121 N. Y. 284; Pitcher vs.
Board of Trade, 121 Ill. 412; Nelson
vs. Board of Trade, 58 Ill. App. 399;
Otto vs. Tailors' Union, 75 Cal. 308.

the proceedings, and that they are not subject to review by the ordinary process of appeal, that a total absence of evidence to support the sentence of expulsion should have the same force in a mandamus proceeding, as an absence of jurisdiction to make any inquiry at all.[1]

The case of Moxey's Appeal, decided by the Supreme Court of Pennsylvania, January, 1881,[2] is an adjudication upon this subject.

In that case Moxey, in 1875, became a member of the Philadelphia Stock Exchange, and transacted business therein until July 29, 1876. At or about this time, the firm of B., M. & Co., of which the plaintiff was a member, purchased a large number of shares of a certain company, from different members of the Board. Before the time of delivery, however, Moxey gave written notice to the president of the board of their insolvency, under Section XI. of the rules of the association which we fully quoted before (p. 86), except § 3, paragraph 1, which is as follows : " If any suspended member fail to settle with his creditors, and apply for readmission within one year from the time of his suspension, his membership shall be disposed of by the Committee on Admissions, and the proceeds paid *pro rata* to his creditors in the Exchange. The Governing Committee may, by a vote of two thirds of the members present, extend the time for settlement,

---

[1] People ex rel. Johnson vs. N. Y. Produce Exchange, 149 N. Y. 401; Bishop vs. Cincinnati Chamber of Commerce, 5 Ohio N. P. 365.

The expulsion of a member, nominally for an offence for which such punishment is proper, but in reality for an offence punishable only by fine, is invalid. Otto vs. Tailors' Union, 75 Cal. 308.

Suspension is a judicial act based on something which calls for such suspension. Stack vs. O'Hara, 98 Pa. St. 232.

[2] Week. Notes of Cas. 440; affirming s. c. *sub nom.* Moxey vs. Phila. Stock Exchange, 37 Leg. Int. 82.

and for application for readmission, of such suspended member."

The rules allowed a suspended member, presenting a certificate of discharge under the United States Bankrupt Laws, to become eligible, providing that upon a ballot, where not less than fifty votes are cast, and not more than fifteen blackballs appear against him, he may be reinstated; but such application shall be referred to a standing committee, whose duty it shall be to ascertain that the applicant has settled and arranged his affairs to the satisfaction of his creditors, and that his present situation affords a reasonable security in future transactions; and unless, and until, the said committee report in favor of readmitting the said suspended member, he shall be held to be still in default, and no vote to restore him to his seat shall be had.   On January 15, 1877, plaintiff went into voluntary bankruptcy, and obtained his discharge on December 21, 1877.   On January 15, 1878, he wrote to the Secretary of the Stock Exchange that he had obtained his discharge in bankruptcy, and he received an answer that, if he desired to apply for readmission under the rules of the Stock Exchange, the matter would be immediately referred to the standing committee and be investigated.

The letter also notified him that, as more than a year had elapsed since his suspension, the Exchange considered itself entitled to sell his seat at any time.   No notice was taken of this letter, and on July 5, 1878, plaintiff's seat was sold, on demand of his creditors, at public sale of the board, after posting and notice in accordance with the rules.   At the time he joined the Stock Exchange a Gratuity Fund existed, payable on the death of a full member (whether suspended or not) to his nominee, widow, child, or legal representative.

On November 15, 1877, this was altered so that any suspended member who failed, for three months, to pay in full all gratuity dues and assessments should cease to be a full member for the purposes of the Gratuity Fund. Moxey was notified of the passage of this provision, but failed to pay his dues, and on March 7, 1878, was notified that he was debarred from participating in the benefit thereof.

He filed a bill in equity against the Stock Exchange, alleging that by far the greater part of the indebtedness of B., M. & Co. was merely fictitious, being founded upon contracts for the sale and delivery of certificates of stock which had no real existence; that they constituted gambling transactions, and that the payment of such debts would be in violation of the Bankrupt Act.

The court dismissed the bill, holding that, irrespective of the alleged gambling transactions, the evidence showed a large indebtedness, which plaintiff's firm was unable to meet; that by filing his petition in bankruptcy, the plaintiff had confessed his insolvency, and that he had not shown any offer to liquidate his indebtedness or arrange with his creditors under the rules of the Stock Exchange; and that the plaintiff had been suspended in accordance with the rules, on his own confession and acts, and could not be restored except under the rules, which he had not complied with.

Upon appeal, the judgment of the lower court dismissing the bill was sustained; the appellate tribunal holding that, as the firm of which the plaintiff was a member had admitted their inability to fulfil their contracts, and, under the by-laws of the Stock Exchange, plaintiff was immediately suspended, no trial was necessary in such a case, the member having pleaded guilty. That the bankruptcy had the same effect. The court could see nothing unreasonable in the rule that before such a party could be readmitted he must settle with his creditors who are members of the Exchange. It may give them an advantage over other creditors, but they have a right to stipulate for it, and the appellant was a party assenting to the law. No suggestion appears to have been made that the assignee in bankruptcy, in whom all the assets of the plaintiff had become vested, was the proper party to recover any money or property to which plaintiff might be entitled; but the case was determined upon the grounds just stated.[1]

[1] See also in this connection, MacDowell vs. Ackley, Supreme Ct. Pa. 8 Week. Notes of Cas. 664. A similar rule was held reasonable in Sexton vs. Commercial Exchange, 10 Pa. Ct. C. 607.

As to when an allegation that a contract, in respect of which plaintiff was suspended, was a gambling one, will not avail, see Lewis vs. Wilson, 121 N. Y. 281. In that case it was expressly urged as a ground for the exercise of the equitable power of the court to compel restoration to membership that the contract for the breach of which the member was suspended was of a gambling character and illegal and, therefore, its violation was not a "breach of contract" under the rules of the Exchange. The court ruled against the point and sustained the Consolidated Stock and Petroleum Exchange of New York in suspending the member, holding that whether the contract to which the complaint before the committee related was valid or void was wholly irrelevant, and that the plaintiff could not insist upon re-maining a member of this association while at the same time he repudiated the conditions of membership. That having been suspended in strict conformity with the constitution of the Exchange, and having had an opportunity to be heard, and the charge having been examined by the proper committee, his suspension was valid. The court said: "The members of the association may, if they so agree, say that no associate shall remain a member and enjoy the privileges of the association if he refuses to comply with its rules. It may be true that the committee, if the facts had been presented and proved as there claimed by the plaintiff, would nevertheless have regarded the gambling element as no excuse to the plaintiff for not performing his contract. But whether the committee should decide rightly or wrongly does not change the attitude of the plaintiff as a member of the association, or qualify his obligation to submit to the decision of the agreed tribunal under pain of suspension. . . .

When a rule of an association provided that "any member failing to pay his assessment within thirty days shall be suspended," it was held that the non-payment of an assessment was not of itself a suspension, and that the association should take some affirmative action to make such suspension valid.[1]

Finally, upon this question, it should be stated that, in all cases in which a member is proceeded against with a view to his expulsion, it is necessary that the proceedings should be conducted in accordance with the constitution and by-laws of the association,[2] and that he should be duly notified to appear, and be allowed an opportunity to explain his acts or be heard in his defence,[3] even although the rules of the

---

There is an intimation in the argument of the plaintiff's counsel that the Exchange was organized as a cover for illegal trading. If this was the truth the plaintiff is in the plight of asking the court to exert its equitable powers to reinstate him as a member of this illegal body."

[1] Scheu vs. Grand Lodge, 17 Fed. 214.

[2] People vs. Musical Mutual Protective Union, 118 N. Y. 101.

[3] Ang. & Ames on Corps. (11th ed.) § 420; People ex rel. Johnson vs. N. Y. Produce Exchange, 149 N. Y. 401; Hutchinson vs. Lawrence, 67 How. Pr. 38; Loubat vs. Le Roy, 15 Abb. N. C. 1; 40 Hun, 546; Lewis vs. Wilson, 121 N. Y. 284; Kuehnemundt vs. Smith, 2 N. Y. Supp. 625; Albers vs. Merchants' Exchange, 39 Mo. App. 583; People vs. San Franciscus Benev. Soc., 24 How. Pr. (N. Y.) 216; Stack vs. O'Hara, 98 Pa. St. 213; Fritz vs. Muck, 62 How. Pr. 69.

The failure on his part to request the privilege to be present is no answer to his exclusion, for he is not legally bound to ask such privilege, but the committee taking action upon the evidence obtained, is legally bound to extend and secure the opportunity for a hearing to him, before it can proceed to a hearing and consideration of the case. Loubat vs. Le Roy, 40 Hun, 546.

See, however, Blumenthal vs. Cincinnati Chamber of Commerce, 7 Wkly. L. Bull. 327; 8 Ohio Dec. Rep. 410, where it was held that the Chamber had jurisdiction to try and indefinitely suspend a member for unmercantile conduct although he had not received any notice of the charges preferred against him. A preliminary inquiry into charges by a committee to determine whether charges shall be preferred, without notice to the member concerned, is not improper, since such prelimi-

association do not so provide.[1] In other words, there must be a charge made against him sufficient in form to fairly inform the member of what he is charged;[2] he should be notified of the charge and a time set for its hearing, not too limited to prevent the accused from properly collecting his proofs and producing his witnesses; and the hearing or trial of the charge should include the right to examine his own witnesses and cross-examine those against him, and to present such suggestions as he may deem proper.[3]

nary inquiry is not a trial. Green vs. Board of Trade, 174 Ill. 585.

[1] Fritz vs. Muck, 62 How. Pr. 69.

[2] Hutchinson vs. Lawrence, 67 How. Pr. 38, at p. 52; People ex rel. Johnson vs. N. Y. Produce Exchange, 149 N. Y. 401; In re Haebler vs. N. Y. Produce Exchange, 149 N. Y. 414; Cannon vs. Toronto Corn Exchange, 5 Ont. App. 268. To require technical precision in complaints of this character, drawn by merchants or business men, and to apply to them the strict rules of pleading in an action in a court of law, would greatly embarrass and many times defeat the disciplinary regulations of such associations. People ex rel. Johnson vs. N. Y. Produce Exchange, supra. And even if a complaint be objectionably vague and indefinite, an appearance by the accused without objection to its sufficiency and a trial of the case upon its merits, renders it sufficient and objections thereon on that account must be regarded as waived. In re Haebler vs. N. Y. Produce Exchange, 149 N. Y. 414. But if a copy of the charges are not served upon the member as re-

quired by the by-laws, and his subsequent conduct before the board of directors does not amount to a waiver of the defective procedure, his expulsion is illegal. People vs. Musical Mutual Protective Union, 118 N. Y. 101.

[3] Hutchinson vs. Lawrence, 67 How. Pr. 38, where it was held that a re-examination of complainant in the defendant's absence, and the taking of additional testimony, without opportunity of cross-examination, were improper. The conclusions reached in this case are not entirely satisfactory, because it did not appear that the expelled member had requested to be present and cross-examine the witnesses or that the usages of the Exchange had established any such practice. Moreover the cases relied upon by the learned judge were of a class *where the party expelled had been refused a hearing, or had requested to be further heard*, which was not the fact in the Hutchinson case. Kuehnemundt vs. Smith, 2 N. Y. Supp. 625; Loubat vs. Le Roy, 40 Hun, 546. The right to cross-examine opposing witnesses may

These requirements having been met and the offense being one of which the committee has jurisdiction, a member, by not making his defences then and there, is held to have waived them.[1] It has been intimated[2] that on such a trial the accused member is entitled to be represented by counsel, and Chief Justice Shaw in an early case,[3] reviewing the action of the board of trustees of a corporation, held that to make binding the decision of any tribunal acting judicially upon the rights of others, there should be substantially (1) a monition or citation to him to appear; (2) a charge given him to which he is to answer; (3) a competent time assigned for his proofs and answers; (4) liberty of counsel to defend his case, and (5) a solemn sentence after hearing the proofs and answers. It has been held, however,[4] that a by-law providing that "in investigations before

be waived by neglect to claim it at the proper time. Kuehnemundt vs. Smith, supra.

[1] Bishop vs. Cincinnati Chamber of Commerce, 5 Ohio N. P. 365. See also State vs. Id., 4 Ohio N. P. 244; Lewis vs. Wilson, 121 N. Y. 284.

[2] By Barrett, J., in Gebhard vs. N. Y. Club, 21 Abb. N. C. 248, at p. 252. In Hutchinson vs. Lawrence, 67 How. Pr. 38, it appeared that at a meeting of the governing committee of the Stock Exchange, preliminary to hearing charges against the plaintiff, a motion on behalf of the latter to be defended by counsel was defeated.

[3] Murdock vs. Phillips' Academy, 29 Mass. 263. In Young vs. Eames, 78 A. D. (N. Y.) 229, plaintiff objected that he had no counsel, and the court held that such objection could not be considered as it was

not raised by the pleadings, and (Neukirch vs. Keppler, 56 A. D. 230) because plaintiff had not asked for counsel.

[4] Green vs. Board of Trade, 174 Ill. 585. A by-law of the Merchants' Exchange of St. Louis provided that in investigations before the board, either party should be allowed to be represented by a member, either as professional counsel or as a friend. It was held in Albers vs. Merchants' Exchange of St. Louis, 138 Mo. 163, that the board might be advised by their counsel as to the legality of a by-law under which plaintiff was suspended even though such counsel was a member of the board. The principle of trial by jury is in no way applicable to such trial. People ex rel. Thacher vs. Commercial Assn., 18 Abb. Pr. 271.

the board of directors or any committee of the association, no party shall be allowed to be represented by professional counsel," was not against public policy or unreasonable. The rules, the court said in that case, " provide a tribunal and procedure, voluntarily chosen to determine questions arising between the association and its members, to which the members assented on being admitted." In fine, he should be allowed a full and fair opportunity of defending himself.[1]

The fact that the charges are preferred by a member of the committee which is to try the same is not a cause for interference by injunction to prevent the trial.[2]

This question of notice was considered by the Court of Appeals of New York, in Wachtel vs. Noah Widows and Orphan's Benevolent Society;[3] and it was held that an association whose members become entitled to privileges or rights of property therein cannot exercise its powers of expulsion without notice to the party charged or without giving him an opportunity to be heard; and that where the charter of a beneficiary association provided that the secretary should give to a member who is six months in

---

[1] And the accused member is not merely entitled to be present at the taking of the evidence but also at the rendition of the judgment. Loubat vs. Le Roy, 40 Hun, 556.

[2] Green vs. Board of Trade, 174 Ill. 585. The presumption cannot be entertained that the board would not give the member a fair trial. Ibid. See also Jackson vs. South Omaha Live Stock Exchange, 49 Neb. 687, and compare Temple vs. Toronto Stock Exchange, 8 Ont. 705

That the charges on which a member has been suspended after due notice and a fair trial were preferred by an employee not a member of the Exchange, will not invalidate the proceeding. Albers vs. Merchant's Exchange, 39 Mo. App. 583.

[3] 84 N. Y. 28. For other cases relating to power of unincorporated associations to expel a member, see preceding subdivision, p. 59 ; Foster vs. Harrison, Week. Notes of Cas. 171.

arrear a written notice of the fact, and that "he shall be
stricken from the roll if he does not pay his dues within
thirty days," a notice was essential to deprive the member
in arrears, or his representative after his death, of the benefits of membership in the society; and that the fact that
the member had changed his place of residence, without
notifying the society, was not an excuse for a failure to
serve a notice upon him, especially when there was a specific penalty imposed in the by-laws of the society upon a
member changing his residence without giving notice.[1]

In the celebrated case of Labouchere vs. Earl of Wharncliffe[2] several important questions relative to the expulsion
of members of voluntary associations were considered. One
of the rules of the club, of which plaintiff was a member,
provided that " in case the conduct of any member, either
in or out of the club, shall, in the opinion of the committee,
after inquiry, be injurious to the welfare and interests of
the club, the committee shall call on him to resign."

The court held that the words "after inquiry" did not
mean that the committee might take up a newspaper, see
in it that Mr. A. B. has written an objectionable letter, or
has been brought up at a police-court for drunkenness, and
then expel him; but that the inquiry should be a fair one
into the truth of the alleged facts. That where the conduct of a member is impugned, such conduct should be
inquired into; and the committee making the inquiry ought
to see what excuse or reason the accused member can give
for it, and they ought to give him notice that his conduct is

---

[1] See also Bartlett vs. Med. Soc.,
32 N. Y. 187; Commonw. vs. Penns.
Benev. Soc., 2 S. & Rawle, 141;
Innes vs. Wylie, 1 C. & K. 257.

Consult also Olery vs. Brown, 51
How. Pr. 92.
[2] L. R. 13 Ch. Div. 346.

about to be investigated, and afford him an opportunity of stating his case to them. And the notice should not be ambiguous, but should clearly inform the member that his conduct was to be investigated. At a special meeting of the committee, held on the 16th of October, 1879, it was resolved that the plaintiff be called upon to resign in accordance with the above rule. This he refused to do. Rule 31 of the club provided that the committee should, at any time, have power to call a general meeting on giving a fortnight's notice. On the evening of the 31st of October an adjourned meeting of the committee was held, which continued in session into the following morning; at which meeting it was resolved to call a general meeting of the club to consider the expulsion of the plaintiff. Notice was posted in the club-house at 3. A. M. of the same morning, the 1st of November, calling such a meeting to be held on the 14th of November; and, in the course of the 1st of November, notices were mailed to the members of the club. According to the statement of the secretary of the club, the notice posted in the club-house at 3 A. M. on the morning of the 1st of November would be reckoned, having regard to the custom of the club, as being done on the 31st of October, on which day the notice was dated. On the 14th of November the general meeting of the club was held. There were one hundred and seventeen members present, all of whom voted, except the plaintiff and one other; of whom seventy-seven voted for the committee, and thirty-eight for the plaintiff. The plaintiff was present, addressed the meeting, and protested against his expulsion; but made no objection to the proceedings on the score of irregularity or the insufficiency of the notice.

In respect to the sufficiency of the notice, the court held

that, the notice having been first posted on the 1st of November, it was not a fortnight's notice, and that, therefore, the meeting was irregularly called. That a fortnight had a definite legal meaning, and was not affected by the secretary's notion of the club-day. It was further held that the plaintiff had not waived the irregularity by addressing the meeting; that the plaintiff had said that he protested against his expulsion, and that was sufficient. In respect to whether plaintiff had been expelled by a two-thirds vote of "those present," the court said: "The rule of the club was to the effect that, in the event of a member refusing to resign, a general meeting of members should be called, at which it should be competent for two thirds of 'those present' to expel him. Now, Mr. Labouchere has stated that there were one hundred and seventeen persons present, of whom one hundred and fifteen voted; that he himself was present, but did not vote; and that the number who voted for his expulsion was seventy-seven. It is clear, therefore, that if there were one hundred and seventeen persons present, seventy-seven were not two thirds of the number. The expulsion was, therefore, irregularly made.

" When a resolution is put to a meeting, the persons present may take one of these courses: they may vote for or against it; or, not wishing to express a positive opinion on the question, refrain from voting at all. This being so, those who do not vote may, by not doing so, turn the scale in favor of the accused member of the club. It was, therefore, the duty of the secretary to ascertain, first, how many persons were present when the question was put, and, secondly, how many of those present had voted for the resolution; but no such course has been adopted in this instance. It appears to me, then, that this also is a fatal objection."[1]

So, in Fisher vs. Keane,[2] in an action against the Trustees and Committee of the Army and Navy Club, asking for a declaration that a resolution purporting to expel the plaintiff from membership in the Army and Navy Club was null and void, Jessel, M. R., construed the rule under which the plaintiff was expelled, and held that the action of the committee was irregular, and, further, decided that a committee of a club, acting under its rules, is bound to act according to the ordinary principles of justice, and cannot convict a man of a grave offence, warranting his expulsion, without fair, adequate, and sufficient notice, and an opportunity of meeting the accusations brought against him; he should be given an opportunity of either defending himself or palliating his conduct.

The question also came up in New Jersey, in the case Sibley vs. Carteret Club of Elizabeth.[3] In that case the club was incorporated, and possessed power, in virtue of its charter, to make regulations and by-laws for the admission, suspension, and expulsion of members. Under one of the sections of the constitution it was provided that, if a member remained in default of his indebtedness after fifteen days of posting, he should forfeit his membership in the club, etc.

---

[1] Where a two-thirds vote of a committee consisting of twenty-four members is expressly required to expel, only an affirmative vote of two thirds of the full committee will suffice, and therefore, when at the time of the expulsion proceedings the committee had become reduced to twenty members, of whom there were present at the meeting eighteen members, of whom fourteen voted for the expulsion, the other four being opposed to it, it was held that the expulsion was irregular, as sixteen of the members should have voted therefor. Loubat vs. Le Roy, 40 Hun, 546.

[2] 41 L. T. 335; s. c. L. R. 11 Ch. Div. 353; 49 L. J. Ch. 11.

[3] 40 N. J. L. Rep. 295.

The Board of Managers, upon failure of the relator to pay after posting, resolved that he ceased to be a member; whereupon the relator sued out a writ of mandamus, commanding them to cause his name to be replaced upon the roll of members. The writ was granted, the court holding that there could be no forfeiture by a mere failure to pay dues, unless there was a determination of that fact by the Board of Managers, upon notice to the member charged; that the right of membership in a club is one which the courts will protect; and that an irregular removal will warrant the use of the writ of mandamus to effect a restoration of the expelled member to his rights.[1]

And a contract made between a Broker and his Client, that if the former would refuse to appear before the Arbitration Committee and suffer suspension, the latter would reimburse him for all losses incident to giving up his business, is good, and damages may be recovered for its breach.[2]

A club cannot recover dues from a member during his suspension from the club, unless the by-laws to which the member has subscribed contain an express or implied contract to pay dues during suspension.[3] And it seems that where the by-laws of a club provide that a member may be expelled for not paying his dues or indebtedness, the expulsion of the member is an election as to remedies, and,

---

[1] 40 N. J. L. Rep. 295. In N. Y. Protective Association vs. Mc-Grath (23 N. Y. St. Rep. 209), a by-law of an incorporated association was held to be void because it provided that on the expulsion of a local assembly, all of its members should be deemed to have voluntarily withdrawn, and in Wicks vs. Monihan (54 Hun, 614), a by-law decreeing a forfeiture of the right of members in property of a local assembly without judicial process was held void. To same effect is Austin vs. Searing, 16 N. Y. 112.

[2] White vs. Baxter, 71 N. Y. 254, aff'g 9 J. & S. (N. Y. Superior Ct. Rep.) 358.

[3] The Carteret Club vs. Florence, 3 N. J. L. Jour. (1880) 208.

after expulsion takes place, action will only lie where he has received some consideration after his suspension or expulsiou.[1]

But before a member of a corporation or an unincorporated association can appeal to the courts, it must appear that he has exhausted all of the remedies provided for by the constitution and by-laws of the association.

The question arose in White vs. Brownell,[2] as to an unincorporated association, viz., The New York Stock Exchange, and the court held that, before it would examine into any proceedings of the committee of the Stock Exchange, it must appear that the plaintiff had exhausted all of the remedies provided for in the constitution and by-laws, the court saying : " The by-law having provided a mode for reviewing and correcting any error or injustice on the part of the committee on membership, in reporting to the president that the plaintiff was in default he was bound to avail himself of the remedy provided by the constitution and by-laws of the body of which he had 'become a member, before he can ask a court of equity to investigate a proceeding not necessarily final in the body itself, but which was there subject to review, and might be annulled by the action of a committee expressly clothed with authority to investigate it (Carlen vs. Drury, 1 Vesey & B. 154)."[3]

[1] The Carteret Club vs. Florence, 3 N. J. L. J. 208.

[2] 4 Abb. Pr. (n. s.) 162.

[3] Id. 199; Lafond vs. Deems, 81 N. Y. 507; see also Soc. for Visitation of Sick vs. Commonw. ex rel. Meyer, 52 Pa. St. 125; Strempel vs. Rubins, 21 N. Y. St. Rep. 483. In Olery vs. Brown, 51 How. Pr. (N. Y.) 92, it appeared that plaintiff had exhausted his remedies in the association, and his appeal to the courts was upheld. Gebhard vs. New York Club, 21 Abb. N. C. 248; Baum vs. N. Y. Cotton Exchange, 21 Abb. N. C. 253; Lewis vs. Wilson, 2 N. Y. Supp. 806, aff'd in 121 N. Y. 284; Loubat vs. Le Roy, 40 Hun, 549.

He is not, however, obliged to follow the possible relief under a by-law which provides, not for an appeal from the trial body, but for a rehearing by that body itself. The probability in that case, of favorable reconsideration, is so slight, that the court will not compel a member to seek it before applying to the courts.[1]

And if he has been unlawfully expelled, it has been held that he is not obliged, before resorting to mandamus, to exhaust the means for reinstatement provided by a by-law authorizing the society to reinstate one expelled, by a two-thirds majority of all members present, after having paid all dues and fines, and an extra fine of fifty dollars, and after having passed the examination required for original membership, as the by-law related to cases of lawful expulsion, and where the appeal was to the discretionary power of the society.[2]

But the courts will not review and set aside proceedings of a society, taken under the authority of its articles of association assented to by its members, for the expulsion of a member upon notice of charges presented, and a hearing according to the by-laws, either because the charges were insufficient or the proceedings irregular, *unless* injustice has been done, which the party charged, tried, and expelled could not have objected to in the society or committee meeting.

Proceedings to expel a member under charges presented, notice given, and a hearing afforded, in conformity with articles of association agreed to by all the members, are to be considered without too much regard to any technicali-

---

[1] Loubat vs. Le Roy, 40 Hun, 546

[2] People vs. Musical Mutual Protective Union, 118 N. Y. 101

ties. Substantial justice is to be followed rather than form.[1]

So, where a committee of a club have power to expel any member whose conduct is, in their opinion, injurious to the interests of the club, and they exercise this power, all that is required is that the committee should form their opinion in a *bona fide* way, and the question whether their opinion is just or unjust is immaterial. The court will not interfere with the authority of the committee unless it appear that their decision has been arrived at dishonestly, or through caprice or improper motives.[2] But if the managers of a corporation exceed their authority, and their decision therefore cannot be enforced, a payment made in pursuance of such decision, cannot be recovered. Accordingly, when a by-law of the New York Coffee Exchange provided for a member's suspension on his insolvency, and the managers proceeded to settle a dispute between members by declaring that one of them, who was solvent, was in default on his contracts, if such solvent member makes a payment to the other, under the ruling of the managers, he does not do so under duress, as the decision could not be enforced by his suspension, and he cannot recover back the money so paid.[3]

In respect to the form of the remedy which a member of one of these associations should adopt to prevent an inter-

---

[1] People ex rel. Johnson vs. N. Y. Produce Exchange, 149 N. Y. 401, at p. 413; Albers vs. Merchants' Exchange of St. Louis, 39 Mo. App. 583, at p. 587; State vs. Cincinnati Chamber of Commerce, 4 Ohio N. P. 244; People vs. The St. George's Soc. of Detroit, 28 Mich. 261.

[2] Gardner vs. Fremantle, 19 W. R. 256; Hopkinson vs. Marquis of Exeter, 5 Eq. L. R. 63–66; Lyttleton vs. Blackburn, 33 L. T. Reps. 641. But see Evans vs. Phila. Club, 14 Wright (Pa.), 107. The jurors provided by the organic law are not to be lightly set aside. Gebhard vs. New York Club, 21 Abb. N. C. 248, at p. 251.

[4] Sawyer vs. Gruner, 17 N. Y. Supp. 465

ference with his membership or with his rights in the body, the question seems to have been generally raised by injunction. In the case of Leech vs. Harris,[1] where the plaintiff had prayed for an injunction to restrain the Board of Brokers from acting on a report of a committee by which he would be expelled, the defendants contended that the plaintiff's action was premature, and " that the board must first decide whether the case was within its jurisdiction before a court can interfere." The court, upon this point, said: " But whether this be so or not, equity prevents mischief. It does not wait until it is consummated. It does not even measure the paces by which it advances. It meets it at the threshold, and seeks to prevent a meditated wrong more often than to redress an injury already done. Courts of equity constantly decline to lay down any rule which shall limit their power and discretion as to the particular cases in which special injunctions shall be granted or withheld (2 Story's Eq. Juris. §§ 862, 959 b)."[2]

---

[1] 2 Brews. (Pa.) 571.

[2] To same effect, Powell vs. Abbott, 9 Week. Notes of Cas. 231. Lowry vs. Reed, 3 Brews. (Pa.) 452. An injunction *pendente lite* restraining the Exchange from asserting a resolution of expulsion against the expelled member, was granted in Hutchinson vs. Lawrence, 67 How. Pr. 38. But see, in this connection, Rorke vs. Russell, 2 Lans. (N. Y.) 244. See also, as to general power of court to interfere by injunction in cases of unincorporated associations like clubs, Joyce on Injunctions, 748, 751; Heath vs. Prest. of the Gold Exchange, 7 Ab. Pr. (n. s.) 251. In the following cases the injunction was denied on the merits, but not on the ground that the remedy invoked was improper; Sonneborn vs. Lavarello, 2 Hun, 201; Rorke vs. Russell, 2 Lans. (N. Y.) 244; Sewell vs. Ives, N. Y. *Daily Reg.* Feb. 11, 1879; Lewis vs. Wilson 121 N. Y. 284; Moxey's App., 9 Week. Notes of Cas. 440, affirming s. c. *sub nom.* Moxey vs. Phila. Stock Exchange, 37 Leg. Int. 82, and in Baum vs. N. Y. Cotton Exchange, 21 Abb. N. C. 253; an injunction against the defendant, a corporation, was denied on the merits. See also Cannon vs. Toronto Stock Exchange 5 Ont. App. 268; Kuchnemundt vs. Smith, 2 N. Y. Supp. 625 But in

And in a recent case in Wisconsin the Milwaukee City Chamber of Commerce was temporarily enjoined from suspending or expelling plaintiffs, on the ground that their complaint stated good grounds of relief, and as there was a probability that complainants were entitled to a permanent injunction, they were entitled as a matter of right to a temporary injunction, as, if the Chamber of Commerce were allowed to do the mischief threatened, it was reasonably certain that the object of the suit would be in a great

Massachusetts it has been held that where the charter of a corporation gives it power to suspend or expel members, there was conferred upon the corporation a special and limited judicial power, and that a court of chancery could not interfere with its action in the contemplated expulsion of a member. Grigg vs. Medical Society, 111 Mass. 185.

In Fritz vs. Muck, 62 How. Pr. 69, Merwin, J., said: "Cases are cited showing that the proper remedy is by mandamus where parties seek restoration to the membership of a corporation, but this does not, I think, apply to an unincorporated association (see White vs. Brownell, 2 Daly, 329, 358). Here if the party has any remedy it is by suit," and he held that plaintiff was entitled to a judgment declaring his expulsion invalid and restoring him to all his rights as a member.

The expelled member may, after the expulsion has been declared void, recover the value of his seat, in an action of conversion, if the Exchange has sold it and retained the proceeds. Sewell vs. Ives, 61 How. Pr. 54; Cecil vs. Simmons, N. Y. *Daily Reg.* March 17, 1886. Or

in the case of a certificate of membership the value of the right of which it is evidence of title, without interest. Olds vs. Chicago Bd. of Trade, 33 Ill. App. 445. Or may recover damages for any wrong to him consequent upon the wrongful expulsion. Burt vs. Grand Lodge, 66 Mich. 87. A mandamus against an unincorporated association was granted in the case of Otto vs. Tailors' Union, 75 Cal. 308.

In Illinois it has been held that injunction is a preventive, and not an affirmative, remedy and, therefore, a court of chancery cannot by injunction restore an improperly expelled member to membership. Fisher vs. Bd. of Trade, 80 Ill. 85; Baxter vs. Bd. of Trade, 83 Ill. 146. Nor can injunction issue to restrain a threatened expulsion. Sturges vs. Board of Trade, 86 Ill. 441, or where the expulsion has been legally effected. Pitcher vs. Board of Trade, 121 Ill. 412. And see Rex vs. Richardson, 1 Burr. 539; Murdock vs. Phillips Academy, 12 Pick. (Mass.) 244; Beach on Injunctions, p. 1362; Spelling on Injunctions. p. 633.

measure defeated. A judgment in their favor, if the *status quo* was not preserved during the litigation, would leave them irreparably injured, while, if it was preserved, no damage of a serious character could accrue to the Chamber if it finally prevailed, certainly none that could not be adequately guarded against by security.[1]

In a similar case in New York, where a member of the New York Produce Exchange sought to restrain the Exchange from investigating charges brought against him by another member, an order granting a temporary injunction was dissolved, as a majority of the court was in favor of reversal of the order granting it. Three of the judges were in favor of reversal on the ground that the board had jurisdiction of the complaint, whilst the three dissenting judges held that the board had no jurisdiction. Andrew, J., concurred for reversal on the ground that, upon the facts, the remedy by injunction would not lie, as no violation of plaintiff's rights had happened, or might ever happen, and no injury thereto was threatened in such a sense as justified a preventive remedy.[2]

But when a member has been expelled from a corporation for no legal cause, mandamus lies against the corporation to compel it to restore him to membership.[3]

---

[1] Bartlett vs. Bartlett, 93 N. W. (Wis.) 473; See Kolff vs. Ex., 48 Minn. 215.

[2] Hurst vs. New York Produce Exchange, 100 N. Y. 605; Greer v. Stoller, 77 F. 1.

[3] High, Extra. Legal Rem. (2d ed.) § 291; State vs. The Georgia Med. Soc., 38 Ga. 608, where there is a review of authorities; Evans vs. Phila. Club, 50 Pa. St. 107; The Carteret Club vs. Florence, 3 N. J. L. J. 208; Commonw. vs. The German Soc., 15 Pa. St. 251; People vs. Mechanics' Aid Soc., 22 Mich. 86; People vs. Med. Soc. of Erie, 24 Barb. (N. Y.) 570; People vs. New York Cotton Ex., 8 Hun, 216; People vs. N. Y. Ben. Soc., 3 Hun, 361; People vs. Am. Inst., 44 How. Pr. 468; People vs. N. Y. Prod. Ex., 149 N. Y. 401; People vs. Society, 24 How. Pr. 216; People vs. Institute, 2 N. Y. Leg. Ob. 170; Nelson

Mr. High says :[1] " The use of the writ of mandamus as
a remedy for the wrongful amotion of a corporator, and to
restore him to the enjoyment of the franchise, of which he
has been wrongfully deprived, is of very ancient origin, and
may be distinctly traced to a period as early as the reign of
Edward the Second.   It was also used for the same purpose
in the time of Henry the Sixth ; and in the reign of Elizabeth it was treated as a well-established jurisdiction."

vs. Board of Trade, 58 Ill. App.
414.

In Albers vs. Mer. Ex., 39 Mo.
App. 583, under the statutes of
Missouri, an injunction against a
corporation was granted restraining
the enforcement of a resolution of
suspension. The remedy by injunction has been also applied in
Pennsylvania and Wisconsin. Kerr
vs. Trego, 47 Pa. St. 295; Roshi's
Appeal, 69 Pa. St. 467; Lutheran
Church vs. Gristgau, 34 Wis. 336.
Mandamus cannot issue to restore
one to membership in an unincorporated Exchange. Weidenfeld vs.
Keppler, 84 A. D. 235; 68 N. E.
1125. The proper proceeding in
such case is by equitable action.
Fritz vs. Muck, 62 How. Pr. 69.

It seems that where a member is
expelled and seeks to review the act
of the Exchange in expelling him in
the courts on the ground that it was
unauthorized and illegal, the court
will permit him by order to inspect
and copy the record and proceedings under which he was expelled,
and to examine the President or
other officers upon the subject to

enable him to prepare his complaint. Hutchinson vs. Lawrence,
N. Y. Supreme Ct. Chambers, N. Y.
Daily Reg. Feb. 20, 1883, aff'd
by Gen. Term, 3 N. Y. Civ. Proc.
Rep. 98.   And as to what questions
the President of the Exchange can
be compelled to answer upon such
examination, see elaborate opinion
of Lawrence, J., in Hutchinson vs.
Lawrence, N. Y. *Daily Reg.* April 3,
1883, N.Y. Supreme Ct.   But where
a member of the New York Stock
Exchange is expelled for "obvious
fraud" under its rules and constitution, in an action by such member
against the Exchange, the plaintiff
is not entitled to a bill of particulars of the fraud. Solomon vs.
McKay, 17 N. Y. W. Dig. 229. See
also State vs. Chamber of Comm.,
20 Wis. 68; State vs. Chamber
of Comm., 47 Wis. 670; Delacy
vs. Neuse River Nav. Co., 1
Hawk. (N. C.) 274; Franklin Beneficial Assoc. vs. The Commonw.,
10 Pa. St. 357 ; State vs. Un.
Merchant's Ex., 2 Mo. App. 96;
Savannah Cotton Ex. vs. State, 54
Ga. 668.

---

[1] Extra. Legal Rem. (2d ed.)
§ 291, and see Merrill on Mandamus, § 166; Albers vs. Exchange, 39
Mo. App. 583, at p. 588.

The following are some of the grounds held sufficient for invoking the extraordinary aid of mandamus : Want of notice of proceedings taken for the removal of a member, and want of opportunity of being heard in his defence;[1] where no sufficient cause has been shown for the removal, and where the proceedings have been conducted with irregularity,[2] and in a spirit of malice;[3] and where the member has been illegally removed for violating a rule of the corporation which is in conflict with public policy and the law of the land;[4] or where he has been expelled under an unreasonable by-law;[5] or where the act of the member is not a violation of the charter and by-laws.[6] Where, however, a corporator has been regularly tried in accordance with the rules of the association, which he has assented to by becoming a corporator, and has been expelled in due form, the merits of the expulsion will not be examined in proceedings for a mandamus.[7]

So it would seem that a mere restriction upon the mode

---

[1] Delacy vs. Neuse River Nav. Co. (supra); People vs. St. Franciscus Soc., 24 How. Pr. 216; People vs. Benevolent Soc., 3 Hun, 361; State vs. Chamber of Commerce, 47 Wis. 670.

[2] People vs. New York Cotton Exchange, 8 Hun, 216; People vs. Musical Union, 118 N. Y. 101.

[3] State vs. The Georgia Med. Soc. (supra).

[4] People vs. Med. Soc. of Erie (supra).

[5] Commonw. vs. St. Pat. Benev. Soc., 2 Binn. (Pa.) 442; State vs. Union Mer. Ex., 2 Mo. App. 96. And where an appeal from the committee's decision, on ground of jurisdiction, reserving the merits, has

been denied, Savannah Cotton Ex. vs. State, 54 Ga. 668.

[6] People ex rel. Elliott vs. New York Cotton Exchange, 8 Hun, 216.

[7] High, Extra Legal Rem. (2d ed) § 292, and cases cited; Merrill on Mandamus, § 166; Society vs. The Commonw. 52 Pa. St. 125. Nor will mandamus be issued because of mere irregularity in the expulsion proceedings, if it appears that proper grounds for the expulsion exist and the member may, after the restoration by virtue of the mandamus, again be expelled by proceedings in due form. Merrill on Mandamus, § 170, and cases there cited; see also Black and White Smiths' Soc. vs. Vandyke,

in which the member may exercise his corporate right, and not an actual exclusion from the corporation, affords no ground for a mandamus.[1] And mere informality in the proceedings for the removal of a member, especially where they are carried by his own action, will not justify interference by mandamus, where there was just ground for his removal, and the member has been acting in hostility to the corporation, and threatens to continue his opposition.[2]

The return must set forth distinctly all the facts essential to the conviction, both as to the cause of disfranchisement and the mode of proceeding.[3]

An action for damages may also be maintained by a member who has been unlawfully expelled[4] or indefinitely suspended,[5] or if he is denied the privileges of the Exchange and his means of livelihood as a Broker without actual suspension or expulsion.[6] And the bringing of such an action is a waiver of the right to mandamus.[7]

2 Whart. 309; Sperry's Appeal, 116 Pa. St. 391; also, Commonw. vs. Pike Benev. Soc., 8 W. & S. 247. Mandamus to restore corporator, Franklin Beneficial Assoc. vs. The Commonw. (supra).

[1] High, Extra. Legal Rem. (2d ed.) § 300; Crocker vs. Old South Soc., 106 Mass. 489.

[2] High, Extra Legal Rem. (2d ed.) § 301; State vs. Lusitanian Portuguese Soc., 15 La. An. 73; King vs. Griffiths, 5 Barn. & Ald. 731.

[3] Society vs. Commonw., 52 Pa. St. 125, and cases there cited.

[4] Cannon vs. Corn Ex., 5 Ont. App. 268; Burt vs. Grand Lodge, 66 Mich. 87.

[5] Blumenthal vs. Cincinnati Chamber of Commerce, 8 Ohio Decis. Rep. 410.

[6] Temple vs. Stock Ex., 8 Ont. (Can.) 705.

[7] State vs. Slavonska, 28 Ohio St. 665. As to when not even nominal damages will be given, see Albers vs. Ex., 138 Mo. 140. See also Lurman vs. Jarvie, 81 N. Y. Supp. 468.

(*c.*) *Rule Giving members of Exchange Lien on Proceeds of Defaulting Members' " Seats," etc., in Preference to other Creditors, not Illegal.*

In the case of Hyde vs. Woods[1] it was held that a provision in the constitution of a Stock and Exchange Board (a voluntary unincorporated society, whose members are elected by ballot and are limited in number)—that a member, upon failing to perform his contracts or becoming insolvent, may assign his seat to be sold, and that the proceeds shall, to the exclusion of his outside creditors, be first applied to the benefit of the members to whom he is indebted—is neither contrary to public policy nor in violation of the Bankrupt Act. The reasoning of the court was that the San Francisco Stock and Exchange Board was a voluntary association, and the members had a right to associate themselves upon such terms as they saw fit to prescribe, so long as there was nothing immoral, or contrary to public policy, or in contravention of the law of the land in the terms and conditions adopted. No man was under any obligation to become a member unless he saw fit to do so ; and when he did, and subscribed to the constitution and by-laws, thereby accepting and assenting to the conditions prescribed, he acquired just such rights, with such limitations, and no others, as the articles of the association provided for. The decision was affirmed by the Supreme Court of the United States,[2] where the court, through Mr. Justice Miller, said : " There is no reason why the Stock Board should not make membership subject to the rule in

[1] 94 U. S. (4 Otto) 523, aff'g 2 Sawy. 655. See this case distinguished in Barclay vs. Smith, 107 Ill. 355, in which it was held that a Chicago Board of Trade certificate was not property such as could be sold to pay the holder's debts. But see Weaver vs. Fisher, 110 Ill. 146.

[2] 94 U. S. 523.

question, unless it be that it is a violation of some statute or of some principle of public policy. It does not violate the provision of the Bankrupt Law against preference of creditors, for such a preference is only void when made within four months previous to the commencement of the bankrupt proceedings. Neither the Bankrupt Law nor any principle of morals is violated by this provision, so far as we can see. A seat in this board is not a matter of absolute purchase. Though we have said it is property, it is encumbered with conditions when purchased, without which it could not be obtained. It never was free from the conditions of Article XV., neither when Fenn bought nor at any time before or since. That rule entered into and became an incident of the property when it was created, and remains a part of it, into whose hands soever it may come. As the creators of this right— this property—took nothing from any man's creditors when they created it, no wrong was done to any creditor by the imposition of this condition."

In New York it has also been decided that a person becoming a member, assents to the appropriation of the proceeds of his seat, to the payment of debts on the Exchange.[1]

[1] Weston vs. Ives, 97 N. Y. 222; Bernheim vs. Keppler, 34 Misc. 321; Stonebridge vs. Smith, 55 N. Y. Super. Ct. 294; People ex rel. Krohn vs. Miller, 39 Hun, 557; Hanscom vs. Hendricks, 52 Hun, 80. See also Belton vs. Hatch, 109 N. Y. 593. The constitution of the New York Stock Exchange provides that if a member be suspended, upon insolvency, and fails to settle within one year, his seat shall be disposed of by the committee on admission and the proceeds first applied to his debts in the Exchange. The Governing Committee may extend the time for settlement for periods of not more than one year, and it has been held that when a member is suspended the rights of other members in the proceeds of his seat do not become fixed immediately, unless the seat is then sold, and if the period of settlement is extended, the committee are to determine such rights according to

But if the articles of incorporation, rules, or by-laws of a chamber of commerce do not give the members a lien on the certificate of membership for debts due to them, such debts become barred by the discharge of the debtor in bankruptcy, and mandamus will lie to compel the board to transfer the certificate on its books to one to whom the trustee in bankruptcy had sold it, the sole reason for the refusal of the transfer being the objection of two of the members to the transfer on the ground that debts due to them by the bankrupt were unpaid.[1]

The case of Nicholson, Assignee, vs. Gouch[2] was, in many respects, very much like that of Hyde vs. Woods, the action having been brought to recover certain property that, under the rules of the London Exchange, of which the bankrupt was a member, had been received and paid to his fellow-members. This was asserted to be a preference, void by the Bankrupt Law; and the rules of the Exchange under which it was done were assailed on the same ground taken above. It is true that in the decision of the Queen's Bench in banc, Lord Campbell, the Chief Justice, ruled against the plaintiff, on the ground that the money in question arose out of wagering contracts, which, as they could not have been enforced

the rules existing at the extended time and not as they were at the time of suspension. Haight vs. Dickerman, 18 N. Y. Supp. 559. The constitution of the San Francisco Stock Exchange has a similar provision which has been judicially applied. Rorke vs. San Francisco Stock Exchange Board, 99 Cal. 196. An agreement to invest the purchase price of seats in a proposed Exchange in a trust fund for the security of debts between members, does not contravene the statute forbidding perpetuities. Brown vs. Mutual Trust Co., 22 Weekly Dig. (N. Y.) 394.

[1] State vs. Chamber of Commerce, 79 N. W. (Minn.) 1026.

[2] 5 El. & Bl. 999. In Clarkson vs. Toronto Stock Exchange, 13 Ontario Rep. 213, a by-law giving a preference to claims of the Exchange and its members was sustained.

by the bankrupt, were therefore not subject to the claim of the assignee; but Compton, J., held, also, that the money being received and distributed under the rules of the Stock Exchange, by reason of the bankrupt having become a member subject to said rules, this was a sufficient defence to the party who so received and distributed it.

So, in the State of Pennsylvania, there are several decisions which uphold the right and power of the Board of Brokers to make by-laws by which members of the association are entitled to a preference in the payment of their debts from the proceeds of the sale of an insolvent member's seat over outside creditors.

In the case of Leech vs. Leech [1] an outside creditor sought to reach the proceeds of the sale of his debtor's seat in the Exchange by attachment; but the court held that the claims of the fellow-members of the insolvent should first be paid; that this was the condition upon which the insolvent became possessed of his seat, and it could not be repudiated.[2]

In the case of Singerly vs. Johnson [3] the plaintiff's intestate, at the time of his death, was a member of the Philadelphia Board of Brokers. After his death, his seat was sold by the secretary, under the provisions of the constitution, as follows: " Sec. XII. . . . When a member dies, his seat may be sold by the secretary, and after satisfying the claims of the members of the board, the balance shall be paid to his legal representatives."

The plaintiff's intestate was indebted to another member of the board at the time of his death, which claim was passed upon and allowed by the Arbitration Committee, in

[1] 3 Week. Notes of Cas. 542, note.

[2] This decision was confirmed in

the case of Evans vs. Wister, 1 Week. Notes of Cas. 181.

[3] 3 Week. Notes of Cas. 541.

pursuance of the constitution. On this state of facts, it was held—(1) that the decision of the Arbitration Committee was final and conclusive as to the existence, validity, and amount of the member's claim, and that a court of law has no jurisdiction to go behind or inquire into the finding of said committee ; (2) that the agreement to abide by the arbitration clause, etc., in the constitution, entered into by Singerly, or implied by his membership, was not revoked by his death ; (3) that the plaintiff, as the legal representative of the decedent, was only entitled to recover the balance, if any, after the payment of the member's claim, with interest ; and that such limitation of his right was not affected by the fact that the decision of the Arbitration Committee was made after the commencement of the suit.

This case was followed by Thompson vs. Adams,[1] where the court held, that under the constitution and by-laws of the Philadelphia Stock Exchange, providing that a member may sell his seat if he has no claims against him, and also providing that, in case of death, a member's seat might be sold and the proceeds paid to his representatives, after satisfying claims of members, a secret equitable owner of a seat—one who had advanced the money to the member to enable him to purchase the same—has no right, as against members of the board who are creditors of the legal owner, to share in the proceeds of the sale of the seat on the death of the latter. It was held that the constitution and by-laws have the force of law as to its members. The court said :

"The jurisdiction of the courts cannot be ousted by contract, but any person may covenant or agree that no right of action shall accrue until a third person has decided on

[1] 93 Pa. St. 55.

any difference that may arise between himself and the other party to the covenant. The leading case upon this subject, and followed in Pennsylvania, is Scott vs. Avery."[1] Upon appeal the court said : "There is nothing unlawful or unreasonable in this regulation."[2]

The by-laws may provide that the preference shall extend to all debts incurred in the course of business between the members, though they do not grow out of stock transactions.[3] But the debt must have arisen in dealings on the Exchange of the character specified in the rules or by-laws. The maxim *inclusio unus est exclusio alterius* applies.[4]

A debt due to a firm in which only one of the partners has a seat in the Exchange, is entitled to the same preference as if due to the partner individually. A debt to a firm is a debt to each member of the firm.[5]

[1] 5 House of Lords Cas. 811.

[2] See also Moxey's App, ante, p. 91, where the court again held that such a regulation was not contrary to law.

[3] Sheppard vs. Barrett, 17 Phila. 145, where it was held that the rules included in the preference given, a "friendly loan" which by the custom of brokers was a loan of money or stocks between brokers for business purposes.

[4] Bernheim vs. Keppler, 34 Misc. 321; Cockran vs. Adams, 180 Pa. St. 289. In the first named case it was held that a claim by one member against the proceeds of the sale of the seat of another arising out of transactions prior to the former's admission to membership was properly disallowed.

Although the language of the constitution of the Exchange is that "all contracts, debts or obligations of every description" (art. 13, § 6) due to members are to have preferential payment, the committee on claims has only jurisdiction of claims arising from transactions in the Exchange, viz., those arising on stocks, bonds, bullion, grain or cotton on the Exchange, and if the committee, in investigating these claims, proceeds according to the by-laws and the jurisdiction conferred upon them, their findings will be sustained. In re Hayes, 75 N. Y. Supp. 312.

[5] Sheppard vs. Barrett, 17 Phila. 145. In Cochran vs. Adams, 180 Pa. St. 289, the provision of the constitution considered had a special provision to this effect. And the same has been held to apply in New York, although the member had made a prior general assignment.

By the terms of the constitution and by-laws, the person becoming a member assents, in case of suspension, to the appropriation of the proceeds of his seat in a particular way, and no other appropriation can be made. Even though the decision of the committee making the distribution as to claims is declared to be final, it has no power beyond that given by the contract. It cannot admit a claim which the constitution by its terms excludes, and this is so whether the claim is valid or not.[1]

A Stock Exchange creditor who has taken the benefit of the distribution of the proceeds of the seat, or in England, of the other assets to be distributed under the rules, is not precluded from afterwards taking ordinary legal proceedings, for the recovery of the balance due him, though in England he must give credit for what he has received in the

In re Hayes, 75 N. Y. Supp. 321. Even although the constitution of the New York Stock Exchange does not so clearly indicate, proof of the usage of the Exchange, and of the practical construction put upon the constitution by the parties thereto, will give effect to the constructions thereof as stated in the text. Id.

[1] Weston vs. Ives, 97 N. Y. 222. An amendment to the constitution or by-laws, made after the member had ceased to be such, but pending the distribution of the fund in the hands of the Exchange, and admitting claims to the preference, which were not entitled previously thereto, would be ineffectual in that case. Ibid.

A threat by an officer or member of the Exchange to make an improper distribution, even if such individual were a member of the committee, is not enough to sustain the granting of an *ad interim* injunction, restraining the disposition of the fund. It is to be presumed that the action of the committee will be legal. Stonebridge vs. Smith, 55 N. Y. Super. Ct. 294. See also Hurst vs. N. Y. Produce Exchange, 100 N. Y. 605; s. c. 1 Cent. Rep. 260, in which it was held that it is to be presumed that the committee will deal justly in deciding any question arising under the by-laws.

The committee are all members of the Exchange, and they may have an interest in the matter before them. But the mere fact of having such interest does not disqualify them from taking part in a decision, though the fact that some members have an interest may put the other members of the committee on their

Exchange.[1] In New York, however, it has been held that
when a member of the Stock Exchange makes a general assignment, his membership is an asset of the assigned estate,
subject to the existing constitutional rights therein of the
Stock Exchange creditors, and therefore in the distribution
of the general estate by the assignee, the claims of the Stock
Exchange creditors, without reference to the amounts received by them out of the proceeds of the sale of the seat,
should be allowed as filed, subject to the exception that no
such creditor should receive any sum, as dividend, in excess
of the balance due him upon the full amount of his original
claim, after deducting the amount received by him from the
proceeds of the membership.[2]

Reverting to the question of preference, the law seems
to be differently settled in England,[3] where a member of the
Exchange seeks to prefer his fellow-members to his outside
creditors by *paying money* to the official assignee of the
Exchange. In the case in question it appeared that C.
was a member of the Stock Exchange, and became unable
to meet his Stock Exchange engagements, of which fact he
gave notice to the secretary. In such a case the rules of
the Stock Exchange prescribe the course to be followed.
The defaulter ceases to be a member of the body; two
members of the Exchange act as official assignees of the
defaulter; a meeting of the creditors is called; the defaulter

guard as to how far the opinion of
those members who have an interest is to be considered. Ex parte
Ward, L. R. 20 Ch. Div. 356.

Where the by-laws provided no
means of deciding a contest as to
the propriety of particular deductions, the jurisdiction of the court is
not ousted and a reference will be

made to a master to ascertain what
deductions should, under the by-
laws, be made. Clarkson vs. Toronto Stock Exchange, 13 Ont. 213.

[1] Ex parte Ward, 20 Ch. Div. 356.
[2] In re Hayes, 75 N. Y. Supp. 312.
[3] Tomkins vs. Saffery, 3 L. R.
App. Cas. 213.

(as he is required to do) makes his statement; and, the assembled creditors having decided what is to be done, the official assignees carry the decision into execution. The committee of the Exchange has the power to readmit the defaulter or to refuse him readmission. C. made his statement at the first meeting, declaring at that time he had no debts outside the Stock Exchange. His Stock Exchange creditors then consented to accept a composition, and to provide for a part of it he, at the demand of the official assignees, gave them a cheque for £5000, then standing to his credit in the Bank of England. The official assignees obtained the money and apportioned it among his Stock Exchange creditors. C. afterwards confessed to owing debts to a large amount to outside creditors, and was declared a bankrupt. The trustee in bankruptcy, on behalf of the general creditors, claimed from the official assignees of the Stock Exchange the £5000, and the court decided that the trustee was entitled to claim it, for the action of C. in paying it to the official assignees amounted to a *cessio bonorum*, and constituted an act of bankruptcy; and that the rules of the Stock Exchange as to defaulting members of the body are the rules of a domestic forum, which have no influence on the rights of those who are not amenable as members to the jurisdiction of that body. They cannot, therefore, govern the rights of the general creditors of a defaulting member.

The Lord Chancellor, in delivering his opinion in this case, said : " I can see nothing whatever in those rules which is deserving of any animadversion whatever. They seem to me to be judicious and business-like rules. They do not seem to me to be rules contemplating or intending in any way to warp or strain, or in any way to elude or defeat the operation of the bankruptcy law of the country ; but they are rules which, from the very nature of the case, are and must be subject to one infirmity—namely, that, if they are to be effectual, they must be applicable to the case of a person who not merely is a defaulter upon the Stock Exchange, but who has no creditors outside the Stock Exchange; because if such a person has creditors outside the Stock Exchange, the general law of the country will step in, and must step in, and will give to those creditors rights which these rules cannot take away from them, and which, I am bound to say, these rules do not profess to attempt to take away from them.   Therefore, although everything done in the domestic forum of the Stock Exchange under those rules may be done according to the rules, and may be most wholesome in its operation for the members of the Stock Exchange, still what is done must be subject to the rights of those who are not amenable to the jurisdiction of the Stock Exchange; and when those higher rights come into conflict with these rules, of course these rules must give way to those higher rights."

But in the case of Ex parte Grant, Re Plumbly,[1] the case of Tomkins vs. Saffery was distinguished; and the result shows that the English courts did not mean to condemn all the transactions of an insolvent Broker as void, whereby his fellow-members reaped the benefit of his assets to the exclusion of his outside creditors.

The facts of this case showed that on the 25th of June, 1879, Plumbly, a Stock-jobber, and a member of the London Stock Exchange, having given notice that he was unable to meet his engagements, was declared a defaulter in accordance with Rule 142 of the Stock Exchange.   The same day

---

[1] 42 L. T. R. (n. s.) 387.

he filed a liquidation petition, and a trustee was afterwards appointed. Grant, the official assignee of the Stock Exchange, in obedience to Rule 168, closed all Plumbly's contracts with members of the Stock Exchange, which were open for the next account or settling day, the 27th of June, at the market prices on the 25th of the various stocks and shares contracted for; and called upon those members who on that footing were debtors on their contracts with Plumbly, to pay to the official assignee the differences due from them. On hearing this, the trustee gave notice to the debtors to pay the money to him, instead of to the official assignee. They, however, paid them to the official assignee. The amount of these differences so received was £3957, which sum was, under Rule 168, divisible among those members, of the Stock Exchange who, on the above-mentioned footing, were creditors for differences on their contracts with Plumbly.

The rules of the Stock Exchange apply to Jobbers as well as to Brokers. It appeared to be the practice of Stockjobbers to make two contracts equal and opposite at once, so that a Stock-jobber's legitimate profit is the difference between the buying and selling prices, and the fact of stocks going up or down in price does not affect him. The Jobber does not deal with an outside principal, but only with members of the Stock Exchange.

The trustee in the liquidation claimed the £3957 as part of the assets distributable among Plumbly's creditors. The registrar, being of opinion that the case was within Tomkins vs. Saffery,[1] held that the trustee was entitled to the money. The official assignee appealed, and the judgment was reversed upon the theory laid down by the court, per Baggal-

[1] 37 L. T. R. (n. s.) 758; 3 L. R. App. Cas. 213.

lay, L. J., that the distinction to be drawn between this case
and that of Tomkins vs. Saffery was a very marked one.
Here there is no division of Plumbly's money. The official
assignee holds no private assets of Plumbly, and the fund
which he has collected is a fund collected by virtue of certain
rules of the Stock Exchange ; certain sums ascertained
in a particular way being raised from particular members
of the Stock Exchange, and applied in a particular manner.
These funds can in no respect be regarded as funds belonging to Plumbly; they are voluntary contributions of the
members of the Stock Exchange, to be applied in satisfaction of the Stock Exchange creditors; or, if they are to be
regarded as moneys handed over by persons who had become surety to meet the claims of the Stock Exchange, in
either view of the case they cannot be claimed by the trustee. "It certainly did," says the learned justice, "at one
time occur to me that some injustice might be done to the
general creditors of Plumbly by the official assignee taking
these sums. But the true view of the case appears to me to
be this: As far as regards any losing contracts, entered into
by Plumbly, the trustee in bankruptcy, or in liquidation is
relieved from them ; and if, on the other hand, it is said that
there may be some winning contracts, the answer, as far as
regards them, is, that it would be impossible to realize on
them, because, when the time arrived for the completion of
the contract, Plumbly could not, and would not, have been
ready and willing to perform them. In making these observations, I do not mean to imply that in such cases the
contracts, whether losing or winning, are absolutely void;
but, in regard to the case now under consideration, I am
satisfied that no injury could be done to the outside creditors
by the course pursued."

Upon a first reading, there seems to be very little substantial distinction between the case of Tomkins vs. Saffery and the last one. In both cases the money had been placed in the hands of the official assignee of the Stock Exchange, who had received the same from debtors of the insolvent member,[1] and who had, with knowledge of the latter's insolvency or failure, paid out the money so received to his Stock Exchange creditors. But, in the one case, the official assignee received the money by virtue of a check given by the defaulting Broker upon the Bank of England, an outside debtor; on the other hand, the official assignee received the money from voluntary payments made to him by members of the Stock Exchange who were debtors to the defaulter, but who were under no obligations to pay at the time they did, except by reason of their being such members.

There is nothing unreasonable in annexing to a membership of an Exchange a condition, that, if the member fails to perform his contracts, his seat and the money due him from fellow-members should first go to satisfy the claims of his fellow-members. Such a condition is in the nature of a lien on his property in the Exchange. It is not made secretly, nor with any intent to defraud creditors; nor are the latter injured any more in their rights than they would be in the case of a mortgage. It is upon the faith of this condition that his fellow-members transact any business with him, and it is hard to subscribe to a doctrine which invests subsequent outside creditors with the property of a defaulting member, which he has acquired by reason of his membership in the Exchange.[2]

---

[1] In Tomkins vs. Saffery he received the money from the insolvent's bank. See p. 120.

[2] And since the above was written the private administration by the officers of the Exchange of the as-

It must also be borne in mind, in this connection, that there is a wide difference in the facts of the American, from those in the English, cases upon which we are commenting. In the former cases the creditors sought to reach the seats, or the proceeds of the seats, of members of the Stock Exchange; seats which had been granted to the members with certain conditions attached, which gave a preference to their fellow-members; whereas in the English case of Tomkins vs. Saffery, the Stock Exchange creditors sought to appropriate money in bank, belonging to the insolvent member, in preference to his outside creditors.[1]

But the members of the Exchange have no lien upon the proceeds of a seat illegally ordered to be sold by the association; and in an action by a member whose seat has been so illegally disposed of, against the President of the association to recover damages as for a conversion of his property, the fact that the proceeds have been applied towards satisfying claims against the member whose seat has been sold is not a matter in mitigation of damages, or the proper subject of a counterclaim. These propositions were laid down in the case of Sewell vs. Ives, President.[2]

sets realized as in Ex parte Grant, Re Plumbly, to the payment of debts on the Exchange, accounting only to the trustee in bankruptcy, for the balance, has been uniformly sustained in England. Ex parte Ward, L. R. 20 Ch. Div. 356; King vs. Hutton, L. R. 2 Q. B. D. 1900, 504; Re Woodd; Ex parte King, 82 L. T. N. S. 504.

But the committee is not, as against the trustee in bankruptcy, entitled to balances due the defaulting member from his outside clients, even though the defaulter has in turn become liable on the execution of the same contract, to a jobber member of the Exchange. Re Woodd; Ex parte King, supra.

[1] Tomkins vs. Saffery is so distinguished in Clarkson vs. Toronto Stock Exchange, 13 Ont. Rep. 221

[2] 61 How. Pr. Rep. 54. The measure of damages is the value of the property right at the time of the conversion, with interest. Olds vs. Chicago Open Board Trade, 33 Ill. App. 445.

In that case the New York Stock Exchange, in January, 1878, attempted to expel the plaintiff upon an accusation of "obvious fraud," and in an action between the same parties the court adjudged and decided that his expulsion was illegal and void. The defendant, treating the plaintiff as effectually expelled, under Article XX. of its constitution, in April, 1878, sold his seat, and appropriated the proceeds to the payment of his creditors in the Exchange.

The court held that the seat of a member in the Exchange was property in every proper sense of the term, and could be sold ; and was transferable as any other species of property having actual value as such. The price realized by the defendant was $4000, which is proof of its then value. It was proved, and the court on the former trial found, that the plaintiff paid, on his admission to the board, $2000 for his seat.

Although the plaintiff was a suspended member of the New York Exchange, it having been held and decided that his alleged expulsion therefrom was void and of no effect, it followed that, the sale of his seat by the board having been made solely upon the ground of his wrongful expulsion, the Exchange became by that act responsible to the plaintiff for any injury or damage done thereby.

It was claimed that the proceeds of this sale were applied to the payment of the plaintiff's debts in the Exchange, and that such payment should be received in mitigation of damages, if not in bar to the action. The court said : "If this be so, it must be upon the assumption that the defendant had authority to dispose of the seat, and to receive and appropriate the proceeds of the sale to his creditors." The court held that under the facts in the case, no such authority was shown, nor can any be inferred, as all the proceedings on defendant's part were wholly illegal and void.

The property wrongfully taken or appropriated by the defendant, in satisfaction of a demand against the plaintiff as owner, cannot be set up in bar or in mitigation of damages suffered by him. The first objection urged against the plaintiff's right to recover was that the action was for the conversion of personal property, commonly known as an action of trover. The declaration tersely set out " that the plaintiff was owner, and entitled to the possession, of a seat in the association of the value of $10,000 ; that the defendant wrongfully and unlawfully sold said seat and converted the proceeds to its own use, to the plaintiff's damages." [1]

The court held that it was too late to raise this objection. The defendants treated the seat of the plaintiff as their property, or they could not have undertaken to sell it. They are estopped by their own acts. The amount of recovery in the action, the court decided, was the amount of the proceeds received by the defendant, with interest.[2]

---

[1] A similar complaint was sustained on demurrer in Cecil vs. Simmons, N. Y. *Daily Reg.* March 17, 1886.

[2] Where a certificate of membership has been ordered by judicial decree to be transferred by the person in whose name it stood to the actual owner, and the decree has not been obeyed, on inquisition of damages, the proper measure is its value when it should have been so transferred, and not what it had become, during the delay, by being subjected to debts to members greatly diminishing its value. Jones vs. Fisher, 2 Western Rep. 890.

One of the by-laws of the New York Cotton Exchange provided for the transfer from one member to another of certificates of membership upon ten days' notice of intention so to do, such notice to be posted upon the bulletin board of the Exchange, and upon payment of all claims against the member making the transfer, and it was held in People vs. Miller, 39 Hun, 557, that this by-law should have been strictly complied with by complet-

*(d.) The Stock Exchange cannot Take Cognizance of Matters
Arising outside of, and Disconnected with the Purposes of
its Organization.*

It would seem entirely reasonable to confine and limit the
jurisdiction of the Stock Exchange *to those matters which
arise between its members in the course of their business with
each other as Brokers,* otherwise its judicial powers might
be extended to embrace every affair of human life, which
was never contemplated, and which the law would not permit.[1]

Thus, the wife of a Broker might bring her grievances
before the Board or its Committees, and claim to have them
settled by that tribunal, just as any outside person might
insist upon having an action of assault and battery, alleged
to have been committed upon him by a member of the Exchange, determined by the same forum. For very obvious
reasons the law will not permit any organizations to usurp
the prerogatives of the regularly constituted courts of justice. One of the most important is, that such an organization
has no power to issue subpoenas, or any other compulsory
process, to enforce the attendance of witnesses. It can co-

ing the transfer and obtaining a surrender of the certificate at the end
of the ten days and that a notice of
nearly one year was insufficient, as
the selling member continued to be
such until the certificate was surrendered, and might incur further
liabilities, the lien of which might
not be sufficiently protected by
such an indefinite notice. It was
held in that case also that the purchasing member's remedy against
the corporation was by action at

law for damages, and not by mandamus.

[1] "This proposition is certainly
consistent with the purpose for
which the association was formed,
is patent from a reading of the instrument vitalizing it, and should
not be extended to the detriment of
one of the contracting parties unless the language of the provision
invoked unmistakably intends it."
Per Levintritt, J., Bernheim vs.
Keppler, 34 Misc. 321.

9

erce its own members into attendance by threatening expulsion, but it has no power over outside witnesses.

Another equally important reason is, that the law has prescribed, for the determination of disputes between citizens, regular and well-adapted forms and proceedings, which no one can be deprived of against his will.[1]

And while a voluntary association may adopt rules obligatory upon its own members, by which their rights may be summarily determined as between themselves, such determination has no external force to injure or impair the rights of non-members not voluntarily subject to the jurisdiction of the tribunal.[2]

Chief Justice Tilghman,[3] in speaking of a corporation taking cognizance of matters unconnected with the affairs of the society, said : "So far from its being necessary for the good government of the corporation, it appears to me that taking cognizance of such offences will have the pernicious effect of introducing private feuds into the bosom of the society and interrupting the transaction of business."[4]

In the case of Leech vs. Harris[5] the plaintiff was a member of the Philadelphia Board of Brokers, a private unincorporated association, similar to the New York Stock Exchange. One M. presented a complaint to the board,

---

[1] See, for other cases illustrating this proposition, the next succeeding subdivision (e.).

[2] Morris vs. Grant, 34 Hun, 377.

[3] Commonw. vs. St. Pat. Benev. Soc., 2 Binn. 449.

[4] "The power of a corporation to control the conduct and define the rights of its members, by means of its by-laws, is limited strictly to their rights and conduct as members of the association. With the private affairs of its members, the corporation has nothing to do, and any by-law attempting to interfere with such affairs is necessarily ultra vires and void." Boisot on By-Laws (2d ed.), § 72. See also Green vs. African Methodist Society, 1 S. & Rawle (Pa.), 254.

[5] 2 Brews. (Pa.) 571.

charging the plaintiff with having obtained money from him by falsely pretending that he had paid a large sum of money for certain oil lands, and thus inducing M. to purchase an interest in the same. Thereupon the board appointed a committee to investigate the charges, which it was proceeding to do, when the plaintiff procured an injunction, on the ground that the board had no jurisdiction over the question, and that it would be impossible for him to produce his witnesses without the aid of the process of the courts, which could not be obtained in behalf of defendant's tribunal. The court, after full argument, in a careful opinion granted a perpetual injunction, on the ground that the matter sought to be inquired into was not within the jurisdiction of the board. The court said:

"What the plaintiff really submitted to when he became a member of the Board of Brokers was that the board should take jurisdiction if he should refuse to comply with his stock contracts; not that they should have jurisdiction of his contracts touching houses, lands, leasehold estates, or farming interests. . . . I do not perceive that either by the law of the association, by the law of the land, or by submission to its jurisdiction, the Board of Brokers has acquired any right to arbitrate and settle the matters in dispute between the plaintiff and Mr. Reuben Manley, Jr. The courts of law are open to Mr. Manley to vindicate his rights and to redress any wrongs done to him. But the Board of Brokers cannot erect itself into a tribunal for this purpose. The plaintiff has, in my opinion, a clear right to the protection of a court of equity. He has a valuable interest in his membership in the board, which cost him $2,000. He has an interest, in common with his fellow-members, in the accumulated funds of the association, and in the claim which he would have, in case of necessity, upon the fund set apart to aid poor or distressed members or their families whom the board may think proper to assist. He has a right, also, to be protected in his good name and reputation from unauthorized proceedings against him, in which he cannot have the assistance of a court of law to compel the attendance of witnesses or to obtain testimony from abroad."[1]

A related question is that of the exercise of jurisdiction by a committee of the Exchange, over a matter arising on the Exchange, but beyond the jurisdiction conferred upon the committee by the by-laws. A determination made in the exercise of such unwarranted jurisdiction is wholly nugatory and will not be regarded by the courts.[2] Accordingly a committee empowered to pass upon the regularity and genuineness of the form of securities dealt in, has no jurisdiction to adjudge the legal rights of the parties to a transaction where the regularity or genuineness of the securities are not involved, and if it relieves a vendee from the obligations of a contract of sale, enforceable in law, the determination will be set aside by the courts.[3]

(c.) *Members not Bound by Rules which Prevent Recourse to Courts of Law.*

This subject is closely connected with that which has been briefly discussed under the preceding subdivision.

---

[1] Examine, in this connection, rule of Stock Exchange as to paying debts, submitting differences, etc.

[2] Morris vs. Grant, 34 Hun, 377; Sawyer vs. Gruner, 17 N. Y. Supp. 465.

[3] Morris vs. Grant, supra. So, too, where there was no jurisdiction under the charter or by-laws of an incorporated Exchange to determine who was the owner of a disputed right of membership, a member is not guilty of improper conduct warranting his expulsion for resorting to the courts to prevent the corporation from disposing of

It is a well-recognized principle of law appertaining to incorporated bodies that where their by-laws prohibit the members from pursuing their legal remedies beyond the jurisdiction of the corporation, such by-laws are void.[1] The theory being that no power less than that of the Legislature can exclude the subject or citizen from his right to legal redress.[2]

There is no substantial reason why this principle should not be applied to the by-laws or rules and regulations of unincorporated associations, and the precedents are directly that way.

In Austin vs. Searing[3] the question discussed was as to the validity of a by-law which undertook to confer judicial powers upon a body of officers of the association, with power to adjudicate upon alleged violations of rules, and to decree a forfeiture of the rights to such property as the parties violating the rules were possessed of as members of the association. The court said : " But, were it distinctly averred that the defendants had subscribed the constitution of the grand as well as of the subordinate lodge, I should still be of the opinion that public policy would not admit of parties binding themselves by such engagements. The effect of some of the provisions of these constitutions is to create a tribunal having power to adjudicate upon the rights of property of all the members of the subordinate lodges, and to transfer that property to others ; the mem-

such a right claimed by him. People ex rel. Elliott vs. New York Cotton Exchange, 8 Hun, 216.

[1] Ang. & Ames on Corp. (11th ed.) § 341.

[2] Player vs. Archer, 2 Sid. 121; London vs. Bernardiston, 1 Lev. 11;

Ballard vs. Bennett, 2 Burr. 778; Middleton's Case, Dyer, 333 (a); State ex rel. Kennedy vs. Union Merchants' Exchange, 2 Mo. App. 96, at p. 101.

[3] 16 N. Y. 123; s. c. annotated, 69 Am. Dec. 670.

bers of this tribunal being liable to constant fluctuations, and not subject in any case to the selection or control of the parties upon whose rights they sit in judgment."

To create a judicial tribunal is one of the functions of the sovereign power; and although parties may always make such tribunal for themselves, in any specific case, by a submission to abitration, yet the power is guarded by the most cautious rules. A contract that the parties will submit confers no power upon the arbitrator; and, even where there is an actual submission, it may be revoked at any time. The law allows the party up to the last moment to ascertain whether there is not some covert bias or prejudice on the part of the arbitrator chosen. It would hardly accord with this scrupulous care to secure fairness in such cases that parties should be held legally bound by an engagement, by which the most extensive judicial powers are conferred upon bodies of men whose individual members are subject to continual fluctuations.[1]

So, in the case of Heath vs. President of the Gold Exchange,[2] the effect of a clause in the constitution of an unincorporated association was considered, providing that "it shall be the duty of said committee (arbitration) to take cognizance of, and exercise jurisdiction over, all claims and matters of difference between the members of the board, and their decision shall be binding." The plaintiff, at the commencement of his action, was a member of the Gold Exchange, and sought to restrain the defendant, by injunction, from proceeding to hear and determine, under such

[1] See also White vs. Brownell, 3 Ab. Pr. (n. s.) 318; s. c. on appeal, 4 id. 162, 198; Savannah Cotton Exchange vs. State, 54 Ga. 668; Dennis vs. Kennedy, 19 Barb. (N. Y.) 527.
[2] 7 Ab. Pr. (n. s.) 251.

clause, a dispute between himself and other members of the body. Subsequent to the suit, and before the argument for a perpetual injunction had been heard, the plaintiff resigned his membership in the Exchange.

It was held : 1. That before a member could be bound by the constitution and by-laws of such a body, it must appear that he personally assented to the same.[1] 2. That the most that could be claimed for the arbitration clause in question was, that it should have the same force and effect as an agreement in writing, made by persons to submit to the decision of one or more arbitrators any controversy existing between them, and that the plaintiff had the right to revoke and annul the power to arbitrate ; that by resigning from the board this was conclusively established ; and that any attempt afterwards to arbitrate claims by the board was null.

The decision was placed upon the ground that the enforcement of arbitration agreements was against public policy ; and that, as courts of justice are presumed to be better capable of administering and enforcing the real rights of the parties than mere private arbitrators, such agreements would not be enforced either in law or equity.[2]

---

[1] Austin vs. Searing, 16 N. Y. 112. But see as to this White vs. Brownell, 4 Ab. Pr. (n. s.) 162, 193.

[2] The following cases were cited on the last point: Russell's Arbitrator, 147; 2 Story Eq. Jur. § 1457; 1 id. § 607; Kill vs. Hollister, 1 Wils. 129; Street vs. Rigby, 6 Ves. 818; Agar vs. Macklew, 2 Sim. & S. 418; Milnes vs. Gery, 14 Ves. 408; Thompson vs. Charnock, 8 Term, 139; Haggart vs. Morgan, 5 N. Y. (1 Seld.) 422. See also Lloyd vs. Loaring, 6 Ves. 772;

Mitchell vs. Harris, 2 Ves. Jr. 129, and N. Sumner's ed.; Simmons vs. Monier, 29 Barb. 419; Smith vs. Compton, 20 id. 262. See also State ex rel. Kennedy vs. Union Merchants' Exchange, 2 Mo. App. 101, and the many cases cited in 2 Am. & Eng. Ency. of Law (2d ed.), 570.

The distinction attempted in the case of Farmer vs. Board of Trade, 78 Mo. App. 567, that the association may rightfully enforce, not the

Upon this question of the right of a member to apply to the courts, there is another article of the constitution of the New York Stock Exchange which is important to be considered.

By the 22d article[1] of that constitution it is declared that "any member of the Stock Exchange who shall himself, or whose partner or partners shall, apply for an injunction or legal instrument restraining any officer or committee of the

agreement to arbitrate, but the penalty of expulsion for refusal to arbitrate, is not unsound and that case itself is opposed to the earlier case in the same state. Cf. State ex rel. Kennedy vs. Union Merchants' Exchange, 2 Mo. App. 96. It has been said by an able judge that it was difficult to assign any good reason at this day why an executory contract for the amicable adjustment of any differences that may arise, either by arbitration or otherwise, made by parties standing upon an equal footing and intelligently and deliberately, should not stand and the parties made to abide by it and the judgment of the tribunal of their choice, and that the tendency of the more recent decisions is to narrow rather than enlarge the operation and effect of prior decisions. The rule that an agreement to arbitrate all questions that may arise will not oust the courts of jurisdiction, is not to be extended or applied to new cases not coming within the letter and spirit of previous decisions. Allen, J., in President, etc., Del. & Hudson Canal Co. vs. Pa. Coal Co., 50 N. Y. 250, at 258-259. And a provision in the charter of

an unincorporated Board of Trade and by-laws pursuant thereto, authorizing and indeed, requiring the settlement of all questions of dispute between members, by committees of arbitration, was judicially commended in Vaughn vs. Herndon, 91 Tenn. 64, "as wise legislation, that will operate to prevent much needless and expensive litigation as well as promote the welfare of commerce, if correctly enforced."

The fact that a member is given by the by-laws an opportunity to arbitrate or conciliate his differences where a complaint has been made, before it shall be referred to the board of managers, does not make the by-law under which the complaint is made coercive or invalid as repugnant to public policy on the ground that it gives the board power to punish only when the member refuses to arbitrate. Such a by-law does not compel the member to submit to arbitration but permits him to do so or not as he chooses. In re Haebler vs. N. Y. Produce Exchange, 149 N. Y. 414; Hurst vs. N. Y. Produce Exchange, 100 N. Y. 605; s. c. fully reported, 1 Cent. Rep. 260.

[1] This article has been rescinded.

Exchange from performing his or its duties under the constitution and by-laws, shall by that act cease to be a member of the association."

The general effect and meaning of a provision similar to the above has been before the courts on several occasions. If the intention of the enactment is to prevent a member from appealing to the courts from an arbitrary and illegal decision against his rights and privileges as a member of an association, which he otherwise would be deprived of, it seems that such provision would be abortive and illegal.[1]

In the case of Sewell vs. Ives, heretofore referred to,[2] this provision was invoked by the Exchange against the plaintiff, but the court passed it without notice, and determined the case upon other grounds. So, in Leech vs. Harris,[3] it was said: " It is not alleged that he has in any manner offended against the rights or interests of the Board of Brokers, or failed in his duty as a member thereof, unless his refusal to submit to its claim of authority in this case can be construed into an offence against his duty as a member of the board. If he is right in resisting the authority which the board claims over him, then he has committed no offence against his duty as a member. In such case his right of self-protection justifies him in his action, and he more faithfully dis-

[1] Austin vs. Searing, 16 N. Y. 123; Heath vs. President, etc., of Gold Exchange, 7 Ab. Pr. (n. s.) 251; White vs. Brownell, 4 Ab. Pr. (n. s.) 162.

A member is not guilty of "improper conduct" warranting his expulsion, in applying for an injunction restraining the Exchange from proceeding in a matter over which, under its charter and by-laws, it had no jurisdiction. Peo-ple ex rel. Elliott vs. New York Cotton Exchange, 8 Hun, 216. And where the rules provide a remedy which does not assume to exclude the jurisdiction of the courts, the parties to contracts made with reference to such rules are not to be restricted to the remedy so provided. Clows vs. Jamieson, 182 U. S. 461, at p. 495.

[2] Ante, p. 80.

[3] 2 Brews. (Pa.) 571.

charges his duty as a member of the board in resisting its encroachments than he would in submitting to its unlawful authority. He becomes not only the vindicator of his own rights, but the vindicator and defender of the rights of every member of the board, and of the well-being and integrity of the board itself."

The English courts have also emphatically, through James, L. J.,[1] endorsed this view. "The Stock Exchange is not an Alsatia. The Queen's laws are paramount there, and the Queen's writ runs even in the sacred precincts of Capel Court."

But where the association, in expelling or disciplining a member, acts within the sphere of its authority in enforcing rules which are not contrary to law or public policy, the courts will not interfere.[2]

So where a member of a Stock Exchange signs or agrees to a constitution in which is contained a provision referring all differences between members to an Arbitration Committee, and such committee proceeds in the mode pointed out by the organic law, giving full notice and ample opportunity to be heard, it has been held that a member is bound by the result, and a court will not interfere in the matter.[3]

In the case of Sonneborn vs. Lavarrello[4] the plaintiff and defendants, members of the New York Produce Exchange, had voluntarily submitted to the Arbitration Committee there-

[1] Ex parte Saffery, 4 L. R. Ch. D. 561.

[2] See cases cited, ante, under sub. (b.) of § 8, ch. 2; Vaughn vs. Herndon, 91 Tenn. 64.

[3] But if the committee on appeals, of the Chicago Board of Trade, simply reverses an award of the committee on arbitration, the parties are simply left as they were, and one of them may sue the other in the courts. There should be reasonable certainty in an award to make it conclusive upon the rights of the parties. Redmond vs. Bedford, 40 Ill. 267.

[4] 2 Hun (N. Y.), 201.

of (chosen in pursuance of § 5 of ch. 359, Laws of 1862) a dispute arising out of a transaction in petroleum. The committee having decided in favor of the defendants, the plaintiffs brought this action to restrain them from entering judgment on the award, on the grounds that the arbitrators had not been sworn, and that they had received illegal evidence. It was held that the plaintiffs, by appearing before the committee, making their statements, discussing their case and the whole controversy, and interposing no objection to the proceedings in any respect, had waived any such irregularities on the part of the arbitrators. The power to adjourn rests in the sound discretion of the committee; but its proceedings in this respect are nevertheless subject to review, and may be annulled if it appear that the discretion has been abused.[1]

So when a member of the New York Stock Exchange cited by another member to account for a sum of money claimed, voluntarily pays the same with full knowledge of all the facts, he cannot recover back the money. Fear of the Arbitration Committee before which the claim was adjusted is not duress.[2]

---

[1] See also Lafond vs. Deems, 81 N. Y. 507, at 514, per Miller, J. In arbitrations generally the refusal of the arbitrator to hear testimony, pertinent and material, is sufficient to set aside the award. Halsted vs. Seaman, 82 N. Y. 27; s. c. 37 Am. Rep. 536. And this also is the rule appertaining to the trial of disputed questions before committees of Exchanges. Ryan vs. Cudahy, 157 Ill. 108, at p. 120. See Waite vs. Bartlett, 17 Chic. L. J. 636, and article on "Power of Board of Trade

to settle business disputes between its members under its by-laws." Id. The case of Vaughn vs. Herndon, 91 Tenn. 64, does not conflict with this view, as a reading merely of its headnote might indicate.

[2] Quincey vs. White, 63 N. Y. 370; reversing 5 Daly, 32. Nor is a payment made under an unfounded fear that the board of managers would order suspension in case of non-payment, recoverable, when, in fact, the board had no jurisdiction or authority at all in the

But in a recent case in which plaintiffs sought to enjoin the Chamber of Commerce of the city of Milwaukee from expelling or suspending them, it was held that if the board of

matter. Sawyer vs. Gruner, 17 N. Y. Supp. 465. In Scott vs. Avery (5 House of Lords Cas. 845), the Lord Chancellor (Cranworth), after stating the nature of the action and the pleadings, said, "There is no doubt of the general principle which was argued at your lordship's bar, that parties cannot by contract oust the ordinary courts of their jurisdiction. That has been decided in many cases. Perhaps the first case I need refer to was a case decided about a century ago—Kill vs. Hollister (1 Wils. 129). That was an action on a policy of insurance, in which there was a clause that, in case of any loss or dispute, it should be referred to arbitration. It was decided there that an action would lie, although there had been no reference to arbitration.

"Then, after the lapse, of about half a century, occurred a case before Lord Kenyon, and, from the language that fell from that learned judge, many other cases had probably been decided which are not reported; but in the time of Lord Kenyon occurred the case which is considered the leading case upon this subject, the case of Thompson vs. Charnock (8 T. R. 139). That was an action upon a charter-party in which there was a stipulation that if any difference should arise it should be referred to arbitration. That clause was pleaded in bar to the action which had been brought upon a breach of the covenant with

an averment that the defendant had been, and always was, ready to refer the matter to arbitration. That was held to be a bad plea, upon the ground that a right of action had accrued, and that the fact that the parties had agreed that the matter should be settled by arbitration did not oust the jurisdiction of the courts.

"Just about the same time occurred a case in the Court of Common Pleas, when that court was presided over by Lord Eldon—the case of Tattersall vs. Groote (2 Bos. & P. 131). That was an action by the administratrix of a deceased partner against a surviving partner for not naming an arbitrator, pursuant to a covenant in the deed of partnership. To that action there was a demurrer, and the demurrer was allowed. But that case, I think, can afford very little authority in the present action, or in actions similar to the present, because there the covenant was only that if any dispute arose between the partners, they would name an arbitrator. One of the partners died, and his administratrix brought an action, and Lord Eldon pointed out that the covenant did not apply to a case where one of the partners was dead and an action was brought by his representatives. Therefore, in truth, that amounts to no decision whatever upon the general question. There was then a case before Sir Lloyd Kenyon at the Rolls, of Half-

arbitrators went outside the scope of the submission or were guilty of palpable misconduct, their award was defective for jurisdictional error.[1]

In that case a temporary injunction was granted. When a statute under which a Chamber of Commerce was organized conferred upon it the right to make membership conditional upon the submission of business disputes to arbitration, a by-law, providing for expulsion if a member did not submit a business dispute to arbitration, is not against public policy nor does it oust the court of jurisdiction.[2]

A dispute between an association and a party claiming to be a member, as to whether such party is a member or not, is not a dispute between the association and such a person, *as member*, and consequently is not a case within a by-law, or statutory provision requiring disputes between a member and the society to be decided by arbitration.[3] And

hide vs. Penning (2 Bro. C. C. 336), in which he held a different doctrine. That was a bill for an account of partnership transactions. The plea to that bill was that the articles contained an agreement that any difference which should arise should be settled by arbitration, and the Master of the Rolls allowed that plea. But I think that case cannot be relied upon, because it has been universally treated as having proceeded upon an erroneous principle. There is no doubt that where a right of action has accrued, parties cannot by contract say that there shall not be jurisdiction to enforce damages in respect to that right of action. Now, this doctrine depends upon the general policy of the law, that parties can-

not enter into a contract which gives rise to a right of action for the breach of it, and then withdraw such a case from the jurisdiction of the ordinary tribunals. But surely there can be no principle or policy of the law which prevents parties from entering into such a contract as that no breach shall occur until after a reference has been made to arbitration. It appears to me that, in such cases as that, the policy of the law is left untouched."

[1] Bartlett vs. Bartlett, 93 N. W. 473.

[2] Evans vs. Chamber of Commerce of Minneapolis, 91 N. W. 8.

[3] Prentice vs. London, L. R. 10 C. P. 679. Nor can an Exchange, under its power of "adjusting controversies between its members"

where the trustees or officers of an association deny the right of a person to be a member of the society, they are estopped from saying that the dispute is one between the parties, *as members*, within the rule.[1] The matters in dispute, which are the subject of reference and decision under the constitution and by-laws of associations and in-

and of "inculcating just and equitable principles of trade," and in the absence of any reserved right, try the title to a disputed membership claimed by one member under a bill of sale from another, and expel him for refusing to abide by its decision. "He had no controversy with any member or officer. He said simply: 'You cannot sell the membership because it belongs to me, and I do not admit your authority to dispose of my rights in regard to it.' . . . There is no provision in the by-laws for the trial of the title to a seat, and there is, therefore, on refusing to submit to the decision, no violation of the by-laws." People ex rel. Elliott vs. N. Y. Cotton Exchange, 8 Hun, 216.

In Babcock vs. Merchants' Exchange of St. Louis, 159 Mo. 381, it appeared that plaintiff, who was a Broker, and had deskroom in the Exchange building, with tenants of the Exchange, who were not members thereof, purchased from a member his certificate of membership, but the Exchange had refused to permit him to become a member. Thereafter, notwithstanding a resolution of the Exchange, excluding non-members from the "Curb," a portion of the building where mem-

bers traded with each other after the regular session, he continued, as he had theretofore done, to trade in the "Curb," and at the instance of the committee on irregular trading, was arrested, charged with trespass, and subsequently acquitted. In an action for damages for malicious prosecution, it was held that the right of plaintiff to membership could not be determined in that action. If his application for membership were improperly rejected, the courts were open to him in a proper action, but even if this were done, he could not go upon the premises until his right was established by a competent court.

[1] Prentice vs. London, L. R. 10 C. P. 679.

On the other hand, if one not a member often visits the Board of Trade on a visitor's ticket, and deals with another as if he were a member, he is estopped from denying that he is a member, and he is bound by the board's rules and customs. Chicago vs. Tilton, 87 Ill. 547. And a non-member cannot enjoin an Exchange from fining one of its members for breach of a rule prohibiting members from dealing with non-members. Downes vs. Bennett, 63 Kan. 653.

corporations, as a general rule, are only such matters as are in dispute between the society and its members, *as members,* and not extraneous matters of any kind. Thus, where a building society loaned money to a member on mortgage of leasehold property, and the member covenanted to observe and fulfil the rules of the society, and also to pay the rent reserved by the lease, and the trustees of the society sued for breaches of both those covenants, it was held that as some part of the plaintiff's claim was not a matter in dispute between the society and the defendant, *as member,* but only *as mortgagor,* the society was not bound by its rule to refer to arbitration the subject-matter of the action.[1]

[1] Morrison vs. Glover, 4 Ex. 430, It is not an unusual thing for the statutes incorporating associations to oust the jurisdiction of ordinary tribunals, and to refer all disputes, either between the members themselves or between the members and the association thereof, to certain persons or classes of persons named by the statute, whose jurisdiction is exclusive and whose decision is final. Thus, the statute of 6 & 7 William IV. c. 32, incorporating the provisions of 10 Geo. IV. c. 56, relating to the formation of friendly societies, provides that rules shall be made by such societies directing whether disputes shall be settled either by justices of the peace or by arbitrators; and, when rules have been adopted to that effect, it has been held that any decision made by such justices of the peace, or by such arbitrators, was final, and a rule for a mandamus to compel the judge of the county court to proceed in such an action was denied (Ex parte Payne, 5 D. & L. 679). The same is true under the "Act to Consolidate and Amend the Laws relative to Savings-banks" (9 Geo. IV. c. 92, § 45), by which it was provided that any dispute arising between the bank and the depositor should be decided by arbitrators appointed in the manner provided by the statute. It was held that the right of a depositor to bring an action in a court of law for any matter coming within the purview of the provisions of the statute was barred by the statute; and it was held that the language of the statute, which was that "the matter so in dispute *shall* be referred," etc., gave the arbitrators an exclusive, and not merely concurrent, jurisdiction (Crisp vs. Bunbury, 8 Bing. 394). (This 45th section of the act is omitted in the edition of the Statutes of 1875.) So in the Act relative to Loan Societies (5 & 6 Wm.

IX. Liability of Seats in Exchange to Legal Process.

The general nature of seats in an unincorporated Stock Exchange has already been considered in Section V. of this chapter, and we have seen that its members have no separate or severable interest in its property, and no right to call for an account of the same, or its accumulations, with a view of dividing it, as in the case of ordinary partners.

The question now is, as to the right of outside creditors to attach or seize this seat, upon attachment or execution, to satisfy their claims.[1]

IV. c. 23, § 8), it was provided that all notes and securities entered into for the payment of loans might be prosecuted, upon default, by the treasurer; and that it should be lawful for one or more justices of the peace to summon, etc., the person complained of, etc. In construing this statute, it was held that the jurisdiction of the higher courts was ousted, if not by the express words of the statute, at least by implication (Timms vs. Williams, 3 Q. B. 413; but see, contra, Albon vs. Pyke, 4 M. & G. 421, and note, 426). And where a bill in equity was brought, by a holder of shares in a building society, against the society and its directors, for misconduct, and praying a declaration that the plaintiff was not bound by certain rules, etc., it was held that this was a dispute for the decision of which arbitrators were the proper authority under the statute of the societys' incorporation (6 & 7 Wm. IV. c. 32); and that it was not only provided by the statute that such disputes should be referred to arbi-

tration, but that it was against the policy of the law, as shown by the statute, to drag the disputes of friendly benefit societies into the courts, etc. (Thompson vs. Planet Benefit Building Soc., 15 L. R. Eq. 333). But the jurisdiction of the superior courts is only to be ousted by express words, or by necessary implication (Cates vs. Knight, 3 T. R. 442; Crisp vs. Bunbury, 8 Bing. 394; and Albon vs. Pyke, supra).

[1] The rules of the New York Stock Exchange provide as follows, in relation to seats:

Art. XIII. § 1, states the qualification of the member. Art. XI. § 1, subd. 2, provides for the admission of members by two thirds of the committee on admissions. Any member wishing to transfer his membership shall submit the name of the proposed transferee to the Committee on Admissions; and, on the approval of two thirds of said committee, the transfer may be made, upon payment, out of the proceeds of the transfer, of fines, as-

In the first place, it will be observed that, as between the owner or member and the association, the seat is regarded, and has been recognized, as a right or property of a valuable nature, subject to taxation as personal property,[1] of which the owner cannot be deprived, except in accordance with the rules of the organization, and that a court will interfere by an injunction, or other appropriate legal remedy, to prevent such deprivation.

But, on the other hand, it is equally well settled, as we have seen, that the ownership of a seat in such association is not absolute and unqualified, but it is limited and restricted by the rules of the body issuing the same.[2] The owner cannot sell the seat to a person whom the body will not recognize.[3] He cannot devise or bequeath the same, so that his heirs or personal representatives will be able to use and enjoy it as the testator has, for the seat is a mere personal privilege, dying with the member, and not containing any inheritable qualities.[4] The proceeds of his seat, it is true, may belong to his personal representatives, but

---

sessments and unsettled contracts, due by the member (Art. XV.), the balance, if any, to be paid to the member. Id. Upon the death of a member, his membership may be disposed of by said committee (Art. XV. § 7).

Elaborate provision is also made for the suspension and readmission and expulsion of members.

[1] See post, p. 163.

[2] See ante, p. 31.

[3] White vs. Brownell, 3 Ab. Pr. (n. s.) 318; Leech vs. Harris, 2 Brews. (Pa.) 571. Any disposition of the seat gives merely the rights therein

of the vendor subject to the rules and conditions of the Exchange. And, therefore, if a certificate of membership is transferred, the only way the transferee can avail of it, if refused membership, is by transferring it, for a consideration, to some person desiring membership. American Live Stock Comm. Co. vs. Live Stock Exchange, 143 Ill. 210; Clute vs. Loveland, 68 Cal. 254, and cases cited, ante.

[4] White vs. Brownell, 3 Ab. Pr. (n. s.) 318; Leech vs. Harris, 2 Brews. (Pa.) 571.

the franchise or right of exercising the occupation of Broker in the Exchange is gone.

Moreover, a member may be entirely deprived of the benefits and value of the seat by a violation of the rules of the association.[1]

A seat, therefore, in one of these bodies, is a species of incorporeal property—a personal, individual right to exercise a certain calling in a certain place, but without the attributes of descendibility or assignability which are characteristic of other species of property.[2] It is not a chose in action.[3] It does not, in New York, constitute the working tools of the member so as to exempt it from judgment creditors, and even if it did, it would, under § 1391 of the Code of Civ. Proc., be exempt only to the extent of $250.[4]

By far the most numerous class of cases in which the legal character of seats has arisen are those in which seats have been sought to be attached or seized on execution by creditors of an insolvent member. Carrying out the principles just alluded to, the courts have uniformly[5] held that the

[1] Ritterband vs. Baggett, 4 Ab. New Cas. 67, Sp. T. And the association may then fill the vacancy or not as it pleases. Belton vs. Hatch, 109 N. Y. 593. In that case a distinction is made between the case of an expelled member who is ineligible for readmission, and a member who becomes honestly insolvent and fails to qualify for readmission. In the former case the member is deprived of all claim upon the association, but in the latter, the proceeds of the seat may be paid to the member after all claims of the association are discharged. And a member in good standing may dispose of his seat, subject to the rules.

[2] Compare, as to character of market-stands, Barry vs. Kennedy, 11 Ab. Pr. (n. s.) 421; In re Emrich, 101 Fed. Rep. 231. And as to auction-stand in a real estate Exchange, McQuillen vs. Real Estate Exchange, 15 N. Y. Supp. 206.

[3] London and Canadian Co. vs. Morphy, 10 Ont. 86.

[4] Leggett vs. Waller, 80 N. Y. Supp. 13.

[5] See, however, Leggett vs. Wallers, supra.

right of a member to a seat in a Stock Exchange cannot be attached [1] or seized on execution.[2]

By the rules of the Philadelphia Stock Exchange, it was provided that a member might sell his seat to any person whom the association should elect; that the proceeds of such sale shall belong to the creditors of the owner who are members of the association, and the balance, after paying their claims, shall go to the owner. The court held that such seat was not properly subject to execution in any form. It was a mere personal privilege; perhaps, more accurately, a license to buy and sell at the meetings of the board. It certainly could not be levied on and sold under a *fi. fa.* The sheriff's vendee would acquire no title which he could en-

---

[1] Pancoast vs. Houston, Phila. C. P. 17 Alb. L. J. 172; s. c. 5 Week. Notes Cas. 36. The court held that until all claims of members were settled the seat was the property of the Exchange, and until it was shown that such claims were settled or that none existed, an attachment could not issue. It appeared that some claims existed against the seat, and it might be contended that if no claims existed, the seat could be attached. But in face of the rule of the Exchange that a member could only sell his membership upon condition that the purchaser was first ballotted for and elected, and that all claims of the association had been paid, this contention could hardly be sustained. Quære, Could an intending purchaser at an execution sale, following judgment upon the attachment, be first ballotted for and elected, and then have a transfer of the seat by the sheriff, all claims of

the Exchange having been first paid?

In Bowen vs. Bull, 12 N. Y. Supp. 325, aff'd without opinion, 128 N. Y. 597, it appeared that an attachment had been issued against a seat in the Open Board of Brokers, and the court, without deciding whether a seat in the stock exchange was capable of attachment, held that as there was no proof of the levy, a purchaser at a sheriff's sale could not compel the Exchange to recognize his right to the seat.

[2] Freeman on Executions (3d ed.), p. 422; Pancoast vs. Gowen, 20 Alb. L. J. 414; s. c. 36 Phil. Leg. Int. 86; Lowenberg vs. Greenebaum, 99 Cal. 162; Eliot vs. Merchants' Exchange, 14 Mo. App. 235; Barclay vs. Smith, 107 Ill. 349; Fish vs. Fiske, 151 Mass. 302. The rule also prevails in Canada. London and Canadian Loan Co. vs. Morphy, 10 Ont. Rep. 86. See also Habenicht vs. Lissak, 78 Cal. 351.

force.   Nor is it within either the words or the spirit of the act of June 16, 1836, § 35 (Pamph. L. 767), providing for attachment on judgments.

"Whether," says the court, " the proceeds of the sale of the seat, in the hands of the treasurer of the board, and payable to the defendant, according to the regulations and by-laws of the board, could be thus reached, is an entirely different question.   This, and no more, is what we understand to have been decided by the Supreme Court of the United States, in Hyde vs. Woods,[1] where Mr. Justice Miller says: " If there had been left in the hands of the defendants any balance after paying the debts due to the members of the board, that balance might have been recovered by the assignee in bankruptcy."[2]

The case of Thompson vs. Adams[3] is another interesting case on this subject, holding that a third person, secretly furnishing money to a member to purchase his seat, has no claim for the money until after the debts are paid to the members of the board.   The Supreme Court of Pennsylvania held, in that case, that a seat in the Philadelphia Board of Brokers was not property in the eye of the law, and could not be seized in execution for the debts of the members ; it was the mere creation of the board, and was to be held and enjoyed with all the limitations and restrictions which the constitution of the board have put upon it ; and, under the constitution and by-laws of the Philadelphia Board of Brokers, the secret equitable owner of a seat therein has no right as against members of the board, who are creditors of the legal owner, to share in the proceeds of the sale of the seat on the

[1] 4 Otto, 525.
[2] Pancoast vs. Gowen, 20 Alb. L. J. 414; s. c. 93 Pa. St. 66.
[3] 7 Weekly Notes of Cas. 281.

death of the latter. The plaintiff in that case was not a member of the board, but had furnished the money by which the deceased member had obtained his seat, but plaintiff's name was not known to the board in connection with the seat. The rules of the board provided that all claims upon the seat of a dead member should be decided by the Arbitration Committee, and such claims were so passed upon in this case. The court said: " His [plaintiff's] contention is that he was the equitable owner of the seat, and had title to what was received for it, and that the defendant had no right to apply the proceeds to debts due by Richards to other members, in pursuance of the terms of the constitution of the club. But why not? Richards was the member of the board, the legal owner of the seat, and the plaintiff an entire stranger, unknown to the association. The members gave credit to each other in part, no doubt, upon the faith of the liability of a member's seat to them for his debts. There is nothing unlawful or unreasonable in this regulation."[1]

In Evans vs. Wister[2] the same court held that an attachment would not lie against the Board of Brokers for the proceeds of the sale of a seat of a member, he being indebted to his fellow-members to the amount of the proceeds. In that case one W., being a member of the board, became insolvent. Subsequently he sold his seat, but the purchaser was informed by the secretary that the transfer could not be completed until the price of the seat was paid to

---

[1] In Clute vs. Loveland, 68 Cal. 254, it was held that a member of the San Francisco Stock Exchange had power to pledge or mortgage his seat, and that the lien thereby created may be foreclosed and the seat sold, subject to the conditions imposed by the rules of the association.

[2] 1 Week. Notes of Cas. 181; s. c. 32 Leg. Int. 354; s. c. sub nom. Evans vs. Adams, 81 Pa. St. (32 Sm.) 443.

him, to be held for the creditors of W. in the board. Plaintiff then presented his claim to the Arbitration Committee, but the same was disallowed. He thereupon began a suit, attaching the money in the hands of the secretary, with the above result.[1]

In the suit of the Grocers Bank vs. Murphy, Mr. Justice Van Hoesen, in the New York Court of Common Pleas,[2] passed upon the question whether a seat in the New York Stock Exchange may be regarded as property subject to sale by legal process against the owner. An execution in this case was issued upon a judgment in favor of plaintiff, and subsequently an order was granted requiring the defendant to appear before the court to make discovery on oath concerning his property, etc., under section 292 of the Code of Procedure ; and, it appearing that the defendant possessed a seat in the New York Stock Exchange, plaintiff asked to have it assigned, and the proceeds applied towards the satisfaction of his judgment. The court, in denying a motion requiring defendant to make the assignment, said, " There is no doubt if a seat be sold, the proceeds of the sale, after the payment of claims due to members of the board, may be reached by proper process. This is the view of every court which has had occasion to express an opinion on the subject. It by no means follows, however, that the seat itself may be seized by the sheriff, or taken possession of by a receiver. It may well be doubted if a seat in the Exchange be property.[3] It is true that Mr. Justice Miller, of the

---

[1] This was an affirmance of Leech vs. Leech, 3 Week. Notes of Cas. 542, note.

[2] N. Y. *Daily Reg.* June 14, 1880; reversed on appeal, N. Y. *Daily Reg.* March 12, 1881, where dissenting opinion of Van Brunt, J., is also reported; s. c. 11 N. Y. *Weekly Dig.* 538; 60 How. Pr. 426.

[3] The New York Court of Appeals has, however, since the text was written, held that a seat in the

Supreme Court of the United States, in the case of Hyde vs.
Woods,[1] said that he thought it was property; but the
Supreme Court of Pennsylvania, in two carefully considered
decisions, in which the decision of Mr. Justice Miller was
thoroughly reviewed, came to the opposite conclusion. . . .
A seat in the Exchange does not fall within any of the
classes into which the subjects of property are divided. It
is not capable of manual delivery or appropriation; it is
not a domestic animal, nor a product of labor or skill, nor
a right created by statute.”

But, upon appeal, this decision was reversed by two of the
judges, the third judge dissenting, and coinciding with Mr.
Justice Van Hoesen.[2]

Mr. Justice Beach, in delivering the opinion reversing the
decision of the court below, after reviewing the cases, held
that, under the section of the code in question, the defendant was bound to apply the proceeds of the seat to the satisfaction of his debts; and that if this result were not correct,
the legal principle which makes the debtor's possessions
liable to his creditors would be nullified. “Probably an
order appointing a receiver, containing directions for the
judgment debtor to do whatever may be deemed needful to
transfer the seat under the rules of the Exchange, would
accomplish the result sought.” In another case [3] a peremptory mandamus, directed to the defendant, compelling it to
transfer to the relator, who had purchased the same at a
sheriff's sale, a seat in the Cotton Exchange, was refused

New York Stock Exchange is, in a
certain sense, property and passes
to the member's assignee in bankruptcy. Platt vs. Jones, 96 N. Y.
24, 29, and cases cited.

[1] 94 U. S. (4 Otto) 523.

[2] N. Y. *Daily Reg.* March 12,
1881; 60 How. Pr. 426.

[3] Allen, Jr., vs. The New York
Cotton Exchange, N. Y. Daily
Reg., March 31, 1880.

upon the grounds heretofore adverted to in the preceding cases. If the seat were subject to direct legal process, it is very evident that the whole design of the organization would be thwarted by introducing into the Exchange the purchasers at a judicial sale, without a compliance with the prerequisite rules of admission and against the wish of the regular members. This the courts have uniformly refused to do.[1]

But the courts, through the instrumentality of their equity powers, or by process in aid of execution, will compel an insolvent member to sell his seat to some person whom the association will recognize, and apply the proceeds to the satisfaction of his debts. It would be a failure of justice to allow an insolvent to be the possessor of such a valuable right or property, to the defiance of his just creditors.[2]

So, in a case[3] where a receiver instituted an action to compel a debtor member of a Produce Exchange to convey

[1] See in this connection McCabe vs. Emmons, 109 N. Y. 665.

[2] Text commended, Eliot vs. Merchants' Exchange, 14 Mo. App. 242, 243. These views have also since received confirmation in New York in Powell vs. Waldron, 89 N. Y. 328, and in Illinois in Smith vs. Barclay, 21 Am. L. Rep. (n. s.) 408, where the subject is fully discussed, and the views herein expressed are endorsed.

In the former case Judge Finch in deciding the cause said: "Whether he (the receiver of the member's estate) could make it available, or in what manner convert it into money or how it might prove to be encumbered under the rules of the Exchange, are after questions in

which defendants have no present interest." 89 N. Y. 332, 333. The latter case of Smith vs. Barclay was, however, reversed in Barclay vs. Smith, 107 Ill. 349, in which it was held that a certificate of membership in the Board of Trade was not property. See page 154, note 1, as to criticism of this decision which is contrary to all the authorities. And in a later case the Supreme Court of New Jersey held that courts of law will interpose to control the proceedings of ecclesiastical bodies when a right to property is involved, but in no other instance (State of New Jersey vs. Rector of Trinity Church, 28 Alb. L. J. 111.)

[3] Ritterband vs. Baggett, 4 Ab. New Cas. 67.

his seat to a member-elect, with whom the receiver might contract for its sale, the court said:

"The appointment of plaintiff as receiver of Baggett, made in the supplemental proceedings under the code, vested in him the legal title to all the personal property of Baggett. By force of the statute, Code 298, the receiver of the judgment debtor is subject to the direction and control of the court in which judgment was obtained upon which the proceedings are founded. This action was commenced by leave granted by this court, and the receiver's appointment confers upon him the right to make discovery, on defendant's oath, of all his property. I am of the opinion that the seat in the Cotton Exchange was an incorporeal right which Baggett had at the time he became bankrupt, and was in the fullest sense property, and that the franchise and privileges secured to the Exchange by its charter and high price of the initiation fee show that it was valuable property. Nor can I doubt that had there been no supplemental proceedings under which a receiver was appointed it would have passed, subject to the rules of the Cotton Exchange, to his assignee in bankruptcy; and if there had been left in the hands of the members of the board any balance, after paying the debts due to the members, and all penalties and charges, that balance might have been recovered by the assignee. The question whether the seat in the board was property has been fully settled in a late case, almost if not entirely, identical with the case at bar.[1] The question being settled that the seat in question is property of value, I think it is the duty of the court to enforce its transfer for the plaintiff's benefit in this action, either to a re-

---

[1] Hyde vs. Woods, 91 U. S. (4 Eaton, 91 U. S. 716, followed in Otto) 524. See also Nichols vs. Sparhawk vs. Yerkes, 112 U. S. 1.

ceiver or to a third person qualified to work out the designs of the law. We have seen that the personal estate of the debtor becomes vested in the receiver from the time, and by virtue, of his appointment. The entry of the order appointing the receiver places the title of all the personal property in him. The provisions of the Code relating to supplemental proceedings were enacted for the purpose of making the property of the debtor available assets in his hands to pay his debts. By a by-law of the Exchange this property cannot be assigned to any one but members and to members-elect. It cannot, therefore, be assigned to the receiver, as he is neither a member nor a member-elect. If this property cannot be reached by the receiver unless some mode is presented, the object and intention of the Code become not only a dead letter, but lifeless in spirit. Rights of property, from time immemorial, could be reached by a creditor's bill; and it is now well settled that the same result may be accomplished by proceedings under the Code, which furnish a substitute for that proceeding in chancery. Personal property passes to the receiver without assignment; but if an asssignment be necessary to effect the purpose of the law I do not question the power of the court to direct it to be done. I therefore direct an assignment to be made to Mr. Covas or some other competent and fit member of the Cotton Exchange, with apt and proper directions."[1]

[1] To same effect are Londheim vs. White, 67 How. Pr. 467; Roome vs. Swan, 2 N. Y. Supp. 614; Habenicht vs. Lessak, 78 Cal. 351; Eliot vs. Merchants' Exchange, 14 Mo. App. 234; London and Canadian Loan Co. vs. Morphy, 10 Ont. Rep. 86, and see cases cited post, pp. 156–160, under the bankruptcy law.

A seat in the New York Consolidated Stock and Petroleum Exchange will pass to a receiver in supplementary preceedings. If there are debts due to the members of

The seat may be pledged to secure a loan, and the lien may be enforced without a foreclosure.[1] And if the seat has been pledged as collateral for a loan the receiver has the right to redeem it.[2]

In Massachusetts a creditor may, under Pub. Stat. ch. 151, § 2, cl. 11, and St. of 1884, ch. 285, § 1 (now Rev. L. ch. 159, § 3, cl. 7), bring a bill in equity to reach property which cannot be attached or taken in execution. It has been held that the bringing of a bill in equity under this statute to compel the sale of a seat in the Boston Stock Exchange, did not give the plaintiff such a lien on the property as would prevent it passing to the assignee in insolvency of the debtor,

the Exchange, the receiver takes the equitable interest of the judgment debtor in it. Leggett vs. Waller, 80 N. Y. Supp. 13.

In Roome vs. Swan, supra, it was held that the debtor would not be required to sign a consent that the purchaser take his seat or to formally resign and nominate the purchaser as his successor (these formalities being required by the rules of the Exchange) the sale and purchase at law being equivalent to these, but he would be required to sign a consent that the purchaser be vested with the rights and privileges enuring to membership. And a bankrupt member will be compelled in equity to execute any instrument necessary to complete the transfer of title to a purchaser from the assignee. Platt vs. Jones, 96 N. Y. 24.

In Illinois, however, it has been held that a certificate of membership in a commercial Exchange is not property liable to be subjected by creditor's bill to the payment of his debts. Smith vs. Barclay, 107 Ill. 349; Weaver vs. Fisher, 110 Ill. 146.

The doctrine of these cases is severely criticised in an article in 22 Am. L. Reg. (n. s.) 438, and undoubtedly "the weight of authority and the better reasoning support the proposition that such a seat or membership is property and should be applied as other property of a debtor to the payment of his debts. To hold that it cannot be thus applied would establish a rule giving to the members of such associations the power to invest fortunes under the name of licenses and privileges, and by their constitutions and regulations to establish a law for the exemption of the same." Habenicht vs. Lessak, 78 Cal. 357.

[1] Nashua Savings Bank vs. Abbott, 63 N. E. (Mass.) 1058.

[2] Powell vs. Waldron, 89 N. Y. 328.

and that when the latter made an assignment pending an appeal, the proceeds of the sale of his seat passed to his assignee.[1]

If, however, after the seat has been pledged to secure a loan, and the death of the member, the seat has been sold under the rules of the Exchange and the proceeds paid to the member's administrator, the lien subsists and holds the proceeds of sale in the administrator's hands, when the seat was sold with notice to the Exchange and to the administrator of the claim, and the short statute of limitations did not bar a claim under the lien.[2]

In another case in Massachusetts it appeared that a seat in the Boston Stock Exchange was purchased by a firm of stock-brokers, but the membership was taken in the name of one of the two persons composing the firm, the rules not allowing partnerships to become members. The firm failed, and afterwards the members of it did no business together, but no formal dissolution or settlement of the firm affairs was made. Fifteen years subsequently the member who held the seat, and who afterwards occupied it for the transaction of his private business only, sold the seat, and his former copartner sued him for a moiety of the proceeds, and it was held that the statute of limitations was a bar to the plaintiff's claim.[3]

In the bankruptcy courts the same doctrine has been adopted. In the matter of Ketcham, bankrupt,[4] on an ap-

---

[1] Fish vs. Fiske, 154 Mass. 302.

[2] Nashua Bank vs. Abbott, 63 N. E. (Mass.) 1058.

[3] Currier vs. Studley, 159 Mass. 17.

[4] N. Y. *Daily Reg.* Feb. 9, 1880; s. c. more fully, 9 Rep. 305; 1 Fed. Rep. 840; cited and the conclusions approved in the case of Grocers' Bank vs. Murphy, N. Y. C. P. 11 N. Y. *Weekly Dig.* 538; s. c. in full, 60 How. P. 426; N. Y. *Daily Reg.* March 12, 1881. See also Scott vs. Ives, N. Y. *Daily Reg.* July 24, 1879,

plication for an order requiring the bankrupt to make transfer of his seat in the New York Stock Exchange to the assignee in bankruptcy, or to such person as the assignee might procure as a purchaser of the seat, Judge Choate, in the United States District Court, in a lengthy decision, said : " The real question is whether the right or privilege which the bankrupt holds as a member of this Stock Exchange is to be regarded as property which passes to his assignee in bankruptcy, under the Bankrupt Law, for the benefit of his creditors. If it is, then whatever it may be necessary for the bankrupt to do to make the right available to the assignee, he will be required to do. The seat, however, has an actual pecuniary value which the rules of the society, as interpreted and applied in practice, permit the holder to realize by a sale and transfer. There is no practical difficulty in effecting a transfer of this right or interest, for a pecuniary consideration, subject to the condition that the debts of the present holder to members are first paid, and the right or privilege is, to all intents and purposes, a business right, or privilege for business purposes only. I see nothing in the rules of the Exchange which renders it impossible for a seat to be disposed of by the assignee with the co-operation of the bankrupt, subject to the condition above mentioned. This seat in the board was actually used as a part of the business capital of these bankrupts as Stock-brokers. To suffer the bankrupt still to hold it virtually withdraws several thousand dollars in value of his business assets from his creditors." The court reviewed several cases somewhat analogous, one of

where the court denied an applica- Exchange from disposing of, or in-
tion for an injunction to restrain terfering with, the proceeds of a
the president of the New York Stock member's seat in the Exchange.

which was touching a stall in a market, in which it was determined that the transfer could not be made without the consent of the city authorities, and concluded as follows: "The controlling consideration is, as it seems to me, that practically, and whatever its form or incidents with respect to other matters may be, it is a part of the bankrupt's business assets, or, more generally, of his property, which it was the primary design of the Bankrupt Law to distribute among his creditors; and that the peculiarities which distinguish this from other property are, in view of the evident purpose and scope of the Bankrupt Law, unessential, mere technical cobwebs which the law is strong enough to break through." An order was directed to be entered requiring the bankrupt to execute any transfer, assignment, or other instrument necessary for the purpose of vesting the title of his seat in the New York Stock Exchange in such person as the assignee in bankruptcy might procure.[1]

---

[1] Contra, In re Sutherland, 6 Biss. 526, but the doctrine of In re Ketchum, supra, has since entirely prevailed. Matter of Werder, 15 Fed. 789; Platt vs. Jones, 96 N. Y. 24; McCabe vs. Emmons, 109 N. Y. 665; Powell vs. Waldron, 89 N. Y. 328; People ex rel. Lemmon vs. Feltner, 167 N. Y. 1. So, too, under the bankruptcy act of 1898. In re Gaylord, 111 Fed. Rep. 717. In that case it appeared that the bankrupt member had been expelled for fraud, and the St. Louis Stock Exchange sought to retain the proceeds of the sale of the seat on the ground that the expulsion of the member had worked a forfeiture of the proceeds to the Exchange, as held in Belton vs. Hatch, 109 N. Y. 593, but the court held that as the rules of the Exchange merely provided for the sale of the seat of an expelled member, and were silent as to the disposal of the proceeds, the member could not be deprived of the property right in his seat, and that after paying any debts due to the members or to the Exchange, the balance constituted part of the bankrupt's estate to which his trustee became entitled. Id.

The title to the seat is vested in the assignee by the assignment in bankruptcy and the assignor may be compelled by order of the court having jurisdiction of the bankruptcy proceedings to execute the necessary assignments, transfers,

It has been also recently decided by the United States Supreme Court in the case of Page vs. Edmunds,[1] that a seat in the Philadelphia Stock Exchange is property within the meaning of the Bankruptcy act, as a bankrupt member might have transferred it prior to the filing of the petition (Act of 1898, section 70, subdivision 5), subject, however, to the payment of any debts due to the Stock Exchange creditors, and when there are no such debts, it passes to the bankruptcy trustee.

etc., to pass the seat to such person as the assignee might procure. Matter of Ketchum, Platt vs. Jones, supra.

"In an unreported case Judge Blatchford refused to make an order for the sale, at auction, of a seat in the Stock Exchange, solely because he would not permit a public sale to be made under the sanction of the court, in a case where the assignee could not undertake with the purchaser to deliver the thing sold." In re Gallagher, 16 Blatch. 417. The assignee in bankruptcy, however, is not bound to accept property of an onerous or burdensome nature, and may elect to accept or not a seat encumbered with debts to members of the Exchange. Twelve years of "masterly inactivity" while the bankrupt was by his own efforts discharging his debts within the Exchange, was sufficient ground upon which to decide that the assignee had elected not to take. Sparhawk vs. Yerkes, 142 U. S. 1. The authority of the court of bankruptcy ceases at the discharge and the former bankrupt cannot after that be compelled by such court to execute such instruments.

He has then ceased to be either "debtor" or "bankrupt." Matter of Nichols, 1 Fed. 842; Platt vs. Jones, supra. Nor will a court of equity under such circumstances interfere by injunction, at the instance of the assignee or a purchaser from him who has not been admitted to the Exchange, to restrain the former bankrupt from using the untransferred seat or the Stock Exchange from allowing him to do so. The membership of the Exchange being unlimited and the assignee or vendee not being admitted, there is no injury done him by allowing the former bankrupt to continue his use of the seat. When the vendee of the assignee had applied to the Exchange to have his right recognized, or when he had been legally nominated and elected to the Exchange, then undoubtedly the jurisdiction of a court of equity might be invoked to compel the former bankrupt, in case of his refusal, to execute any paper that might be necessary to vest a complete title in the applicant. McCabe vs. Emmons, and Platt vs. Jones, supra.

[1] 187 U. S. 596. See also In re Neimann, 124 Fed. 738.

From the evidence it appeared that the seat had a decided value, as the bankrupt had paid $5500 for it, and he testified that the last price he had heard paid for a seat was $8500. Upon the question of value the court said: " The contingencies which may defeat or affect its title, or its enjoyment, will be reflected in its price, and if, notwithstanding them, a seat has a vendible value of from $5000 to $8000, it would seem that the law should have some process to reach it for the benefit of creditors.   And the bankrupt act supplies the process."   The court also declined to follow the cases of Thompson vs. Adams and Pancoast vs. Gowen, in so far as it might be gathered from them that a seat in the Stock Exchange was not property which might pass to a trustee in bankruptcy, as these decisions were not interpretations of a state statute, but were declarations of general law— mere definitions of property—as to which the court might dispute their conclusions, if their reasoning did not persuade. And an order directing the trustee to sell the seat at public auction, subject to the by-laws of the Exchange, was approved.

Whether the Exchange should be joined as a party in such proceedings has been mooted.   In the case of Campbell vs. The New York Cotton Exchange,[1] in the New York Supreme Court, Special Term, the plaintiff, a receiver, set up a judgment in favor of one Weeks vs. Talcott; the ownership by Talcott of the certificate of a seat in the Cotton Exchange; that the by-laws provide that on the surrender by a member of his certificate to the treasurer of the Exchange, "a transfer should be made by him to a member or member-elect only ;" and that " any member may purchase

---

[1] N. Y. *Daily Reg.* Jan. 11, 1881; s. c. 47 N. Y. Super. Ct. 558.

said rights of membership of any other member, which shall give him the right to sell the same to any other member or member-elect;" that plaintiff, as receiver in Weeks vs. Talcott, prior to the commencement of this action, received an offer from one M., a member, in good standing, of the Exchange, of $1000 for said seat; that Talcott refused to excute the necessary transfers, and the suit is brought to compel such transfers, it being alleged that Talcott has no other property. The corporation demurred to the complaint, claiming that it was improperly joined as defendant, there being no suggestion that the Exchange would refuse to abide by its rules and by-laws, and that the court was bound to assume that when the time came and the necessary conditions precedent were performed, the Exchange would do what it ought to do.

But the demurrer was overruled on the ground that the plaintiff's equitable cause of action comprehended a consummated assignment of the seat; or, in other words, a complete vesting of the right to a seat, which could not be accomplished without the defendant, the New York Cotton Exchange's co-operation. It is therefore a necessary party to the action. There is no more trouble substantially connected with the defence of the action than would be involved in the defendant's scrutinizing any set of circumstances which would be presented to it with a demand of transfer under the rules.[1]

---

[1] It has not, however, been the practice to join the Exchange as a party, and in Londheim vs. White, 1 N. Y. City Court, Special Term, 67 How. Pr. 467, where the objection of non-joinder of the Exchange was raised in opposition to a motion to compel the debtor to assign his seat to a receiver in supplementary proceedings, it was held that as all the rights and interests of the Exchange in the membership are fixed and the transferee takes it with the burden of these rights, which could not be

The following propositions may be deemed as settled :

1. That in the disposition of a seat, or the proceeds thereof, the members of the Exchange will be preferred to outside creditors.

2. That the seat is not the subject of seizure and sale on attachment and execution.

3. That the proceeds of the seat, in the hands of the Exchange or its officers, are capable of being reached, after the claims of members have been satisfied, to the same extent and in the same manner as any other money or property of a debtor.

4. That a person owning a seat in the Exchange can be compelled, by proceedings subsequent to execution, or under the direction of a receiver, to sell his seat to a person acceptable to the Exchange, and devote the proceeds to the satisfaction of his judgment debts. How far the Exchange may go in deciding that such a person is not acceptable to it has not been decided. The Court of Appeals said,[1] there is " no case where the Stock Exchange has admitted to membership the purchaser at a judicial sale. The court has no power to compel such action and the probability of a creditor reaching a favorable result by selling the seat of a member is, to say the least, exceedingly remote." But it *seems* that the

divested by any order of the court, the Exchange was not a necessary party. It certainly does not seem proper to submit the Exchange to the annoyance of being joined as a party in every such proceeding where its own interests cannot be infringed and where there is no claim that it will infringe the interests of others.

[1] People ex rel. Lemmon vs. Feit-

ner, 167 N. Y. 1. See also American Live Stock Co. vs. Chicago Live Stock Exchange, 143 Ill. 210, at pp. 228, 229. The New York Court of Appeals has decided that a patent may be reached by a creditor's bill, and the debtor cannot set up that it is invalid for want of utility, and therefore not property. Gillett vs. Bate, 86 N. Y. 87.

Exchange could not wantonly refuse a member leave to sell to a proper person, and *semble* also to one proposed by a sequestrator.[1]

X. Liability of "Seats" to Taxation.

The value of a seat in the Stock Exchange is, with some judicial dissent, recognized to be capital invested in business[2] and as such liable to the operation of any tax law which reaches personal property either in the usual acceptation of that term, or as it may be defined by statute, such for instance as the Transfer or Inheritance Tax.[3]

[1] London and Canadian Loan Co. vs. Morphy, 10 Ont. 86, at p. 99. The question as to how a seat in the Stock Exchange should be regarded in the settlement of the affairs of a partnership, has never apparently directly arisen. It seems that there can be no objection to partners, only one of whom is a member of the Exchange, making any bargain they please between themselves about the seat of the Exchange partner and about the price or value of it, subject of course to the superior rights of the Exchange. London and Canadian Loan Co. vs. Morphy, 10 Ont. 86, at p. 101.

An action cannot be maintained which is one at law to recover judgment for debt against three of four defendants, and a creditor's bill as to the other defendant, to reach an Exchange membership in the latter's name, but alleged to have been purchased with money belonging to a copartnership of the three other defendants and in equity to belong to them, as a judgment for debt must always be secured before the property to pay that debt can be pursued. An injunction will not be granted restraining the transfer pendente lite of such seat. First Nat. Bk. vs. Miller, *Daily Reg.* Oct. 25, 1882; 4 Mo. L. Bull. (N. Y.) 92.

[2] People ex rel. Lemmon vs. Feitner, 167 N. Y. 1; Matter of Glendinning, 68 App. Div. 125, aff'd without opinion, 64 N. E. 1121; Austen vs. Brigham, 67 N. Y. Supp. 891. See also Matter of Curtis, 31 Misc. 83.

Money is capital and when money is invested in facilities or appliances to do business with, it is capital invested in that business; instances being money expended for the library of a lawyer, the implements of a surgeon, the patent rights of a manufacturer. The money expended in buying a seat in the Stock Exchange is paid for property of great value and which is the main instrumentality for carrying on the member's business. Per Vann, J., in People vs. Feitner, 167 N. Y. 1.

[3] Matter of Hellman's Est., 174 N. Y. 254, rev'g 77 A. D. 355; Mat-

It has been held in New York that the definition of the personal property upon which the latter tax is imposed is that contained in section 242 of the Tax Law (Laws, 1896, ch. 908), and not in that of subdivision 5 of section 2 of the same statute.[1]

A membership in the Stock Exchange is not, however, considered to be personal property under the special and limited definition of that species of property, given by the last cited section (subdivision 5 of section 2),[2] and, therefore, the value of a seat in that State, whether owned by a resident or non-resident of the State, is not liable to the general tax applicable to county, town, and municipal purposes, imposed upon property by the Tax Law (Arts. 1–9).[3]

In California it has been held that as a seat in the Stock Exchange is a mere personal privilege to belong to an association with the latter's assent, it is not liable to city, county, or state taxes.[4]

XI. Gratuity Fund—Life Insurance.

The constitutions of both the New York and the Philadelphia Stock Exchanges make provision for the families or representatives of deceased members. The New York Produce Exchange has, by its by-laws, made similar provision in accordance with express authority in its charter,[5]

ter of Glendinning, 64 N. E. 1121, aff'g 68 App. Div. 125; Matter of Curtis, 31 Misc. 84; 64 N. Y. Supp. 574.

[1] Matter of Hellman, 174 N.Y. 254.

[2] L. 1896, ch. 908, § 2, subd. 4, made subd. 5 by L. 1901, ch. 490.

[3] People ex rel. Lemmon vs. Feitner, 167 N. Y. 1, which must be considered as overruling Austen vs. Brigham, 67 N. Y. Supp. 891, so far as it decides to the contrary.

[4] San Francisco vs. Anderson, 36 Pac. 1034; San Francisco vs. Wangenheim, 37 Pac. 221. See also City of Baltimore vs. Johnson, 54 Atl. 646.

[5] Laws, 1882, ch. 36; Kemp vs. N. Y. Produce Exchange, 34 App. Div. 175.

and it has been held that it could not divert the fund which it had accumulated to meet death losses, and destroy the vested rights of members therein, by so amending its by-laws as to provide for its distribution among the living subscribing members. The power of such a corporation to amend its by-laws is a power to regulate, within reasonable bounds, not a power to destroy the contract rights of its members.[1]

[1] Parish vs. New York Produce Exchange, 169 N. Y. 34. The gratuity fund of this Exchange exists by virtue of a provision in the charter of the Exchange, and an additional reason given by the court for its decision was that the statute of incorporation did not confer upon the members of the Exchange the power to create a fund by assessment for distributing among the subscribing members thereof. Had a by-law with that purpose been enacted in the first instance it would have been without authority in the charter, which did not attempt to confer the power to create a gratuity fund for distribution among the members of the Exchange, but instead limited its scope to that of provisions for the widows and families of deceased members or other persons dependent upon a deceased member.

It has, however, been since held by the Supreme Court, Special Term (French vs. Commercial Exchange, N. Y. L. J. July 25, 1902) that an amendment to the by-laws of the New York Mercantile Exchange (which is an incorporated association), permitting the withdrawal of a member holding a certificate in the participating class, upon giving notice and relinquishing his claim upon the gratuity fund, was not unreasonable, as it did not undertake to dispose of the funds on hand, or any assessments which had accrued, and that, therefore, it did not interfere with the vested rights of plaintiff (a participating member) under the agreement by which the participating membership was formed. It is doubtful, however, if the doctrine of this decision can be upheld in view of the decision of the Court of Appeals, just cited (Parish vs. N. Y. Produce Exchange, 169 N. Y. 34). If all the participating members of the Mercantile Exchange should, immediately after the passage of the by-law, elect to avail of its provisions, and withdraw from the participation, the object for which the fund was established could not be fulfilled, viz: the making provision for the widows and children, etc., of such members, except to the extent of the fund then existing, and even as to that fund, it could scarcely be made available for the beneficiaries under the by-laws, in view of such general withdrawal.

The question has arisen, in Pennsylvania, in regard to the right of the representatives of a deceased suspended member to recover the fund.

In this case[1] the facts were these: One MacDowell, the father of the plaintiff, purchased a seat in the Exchange, and was elected a member August 28, 1865. In December, 1875, while MacDowell was still a member, an amendment to the constitution of the Exchange was passed, providing substantially as follows: *That every full member of the Exchange should, in addition to all other payments required of him at the time of his admission, pay into the hands of the trustees $15, and the further sum of $15 annually, on December 1, and also the sum of $10 upon the death of any full member. Said payments were to be charged and collected in the same manner as all other dues to the Exchange. Said trustees were to set apart the fund arising from such payments as the " Gratuity Fund," and were to pay therefrom, within thirty days after the death of any full member, the sum of $2000 to his nominee, widow, children, or legal representatives.* A full member was one owning a seat in the Exchange, whether suspended or not.

After the passage, MacDowell paid all assessments except those stated hereafter.

On November 17, 1877, the following amendment to the constitution was adopted:

" *That any suspended member who shall have failed for three months to pay in full all gratuity dues and assessments, shall forthwith cease to be a full member for the purposes of this section ; such member may be restored to such full membership by a favorable report of the Standing Committee,*

---

[1] MacDowell vs. Ackley, 8 Week. Notes Cas. 464.

upon paying in full all arrears of gratuity dues and assess-ments."

It was not shown that MacDowell ever expressly assented or agreed to this amendment. He failed to pay his regular quarterly dues for 1877 and for some parts of the year 1878, and several assessments due from him to the Gratuity Fund, by reason of the deaths of members, in 1877 and 1878, and continued indebted in these amounts to the Exchange until his death. In April MacDowell became hopelessly insane, and he was subsequently, in August, duly suspended in ac-cordance with the rules for non-payment of dues, after which no further dues or assessments were imposed upon him. In November, 1878, he died, leaving one child, the plaintiff, his sole heir, and having designated no person to whom the gratuity from the Exchange should be paid.

After his death his seat was sold under the rules, but suffi-cient was not realized to pay the claims of the members of the Exchange. A portion of the proceeds of the sale of the seat were applied to the payment of said dues and assess-ments; said proceeds were not distributed, however, but were held by the treasurer of the Exchange. This action was brought by the guardian of the heir of MacDowell against the officers, etc., of the Exchange to recover the sum of $2,000 above provided for. Judgment was rendered for the defendant, which was affirmed by the Supreme Court, where it was held that the right of MacDowell in this Gratuity Fund was grafted on his existing membership in the Stock Exchange, and that he was bound by the amend-ment which had been regularly adopted. The court further held that his absence when the amendment was adopted, even if shown, could not avail; that even if he had dis-sented therefrom he could not have been relieved from its obligation ; for, having subscribed to the constitution and by-laws, and the change having been made in accordance therewith, he could not be permitted to question its validity ; he could not enjoy the benefits of the fund without perform- ing his part towards creating it ; and that his subsequent mental incapacity did not relieve him from the effect of previous neglect and refusal to discharge his legal and just duty.

Article XVIII. of the constitution of the New York Stock Exchange, establishing the gratuity fund, will be found in the appendix, and the by-law of the Produce Exchange is substantially the same.[1]

The agreement of the Stock Exchange, expressed in its constitution, does not bind that body to pay upon the death of a member the full sum named, but only to pay that sum or such part thereof as shall be yielded by levy and assessment upon surviving members.[2] While it is called a gratuity it is beyond the power of the Exchange itself to withhold it, after collection, against those beneficially inter- ested.[3]

The right to the gratuity fund falls with the loss of membership or the non-payment of subscriptions in accord- ance with the constitution and by-laws.[4]

The provision in the plan against assignability for debts has been sustained by the courts. The gratuity is "in- capable of assignment. It was the intention to create pro- vision for the family of the deceased member which should

[1] Kemp vs. New York Produce Exchange, 34 App. Div. 175; Mc- Cord vs. McCord, 40 App. Div. 275.

[2] Matter of Noyes, 5 Dem. 309, at p. 317.

[3] Webb vs. Meyers, 67 Hun, 11. See also Matter of Noyes, 5 Dem. 307.

[4] MacDowell vs. Ackley, 93 Pa. St. 277; Matter of Fay, 25 Misc. 469.

be beyond the hazard of loss from pecuniary misfortune."[1] It is not liable to the payment of debts or legacies[2] and even an assignment made during the life of a member, by his wife, who was the sole beneficiary of the fund, in which assignment the husband joined, would not vest in the assignee any interest in the fund.[3]

In the last cited case the court based its conclusion "upon the broad ground that it would not only be against public policy to uphold the assignment, but it would be subversive of the entire plan of beneficence as embodied in the constitution and by-laws of the Exchange."[4]

Nor does the fact that, with the consent of a creditor to whom a seat in the Boston Stock Exchange was assigned to secure a loan, part of a gratuity fund paid to the assignor's widow, was applied in part payment of the loan, preclude the creditor from enforcing his lien against the proceeds of the sale of the seat, as the gratuity was not a right, but merely a gift from the other members to the widow.[5]

Nor has the member any such property right in the gratuity fund as would enable him to change the beneficiary while living or alter the disposition of the fund by his will.[6] And it is not taxable under the Transfer or

[1] Kemp vs. New York Produce Exchange, 34 App. Div. 175.

[2] Matter of Fay, 25 Misc. 468.

[3] McCord vs. McCord, 46 App. Div. 275.

[4] Id. The argument upon the ground of public policy is based upon the similarity of the gratuity fund to ordinary life insurance policies for the benefit of those dependent upon the insured, which in New York are generally non-assignable. Id.

[5] Nashua Bank vs. Abbott, 63 N. E. (Mass.) 1058.

[6] Webb vs. Meyers, 64 Hun, 11. Yet, where in making a particular legacy to his next of kin, the testator manifests his intention that the amount of the gratuity fund shall form part thereof, as by directing his executors to collect it and apply it on the legacy, the legatee is deemed to take the gratuity as pro tanto in satisfaction of the legacy,

Inheritance Tax, as assets of the deceased, as it passes not by virtue of his will, or the administration of his estate, but by the contract of the deceased with the Exchange.[1]

The fund is to be paid to the widow, descendants, children, adopted children, or next of kin,[2] but under by-laws wherein children and not adopted children were mentioned, an adopted child, in view of the statutes giving to such all the rights of a child including that of inheritance, was held entitled to share in the fund and this, it was said, would be so even if the deceased adopted the child, for the very purpose of enabling the adopted child to obtain the fund.[3]

The meaning of the term "next of kin" as used in the gratuity fund article is to be determined according to the law of the State at the time the fund becomes payable.[4]

It is provided that, "In all cases a certified copy of the proceedings before a Surrogate or Judge of Probate shall be accepted as proof of the rights of the claimants, be deemed ample authority to the Exchange to pay over the money, shall protect the Exchange in so doing, and shall release

under the familiar doctrine in the law of wills, that a beneficiary who accepts the bounty of a testator must do so upon such terms as the testator has imposed. Matter of Noyes, 5 Dem. 309. And if an executor collects the gratuity, and treats it as part of the estate, and his account is adopted as rendered, the surrogate has no jurisdiction to reopen the decree for the purpose of having the amount thereof deducted from the estate. Watt's Estate, 20 N. Y. Supp. 63.

[1] Matter of Fay, 25 Misc. 468.

[2] Article XVIII. § 5, as amended to April, 1903. Should there be none of these, it shall be credited to the members against whom the assessment shall have been levied.

[3] Kemp vs. New York Produce Exchange, 34 App. Div. 175.

Semble that the adopted child might, under the statutes of New York, claim the fund, as next of kin, if not considered as the child of the deceased within the by-law. Ibid.

[4] Kemp vs. New York Produce Exchange, 34 App. Div. 175.

the Exchange forever from all further claim or liability whatsoever."[1]   And payment so made, though to persons not justly entitled thereto, discharges the Exchange from any liability to again pay it over, even to the rightful owners thereof.   This protection, however, to the Exchange does not affect the right or title of those legally entitled to the fund to recover the amount from the person to whom it was paid, as money had and received to their use.[2]

All interested beneficially in the fund should join in any action for its recovery from the Exchange.   It cannot be sued therefor piecemeal.[3]

In concluding this review of the general legal character of unincorporated Stock Exchanges, we find that the subjects discussed are comparatively new in the law, and hence we have, at great labor and expenditure of time, set forth the most important adjudications in full ; from which it appears that the courts have treated these novel questions in a spirit of great fairness, and that, when analogous branches of the law have failed to furnish precedents, they have been determined upon general principles of justice and good sense.

---

[1] Art. XVIII. § 5.

[2] Webb vs. Meyers, 64 Hun, 11.

[3] Diepenbrock vs. N. Y. Produce Exchange (Special Term, N. Y.), N. Y. *Law Journal*, July 11, 1901.

CHAPTER III.

ANALYSIS OF TRANSACTIONS BETWEEN BROKER AND
CLIENT UPON PURCHASE OR SALE OF STOCKS IN THE
UNITED STATES.

I. Stock-Brokers and Stock Exchanges—License.

In the United States the business of buying and selling stocks and other securities is generally transacted by Brokers for a commission agreed upon or regulated by the usages of the place ; and although any person may enter into such an occupation[1] upon his obtaining a license for

---

[1] A national bank, however, is not by its charter, or incidentally, authorized to act as broker in the purchase or sale of bonds and stocks. First National Bank vs. Charlotte, 92 U. S. (2 Otto) 122; Bank of Allentown vs. Hoch, 89 Pa. St. 324; Wickler vs. First National Bank, 42 Md. 581, and cases cited. But it is within the incidental powers of a national bank, as part of the business of banking, to sell securities for a customer, where such sale is simply for the purpose of increasing the customer's deposit account with the bank. Williamson vs. Mason, 12 Hun, 97.

that purpose, when he intends to carry on the business of a Stock-broker in a State whose legislation makes a license a prerequisite, such business is now generally restricted to Brokers who are members of Stock Exchanges.

In Pennsylvania the occupation of Stock-broker is regulated by statute, the substance of which is here given:

1. Stock-brokers to be licensed, etc.

5. License to be renewed annually, etc., to enure for the benefit of assignees or legal representatives. Proceedings in such cases: Brokers not to use more than one place of business. The same person may be licensed as stock, exchange, and bill Broker.

6. Penalty for acting without license.

9. Tax on Broker's license. Three per cent on commissions, etc. (Stock, bill and exchange Brokers were relieved from license tax by the Act of June 7, 1901, P. L. 254.)

10. To be appraised.

11. How classified.

12. To make annual returns on oath.

13. Statement of name of Broker or firm, location of business, and amount of capital engaged to be reported to the auditor-general.

14. Penalty for neglect.

15. Power of auditor-general in relation to penalties.

16. Tax on receipts to be additional to license. (This tax was reduced from three to one per cent by the Act of June 13, 1901, P. L. 266.)[1]

---

[1] See 1 Pepper & Lewis's Digest of the Laws of Penna. tit. "Brokers," where the cases arising under the statute are given. See also P. L. 1899, p. 184, and Opinion of Attorney General of Penna., 9 Dist. Ct. Rep. 166.

Under authority of the legislature, Chicago has enacted an ordinance making it unlawful to follow the business of a Broker generally, without a license therefor. The text of the statute and the ordinance may be found in the cases hereinafter cited.

The constitutionality of this license tax was attacked in Illinois, but unsuccessfully, the supreme court holding that a tax upon occupations or employments whether for revenue or as an exaction for the privilege of pursuing a calling may be imposed in the form of a license tax and that the legislature is not restricted therein to occupations or businesses which are immoral, vexatious or injurious to the well-being of society, nor is it necessary that before a business can be regulated or burdens imposed upon its exercise, that there should be power to suppress it. " It is true that in order to be effectual, a license must confer authority to do that which without the license would be illegal but . . . the occupation may be lawful in itself and not subject to prohibition or regulation by the State, yet it may be prohibited in order to compel the taking out of a license if the purpose is to raise revenue by means of license fees. Cooley on Taxation, pp. 595, 597." The constitutional requirement of uniformity in taxes is met by a uniform operation upon all within the class to be taxed, and the taxing or licensing power may be delegated by the State to its municipalities.[1]

The ordinance defines a Broker as " one who for commission or other compensation is engaged in selling or negotiating the sale of goods, wares and merchandise, produce or grain belonging to others " and the phrase " goods, wares and

[1] Banta vs. Chicago, 172 Ill. 204; s. c. 40 L. R. A. 611; Braun vs Chicago, 110 Ill. 186.

merchandise " includes shares in the stock of incorporated companies and other securities which are the subject of common barter and sale, and which are given visible and palpable form by means of certificates, bonds, or other evidences of indebtedness.[1]

Brokers in mining stocks are also included in the words quoted, and a Broker who has dealt in stocks for a third party in violation of the ordinance cannot maintain an action for his commission.[2]   But in Indiana, where there is also a licensing statute (§ 5269, Horner's Stats. 1902 ed.), an unlicensed person not engaged in " the regular brokerage business," to which regular business the statute only applies, was not debarred from maintaining an action for compensation for effecting the sale of stock.[3]   And the statute does not apply to persons dealing in stocks, etc., on their own account.[4]

In Colorado cities are empowered to license Brokers. Mill's Ann. Stats. § 4403, cl. 61.

In Kansas cities may collect a license tax from keepers of " bucket " shops and option dealers.   Gen. Stats. (Dassler) § 727.

In Maryland Stock-brokers were required to be licensed, Public Gen. Stat. art 56, § 12, but this section was repealed by L. 1896, ch. 144.

In Missouri money Brokers and exchange Brokers must be licensed. Rev. Stats. § 5203.   A savings bank whose president acts on behalf of the bank as a money Broker and exchange dealer need not be licensed.[5]

---

[1] Banta vs. Chicago, supra.
[2] Hustis vs. Pickands, 27 Ill. App. 270.
[3] Johnson vs. Williams, 36 N. E. Rep. 167. See also O'Neill vs. Sinclair, 153 Ill. 525.
[4] Henderson vs. State, 50 Ind.
[5] State vs. Field, 49 Mo. 270. For other cases on this subject, see footnote to Missouri Rev. Stat. pp. 1212, 1213.

Iń Michigan, Brokers and exchange dealers shall not engage in such business until a verified certificate giving certain particulars is first filed with the county clerk. Comp. Laws, §§ 5271–5276.

Coupon Brokers must be licensed in Virginia. Code, § 402, L. 1883–4, § 65 ; also Stock-brokers. L. 1883–1884 §§ 58–60.[1]

All the foregoing enumerated States (nine in number) comprise some of the sixteen States in the principal cities of which stock exchanges have been organized. The remaining seven States have not enacted any licensing laws as to Stock-brokers.

Other States (in which stock exchanges have not been organized) also provide for the licensing of Stock-brokers. In Tennessee, a Broker's privilege tax is not payable by one who sells stocks or bonds purchased with his own moneys.[2]

In West Virginia Stock-brokers must be licensed. Code, ch. 32 ; § 2.

The city of Little Rock in Arkansas has power under an act passed in the year 1875 (§ 12) to license Brokers who buy or sell scrip, bonds or exchange.[3]

Under the United States Internal Revenue Act of 1864 (now repealed), bankers as such, Brokers, and bankers doing business as Brokers were required to pay certain taxes upon their transactions.[4]

---

[1] Com. vs. Lucas, 84 Va. 303.
[2] State vs. Duncan, 84 Tenn. 75.
[3] City of Little Rock vs. Barton, 33 Ark. 436.
[4] Clark vs. Gilbert, 5 Blatch. 330; United States vs. Cutting, 3 Wall. 441; United States vs. Fisk, 3 Wall. 445; Northrup vs. Shook, 10 Blatch. 243; Clark vs. Bailey, 12 Blatch. 156; s.c., aff'd 21 Wall. 284; Bankers' Cases, 11 Op. Atty. Gen. 482; Selden vs. Equitable Trust Co., 91 U. S. 419; Warren vs. Shook, 91 U. S. 704, followed in State vs. Duncan, 16 Lea (Tenn.), 75.

By the act of June 13, 1898 (30 U. S. Stats. at Large ch. 448), commonly spoken of as the War Revenue Act, an annual special or license tax of $50 was imposed upon bankers and a similar tax upon stock and bill Brokers, and in the case of sales of stocks the seller was required to deliver to the buyer a memorandum of the sale, showing the date of the sale, the name of the seller, the amount of the sale or the matter or thing to which it referred. A tax of two cents for each $100 of the face value of the sale was imposed by the act, and adhesive stamps denoting the amount of the tax were required to be affixed to such memorandum.

A memorandum and stamps were also required upon each sale or agreement to sell any products or merchandise at any exchange, board of trade, or similar place.

The constitutionality of the provision requiring such memorandum and stamping has been upheld in Nicoll vs. Ames,[1] but since these provisions were entirely repealed by the act of April 13, 1902 (32 Stats. at Large, ch. 500), it is not deemed necessary to do more than mention the cases. The War Revenue Act was also considered in McClain vs. Fleshman.[2]

The question of the taxability of seats in the Stock Exchange is taken up in another place (*ante*, pp. 163–4).

Stock Exchanges have been organized in the following cities of the United States, viz.: New York, Philadelphia, Chicago, Boston, St. Louis, San Francisco, New Orleans, Denver, Baltimore, Cleveland, Cincinnati, Detroit, Kansas,

---

[1] 173 U. S. 509. Also in United States vs. Thomas, 115 Fed. 207. Fed. 880. Also in White vs. Treat, 100 Fed. 290.

[2] 105 Fed. 610; s. c. on appeal, 106

Providence, Indianapolis, Richmond, Washington, Pittsburg, and Los Angeles.

About twenty per cent of the members of the New York Stock Exchange are known as " Room Traders," i. e. they devote themselves exclusively to dealing in securities on their own account, and in this respect they resemble the London Stock Jobbers. See chapter IX.

Other members of the various Stock Exchanges buy and sell securities for themselves, besides transacting brokerage business for their clients.

II. Legal Relation of Stock-broker to his Client.

Considerable discussion has arisen in the cases, especially those in the State of New York, as to the precise relation which exists, where a Broker with his own money purchases or sells stocks, etc., for his Client, for the purposes of speculation.

Does the Stock-broker in such a transaction, in the absence of an express agreement defining the relation, unite in himself the characters of " Broker," " pledgee," and " trustee ? "

The importance of this question is obvious, because, if it be answered affirmatively, it would seem to follow that all of the incidents and consequences of those characters would attach to the Broker, in his dealings with his Client; but, on the other hand, if the question be answered negatively, the simple relation of debtor and creditor, arising out of a breach of contract, would exist.

The embarrassment of the question arises from the fact that, in the case of an ordinary purchase of stocks for speculation, on a margin, the Stock-broker, without literally

filling the technical definitions of " Broker," " pledgee," or
" trustee," comes within the purview of all of those terms.

He is a Broker because he has no interest in the transaction, except to the extent of his commissions;[1] he is a pledgee, in that he holds the stock, etc., as security for the repayment of the money he advances in its purchase;[2] so he is a trustee, for the law charges him with the utmost

---

[1] Hays vs. Currie, 3 Sand. Ch. Ketchum's ed. 638 (marginal paging 585).

[2] The question of a Stock-broker's relation to a client for whom he makes advances, on stocks purchased by, and held by, him as security for his advances, came in question incidentally in a recent case (People ex rel. Sands vs. Feitner, 76 App. Div. 620; 79 N. Y. Supp. 1143, no opinion, aff'd 173 N. Y. 647). The relator contended (see New York L. J. November 8, 1902, giving the arguments of counsel) that a large sum alleged to be due by him to his Stock-brokers, should be allowed as a deduction in assessing his personal property for tax for the year 1901, on the ground that his relation with his Broker was that of pledgor and pledgee, and that he absolutely owned the stocks purchased for him, and owed the Brokers, as pledgees, the amount of their advances. The claim of the tax commissioners was that as the only liability of relator was contingent on a fall in the price of the securities, he had shown no present liability under the contract with his brokers, and as it was uncertain what, if anything, would ever become due from him to his Brokers, the deduction should not be allowed. The question was decided at Special Term adversely to the relator's contention, and this decision was unanimously affirmed by the Appellate Division, whose decision was affirmed by the Court of Appeals on the ground that the question of fact thus passed upon was not reviewable.

In a prior case in the Surrogate's Court it was held, in a similar state of facts, that the client's title to the stocks was not absolute but he held merely the rights of a pledgee with relation to it, the Brokers being the owners of the property at law, subject to the client's right to redeem upon paying the entire amount of the debt, and, therefore, on the client's death, when the securities were sold by the Brokers for a sum less than what was due them, the value of the stocks sold was not part of the decedent's estate for the purpose of transfer tax. In re Havemayer, 32 Misc. 416. If a Broker sells stock on his own account to his client, the mere fact that he acts as a Broker in other transactions, does not convert the former stock into a pledge. The relation of the parties as to that stock is that of vendor and vendee.

honesty and good faith in his transactions; and whatever benefit arises therefrom enures to the *cestui que trust*.[1]

The circumstances attendant upon an ordinary transaction between a Broker and his Client in a stock speculation are carefully described by Hunt, Ch. J., in a leading case in the State of New York.[2]

" The customer employs the Broker . . . to buy certain stocks for his account, and to pay for them, and to hold them subject to his order as to the time of sale. The customer advances ten per cent. of their market value, and agrees to keep good such proportionate advance, according to the fluctuations of the market. . . .

"The Broker undertakes and agrees:

" 1. At once to buy for the customer the stocks indicated.

" 2. To advance all the money required for the purchase, beyond the ten per cent. furnished by the customer.

" 3. To carry or hold such stocks for the benefit of the customer, so long as the margin of ten per cent. is kept good, or until notice is given, by either party, that the transaction must be closed. An appreciation in the value of the stocks is the gain of the customer, and not of the Broker.

" 4. At all times to have in his name, or under his control, ready for delivery, the shares purchased, or an equal amount of other shares of the same stock.

" 5. To deliver such shares to the customer, when re-

Leahy vs. Lobdell, 80 Fed. Rep. 665.

[1] That the position which a Stock-broker occupies in relation to his principal is that of a trustee has been held in Taylor vs. Plumer, 3 M. & S. 562; Ex parte Cook, 4 Ch. Div. 123.

[2] Markham vs. Jaudon, 41 Y. N. 235. This analysis of the obligation of the parties to a purchase of stocks on margin was adopted by the Connecticut Supreme Court. Skiff vs. Stoddard, 63 Conn. 198; 21 L. R. A. 113.

quired by him, upon the receipt of the advances and commissions accruing to the Broker ; or,

" 6. To sell such shares, upon the order of the customer, upon payment of the like sums to him, and account to the customer for the proceeds of such sale.

" Under this contract the customer undertakes :

" 1. To pay a margin of ten per cent. on the current market value of the shares.

" 2. To keep good such margin according to the fluctuations of the market.

" 3. To take the shares so purchased on his order whenever required by the Broker, and to pay the difference between the percentage advanced by him and the amount paid therefor by the Broker." [1]

It may be well to set forth the history of an ordinary transaction between a Client and Broker, even with a little more detail than that contained in the foregoing extract. The ordinary margin paid on opening an account with a Broker—that is, in ordering him to buy or sell securities—is ten per cent.[2] The margin may be less than this, or frequently none is advanced, according to the confidence which the Broker has in the ability of the Client to respond to ultimate loss.   But, whether the Broker advance all or only the principal portion of the sum invested in the securities, the relation of the parties is unchanged.   The fact exists that the Broker looks to the principal for an indemnity upon the entire transaction.   The Client, having given the Broker an order to buy or sell, either in writing or verbally, the next step in the transaction is, that the Broker goes into the

[1] See also Brass vs. Worth, 40 Barb. 648.   [2] Markham vs. Jaudon, 41 N. Y. 235.

Stock Exchange and executes the business, making a verbal contract therefor with another Broker. Frequently the Broker, upon receiving an order, deputes another, or subordinate, Broker to do the business. This is contrary to the general principal of law, that an agent cannot delegate his business to another—" *delegata potestas non potest delegari;* "[1] but it is justified by the general usage of Wall Street, of which the Client has express or implied knowledge.[2]

The exact transaction in the Stock Exchange is as follows:

The selling Broker offers for sale his securities, and if there is a Broker present who wishes to purchase, the contract is completed, upon his assenting to the terms mentioned.

All offers to buy or sell securities shall be for 100 shares of stock, or for $10,000 par value of bonds, unless otherwise stated.[3]

Some rules of the Stock Exchange are here given which further illustrate the transaction in the Stock Exchange.

All bids and offers made and accepted in accordance with the rules of the Stock Exchange shall be binding.[4]

Bids and offers may be made only as follows:

(*a*) " Cash," i. e. for delivery upon the day of contract.

(*b*) " Regular way," i. e. for delivery upon the business day following the contract.

(*c*) " At three days," i. e. for delivery upon the third day following the contract.

(*d*) " Buyer's," or " Seller's " options for not less than four days, nor more than sixty days.

---

[1] Leake's Dig. Law of Cont. 482.
[2] See on this subject, subdivision X., "When Broker can act by substitute," p. 391.
[3] Constitution of the New York Stock Exchange, Rules for the transaction or conduct of business, Art. XXIII. § 2.
[4] Id. § 1.

Bids and offers under each of these specifications may be made simultaneously as being essentially different propositions, and may be separately accepted without precedence of one over another.

Bids and offers made without stated conditions shall be considered to be in the "regular way."

On transactions for more than three days written contracts shall be exchanged on the day following the transaction, and shall carry interest at the legal rate, unless otherwise agreed; on such contracts one day's notice shall be given, at or before 2:15 P. M., before the securities shall be deliverable prior to the maturity of the contract.

On offers to buy "Seller's Option, or to sell "Buyer's Option," the longest option shall have precedence. On offers to buy "Buyer's Option," or to sell "Seller's Option," the shortest option shall have precedence.[1]

No party to a contract shall be compelled to accept a substitute principal, unless the name proposed to be substituted shall be declared in making the offer, and as a part thereof.[2]

When a disagreement arising from a transaction in securities shall be discovered, the money differences shall forthwith be established by purchase or sale by the chairman, or by mutual agreement.[3]

All deliveries of securities must be made before a quarter after 2 o'clock P. M., otherwise the contract may be closed "under the rule," in the manner provided by Art. XXVIII.[4]

On half holidays securities sold for "cash" must be delivered and received at or before 11:30 o'clock A. M.,

[1] Id. § 3.　　　　　　　　　[3] Id. Art. XXX.
[2] Id. Art. XXIV. § 9.　　　　[4] Art. XXVI. § 1.

otherwise the contract may be closed "under the rule" (Art. XXVIII.), after 11:40 o'clock A. M.[1]

In all deliveries of securities, the party delivering shall have the right to require the purchase money to be paid upon delivery; if delivery is made by transfer, payment may be required at time and place of transfer.[2]

But to continue: the Brokers, in making transactions with one another, do not know for whom they are made, the names of the principals being jealously concealed. One Broker looks to the other contracting Broker to carry out the transaction, and in practice there is no attempt made to enforce any liability against the principal should he become known. Here another question arises, whether there is any liability on the part of the unknown principal for the default of his Broker? Is there any privity between him and the other contracting Broker? We shall not attempt to answer these questions in this place, but they are suggested as they arise in the history of the transaction.[3]

In transactions for three days or less, there is no written contract as a general rule between the Brokers, each one merely dotting down the transaction made. On transactions for more than three days written contracts must, as already stated, be exchanged on the following day. But as to every transaction it is the duty of every member to report each of his transactions as promptly as possible at his office, where he shall furnish opportunity for prompt comparison.[4] If there is no written contract the contract is invalid in a majority of the States under the Statute of Frauds.[5] But the rules (Art. XXIII. § 1) make them

[1] Id. § 5.
[2] Id. Art. XXV. § 1.
[3] See this subject considered, ch.
VII.
[4] Art. XXIV. § 1 et seq.
[5] See post, ch. VII. tit. "Statute of Frauds."

inviolable between the members in the tribunal known as the "Arbitration Committee."

On the following day, if the transaction is made "in the regular way," the stocks are duly delivered at the office of the purchasing Broker by the selling Broker, who receives payment for them. If the sale be made on time, the transaction is completed when the time expires. The stock, when received, remains in the office of the purchasing Broker to await the further orders of the Client. Sometimes the stock is held by the Broker with merely a general power of attorney in blank attached to or endorsed on it.

The receiver of the shares of stock shall have the option of requiring the delivery to be made either in certificates therefor or by transfer thereof; except that in cases where personal liability attaches to ownership, the seller shall have the right to make delivery by transfer. The right to require receipt or delivery by transfer shall not obtain while the transfer books are closed.[1]

Deliveries of securities on contracts subject to the rules of the Exchange shall in all cases conform to the requirements for regularity which may be made from time to time, by the committee on securities.[2]

The buyer must, not later than 2:15 o'clock P. M., accept and pay for all or any portion of a lot of stock contracted for, which may be tendered in lots of one hundred shares, or multiples thereof; and he may buy in "under the rule" the undelivered portion, in accordance with the provisions of Article XXVIII. This rule shall also apply to contracts for bonds where tender is made in lots of $10,000, or multiples thereof.[3]

[1] Constitution, Art. XXV. § 2.   [3] Id. § 4.
[2] Id. § 3.

Usually the stock is transferred on the books of the Company in the name of the Broker, rarely in the name of the principal. This stock is considered as the Client's, subject only to the lien of the Broker for advances and commissions. The Broker collects the dividends, and pays assessments upon it, if any be levied, and the same remains in his hands through the whole transaction until it is sold, the Client never having possession of, and rarely ever seeing, the stock. Upon the purchase of the stock, the Broker sends a notice to his Client giving the price *and the name of the Broker from whom he has purchased.* What effect this would have upon a contest between the unknown principal and the other, or selling, Broker is still another question. Frequently a Broker is himself a speculator, and, in executing an order for his principal, unites a purchase or sale on his own account. Finally, the Broker in many instances may have two Clients, who, at the same time, give him counter-orders, the one to buy and the other to sell, which the Broker frequently executes at the market price, but without any real sale or purchase, merely making cross-entries in his books. In the absence of any fraud or any damage to the Clients, can such transactions stand? During the time the stock or securities remain in the possession of the Broker, he uses them to raise money with which to carry on his business, and no attempt is made to keep the stocks separate, or to keep the identical certificates on hand, the Client usually being satisfied if the Broker is able to deliver the number of shares purchased, without any regard to particular certificates. According to the strict legal definition, it is manifest that a Stock-broker, in transactions such as those described above, is not embraced within the term " Broker."

" Brokers " have been defined by a standard legal lexicographer to be "those who are engaged for others in the negotiation of contracts relative to property with *the custody of which they have no concern;* "[1] and "Stock-brokers" as "those employed to buy and sell shares of stocks in incorporated companies and the indebtedness of governments."[2]

The distinctions between a Stock-broker and an ordinary Broker are tersely summarized by Woodruff, J., in his dissenting opinion in the well-known case of Markham vs. Jaudon,[3] in this language: "In the first place, the Stock-dealer who is employed, though called a Stock-broker, does not act as Broker in this transaction. It is no part of the office or duty of a Broker to pay the price. It is no part of the office or right of a Broker to receive the property, still less to take the title to his own name.[4] In this transaction he acts in a peculiar business, in his own name and on his own responsibil-

---

[1] 1 Bouv. L. Dict. Rawle's Rev. title "Broker"; Ewall's Evans on Agency, Bedford's American ed. p. 36; Mechem on Agency, §§ 13, 927, 936; Reinhard on Agency, § 21; Huffcut on Agency, § 112; Tiffany on Agency, p. 224; Braun vs. City of Chicago, 110 Ill. at p. 194.

[2] Ibid.; Anderson's Law Dict. title "Broker"; Black's Law Dict. same title. See also Clark vs. Powell, 1 Nev. & M. 494, arguments of counsel pro and con.; Ab. L. Dict. title "Broker"; Banta vs. Chicago, 172 Ill. 204; s. c. 40 L. R. A. 611. "A Broker is an agent simply. He transacts business not for himself, but for another. He is a middleman, a negotiator between other persons for a compensation. A Stock-broker deals in stocks of moneyed corporations and other securities for his principal. It is a

calling of great responsibilities, in which punctuality, honesty, and knowledge are required." Per Van Vorst, J., White vs. Brownell, 3 Ab. (N. Y.) Pr. (n. s.) 326.

[3] 41 N. Y. 256; Northrup vs. Shook, 10 Blatch. 243.

[4] A Broker has not the custody of the goods of his principal; he is merely empowered to effect the contract of sale or purchase on his behalf. Chitty on Cont. (11th Am. ed.) 274; Paley on Ag. 13; Story on Ag. (9th ed.) § 28 et seq. The functions of a Stock-broker are thus broader than those of the ordinary Broker; some of these broader functions pertain more nearly to the functions of factors or bankers, but their exercise does not make the Stock-broker any the less such. Banta vs. Chicago, supra.

ity, protected against loss by the indemnity furnished, or by the agreement to be furnished to him. The idea of mere agency ordinarily suggested by the name Broker does not, therefore, arise out of the fact that the dealers in stocks for account of others, as to profit and loss, are called Stock-brokers. In the next place, the transaction, according to the intent and purpose of the employment of the Broker, does not contemplate that the customer will ever receive the stock, or own it. It may be that if the Broker desires to close his connection with the transaction, the customer, if he pays the cost, interest, and all commissions which the Broker has earned, or is entitled to earn, will receive the stock. Whether he may so insist or not is a collateral question ; and, if he be so entitled, it will nevertheless be true that this is not in pursuance of the arrangement, but a departure from it ; for the intent is, that the stock shall be carried by the Broker until directed to be sold, the customer never having the title to the stock at all. And, finally, in my opinion, the transaction is an executory agreement for a pure speculation in the rise and fall of stock, which the Broker, on condition of perfect indemnity against loss, agrees to carry through in his own name and on his own means or credit, accounting to his customer for the profits, if any, and holding him responsible for the loss. "

Notwithstanding these technical differences, the decided inclination of the courts has been to visit a Stock-broker with all of the responsibilities of a Broker and pledgee, and, as we shall hereafter see, to confer upon him all the advantages of those relations.

It is impliedly conceded by Mr. Justice Woodruff, and all the advocates of his view of the law, that where the Stock-broker makes purchases of stock, etc., for his principal *for investment,* with money furnished by the former, the relation of pledgor and pledgee exists.[1]

It is also conceded that when stock, etc., is purchased on a margin for the Client, although it does not become the property of the latter,[2] together with all its future dividends and earnings;[3] yet that the Client is entitled to the possession of such stocks, etc., upon paying the money represented in their purchase, with the commissions of the Broker.[4]

So it has been decided that a pledgee of stock is not liable for a loss occasioned by his neglect to sell the stock, it having depreciated in his hands till it became worthless, when, by the contract between the parties, the right to sell the stock had been conferred upon the pledgee or a third person; and the pledgee has never refused to transfer the stock for the purpose of a sale, and the pledgor has never requested that a sale, should be made.[5]

It has been also held that a Stock-broker is not liable where spurious securities are purchased by him for a Client in the regular course of business. And if he sell stocks or securities for his principal, which turn out to be spurious, and the Broker, in consequence, repays the purchase-money to the buyer, he can recover the same from the principal.[6]

So if the pledge be stolen from the Broker, he is not liable unless the theft arose from, or was connected with, a want of ordinary care on his part.[7]

[1] Markham vs. Jaudon, 41 N. Y. 133; at 257 and 258; also Grover, J., s. c. at 247. See also Baker vs. Drake, 53 N. Y. 211, at 216.

[2] Id.

[3] Id.

[4] Per Grover, J., Markham vs. Jaudon, supra, p. 247.

[5] Howard vs. Brigham, 98 Mass.

O'Neill vs. Whigham, 87 Pa. St. 394.

[6] Lamert vs. Heath, 15 M. & W. 486; s. c. Lambert vs. Heath, 15 L. J. Exch. 298; Mitchell vs. Newhall, 15 M. & W. 308; Westropp vs. Solomon, 8 C. B. 373.

[7] 2 Pars. on Cont. (8th ed.) vol. 2, p. 119 (bottom paging); Abbett vs.

Again, if assessments or "calls" are made upon stocks which a Broker holds for a Client, the liability to pay them, if any, is that of the principal, and not the Broker.[1] In fine, all of the benefits, liabilities, and disadvantages of ownership are attached to the principal, while the Broker has no interest in the transaction except to the extent of his commissions.[2]

In view, therefore, of these considerations, the better doctrine would seem to be to hold the Broker to the responsibilities of that relation ; in fact, it appears difficult to conceive of any other relation which could so fully harmonize with the circumstances as that of Broker and pledgee.[3]

The leading case of Markham vs. Jaudon was expressly overruled on the question of the measure of damages in an action for the conversion of stocks by a Broker.[4] It should also be noticed that there were two elaborate dissenting opinions by Woodruff and Grover, JJ., on the question of the relation which existed between the Broker and the Client, the two judges just mentioned holding that the Brokers were not pledgees, but that they held the stock under a contract which enabled them to sell upon the failure of the Client to furnish margins. When this question came again before the court of last resort in New York,[5] Commissioners Earl and Reynolds both wrote opinions affirming the judgment on the specific ground that the Brokers were pledgees. But in the case of Baker vs. Drake[6] (which was not adverted to in the preceding case), overruling Markham vs. Jaudon

Frederick, 56 How. Pr. (N. Y.) 68. See Arent vs. Squires, 1 Daly, 347.

[1] McCalla vs. Clark, 55 Ga. 53.

[2] See the above questions considered at pp. 218, 261.

[3] See, however, the New York doctrine criticised in In re Swift, 112 Fed. Rep. 318.

[4] Baker vs. Drake, 53 N. Y. 211.

[5] Stenton vs. Jerome, 54 N. Y. 480.

[6] 53 N. Y. 211.

upon the question of the measure of damage, Mr. Justice Rapallo, in alluding to the latter case, said : "It seems to me, after as full an examination of the subject as circumstances have permitted, that the dissenting opinions (per Woodruff and Grover, JJ., alluded to above) embody the sounder reasons." Yet, when Baker vs. Drake came before the Court of Appeals again in September, 1876,[1] the court expressly reiterated and reaffirmed three propositions laid down in the case of Markham vs. Jaudon, the principal one being that "the relation of Broker and Client, under the ordinary contract for a speculative purchase of stock, is that of pledgee and pledgor." From this view Rapallo and Allen, JJ., dissented.

The doctrine of Markham vs. Jaudon was again distinctly reaffirmed in the last-mentioned respect in Gruman vs. Smith,[2] and in several later cases.[3] And this now seems to be the established law in New York,[4] and is sustained

---

[1] 66 N. Y. 518.

[2] 81 N. Y. 25, reversing 12 J. & S. 389.

[3] See cases cited in following note.

[4] Gruman vs. Smith, 81 N. Y. 25; Markham vs. Jaudon, 41 N. Y. 235; Morgan vs. Jaudon (Ct. of App.), 4 How. Pr. (N. Y.) 366; Stenton vs. Jerome, 54 N. Y. 480; Baker vs. Drake, 53 N. Y. 211; id. 66 N. Y. 518; Ritter vs. Cushman, 7 Robt. (N. Y.) 294; Read vs. Lambert, 10 Ab. Pr. (n. s.) 428; McNeil vs. Tenth National Bank, 55 Barb. (N. Y.) 59 (reversed on other points in 46 N. Y. 325); Clarke vs. Meigs, 22 How. Pr. (N. Y.) 340; Brass vs. Worth, 40 Barb. (N. Y.) 648; Andrews vs. Clerke, 3 Bosw. 585; Taylor vs. Ketchum, 5 Robt. (N. Y.) 507; Capron vs. Thompson, 86 N. Y. 418; Gillett vs. Whiting, 120 N. Y. 402; Douglas vs. Carpenter, 17 App. Div. 329; 45 N. Y. Supp. 219; Zimmerman vs. Heil, 33 N. Y. Supp. 391, aff'd 156 N. Y. 703. Contrary to this view in addition to the cases cited, supra, are Hanks vs. Drake, 49 Barb. (N. Y.) 186; Schepeler vs. Eisner, 3 Daly, 11; Sterling vs. Jaudon, 48 Barb. (N. Y.) 459, which have all been expressly overruled in the State of New York.

Whether the relation is that of pledgor and pledgee, or that of a special contract under which the Broker holds the stock, the Broker's obligation to keep the same or an

in the United States generally by the weight of authority.[1]

The theory that the relation which exists between a Stock-broker and his Client in an ordinary speculative transaction is not that of pledgor and pledgee, is mainly based upon the argument *ab inconvenienti.* It is said that as stocks are a fluctuating species of property, whose value is liable to be wiped out in a moment, the burden should not be put upon a Broker to give his Client notice of a decline or rise, as the case may be, and to make a demand for further margins. But this argument is just as forcible when applied to the undisputed case of a pure pledge, where it is conceded that there must be notice to the pledgor before a sale can be made, as where the owner of stocks pledges them to secure borrowed money. In this instance, although the stocks are liable to decline and leave the lender without

equal quantity of stock in his possession, is the same. Taussig vs. Hart, 58 N. Y. 425.

[1] Skiff vs. Stoddard, 63 Conn. 198, 222; 21 L. R. A. 112; Thompson vs. Toland, 48 Cal. 99; Cashman vs. Root, 89 Cal. 373; Kenfield vs. Latham, 2 Cal. Leg. Rec. 235; Brewster vs. Van Liew, 119 Ill. 551; Gilpin vs. Howell, 5 Pa. St. 41; Wynkoop vs. Seal, 64 Pa. St. 361; Esser vs. Linderman, 71 Pa. St. 76; Maryland Fire Ins. Co. vs. Dalrymple, 25 Md. 212; Baltimore Ins. Co. vs. Dalrymple, id. 269; Child vs. Hugg, 41 Cal. 519; Chew vs. Louchheim, 80 Fed. Rep. 500 ("The relation of the parties was that of bailor and bailee"). The same rule would seem to exist in England: Brookman vs. Rothschild,

3 Sim. 153, aff'd by House of Lords in 5 Bli. (n. s.) 165. The text writers also have adopted this view. See works cited in Skiff vs. Stoddard, supra, at p. 222.

In the carrying of executory contracts for the future delivery of grain, when neither the grain nor warehouse receipts are delivered, the Broker is not a pledgee, and the distinction between such a case and the case of a carrying of stock on a margin is this: The stocks are delivered into the actual possession of the Broker who claims it as the pledge, while the grain bought for his customer or any evidence of title thereto is not delivered to the commission merchant. Corbett vs. Underwood, 83 Ill. 324.

13

security, it is clear that, in the absence of express agreement, they could not be sold without legal notice.[1] So it has been held that where, instead of money, the Client deposits stock, etc., as margin, the relation of pledgor and pledgee exists.[2]

The Broker may always, in the outset, protect himself against the fluctuations of an advance or decline in the market by exacting sufficient margins to meet the contingencies of speculation and if he neglect to do this, he should not expect the law to aid him.

But finally, the Broker may always fully insure himself by making a special contract with his Client,[3] which will enable him to dispose of securities in any manner and at any time that may be agreed upon without notice, and such contracts the law will uphold and carry out.[4]

A different result has been reached in Massachusetts. There it is held that the transaction between a Broker and his Client on a marginal purchase of securities stands on the footing of a contract by the Broker to deliver the shares on the payment by the Client of so much money. This doctrine is probably peculiar to cases arising in Massachusetts [5] and was first promulgated in the case of Woods vs. Hays.[6]

---

[1] Schouler on Bailm. (3d ed.) § 229.

[2] Lawrence vs. Maxwell, 53 N. Y. 19. See also Vaupell vs. Woodward, 2 Sandf. Ch. 143; De Cordova vs. Barnum, 9 N. Y. Supp. 237, aff'd 130 N. Y. 615; Mattern vs. Sage, 16 Daly, 142.

[3] See in this connection remarks by Hunt, Ch. J., Markham vs. Jaudon, 41 N. Y. 244.

[4] Post, subd. (VI.) of this chapter, p. 306.

[5] In re Swift, 112 Fed. Rep. 318; Skiff vs. Stoddard, 63 Conn. 214; 21 L. R. A. 111. A later decision in Massachusetts, however, affirms that the English doctrine on the subject is the same as that of Massachusetts, citing Bentinck vs. Bank (1893), 2 Ch. Div. 120, 140; Chase vs. Boston, 180 Mass. 458.

[6] 81 Mass. 375.

While that case did not in its facts present a marginal purchase at all, and if it stood alone might not be decisive,[1] it has in subsequent decisions of the same court received the interpretation indicated above.[2] These subsequent cases[3] have been held by the United States courts to declare the rule in Massachusetts in cases arising in that State, and therefore to be governed by its law.[4]

And a recent Massachusetts decision holds that the legal title is in the Broker, and he is liable to pay municipal tax on the value of stocks, carried by him on margins.[5] The question of the Broker's relation to his customer also came up in the case of Rice vs. Winslow,[6] in which the latter sought to recover margins deposited with his Broker to secure the purchase of securities bought and afterwards sold by the defendant, on the ground that, under the cases cited, the relation was a contractual one, and, that being so, the Broker ultimately sells to the customer, and that sale brought the transaction within the first clause of § 2, of the gaming statute—L. 1890, ch. 437 ; but the court held that such a construction was a mistake. The

---

[1] In re Swift, 105 Fed. Rep. 496; Jones on Collateral Securities (2d ed.), § 498, note.

[2] See next note, 3.

[3] Covell vs. Loud, 135 Mass. 41; Jordan vs. Weston, 168 Mass. 401. In this latter case, while the court recognized the rule declared in Covell vs. Loud, there was apparently some doubt in its mind of the correctness of the rule. See In re Swift, 105 Fed. Rep. 496. But a later decision affirmed the doctrine. Chase vs. Boston, 180 Mass. 458.

[4] In re Swift, 105 Fed. Rep. 493; s. c. aff'd 112 Fed. Rep. 319. It was suggested in the last-named case that the difference in the doctrines of the New York and Massachusetts courts was one of name only and not of substance. There are, however, differences of substance which become apparent when the remedies respectively for conversion and for simple breach of contract are considered.

[5] Chase vs. Boston, 180 Mass. 458.

[6] Rice vs. Winslow, 180 Mass. 500.

relation of the Broker to the customer was that of an agent, and when the Broker actually bought and received the securities, there was no violation of the statute. The contract referred to in the statute was the contract to buy, not the contract to carry, the securities.

Upon the whole, while it must be conceded that there are apparently some incongruous features in the relation,[1] there seems to be neither difficulty nor hardship in holding that a Stock-broker is a pledgee; for, although it is true that he may advance all or the greater part of the money embraced in the speculation, if he acts honestly, faithfully, and prudently, the entire risk is upon the Client, and may be enforced against him as a personal liability, irrespective of the value of the securities, which are the subject of the transaction. To introduce a different rule would give opportunities for sharp practices and frauds, which the law should not invite; and if it be true, as Mr. Justice Woodruff[2] puts it, that "the transaction is an executory agreement for a pure speculation in the rise and fall of stock, which the Broker, on condition of perfect indemnity against loss, agrees to carry through in his own name and on his own means," accounting to the Client for the profits, it is very questionable whether all the transactions of Wall Street could not be set aside as mere wagers.[3] But, as we have seen, the cases most emphatically condemn this view, except those in Pennsylvania, in one of which —viz., North vs. Phillips[4]—the Supreme Court of Penn-

---

[1] Markham vs. Jaudon, supra; dissenting opinions. In re Swift, 105 Fed. Rep. 498; 112 Fed. Rep. 318. See also Skiff vs. Stoddard, 63 Conn. 217 et seq; 21 L. R. A. 112, 113.

[2] Markham vs. Jaudon, 41 N. Y. 256; ante, p. 189.

[3] See cases cited in chapter on "Stock-jobbing."

[4] 89 Pa. St. 250.

sylvania held that the peculiar facts there developed showed that the dealings between the Client and the Brokers were in "differences" and "margins," and the purchase and sale of the stock were a mere pretence; but it is plain, from reading the opinion of the learned judge in that case, that not only was no effect given to the verdict of the jury, which found that the purchases of stocks had been made *bona fide*, but the different elements which made up the transaction between the Brokers and their Client were completely overlooked—viz., that stock was actually purchased for the Client; that it was held subject to his orders; that he would have been entitled to the dividends thereon; that he could have insisted upon the instantaneous delivery of the stock to him upon tendering the purchase-money remaining due; that, if the Brokers had failed, the stock would not have passed to their assignees; and that, in fine, the Brokers were only interested in the transaction to the extent of their commissions. With great respect, therefore, we think that this case is not entitled to rank as an authority upon the question involved, especially as it appears to be directly opposed to the previous cases of Esser vs. Linderman[1] and Wynkoop vs. Seal,[2] where similar transactions were upheld.[3]

---

[1] 71 Pa. St. 81.

[2] 64 Pa. 361.

[3] See this question fully discussed in chapter on "Stock-jobbing," under head of "Wagers." The case cited must be considered as substantially overruled in Pennsylvania. Since the text was written the Supreme Court of Pennsylvania in speaking of the class of cases of which North vs. Phillips was one, has said: "In dealing with stock transactions falling within or in any way connected with wagering contracts, the law of Pennsylvania is of exceptional and . . . of illogical and untenable severity in its interference with the business affairs of parties sui juris and entirely competent to manage their own affairs." "A purchase of stock for speculation even when done merely on margin

Some cases have also been decided in New York involving the question of a Stock-broker's character as a trustee. In McBurney vs. Martin [1] the complaint set up a refusal by the defendant Stock-broker to pay money claimed to have been received by him in a *fiduciary* capacity, and the court in vacating an order for defendant's arrest, held that the 179th section of the Code did not include, in the class of persons liable to be arrested, any one except those who received moneys purely in a fiduciary capacity as simple agents, to apply it as directed, and therefore it excluded all those who had a personal interest in such money, or its use. In the case under consideration the defendant had sold stock "short" for plaintiff's assignor, who had deposited money with defendant as "margin," and defendant borrowed stock to deliver to the purchaser, and with plaintiff's assignor's assent, retained the purchase money to indemnify him against any appreciation in the borrowed stock, for which he was personally responsible. In violation of his agreement with plaintiff's assignor to *keep* the stock *borrowed*, and not to buy in and close the transaction until so instructed, defendant bought in stock and delivered same to the lender, whereas if he had waited nine days subsequently, he could have purchased the stock, which had de-

---

is not necessarily a gambling transaction. If one buys stock from A and borrows the money from B to pay for it, there is no element of gambling in the operation, though he pledge the stock with B as security for the money. So, if instead of borrowing the money from B, a third person, he borrows it from A, or in the language of Brokers procures A to 'carry' the stock for him, with or without margin, the transaction is not necessarily different in character." Peters vs. Grim, 149 Pa. St. 163; Hopkins vs. O'Kane, 169 Pa. St. 478; Wagner vs. Hildebrand, 187 Pa. St. 136; Estate of Taylor, 192 Pa. St. 304, 309, 313; Smyth vs. Glendinning, 194 Pa. St. 550.

[1] McBurney vs. Martin, 6 Rob. (N. Y.) 502.

clined, at a much lower figure. The court held, as already stated, that the defendant had an interest in the moneys retained by him, as he was personally liable to the lender of the stock, and therefore the moneys were not held by him as a trustee. But if the stocks to be sold belong to the plaintiff, and are actually delivered to the Broker, the latter is a trustee of the purchase price. So held in Waters vs. Marrin,[1] which distinguishes the last cited case. In a state of facts similar to those in McBurney vs. Martin, *supra*, the Supreme Court, however, subsequently held that a case of *agency* was disclosed showing that money received by defendant Stock-broker as " margin " was held by him as a trustee, and an order for his arrest was granted.[2] But the doctrine enunciated in McBurney vs. Martin, *supra*, seems to be more reasonable, and it was followed in Mann vs. Sands,[3] where it was held that if moneys are deposited as margins and settlements are had by balances struck, the relation thus formed becomes that of debtor and creditor, and a failure by either party to pay the balance due does not furnish the other with a ground of arrest. This, like every other loan or deposit, may, to a limited extent, imply a trust and confidence, but it does not necessarily create that fiduciary relation which subjects the party who makes default in paying such balance to arrest. As stated in the last cited case, the general rule is that if a Broker is given money to buy a particular stock, he becomes a trustee as to both stock and money. If he sells a particular stock belonging to a client, he becomes a fiduciary as to such stock

---

[1] Waters vs. Marrin, 12 Daly, 145.

[2] Clark vs. Pinckney, 50 Barb. 226.

[3] Mann vs. Sands, 2 City Ct. Rep. 25.

and its proceeds. For a breach of duty in either case he is liable to arrest. But as to money deposited on "margin" to cover the fluctuations of the market, and where settlements are had by the balances struck, he is merely a debtor to his client, and a failure to pay a balance due by him does not authorize his arrest.

It was held in Hoffmann vs. Livingston[1] that the agreement made by the parties disclosed a *fiduciary* relation. In that case the Broker asked his Client, a woman not accustomed to dealing in stocks, whether she wanted to trust' him as to the amount of stocks to be bought and sold for her, and she replied that she left it to his own judgment, and the court held that the relation established largely imposed confidence and good faith in the discharge of the duties assumed by the Stock-broker.

III. Definitions of Terms Used.

There are a number of technical or well-known terms used in Wall Street which should be defined preliminarily to a discussion of this chapter.

When a person is said to be "long" of stocks, it is meant that he has purchased stocks through his Brokers or otherwise, in the expectation of a rise or advance in the market; he is then called a "bull."

To be "short" of stocks is where one sells stocks which

---

[1] Hoffman vs. Livingston, 14 J. & S. (N. Y.) 552. See also the recent English cases of King vs. Hutton, 69 L. J. Q. B. D. 786; Re Woodd, Ex parte King, 82 L. T. R. 504 (and cases cited), which distinguish transactions in which a Broker becomes a trustee for his Client, and in which the relation merely of debtor and creditor exists between them. See also as to what constitutes a breach of trust, In re Jamison, 29 Atl. Rep. (Pa.) 1001; People vs. Thomas, 83 A. D. 226. And see post p. 779.

he does not own or possess, and borrows the number of shares which he has sold from some third person to deliver to his vendee, expecting to be able to buy the stocks at a lower figure, and then return them to the person from whom he has borrowed them; he is called a "bear."[1]

To "carry" stocks means where a Broker or other person advances the money, or a principal part thereof, with which to purchase stocks, and holds the same subject to the orders of his Client.[2]

"Margin" is the security against loss on the part of the Broker while he is carrying stock for his customer.[3]

"Net balance," as applied to the proceeds of the sale of stock, means, the balance of the proceeds after deducting the expenses incident to the sale.[4]

"Stop Order," an order given to a Broker to await a certain figure in the price of a particular bond or stock before he buys or sells it, and then to "stop" the transaction by then buying or selling as the case may be, as well as possible.[5]

---

[1] White vs. Smith, 54 N. Y. 522; Knowlton vs. Fitch, 52 N. Y. 289; Cameron vs. Durkheim, 55 N. Y. 425; Hess vs. Rau, 95 N. Y. 359; Sistare vs. Best, 88 N. Y. 533. The sale of stocks "short" was legalized by statute in New York State, L. 1858, ch. 134, repealed by and re-enacted in the Personal Property Law, § 22. It is illegal by statute in Massachusetts and Illinois, and was illegal in New York (1 Rev. Stat. 710, § 6) prior to the passage of L. 1858, ch. 134. See Birdseye's Stats., vol. 2, p. 2635, and cases noted under sec. 22, Per. Prop. Law. See Ch. on "Stock-jobbing."

[2] Price vs. Gover, 40 Md. 102; Saltus vs. Genin, 3 Bosw. (N. Y.) 250, 260.

[3] McNeil vs. Tenth National Bank, 55 Barb. 59, 64; Markham vs. Jaudon, 41 N. Y. 235; Hatch vs. Douglas, 48 Conn. 116, 128; McClain vs. Fleshman, 106 Fed. Rep. 880, 882.

[4] Evans vs. Waln, 71 Pa. St. 69, 74.

[5] Porter vs. Wormser, 91 N. Y. 413; Wronkow vs. Clews, 52 N. Y. Super. Ct. 176. As used in a letter

" Dividend on," means that a dividend goes to the buyer of stock.

"Ex-dividend," means that the seller retains a dividend.

In connection with these terms, Art. XXXII., § 1 of the constitution of the New York Stock Exchange may be quoted. "On the day of closing of the transfer books of a corporation for a dividend upon its shares, all transactions therein for 'cash' shall be 'dividend on' up to the time officially designated for the closing of transfers ; all transactions on that day other than for 'cash' shall be 'ex-dividend.' Should the closing of transfers occur upon a holiday or half holiday, observed by the Exchange, transactions on the preceding business day, other than for 'cash,' shall be 'ex-dividend.'" [1]

A "corner" in stocks is where the owners or holders (i. e. bulls) refuse to loan stocks to the "bears," with which to carry out their short contracts, in which event the "bears," being unable to deliver, are compelled to go into the market or Exchange and buy the stocks at any price at which they can obtain them.[2]

A "pool" means that individuals have combined together

by a Broker to his principal then abroad, in which the Broker called for more margin, it means that the Broker would "stop" entirely in everything, i. e., keep the transaction in statu quo, till he heard from his principal. Id.

[1] See Chap. IV., "Usages of Stockbrokers."

The following request by a customer to his Brokers directing a sale of government bonds carried by them for him "or at your discretion 'stop order' $500,000 United States four per cent. bond at 100¼ ex. July coupons and accrued interest; $500,000 do. at 100¼ do., do.," means that the Brokers were required to sell when the market price should decline to 100¼ or 100¼ without the July coupons, or if sold after July 1st when the market price should equal 100¼ and 100¼, plus the accrued interest from that date. Porter vs. Wormser, 94 N. Y. 431, 443.

[2] Cameron vs. Durkheim, 55 N. Y. 425, 438. See also chapter on "Stock-jobbing."

in buying and selling stocks, and dividing the profits or loss in agreed proportions.[1]

" Wash sales " are not real sales, but are made by persons interested in each other, for the purpose of giving a fictitious value to the stock.[2]

A " shave " is a consideration for carrying stock for a certain time.[3]

A " call " is a contract by which the party signing or making the same agrees, in consideration of a certain sum, to deliver, at the option of a party therein named, or his order or bearer, securities therein mentioned, at a certain day for a certain price.[4]

A " put " is also an option contract, except the party holding the same has the option of delivering securities to the maker.[5]

---

[1] Kilbourn vs. Thompson, 103 U. S. 195; Myers vs. Paine, 13 App. Div. 332; aff'd 57 N. E. Rep. 1118; Leonard vs. Poole, 114 N. Y. 371. One action against two "pool" partnerships cannot be maintained when the members of each are not the same. Earle vs. Scott, 50 How. Pr. 506.

[2] Bryan vs. Baldwin, 52 N. Y. 232, 236; aff'g 7 Lans. (N. Y.) 174; Secor vs. Goslin, N. Y. L. J. March 26, 1901, p. 2310. Rosenberg vs. Meyer, N. Y. L. J. June 10, 1902, p. 922. The price at a wash sale is not evidence of the real market value of the stock with a view to assessing damages. Bryan vs. Baldwin, supra.

[3] North vs. Phillips, 89 Pa. St. 250-255.

[4] The following is a copy of the call commonly used:

"New York, , 1881.

"For value received, the bearer may call on me for shares of the common stock of the Railroad Company at per cent., any time in days from date. The bearer is entitled to all dividends or extra dividends declared during the time.

"Expires 1881, at 1¾ P. M.

"Signed, ."

By the usage of Brokers, it is negotiable, and it has been declared valid by certain courts. See title "Stock-jobbing," under head of "Wagers."

[5] Hopper vs. Sage, 112 N. Y. 530; Bigelow vs. Benedict, 70 N. Y. 202; Ex parte Young, 6 Riss. 53; Gilbert vs. Gaugar, 8 id. 218; Pixley vs. Boynton, 79 Ill. 353; Pearce vs. Foote, 113 Ill. 231; Anderson's Law

A "straddle," or "spread-eagle," combines the advantages of a "put" and a "call," being a contract by which the holder has the right or option either to deliver or have delivered to him certain stocks at prices designated in the writing.[1]

A purchase or sale of stock "for the account" means a purchase or sale of stock to be received or delivered at a future time. Transactions "for the account," have been practised on the London and New York and other Stock Exchanges for many years.[2]

Dict. title "Put." It is as follows:

    "NEW YORK,   1881.
"For value received, the bearer may deliver me   shares of the common stock of the   Railroad Company at   per cent., at any time in   days from date. The undersigned is entitled to all dividends or extra dividends declared during the time.
  "Expires   at 1¾ P. M.
    "Signed,   ."

[1] Harris vs. Tumbridge, 8 Ab. New Cas. 291; aff'd 83 N. Y. 92, where the court, in speaking of a "straddle," said: "The word, if not elegant, is at least expressive. It means the double privilege of a 'put' and a 'call,' and secures to the holder the right to demand of the seller at a certain price, within a certain time, a certain number of shares of specified stock, or to require him to take at the same price, within the same time, the same shares of stock." See also Van Norden vs. Keene, 55 N. Y. Super.

Ct. 67; Story vs. Salomon, 71 N. Y. 420.

The following is the form of a "straddle:"

    "NEW YORK,   1881.
"For value received, the bearer may call on the undersigned for   shares of the common stock of the   Railroad Company at   per cent., any time in   days from date. Or the bearer may, at his option, deliver the same to the undersigned at   per cent., any time within the period named. All dividends or extra dividends declared during the time are to go with the stock in either case; and this instrument is to be surrendered upon the stock being either called or delivered.
  "Expires   at 1¾ P. M.
    "Signed,   ."

[2] Clews vs. Jamieson, 182 U. S. 461, 487. In that case transactions of this kind as practised on the Chicago Stock Exchange are explained in full detail. See also Chap. X.

IV. Purchase on "Long" Account.

We have already seen what the relation is where a Stock-broker contracts to buy stocks for a Client on a margin[1] for speculation, and advances all or the greater portion of the purchase-money, and that, after such purchase, the Broker immediately acquires a lien upon the stocks, for the balance of the purchase-money in excess of the margins received, which he has advanced to pay for the stocks, and becomes, in relation thereto, a pledgee, with the full powers and responsibilities of that position.[2]

It is proposed to examine, under this subdivision, with some detail, the duties of the Broker in respect to the pur-

---

p. 987, et seq. as to such trading on the London Stock Exchange.

An interesting question was raised in Clews vs. Jamieson, supra, as to the privity of contract between undisclosed principals in sales "for the account." In that case Brokers on the Chicago Stock Exchange had sold, on the 3d of August, 1150 shares of stock belonging to different owners for delivery on the 31st of August. Included in the shares sold were a large number (700) belonging to plaintiffs. Settlements were had as to all the shares except those belonging to plaintiffs. It was held that the fact that there were, in the sale of August 3, other shares than the 700, and that, in regard to those others, some had been sold originally by complainant's Brokers to other and different Brokers than defendant's, would not prevent the contract as to the 700 shares from being enforced against the defendants, although, but for such settlement, there might have been some embarrassment in maintaining a suit against the latter for a portion only of the total shares sold them, while the other portion was represented by different clients of complainants' Brokers.

In England, however, a Broker may make one contract with a jobber as to shares in the same undertaking owned by several clients, and a usage to that effect is valid. Scott vs. Godfrey, 2 L. R. K. B. (1901) 726. For other English cases on this subject, see Chap. X.

[1] See cases cited in this chapter, § II.

[2] Id.; Brookman vs. Rothschild, 3 Sim. 153, aff'd in House of Lords, 5 Bli. (n. s.) 165; Gruman vs. Smith, 12 J. & Sp. (N. Y.) 389; aff'd 81 N. Y. 25.

chased stock, from the inception to the termination of the business.[1]

(a.) The Order to Purchase, Price, and Number of Shares to be Bought.

If the order to purchase is ambiguous or fairly susceptible of two constructions and the Broker honestly and fairly acts on that not intended by the Client, the latter must bear any loss.[2]

If the technical terms of the stock market are used in the order of the Client, he cannot afterwards claim that he intended them to have other than their customary meaning.[3]

A Broker is not obliged to accept a proposition that he act as such, nor is he necessarily bound to communicate his declination to the proposer,[4] but the rule of law is that having entered into the relation, he is, when directed to buy or sell, bound to follow the directions of his principal, or give prompt notice that he declines to do so.[5]

If the order is to purchase he must actually execute it.[6] If the Broker fails to execute the order in the expectation of making a profit for himself through the fluctuation of the

---

[1] See also Mr. Eliot Norton's essay on "A simple purchase and sale through a Broker" (8 Harvard L. Rev. p. 435), afterward amplified and published under the title "On Buying and Selling Securities through a member of a Stock Exchange," N. Y. 1896.

[2] Ireland vs. Livingston, L. R. 5 H. L. 395; 41 L. J. Q. B. 201; Coquard vs. Weinstein, 16 Mont. 312, and cases cited. See also Tallentine vs. Ayre, 1 T. L. R. 143; Loring vs. Davis, 32 Ch. D. 625.

[3] Hatch vs. Douglas, 48 Conn. 116.

[4] Mechem on Agency, § 108.

[5] Galigher vs. Jones, 129 U. S. 193. The declination to execute the order should be by means as speedy as the circumstances require. Ibid.

[6] Skiff vs. Stoddard, 63 Conn. 198; 21 L. R. A. 110, overruling Ingraham vs. Taylor, 58 Conn. 503; Prout vs. Chisolm, 21 App. Div. 54; Zimmerman vs. Heil, 86 Hun, 114; aff'd 156 N. Y. 703; Allen vs. Mc-

market, he is guilty of fraud in morals as well as law.[1] Making a contract with a third party whereby he can get the stock by paying for it, but which he does not obtain, is not enough.[2]

If the order is to buy at a fixed price he must buy at the best price obtainable not exceeding that price. He is not entitled to buy at a lower price and re-sell to the Client at the price named, although he does not charge commission.[3] If the Broker disobeys his Client's orders, and the result is a loss which the Broker promises to pay, the fact that the Broker, with the consent of the Client, continues to speculate, and the Client's entire deposit is thereby lost, does not relieve the Broker from liability as to the first loss which he promised to repay.[4]

Agents constituted for a particular purpose, and under a limited and circumscribed power, cannot bind their principal beyond their authority.[5] Accordingly an order to buy stocks " regular " is not fulfilled by a purchase by the

---

Gonibe, 124 N. Y. 342. Proof that the Broker employed other Brokers to make the purchase and that the latter reported that the purchase had been made, is not sufficient. Sweeney vs. Rogers, 10 Daly, 469.

[1] Prout vs. Chisolm, supra.

[2] Smith vs. New York Stock and Produce Exchange, 25 N. Y. Supp. 261.

[3] Thompson vs. Meade, 7 T. L. R. 698.

[4] Hollingshead vs. Green, 1 Cin. Super. Ct. R. 305. If a Broker is intrusted with money to buy stocks for plaintiff, he does not execute his duty as agent by purchasing the stocks in his own name, and the customer may either sue for a non-delivery of the stock, or for a return of his deposit with interest. Larrabee vs. Badger, 45 Ill. 440.

[5] Genin vs. Isaacson, 6 N. Y. Leg. Obs. 213; Bush vs. Cole, 28 N. Y. 261, and cases cited; Delafield vs. State of Ill., 26 Wend. 221; Galigher vs. Jones, 129 U. S. 193; Story on Ag. 9th ed. § 126; Wharton on Ag. § 712; Maxted vs. Paine, L. R. 4 Ex. 81; Maxted vs. Morris, 21 L. T. (n. s.) 535. Nor is this rule affected by the fact that the contract made is more advantageous for the principal. Nesbitt vs. Helser, 49 Mo. 383; Smith vs. Bouvier, 70 Pa. St. 325; Borham vs. Godfrey, 1 Knapp, 381.

Broker at "seller's option, thirty days." [1]   An order to purchase at 57¼ is not fulfilled by a purchase at 57⅞ or 58.[2]

So an order to a Broker to buy 500 shares of stock, buyer's option in 60 days, at $2 per share, is not fulfilled by the Broker's buying the same at $1.62½ per share, at 30 days, buyer's option, and then charging $1.75, 60 days ; and the Client is not liable, therefore, even though he give a note, without knowledge of the facts.[3]   If the Broker is merely directed to buy, without any price being designated, he can make the purchase at the market price.[4]

In respect to the amount or number of shares which the Broker may buy, he is, of course, restricted to the order. But if he cannot purchase the whole amount stated, he may purchase a less number of shares; and where a Broker receives an order to purchase securities, his undertaking is not to deliver the whole absolutely, but to buy as many of them as could be bought in the regular way, below or at the limit,[5] unless there is something in the circumstances to show the intention of the Client to do otherwise.   If an unforeseen emergency arise, such as for instance an extraordinary advance in the price of the securities ordered to be purchased before the completion of a direction to invest a certain sum therein, the Broker is justified if acting in good

---

[1] Taussig vs. Hart, 58 N. Y. 425–428.

[2] Genin vs. Isaacson, supra.

[3] Day vs. Holmes, 103 Mass. 306; Pickering vs. Demeritt, 100 Mass. 416.   An order to buy "five December barley" is not fulfilled by buying "five January barley," although the latter purchase might have been as advantageous. McDermid vs. Cotton, 2 Ill. App. 297.

[4] As to how far the usages of the business affect the orders of the Broker, see chapter on "Usages." It has been held, however, that no usage will authorize a factor or agent to depart from positive instructions (Barksdale vs. Brown, 1 N. & McC. [S. C.] 517).

[5] Marye vs. Strouse, 5 Fed. Rep. 483; Leddy vs. Flanagan, 3 Phila. 355; Marland vs. Stanwood, 101 Mass. 470.

faith in writing and waiting for further instructions of the Client.[1] An order to purchase stock to a certain amount must be carried out and an error in regard to the par value must be borne by the Broker.[2]

An ordinary Broker's contract for the buying of stock, every share of which has a distinct and independent value, cannot be regarded as an entire contract.[3]

Accordingly, it was held[4] that where a Client ordered Mining Brokers to buy 500 shares of the Franklin Mining stock at the San Francisco Stock Board, and the Brokers purchased 125 shares at the latter place, and delivered 375 shares to their firm of the said stock belonging to one of the members of the firm, which was placed in the Client's account as a fulfilment of his order, without his knowledge, the Client was to be held for the 125 shares regularly purchased, the other shares being stricken from the account upon the familiar ground that an agent employed to buy cannot become the seller.[5]

So, in regard to the place where the securities are to be purchased, the Broker is justified in acting according to the course of trade and the regular usages of business.

Therefore, where a Client residing in Baltimore directs his Broker, residing in the same place, to purchase stock—the order being in general terms, and not directing the purchase to be made at any particular place or mode, and not containing any restrictions as to price—the Broker, in the full exercise of his discretion, and acting in good faith, may make the pur-

---

[1] Bernard vs. Maury, 20 Gratt. 434; Story on Agency, § 193.

[2] Linden vs. Silverston, Q. B. D. June 22, 1899.

[3] Marye vs. Strouse, 5 Fed. Rep. 483.

[4] Id.

[5] Nor is there any absolute engagement on the part of Broker to carry out the order at all events (Fletcher vs. Marshall, 15 M. & W. 755).

14

chase in New York through correspondents' Brokers or sub-agents residing and doing business in that city.[1] The transaction is governed by the law of the place where it is to be performed.[2]

So, as to the length of time within which the Broker should execute his orders, the question depends upon the circumstances of each case. The general rule is, in the absence of express restrictions or limitations, that the authority of an agent continues until countermanded[3] and that the principal may terminate the relation at any time.

But the previous dealings between the parties, the usages of Brokers, the fluctuating and uncertain value of the securities dealt in on the Exchange, may all be appealed to to vary the general rules of law in this respect and establish a different principle.

In England it has been held that where an order has been given to a Broker to deal in a current security, a jury would be authorized to consider the usage of the Stock Exchange to deal for the coming settling day, and to find that when that day arrived a reasonable time had elapsed for carrying out the order, and that the authority of the Broker was at an end.[4]

Until the Broker has acted upon his authority to buy

---

[1] Rosenstock vs. Tormey, 32 Md. 69; Billingslea vs. Smith, 77 Md. 504; Taylor vs. Bailey, 48 N. E. Rep. (Ill.) 200. Evidence as to entries contained in the books of the correspondent Broker is not admissible against the client to show that the stocks had been purchased. Boyd vs. Yerkes, 25 Ill. App. 527.

[2] In re Swift, 112 Fed. Rep. (Mass.) 315.

[3] Burkitt vs. Taylor, 13 W. D. 75; aff'g s. c. sub nom. Bickett vs. Taylor, 55 How. Pr. 128.

[4] Maxted vs. Paine, L. R. 4 Ex. 81; see also Maxted vs. Morris, 21 L. T. (n. s.) 535; Lawford vs. Harris, 12 T. L. R. 275.

shares, it may be revoked;[1] and if any money has been given him, in order to enable him to pay for them, it may be demanded back.[2] But this cannot be done after he has entered into a contract for purchase and become personally responsible for the due performance of that contract.[3]

And if after a Stock-broker has received instructions to sell certain shares, and before rescission of the instructions, he receives notice from a third party claiming the shares, the Brokers, having no interest, are entitled to interplead.[4]

In order to charge a defendant in an action for money paid for the purchase of stock on his account, and by his order, the plaintiff must clearly show the authority under which he acted, and prove that he was instructed by the defendant to make the purchase. And where the proof is so defective that the jury will be compelled to infer such authority from conversations and admissions of the defendant, which are neither explicit nor satisfactory, the plaintiff will be non-suited.[5] While ordinarily it is the principal's judgment, and not the Broker's, which is to control in the purchase and sale of stocks,[6] in some cases Clients, by special agreement, give to the Brokers general authority to buy and sell for the Client at the Broker's own discretion as to stock and price.[7] If a Broker guarantees

[1] Sibhall vs. Bethlehem Iron Co., 83 N. Y. 378.

[2] Fletcher vs. Marshall, supra; Rees vs. Pellow, 97 Fed. Rep. 167.

[3] McEwen vs. Woods, 11 Q. B. 13; Sutton vs. Tatham, 10 Ad. & E. 27; Read vs. Anderson, 13 Q. B. D. 779.

[4] Robinson vs. Jenkins, 24 Q. B. D. 275.

[5] Ward vs. Van Duzer, 2 Hill (N. Y.), 162. When the client is asserting that the Broker has been ordered by him to make certain transactions, then the burden of proof to show the receipt by the Brokers of such orders is upon him. Proof of mailing the order, without proof that such mailing was timely, is not enough. Birnbaum vs. May, 58 A. D. 76.

[6] Galigher vs. Jones, 129 U. S. 193.

[7] Proof that the customer told the Broker that he would like to make a

the return of money deposited with him to buy and sell stocks with interest, and any profits he may make, the mere fact that the profits were carried to a new account and left on the Broker's hands did not show that he also guaranteed the security thereof; and if the Broker, acting in his discretion and in good faith, subsequently loses these profits in further speculation, the Client must bear the loss.[1] But if the transactions are so conducted by the Broker that through his want of that degree of diligence and skill which the Client might expect at his hands, no benefit results, this, it is said, constitutes a defence, to a suit for commissions.[2]

A Client may ratify an unauthorized purchase of his Broker, and then the position is the same as if the Client had given an original authority. The ratification relates back to the time of the act which is ratified.[3]

Before one is called upon to ratify any unauthorized transaction, he is entitled to have all the facts before him and to have a reasonable time in which to act in regard to the transaction.[4]

The question is one for the jury, and the burden of proof

dollar if he could, and that if the Broker could help him he would like to have him do so, is not, however, sufficient authority for the Broker to enter into "discretionary" speculative transactions for the client. Hopkins vs. Clark, 7 App. Div. 207; aff'd 158 N. Y. 299.

[1] In re Vermilye, 43 N. J. Eq. 146; 10 A. 605, and evidence as to the intrinsic value of the securities dealt in, is admissible upon the question of good faith and wise exercise of such discretion. Hopkins vs. Clark, 158 N. Y. 299.

[2] Hoffman vs. Livingston, 14 J. & S. 552.

[3] Campbell vs. Brass, (1891) 7 T. L. R. 612; Clews vs. Jamieson, 182 U. S. 461. As to when the burden of proof to show ratification rests upon the Stock-broker, see Hopkins vs. Clark, 7 App. Div. 461; McGeoch vs. Hooker, 11 Ill. App. 640.

[4] See cases cited in note 3, supra; Harris vs. Tumbridge, 83 N. Y. 92,

rests upon the Brokers.[1] Ratification may be proved by the acceptance of an account showing the unauthorized transaction, and a promise to pay the balance due upon that account.[2] But mere retention of such an account is not enough as matter of law to operate as a ratification.[3]

It is the custom in the Stock Exchange when orders have been executed, for the Broker to give prompt notice to his Client of that fact, stating the number of shares purchased or sold, the price received or paid and the name of the opposite Broker,[4] and obedience to that custom in transactions in the Exchange is the Broker's legal duty.[5]

99. A client is not chargeable with a price which the stock directed to be purchased may have had prior to the time that the order was given, and greater than it then had, unless she consents to adopt such greater price. Day vs. Jameson, 33 N. Y. St. Rep. 375, 377.

[1] See cases cited in note 3, supra. See also Day vs. Jameson, 33 N. Y. St. R. 375, 377; Harris vs. Tumbridge, 83 N. Y. 92, 99. See also Genin vs. Isaacson, 6 N. Y. Leg. Ob. 213; and cases cited in notes 4 and 2, supra.

[2] Gillett vs. Whiting, 55 N. Y. Super. Ct. 187, reversed on other grounds, 120 N. Y. 402.

[3] Burhorn vs. Lockwood, 71 App. Div. 301, aff'd 177 N. Y. 17, 32; Hansen vs. Boyd, 161 U. S. 397. As to how far the letters between the parties and diary entries are admissible in evidence and the weight that should be attached to them, see Whitaker vs. White, 69 Hun, 258; Hopkins vs. Clark, 7 App. Div. 207.

[4] See Hoffman vs. Livingston, 14 J. & S. 552; Skiff vs. Stoddard, 63 Conn. 204; 21 L. R. A. 102; Finney vs. Gallaudet, 2 N. Y. Supp. 707; Tuell vs. Paine, 80 N. Y. S. 956.

[5] Hoffman vs. Livingston, supra; Rosenstock vs. Tormey, 32 Md. 178; Prout vs. Chisolm, 89 Hun, 108; s. c. 21 App. Div. 54; Bate vs. McDowell, 17 J. & S. 106.

In Delenne vs. Haight & Freese Co., N. Y. L. J. May 23, 1903, it was held that it was the duty of defendant Broker to give to its principal, the plaintiff, the names of the Brokers from whom it bought and sold stock for plaintiff and the prices at which such stock was bought or sold and it will be compelled to deposit its books and papers in court, or have them examined by a referee at its expense, for the purpose of eliciting such information.

Bought and sold notes sent by a Broker to the buyer and seller, the execution of which is not denied, constitute the contract between the parties. Murray vs. Doud, 63 Ill. App. 217. But a "sold" note giv-

His refusal to furnish information as to the time or times of sale, and the amount realized by the sale or sales, raises a presumption authorizing the strictest construction against him as to amount, value and price.[1] And it was decided in Hoffman vs. Livingston,[2] that a failure of the Broker to give this notice was such negligence as to preclude him from recovering his commissions. Where such notices are rendered by the Broker to the Client, who relies thereon, the Broker is afterwards estopped from denying the truth thereof.[3] It is for the jury to decide whether a Broker should keep accounts showing the names of persons with whom he deals for his principal.[4] Where the transaction reported was in fact never made, the Brokers are guilty of fraud.[5]

Speculations in stocks are frequently made by agents of the Client with the Broker, and the authority of the agent is denied.[6] So cases may arise where a speculative transaction is made between a Client and a clerk or agent of the Stock-broker, and the authority of the clerk is disputed or his acts disowned by the Stock-broker.[7] Sometimes, too,

---

ing the name of the opposite principal, on the assumption that the latter's Brokers had authority from him, does not constitute a contract between principal and Broker, so as to render the latter liable for negligence, when the opposite principal repudiates the contract. Pim vs. Wait, 32 Fed. Rep. 744. See Simmons vs. More, 100 N. Y. 140.

[1] Bate vs. McDowell, supra.

[2] 46 N. Y. Super. Ct. 552.

[3] Matter of Pierson, 19 App. Div. 478.

[4] Prout vs. Chisolm, 21 A. D. 54

[5] Id.

[6] See Finney vs. Gallaudet, 2 N. Y. S. 707. As to when one partner becomes the agent of another in the purchase of stocks, see Rand vs. Whipple, 71 A. D. 62. See also Martin vs. Peters, 4 Rob. (N. Y.) 434.

[7] The ordinary presumption is that the party in whose name an account stands is the party in interest from whom instructions are to be taken. Timpson vs. Allen, 149 N. Y. 513, 519. Where a transaction is made prior to the partnership by an individual member of a firm of Brokers for his own client,

dealings are had between Broker and Client, through an intermediary, and each side asserts that such intermediary is the agent of the other.[1]

In one case in Nevada it appeared that R. & P. were Stock-brokers, and R. was also agent and P. cashier of the express and banking business of W. F. & Co. One W. called at the banking department and asked R. how much interest W. F. & Co. would charge to buy for him certain shares of stock. The interest was agreed on, and R. and P. ordered the stock through their Brokers in San Francisco, and sent W. notice of the purchase in their own firm name of R. & P. The next day W., at R.'s request, executed his note to W. F. & Co. for the amount of money it took to purchase the stock. The stock was never delivered to W., but the latter was credited upon the books of R. & P. with the stock and the amount of purchase-money stated in the note. R. & P. received credit with W. F. & Co. for the same amount as so much money deposited. R. & P. subsequently failed. W. F. & Co. brought suit against W. on the note, and the question was whether the transaction was only a loan, as claimed by W. F. & Co., or a contract to procure the stock as claimed by W. The jury having found a verdict for W. on the ground that R. & P. acted as agents of W. F. & Co., the court upon

---

and the firm renders an account of such transaction in its own name charging themselves with the whole transaction, they will thereby be held to have adopted the act of the individual partner, as to any benefit to be derived therefrom, and as to responsibility for loss. Bate vs. McDowell, 17 J. & S. 106. See also Wells vs. Welter, 15 Nev. 276. As to when a Broker is liable for the acts of a "correspondent," see Smith vs. New York Stock &c. Ex., 25 N. Y. S. 261.

[1] Timpson vs. Allen, 149 N. Y. 513; Wolff vs. Lockwood, 75 N. Y. Supp. 605; Boyd vs. Yerkes, 25 Ill. App. 527.

appeal refused to disturb it,[1] on the ground that R. & P. acted as agents of W. F. & Co. In all such cases, where the authority of the agent is denied, the question is one of fact, and the proof must be the same as would exist in an ordinary case between a third person seeking to charge the principal for the acts of his agent, and the burden would be upon the party asserting the fact. Authority in an agent may be implied from circumstances, and a customer has a right to rely upon the apparent authority of the Broker's agent.[2]

The agency being proven, the general rule applies in all such cases that a party who employs an agent to transact business with third parties cannot be relieved from liability for the misdoings of such agent in the absence of neglect or want of ordinary care on the part of the party injured. When one of two innocent parties must suffer from the act of a third person, he shall sustain the loss who enabled the third party to do the injury.[3] And the general rule that, if an agent has limited authority to contract, a party without notice of such limitation is not bound to inquire as to the extent of such authority, is also applicable,[4] but if the party has notice he is put upon inquiry.[5]

When therefore a principal imposes a limit upon his Broker, the former is liable if the Broker exceeds the limit.[6] But if the Broker makes an unauthorized contract (i. e. when

---

[1] Wells vs. Welter, 15 Nev. 276.

[2] Kratt vs. Hopkins, 78 N. Y. S. 1012; Briggs vs. Kennett, 8 Misc. 264; aff'd (without opinion) 149 N. Y. 577.

[3] Andrews vs. Clark, 72 Md. 396; Caswell vs. Putnam, 120 N. Y. 153, 158, and cases cited in note 1, supra.

[4] Rimmer vs. Webster, (1902) 2 Ch. 163; Robinson vs. Brewing Co., (1896) 2 Ch. 841; Bentinck vs. Bank, (1893) 2 Ch. 120.

[5] Nester vs. Craig, 69 Hun, 543.

[6] Crabb vs. Miller, 24 L. T. 219; Coles vs. Bristowe, L. R. 4 Ch. 14.

instructed to buy the shares of one company, by mistake, purchases those of another), he is personally liable, on the ground of misrepresentation of authority, for the fulfilment of the contract, and if the shares are unsalable, the damages will be the full price named in the contract.[1] If no limit is placed upon the Broker, he has implied authority to contract subject to the rules of the Exchange and reasonable customs (see chapter on Usages), but a vendor's Broker has not implied authority to receive the purchase money unless it may be presumed from the vendor's acts, i. e. when he gives the Broker share certificates or a transfer.[2]

A Broker or Client dealing with an agent within the limit of his authority has the right to assume if not otherwise informed that the authority of the agent is unlimited, and when the dealing continues after the authority is revoked the principal is bound unless notice of the revocation is brought home to the opposite party.[3] But where the agent or office manager of the Broker is given general authority by the Client to make purchases and sales for his account, notice by the Client to such agent to cease, is binding upon the Broker, his principal, within the rule that notice to an agent touching the subject-matter of his agency is notice to the principal, this rule applying even where the agent represents both parties at one time.[4]

---

[1] Ex parte Panmure, 24 Ch. Div. 367.

[2] McDevitt vs. Connolly, 15 L. R. (Ir.) 500.

[3] Andrews vs. Clark, supra. When changes are made in a brokerage business whereby a former clerk becomes the proprietor, it is a mixed question of law and fact to be determined by the court, whether the changes are enough to put a customer on inquiry as to with whom he is dealing. Lines vs. Shepard, 16 Daly, 471.

[4] Boyd vs. Yerkes, 25 Ill. App. 527.

(b.) Duty and Liability of Broker in Purchasing; Right to Indemnity.

Brokers or factors are required to act with reasonable diligence and prudence in their employment,[1] and to exercise their judgment and discretion to the best advantage of the principal. This means that those who deal with them, contract for, and have a right to expect, a degree of care commensurate with the importance and risks of the business and a skill and capacity adequate to its performance. That care and skill is different in kind from the ordinary diligence and capacity of the ordinary citizen, and the Broker is employed for that reason.[2]

These requirements apply in all cases, where an order to purchase is given to a Broker, whether the transaction is to be executed at a fixed price, or at the market price, or at his discretion, and whether the Broker is acting for compensation or gratuitously.[3]

A commission merchant or Broker must also in his dealings with his Client act in entire good faith,[4] and he has no right to conceal any portion of his transactions and dealings in relation to the property alleged to have been bought or

[1] Prout vs. Chisolm, 21 App. Div. 54; Bate vs. McDowell, 17 J. & S. 106, 111; Speyer vs. Colgate, 4 Hun, 622; Leveson Gower vs. May, 7 T. L. R. 696; Boyle vs. Henning, 121 Fed. Rep. 376; In re Vermilye, 43 N. J. Eq. 146; 10 A. 605. If the Broker acting in good faith, and within the line of his duty, incurs damages, his principal is liable. Maitland vs. Martin, 86 Pa. St. 120, 124.

[2] Isham vs. Post, 141 N. Y. 100, 105; Boyd vs. Barrett, 16 Phila. 653.

[3] Isham vs. Post, supra. If a Broker has a general discretion as to purchase of securities, and gives evidence to prove a proper exercise of such discretion, his client may introduce evidence contra. Hopkins vs. Clarke, 158 N. Y. 299.

[4] When a sale of stock is actually made by Brokers, and there is no evidence to show that they acted in bad faith, it is error to submit the

sold.[1] His duty to keep and render just and true accounts is "plain to the last degree."[2]

A Broker who is the agent of his Client is, and ought to be, required to show fully and specifically each item of the account which he charges against his Client. Furnishing a gross sum is insufficient. Each of the parties to an account is entitled to know and to have presented to him, when a demand is made for a loss, supposed or real, the items which make up such loss, and to be given an opportunity not only to inspect and ascertain the correctness of the same, but to controvert such items whenever it becomes necessary.[3] A presumption against the Broker's good faith and honesty can be drawn from his omission of these duties.[4]

When the Broker withholds the fullest information in this respect, the right to examination before trial, in an action brought to recover alleged profits or to adjust the unsettled accounts, should be fully accorded.[5] His refusal to give such information without compulsion raises a presumption authorizing the strictest construction of the evidence against him.[6]

question of their good faith to the jury. Day vs. Jameson, 33 N. Y. St. Rep. 375, 379.

[1] Miller vs. Kent, 59 How. Pr. 322, 325; Marvin vs. Buchanan, 62 Barb. 468; Talbot vs. Doran & Wright Co., 9 N. Y. Supp. 478; Drake vs. Weinman, 33 N. Y. Supp. 177; Drake vs. Thompson & Deer Co., 33 N. Y. Supp. 180, and cases cited in succeeding notes.

[2] Prout vs. Chisolm, 89 Hun, 108; s. c. 21 App. Div. 54; Bate vs. McDowell, 17 J. & S. 106; Miller vs. Kent, 10 Weekly Digest, 362; s. c. 23 Hun, 657; Duff vs. Hutchinson, 19

N. Y. Weekly Dig. 20, but when an accounting is demanded, a discovery of the Broker's books will not be granted to enable the client to prepare his complaint. Id. N. Y. Daily Reg. Nov. 27, 1882; 5 Monthly L. Bull. 4.

[3] Miller vs. Kent, supra; Harding vs. Field, 46 N. Y. St. Rep. 628, and cases supra.

[4] Prout vs. Chisolm, 21 App. Div. 54.

[5] See post, p. 770, where the remedy is more fully discussed.

[6] Bate vs. McDowell, supra; Gray vs. Haig, 20 Beav. 219.

A Broker has no right to adopt methods of business that are so intricate or tortuous that they are incapable of being explained to the full comprehension of an ordinarily intelligent jury.[1]

The known usages of trade and business enter into such employment; and if he conducts his business with diligence, care and good faith according to such usages, he will be exonerated from all responsibility.[2]

But a Stock-broker cannot bind his Client by anything done under a rule of the Exchange which was not made until after the instructions were given to him.[3]

---

[1] Oldershaw vs. Knowles, 101 Ill. 117.

[2] Bibb vs. Allen, 149 U. S. 481; Clews vs. Jamieson, 182 U. S. 461; Hausen vs. Boyd, 161 U. S. 403; Phillips vs. Moir, 69 Ill. 155; Deshler vs. Beers, 32 Ill. 368; Paton vs. Newman, 51 La. Ann. 1428; 28 So. Rep. 576; Skiff vs. Stoddard, 63 Conn. 198; 21 L. R. A. 102. Mitchell vs. Newhall, 15 M. & W. 308; Westropp vs. Solomon, 8 C. B. 345; Pollock vs. Stables, 12 Q. B. 765; Tempest vs. Kilner, 3 C. B. 253; Bayley vs. Wilkins, 7 C. B. 886; Hunt vs. Gunn, 13 C. B. (n. s.) 227; Taylor vs. Stray, 2 C. B. (n. s.) 175; Lamert vs. Heath, 15 M. & W. 486; 15 L. J. Ex. 298; Morrice vs. Hunter, 14 L. T. 897; Inchbald vs. Neilgherry Coffee Co. 34 L. J. (C. P.) 15; Forget vs. Baxter, L. R. A. C. (1900), 467; s. c. 82 L. T. R. 510; Harker vs. Edwards, 57 L. J. Q. B. 147; Peckham vs. Ketchum, 5 Bosw. (N. Y.) 506; s. c. less fully, 10 Ab. Pr. (N. Y.) 220; Van Dusen-Harrington Co. vs. Jungeblut, 77 N. W. Rep. 970; Gheen vs. Johnson, 90 Pa. St. 38; Sutton vs. Tatham, 10 Ad. & E. 27; Smith vs. Lindo, 5 C. B. (n. s.) 587; Rosewarne vs. Billing, 15 C. B. (n. s.) 316; Remfry vs. Butler, 1 E. B. & E. 887; Biederman vs. Stone, L. R. 2 C. P. 504; Chapman vs. Shepherd, Whitehead vs. Izod, L. R. 2 C. P. 228; Webb vs. Challoner, 2 F. & F. 120; M'Ewen vs. Woods, 11 Q. B. 13; Bayliffe vs. Butterworth, 1 Ex. 425; Patterson vs. Keys, 1 Cin. Super. Ct. Rep. (Ohio) 94. As to knowledge of the usage by the client, see Blakemore vs. Heyman, 23 Fed. Rep. 648; Higgins vs. McCrea, 23 Fed. Rep. 782. If the Broker's agent receives an order forbidden by the Stock Exchange rules, the broker is liable. Newman vs. Lee, 84 N. Y. Supp. 106. See also chapter on "Usages."

[3] Westropp vs. Solomon, 8 C. B. 345. As to when evidence of Board of Trade custom is admissible, see Ayer vs. Mead, 13 Ill. App. 625.

If a rule of an Exchange requires a vendor, on receiving written no-

The Broker should hand over to his principal money or securities as soon as he has received them, but the Client cannot insist on delivery, at the time of the payment of the purchase money, if this obliged the Broker himself to advance the purchase money, as the Broker is under no obligation to pay the price.[1]

In respect to the character and kind of stocks or securities which the Broker may buy, he is bound to purchase the kind designated by the Client.[2] But if he exercises prudence and care, he is not liable, although the securities purchased by him in the regular course of business prove spurious.

In the case of Westropp vs. Solomon[3] the plaintiffs were Stock-brokers, and were employed by the defendant to sell certain scrip which turned out to be invalid. The certificates were such as to deceive everybody who dealt in them. There was no fraud or negligence on either side. The Brokers paid the purchase money back to the vendors, as also a certain sum which, under the rules of the Stock Exchange, had been prescribed to be paid in such cases. They

---

tice that a default is intended, to sell on or before the first open board thereafter, he must on receiving a notice that, for the reason given "the deal is off," strictly comply with the rule, quite irrespective of the reasons given. Gill vs. O'-Rourke, 6 Pa. Super. Ct. Rep. 605.

[1] Stock Co. vs. Galmoyle, 3 T. L. R. 808.

[2] If the Client instructs his Broker to purchase and sell grain on the Chicago Board of Trade, but it appears that the purchases and sales were not made on the Chicago Board of Trade but were fictitious or "bucket shop" transactions made in the Broker's own office, the Client may recover the amount of margins deposited by him with the Broker. Mellott vs. Downing, 64 Pa. St. 393. A Stock-broker is an "agent" within the meaning of Comp. Laws, Michigan, § 11572, making an agent criminally liable for misapplying money sent to him with written instructions as to its application. People vs. Karste, 93 N. W. Rep. 1081.

[3] 8 C. B. 346.

then sued their principal, who did not contest the right of
plaintiff to recover the principal sum, but defended as to
the additional sum, as to which the defendant succeeded.
In Mitchell vs. Newhall[1] the defendant gave the plaintiff,
a Broker on the Stock Exchange, an order to purchase for
him fifty shares in a foreign railway company. At that
time no *shares* of the company were in the market, the
foreign government not having yet authorized its establishment; but *letters of allotment* for shares were then, according to the evidence of persons on the Stock Exchange, commonly bought and sold in the market as shares. The
plaintiff bought for the defendant a letter of allotment for
fifty shares, and it was held, that a jury might well find
that this was a good execution of the order.[2]

In Lamert vs. Heath,[3] where a Broker was instructed to
purchase "Kentish Coast Railway Scrip," and he bought
what was known as such and was paid for it, it was held that
he was not liable to refund the money he had received; although it turned out that he had bought scrip issued without due authority, and, in fact, utterly worthless.

So in Young vs. Cole [4] a Broker brought an action against
his Client to recover the proceeds of Guatemala bonds which
he had sold for his Client on the Exchange. The bonds,
after being a short time in the purchaser's possession, were
discovered to be unmarketable for want of stamps, and they
were returned to the Broker, who indemnified the purchaser
without consulting with his Client. The court held, upon
the authority of Child vs. Morley,[5] that the Broker was en-

---

[1] 15 M. & W. 308.

[2] Tempest vs. Kilner, 3 C. B. 253;
Hunt vs. Gunn, 13 C. B. (n. s.) 227.

[3] 15 M. & W. 486. See Luffman

vs. Hoy, 13 N. Y. *Weekly Dig.* 324;
aff'd 94 N. Y. 626.

[4] 3 Bing. (N. C.) 724.

[5] 8 T. R. 610.

titled to recover from his client the sum previously paid to him, on the ground that the consideration on which it had been paid over had failed, the Client having delivered something which, though resembling the article contracted to be sold, was of no value; and that the repayment made by the Broker to the purchaser was necessary, according to the custom of the Stock Exchange, which treated a Broker dealing with foreign stock as a principal, and made him liable to expulsion if he did not make good his differences.

In the case of Peckham vs. Ketchum,[1] a case almost similar to Lamert vs. Heath, the court held that a Broker who is employed to purchase stock, and who in good faith, and in accordance with the custom of the market, makes the purchase in his own name, and transfers the stock bought to his principal, is not liable to the principal if the stock prove to be spurious. In that case the plaintiff called at the office of defendants and ordered them to buy ten shares of railroad stock at a certain price. On the same day the defendants sent to the plaintiff a memorandum of the purchase, who sent his check for the same, the defendants stating that they would transfer the stock referred to into his name on the books of the company that day, but that the certificate would not be ready until the next day. At the time mentioned they delivered to him a certificate in due form for said stock, signed by one Schuyler, the transfer agent of said railroad company, who was the proper officer to issue the same. In the purchase of the stock the defendants acted in good faith "in the mode usual and customary among Stock-brokers in

---

[1] 5 Bosw. (N. Y.) 506; s. c. less fully, 10 Ab. Pr. (N. Y.) 220.

the city of New York, among whom it is not usual to disclose
the names of their principals to persons with whom they
dealt," and defendants paid for the stock upon receiving the
certificate from the selling Broker. The certificate issued
and delivered to the plaintiff did not represent actual stock,
and was valueless ; and, upon the discovery of this fact, in due
time the plaintiff tendered the same to defendants and demanded a return of his money, which was refused, and the
action was brought to recover the same. In an opinion giving judgment for the defendants, Hoffman, J., after reviewing the English authorities upon the subject, concluded that
the plaintiff, having contracted with defendants as Stock-
brokers, was bound by the custom 'which prevailed in relation to that species of business, and especially by the usage
by which Brokers only, and not their Clients, are known
in their dealings with each other, and that such a custom
put the plaintiff in the same position as in the case of a contract made distinctly with one as the agent of a known or
disclosed principal. The court also held that the employment of the defendants could not be justly treated as an employment to purchase genuine stock to the extent and import of making them guarantors of the validity of that
which they should purchase ; *it was rather to purchase what
in the market was passing as stock of this description,
and that an agent employed to purchase a commodity of a
particular character or quality is only bound to use all the
circumspection and diligence which a prudent purchaser
himself would exercise.*

The conclusion reached in this case is in accord with the
English authorities, and is entirely sound upon principle,
there being no just distinction in this respect between

the employment of a Stock-broker and any other kind of agent.[1]

So where a person employing a Broker to sell shares directed him by mistake to sell 250, when he intended to sell and had only 50 shares, and the Broker sold the shares in accordance with his directions, the Client was held bound to pay the difference which, under the rules of the Stock Exchange, the Broker had been compelled to pay to the Broker to whom he had sold the same.[2]

And the case of Morrice vs. Hunter[3] furnishes still another illustration of the general rule. There the defendant instructed his Brokers to buy 10 Agra & Masterman's

---

[1] Within the principles of the cases cited in the text, the Broker is not to be held to any of the warranties implied on the sale of securities and which would obtain between his Client and the opposite party.

Between the principals the rule is that "the seller is liable ex delicto for bad faith, and ex contractu there is a warranty implied on his part that the securities belong to him and are not forgeries. Where there is no express stipulation, there is no liability beyond this." Otis vs. Cullum, 92 U. S. 447. There is no implied warranty of the solvency of the corporation, or that the stock sold is not part of a fraudulent overissue. People's Bank vs. Kurtz, 11 W. N. C. 225. Or that the stock sold is of a corporation de jure, Harter vs. Eltzroth, 111 Ind. 159. Or that it has good title to its property, or as to its value. State vs. R. R. Co., 34 La. Ann. 917. Neither is there any implied warranty that bonds of a state are constitutionally issued. Otis vs. Cullum, supra. See also Ætna Life Ins. Co. vs. Middleport, 124 U. S. 534. The decision in Bischoffsheim vs. Baltzer, 20 Fed. Rep. 890, to the contrary, might better have rested on the fact that there the vendor of the unconstitutionally issued bond, was really acting as Broker for the vendee and was selling him his own securities. But see Ex parte Panmure, 24 Ch. D. 367.

[2] Sutton vs. Tatham, 10 Ad. & E. 27; see also, to same effect, Child vs. Morley, 8 T. R. 610; Lightfoot vs. Creed, 8 Taunt. 268; s. c. 2 Moo. 255. But see Bowlby vs. Bell, 3 C. B. 284; Fletcher vs. Marshall, 15 M. & W. 755; Stewart vs. Cauty, 8 M. & W. 160. As to liability of Broker for stocks lost by or stolen from him, or for losses occasioned in the exercise of his employment, see post, subdivision (c.), p. 241.

[3] 14 L. T. 897.

shares, which the Brokers' manager by mistake described as £25 shares in place of £50 shares with £25 paid, on which ground the defendant attempted to repudiate the transaction. In an action by the Brokers to recoup themselves for payments made on the Stock Exchange, Mr. Justice Wiles left it to the jury to say whether the order given depended on there being £25 shares, or whether the plaintiffs had bought what they agreed to buy for the defendant.

The care incumbent upon a Broker, it would seem, does not require him to present the purchased certificates of stock at the office of the corporation for verification of their genuineness if there is nothing on their face to arouse suspicion.

It was so held in respect to a loan by a banker of his customer's money upon the security of certificates of stock,[1] and the reasoning of that case seems equally applicable to an ordinary purchase by a Broker, particularly as the Broker ordinarily is under no duty to have the purchased stock transferred at the company's office into his Client's name.

Fuller mention of the case of Isham vs. Post, above referred to, is pertinent here, for the transactions therein considered, i. e., loaning the Client's money upon the collateral security of shares of stock, are more or less common to all stock-brokerage offices. It was held that it is not the duty of the Broker to inquire into the solvency of borrowers reputed to be responsible, particularly where there is no proof that inquiry would have developed any doubt of solvency. Where the stocks upon pledge of which the loan

[1] Isham vs. Post, 141 N. Y. 100.

is made prove to be forgeries and a question is raised as to
whether the Broker gave the certificates an examination
reasonably careful under the circumstances, he is entitled to
show that the forgery was so deft as to deceive the reasonable scrutiny of other careful bankers, and that for an extended time the same forged certificates have been commouly received on the Street among such bankers and
Brokers as collateral for loans. He may also show upon
this point that he has himself loaned his own money on
similarly forged certificates.[1]

But it is not enough to state that he had " carefully "
examined the certificates, without showing in what that
care consisted, or that he was possessed of any information
which would make his inspection anything of a safeguard;
or that loans upon similarly forged certificates had been
made by other bankers and Brokers apparently equally as
careless as himself.[2]

Where a Broker acts in pursuance of his authority, according to the usages of the Stock Exchange or of his
fellow-Brokers, and in good faith and with prudence, he is
entitled to a full indemnification for any outlays and
losses which may occur in the transaction of the business.
His employment implies an undertaking to this effect on
his employer's part. The general rule, in respect to the relation between principal and agent, being thus;—a request to undertake an agency or employment, the proper
execution of which does or may involve the loss or expenditure of money on the part of the agent, operates as an implied request on the part of the principal to reimburse him

---

[1] Isham vs. Post, supra.   App. Div. 605; 64 N. Y. Supp. 1137;
[2] Isham vs. Post, on new trial, 51   aff'd 167 N. Y. 531.

for such losses as may result from the performance of his
agency.[1]

The language of Mr. Justice Blackburn in Duncan vs.
Hill[2] is strong and apposite upon this question of the
Stock-broker to receive indemnity for acts performed in
the business of his Clients. "It must be admitted that
the plaintiffs were authorized by the defendants to enter
into contracts in their behalf according to the rules of the
Stock Exchange. It must be admitted that for any loss
incurred by the agent by reason of his having entered
into such contracts according to such rules, unless they be
wholly unreasonable, and where the loss is without any
personal default of his own, he is entitled to be indemnified by his principal upon an implied contract to that
effect." And the case of Marten vs. Gibbon[3] carried
the doctrine still further; for in that case where a Broker
at the request of his Client made a sale on the Exchange
to a jobber of the prospective dividends of shares in a
railway company—dealings in which, by a rule of that
body, will not be recognized—and the Broker subsequently paid differences to the jobber, it was held, notwithstanding the aforesaid rule, that the Client was bound
to refund these differences to the Broker, on the ground
that the rule did not affect the general liability of the

---

[1] Bibb vs. Allen, 149 U. S. 481,
499; Bennett vs. Covington, 22 Fed.
Rep. S16, 819; Bartlett vs. Smith,
13 Fed. Rep. 263; Arnold vs. Smith,
85 Ga. 510; Perin vs. Parker, 18 N.
E. Rep. 747; Knapp vs. Simon, 96
N. Y. 284; Maitland vs. Martin, 86
Pa. St. 120; Duncan vs. Hill, 29 L.
T. R. 268; Thacker vs. Hardy, 4 Q.
B. D. 685; Smith vs. Reynolds, 66
L. T. R. (n. s.) 808; Hartas vs. Rib-
bons, 22 Q. B. D. 254; Ellis vs. Pond,
L. R. 1 Q. B. D. (1898) 426; Harker
vs. Edwards, 4 T. L. R. 92. See for
further English cases, Stutfield's
Rules and Usages of the Stock Ex-
change, 172.

[2] 8 L. R. Ex. 242; rev'g 6 L. R.
Ex. 255.

[3] 33 L. T. N. S. 561.

members towards each other for contracts made on the Exchange. Where a customer refuses to deliver stock which his Broker sells pursuant to contract, the latter may buy it for delivery at the best price he can and hold the former for the loss.[1] And a purchaser is bound to indemnify a Broker who pays for and takes a transfer of shares in a company after commencement of the winding up.[2]

If the Broker held collateral security of the Clients against the loss, he is not required, in the absence of a special agreement, to realize thereon, or to return the same to the customer before bringing action to recover the

---

[1] Baily vs. Carnduff, 59 Pac. Rep. 407.

[2] Chapman vs. Shepherd, L. R. 2 C. P. 228; Whitehead vs. Izod, id.; Emmerson's case, L. R. 1 Ch. App. 433. A very interesting question arose in the case of Mewburn vs. Eaton (20 L. T. Rep. 449) between a Broker and his Client. In that case the Broker had sold certain shares for his Client on the Stock Exchange, and the latter had executed the transfers and received the purchase price. Subsequently, however, the transfers were returned to the Broker by the ultimate purchaser for some trifling corrections in the spelling of names, and the Broker delivered the same to his Client for that purpose. The latter, however, refused to "initial" the corrections unless the Broker paid him the price mentioned in the transfers to the ultimate purchaser, which was higher than the price at which his shares were originally sold. In consequence, the shares were bought in, and the Broker, un- der the rules of the Stock Exchange, was compelled to pay the differences to the jobber. And the court held that the Broker was entitled to recover the sum which he had so paid out by reason of the conduct of the Client. The court did not pass upon the question as to whether a vendor was bound to sign a transfer to the ultimate purchaser in which the consideration was stated at a price greater than that which he had received for the shares; but the intimations were that he would not be so compelled. It was held that this objection had been waived by the Client in originally signing the transfers. In Hawkins vs. Maltby, (L. R. 6 Eq. 505; 4 Ch. App. 200), the specific performance of a contract was refused, on the technical ground that the bill called for the enforcement of a contract for a different consideration than that actually agreed upon. But subsequently the Broker was held entitled to an indemnity.

amount lost.[1] This right to indemnity is not lost by a wrongful termination of the transaction by the Broker. It is simply to be diminished in its amount by the damage to the Client. Thus the mere fact that the Broker sells, without due notice to his Client of the time and place of sale, and by such act commits a conversion, does not preclude him from bringing an action against his Client to recover the debt arising out of the advance made by the Broker to purchase the stock. This must be deemed the settled rule, despite some contrariety in the decisions in New York State and some opposing authorities elsewhere.

The point first arose in Gruman vs. Smith,[2] where the action was brought by the plaintiff as the assignee of F. & Co., Stock-brokers, to recover a balance due the latter from the defendant, growing out of a stock transaction. After the stock was purchased, the defendant, besides leaving some money as a margin, deposited the stock in question with the Brokers as collateral security. The margin having become exhausted by a sudden decline of the stock in question, the collateral was sold without the due notice of the time and place of sale. A technical conversion was conceded. The action was subsequently brought to recover the above balance, the defendant having been first credited with the proceeds of the sale at 90.

At the trial, the court nonsuited the plaintiff on the ground that the assignee represented the Brokers, who were the wrongdoers. The plaintiff claimed that this cause of action grew out of the original purchase of the stock in the

---

[1] De Cordova vs. Barnum, 130 N. Y. 615.   [2] 81 N. Y. 25.

first place, and not out of its wrongful conversion after it became a collateral. But in the Court of Appeals this judgment was reversed and a new trial ordered, on the ground that a technical conversion of the collateral did not of itself work an extinguishment of the original claim, and that the defendant was only entitled to damages actually sustained. In support of this view, Baker vs. Drake[1] and Markham vs. Jaudon[2] were cited.

The action was not based upon the wrongful sale, but upon the debt for the advance made by the Brokers to purchase the stock. The title of the stock when purchased was in the defendant; the advance of the whole or a portion of the purchase-money created the relation of debtor and creditor; and the stock put up as security, together with any additional amount called a margin, was a pledge to secure the debt.

The defendant was not bound by the sale for want of notice, and might insist upon full indemnity for his loss or injury; but such loss was not necessarily the whole amount of the plaintiff's claim.

The court, by Church, C. J., upon this latter point said: "The stock sold at 90. Suppose that was then its full value, and it had gone down to 50 and remained there, it is very clear that, so far from being injured, the defendant would have been benefited by the sale. The defendant cannot claim a greater benefit than would have been derived if the act complained of had not been committed. The defendant might have shown that the market value of the stock at the time of the sale exceeded the price for which it was sold, and he was entitled to a reasonable time after

---

[1] 53 N. Y. 211. [2] 41 id. 435.

notice of the sale to replace the stock; and if in the meantime it had advanced in price, the defendant would have
been entitled to the difference. Beyond this, he was not
legally injured."

And these propositions were again confirmed by the
New York Court of Appeals in Capron vs. Thompson.[1]

But later the Second Division of the Court of Appeals in
Gillett vs. Whiting,[2] referring to the language of the lower
Appellate Court, that the fact of conversion did not go to
the whole damages asked by the Broker but entitled the
Client to a reduction of the Broker's demand by the amount
proven to have been suffered by the conversion, and that
no such amount was proven,[3] said "We do not understand this to be the law. This action was based upon the
performance of the agreement by the plaintiffs, in which
they undertook to carry for the defendant the stock purchased, and if, instead of performing the contract on their
part, they converted the stock to their own use, they had no
ground of complaint or cause of action against the defendant." There was no mention in the briefs of counsel or
in the opinion of the court, of the cases of Gruman vs.
Smith and Capron vs. Thompson, and the court assumed
that the only basis for the decision of the General Term
was the case of Baker vs. Drake, which was held to be distinguishable. This view was then followed by the General Term of the Supreme Court in Minor vs. Beveridge,[4]
but when these two cases came again to the Court of Appeals,[5] the court re-declared the doctrine of Gruman vs.

---

[1] 86 N. Y. 418.

[2] 120 N. Y. 402.

[3] 23 J. & S. 187, 188.

[4] 67 Hun, 1.

[5] Gillett vs. Whiting, 141 N. Y. 71; Minor vs. Beveridge, 141 N. Y. 399.

Smith and Capron vs. Thompson and said that the remarks on the first appeal in Gillett vs. Whiting were *obiter* and not necessary to the decision of that appeal.

Bartlett, J., said, in the second appeal in Minor vs. Beveridge: "We think the trial Judge should have submitted these questions (viz., whether the Client sustained loss on the sale, and as to whether he could have replaced the stocks sold within a reasonable time) to the jury under the settled law of this court that even where a Stock-broker sells without due notice stock purchased by him for a customer, on a margin, and held in pledge to secure the advance made by him for the purchase, he does not thereby, as matter of law, extinguish his claim against the customer for the advance, but the customer is entitled to be allowed as damages the difference between the price for which the stock sold and for which he received credit, and its market price then, or within such reasonable time after notice of sale, as would have enabled him to replace the stock in case the market price exceeded the price realized."[1]

In certain other jurisdictions, however, the doctrine stated in Gillett vs. Whiting, *supra*, is in effect adopted. These cases are referred to in note.[2]

So when Stock-brokers are sued for illegally converting

See also Quinlan vs. Raymond, N. Y. *Daily Reg.* July 29, 1886; aff'd 3 N. Y St Rep. 573.

[1] 141 N. Y. at 403.

[2] Bail vs. Clark, 28 Fed. Rep. 179; Denton vs. Jackson, 106 Ill. 433, 437; Larminie vs. Carley, 111 Ill. 196, in which case it was also held that the margins deposited might be recovered under the common counts in assumpsit. Ellis vs. Pond, 1 Q. B. D. (1898) 426. In this latter case, however, there was a dissenting opinion and the case is elaborately considered and criticised in an article in 23 L. M. and Rev. p. 355. See also Lacey vs. Hill, Scrim. Cl. L. R. 8 Ch. 921.

plaintiff's stocks, they may interpose a counterclaim for the deficiency on such sale.[1]

But the Broker has no right to recover indemnity for acts beyond the scope of his authority.[2] This proposition is well illustrated in the case of Bowlby vs. Bell.[3] In that case a Broker was employed to sell shares, and made a bargain on the Stock Exchange for the purpose. The scrip having been sent to the company's office for registration, the Broker failed to deliver registered shares, and, after notice from his Client not to do so, paid the difference due on a "buying in" of other shares at an advanced price against him. He claimed to recoup the same as money paid to the Client's use. The price of the shares had not been paid to the latter, and no transfer had been tendered by the purchaser; and the court was of the opinion that, as the Broker of the purchaser had made no such tender, he was not in a position to take any steps against the Broker of the vendor; and, therefore, the difference paid by the latter was paid in his own wrong, and could not be recovered from his principal. In this case it appeared that the contract made by the selling Broker was for the sale of registered shares. Upon this point the court said: "If the contract was for unregistered shares, it may be collected from the correspondence that the defendant did not authorize the plaintiff to make such a contract; and if he did make it, and thereby incurred a liability to have shares bought in

---

[1] Wicks vs. Hatch, 62 id. 535. To same effect, Work vs. Bennett, 70 Pa. St. 484.

[2] As to when a Broker is within his authority if he acts in good faith, see Matthews vs. Fuller, 123 Mass.

446. See also cases heretofore cited under this head.

[3] 3 C. B. 284, decided on the authority of Stephens vs. De Medina, 4 Q. B. 422.

against him, he cannot charge the defendant with the loss sustained."

A similar result was reached in Fletcher vs. Marshall,[1] where the plaintiff employed the defendants as Brokers to buy shares for him to be delivered within a " reasonable time; " and the defendants made a bargain for the next settling-day with H., who did not then deliver, yet they paid the purchase-money ; and it was held by the Court of Exchequer that the words " reasonable time " were rightly interpreted by the usages of the Stock Exchange, and that on non-delivery of the shares on the settling-day the defendants ought not to have paid the money, and that an action would lie against them by the plaintiff to recover it.

So authority to a Broker to invest a sum of money deposited with him for the purpose, in certain stocks, does not authorize a larger investment, and the Client may recover the value of the stock ordered, in an action on an account.[2] Nor can the Broker recover where the loss is caused by his own default.[3]   But he cannot be deprived of his indemnity for commissions and expenses on the ground that he has not avoided a contract which was not in strict conformity with the statute of frauds, in the absence of any instructions of his principal not to comply therewith.[4]

---

[1] 15 M. & W. 755; consult also, in this connection, Stewart vs. Cauty, 8 M. & W. 160.

[2] Bradfield vs. Patterson, 106 Ala. 397.

[3] Duncan vs. Hill, L. R. 8 Ex. 242, unless the Client elects to become bound therefor by ratification. Hartas vs. Ribbons, 22 Q. B. D. 254.

[4] Bibb vs. Allen, 149 U. S. 481.

As to when it is error to direct a money verdict for a Client for an amount admitted by the Brokers to be due, when it appears that the husband of the Client advanced more than the amount due, upon his wife's account, conditionally upon the latter's account being liable to indemnify the husband's account for the amount so advanced,

As the object of carrying stock on a margin is to enable the customer to realize a profit if there is an advance, or to permit the Broker to close the transaction if there is a depreciation exhausting the margin, and the customer does not respond to a call for further margins, the Client need not pay a balance due in the transaction until a request for payment has been made[1] and the statute of limitations accordingly does not run till such demand by the Broker.[2] And a Broker must not incur any expense on the principal's behalf which the Broker can avoid. Accordingly, where— acting on the supposed instructions of his principal, who wished to repudiate a contract for the purchase of shares— a Broker defended an action which was virtually without legal merit, and sued his principal for the price of the shares and costs of the former action, the price having been paid into court, the trial justice directed a non-suit.[3]

A principal in a stock transaction cannot avoid his liability to his Brokers for a loss by setting up the guaranty of a third party. In Lee vs. Gargulio[4] the plaintiff, it appeared, had certain stock transactions in which defendants acted as his Brokers, in which there was a loss. He sought to avoid this loss by introducing a guaranty signed by one F., which was enclosed in a letter to defendants. The letter began, "Yours, notifying me of acceptance of my offer by customer at 35, at hand. I accept his conditions as set forth in your letter, and enclose guaranty, etc." The guaranty enclosed was in these words: "For and in consideration of one half

---

see Boody vs. Pratt, 45 Atl. Rep. 598.

[1] Kennedy vs. Budd, 5 App. Div. 140.

[2] Id.

[3] Clegg vs. Townsend, 16 L. T. 180.

[4] 45 N. Y. Super. Ct. (13 J. & S.) 595.

the profit on 800 shares, etc., I hereby guarantee the holder of said 800 shares against all or any loss whatsoever ; and further agree, in case of decline of said stock below 35, to deposit margin, if called on to do so, to cover all or any decline as fast as it may be made in said stock. Orders to sell and repurchase said 800 shares, or any part thereof, to be given exclusively by me, the undersigned, for a period of sixty days from the date hereof." Held, that by accepting the guaranty the Broker did not discharge the principal, and that it was not inconsistent with the original agreement.

Where a promise that a guarantor will become liable, is part of the inducement on which the Broker acts, there is sufficient consideration for the subsequently signed contract of the surety.[1]

But in an action against a surety who has agreed in writing to indemnify a Stock-broker against losses in any stock speculations which the Broker might make for his Client, the accounts rendered to the latter by the Broker, which showed a loss, and were admitted to be correct by the Client, are not admissible against the surety. In such a case, the party holding the indemnity claiming loss against his indemnitor must prove it by evidence competent against him. He cannot prove it by the mere admissions or statements of the principal, however formally made. The admissions of the Client are no part of the *res gestæ* so as to be binding upon the surety.[2]

---

[1] Oppenheim vs. Waterbury, 86 Hun, 122; 33 N. Y. Supp. 183; Brandt on Suretyship, 2d ed. § 17.

[2] Hatch vs. Elkins, 65 N. Y. 489. If a note is given to secure the Broker against loss on carrying stocks for a certain time or until a certain price is reached, he may recover upon it at its maturity and hold the proceeds against loss on the closing of the transaction, and this irrespective of whether he had

A guaranty against loss on the purchase of certain shares is not a continuous guaranty against loss on subsequent transactions in buying and selling shares of the same stock where they are so intermingled that it is impossible to say whether or not there was a loss on the shares originally purchased.[1]

A Broker also is not entitled to indemnity for losses on transactions for a corporation acting *ultra vires*. This conclusion was reached *in re* London, Hamburg, and Continental Exchange Bank—Zulueta's Claim.[2] That case arose in the winding-up of a banking company. It appeared that the directors of the bank had given orders to their Broker to buy for the bank a large number of their own shares for the purpose of keeping up the price. Although the order was *ultra vires*, it was executed by the Broker in due course, some of the shares being taken and paid for by the directors and their friends, and the balance was transferred to a trustee for the company; and the Broker's account with the bank was credited with the price. The question was whether the Broker was at liberty to prove for this amount in the winding-up of the company. Lord Romilly, the Master of the Rolls, held the proof should be admitted, on the ground that it was not the duty or business of the Broker to decide whether the directors were or were not exceeding their powers; and as the transaction was concluded, and the Broker's account with the bank credited with the price of the shares—which, in the opinion of the Master of the Rolls, was equivalent to the payment of money —the only remedy of the shareholders should be to require

suffered loss at the time of suing on the note. Hertzfield vs. Aaron, 17 W. D. 309.

[1] Strong vs. Lyon, 63 N. Y. 172.
[2] L. R. 9 Eq. 270.

the directors personally to refund it. But this decision was reversed on appeal,[1] and the transaction held to be wholly void ; and the Broker was held bound to know that the directors were acting *ultra vires*—the court intimating that even if the money had been actually paid over to the Broker by the directors, he would have been liable to refund it.[2] But where an application was made by Stock-brokers to be declared creditors of a company, and it appeared that the manager and certain directors, having associated themselves together in a body, called a " syndicate," for dealing in shares of the company, employed the applicants to borrow money for them on the security of shares of the company, which the applicants effected by lending shares on several occasions to dealers on the Stock Exchange, who advanced the market value of the shares until a subsequent account-day. In the interim a call was made on 820 shares thus lent by the claimants, which they paid ; and the value of the shares falling, and their principals not giving them instructions to renew, the applicants at the end of the period sold the shares at a loss, and repaid the lenders of the cash. The balance of sums due the applicants on these accounts was the sum claimed. One of the " syndicate " was a brother of the applicant B ; but the applicants deposed that they had no knowledge of the existence of this body, and believed throughout that they were dealing with property of the company by the direction of its authorized agents. It was objected that the claim was illegal, upon the ground that the applicants knew that these transactions were effected without the knowledge of the shareholders ; and, if not,

[1] S. c., rev'd L. R. 5 Ct. App. 444.

[2] See also, in this connection, Josephs vs. Pebrer, 3 B. & C. 639.

the transactions were beside the company's powers : they must show that they held these shares as a security ; and, if they did, that they have a right to be indemnified. But the vice-chancellor said the applicants had dealt with ostensible managers of the company in a regular way. If the articles had strictly forbidden the raising of money on behalf of the company by this means, there might have been a question as to whether the Brokers were not bound to take notice of such a provision ; but, in fact, there was no such prohibition. No question as to the *bona fides* of the transaction could arise ; for it seemed that these transactions were examined by the directors from day to day. The question resolved itself simply into one of indemnity, and the rule that it is the duty of principals to indemnify their agents must prevail. The mortgage might have been effected by some other means than by the loan of shares and then no question as to the right to be repaid could have been raised. The claim was accordingly allowed.[1]

So, too, where a savings-bank, having taken certain shares of stock to secure a loan, resolved that it should be sold by the president for the best interest of the bank. The president sold a part of the stock, and directed the plaintiff, a Stock-broker, to sell the remainder at a price named at the New York Stock Exchange; which he did, and so advised the president, whereupon the latter informed him that he had himself previously sold the stock. Plaintiff, being unable to deliver the stock to the Broker to

[1] In re Imperial Mercantile Credit Assoc., 2 Week. Notes (1867), 131. A bill lies by Stock-brokers to compel the defendant to accept the transfer of shares, bought for him, and to repay plaintiffs for calls on the shares (Robins vs. Edwards, id. 197). First Nat. Bank vs. Hoch, 20 Alb. L. J. 215; Pa. St. May, 1879.

whom he had sold it, was compelled to pay the purchaser · differences. In an action against the receiver of the bank to recover the amount so paid—held, that the bank was liable to the plaintiff for the damage occasioned by the act of its president; and that the liability of the bank was not affected by the fact that it was forbidden by statute to loan money upon personal security, such a transaction being not void but merely voidable by the borrower.[1]

(c.) Disposition of Stock when Purchased ; Safely Keeping same ; Liability to Keep Identical Stock Purchased, etc.

After the stock has been purchased and paid for by the Broker, several questions arise respecting the care and disposition thereof.

With respect to the care which the Broker should exercise in keeping the securities of his Clients, it seems to be settled that if the securities be stolen from or lost by the Broker he is not liable unless the theft or loss arose from or was connected with a want of ordinary diligence or care on his part.[2]

In the case of Abbett vs. Frederick[3] it was held that a pawn-broker, where his place of business was broken into and articles pledged taken therefrom, was not liable if he exercised ordinary diligence. The court said : "The rule laid down in the case of Arent vs. Squires,[4] that in cases of

---

[1] Sistare vs. Best, 16 Hun, 611; aff'd 88 N. Y. 527.

[2] 2 Pars. on Cont. 8th ed. vol. 2, p. 117 (bottom paging), and cases cited; 1 Inst. 89 a; 4 Rep. 83 b; Abbett vs. Frederick, 56 How. (N. Y.) Pr. 68; Third Nat. Bank vs. Boyd, 44 Md. 47; Jenkins vs. Nat. Village Bank, 58 Me. 275; Dearborn vs. Union Nat. Bank, 58 id. 273; 61 id.

[3] Supra. To same effect, Laing vs. Blumauer, 1 City Court (N. Y.), 238.

[4] 1 Daly, 347.

16

pawn or pledge all that has ever been required since the
days of Bracton, by the common-law, on the part of the
pawnee, has been that which is required of warehousemen,
the exercise of ordinary diligence, is the law which must
govern this case." So where a bank receives stocks or bonds
as collateral security for the repayment of a loan, it is not
liable for their loss unless there has been an absence of proper
and sufficient care on its part, and this is a question for the
jury.[1]

Lord Holt quotes Bracton to the effect that, if a creditor
takes a pawn, he is bound to restore it upon payment of the
debt ; but if the pledge be lost while in the possession of the
pledgee, and the latter has used due diligence, he will be indemnified notwithstanding the loss, and he may resort to the
pledgor for the debt.[2] But in the case of Cutting vs. Marlor[3]
it was held that a corporation is liable for stocks and bonds
deposited with it as collateral security for a loan which have
been abstracted and misappropriated by one of its officers
who was permitted to have unrestrained control of the
affairs and assets of the corporation, and where the trustees

[1] Third Nat. Bank vs. Boyd,
supra.

[2] Bracton, 99 b; see also Schouler
on Bailm. 3d ed. § 204 et seq., and
cases cited; Third Nat. Bank vs.
Boyd, supra. The liability of trustees does not extend to cases of
robbery or fraud beyond the care
which a prudent man would take
of his own property (Morley vs. Morley, 2 Ch. Cas. 2; Jones vs. Lewis, 2
Ves. Sen. 240; Exp. Belchier, Amb.
218; and see Bostock vs. Ployer, L.
R. 1 Eq. 26). As to precautions
which trustees of shares payable to
bearer should take with regard to

the safety of securities transferable
by delivery, and as to shares which
a company requires to be registered
in a single name, see Consterdine
vs. Consterdine, 31 Beav. 330. See
also Speight vs. Gaunt, 9 App. Cas.
1 (in which a trustee was held not
liable to his cestui que trust for
misappropriation of the purchase
price of trust securities by a Stock-
broker) and Magnus vs. Bank, 37
Ch. Div. 476 (to the effect that
trustees may render themselves
liable through negligence).

[3] 8 N. Y. *Weekly Dig.* 345; aff'd 78
N. Y. 454.

omitted to exercise a proper oversight over the conduct of such officer. And this case is equally applicable to Stock-brokers who receive stocks of their Clients as collateral or otherwise, and, through fraud or negligence, allow them to be lost or misappropriated.[1] This principle has also been extended to a case where a firm, in the course of its business, received money belonging to third persons, and one of the partners misapplied it while it was in the custody of the firm ; and it was held that the latter must make it good.[2]

And the cases just cited directly hold that where stocks or money are received or held by a firm of Stock-brokers for its Clients, and an individual member converts or mis-applies the same, the remaining partners are liable to the Clients, although they had no knowledge of the conversion or misapplication.

Brokers, too, are liable to a Client, where their Clerk converts the securities purchased and delivers forged certif-icates to the Client in their place, unless the wrong doing might have been prevented by ordinary care on the part of the Client, and even then if, by the exercise on the part by the Broker of due and reasonable care as to the duties of the clerk, the loss would not have occurred.[3]

---

[1] If a Stock-broker receives a se-curity from the owner for safe-keep-ing, and without authority delivers it to the corporation by whom it is cancelled, and a new certificate issued to another, he is liable for converting the stock. Hubbell vs. Blandy, 87 Mich. 209.

[2] 1 Lindley on Part. 6th ed. p. 167 et seq., and cases cited; Devaynes vs. Noble (Baring's case), 1 Mer. 611; Sadler vs. Lee, 6 Beav. 324; De Ribeyre vs. Barclay, 23 Beav. 107; Stone vs. Marsh, 6 B. & C. 551; and Ry. & Moo. 364; see also, in this connection, Butler vs. Finck, 21 Hun (N. Y.), 210; Briggs vs. Ken-nett, N. Y. L. J. May 10, 1894; 8 Misc. 264. As to liability of corpo-ration for act of its officers in fraudulently and illegally issuing stock certificates, see post, p. 739 et seq.

[3] Andrews vs. Clark, 72 Md. 396.

In a case in Pennsylvania[1] the question was discussed as to the liability of a Stock-broker for margins which he had placed in the hands of a fellow Broker to cover transactions of his Client. The court laid down the rule that where the Broker acted in good faith, and in accordance with the usages of Stock-brokers, he was not liable for the loss of the margins caused by the insolvency of his fellow Broker. The court said : " The law implies a promise from Brokers, bankers, or other agents that they will severally exercise competent skill and proper care in the service they undertake to perform; but it neither implies nor requires more than this." Accordingly, where G., a Stock-broker, deposited a margin with B., another Broker, to cover a short sale made by G., on account of one J., and did not demand security therefor, but, according to the custom of Brokers, it was optional with G. to do so, he acting in good faith ; and when the deposit was made with B., the latter was in full credit—held, that there was no evidence of negligence such as would make G. responsible for a loss occurring through B.'s insolvency.[2]

Another question arises as to the transfer of the stock.[3] A Broker is under no obligation to have stocks purchased on margin transferred into the name of his Client.[4] As we have shown,[5] his duty is fully performed if he at all times has stock in hand to meet the demands of the Client whether

---

[1] Gheen vs. Johnson, 90 Pa. St. 38.

[2] Wykoff vs. Irvine, 6 Minn. 496; Sadler vs. Lee, De Ribeyre vs. Barclay, supra.

[3] As to liability for "calls" or "assessments" upon stocks, see post, p. 265.

[4] Caswell vs. Putnam, 120 N. Y. 153; Brewster vs. Van Liew, 119 Ill. 554, 563; Harding vs. Field, 1 App. Div. 391, 393; Douglas vs. Carpenter, 45 N. Y. Supp. 219, 220, and cases cited.

[5] Post, p. 252.

or not it is the particular shares purchased in the execution of the Client's order.[1]

It also follows from this, and it is well settled that the Broker is entitled to have the stock transferred into his own name, or those of his clerks, so that he may be able to secure himself for the amount of the advances made by him. In Horton vs. Morgan[2] the court said : " As he [the Broker] was to hold the shares as security for the balance of the purchase-money, which he had advanced, it was proper and entirely consistent with the nature of the transaction that he should take the title in his own name ; . . . and we do not see anything unlawful in his transferring it to his clerks if it remained under his control, and if he was ready when called on by the plaintiff to transfer it to him upon the advance being paid."[3] Whether the Broker has the right or authority to transfer the purchased stock into his Client's name, is a question which has not directly arisen. It would seem that he may do so if necessary for his own protection, as for instance, where a call is to be made upon stockholders of record and his Client's stock stands in his name. But where one Broker acting as such, executes his Client's orders through another Broker, there is no implication of authority to the latter to transfer the stock into the name of the first Broker. In such a case each Broker knows that the other is only acting as a middleman and without any intention of

[1] Harding vs. Field, supra, and see cases cited, post, p. 252.

[2] 19 N. Y. 170, followed in cases cited in note 4, p. 244.

[3] To same effect, Genin vs. Isaacson, 6 N. Y. Legal Obs. 213 216; see also Nourse vs. Prime, 4 Johns. Ch. 490; s. c. 7 id. 69; Morgan's Estate, 11 Pa. C. C. Rep. 536, 540; Skiff vs. Stoddard, 63 Conn. 198; 21 L. R. A. 102; Hubbell vs. Drexel, 11 Fed. Rep. 115. The same rule exists in the case of a pledge, the law being that the pledgee may transfer the securities into his own name (Schouler on Bailm. 3d ed. 182, 200; Tyler on Usury, 507).

himself becoming a stockholder. And the Broker into whose name the stock has so been transferred cannot be made liable by the corporation or its creditors for an unpaid assessment upon such stock.[1]

There is an intimation in Horton vs. Morgan that when the purchase price of the stock is fully paid by the Client and the certificates are to be delivered to him, it is the duty of the Broker to have same transferred into the Client's name, but even in such a case the Broker is not bound to procure a transfer of the stock for the principal, where the office of the company is removed from the city where the Broker lives and the company is insolvent.[2]

As between Brokers, fellow-members of the New York Stock Exchange, the rules formerly provided that, " in the delivery of stock the Receiver shall have the option of receiving said stock by certificate and power irrevocable, in the name of, witnessed or guaranteed by, a member of the Exchange, or a firm represented at the Exchange, resident, or doing business in New York, or by transfer thereof ; but in all cases where personal liability attaches to ownership, the seller shall have the right to deliver stock by transfer." The purpose of the first part of this rule was to give to the " Receiver " or purchaser the security of the endorsement or guarantee of a member of the Exchange, the selling Broker becoming a surety for the genuineness of the signature. The last part of the rule giving the seller the right to deliver stock by transfer in the case stated, simply expresses a rule of law. Webster vs. Upton, *supra*.[3]

[1] Glenn vs. Garth, 133 N. Y. 18. There is, however, implied authority in the vendor of stocks to transfer the same into the name of his vendee. Webster vs. Upton, 91 U. S. 65; cf. Glenn vs. Garth, supra, at p. 39.

[2] Horton vs. Morgan, supra.

[3] The rule as amended merely gives the receiver the option of re-

The question as to how far the pledgor's right to vote the stock is affected by the hypothecation, and by the Broker's right to transfer it to his own name, will now be considered. By the Revised Statutes of New York (1 Rev. Stat. 596, ch. 18, § 37), it was provided that the pledgor of stock in moneyed corporations (i. e. banking or insurance corporations, § 51), created after January 1, 1828, could not vote upon the stock, but this chapter was repealed by the Repealing Act of 1882, and the General Corporation Law. As to all other corporations, except libraries and religious societies, it was provided by 1 Rev. Stat. 603-4, §§ 6, 8, that the transfer books should be conclusive upon the inspectors of election, but section 5 conferred upon the Supreme Court summary powers to review and, in a proper case, to set aside an election. In an application under this section[1] it was held that while the stock remained in the pledgor's name, he was entitled to vote the stock, and this decision was followed in Matter of Barker,[2] in which case it was also held that, although the corporation was an insurance company, § 37, of ch. 18 of the Rev. Stats., *supra*, had no application, as the corporation was created prior to January 1, 1828.

---

ceiving certificates, or a transfer. Art. XXV. sec. 2, Const. N. Y. Stock Exchange. Ordinarily the selling Broker is under no duty to the opposite Broker or principal to procure registration or transfer of stock on books of company, nor does the sale by him import an undertaking that the company will make the transfer, where it has a discretion in the matter. See Stray vs. Russell, 1 El. & E. 888; 917; Taylor vs. Stray, 2 C. B. (n. s.) 175, aff'd id. 197; Humble vs. Langston, 7 M. & W. 517; London Founders' Assn. vs. Clarke, L. R. 20 Q. B. D. 576. Whether he would be liable to his own Client for any call which such Client would have to pay by reason of the Broker's failure to transfer the stock into the name of the vendee, was suggested but not decided in Neilson vs. James, 9 L. R. Q. B. D. 546.

[1] Ex parte Willcocks, 7 Cow. 402, 411.

[2] 6 Wend. 509.

In Matter of Cecil [1] it was held that inspectors of election had no power in the case of a non-moneyed corporation when a stockholder was voting personally or by proxy, to require an affidavit that the stock was not pledged, as a proceeding under § 5 of 1 Rev. Stats. 603-4, *supra*, could not be had under the act in relation to moneyed corporations, but it was within § 5, *supra*, which applied to all other corporations, except libraries and religious corporations. This decision did not refer to the General Manufacturing Act of 1848, ch. 40, § 17, of which provided that the pledgor had the right to vote upon the stock, notwithstanding the pledge. It was held in Strong vs. Smith [2] that, as to a corporation organized under that act, the Supreme Court had power under §§ 5 and 6, *supra*, to go behind the transfer books of the company, and determine whether a transfer on the books was a sale or pledge, and in the latter case to enable the pledgor to vote, although the name of the pledgee appeared on the books.

The equitable powers of the Supreme Court have been also invoked to restrain, by injunction, the pledgee from voting the stock when it has been transferred to his name, [3] but the pledgor must show that his rights will be prejudiced. [4]

The provisions of the Revised Statutes referred to (1 Rev. Stats. 603, §§ 5, 6, 8) and the Act of 1848, were repealed by the General Corporation Law (L. 1890, ch. 563) and have been re-enacted, in amended form, in the latter law (as amended by L. 1901, ch. 355, §§ 20-7). [5] The effect

[1] 36 How. Pr. 477.

[2] 15 Hun, 222.

[3] McHenry vs. Jewett, N. Y. Daily Reg. October 19, 1881; aff'd 26 Hun, 453.

[4] S. c. 90 N. Y. 58.

[5] See Cumming & Gilbert's Gen. Laws, title "Corporations."

of § 20 of the General Corporation Law seems to be, that only the holder of record is entitled to vote, but if the stock has been pledged, the pledgor may demand from the pledgee a proxy to vote upon the stock upon payment of the necessary expenses thereof. It would seem, therefore, that in the State of New York, the pledgor may vote the stock whilst it remains in his name, but the Stock-broker may, if he has transferred the stock to himself, vote upon the stock, subject to the summary power of the Supreme Court (under § 27), and to the general equitable powers of that court to set aside the election, and also to the right of the pledgor to demand a proxy.

In Massachusetts it is provided by statute that a certificate of stock issued as a pledge shall state that fact in the body of the certificate, and it has been held that in such case the pledgor may vote upon the stock, but in other cases the corporation need not accept the vote of the pledgor, although the pledgee may be compelled in equity to give a proxy.[1]

The statutes of some of the States provide that the pledgor may vote his stock.[2] And it may be stated as a general proposition that equity will intervene to protect the right of the pledgor.[3]

---

[1] Wentworth Co. vs. French, 176 Mass. 442.

[2] See as to Colorado, National Bank of Commerce vs. Allen, 90 Fed. Rep. 545; Miller vs. Murray, 17 Col. 408. As to Rhode Island, see Sayles vs. Brown, 40 Fed. Rep. 8.

[3] Where shares of stock are pledged as collateral, the pledgee reserving the right to sell in case of default, and the pledgee causes a transfer to himself to be recorded on the books of the corporation, until the pledgor's rights shall have been foreclosed by a sale, etc., the pledgor and not the pledgee is entitled to vote on the stock in the absence of a statute providing otherwise. State ex rel. Reed vs. Smith, 15 Ore. 98; 15 Pac. Rep. 386; 36 Alb. L. J. 486. See also McHenry vs. Jewett, N. Y. *Daily Reg.* Oct. 19, 1881; aff'd 26 Hun, 453; s. c. 90 N. Y. 58.

Another important question should be alluded to in this connection, viz., as to the use which the Broker may make of securities held by him on margin.

Although in law these securities are regarded as the Client's, the Broker's money has paid for them. Can the latter, therefore, use the same in his business? Can he hypothecate them? Both reason and the precedents hereinafter alluded to seem to require these questions to be answered affirmatively. In the case of an ordinary pledge of personal property, the general rule seems to be, that the

It is undisputed, as said by Judge Barrett in McHenry vs. Jewett, supra, that the corporation can only look to its transfer books in determining who is entitled to vote (see cases cited In re Argus Printing Co., 12 L. R. A. 781). The pledgee after a transfer to him on the books has the legal right to vote and the rights of the pledgor are then solely in equity, and he may in a proper case compel the pledgee by bill in equity, to give him a proxy or perhaps such a transfer of the stock as would allow him to vote upon it. Scholfield vs. Union Bk., 2 Cranch C. C. 115; Vowell vs. Thompson, 3 id. 428; Hoppin vs. Buffum, 9 R. I. 513; In re Argus Printing Co., 12 L. R. A. 781, citing other cases to same effect. But equity will not interfere with the result of an election, when the pledgor has slept on his rights for years. Hoppin vs. Buffum, supra. At common law there is no right in a shareholder to vote by proxy, independently of the contract between the shareholders, and the form prescribed in the articles of association must be strictly complied with or the proxies will be a nullity; and in Harben vs. Phillips, 48 L. T. Rep. 334, they were held to be null, because not "attested by one or more witnesses."

As to rights of stockholders when the right to vote is given by pledgor and pledgee to third parties, see Shelmerdine vs. Walsh, 20 Phila. Rep. 199. If the pledgee, however, votes, he is not guilty of conversion. Heath vs. Silverthorn Lead Co., 39 Wis. 146. See also In re St. Lawrence Steamboat Co., 44 N. J. L. 529, 540; Allen vs. Hill, 16 Cal. 113; Re Argus Printing Co., 1 N. D. 434; McDaniels vs. Flower Co., 22 Vt. 274; Ayer vs. Seymour, 5 N. Y. Supp. 650; Spreckels vs. Nevada Bank, 113 Cal. 272; Schouler on Bailments, 3d ed. § 216; Edwards on Bailments, 3d ed. § 219. But see Com. vs. Dalzell, 152 Pa. St. 217; Hinckley vs. Pfister, 83 Wis. 64. The pledgor may demand a proxy to vote the stock if his right to do so is protected by special agreement. Pennsylvania R. R. Co. vs. Pennsylvania Co., 54 Atl. (Pa.) 783.

pledgee has the right to use the pledged property, unless prohibited either by the nature of the thing pledged or by agreement,[1] the pledgee accounting to the pledgor for the benefits or profits less the amount properly expended in the use of the thing.[2]

The authorities, however, do not all accord upon this subject; but whatever doubt there may be in relation to other kinds of personal property, it seems to be clear that, in case of stock purchased on margin by a Stock-broker, the latter would have the right to use it in his business. And this follows from the peculiar nature of the stock, and from the circumstances attending an ordinary speculative transaction in the same.

In the first place, a Stock-broker, when he makes a purchase of stocks on the order of his Client, receives the same directiy from the selling Brokers in the shape of a certificate with a blank assignment and irrevocable power of attorney authorizing its transfer on the books of the particular company, and the stock generally does not pass through the hands of the Client at all. By advancing the purchase-money for the stocks, the law gives the Broker a lien for the same, and establishes the relation of pledgor and pledgee.

In the second place, the money which the Broker advances is a part of his capital, upon which he relies to carry on his business ; accordingly, he is compelled to use the stocks of his Client to borrow money upon, which he does from banks or capitalists, and he is thus enabled to get back the whole or some part of the money originally invested, with which he continues to transact his business.

---

[1] Schouler on Bailments, 3d ed.   [2] Id.
§ 211; Levy vs. Loeb, 85 N. Y 370.

If it were held that the Broker was bound to keep on hand the identical stock purchased for a Client, and that he could make no other use or disposition of the same, it is apparent that his business would be stopped, for no private fortune would be adequate to make many purchases.[1]

None of the questions which arise out of a pledge of ordinary personal property, capable of being handled and of manual delivery, can apply to a pledge of stock. The latter cannot be handled or worn or used ; it is nothing but an incorporeal right, and the certificate merely represents the interest which the owner has in the whole capital—the right to share in the profits and property when they are divided.

Nor is this question affected by the rule applied in the case of Langton vs. Waite,[2] where the plaintiff borrowed from the defendants, who were Stock-brokers, a certain sum of money, and deposited with them certain railway stock, which the defendants subsequently sold, and, repurchasing the same at a lower price, delivered the latter stock to the plaintiff upon the payment of his loan.

In that case it did not appear that the defendants kept on hand a sufficient or any quantity of the stock of the kind deposited with them by the plaintiff ; and the court, in accordance with the rule laid down in the American cases hereafter referred to,[3] charged the defendants with the price at which they sold the same.

The doctrine may be asserted as well settled, that a

[1] See Price vs. Gover, 40 Md. 115. In Skiff vs. Stoddard, 21 L. R. A. 102, 112, it was held that although the right to repledge did not exist at common law, it was sanctioned by the usage of the Stock Exchange even to the extent that the securities might be pledged en bloc with those of other customers.

[2] 6 L. R. Eq. 165.

[3] Post, p. 255.

Broker holding stocks for his Client on margin for speculation is not bound to keep on hand the identical shares purchased ; but he answers all of the duties of his employment,
by having ready for delivery to his Client shares of the
same description and amount.   Shares of stock have no ear-
mark ; and one share being of equal value with every other
share of the same stock, the Brokers are not bound to deliver, or to have on hand for delivery, any particular shares,
or the identical shares purchased, for a Client.

This principle was first laid down in the State of New York
in the year 1820 by Chancellor Kent, in the well-known case
of Nourse vs. Prime.[1]   In that case the defendants, who were
Stock-brokers, had purchased various shares of United States
bank stock for the plaintiff, and rendered him an account
thereof, by which it appeared that the latter was indebted to
defendants in a large sum of money, for which he gave his
promissory note, the defendants retaining the shares as collateral security, and giving therefor to the plaintiff the following
receipt : " We acknowledge to hold 430 shares of the stock of
the United States Bank as collateral security for the payment
of the said note, dated the 24th of December last, for $54,200,
payable on the 10th of January next, with interest at 7 per
cent, etc.; on the payment of which note and interest we
engage to retransfer the said 430 shares to the said C. J. N.
or his order, accounting with him for the dividends that
shall become payable on the same ; and in case the note
and interest are not duly paid, we are at liberty to make an
immediate sale of the said shares, accounting with him for
any surplus, and holding him responsible for any deficiency.
Dated New York, 11th Feb., 1818."   Upon a bill in Chan-

---

[1] 4 Johns. Ch. 490, and 7 id. 69.

cery to restrain the defendants from proceeding with a suit
at common-law on the note, and to compel defendants to
account to the plaintiff for the highest market price at which
the defendants had sold any United States Bank stock inter-
mediately, the Chancellor held—treating the question as an
original one, to be decided upon general principles—that, as
the plaintiff dealt with the defendants in their character as
Stock-brokers, and the shares in question were not defined
and designated so as to be distinguishable from other shares
in the same bank, under the receipt in question the defendants had performed their whole duty in the premises by
having on hand or under their control shares to the amount
in question, which they were ready, able, and willing to
account to the plaintiff for; and that, in the absence of express stipulation, they were not bound to hold the identical
shares purchased for plaintiff or referred to in the receipt.
This case again came before the court upon the pleadings
and proof, the former opinion having been delivered by the
Chancellor in dissolving an injunction, and the opinion previously given was fully endorsed ; and it was expressly decided that, considering the established usage of Brokers in
similar cases, there was an implied authority from the plaintiff to the defendants to sell or pledge the stock to raise
money to meet their advances in respect to the transaction
with the plaintiff, and that the plaintiff only reserved to
himself a right to call for a retransfer to him of a similar
number of shares on payment of his note.

The case of Nourse vs. Prime was cited by the Supreme
Court of Pennsylvania, in the year 1846, in Gilpin vs.
Howell,[1] and the principle there laid down fully confirmed.

[1] 5 Pa. St. 41.

Again, in 1859, the New York Court of appeals, in Horton vs. Morgan,[1] said : "The plaintiff had no interest in having his shares kept separate from the mass of the defendant's stock. One share was precisely equal in value to every other share."[2]

The same doctrine was laid down in England early in the reign of George the First (1722) by the Court of Chancery, in the case of Le Croy vs. Eastman.[3] In that case plaintiff bought £990 of South Sea stock of one Le G. ; but, not caring to have this stock in his own name, it was, at his desire, transferred to the defendant, from whom the plaintiff took

---

[1] 19 N. Y. 170.

[2] See also, confirming the above proposition, Markham vs. Jaudon, 41 N. Y. 235; Horton vs. Morgan, 19 N. Y. 170; Genin vs. Isaacson, 6 N. Y. *Legal Obs.* 213; Saltus vs. Genin, 7 Ab. Pr. (N. Y.) 193; s. c. 3 Bosw. 250; Stewart vs. Drake, 46 N. Y. 449; Levy vs. Loeb, 85 N. Y. 365, applying the rule to government bonds; Lawrence vs. Maxwell, 58 Barb. 511; 6 Lans. 469; 53 N. Y. 19; Taussig vs. Hart, 58 N. Y. 425; Rogers vs. Gould, 6 Hun (N. Y.), 229; Barclay vs. Culver, 30 Hun, 1; Thompson vs. Toland, 48 Cal. 100; Marston vs. Gould, 69 N. Y. 220, at p. 226; Chamberlin vs. Greenleaf, 4 Ab. New Cas. (N. Y.) 178; Capron vs. Thompson, 86 N. Y. 418; Caswell vs. Putnam, 120 N. Y. 153; Mayo vs. Knowlton, 134 N. Y. 250; Smith vs. New York Stock and Produce Clearing House, 25 N. Y. Supp. 261, 263. Applying the rule to "discretionary" transactions. Harding vs. Field, 1 App. Div. 391; Douglas vs. Carpenter, 45 N. Y.

Supp. 219; Baker vs. Drake, 66 N. Y. 522; Gruman vs. Smith, 81 N. Y. 28; Boylan vs. Huguet, 8 Nev. 345; Hubbell vs. Drexel, 11 Fed. Rep. 115; Haynard vs. Rogers, 62 Cal. 348; Skiff vs. Stoddard, 63 Conn. 198; 21 L. R. A. 102, overruling Ingraham vs. Taylor, 58 Conn. 503; Rothschild vs. Allen, 86 N. Y. S. 42. See also Wynkoop vs. Seal, 64 Pa. St. 361; Wood vs. Hayes, 81 Mass. 375; Atkins vs. Gamble, 42 Cal. 86; Hawley vs. Brumagim, 33 Cal. 394; Le Croy vs. Eastman, 10 Mod. 499; Mocatta vs. Bell, 27 L. J. Ch. 237; Berlin vs. Eddy, 33 Mo. 426; Price vs. Gover, 40 Md. 102; Worthington vs. Tormey, 34 Md. 193. See also, upon this head, Clarke vs. Meigs, 13 Ab. Pr. (N. Y.) 467; 22 How. Pr. (N. Y.) 340, rev'g 12 Ab. Pr. 267, and 21 How. Pr. 187; Also Taylor vs. Ketchum, 5 Robertson (N. Y.), 507; s. c. 35 How. Pr. (N. Y.) 289, overruled by the above cases.

[3] 10 Mod. 499.

a note, declaring that he was a trustee of this stock for the plaintiff, and that he would be accountable to him for the stock and produce. Afterwards, when the stock sold at about 600 per cent, the plaintiff desired that the defendant would transfer the £990 of stock to him; the defendant accordingly transferred £500 of this stock, and informed the plaintiff that it would be inconvenient to him, at that time, to transfer more, but that it was all one, for he would be accountable for the stock. Subsequently the stock fell, and the plaintiff brought a bill against the defendant, praying that he might account for the £490 stock at the price the stock was at the time he requested defendant to deliver the same—viz., at £600, insisting that the defendant, by agreeing to be accountable, had assumed to pay at the price it then was. There was no question of conversion in the case. The defendant had, for some time after he became trustee as above, £1,000 of the stock, which he had mortgaged, and he afterwards sold all the stock he had in his own name, except £80; but he had more than stock enough in another person's name to have answered the trust, if the plaintiff had insisted upon a transfer, and he offered to transfer the £490 stock and produce. Parker, Lord Chancellor, held that it was not material at what the defendant sold the stock, for the sale was at his own risk. If the stock had risen, he would still have been accountable for the same; and, therefore, as he must have stood to the loss in case of the rise, it was reasonable that he should reap the advantage of a fall.

The Lord Chancellor said: " I take it to be very plain that the defendant has not sold, but mortgaged, the trust stock. *For since there is no specificating £100 South Sea stock from another*, ... therefore the stock mortgaged must be esteemed the stock of the plaintiff, the stock sold that of the defendant. The defendant must only account for the stock and produce."

So it is within the scope of the implied authority of a member of a Stock Exchange, when securities are deposited with him for the purpose of his advancing money upon them, to pledge those securities to some other person for that purpose.[1]

But, where a Client delivers a specified quantity of stock to a Stock-broker for sale, and the Broker transfers part of the same to a third person, and part to himself, the Client can treat this as a sale of his stock; and it is no defence, that it is a custom among Brokers to place the stock sent them for sale to their own names on the books of the company, and, in making transfers, to do so indiscriminately, without regard to the person from whom the stock was received, or for whose account the same was sold. A Broker, in such a case, has no right to pledge or do anything else with the stock except to sell it.[2]

And the Broker must at all times have on hand stock sufficient in quantity to deliver the same to his Client upon the payment by the latter of the amount due thereon. The most he can claim is that, so long as he has on hand shares similar in kind, etc., to those he has purchased for his Client, he has performed his contract; but when he denudes himself of the quantity sufficient to answer his Client's demands, he is guilty of a conversion, and the latter may assume that the sale by which the Broker dispossessed himself of the stock was made for his benefit, and re-

---

[1] Mocatta vs. Bell, 27 L. J. Ch. 237.   [2] Parsons vs. Martin, 77 Mass. 111.

17

cover the price of the shares on the day the sale was made.[1]

The language of the New York Court of Appeals, in the case of Taussig vs. Hart,[2] is interesting upon this question : "The subsequent acquisition, by the plaintiffs after the stock had fallen to a very low figure, of a sufficient number of shares to replace those which they had held for account of the defendant, did not relieve them from liability. Such re-acquired stock was never accepted by the defendant, and he was, in fact, ignorant of the transactions. To allow a Broker to sell his customer's stock without authority, and speculate upon it, replacing it at a lower price, would be encouraging speculations by agents at the risk of their principals, and is totally inadmissible under familiar rules. Should the stock rise largely in price, after the Broker had thus divested himself of all control over the shares which he had purchased on the order of his principal, the Broker might be unable to replace the shares, and the principal

---

[1] See, as to this point, Langton vs. Waite, 6 L. R. Eq. 165, and cases cited supra. Whether a custom of the market which authorizes a pledgee in a margin buying transaction, temporarily, to effect short sales, to reduce his carrying of any stock, below the amount required to meet the demands of all his customers, will be sanctioned, quære. Skiff vs. Stoddard, 63 Conn. 198. If the Broker mingles his client's securities with those of other customers and pledges the entire for an amount greater than the indebtedness of his Client, he is liable for conversion, if he does not keep in his possession other securities of a like kind and amount. Douglas vs. Carpenter, 17 App. Div. 329. See this case criticized by Mr. Eliot Norton in an article on "The right to pledge securities carried on a margin," in "The American Lawyer," vol. 5, p. 573, in which he says that if the decision is strictly followed by Stock-brokers it will be difficult for them to do their business conveniently, or, in some cases, not at all, and recommends that the consent of the customer should be obtained to this method of doing business. See also Conwell vs. Harris, N. Y. L. J. March 17, 1897.

[2] 58 N. Y. 425.

would have no remedy except a personal claim against the Broker. This, clearly, is not what is contemplated under an agreement to buy and carry stocks. The customer does not rely upon an engagement of the Broker to procure and furnish the shares when required, but upon his actually purchasing and holding the number of shares ordered, subject only to the payment of the purchase price." [1]

So it has been held in England that where money was borrowed from a Stock-broker for a certain period, and railway stocks deposited with him as collateral for its repayment, the Stock-broker was not justified, either in law or by the custom of the Stock Exchange, in parting with the

[1] To same effect, Lawrence vs. Maxwell, 53 N. Y. 19, where the stock had been hypothecated. Here the court said: "Conceding the right to use the stocks pledged by way of hypothecation or otherwise, as claimed, and that it was at the time of the tender and demand lawfully out of the actual possession of the defendant, it was his duty at once to regain the possession and restore the same to the plaintiff. . . . It is immaterial whether the stock was hypothecated by the defendant upon a loan of money for the benefit of the plaintiff's transactions or for his own purposes." The doctrine of Lawrence vs. Maxwell, 53 N. Y. 19, is followed by the United States Circuit Court in Oregon & Transcontinental Co. vs. Hilmers, 20 Fed. Rep. 717, where it was held that when the owner of securities pledges them to a Stock-broker as collateral to a loan, the latter has no right to rehypothecate them in such a way that they can-not be restored to the owner upon payment of the loan, although both parties understood that the Broker would have to use the securities to obtain the loan. So held also in Van Voorhis vs. Rea, 153 Pa. St. 19; Cass vs. Higenbotam, 100 N. Y. 248; N. Y. L. E. & W. R. Co. vs. Davies, 38 Hun, 477; Muller vs. Legerdre, 47 La. Ann. 1017. See also as to right of pledgee to part with stock, under a written instrument conferring general authority to use, etc., Ogden vs. Lathrop, 65 N. Y. 158. See also, in same connection, Dykers vs. Allen, 3 Hill (N. Y.), 593, aff'd by Court of Errors, 7 id. 497. But parol evidence in the case of a pledge of stock, that the pledgee may use the same, is not admissible, where a written instrument has been given by the pledgee, in which he states that he holds it as collateral security, and may sell "on one day's notice." Fay vs. Gray, 124 Mass. 500.

security during the pendency of the loan, but was bound
to return the identical stock pledged; and that the person
to whom the loan was made was entitled to recover from
the Broker the amount of profits realized by the dealings
in his stocks by the latter.[1] The court said that "in the
absence of express contract, the pawnee of property cannot sell it until the debt for which it is pledged becomes payable; and if he does so, the owner has the
right to charge the pawnee with the price he gets for the
property if he finds it to his interest to do so." The
court also, while finding that there was, in fact, no custom
of the Stock Exchange which varied the rule above laid
down, declared that such a custom would be manifestly
unjust; the borrower would be completely at the mercy of
the lender, who might convert the security and appropriate
the proceeds to his own use, and at the expiration of the
period of the loan be wholly unable to return to the borrower what belonged to him.[2]

But the owner of stocks pledged as collateral for the
repayment of borrowed money may deprive himself of
any remedy by dealing with the property when retransferred
to him[3] on repayment of the loan.

As incident to the Broker's rights in stock carried on

[1] Langton vs. Waite, L. R. 6 Eq.
165.

[2] See also Ex parte Phillips, Ex
parte Marnham, 30 L. J. Bk. 1; 2
De G. F. & J. 634; Phené vs. Gillan,
5 Hare, 1; Allen vs. Dubois, 75 N.
W. 443; 1 Story's Eq. Jur. 714,
note 1. A sheriff having an execution against the pledgor may take
the property from the pledgee and
sell the same on such execution, but
after the sale the property should be
returned to the pledgee to be redeemed by the purchaser. Stief vs.
Hart, 1 N. Y. 20. As to general
duties of pledgee when promissory
notes and stocks are pledged as
collateral security, see article, 17
Western Jurist, Jan. 1883, p. 1.

[3] See Langton vs. Waite, L. R. 4
Ch. App. 402.

margin there would seem to be no good reason in law why he should not have the right—possessing as he does the power to dispose of the securities—to maintain an action for their recovery against any person wrongfully holding the same, notwithstanding the technical ownership of them is in his Clients.

But the rule that the Broker is not bound to keep on hand the identical stock or bonds purchased only applies in the absence of agreement. Where the parties agree that the original bonds shall be carried, the Broker must keep them on hand in the identical shape in which they were purchased. And where the Broker sells or disposes of the bonds in breach of such an agreement, he cannot recover from his Clients any loss arising upon a sale of other bonds substituted for the original, although the Broker shows that he had constantly on hand during the relation other bonds sufficient to meet the demands of his Clients.[1] Before a Broker can recover in such a case, he must show that he has performed substantially all the conditions precedent which are embraced in the contract.[2]

These questions arose in the case of Levy vs. Loeb.[3] There the defendants, bankers and Brokers, bought for account of the plaintiff certain bonds of the United States upon an agreement that the defendants were to advance the purchase price in the form of a loan, upon which interest at the rate of four per cent was to be allowed, the bonds meanwhile being held as collateral to the loan, but to be carried by the defendants, for plaintiff's account. The bonds were accordingly purchased by the defendants, but

[1] Levy vs. Loeb, 85 N. Y. 365.   tion, Hardy vs. Jaudon, 1 Robt.
[2] Id.   261, aff'd 21 N. Y. 619.
[3] Supra.   See also, in this connec-

were charged to the plaintiff at a higher price than the amount paid for them, and other improper items were also included in the price. Plaintiff made a payment on account of these purchases of over $10,000, in consideration of which defendants agreed to carry the bonds purchased for a certain period, which was afterwards extended. Before the maturity of the loan, and while the contract to carry was in force, the defendants for their own account, without the knowledge and consent of the plaintiff, sold the whole lot of original bonds. At the maturity of the loan the plaintiff was called upon to pay the alleged indebtedness, or be sold out—the amount demanded including the excess charged over the actual cost. Upon refusing, the defendants sold other and substituted bonds, and this " vicarious " sale demonstrated a large deficiency ; whereupon the plaintiff brought an action to repudiate the alleged purchase and to recover the money paid upon it. The defendants set up a counterclaim for the deficiency. The Special Term disallowed the counterclaim and directed judgment for plaintiff for $713.77, the amount of the illegal charges made by defendants. Plaintiffs appealed from that portion of the judgment which disallowed them the $10,000 paid by them. Defendants appealed from that portion of the judgment which disallowed their counterclaim. In the Court of Appeals, on the hearing of defendants' appeal, the counterclaim of defendants was rejected upon the grounds before stated. This case came before the Court of Appeals for a second time on plaintiff's appeal and the principles first laid down were reiterated, and the plaintiff was further held to be entitled to recover back the money paid by plaintiff in consideration that defendant's bankers would carry the bonds for plaintiff, for a limited time, and which the defendants failed to do.[1] It does not appear from the reports whether defendants on the first sale of the bonds (i. e., that before the time limited for carrying them had been reached) sold them at a profit or a loss. But even if they had sold them at a loss, it is difficult to see how they could have recovered such loss, or that the plaintiffs would not be entitled to repudiate the contract. The court (per Miller, J.), on the hearing of the second appeal, said : " Looking at the transaction in the light most favorable for defendants, they stood in the position of vendors. Where the vendor of property, who has received a portion of the purchase-price, on agreement to hold and deliver the property to the vendee on payment of the balance, without notice to the vendee disposes of the same, he may be treated as wrongly rescinding the contract on his part, and the vendee may maintain an action to recover the money paid in part performance of such contract." The court also distinguished the case from Capron vs. Thompson,[2] and Gruman vs. Smith,[3] wherein it was held that the unauthorized sale by a Broker of stock purchased and carried on a margin was not a breach of a condition precedent which prevented the Broker from charging for the money paid by him for stock, although he was liable in damages for the unauthorized sale. In the case under review there was a breach of a condition precedent, viz., an agreement to carry the bonds for a stipulated time, and the failure of defendants so to do operated as a rescission of the contract, rendering them liable to refund the money paid by plain-

[1] Levy vs. Loeb, 89 N. Y. 386. [3] 81 N. Y. 25.
[2] 86 N. Y. 418.

tiffs.   And if there be two different kinds of stock of the
corporation, a pledgee must restore the same kind originally
pledged with him.   Accordingly, a pledge of fifty shares
of " consolidated " Erie stock, cannot be restored or made
good to the pledgor by assigning to him the same number
of shares of " converted " stock.   The pledgees are at least
bound to restore stock of the identical kind pledged.[1]

The Broker need not keep the property of his principal
unmixed with his own or the property of other principals.
But where such intermingling takes place and dispute
arises, the Client is entitled to the most favorable presumption that can be drawn from the evidence.[2]

(d.)   *Dividends, Profits, Assessments, Calls, Interest.*

As a consequence of the declaration of the law that the
stock as soon as it is purchased becomes the property of the
Client,[3] it follows that all of the benefits in the way of ac-

---

[1] Wilson vs. Little, 2 N. Y. 443,
449.   The pledgee meets this requirement if he restores stock in the
same company, equivalent in value
to and representing the stock
pledged.   Thus where a corporation, by legislative authority and
for the purpose of re-organization,
reduced its capital stock and so
proportionally reduced the nominal
value of each share, it was held that
the surrender by the pledgee of the
pledged certificate of old stock and
the acceptance of a certificate for
the same number of shares of the
new stock was not a conversion.
The new certificate represented the
same proportional share in the
company's assets as did the pledged

certificate and was its exact equal in
value.   Donnell vs. Wyckoff, 49 N.
J. L. 48.

[2] Harding vs. Field, 1 App. Div.
391; Bate vs. McDowell, 17 J. & S.
106; Gray vs. Haig, 20 Beav. 219.

[3] Gruman vs. Smith, 81 N. Y. 25;
rev'g 12 J. & S. 389, and cases cited,
ante, p. 192.   The legal title to the
stock pledged remains in the pledg-
or, the pledgee having the right to
retain them until the debt is discharged, and while so holding them
he cannot claim adversely and thus
obtain a title under the statute of
limitations.   Cross vs. Eureka Lake
Canal Co., 73 Cal. 302.   See also
Boyd vs. Conshohocken Mills, 24
Atl. Rep. 287.

cretions, interest, dividends, or profits which result there-from belong to the latter.[1]

Under this rule, all profits or benefits of any description which the Stock-broker may derive from the loan or use of his Client's securities would, in the absence of agreement, belong to the latter.

But the Broker as pledgee of securities has the right to collect the dividends or interest thereon,[2] it being reasoned that any increase of the pledged property is likewise pledged.[3]

The securities also are in his possession and he has, as we have seen,[4] a right to have them transferred into his name upon the books of the company.

He has, however, no right to apply the proceeds of the pledged property to the re-payment of his advances, until after default in its payment.[5]

If, therefore, a pledgor of stock receives the dividends from the company, an action lies by the pledgee against him to recover the same.[6] And in the case of the Andros-coggin Railroad Company vs. Auburn Bank[7] the court held that where a bond with interest coupons attached was the subject of the pledge, there was an implied authority in the pledgee to collect the interest thereon.

On the other hand, the Client is subjected to all of the

---

[1] Markham vs. Jaudon, 41 N. Y. 235; Briggs vs. Kennett, 28 N. Y. Supp. 740; see also Gates vs. Halliday (Mo. Ct. of App.), 1 Am. Law Review (n. s.), 172, as to right of pledgee to receive dividends. See further as to dividends, post, Ch. IV. The same rule is applicable to a pledge—viz., that all the profits, etc., belong to the pledgor (Schouler on Bailm. 3d ed. § 212).

[2] Gates vs. Halliday, supra; Androscoggin Railroad Co. vs. Auburn Bank, 48 Me. 335; Husbrook vs. Vandervoort, 4 Sand. 74.

[3] Herrman vs. Maxwell, 47 N. Y. Super. Ct. 347.

[4] Ante, p. 245.

[5] Farwell vs. Importer's, etc., Nat. Bk., 90 N. Y. 483.

[6] Gates vs. Halliday, supra.

[7] Supra.

responsibilities of pure and absolute ownership; and he is liable, and not the Broker, for all assessments or calls of any kind made upon the stock while he is the owner thereof, although the Broker may have paid them, in the first instance, by reason of the stock being transferred on the books into his own name, in accordance with the usages of the business.[1] The general rule being that a pledgee of stock who has transferred the same on the books of the company is subject to all of the liabilities of a stockholder,[2] except where statutes have provided, as in New York, § 16 of the General Manufacturing Act (1848), of which State provides that no person holding stock as executor, administrator, guardian, or trustee, or as collateral security, shall be personally subject to any liability as stockholder of such company.[3] In Robins vs. Edwards,[4] where it appeared that a Broker, at the request of his principal, continued shares in his own name, the Master of the Rolls ordered the principal to repay to his Broker a call which he had paid, and to procure, as far as possible, that the shares should be registered in his own name.[5]

Another element of the transaction should be here noticed. The selling Broker is bound to deliver, upon receiving from

[1] McCalla vs. Clark, 55 Ga. 53; Marshall vs. Levy, 66 Cal. 236; Whitney vs. Page, 1 How. Pr. (n. s.) 389.

[2] National Bank vs. Case, 99 U. S. 628; Pullman vs. Upton, 96 id. 328; Wheelock vs. Kost, 77 Ill. 296; In re Empire City Bank, 18 N. Y. 199; Holyoke vs. Burham, 11 Cush. 183.

[3] This act was repealed by the General Corporation Law, and its provisions have been re-enacted in § 54 of the Stock Corporation Law,

with the additional provision that if the executor, administrator, guardian or trustee voluntarily invested the trust funds in such stocks he shall be personally liable as a stockholder.

[4] 15 W. R. 1065.

[5] To same effect, Taylor vs. Stray, 2 C. B. (n. s.) 175; Chapman vs. Shepard, L. R. 2 C. P. 228; Whitehead vs. Izod, id.; Emmerson's case, L. R. 1 Ch. App. 433.

the purchasing Broker the price agreed upon, a certificate of stock (if stock be the subject of the sale) for the number of shares purchased. This certificate must be in every respect proper and legal. It must be issued by the company, or its authorized officers or agents, and must show, on its face, that the person therein mentioned is entitled to so many shares in the capital stock of the corporation. Usually certificates of stock have forms of assignment endorsed on them, together with irrevocable powers of attorney, authorizing the officers of the corporation to transfer upon the books of the company the number of shares represented in the certificate to the person therein named. It is the duty of the selling Broker to procure this assignment to be duly executed by the person named in this certificate, as the sale would not be complete without it, although there might arise a case where this rule would not prevail.[1]

Upon the point as to what a Broker of a vendor sells on the Stock Exchange, the remarks of Lord Campbell, C. J., in Stray vs. Russell[2] are pertinent: " According to these usages, the price of the shares is payable on the one Broker handing over to the other the transfers and certificates. *What does the vendor contract to sell and deliver ? Genuine*

---

[1] See as to duty of selling Broker, on London Stock Exchange, Ch. X.

[2] 1 El. & E. 888, at p. 900. Where a Note-broker sold a note to another Note-broker without knowledge of the latter that it was worthless, and he is compelled to take it back from his principal, the buying Broker is entitled to recover the amount paid to the selling Broker therefor. Stewart vs. Orvis, 17 How. Pr. 518. And where a Stock-broker had sold upon the order of A to plaintiffs, railway debentures belonging to A, B, and C, A having forged the signatures of B and C to the transfer, the plaintiffs were entitled to recover the sums paid by them for the debentures with interest, they having been compelled by suit in equity to restore the debentures and interest to B and C. Royal Ex. Assn. Co. vs. Moore, 8 L. T. N.. S. 242.

transfers and certificates, with the interest and rights which they convey. There might be a condition subsequent, imposing upon the vendor the onus of procuring the consent · of the directors to the transfer, but I find no evidence of such a condition."[1] And the point was directly passed upon in the last-named case,[2] that the selling Broker is not bound to procure a transfer or registration on the books of the company.

In practice, generally, this assignment is executed in blank by the person in whose name the shares stand on the books of the company, leaving the purchaser to fill in any name and to effect the transfer upon the books, if he so desire it.

Frequently, however, a certificate of stock, with the power of attorney executed in blank attached thereto, is passed from hand to hand, and is used in several different transactions before there is an actual transfer of the shares on the books of the company. But, by executing the certificate to the purchaser as between the latter and the seller, the purchaser becomes the owner of the shares.[3] Although, until the same is transferred on the books of the company, the seller is liable for any "calls" or assessments.[4] So a person is liable to the company for the amount of his subscription, although after calls were made,

---

[1] See also, to same effect, Taylor vs. Stray, 2 C. B. (n. s.) 175; aff'd in Exch. Chamber, id. 197.

[2] Supra.

[3] Lindley on Company Law (5th ed.), 505 et seq; Shellington vs. Howland, 53 N. Y. 372.

[4] Id.; Magruder vs. Colston, 44 Md. 349; Johnson vs. Underhill, 52 N. Y. 203. Yet where there has been no transfer on the books, and

the charter does not require entry on the books, the corporation may recognize a purchaser as a stockholder in such a way as to preclude it from demanding assessments or calls from the seller, as by paying the dividends to the purchaser. Cutting vs. Damarel, 88 N. Y. 410. See also Loring vs. Davis, 32 Ch. Div. 625.

and before they were payable, he assigned his stock to a responsible party.[1] And if the purchaser does not procure the transfer upon the books of the company, and, in consequence, the seller is made liable for assessments or calls, the purchaser is bound to indemnify the seller in respect thereto, and from all liability accruing to the shares since the time they were sold.[2] On the other hand, the purchaser can compel the seller to execute a proper transfer, and to account for all dividends received by him since he ceased to be the equitable owner of the shares.[3]

In the United States this question of transferring stock upon the books of the company has not received the attention which it has in England, because in the latter country, where most commercial corporations are organized by the payment of only a limited amount of the fixed capital, calls can be, and are generally, made upon the stockholders of record, and if the registration of the shares is not attended to, the shareholder of record may be compelled to pay the same, although he may have long since parted with his stock. The rule is the same in this respect in the United States.[4] But with us, corporations have either paid up

[1] Schenectady R. R. Co. vs. Thatcher, 11 N. Y. 102.

[2] 1 Lindley on Company Law (5th ed.), 492, 505. If a Broker is the purchaser and he does not disclose his principal, the former is, under the general law of agency, bound to indemnify the seller against the payment of calls. Lichten vs. Verner, 8 Pa. Dist. Rep. 218. As to the effect of the company's insolvency, see Crabb vs. Miller, 24 L. T. 219; Bowring vs. Shepherd, L.

R. 6 Q. B. 323; Neilson vs. James, 9 Q. B. D. 553.

[3] 1 Lindley on Company Law 490. To constitute a person a stockholder and as such liable to creditors of the corporation, it is not necessary that a certificate should be issued to him, or payments made by him. A subscription for stock and a recognition of him by the company as a stockholder are sufficient. Wheeler vs. Miller, 90 N. Y. 353.

[4] Shellington vs. Howland, supra.

their capital in cash, or its equivalent, pursuant to statutory enactment, and the stockholders are not generally liable for future calls. But the increasing number of corporations, and the frequent evasions of the requirements of the statutes authorizing the issuance of the entire capital for property by placing a fraudulently extravagant value thereon, may, and doubtless will, render the question of calls or assessments, and the necessity of seeing that a transfer or registration is made upon the books of the company when a sale is made, as important and essential as it is in England.[1]

In respect to the liability of the Client to pay interest, it is a well-understood rule of Stock-brokers to charge him legal interest upon the amount advanced by the Broker in the purchase of the stock ; it is also the usage of the Brokers to charge the Client with an extra interest which the Broker is compelled to pay for carrying the stocks of the former caused by a stringency of the money market.

---

[1] For the subject of the liability for calls in England, see post, Ch. X. Where shares in a bridge company were issued as paid-up shares, which were not fully paid up, the transaction, though a fraud in law upon the creditors of the company, was made apparently in good faith by the company, and on its face was formal and regular, the shares appearing on the books as paid, and nothing appearing to apprise a purchaser that such was not the fact; a purchaser to whom the shares had been transferred without notice was not required to suspect fraud or institute inquiries where all seemed to be lawful and regular; and if he paid full value for the shares as paid up, he is not liable to the creditors of the corporation under the statute for the amount actually unpaid on the shares. In order that the shares should be regarded as paid-up shares in the hands of an innocent purchaser, it is enough that they were in the usual form; it is not necessary that they should express upon their face that they were fully paid. Keystone Bridge Co. vs. Mc-Cluney, Mo. Ct. of App., decided March 30, 1880; 1 Am. L. Rev. 395. As to when a transferee is liable under an implied promise to pay call, see Sigua Iron Co. vs. Brown, 171 N. Y. 488.

Both of these usages are reasonable, and it does not seem to be difficult to sustain them by authorities.

Thus it has been held that an agreement for interest may be inferred from the course of dealing between the parties; as where interest has before been charged and allowed under the like circumstances.[1] Also, when the creditor has a uniform practice of charging interest, which was known to the debtor at the time of the dealing. And where there is a general usage in any particular trade or branch of business to charge and allow interest, parties having knowledge of the usage are presumed to contract in reference to it; and if the usage does not conflict with the terms of the contract, it will be deemed to enter into and constitute a part of it. Knowledge of the usage may be established by presumptive as well as by direct evidence. It may be presumed from the fact that both parties are engaged in the particular trade or branch of business to which the usage relates, and also from other facts, as the uniformity, long continuance, and notoriety of the usage.[2]

In the case of Robinson vs. Norris[3] the question of the liability of a Client to pay interest which the Broker had been compelled to pay, beyond the rate established by law, was raised and indirectly sustained. There a Broker, authorized by his principal to borrow money in order to carry stocks for him, rendered an account to the latter by which it appeared that in borrowing money he had been compelled to pay to other persons, as commissions, sums

---

[1] Easterly vs. Cole, 3 N. Y. 503. Godby, 4 Taunt. 346; Eaton vs.
[2] Id.; Hatch vs. Douglas, 48 Conn. Bell, 5 B. & Ald. 34; Ikin vs. Brad-116; Calton vs. Bragg, 15 East, 223; ley, 2 Moo. 206.
Bruce vs. Hunter, 3 Camp. 467; [3] 6 Hun (N. Y.), 233.
Denton vs. Rodie, id. 496; Gwyn vs.

exceeding the amount allowed by the laws of the State of New York[1] for effecting loans, and it was held that it was the duty of the principal promptly to object to the payment of such commissions; and in case he failed so to do, he cannot, in an action by the Broker to recover a balance due to him, insist that such payments were illegal and unauthorized.

And a charge made by a Broker for extra and usurious interest paid to enable him to carry his Client's stock was sustained,[2] on the ground that the Client had authorized the Broker to pay the same.

Where, however, the Broker is himself the lender of the money, he cannot charge a rate of interest beyond that allowed by statute; and the assent of the client to the payment of such excess of interest cannot affect the operation of the laws forbidding usury.[3] But, where a statute does not more than prohibit a recovery of interest in excess of 10 per cent, unless the contract is in writing, and does not otherwise make the rate of interest unlawful, interest in excess of that rate may be charged in an account stated; and money paid on account by the debtor may be applied to the payment of such interest by the creditor, in the absence of any appropriation by the debtor.[4]   This proposition is laid down in Marye vs.

---

[1] 2 Rev. Stat. (5th ed.) 979. By Laws of N. Y. of 1850, c. 172, corporations may not interpose the defence of usury. The effect of this statute is to repeal the Statute of Usury so far as it applied to corporations. Curtis vs. Leavitt, 15 N. Y. 85, 155; Belmont Bank vs. Hoge, 35 N. Y. 65. A similar effect was produced by the enactment of L. 1882, c. 237, upon all demand loans of $5,000 and upwards, secured by the pledge of negotiable instruments. Hawley vs. Kountz, 6 App. Div. 217.

[2] Smith vs. Heath, 4 Daly (N. Y.), 123. A Stock-broker is entitled to charge upon all accounts due previous to any statutory change in the interest rate, in accordance with the old rate. Reese vs. Rutherford, 90 N. Y. 644.

[3] See last preceding note.

[4] Marye vs. Strouse, C. C. U. S.

Strouse, a case which arose out of dealings in certain mining stocks. In that case it appeared that the Broker had
a book called a " Broker's Pass-book," which contained an
account of all the transactions between himself and his
Client (being a copy of the Broker's ledger), the Client having possession of the book at all times, save when it was
being " written up," after which it was again returned to
him. The statute of Nevada[1] provides that " when there.
is no express contract in writing fixing a different rate of
interest, interest shall be allowed at the rate of 10 per cent
per annum for all moneys. . . . Parties may agree in
writing for the payment of any rate of interest whatever
on money due or to become due." The Broker, without
any agreement in writing, charged his Client with interest
at the rate of 2 per cent per month, which sums were duly
entered in the " pass-book " and known to the .Client. Interest on all advances during the month, as well as on the
balance brought forward from the preceding month, was
charged at the same rate at the end of each month, and
went into the balance struck. No objection was ever raised
to these charges by Client, and the court held that the
facts constituted an account stated; and the agreement being fair and perfectly understood, and nothing in it opposed
to the policy of the State or good morals, such interest could
be included in the balance agreed to in stating the account.

And a right may be made to charge compound interest,
either by express contract, or it may be implied from the
mode of dealing with former accounts or custom;[2] but a

(Nevada) 5 Fed. Rep. 483. See 2746, Cutting's Comp. Laws, ed.
also Isett vs. Ogilvie, 9 Iowa, 1900.
313. [2] Fergusson vs. Fyffe, 8 C. & F.
[1] Comp. Laws, § 32, now §§ 2745– 121, 140.

18

Client is not bound, or affected by the practice of his bankers, to charge interest upon interest by making rests in their accounts at stated intervals, unless it be proved that he was aware that such was their custom.[1] He cannot, however, object to such method of charging interest, or indeed to any method claimed to be unlawful, in his own action for conversion of stocks sold for default of margin, where it does not appear that the excessive charges would equal the deficit in margins.[2]

And where the taking of compound interest is usury, it does not affect a contract for the purchase and sale of the stock. The charging of interest is outside of that contract and may be disallowed by the court.[3]

Any other expenses or actual disbursements which a Stockbroker makes for his Client, in pursuance of agreement or usage, would seem to be recoverable upon the principles laid down in the preceding cases; but it should be shown that the expenses have been actually incurred. Thus, in Marye vs. Strouse,[4] the Brokers sought to recover money laid out for telegrams. The Brokers were in the habit of receiving orders daily for the purchase and sale of mining stocks. It often happened that a number of orders would be sent to San Francisco in one despatch; in such case the practice was to charge each Client having an order thereon seventy-five cents (that being the proper charge for a single telegram of

---

[1] Moore vs. Voughton, 1 Stark, 487; Leake's Dig. Law of Cont. 1107; Chitty on Cont. (11th Am. ed.) 957, note (h), and cases there collected; 13th Eng. ed., p. 545, and cases cited.

[2] Gould vs. Trask, 10 N. Y. Supp. 619.

[3] Hatch vs. Douglas, 48 Conn,

116. In that case the Brokers waived their claim for compound interest and charged simple interest only, so that the question whether that part of a custom contravening the policy of the law would be enforced was not before the court. Id.

[4] 5 Fed. Rep. 483.

ten words), although such Client's proportion of the actual cost was often, if not always, less. But no effort was made to keep an account of the sums actually paid out for telegrams about the business of the particular Client sought to be charged. The Brokers, however, relied for recovering such charges on the ground that they were in accordance with an established usage of mining-stock Brokers; but the court rendered judgment against them on his point, holding that a custom or usage like the one in question, of charging not merely the actual cost of telegrams, but an arbitrary price, if it can be considered as reasonable, should be established by showing that both parties had knowledge of it.

(e.) *Right of Client to Control and Take up Stock.*

Although, as we have seen, the stock in an ordinary speculation upon margin remains in the possession of the Broker, it is at all times, in the absence of express agreement to the contrary, subject to the orders of the Client.

The latter has the right to demand possession of the stock upon payment of the purchase price and the commissions and proper expenses.[1]

---

[1] Markham vs. Jaudon, 41 N. Y. 235, at 247. This proposition is conceded even by Mr. Justice Grover in his dissenting opinion in that case. See also, as to right of Client to direct the stock to be bought in on a short sale, Knowlton vs. Fitch, 52 N. Y. 288, rev'g 48 Barb. 493. The same rule exists in the case of a pledge; the pledgor having the general property in the pledge may sell it, and compel its restoration upon paying the debt secured (Rozet vs. McClellan, 48 Ill. 345). In an action against a corporation by one to whom certain of its bonds had been pledged, to be declared the owner of such bonds and registered as such, the pledgor, although not opposing this demand of the pledgee, is a necessary party to the action, because he has a right of redemption by paying his debt and an interest in any proceeds after satisfaction of his debt. Newcombe vs. Ry. Co., 8 N. Y. Supp. 366. And it seems that

And where the Broker sells the stock without authority, a demand therefor is not necessary to maintain an action for conversion, and such action may be maintained although they were purchased in the name of plaintiff's agent.[1]

Where the Broker has deprived himself of the power of delivering the stocks to his Client by selling them, or otherwise disposing of them without, or contrary to, the instructions of his Client, an offer by the Broker to replace the stock does not bar the right of action of the Client, because where an agent has violated his duty or instructions, and made himself liable to an action for damages, nothing but payment of the damages, and accord and satisfaction, or a release, is a bar to the same. The offer of the Broker to replace the stock, so long as it is unaccepted, affects neither the principal's right to recover nor the measure of damages.[2]

If the Broker wrongfully hypothecate the stock, his Client can follow the same, and, upon payment of the amount due, compel the delivery of the stock to himself;[3] and if the Client be compelled to pay to the third person an amount greater than that which he owes upon the same to the Broker, he can recover the surplus from the latter or his estate.[4]

where stocks are pledged as collateral security that the pledgee cannot, whilst his debt remains unsatisfied, acquire a title to them by virtue of the statute of limitations. Cross vs. Eureka Lake, etc., Canal Co., 73 Cal. 302.

[1] Cunningham vs. Stevenson, 20 W. D. (N. Y.) 82.

[2] Clarke vs. Meigs, 10 Bosw. (N. Y.) 337, 338; s. c. 22 How. Pr. (N. Y.) 340; Gruman vs. Smith, 12 J. & S. (N. Y. Sup. Ct.) 389; rev'd, on another ground, 81 N. Y. 25.

[3] An unauthorized hypothecation of stocks by a Broker is a conversion, but it does not destroy the original contract of pledge so that the pledgor may demand a return of the stocks without tender or payment of the debt. New York, L. E. & W. R. Co. vs. Davies, 38 Hun, 477.

[4] And when the Broker's assigned estate is benefited, he is entitled to

Where plaintiffs, Stock-brokers holding stock for differrent Clients on margin, in speculative transactions, pledge the same to outside Brokers, who in turn repledge or rehypothecate the stock with a bank, and subsequently the latter claims to appropriate and hold them as security for other distinct loans made to the outside Brokers, and in consequence thereof the plaintiffs are compelled, under duress, to pay an excessive amount to release the stocks, the plaintiffs have the right to maintain an action against the bank to recover such excessive sum. The stocks being the property of the Clients and having been released, the extra sum paid to obtain the custody of the same being the money of the plaintiffs, the latter have the exclusive right to recover the same.[1]

In London Joint Stock Bank vs. Simmons[2] it appeared that a Stock-broker in fraud of his pledgor had repledged negotiable instruments (Cedulas bonds) *en bloc* with securities belonging to other persons for an advance to him, and then absconded. The bank had no knowledge whether the bonds belonged to the Broker or whether he had any authority to deal with them, and it had made no inquiries on these points. In an action brought by the owner of the bonds it was held : That as there were, as matter of fact, no circumstances to create suspicion as to the Broker's authority and power, the bank was entitled to retain and realize on the bonds, they being negotiable instruments taken for value and in good faith. And the mere fact that

---

a preference over the other creditors in the payment of such surplus. Matter of Price, 171 N. Y. 15.

[1] Gould vs. Farmer's Loan and Trust Co., 23 Hun, 322, at p. 326.

[2] L. R. A. C. (1892) 201; rev'g s. c. (1891) L. R. 1 Ch. Div. 270. See the lower court decision criticized in 18 Wash. L. R. 293. See also Wookey vs. Pole, 4 B. & Ald. 1.

a bank knew that the pledgor was a Broker is not sufficient to charge the bank with knowledge.[1]

This case was followed in Bentinck vs. London Joint
Stock Bank,[2] in which stocks had also been repledged with
the Bank by a Stock-broker *en bloc* with others as security
for a loan to him, and transferred and registered in the
names of the bank directors, some by the Client himself,
some by the Broker and some by the parties from whom the
Broker had purchased. The Client, asserting that he had
only authorized the Broker to repledge for the same amount
as he was indebted to the Broker, claimed to be entitled to
redeem from the bank on payment of that amount. The
court denied this claim, holding that as upon all the evidence and especially upon that relating to the "contango"
system under which the Broker had purchased the stock,
there was nothing to lead the bank to suppose that the securities were not the Broker's own property, it was entitled
to be treated as a *bona fide* holder for value without notice; its legal title to the securities could not be impeached,
and the Client could not redeem without paying the full
amount due to the Bankers by the Brokers.

In both these cases the court carefully distinguished Sheffield vs. The Banks,[3] where the banks had either actual

---

[1] Baker vs. Bank, 60 L. J. Q. B.
542. See also Goodwin vs. Roberts, L. R. 1 App. Cas. 476; Rumball vs. Bank, L. R. 2 Q. B. D. 194;
Hone vs. Boyle, 27 L. R. (Ir.) 137;
Marshall vs. Bank, 61 L. J. Ch. 465.
When the Broker is apparently the
owner, the subpledgee may compel
registration in his, the subpledgee's,
name, In re Tahiti Cotton Co., L.
R. 17 Eq. 273, but the subpledgee is
liable if the circumstances are such
as to put it upon inquiry. Mulville
vs. Bank, 27 L. R. (Ir.) 379. As
to what will constitute notice, see
London and Canadian Loan and
Agency Co. vs. Duggan, (1893) A.
C. 506.

[2] L. R. (1893) 2 Ch. Div. 120.

[3] 13 A. C. 333. See article
"Fraudulent dealing with client's
securities" in 27 Ir. Law Times,
167, 181, commenting on the English
cases cited in the text, and also on

knowledge or reason to believe that the person pledging negotiable and non-negotiable securities to them, and who was a money lender with the course of whose business they were familiar, had no further authority to repledge other than for the same sum which he himself had loaned. The banks in this case made no inquiry as to that amount, but choose to rely on the money lender not to repledge beyond it, and it was properly held that they therefore were not purchasers for value, without notice, and that the owner of the securities was entitled to them or their proceeds upon payment to the banks of the amount of his debt to the money lender.

If a Broker pledges a blank transfer signed by the owners of the certificates it is constructive notice to the pledgee, who should have inquired into the Broker's authority.[1] The tender by the pledgor of a larger amount then is justly due to the pledgee upon stocks pledged by his Broker is not an admission that the pledgor owes the amount tendered, nor is it an estoppel to that effect.[2] This conclusion proceeds upon a like principle to that obtaining where a tender is made for the purpose of obtaining property sold and in the hands of the tendee claiming to own the same and the tender is accepted, in which case the rule is undoubted that the money may be recovered back.[3]

In the case of Smith vs. Savin,[4] after the decision cited at p. 291, note 1, the plaintiff becoming apprised of the facts stated below, amended his complaint so as to make his

several Irish cases decided about the same time.

[1] Colonial Bank vs. Cady, 15 App. Cas. 267; Fox vs. Martin, 64 L. J. Ch. 473.

[2] Talmage vs. Bank, 91 N. Y. 551.

[3] Briggs vs. Boyce, 56 N. Y. 289; Scholey vs. Mumford, 60 N. Y. 498.

[4] 141 N. Y. 315.

action in effect one for conversion. On May 8, 1894, plaintiff had deposited with B. & Co., New York bankers, 100
shares of a stock as security for any indebtedness which he
might incur to that firm. On that day B. & Co., without
plaintiff's knowledge, pledged this stock with other stocks
as security for a loan with S. & Co. Both firms were
members of the Stock Exchange and the loan was made
subject to its rules. S. & Co. were *bona fide* holders without knowledge that B. & Co. were not the real owners of
the stocks pledged. On May 14 B. & Co. assigned, and
plaintiff then learning of the pledge of his stocks notified
S. & Co. of his interest, and requested a statement of the
amount for which his stock was held. S. & Co. refused all
information or to recognize plaintiff's rights, and on the
same day, without notice to him or to B. & Co., and in
violation of the rules of the Exchange, sold all the stock
pledged, realizing thereby more than the debt of B. & Co.
to them, but excluding the price of plaintiff's stock, not
enough to discharge that debt. Plaintiff did not learn of
the sale of his stock until June 21, at which time his stock
had reached par, and the other stocks had so far advanced
that if then sold the proceeds would have entirely repaid
the loan, leaving plaintiff's stock free from any claim.
The Court of Appeals affirmed the judgment of the General
Term,[1] and seems to proceed on the same theory, i. e., that
the plaintiff being the undisclosed principal of his agents,
B. & Co., had the right to ratify their wrongful pledge and
maintain an action for conversion of his property against
S. & Co., subject to their claim on the proceeds of his stock
for the balance of the loan after first selling the stocks

---

[1] 69 Hun, 311.

pledged belonging to B. & Co., and without any right in them to apply the surplus on any other loan to B. & Co.

Cases have arisen when the order given to one firm of Brokers was by them executed through a second firm without the knowledge of the real purchaser, and with whom the stocks purchased were pledged as margin for their general account with the first Brokers. On the insolvency of the first Brokers, the second Brokers, even if then informed of the purchaser's claim, are in such equity as entitle them to sell the stock for the purpose of paying the balance of indebtedness on the general account for which they held the stock on pledge.[1] But if any surplus remains that belongs by right to the original purchaser, and the second Brokers by having presumptive knowledge of his legal right thereto, are liable to him for its amount if they pay it to the assignees of the first Brokers.[2]

The one to whom the Broker has hypothecated his Client's stock is a *bona fide* holder in two classes of cases, and as such entitled to have his claim against the Broker paid before he delivers the stock to the Client. These cases are as follows:

1. Where no hypothecation has been authorized by the Client, but the Broker is apparently the owner of the stock, and the pledgee has no notice that actually he is not such owner.[3]

2. Where the power to hypothecate for the general purpose of the Broker's business is expressly or impliedly given.[4]

---

[1] Willard vs. White, 56 Hun, 581; Le Marchant vs. Moore, 79 Hun, 352; aff'd 150 N. Y. 209.

[2] Id.

[3] Willard vs. White, 56 Hun, 581; Skiff vs. Stoddard, 63 Conn. 198;

Smith vs. Savin, 141 N. Y. 315; Le Marchant vs. Moore, 79 Hun, 352; aff'd 150 N. Y. 209, and cases cited.

[4] Skiff vs. Stoddard, supra; Talmage vs. Bank, 91 N. Y. 543.

The difference in the position of one who has not authorized hypothecation and one who has, is this : If the stocks of both such Clients be hypothecated for the same loan, the former has the right to demand that all the stock of the latter be so applied as to extinguish all the pledgee's claim before resort is made to his.[1]

He stands, after informing the pledgee of his rights, merely as a surety for the repayment of the loan to his Broker.[2]

In either class of cases the Client's title is no further affected by the hypothecation than so far as the pledgee acquires the right to secure by it the repayment of the amount advanced by him.[3]

And if the stocks hypothecated have been sold by the pledgee, the surplus is to be distributed to the owners of the stock, preference in such distribution being given to those who have not authorized the hypothecation.[4]

If several loans have been made to the Broker, the pledgee is a holder for value only to the extent of the particular loan upon the particular stocks,[5] unless the loans are made generally upon all the stocks.[6]   And a Client whose stocks, together with others belonging to his Broker, have been, without his authority, hypothecated as security for a loan to his Broker, made subject to the rules of the Stock Exchange, after he has informed the pledgee of his ownership, has the right to demand that these stocks be

[1] Willard vs. White; Skiff vs. Stoddard, supra.

[2] Farwell vs. Bank, 90 N. Y. 483; Smith vs. Savin, 141 N. Y. 315.

[3] Willard vs. White ; Skiff vs. Stoddard; Le Marchant vs. Moore; Smith vs. Savin, supra, and Mackie vs. Requa, N. Y. L. J. July 6, 1892.

[4] Willard vs. White ; Skiff vs. Stoddard, supra.

[5] Smith vs. Savin, 9 N. Y. Supp. 106; Talmage vs. Bank, supra.

[6] Willard vs. White ; Le Marchant vs. Moore, supra.

sold in accordance with the rules of the Exchange, and may treat an unauthorized sale as a conversion. Therefore, after the proceeds of the sale of the other stocks have been applied to the payment of the loan, he is entitled to the highest price which his stock reached within a reasonable time after its illegal sale, and to judgment for that sum, deducting therefrom the balance due the pledgee after such application. In regard, however, to the other stock not belonging to him, he is not entitled to charge the pledgee with the highest price because of the illegal sale, provided they sold at the full market value on the day of the sale. He then could have no cause of complaint.[1]

The Client, in order to maintain an action for the recovery of the pledged property, is bound to show that no title passed to the pledgee, or that at some time prior to the commencement of the action he had become entitled to the property pledged, which may be shown by proof that the debt for which it was pledged had been discharged, or that a tender had been made of a sufficient amount to discharge it.[2]

When a Stock-broker pledges his customers' securities *en bloc* with a bank even to an amount beyond his indebtedness to them, it was held that as the transfer appeared to be absolute, the bank took good title to hold the securities as collateral for the Broker's indebtedness to it, and after payment thereof, the proceeds of sale belonged to the customers *pro rata.*[3]

[1] Smith vs. Savin, supra. See also Talmage vs. Bank, 91 N. Y. 537.

[2] Thompson vs. Bank, 113 N. Y. 333.

[3] Whitlock vs. Bank, 2 Misc. 81. In such case so much of a Client's securities as remain with the bank after payment of their claim out of the proceeds of the other securities will be directed to be sold, and the broker cannot object to a present

And where the security deposited as collateral is sold by the Broker to a *bona fide* purchaser without notice, there must be a tender to the latter of the amount due by the pledgor, before there can be a recovery.[1]

In German Saving's Bank vs. Renshaw [2] it appeared that Stock-brokers had hypothecated with defendant bank, securities deposited with them as collateral security for stock purchased by them for plaintiff. The assignments and power of attorney endorsed authorized a *sale* only of the securities. This sale was to be made, if necessary, to cover the Client's indebtedness in connection with the stock dealing transactions. And it was held that as the bank had notice that the securities were only for *sale*, and that the endorsed assignment did not authorize a *pledge*, it stood merely in the place of the original pledgee, and as nothing was due to the latter by the pledgor, it was bound to restore the stock to the owner and that a tender of the original debt was not necessary. So if the stock belonging to the Client be in the hands of a receiver or assignee of an insolvent Broker, the Client can recover the same upon payment of the amount due thereon.[3]

The assignee of a Broker stands in the same relation to stocks hypothecated by the Broker as his assignor stood, and so is not a *bona fide* purchaser for value as against customers of the firm for whom the stocks had been purchased.[4]

sale on the ground that the market is low; s. c. N. Y. L. J. April 20, 1898.

[1] Talty vs. Freedsman's Bank, 93 U. S. 321.

[2] 78 Md. 475. To same effect are Taliaferro vs. First National Bank, 71 Md. 209; and usage cannot control. First National Bank vs. Taliaferro, 72 Md. 164.

[3] Demand and tender are not necessary. In re Swift, 112 Fed. Rep. 315.

[4] Willard vs. White, 56 Hun, 581. Le Marchant vs. Moore, 79 Hun, 352; Skiff vs. Stoddard, 63 Conn. 198.

Prior to the insolvency the general creditors of the Broker had no right to appropriate such stocks to the payment of their claims, and, after the assignment, the purchasers may redeem the stocks and the creditors are not thereby deprived of any right or advantage they ever had. Nor does the fact that the insolvent Broker had the stocks transferred to his own name on the corporate books confer any such right on the general creditors.[1] Nor can the purchasers be deprived of their right to redeem, and hold to themselves the surplus after redemption, by the act of the pledgees (the agents of the purchaser's Brokers) in selling the stocks without their knowledge and immediately turning over the surplus after payment of their claim to the assignee of the purchaser's Brokers. In such a case the pledgees are liable to the purchasers to the amount of such surplus.[2]

The presentation to the assignee by the customer of a claim against the Broker's estate is not an election to hold the estate and release the stocks. He may still claim them if he can find them.[3]

The assignee, therefore, not being allowed to retain the stocks, but they, or their proceeds, if they have been sold, being subject to redemption by the customers for whom they were held, interesting questions arise as to marshalling the securities or proceeds between the customers and as to the rights of the sub-pledgee if the stocks have been hypothecated by the insolvent Brokers. In Willard vs. White and Skiff vs. Stoddard such questions arose, and in Skiff vs. Stoddard are very ably treated and disposed of. In the latter case it appeared that the Brokers, who carried on business in New

---

[1] Skiff vs. Stoddard, supra.   [3] Mackie vs. Requa, N. Y. L. J.
[2] Le Marchant vs. Moore, 79 Hun,   July 6, 1892, p. 842.
352; aff'd 150 N. Y. 209.

Haven, bought and sold stocks upon their own account, and for others. The largest part of their business consisted in buying and selling upon margins for customers. At the time of their assignment they were in some manner carrying various stocks and securities. A few of them were in their own hands, others in the hands of pledgees from them, and others still in the hands of their New York agents, who held them as security for advances to the insolvent firm. The accounts of nearly all the customers showed an indebtedness to the Brokers, but the stocks carried as aforesaid were not sufficient to fill all the orders. The plaintiffs desired to pay their debit balances and redeem their securities. The defendant (trustee in insolvency) disputed their right so to do.

Prentice, J., in an opinion which is given at length because nearly every possible contingency as to these questions is explained, said (p. 224): " An attempt on the part of the several plaintiffs to redeem, raises legal questions which demand consideration. These questions relate to the necessity of identification and the character and extent of that identification. The pledge relation implies the possession by the pledgee of some property to which the pledge attaches. A pledgor seeking to retake his own must be able to identify it. The burden is upon him, not only to establish the contract relation, but to point out the property of which the contract gives him the right to repossess himself upon redemption. In ordinary cases of pledge, where the property given in security is corporeal, or consists of certain kinds of choses in action, the means of strict identification are usually at hand. In cases like the present, where the pledged property is made up largely of stocks, the problem of identification becomes complicated by reason of the right in the pledgee to take out in his own name a new certificate, and to preserve no separation of particular shares from other like shares held by the pledgee. A strict identification of precise shares is thus oftentimes rendered impossible. Nevertheless, both in law and in fact, shares are being held in pledge. Evidently the rule which demands identification as a prerequisite to repossession must, when such conditions are encountered, receive such reasonable construction and application as will, upon the one hand, satisfy the purpose of the rule, and upon the other hand do justice to the parties. It will not do to dispense with the necessity of identification. Neither will it do to permit a permissible practice on the part of the pledgee to deprive a pledgor of his property."

"If we look at the conditions which the claims of the several plaintiffs present, we find that nearly every possible contingency exists. These may be classified as follows:

"Class 1. Where it can be shown that the precise certificates of stock or evidences of title originally purchased in the execution of a plaintiff's order were held for him by the Brokers at the time of their assignment.

"Class 2. Where it appears that certain particular certificates of stock or evidences of title were by the Brokers being carried in fulfilment of a plaintiff's order, although it may be impossible to establish that such certificates or evidences of title were the precise ones originally purchased in the execution of that order.

"These classes present no difficulty. The plaintiffs making such identification are clearly entitled to redeem. This identification being a strict one of precise property, it, of course, follows that it must take precedence of any general identification such as remains to be considered, and gives to the fortunate pledgor the first right to that which is so identified."

"Class 3. Where no more precise identification is possible than that the Brokers were carrying a block of stocks of a particular kind sufficient to satisfy the demands for that kind of stock of all their customers, including themselves."

"The problem of identification and distribution as related to class three is not a difficult one. If the Brokers were at the time of their failure carrying a block of certain stock, and the orders of their customers taken together called for them to carry that amount of stock, the identification of that stock as being stock carried for these customers, the requisite amount for each, is clearly reasonable and sufficient. The shares being all alike and merely representing an ownership of a certain undivided interest in a corporation, the interests of all concerned are satisfied by a distribution to each pledgor of his proper number of shares."

"Class 4. Where it appears that the Brokers were carrying a block of stocks of a particular kind not capable of the precise identification contemplated in classes 1 and 2, and the whole amount of unidentifiable shares is insufficient to satisfy the demand of all their margin buying customers, including themselves, but sufficient to satisfy the demands of all such customers, exclusive of themselves, either as individuals, or as a partnership.

"This class presents the same problem as class 3, modified only by the additional factor that the shares in the Broker's hands were insufficient to meet the demands of their customers and themselves together. The Brokers had the right to do as they pleased with their own. For their customers they were bound to hold and carry the requisite

stocks. If they did not have on hand what was called for
by their customers' contracts and their own purchases, it
will be presumed in the absence of evidence to the contrary
that the situation arose in a way consistent with their right
and duty and that the stocks on hand were held for their
customers. This presumption, however, must yield to the
fact. If it appeared that certain shares were at the time of the
assignment specifically held by the insolvent firm upon the
purchases of, or for itself, or its members, and thus, and not
otherwise, actually carried, the right thereto of the trustee
or administrator of such purchaser and owner would be as
clear as that of a plaintiff who is able to make a like strict
identification. Should the exercise of this right by the defendant as trustee of the insolvent Broker reduce the
amount of any kind of stock remaining below that required
to satisfy the demands of customers, the distribution would
fall under the principles of class 5 to be considered. Otherwise each customer would take his full quota of stock."

"Class 5. Where it appears that the Brokers were carrying a block of stocks of a particular kind not capable of the
precise identification contemplated in classes 1 and 2, and
the whole amount of such unidentifiable shares is insufficient to satisfy the demands of all their margin buying customers exclusive of themselves either as individuals or as
partners.

"Our previous discussion has eliminated certain of the
features of this class. There remains the single question as
to what shall be done when it appears after all efforts at
precise identification have been exhausted, and after the
claims of the Brokers as purchasers have been cut off, that
there remains a block of stock insufficient to meet the demands of all the pledgors of that stock. There is a short-
19

age which must fall to the loss of somebody. . . . It is not possible to show to whom it, share by share, does belong. The shares are all alike. We think that the identification is sufficient to justify, and that equity requires, the division of the stock *pro rata* among all those for whom the Brokers were holden to carry such stock. This course fully protects the creditors of the Broker. No stock is taken from the assets of the firm to which it was ever by any possibility entitled. It gives the pledgors their rights so far as may be and in an equitable manner." [1]

But where the Broker has so mixed the stock he has bought for his Client, in hypothecating it with several pledgees on separate loans by each, that no Client can identify any of the stock in the hands of any pledgee as the stock bought on his order, he cannot say it is his stock. And if, notwithstanding such hypothecation, the Broker had continued to hold stock enough to deliver to each Client all to which he might be entitled on paying the amount due from him to the Broker, the Client could not claim any right to the hypothecated stock; and this results from the rule heretofore referred to, that the Broker is not bound to keep on hand the identical stock purchased, but his obligation to his Client is fulfilled if he keep on hand sufficient like stocks, and be ready to deliver the same to his Client at any time that they are demanded. These positions were enforced in Chamberlin vs. Greenleaf.[2] A pledgee, with whom securi-

---

[1] See also Mutton vs. Peat, 2 Ch. Div. (1900) 79; In re Graff, 117 Fed. Rep. 343; Sillcocks vs. Gallaudet, 66 Hun, 522; Matter of Pierson, 19 App. Div. 478.

[2] 4 Ab. New Cas. (N. Y.) 178; and consult this case also for the meas-

ure of damage in a case where a Broker hypothecates stocks belonging to his general Clients and which cannot be identified by any particular one. See also Gould vs. The Central Trust Co., 6 id. 381, for principle of marshalling assets real-

ties belonging to several persons are pledged as collateral security for a loan made thereon to one having all the securities in his possession, and who wrongfully re-pledges or re-hypothecates them, should proceed *pari passu* in the application of the securities to the satisfaction of the loan, so that whatever loss should be occasioned to the parties whose stocks are wrongfully pledged shall fall on them ratably. Accordingly, if the pledgee, without notice of the claims of the true owners, sells the securities of one, thus realizing sufficient in amount to repay his loan on all the securities, and leaving in his hands as surplus the securities of the others, a court of equity will order such surplus securities to be sold, and the proceeds applied so that the burden of the loan will be borne by all in equitable proportions.[1] And where a draft for money was intrusted to a

---

ized from sale of pledged stocks which have been re-hypothecated. See also Rich vs. Boyce, 39 Md. 314. But although a Stock-broker had surrendered the pledged certificate and obtained a new certificate in his own name, and the certificate sub-pledged to defendant bank bore a different number from the Client's stock, the latter may nevertheless recover the certificate from the bank when the weight of evidence shows that it is his, Mould vs. Importer's & T. N. Bank, 72 App. Div. 30, even although he has presented a claim to the trustee in bankruptcy of the Broker. Id.; Rhinelander vs. Bank, 36 App. Div. 11. As to the rights of customers whose stock was merely on deposit for sale and of those whose stock was pledged to the Broker, see last cited case. An assignee will be enjoined pendente lite from paying

to preferred creditors the proceeds of the sale of a customer's stocks, after payment of the amount due by the customer, in an action by the latter to recover such sum. Adams vs. Ball, 24 App. Div. 69. When one of three notes with some bonds which with other bonds were deposited as collateral have been sub-pledged, the original pledgors may redeem same from the sub-pledgee on payment of the amount of the note. McDonald vs. Grant, 69 St. Rep. 48. As to when interpleader will be refused as between the original pledgor, the assignee of the pledgee, and the sub-pledgee, see Dodge vs. Lawson, 19 N. Y. Supp. 904. And as to indemnity to sub-pledgee, see Union Pac. R. Co. vs. Schiff, 74 Fed. Rep. 674.

[1] Gould vs. Central Trust Co., 6 Ab. New Cas. (N. Y.) 381. If,

Broker to buy Exchequer bills for his principal, and the Broker received the moneys and misapplied it by purchasing American stock and bullion, intending to abscond with it and go to America—and did accordingly abscond, but was taken before he quitted England, and thereupon surrendered to the principal the securities for the American stock and the bullion, who sold the whole and received the proceeds—held, that the principal was entitled to withhold the proceeds from the assignees of the Broker, who became bankrupt on the day on which he so received and misapplied the money.[1]

And where bankrupts, in their character of Stock-brokers,

pledged with the stocks of the Clients, are also some stocks of the Brokers themselves, as between the Clients and the Brokers, equity would doubtless apply the Brokers stocks to the extinguishment of the debt before resort is made to the stocks of the Client, but where the Brokers have become insolvent and the rights of other creditors have intervened, the Clients are not entitled to such relief. It would in effect give them a priority over other creditors. Skiff vs. Stoddard, 63 Conn. 198. See also Van Woert vs. Olmstead, 71 N. Y. Supp. 431. Where there has been a series of loans and stock of various owners has been pledged to secure each loan, a surplus arising on the sale of the stocks pledged on one loan will not be applied to a loss arising on a sale of the stocks pledged on another. The pledgee is a holder for value only to the extent of the particular loan upon the particular stocks. Smith vs. Savin, 9 N. Y.

Supp. 106. See this case on second trial, 141 N. Y. 315. Where defendants holding certain stocks as collateral security which had subsequently been assigned to the plaintiff, sold the same with the assent of the assignees; held, in an action by the assignees against the defendants to recover the surplus proceeds of the stock, that the defendants could claim, against such surplus, only such an amount as, if tendered by the plaintiffs at the time of the assignment, with interest and expenditures, would have cancelled and discharged the claims of defendants as pledgees of the stock; that the title to the surplus moneys at the time of the sale was vested in the assignees; and consequently the defendants could set off no claim which they at that time held against the plaintiff's assignors. Van Blarcom vs. Broadway Bank, 37 N. Y. 540.

[1] Taylor vs. Plumer, 3 M. & S. 562.

received dividends on dividend warrants intrusted to them, and pledged the dividend warrants for their own debt, they were ordered to be delivered up to trustees who had employed the bankrupts as their Brokers.[1]

And although Brokers are within the list of traders in the English Bankruptcy Acts of 1861 and 1869,[2] yet, in the event of such bankruptcy, a sum of stock or shares which the Broker has bought for his principal and taken into his own name are not in his order and disposition so as to pass to his assignees or trustee.[3] The theory of the law is, that the property of a principal, intrusted by him to his factor or Broker for any special purpose, belongs to the principal, notwithstanding any change which that property may have undergone in point of form, so long as such property is capable of being identified and distinguished from all other property, and that all property thus circumstanced is equally recoverable from the assignees of the factor, in the event of his becoming a bankrupt, as it was from the factor himself before his bankruptcy. And if the property in its original state and form was covered with a trust in favor of the principal, no change of that state and form can divest it of such trust, or give the factor or agent, or those who represent him

---

[1] Exp. Gregory vs. Wakefield, 2 M. D. & DeG. 613. As to doctrine of subpledging and re-hypothocation, see p. 276, et seq.

[2] Taylor vs. Plumer, supra.

[3] Id. In Massachusetts it has been held that if a Broker purchases shares for a customer on a margin, and on account of his insolvency is unable to deliver them, and eventually purchases them on the market for a price higher than the customer contracted to pay for them and delivers them to the customer on receipt of the contract price, the transaction is a preference in violation of the insolvent law (Pub. St. ch. 157, § 96) to the extent of the excess in value over the contract price. Weston vs. Jordan, 168 Mass. 401. When a Client becomes bankrupt, see as to right of lien of owner of property left with the Client for sale, as against the trustee, In re Mulligan, 116 Fed. Rep. 715.

in right, any other more valid claim in respect to it than they respectively had before such change. An abuse of trust can confer no rights on the party abusing it, nor on those who claim in privity with him.[1] The case of Tayler vs. Plumer was directly endorsed in Ex parte Cook.[2] In that case C., a trustee, employed a Stock-broker to make purchases of certain railway shares, informing him that it was for a certain trust fund in which he was interested. C. left the money with the Broker to make the purchase, which was duly made on the Exchange in the usual way for the next settling-day, the Broker in the meantime depositing the money in bank. Before the settling-day, however, the Broker failed, and moved for a declaration in the Bankruptcy Court that a portion of the money in the hands of the bankruptcy trustees belonged to C. This was refused by the registrar, on the ground that the transaction constituted the relation of debtor and creditor between C. and the Stock-broker, and not that of trustee and *cestui que trust*. But this decision was reversed on appeal, the appellate court holding that the Stock-broker had notice that the money belonged to a trust fund, and that the money could be traced. And the court also expressly said that, even if there had been no notice, the relation of the Stock-broker and C. was of a fiduciary character, so as to make the case undistinguishable from

---

[1] Taylor vs. Plumer, supra. Where one executor has wrongfully and for his own use, pledged securities belonging to the estate, his coexecutor may pay the amount for which they were pledged and regain possession of the bonds. Newcombe vs. R. R. Co., 8 N. Y. Supp. 366. And if an executor has, in abuse of his trust, and with the pledgee's knowledge, pledged securities, the pledgee can only relieve himself from liability by showing that the money loaned was applied for the benefit of the estate. Moore vs. American Loan & Trust Co., 115 N. Y. 65.

[2] In re Strachan, L. R. 4 Ch. Div. 123.

Taylor vs. Plumer.[1] But a pledgor cannot follow the securities which he has placed with a pledgee in the hands of a purchaser in good faith from the pledgee, purchasing without notice of the pledge.[2]

An important question in the law of pure pledge is as to the time when the pledgor may be called upon to redeem. When is the debt due? This depends upon the circumstances of the contract. By the pledge the title does not pass to the pledgee, but remains in the pledgor until divested by a sale upon notice or by judicial proceedings.[3]

If no time of redemption be fixed by the terms of the

[1] See further, upon the subject of commingling funds and right of principal or cestui que trust to follow property, note to Hooley vs. Gieve, 9 Ab. New Cas. (N. Y.) 8, at p. 41. And the United States Supreme Court, in the case of The Central National Bank of Baltimore vs. Conn. Mutual Life Ins. Co., 104 U. S. 54, has decided that if money held by a person in a fiduciary capacity, though not as trustee, has been paid by him to his account at his banker's, the person for whom he holds the money can follow it, and has a charge on the balance in the banker's hands, although it is mixed with his (the depositor's) own moneys; and that the bank cannot be permitted to assert its own claim to the balance of an agency account as against the beneficial owner when the bank has notice, either actual or constructive, of such equity. This view is also endorsed in the case of Baker vs. N. Y. Nat. Bank, decided by the N. Y. General Term, Oct. 1881. N. Y. *Daily Reg.* Nov. 9, 1881, s. c. 25 Hun, 453; aff'd on new trial, 100 N. Y. 31; 16 Abb. N. C. 458. In Butler vs. Sprague, 66 N. Y. 392, where special deposits were sought to be reclaimed, the court held that unless the depositor could trace the identical money, he could not stand on any better footing than any ordinary creditor. Compare Le Roy vs. Mathewson, 47 N. Y. Super. Ct. 389, and see generally People vs. City of Rochester, 93 N. Y. 582.

[2] Little vs. Barker, Hoff. Ch. (N. Y.) 487; Strickland vs. Leggett, 21 N. Y. Supp. 356. Nor can he follow them into the hands of a bona fide pledgee of his pledgee, unless the debt of the latter is paid or its amount tendered. Thompson vs. Nat. Bk., 113 N. Y. 325; Work vs. Tibbets, 87 Hun, 352. See also Thomson vs. Bank, 18 A. C. (1893) 282, and cases cited.

[3] Markham vs. Jaudon, 41 N. Y. 235; Sterns vs. Marsh, 2 Denio, 230; Brownell vs. Hawkins, 4 Barb. 491; Gruman vs. Smith, 81 N. Y. 25; Bailey vs. Drew, 17 N. Y. St. Rep. 185.

contract of pledge, the pledgor may redeem at any time, and although a day of payment be fixed he may redeem after that day. He has his whole lifetime to redeem, provided the pledgee does not call upon him to do so, as he has a right to do, at any time in his discretion, and if no such call be made, the representatives of the pledgor may redeem after his death.[1]

Until his title is divested by sale or judicial proceedings the pledgor's right to redeem is a continuing one, and as an incident to this right of redemption he may at any time during its continuance invoke the aid of a court of equity and ask to have the amount of his debt ascertained, if uncertain.[2]

This cause of action does not depend upon the rights of the parties as they existed at the time of the pledge, but depends upon the rights of the pledgor to redeem at the time his bill is filed and the cause of action upon which such bill is founded accrues, not when the collateral security was first pledged, but when the right to redeem was first insisted upon, namely, upon the filing of the bill, and so the statute of limitations is no bar to the action.[3]

---

[1] 4 Kent's Com. (14th ed.) 138.

[2] Kent vs. Westbrooke, 1 Vesey, 278; Bailey vs. Drew, supra.

[3] Bailey vs. Drew, supra; Bowman vs. Close, 20 N. Y. Supp. 415; N. Y. L. J. August 11, 1892. This rule is also applicable in an action for the conversion of the pledge. A mere omission of the pledgee to return the pledge after the payment of the debt is not a conversion. No conversion is committed until there has been a demand for the return of the pledge and a refusal to return. Roberts vs. Berdell, 15 Ab. N. S. 183; Purdy vs. Sistare, 2 Hun, 126. The case of Roberts vs. Sykes, 30 Barb. 173, to the contrary must be looked upon as overruled. Miner vs. Beekman, 50 N. Y. 342; Bailey vs. Drew, supra.

The question whether collateral security for a time note is entitled to days of grace as well as the note has been answered in the negative. Rankin vs. McCullough, 12 Barb. 103.

The same principle also applies to an action by the pledgee to foreclose his lien.[1]

V. Duty of Broker to Sell—"Stop Order."

The Broker, when directed to sell, is bound to comply with the order, and to sell the stocks at the price named or at the market price, if that be the instruction. This consequence flows from the ownership of the stock.[2]

Nor does the Client lose the right to order a sale when his margin is exhausted. His orders to sell the securities must still be obeyed. Any other rule would permit an agent to speculate at the risk of his principal.[3] So a Broker cannot refuse to sell stocks and invest the proceeds in the purchase of others, because the balance due him for advances exceeds the value of the stocks ordered to be sold, particularly if the conversion requires no further advance from him ;[4] and where a Client delivers a specified quantity of stock to a Stock-broker for sale with instructions to sell when the market value should "go up," and the Broker transfers part of the same to a third person, and part to himself, the Client can treat this as a sale of his stock ; and it is no defence, that it is a custom among Brokers to place the stock sent them for sale to their own names on the books of the company, and, in making transfers, to do so indiscriminately, without regard to the person from whom the stock was received, or for whose account the same was sold. A Broker, in

[1] Bowman vs. Close, supra.

[2] Galigher vs. Jones, 129 U. S. 193.

[3] Zimmerman vs. Heil, 33 N. Y.

Supp. 391; aff'd without opinion, 156 N. Y. 703.

[4] Galigher vs. Jones, supra.

such a case, has no right to pledge or do anything else with the stock except to sell it; and the Client is entitled to recover the market value of the stock at the time of its transfer, and cannot be compelled to accept from the Broker a certificate of an equal number of such shares of stock.[1]

As to the duty of the Broker, the general rules are the same as in the case of an order to purchase—viz., that the Broker is bound rigidly to carry out the directions in respect to time, price, number of shares, manner, and place, and to act with prudence and caution and the utmost good faith.[2] An agent with express authority to sell has no implied authority to warrant, when the property is of a description not usually sold with warranty. One employed to make a sale of bank stock is not presumptively empowered to warrant it in the name of the principal, and the receipt of the proceeds by the owner of the stock, in ignorance of an unauthorized warranty by the agent, is not a ratification of the unauthorized engage-

---

[1] Parsons vs. Martin, 77 Mass. 111.

[2] See these questions discussed, ante, p. 205; Bush vs. Cole, 28 N. Y. 261; Taussig vs. Hart, 58 id. 425, 428; Ryder vs. Sistare, 15 Daly, 90; Day vs. Jameson, 33 N. Y. St. Rep. 379; Smith vs. Bouvier, 70 Pa. St. 325; Jones vs. Marks, 40 Ill. 313; 1 Lindley on Company Law (5th ed.), p. 511 et seq., and cases cited; Pulsifer vs. Shephard, 36 Ill. 513; Hollingshead vs. Green, 1 Cin. Super. Ct. 305; 13 Ohio Dec. Rep. 565. Where it is established that he has actually made the sale at a specified price, it must appear that a greater price could have been obtained or some other such fact must be shown in order to rebut the presumption of the Broker's good faith. Day vs. Jameson, supra. Where a Broker is invested with discretionary powers as to whether a sale should be made or not, he must exercise his discretion before selling. But, having determined upon a sale he has exercised his discretion, and the execution of the order involves no discretion whatever. He is not obliged to personally make the sale, and he may, for that purpose, employ a sub-agent. Sims vs. May, 16 N. Y. St. Rep. 780.

ment.[1] An authority to sell exists until countermanded or
revoked by implication; but the question is greatly governed by usage and the course of dealings between the parties. Accordingly, where the defendants, Stock-brokers,
were carrying certain stock for plaintiff on margin and the
latter, on Sept. 12, 1867, wrote to them, that "in case the
stock should look like reaction, or weaken, or have a down-
ward look, they should sell for him 50 or 100 shares, as
the case might look;" to which letter, two days later, the
defendants replied that they thought the market would recover from its present depression. On Sept. 17 the plaintiff
ordered the defendants to purchase 100 shares, if the stock
looked like rising. On the 18th the defendants bought for
the plaintiff 50 shares, and on the 20th, the market falling
rapidly, they sold all the plaintiff's stock without notice to
him. Held, that the direction contained in the plaintiff's
letter of the 12th was not revoked by what subsequently
took place, and defendants were justified in selling upon the
fall in the market.[2]

Where, however, an order has been given, in writing,
to sell stock at a certain designated figure, evidence is
admissible to show that the written order was subsequently
modified by an oral understanding.[3] The question of modification or waiver is for the jury.[4] Parol evidence is also

[1] Smith vs. Tracy, 36 N. Y. 79.

[2] Davis vs. Gwynne, 4 Daly (N.
Y.), 218; aff'd 57 N. Y. 676.

[3] Clarke vs. Meigs, 10 Bosw. (N.
Y.) 337. And where it appears that
the Client verbally agreed with the
Broker's clerk to sell certain securities at 105 or within a small frac-
tion of that figure, but the written
order of the Client merely directed a
sale of the stock without mention-
ing the figure, and the broker subsequently sold the greater part of
the stock at 102, and sued the
Client for the loss, it was held error
to exclude evidence of the verbal
agreement, as part only of the contract was in the written order.
Fisher vs. Moller, 17 N. Y. Supp. 831.

[4] Stone vs. Lathrop, 109 Mass. 63.

admissible to explain a Broker's contract for the sale of stock, acknowledging the receipt of the first payment of the margin.[1]

A Broker is not authorized to sell stock, standing in the name of two trustees, upon an order of one who undertakes to procure his co-trustee to join in the transfer, unless such co-trustee authorized or concurred with the other in making the transfer.[2]

If the Broker fails to sell when directed, the principal may recover back, in an action of assumpsit on the common counts, the margin originally deposited by him with the Broker.[3]

With respect to the terms upon which the Broker is authorized to sell, he is likewise bound by the direction of the Client. If no directions are given, he is entitled to make the sale in accordance with the general usage of Brokers.[4]

The general rule is, that it is no part of the duty of a selling Broker to his employer to procure payment of the price,

As to when a written memorandum made by a Broker is inadmissible. Gurley vs. McLennan, 17 App. Cas. (D. C.) 170.

[1] Winans vs. Hassey, 48 Cal. 634.

[2] Leyton vs. Sneyd, 2 Moo. 583. See also post, "Joint Adventures in Stocks," p. 313. In England it has been held that upon an investment of capital moneys arising under the Settled Land Acts, a tenant for life is not entitled to direct the trustees to employ a particular Stock-broker chosen by himself. Re Duke of Cleveland's Settled Estates (1902), 2 Ch. Div. 350.

[3] Jones vs. Marks, 40 Ill. 313.

[4] Ch. IV., "Usages." See also Cothran vs. Ellis, 107 Ill. 413;

Williams vs. Aroni, 35 La. Ann. 1115. If the sale is cancelled by the Exchange for no fault of the Broker, the Client cannot hold him for damages resulting from failure to carry out the sale. Smith vs. Pryor, 26 N. Y. St. Rep. 928. As to the effect of a usage of the Peoria Board of Trade, see Rugg vs. Davis, 15 Ill. App. 647. Where a statute invalidates a sale of stock, unless its requirements are complied with, the Broker cannot escape responsibility in loss resulting to his Client by showing a custom of the Exchange to disregard the statute, such custom being illegal. Neilson vs. James, 9 L. R. Q. B. D. 546.

nor to procure the execution by the purchaser of a transfer of the shares, nor to procure the registration thereof.[1]

But this question is greatly influenced by usage, especially as to the duty of the Broker to receive payment for the stock sold; and we understand the usage of Wall Street to be decidedly in that way, and as establishing a uniform and unassailable practice on the part of the Broker to receive payment for securities sold, especially as the latter is invested with the possession of the stocks, and is clothed with the apparent ownership upon which purchasers rely, who do not even know the principal.[2] It has been held, however, that a Stock-broker cannot sell upon credit, for that is not the usual course of his business.[3] And where it appears that stocks are usually sold for cash, the Broker is liable for any loss which may occur by his selling on credit, although he may have been acting *bona fide*, and with the object of benefiting his principal.[4]

So also a Broker employed to sell shares, who renders a sales note to the purchaser or his agent, in his own name, is liable as a principal, although known to be a Broker. Evidence that it is the custom in the place where the transaction is made to send in Broker's notes without disclosing the principal's name is properly rejected; and the subsequent

[1] Booth vs. Fielding, 1 Week. Notes, 245; Clark's Law of Joint-stock Companies (Scotch), 145; Lindley on Company Law (5th ed.), p. 511.

[2] Clarke vs. Meigs, 10 Bosw. (N. Y.) 337.

[3] 2 Kent's Comm. 1024, *622 (14th ed.), note (b); Baring vs. Corie, 2 B. & Ald. 137, 113, 148; Wiltshire vs. Sims, 1 Campb. 258; State of Illinois vs. Delafield, 8 Paige (N. Y.), 527; s. c. 26 Wend. 192.

[4] Brown vs. Boorman, 11 Cl. & Fin. 1. But see as to Brokers generally, where usage justifies a sale on credit, Goodenow vs. Tyler, 7 Mass. 36; Clark vs. Van Northwick, 18 id. 313; Van Alen vs. Vanderpool, 6 Johns. (N. Y.) 69; Douglass vs. Leland, 1 Wend. (N. Y.) 490.

rendering of a different note describing the true purchaser will not alter this rule.[1]

If, however, a Broker is employed to sell shares at a certain figure and he does so, but his Client refuses to deliver the stock, the Broker, who, under the rules of the Exchange, becomes personally liable to the purchaser, is entitled to go into the market, and buy the shares at the best price possible, and if at a loss, he may recover the loss from his Client, and the latter cannot say that he was not bound to deliver the stock until he was paid the price, unless it should appear that the Broker was himself the purchaser.[2]

In this connection a practice of Wall Street should be adverted to and explained. Frequently a Client wishes to limit a loss upon stocks, in which case he gives his Broker what is called a "*stop order*," which authorizes and directs the Broker to sell the stocks (or to buy them in, as the case may be) when they arrive at a certain price, in which event the Broker must sell or buy when the price reaches his limit; with this reservation, however, that the price at which the Broker is directed to sell or buy must be made by some third person.[3] This may be illustrated by the following example :

[1] Magee vs. Atkinson, 2 M. & W. 440. And when a Broker assumes to make a contract on behalf of a principal when he is not really authorized to make the contract, he is liable in damages to the party injured by his assuming to have authority even although he does so by mistake. In such a case the Broker warrants that he has authority and thereby contracts that he has authority. The contract, therefore, is that he had the authority which he represents that he had. In re National Coffee Palace Co., Ct. App. Ch. Div., Aug. 1883; 32 *Weekly Rep.* 236; N. Y. *Daily Reg.* April 9, 1884, where the cases upon this subject are referred to.

[2] Baily vs. Carnduff, 59 Pac. Rep. (Colo.) 407.

[3] Anderson's Law Dict., title "Order," p. 738; Porter vs. Wormser, 94 N. Y. 431–443; Campbell vs. Wright, 118 N. Y. 594–598; Wronkow vs. Clews, 20 J. & S. 178.

If A., being the owner of 100 shares of New York Central R. R. stock, should direct his Broker to sell the same when the stock should reach or be quoted at 99, in this event it is the duty of the latter to sell at that price ; not, however, until some other Broker, by a distinct transaction, has made the stock sell at 99, it being the understanding that a Broker cannot make that price himself by the sale of the stock. If, however, the Broker, when the stock reaches 99, is unable to sell at that price, it seems, by the usage of Wall Street, that he can sell at the next figure below 99.

Conclusions rather antagonistic to the above view seem to have been drawn in the case of Smith vs. Bouvier.[1] In that case the order was made by the Client in a transaction in which he was short of stocks, and was as follows : " Buy for my account 2,000 shares, New York Central, at 166 ; or, in event of that stock going against me, take the 2,000 shares in at 175." A Broker testified that " take in " means to buy. The Brokers acting under this order bought in the shares at an average of $174\frac{5}{8}$, or $\frac{3}{8}$ below the price mentioned in the order. The question was squarely raised in the case as to whether this was an execution of the order ; and the court said upon that point, in charging the jury, that " if the contract of the plaintiffs with the defendants was an absolute one, that they were not to buy in the stock until it reached 175 ; and if they had no discretion in the premises whatever, then, of course, they had no right to buy it at a less price and the plaintiff's third point would be well taken ; but is that a reasonable supposition ? Is that the contract which was entered into ? Was it not rather that the plaintiffs (as one of the Brokers testified to) were not to let the stock go

[1] 70 Pa. St. 325.

beyond 175 before buying it in ? and is not that a reasonable interpretation of the written order, in view of what was plainly the interest of the defendants, and of what occurred at that time?"

It will be seen that the learned judge left the question of the construction of the order to the jury, and did not pass upon it himself. The jury found for the Brokers, and, on appeal, the decision was affirmed, no allusion being made to this important question. Although the act of the Brokers in "buying in" the stock at 174⅝ might have been advantageous to their Client, it was not in accordance with the stop order, which gave them the right to act only when the stock reached 175. As we have seen, an agent or Broker must obey strictly his instructions, and it is no answer in his mouth to say that by disobeying them an advantage accrued to his principal.[1]   Suppose the stock had never reached 175, but, after selling at 174⅝, it declined until it reached 166? Here would have been a loss to the Client from which it seems the Broker could not have escaped responsibility by showing a sale at 174⅝.

Thus in a later case a stop order was entered to buy in or cover a short sale at 93⅜, which price was never actually realized. The Broker, however, bought in at 91⅜, which the Client repudiated, and, the price then rapidly falling to 87⅜, ordered the Broker to buy in at that price, which the Broker refused to do, setting up the purchase at 91⅜, as the termination of the transaction. It was held that the Client was entitled to recover the amount that would have been realized had the Brokers made the purchase at 87⅜ as or-

---

[1] See cases cited ante, p. 205. of law.   Davis vs. Gwynne, 57 N. Construction of writings a question   Y. 676.

dered, and that his right to order a purchase at that price was not affected by the unauthorized sale at 91⅜. A Client has the right to designate a limit, at which the transaction is to be terminated, within that which his margin will cover,[1] and a sale by the Broker before the point limited is reached is unauthorized.[2]

Where a principal gives his Broker orders to sell gold for him if it reach a certain price, and that price is reached, and the Broker does not sell, but holds on, hoping in good faith to realize a still higher price for his principal, which is impliedly assented to by the latter, but, owing to a sudden fall, a sale at a lower price is finally made, the Broker is liable only for the actual loss sustained. He cannot be charged with any loss from a neglect to sell at the highest point reached.[3] In England it has also been held that an order to sell stocks at a particular price must be obeyed when the stock reaches that price, and if the Broker did not sell when he might have done, he would in equity be held to have made the stock his own from that time and ordered to account to his Client at the price named.[4]

---

[1] Campbell vs. Wright, 118 N. Y. 594; reported below, 8 N. Y. St. Rep. 474.

[2] Campbell vs. Wright, supra; Porter vs. Wormser, 94 N. Y. 431; Gould vs. Trask, 10 N. Y. Supp. 619. A stop order may describe the price limited by referring to conditions and contingencies. It is not essential that a definite price be named. Wronkow vs. Clews, 20 J. & S. 176. For construction of stop order where Broker is instructed to sell when margin should fall below 5 per cent, see Wicks vs. Hatch, 62

N. Y. 535, and for construction of stop order to sell bonds "at 100¼ and 100¾ ex-coupons and accrued interest," see Porter vs. Wormser, 94 N. Y. 431, where it was held that the sale was authorized when such bonds had sold in the market for a flat price which after deduction of the coupons and accrued interest would leave the figure at which the sale had been ordered.

[3] Hope vs. Lawrence, 50 Barb. 258.

[4] Bertram vs. Godfray, 1 Knapp P. C. 381.

Receipt by the Client of dividends on the stock after the limit of a stop order to sell had been reached to his knowledge would be evidence of a waiver of the stop order.[1]

The term "stop order" may be used, of course, in other then its ordinary sense. Thus when a Broker writing to his Client, then abroad, for margin, adds, "in the meantime we enter stop order," the term may not have its ordinary meaning, but that the Broker will stop entirely and hold the transaction in *statu quo* till he hears from his Client.[2]

When therefore the Broker in his letter of May 12th, quoted the price of certain stock at 105⅝, and requested further margin, and the Client on May 24th cabled the Broker to sell such stock, which the Broker did the same day at 95, it was held that the Client could not make the Broker liable for the difference.[3]

VI. Special Contract with Client—Joint Adventures in Stocks.

But the usual and customary obligations of a Broker may be varied and controlled by special agreement with his Client, it being established that the former may by special contract limit his liability in any respect.[4]

---

[1] Bertram vs. Godfray, supra.

[2] Wronkow vs. Clews, 20 J. & S. 176.

[3] Id.   Compare this case with Gould vs. Trask, 10 N. Y. Supp. 619, in which case the Brokers notified their Clients that they would enter a "stop order" the next day, on securities carried by them on margin, at certain specified prices, meaning that unless the Client meanwhile deposited sufficient margin they would sell when the limit of the stop orders had been reached. And see also Harris vs. Pryor, 18 N. Y. Supp. 128, where although the Client authorized stop orders at 1 per cent above the market, the Brokers were held justified in closing at their own stop order of half a point from the market, when they did not agree to the stop order of the Client, who had failed to furnish margins.

[4] Milliken vs. Dehon, 27 N. Y. 364; Baker vs. Drake, 66 id. 518;

In the case of Milliken vs. Dehon [1] special authority was given to sell cotton " at public or private sale or otherwise, at his option, for the most that it would bring." The court held that such a contract authorized the pledgee to sell at private sale without notice, and modified the ordinary rights of a pledgor to have notice of the time and placed of sale; and that these general rules could be legally modified or waived by agreement. To the same effect was Baker vs. Drake,[2] where it was held that by a special contract a Client might agree that his business should be conducted in accordance with the usage of a particular office, and that if such usage justified a sale of stocks where the margins were exhausted, without notice, the Client would be bound thereby. But a provision in an agreement of pledge by which the pledgor waives *notice* of sale is not a waiver of *demand* of payment before sale.[3]

Wicks vs. Hatch [4] is another case illustrating a dealing where there was a special contract. In that case, it appeared the plaintiff executed to G. A. W. a power of attorney empowering him to buy and sell gold, stocks, and bonds, and to execute for her, and in her name, " all orders, checks, or other

Markham vs. Jaudon, 41 id. 235, at p. 244; Wicks vs. Hatch, 62 id. 535; Stenton vs. Jerome, 54 id. 480; Hyatt vs. Argenti, 3 Cal. 151; Robinson vs. Norris, 51 How. Pr. (N. Y.) 442; aff'd 6 Hun (N. Y.), 233.

[1] 27 N. Y. 364.

[2] 66 id. 518.

[3] Cortelyou vs. Lansing, 2 Cai. (N. Y.) Cas. 200; see as to this case Barrow vs. Paxton, 5 Johns. (N. Y.) 260, by which it is explained by Kent, Ch. J., that it was never decided; see also Wilson vs. Little, 2 N. Y. 443. An agreement to carry wheat until a specified date without further margin, no sale to be made until ordered by the Client, does not mean that the wheat is to be carried indefinitely without further margin until such time as the Client orders a sale, but simply that a sale could not be made prior to the specified date without his order. Amsden vs. Jacobs, 75 Hun, 311.

[4] 62 N. Y. 535; aff'g 6 J. & S. (N. Y.) 96.

instruments in writing whatsoever," which might, in his discretion, be necessary in the business, with power of substitution, etc. G. A. W. employed defendants as Brokers, depositing a sum as a margin. He gave to them a writing signed
by him, as attorney for plaintiff, authorizing them to sell, in
their discretion, at public or private sale, without notice, the
stocks which they might be carrying for her, whenever the
margin should fall below 5 per cent. In an action to recover
damages for sales made at the Board of Brokers in pursuance of this authority, defendants set up as a counterclaim
a deficiency arising on the sales after exhausting the margin.
The court held that it was within the authority of G. A. W.
to execute the writing, and defendants were authorized to sell
at the Board of Brokers without notice, when in good faith,
and in the exercise of a sound discretion, they deemed the
state of the market justified it; that plaintiff was liable for
any loss on sales beyond the amount of the margin ; and that
the same was proper as a counterclaim. The court charged,
among other things, that defendants had a right to sell when
the market rendered it prudent, either for the benefit or protection of their principal or for their own protection. Held,
no error, that from their peculiar relations as Brokers, holding stock paid for, mainly out of their own funds, defendants
were authorized to act, and necessarily in making sales acted,
for the protection of their own interest as well as that of
their principal.

The case of Harris vs. Tumbridge[1] illustrates a special
contract with Brokers growing out of a "straddle." In
that case, the plaintiff purchased through defendant, a
Broker, a 60 days' "straddle"—viz., a contract by which the

---

[1] 8 Ab. New Cas. 291; aff'd 83 N. Y. 92.

plaintiff had the option to either receive or deliver 100 shares of Lake Shore stock at 62¾ for sixty days, the defendant further guaranteeing that the stock should fluctuate at least 8 per cent. The "straddle" remained in the hands of the defendant. The day after the making of this contract, the defendant, without express authority, sold "short" 100 shares of Lake Shore stock against the "straddle," and closed out the contract eventually at a loss to the plaintiff.

Immediately after the contract, Lake Shore began to advance in price, and reached 73⅝ a short time afterwards. The plaintiff, in an action on the "straddle," recovered a judgment; and the court held that the subsequent action of defendant in purporting to sell "short" against the "straddle" was nugatory. It was his duty to have closed the "straddle" contract by exercising the option at a most favorable time within the sixty days; and a failure to do so made him liable for what plaintiff lost by his neglect, and that this result could not be affected by an alleged custom of Brokers not known to the plaintiff.

And where a Client, at the commencement of his dealings with a firm of Brokers, deposits with them money with an order to purchase stocks on his account, and receives from them an agreement for his signature, saying " We herewith enclose our usual customer's agreement for your signature," and he signs and returns the same to them—which agreement authorizes the Brokers to sell, at their discretion, at the Brokers' Board or elsewhere, or at public or private sale, with or without advertising, and without prior demand of any kind, upon a notice to the Client of the time and place of sale, of all or any gold, stocks, property, things in action, or collateral securities held by them and belonging to the Client—the latter is bound by the terms of the agreement;

and would have been bound, though he had never signed it
or given any assent to it, if he subsequently gave orders under it.[1]

But where there is a special contract in writing between
the Brokers and their Client, by which the ordinary principles applicable to such a relation are set aside or modified,
and the dealings under such contract being fully closed, new
transactions are subsequently entered into, the former written contract will not apply unless the parties have specially
agreed thereto.

In Bickett vs. Taylor[2] the Client, in November, 1870,
signed a written agreement in respect to certain stock transactions between him and the Brokers. This agreement
clothed the Brokers with the greatest possible power with
respect to the use and sale of the stock, and subjected the
Client to the most stringent obligations to keep his margin
at all times at 10 per cent. The transactions under this
agreement, and the accounts in respect to them, were fully
closed. More than two years afterwards the Client bought
stock through the Brokers, which the latter sold without
notice for default of Client to keep up margins. Held, that
evidence on the part of the Client to show that the former
written contract was not applicable, but had been superseded
by an oral arrangement, was proper, and the question should
have been submitted to the jury. The court was inclined to
the opinion, that under the circumstances, as *matter of law*,
the previous written contract was ended, and did not apply
to a fresh dealing between the parties.[3]

[1] Robinson vs. Norris, 51 How. Pr. (N. Y.) 442; aff'd 6 Hun (N. Y.), 233.

[2] 55 How. Pr. (N. Y.) 128.

[3] See this case in Court of Ap-peals *sub nom.* Burkitt vs. Taylor, 13 W. D 75, where the above views were fully sustained. See also Winans vs. Hassey, 48 Cal. 634.

Special agreements between the Broker and the Client are sometimes made whereby the former agrees to re-purchase from the Client the securities bought for him, on certain contingencies, usually that of the Client's dissat-isfaction. Such a contract, either between Broker and Client or vendor and vendee, is not a contract for the sale of good, chattels, or things in action, within the Statute of Frauds, but is a provision for the rescission of the entire contract, and is valid though oral.[1] A party does not di-vest himself of an option to return purchased securities at cost price by selling them again with the same option to his vendees, which is exercised.[2] Where the agreement to re-purchase is without express limit as to time, and is there-fore to be construed as running for a reasonable period, a delay not demanding a re-purchase, in one case of three years, and in another of nearly two years, in both cases the vendor having in the interim repeatedly urged the vendee to keep the securities, was held not to be, as matter of law, an unreasonable length of time.[3]

When an option contract provides that notice of intention to require performance of the contract of repurchase is to be given on a specified day, it must be given on that day, al-

---

[1] Johnston vs. Trask, 116 N. Y. 136, and cases there cited; Wooster vs. Sage, 67 N. Y. 67. Nor is an oral contract, whereby a promoter of a company promised plaintiff that if the latter would take two shares in the company and give his promissory note therefor, the former would find some one to take the shares off the hands of plaintiff who would not be put to any expense in the matter, within the provision of the Statute of Frauds declaring that a promise to answer for the debt, etc., of another should be in writing. Green vs. Brookins, 23 Mich. 48.

[2] Wooster vs. Sage, 67 N. Y. 67. As to meaning of agreement to "make good" amount advanced on purchase of stock, see Rowley vs. Swift, 67 Hun, 95.

[3] Johnston vs. Trask, 116 N. Y. 136; Wooster vs. Sage, 67 N. Y. 67. As to transactions between part-ners, see Worn vs. Fry, 84 Cal. 256.

though a holiday other than Sunday, as the Holiday Acts
do not affect such a transaction, otherwise the contract will be
deemed to be at an end, and it cannot be enforced in the
absence of evidence of an agreement reviving it or making a new contract with reference thereto.[1] And a tender
of the stock, and an offer to transfer the same, must
furthermore be made on the day when performance
is due,[2] unless the court can say under all the circumstances that time was not of the essence of the contract,
in which case tender within a reasonable time will suffice.[3]
But a repudiation of the contract before maturity dispenses with the necessity of tender, and the production
upon the trial of the securities, and an offer to deliver
over, is enough.[4]

The vendee is not, upon the trial, bound to prove any
damages, the obligation of the vendor being to repurchase
the securities or to refund the cost. It may be that
when the vendor refuses to accept a return, the vendee
may dispose of the property and sue for the deficiency.

If the securities consist of coupon bonds, and any of the
coupons are removed by the vendee, they must be deducted out of the purchase-money, but any profit in the

---

[1] Page vs. Shainwald, 169 N. Y.
246. If the option is to repurchase at the end of one year after
thirty days' notice, it is not necessary that such notice should be
given thirty days before the expiration of the year. A notice any time
within the year is sufficient. Maguire vs. Halsted, 18 App. Div. 228.

[2] Taylor vs. Blair, 36 N. Y. St.
Rep. 528. Mere non-residence of
the party to whom tender is to be

made, which non-residence also existed at the time the agreement was
entered into, does not dispense with
the making of the tender. Ibid.
See, however, George vs. Braden, 70
Pa. St. 56.

[3] Duchemin vs. Kendall, 149
Mass. 171. If a certificate has no
value, tender at the trial is sufficient.
Lewis vs. Andrews, 127 N. Y. 673.

[4] Maguire vs. Halsted, 18 App.
Div. 228.

transaction stands on a different footing, and cannot be regarded as any part of the property to be returned.[1]

Joint Adventures in Stocks.

There are a few cases which illustrate a dealing in securities for speculation on joint account or for the joint benefit of the parties engaging therein.

It is not an uncommon occurrence in stock operations for the joint account of two or more persons, for one of the parties to furnish the " information," or facts, upon which the transaction is made, and the other person to contribute the capital or means to carry on the operation. And the courts have held, that the contribution of information which is used as a basis for operations in stocks is a sufficient consideration for an agreement to give the party furnishing the same an interest in the profits of the transaction.

In the case of White vs. Drew [2] the plaintiff, being in possession of valuable information in relation to a certain stock, which he proposed to impart to defendant upon condition that, if defendant should consider it sufficiently important to warrant his acting upon it, he (defendant) should hold 5000 shares of such stock at cost for plaintiff's account and at his risk, and subject to his orders for a period of sixty or ninety days, to which defendant assented, and thereupon plaintiff imparted said information, which defendant accepted and acted upon, pronouncing it the best " point ' he had heard of in a long time, the court held that the moment the information was given, and the transaction assented to by defendant, it was an executed contract, and the defendant bore the same relation to the plaintiff in regard to this stock as

---

[1] Wooster vs. Sage, 67 N. Y. 67.   [2] 56 How. Pr. (N. Y.) 53.

Stock-brokers ordinarily bear to Clients for whom they are carrying stocks. The rule, that where one offers a reward for information he is bound by his contract to the one who responds to his offer, applies with equal force to the case where information is proffered by one and accepted by another under a contract by him to carry certain stocks for the benefit and profit of the party imparting the information. And reliable information, as to facts upon which the future price of a stock will depend, is a sufficient consideration to uphold an agreement or contract in relation to such stock. Such information, the court said, being concededly of great value, is just as effective to take the case out of the statute of frauds as if a cash payment had then been made.[1]

In Marston vs. Gould[2] the parties engaged in a joint adventure in the purchase and sale of stock, under an agreement, by which defendant was to furnish the funds, and to bear the loss if the operations should result in loss; the net profits, if any, to be divided in certain proportions. No provision was made fixing a limit of time for the continuance of the operations, or for closing them and settling the accounts. The courts held that the arrangement was terminable at any time at the will of either of the parties, and that either could maintain an equitable action against the other for an accounting or for the adjustment of losses sustained by the misconduct of the other, without regard to the question whether or not they were to be regarded as partners *inter sese*. By arrangement, the Brokers, through whom the joint operations were conducted, kept the account thereof under

---

[1] 56 How. Pr. (N. Y.) 53. Information furnished by one Broker which enables another to effect a sale or purchase and thereby earn commissions is a sufficient consid- eration for a promise to divide such commissions. McLaughlin vs. Barnard, 2 E. D. Smith, 372.

[2] 69 N. Y. 220.

the letter " M." By direction of defendant this account was closed, and the stock on hand, purchased under the agreement, was transferred to his individual account. It did not appear that the certificates of the stock were disturbed. In January, 1872, there was a sudden rise in the market, when plaintiff made a formal call upon defendant to sell the stock and account to plaintiff for his portion of the profits; and, upon his failure to comply, brought this action. Upon the trial, defendant offered to prove that he sold all of the stock held on " M " account before January 9, 1872. This was excluded solely because not connected with an offer to prove that the sale was made avowedly on joint account. Held, error; that if defendant had authority to sell, it was not necessary to make known at the time of the sale that it was made on joint account; and if he made the sale in good faith in the ordinary way, plaintiff was bound.[1]

So in an action for an accounting on the purchase of stock, where the only question between the parties is, whether the purchase was joint or several, and the testimony is conflicting between them, the point will be considered settled in favor of the plaintiff, as a joint purchase, where it appears that the defendant had previously rendered an account to the plaintiff for the latter's share, adding interest and commission to that date, stating that the purchase was joint and containing the actual interest of each of them in the enterprise.[2]

[1] 69 N. Y. 220.

[2] Crosby vs. Watts, 49 How. Pr. (N. Y.) 364; aff'd 41 N. Y. Super. Ct. 208. And where plaintiff with others, advanced a sum of money to defendant to be used in purchasing certain stocks and bonds, the plain- tiff to receive a specified amount thereof. In an action to compel specific performance, held that a trust was created, involving an obligation to use the funds for the purpose for which they were sub- scribed, which the defendant could

Under an agreement for a joint venture in stock, to be held by one party for thirty days, the other party to bear all the loss, if any—held, that the former could not recover the deficiency on a decline in price without proving an actual sale at a loss within thirty days.[1]

So in an action on an agreement to pay a certain portion of the profits of a joint adventure, upon condition that information furnished by the plaintiff should prove true, the burden of proof is on the plaintiff to show that the information was true ; although, if there were no such expressed condition, the burden would be upon the defendant to prove falsity, if he relied upon that defence.[2]

not avoid by showing that he chose to use his own funds, and purchase for himself; that the transaction was not avoided by the statute of frauds; and plaintiff was entitled to a transfer of the portion which fell to him according to his subscription. Johnson vs. Brooks, 46 Super. Ct. (J. & S.) 13. But if the plaintiff upon the joint adventure has received the money, bought and sold the stock, and holds the proceeds, he cannot sustain an action for an accounting. Conger vs. Judson, N. Y. L. J. August 1, 1901. The trust relation must be established and that defendant received plaintiff's money, Schantz vs. Oakman, 163 N. Y. 148, and the burden is upon defendant to show that his trust has been performed. Marvin vs. Brooks, 94 N. Y. 71. The judgment should be against all jointly liable, although some were not served with process. Sternberger vs. Bernheimer, 121 N. Y. 194.

[1] Monroe vs. Peck, 3 Daly, 128.

[2] Strong vs. Place, 4 Robt. 385; s. c. 33 How. Pr. (N. Y.) 114. The case of Luders vs. Rasmus, 14 N. Y. W. D. 221, also arose out of joint adventures in stock. The plaintiff agreed with defendants to purchase bonds and stocks for them, he to receive one third of the net profits and be chargeable with one third of the losses thereon. Certain bonds purchased by him turned out to be counterfeits; the loss thereon was afterwards partially made good and plaintiff was credited with one third of the net amount received. The agreement was thereafter modified so that plaintiff could only draw a certain amount of his share of the profits per month, the excess to be applied on the charge for loss. The following year plaintiff left the business. In an action to recover an amount alleged to be due him, held, that plaintiff having abandoned the means provided by the

An interesting case upon the question of the right to participate in the profits of certain stock is that of Jones vs. Kent.[1] In that case defendant's intestate gave to the plaintiff a paper containing these words: " Received of J. W. Jones, by agreement, one thousand shares of St. Joe Lead stock, for which I paid him $3000. The understanding is that I am to give said Jones one half of whatever price the same is sold for, when sold, over and above that sum." Whereupon the stock was delivered by plaintiff. The latter brought an action to enforce the trust, the stock having increased very much in value; and the court below held that the instrument expressed an absolute purchase and sale free from any trust, and gave exclusive discretion or option to the buyer as to whether he would sell, and, if so, when, subject only to the obligation to pay over one half of any excess in case he should choose to sell, and should sell at an advance. The Court of Appeals reversed this ruling, and decided that it was apparent, from an inspection of the writing, that the last clause was an inducement of the sale and part of the consideration thereof; and, the party making the instrument having died, his representatives would be compelled to carry the same into effect; but that plaintiff could not recover any dividends or other income received by defendant's intestate, the contract not covering the same. A portion of the stock, however, had been exchanged into bonds of the same company, and it was held that plaintiff was entitled to one half interest in the avails of the same, after deducting any money paid to complete the conversion of the stock into bonds.

modified agreement for paying the balance due from him by the application of the surplus profits, his original liability revived and his share of the balance of loss was recoverable by defendants by way of counterclaim.

[1] 80 N. Y. 585, rev'g 13 J. & S. 66.

The court did not pass upon the question whether the intestate had the right to choose the time of sale, so that this discretion could not be interfered with by the plaintiff.   It would seem, however, that such agreements are to be construed according to the circumstances of each case, and that no general rule can be laid down.   But it is clear that the party possessing the discretion cannot seek to exercise it unreasonably against the other party to the agreement.

So in an action to recover, with dividends, certain shares of telegraph stock, claimed to be in defendant's hands, and to belong to plaintiff, as assignee of S. & Co., it appeared that in March, 1854, the stock was placed in defendant's hands, under a contract that he was to do the best he could with it, "and to have one half of the proceeds." At that time the stock was comparatively worthless. Defendant retained the stock, and dividends were made upon it. February, 1865, S. & Co. demanded the stock, which defendant declined to give up.   No request was made to sell the same.   When the demand was made it had reached a higher point than it had touched at any time since it was placed in defendant's hands.

Upon the trial it was adjudged that plaintiff was the owner of the stock and entitled to a transfer thereof, and to the dividends received and interest thereon.   But the judgment in respect to the dividends was modified, and it was held that plaintiff was entitled to the whole of the stock. On appeal this was held, error ; that as no request was made to sell, and as no injury had accrued to plaintiff by the delay, and as there was no failure on the part of defendant to fulfil his contract, he should receive one half of the avails of the stock and of the dividends actually paid to him.[1]

[1] Wight vs. Wood, 12 N. Y. *Week. Dig.* 529, s. c. 85 N. Y. 402.

The case of Butler vs. Finck[1] should also be noticed in this connection, as bearing upon the question as to how far a joint speculation will constitute the parties engaged therein, partners, so as to render one of them liable for the fraud of his co-operator. There the defendant entered into an agreement with his brother-in-law, B., to the effect that he should conduct certain stock speculations for B.'s benefit, collecting information of such a character as to justify the purchase of stocks, and giving his time and attention to the purchase and sale thereof; for these services he was to receive one third of the net profits, the margin to carry the account being furnished by B. The defendant knew that B. was a book-keeper in the employment of the plaintiff, and had no means outside of his salary. On April 23, 1879, the defendant, claiming that his share of the profits amounted to $6818.48, received from B. an order upon his Broker for that sum, which was paid by the drawee. Subsequently B. absconded, and it was then learned that he had stolen bonds from the plaintiff, and pledged them to secure his account with the Broker, by whom some had been sold and others pledged. It appeared that the sum received by the defendant was, in fact, one third of the profits actually made by him while conducting the account, and also that B. had, without his knowledge, speculated on his own account, both before and after the times referred to. It was not shown that the defendant knew that B. had stolen the bonds until after

---

[1] 21 Hun (N. Y.), 210. It was held in Sutton vs. Gray, (1894) 1 Q. B. 285, that an agreement between a member of the Exchange and a non-member, by which the latter, on business introduced by him, was to receive half the Broker's commissions and was to bear half the losses, was not a partnership agreement, and did not come within the 4th section of the Statute of Frauds so as to require the agreement to be in writing.

he had absconded. The defendant having refused to account to the plaintiff for the amounts received by him, an action was brought to recover damages for the conversion of the bonds; and, upon the trial thereof, the court directed a verdict for the plaintiff, for the entire amount lost by the abstraction of the bonds, on the theory that the defendant and B. were co-partners in the transaction, and that the former was therefore liable for the acts of the latter. It was held, that this was error, and that the question as to whether or not a partnership existed between B. and the defendant should have been submitted to the jury. It was doubted whether in any event the defendant was liable for the amount actually received by him from B.[1]

And where an agreement was made between three persons to share the profits and losses of a single transaction, the parties do not become partners so as to render an accounting necessary, and if the speculation has proved a loss, and one of the parties has paid the entire loss, he may recover one third of the loss from the representative of one of the parties who had died, without naming the other as a party to the action.[2]

Where A., in pursuance of a parol authority from B, purchases stock in his own name on the joint account of himself and B., the latter becomes the owner of one half the

---

[1] An agreement by which one party loans money to another to be used in joint-stock speculations, the profits of which were to be equally divided and the money loaned returned, nothing being said as to the losses, constitutes the parties copartners, the copartnership being terminable at will. Sims vs. Vyse, 13 N. Y. St. Rep. 355. Upon the general question as to whether joint operators are partners, see Parsons on Partnership (4th ed.), 50, 51; also as to joint adventures in a purchase or enterprise, see King vs. Wise, 43 Cal. 628; Flagg vs. Mann, 2 Sumner, 486; Reilly vs. Freeman, 1 App. Div. 560.

[2] Burleigh vs. Bevan, 22 Misc. 38.

stock, and liable to pay A. the amount advanced therefor ; and no written assignment of the stock from A. to B. is necessary, to render B liable for his proportionate share of the purchase-money.[1]

---

[1] Stover vs. Flack, 41 Barb. (N. Y.) 162, aff'd 30 N. Y. 64. And if the stock is worthless he is not bound to attempt to sell it in the market before commencing his action. Ibid. Unless otherwise stipulated parties to a joint account are entitled to share in the profits and liable to divide the loss in proportion to the amount of the purchase money each has advanced. Boardman vs. Gaillard, 60 N. Y. 614. See generally on subject of "joint account" and several liability in stock transactions, Quincey vs. White, 63 N. Y. 370, 377, 378; Kimball vs. Williams, 65 N. Y. Supp. 69. In an action to recover capital contributed for the purpose of engaging in joint speculations, a recovery can only be had by proof that there had been no transaction on joint accounts, and where there have been such transactions resulting in total loss of the capital, the complaint must be dismissed. Sims vs. Vyse, 13 N. Y. St. Rep. 355. Joint account may be proved by showing original authority to buy or sell; or if there be no such authority by subsequent ratification. Wheeler vs. Sedgwick, 94 U. S. 1. The sale of stock by one of the parties to a joint account without the knowledge or consent of the others, is a conversion, and the parties not consulted are not liable for any loss occurring thereby. Thompson vs. Brown, 2 J. & S. 1. Where bonds were purchased by plaintiff, there being an agreement that another who did not become part owner of the bonds should share in the profits and losses, but the plaintiff advanced all the money and had the exclusive right of possession, the defendants, Brokers, who acted in the purchase could not, when sued for conversion, set up that such third person was a necessary party; they had no equity to place the latter in any other relation to plaintiff than had been assumed by the parties themselves under the agreement. Wyckoff vs. Anthony, 90 N. Y. 442. A claim for damages growing out of a breach of warranty or fraud by the seller belongs to joint buyers jointly, and cannot therefore be set up in a separate counterclaim of any of them. Hopkins vs. Lane, 87 N. Y. 501. Where in an action for an accounting as to joint transactions in stocks by copartners, the plaintiff's right to an account is established and the referee states such account, and directed further that certain bonds and stocks be delivered by defendant to several persons not mentioned in the complaint, nor parties to the suit, held that the directions of the judgment with reference to these persons not parties to the suit were improper; that the referee should have directed, when he found outside parties had claims against

21

But where two parties agree to operate jointly in stocks, and one of them accordingly opens an account in his own name with a Stock-broker, without disclosing the name or interest of the other party in the transactions, and individually manages and directs the operation, and the Broker has no knowledge of the other person, the latter cannot recover his interest in the profits of specified operations, ignoring the balance of the account. He cannot isolate certain items from the account, and recover them simply for the reason that he had no interest in the other transactions going to make up the whole account from which losses resulted. The Brokers, having dealt in ignorance of the rights of the other owner, may insist that the entire dealings shall be closed, as if the person operating the account were the only one interested.[1] The mere fact that a check, paid out by a member of the firm, is in the name of the firm, is not sufficient notice to the parties receiving it that it is partnership property, nor enough to put them on inquiry before crediting the amount to the private account of the partner of whom they receive it.[2]

Although a Broker may make a hard and unconscionable bargain in a joint speculation in stocks in which he procures from his contractee a guarantee against all losses and that

the firm property, the appointment of a receiver, who should ascertain the valid claims and distribute the same, etc. Mifflin vs. Brooks, 18 N. Y. *Week. Dig.* 531.

[1] Read vs. Jaudon, 35 How. Pr. (N. Y.) 303. See also Jaycox vs. Cameron, 49 N. Y. 645.

[2] Sterling vs. Jaudon, 48 Barb. (N. Y.) 459. Where husband and wife have a bank account in their two names, and each draws and de-

posits moneys in the absence of the other, the husband is presumed, in the absence of evidence, to own half at least of the sum standing to their credit. Gelster vs. The Syracuse Savings Bank, 17 N. Y. *Weekly Dig.* 137. As to effect of joint deposit of money in a savings bank, see Mulcahy vs. Emigrant Industrial Savings Bank, 15 N. Y. *Week. Dig.* 27.

his (the Broker's) profits on the transaction should in any case amount to a certain sum, the parties advancing the capital in about equal shares, the relationship between the parties is that of copartners, and not that of borrower and lender, so as to enable the contractee to interpose the defence of usury.[1]

VII. Sales for "Short Account."

(a.) Nature of "Short Sale."

A "short sale" of stocks has already been defined. By such a sale the Client expects to be able to deliver the stock at a lower price. In case the sale of the stocks is made "regular" (that is, not upon time, seller's option), the party selling is bound to deliver them on the next day after the sale is made, in which case, not having the stocks which he has sold, he is compelled to borrow them, and to deliver such borrowed stocks. If, however, as is frequently the case, the stocks are sold deliverable in the future—that is, "seller's option" or "buyer's option"—then, and in such event, it is not necessary for the vendor to deliver the stocks until the expiration of the option, or until the buyer calls for them, as the case may be.[2] In Knowlton vs. Fitch,[3] Mr. Justice Rapallo defined a "short

[1] Orvis vs. Curtiss, 157 N. Y. 657. See further as to joint adventures in stocks, and as to opening an account stated. Berdell vs. Allen, 22 J. & S. 38; aff'd 116 N. Y. 661.

[2] See, for cases defining "short sales," White vs. Smith, 54 N. Y. 522; Wicks vs. Hatch, 62 id. 535; Knowlton vs. Fitch, 52 id. 288, rev'g 48 Barb. 493; Campbell vs. Wright, 118 N. Y. 594; Lazare vs. Allen, 20 App. Div. 616; Smith vs. Bouvier, 70 Pa. St. 325; Maxton vs. Gheen, 75 id. 166.

[3] 52 N. Y. 288. As to difference between "short sale" and one at seller's option where the seller owns the stock contracted to be sold, see Sistare vs. Best, 88 N. Y. 533. The seller's option here referred to is of a

sale" as follows: "The nature of these sales has, in the
many litigations which have come before the courts concerning them, been frequently proved, and is again explained in
the testimony in this case.   It is proven to be a sale before
purchase, with a view of purchasing at a future time at a
lower price.   It is evident that, to carry out such a speculation, the stock sold must be temporarily procured by the
seller for delivery to the purchaser.   The manner in which
this had been accomplished, in the course of the previous
dealings between the plaintiff and the defendants, is explained in the testimony.   The plaintiff did not furnish the
stock to deliver, but only margins.   The defendants furnished the stock.   They sold in the regular way, which is
deliverable the next day, and then borrowed the stock of
other parties to deliver.   The profit or loss depended upon
whether the stock rose or fell.   The plaintiff had the right

different nature from that referred
to in the text, where the seller need
not possess the stocks at the time of
sale. Requirements of complaint
against Broker for neglect to execute
"short sale" stated in Ryder vs.
Sistare, 15 Daly, 90. When the
complaint does not show that the
stocks ordered bought ever increased in value, or that loss was
caused by any change in the value
of the stocks ordered sold, the plaintiff can only recover nominal damages. Id. As to whether a custom
of Brokers to use stocks carried for
margin buyers in effecting sales for
other "short sale" customers, so
that the amount of certain stocks
carried are at times reduced below
the requirements of the purchasing
customers, is reasonable, quære.
Skiff vs. Stoddard, 21 L. R. A. 102,

113. A contract to sell stocks
"short" which is contrary to public
policy cannot be enforced. Veazy
vs. Allen, 173 N. Y. 359. In that
case the Client's claim was that the
defendant Brokers, in consideration
of his supplying them with information concerning an investigation into the affairs of two corporations
popularly known as the "Whisky"
and "Sugar" Trusts, which he was
to procure to be made by Congress,
would sell the stock of the corporations, and buy them again at a
lower price, the decline in price being caused by the Congressional investigation, and divide with him the
profits so made, and the court held
that such a contract was clearly
against public policy, and unenforceable. Id.

to direct his Brokers at any time to buy in the stock and close the transaction. Until bought in, the Brokers remained bound to the persons from whom they had obtained the stock, to return to them an equal number of shares, whatever might be the market price at the time it was demanded." [1]

A "short sale" was also defined, and the duties of a Broker considered, in the case of White vs. Smith. [2] It was there laid down that where a Stock-broker agreed for a commission to be paid to him, and upon a deposit with him of a stipulated margin, to make a short sale for a Client,

---

[1] A "short sale" of stocks is legal in Pennsylvania (Smith vs. Bouvier, 70 Pa. St. 325; Maxton vs. Gheen, 75 id. 166). In the case of Appleman vs. Fisher (34 Md. 540), a contract to sell gold "short" was upheld as legal. See also Chap. V. "Stock-jobbing."

"About ten years ago it became the practice to rig the market as regards the shares of particular joint-stock banking companies. A party would be formed, perhaps, owning none of the shares of the selected company, and they would proceed to sell considerable quantities of the shares, hoping so to damage the reputation of the company and lower the value of the stock as to be able to buy up enough before delivery would be required. This noxious kind of speculation was checked by an Act of Parliament (30 Vict. c. 29, 1867), which now requires the seller of bank shares to specify the numbers or the registered proprietors of the shares which he is selling for future delivery" (Jevon's Money

and the Mechanism of Exchange, pp. 210, 211). The act of 1867 has been, however, disregarded on the English Stock Exchanges, and it has, to a large extent, failed to attain the object of its enactment, as knowledge by the Client of the custom to disregard it, is sufficient to exonerate the Broker. See Chapter on "Usages"; Brodhurst's Stock Exchange Law, p. 197; Chitty's Statutes, vol. 1, title "Bank," p. 39. It was held in Mitchell vs. City of Glasgow Bank, 4 App. Cas. 624, that entries in the books of the respective Brokers, each entry specifying the name of the Broker for the other party, initialed by him, coupled with the mention of the vendor's name after the sale, was not a compliance with the act. But the practice of selling stocks and securities "short" has prevailed for a very much longer time in this country. As to legality of "short sales," see title "Stock-jobbing."

[2] 51 N. Y. 522.

the agreement is but partially performed by a sale; it is part of the bargain that the Broker shall carry the stock for a reasonable time, as otherwise the object of the transaction would be defeated. The Broker can close the transaction at any time if, upon demand and notice, the margin is not kept good; and he may close it upon notice after he has carried the stock for a reasonable time. He has not the right, unless so expressly agreed, to buy in stock to cover the sale without notice to, or direction from, his Client, and by so doing he becomes liable for any loss he thus occasions his principal. In that case it appeared that on the 18th of October, defendants (Stock-brokers), upon plaintiff's order and on his account, sold 300 shares N. Y. C. "short" at 186. On the 1st of November, without plaintiff's order or knowledge, they "bought in" stock to cover the sale. On the 2d of November, the stock having declined to 180¼, plaintiff ordered defendants to cover their sale, to which no attention was paid. The court held that the plaintiff was entitled to recover, and that the proper measure of damages was the difference between the price at which the stock was sold short, and the market price upon the day when the order was received to purchase, with interest, deducting commissions, etc.[1]

---

[1] See also to same effect, Rogers vs. Wiley, 131 N. Y. 527. The same rule was declared in regard to a short sale of wheat in Campbell vs. Wright, 118 N. Y. 394. The Broker and the customer have mutual and correlative rights and duties. The former undertakes to carry the stock a reasonable time, so as to afford the customer an opportunity to realize the expected profits, while the customer, on his part, is bound to keep his margin good, so as to secure the Broker against loss. But the customer is entitled to notice before the Broker can close him out by buying in the stock on his account. Hess vs. Rau, 95 N. Y. 359, 362, aff'g 17 J. & S. 324; Harris vs. Pryor, 18 N. Y. Supp. 128. But if a Client wishes to "cover" a short sale, he must

(b.) Duty of Broker to Sell at Price Ordered.

The Broker's duty, upon receiving an order to sell stocks short, is analogous to that which he owes in the case of a purchase. Where he is ordered to sell at a fixed price, he must, if possible, sell at such price; if at the market price, he must, as we have seen, sell at the best possible market price, being responsible to his Client for the non-exercise of ordinary care and diligence.[1]

(c.) Nature of Contract made upon " Borrowing" Stock, and from whom the Stock may be Borrowed.

The practice or usage in borrowing stocks is this : A Broker who has sold stocks " short " borrows the number of shares of stock sold from a fellow-Broker who has the stocks to loan, and pays him the market price for them. Although in semblance a sale, the full market price being paid and the stock delivered, it is, in effect, but a loan, and is so registered on the books of the respective Brokers. So, if the borrowed stocks fluctuate widely, either Broker can call upon the other to put up a sufficient margin to guard against loss until the stock is returned.[2]

---

prove that his instructions reached the Broker in sufficient time to make the purchase at the time requested. His evidence that he mailed a letter to his Broker on October 21, 22 or 23, to buy 10 shares of railroad stock at the market price at the opening of the market on October 23, is not sufficient to hold the Brokers liable for not filling the order, unless it is shown that the letter was mailed at such a time that it would have reached the Brokers at the opening of the market on October 23. Birnbaum vs. May, 58 App. Div. 79. If a "short sale" is repudiated by the customer, the Broker is justified in closing, and the Client cannot afterward enforce it. Id.

[1] See ante, § IV., sub. (a.), p. 206. See also Allen vs. McConihe, ante, p. 206.

[2] See Arts. XXXI. and XXVIII. Const. New York Stock Exchange. But the rule to require the lender to

For instance, a stock may be selling for $100 per share when it is borrowed, and afterwards may decline to $50 per share, in which case the borrowing Broker has stock which is only worth one half the amount which he has paid to the lender; in such a case the borrower has the right to call upon the lender to make up the difference by depositing a sufficient margin, and vice versa.[1] So, it seems, that a Broker who is " short" of stock for a Client may borrow the stock belonging to other Clients; no one can object to this arrangement but the Clients themselves whose stocks are borrowed, and it does not lie in the mouth of the person "short" to do it.[2]

Rapallo, J., upon this point, said: "The fact that the shares thus used belonged to a customer of the defendants can make no difference to the plaintiff. The result of the transaction was to leave the defendants liable to their customer as before, to deliver to him an equal number of shares when demanded. Whether or not the defendants were authorized thus to employ the stock of their customer depends upon the arrangements between them." In the case of Dykers vs. Allen [3] Mr. Chancellor Walworth held that an ordinary loan of a given number of shares of stock of a corporation amounts in substance to a sale, to be paid for

put up margins, or a usage to that effect, must be proved, and therefore, if a Stock-broker, at his Client's request, borrows the stocks to cover a short sale, and pays, for such borrowed stock, a greater sum than that received on the short sale, he is not bound to require the lender to put up margins on a decline of the stock, in the absence of a special agreement, or proof of a rule or usage of the Exchange, to that effect. Morris vs. Jamieson, 68 N. E. Rep. 742.

[1] As to the measure of damages for refusal or neglect to return borrowed stock, see chapter "Measure of Damages."

[2] Knowlton vs. Fitch, 52 N. Y. 288, rev'g 48 Barb. 593.

[3] 7 Hill, 497.

in kind and quality, and the title vests in the borrower.[1] If a bonus be declared on stock loaned, while it is in the hands of a borrower, the lender is in equity entitled to the bonus.[2] This law fully accords with the practice of Brokers, who hold all dividends, interest, or other accretions to the stock for the account of the lender.

(d) Duty of Brokers to Close Short Contract by "Buying in" Stock.

As we have seen,[3] the Broker has no right to buy in the stocks with which to cover or conclude a "short" sale, without the order or knowledge of the Client, unless, after notice and demand of additional margin, the latter fails to respond. Upon the order or request of the Client, the Broker must proceed to buy the stocks, and return them to the person from whom they were originally borrowed, and this closes the transaction.[4] If the stocks can be purchased at

---

[1] See also Fosdick vs. Greene, 27 Ohio St. 484; Taylor vs. Ketchum, 35 How. Pr. (N. Y.) 289. The borrower is not bound to return the identical shares borrowed. Any certificate for the same number of shares will suffice, provided the shares continue to represent the same interest in the corporate capital. Barclay vs. Culver, 30 Hun, 1.

[2] Vaughan vs. Wood, 1 M. & K. 403.

[3] White vs. Smith, 54 N. Y. 522; Hess vs. Rau, 95 N. Y. 359; Harris vs. Pryor, 18 N. Y. Supp. 128.

[4] If the Client has died, or becomes incompetent to transact business, a Broker, acting in good faith, may continue a "short sale" contract until the appointment of a legal representative. The Broker has bound himself to return the stock, however, for delivery, and has an interest in the contract, and so the case is within the exception to the rule that the death of a principal revokes the authority of the agent. Hess vs. Rau, 95 N. Y. 359, aff'g 17 J. & S. 321. The court said (p. 363): "As it turned out it would have been to the advantage of the estate if the stocks had been bought in immediately after Rau's (the Client's) death. But if this course had been taken and the market had gone the other way, the Brokers would have been called upon to justify the transaction. We think

a lower figure than that for which they were originally sold, the Client has made a profit; if otherwise, a loss. In the case of White vs. Smith [1] the defendants, Stock-brokers, bought in stocks to complete a short sale without the authority of the plaintiff; and, subsequently, the latter directed them to make the purchase, which the defendants refused to do. The defendants contended that they were not under an obligation to act for the plaintiff, either for any fixed period or to any definite amount. But the court held the rule of law otherwise, and decided that, by the agreement by which the agency was created, no period was fixed for its continuance, and the only limit as to amount was fixed by margin or deposit; and that it could not be revoked by the defendants without notice; and a renunciation without such notice subjected the defendants to a liability for any damages the plaintiff might sustain thereby. [2]

The notice to furnish more margin must be a reasonable notice. As to what is a reasonable notice to justify a Broker

the plaintiffs were not bound to place themselves in this dilemma, but were authorized, acting in good faith, to maintain the existing situation until a representative of the estate should be appointed. . . .

"The act of buying in the stocks on account of the estate, which the executor insists should have been done, would have been a more decisive act of agency than to borrow stocks to replace others previously borrowed, in order to discharge their own obligation. We do not say that circumstances might not exist which would justify a Broker in closing a stock transaction after the death of the principal, without awaiting the appointment of a representative; but however this may be, we think it plain that no exigency existed in the case now under consideration which imposed any such duty upon the plaintiffs."

If the promisor in a stock option contract dies while the contract is executory, a demand for the stock under the contract must be made upon the personal representatives of the deceased promisor and not upon the bank where the contract is made payable. Prince vs. Robinson, 14 Fed. Rep. 631.

[1] 6 Lans. (N. Y.) 5.

[2] This case was affirmed on appeal, 54 N. Y. 522.

to cover a transaction and close the deal, depends upon circumstances.[1] It was held in Lazare vs. Allen,[2] that a notice given at between 10 and 10:30 A. M. to furnish more margin, the stock having been purchased by the Brokers about noon of the same day, was, standing alone, unreasonable in point of time, but in that case the Brokers had testified that on the fourth, third and second days before the sale they had requested more margins from their Client, the stock having gone up, and if the case had gone to the jury they might from the evidence have declined to find that the Client (who had been forty years engaged in stock transactions, and who lived only a block away from the Broker's office) had the necessary margins ready for use on the day of sale. If the purchase had been made four days' subsequently, the customer would, owing to the fall in price of the stock, have made a profit of $925. After the transaction was closed the Brokers had to his credit $64.35, for which sum the jury found for the plaintiff under the direction of the court, and the judgment on such verdict was affirmed by the Appellate Division.

In Knowlton vs. Fitch[3] the plaintiff employed defendants, who were Stock-brokers, to operate for him in stocks. He was to furnish a margin, and keep it good without notice; defendants to care for themselves, if he did not. All the transactions were "short sales," defendants selling, deliverable the next day, and borrowing the stock to deliver until plaintiff directed a purchase to replace the stock borrowed. At the close of a transaction thus conducted, defendants had to the order of plaintiff $1249.19. The latter

[1] See p. 340, and cases cited note 4. [3] 52 N. Y. 288, rev'g 48 Barb.
[2] 20 App. Div. 616. See also 593.
Kanady vs. Burk, 18 Mich. 278.

then directed the sale of 100 shares of Michigan Southern. Defendants sold as ordered on account of plaintiff, borrowing the stock to deliver, and placing proceeds to plaintiff's credit. The stock rising in the market so as to exhaust the margin, defendants notified plaintiff to furnish more, and, upon his failure to comply, bought in, to replace the stock borrowed. In an action brought to recover the $1249.19, held, that the defendants were authorized under plaintiff's order to sell and to borrow the stock for delivery; and, upon failure of plaintiff to furnish the necessary margin, they had the right to buy on his account; that the purchase was so made, and that therefore a finding that such purchase was not made for or on account of plaintiff was error. In the case of Staples vs. Gould[1] the court held that where a Broker is employed to sell "short" certain stock, deliverable at any time within 30 days, at the option of the principal, and the Broker sells the stock as ordered, although the stock advances beyond the extent of the margin deposited with the Broker, the latter cannot buy in the stock, without the authorization of the principal, at any time before the 30 days have expired, the time for delivery limited by the contract. In that case the plaintiff, on the 15th of January, 1851, employed the defendant, a Broker, to sell for him 200 shares of Canton Company stock at $66 per share, deliverable at the plaintiff's option, at any time within 30 days from date. At the same time, he deposited with the defendant the sum of $750 "for the purpose of protecting the defendant against loss or damage in the business of such agency." In pursuance of his employment, the defendant on the

[1] 9 N. Y. 520.

same day made contracts for the sale to two firms specified in the agreement with defendant. The plaintiff did
not at the time own any stock of the Canton Company.
On the 20th of January, 1851, the defendant delivered to
each of the purchasers the 100 shares of stock contracted
to be sold by him, without the knowledge or consent of
plaintiff, the stock on that day selling at $80 and $85 per
share. At the expiration of the 30 days the stock was below $66 per share. The plaintiff brought an action to re-
cover back the money deposited with the defendant, and
the court held that the plaintiff had a cause of action, but
there could be no recovery under the Stock-jobbing Act.

The usage of Wall Street is, that where stock is sold deliverable at a future time, the parties to the contract can
call upon each other for a deposit to meet fluctuations commensurate with the present market price of the stock. This
can be repeated any number of times, so that each party
will remain intact.[1] But it may be contended that the
legitimate effect of the case just cited would be to put the
whole burden of the fluctuations upon the Broker, and to
leave the Client entirely unburdened in a transaction consummated for his sole benefit, after his margin has been
entirely exhausted by the rise in the price of the stocks.
This does not seem to be reasonable, but the only relief
against the decision would seem to be by providing in the
beginning of the transaction, either by a deposit or special
agreement, for the fluctuations of the market. The full
force and influence of this view of the decision in Staples
vs. Gould will be seen by the following illustration : A
Client orders his Broker to sell 100 shares of stock "short,"

---

[1] Arts. XXXI and XXVIII. Const. N. Y. Stock Exchange.

seller 60, at $100 per share. The Broker executes the order upon receiving a 10 per cent margin, or $1000. Ten days after this sale the price of the stock is $120, and fifty days after the sale it has risen to $150. Yet it seems that the Broker cannot call upon his Client for further margin, nor buy in the stock without his consent. This is certainly contrary to the usage of Wall Street; and if the question were to clearly arise again, the courts would have good reason to reject the decision upon the ground that the case of Staples vs. Gould was really decided upon another point, and that it contradicts the law that the Client is impliedly bound to furnish margins to meet the fluctuations of the market.[1] Or, although no reference is made to this point in the opinion, the decision may be supported upon the ground that the plaintiff had the right to recover back his margins because the stock was bought in by the Broker, and the transaction closed, without any notice to him. While the theory of the law in this respect, when applied to general commercial subjects, is correct, that where goods are sold, deliverable within sixty days, at the option of the buyer, there is no liability on the part of the latter until the sixty days have accrued,[2] yet when applied to a Wall Street transaction, where the business is conducted from day to day upon present values, it works manifest hardship and injustice.

VIII. Cumpulsory Sale by Broker.

(a.) *For Failure to Put up Margins to Meet the Fluctuations of the Market.*

It the absence of an express contract providing otherwise, the law will not throw the burden or risk of loss from

---

[1] See, upon this point, next sub. (VIII.), p. 335.

[2] Oelricks vs. Ford, 23 How. (U. S.) 49.

the fluctuations of the market upon the Broker, but will compel the Client, upon a proper demand by the former, to furnish margin sufficient to make the latter safe.[1]

In a stock transaction such as we are treating of, it is expressly or impliedly agreed that the margin shall be replenished, if the stock appreciates or depreciates, as the case may be; and, upon failure of the Client to do so, the stock may be sold upon reasonable and customary notice.[2]

The relation which exists between a Broker and his Client in the purchase of stocks has already been considered,[3] and it follows, from the establishment of the relation, that the Broker cannot summarily, without any previous demand of margin, dispose of his Client's stocks. He is bound to give

[1] The fact that in dealings between members of the Chicago Board of Trade, one member might be able to defeat a call for margins under § 7 of rule 20 of the rules, did not deprive him of the right, when the title to the margins was put in issue, to prove, that the market value of the article sold was no higher on the day of delivery than when it was sold. Ryan vs. Cudahy, 157 Ill. 108, 121.

[2] Gruman vs. Smith, 81 N. Y. 25; 10 N. Y. *Weekly Dig.* 63, rev'g 12 J. & S. (N. Y.) 389; Knowlton vs. Fitch, 52 N. Y. 288; Stenton vs. Jerome, 54 id. 480; Gillett vs. Whiting, 120 N. Y. 402 (in which case it was also held that as there was a breach of contract by the Brokers they were not entitled to any damage), and cases cited at p. 342. See, as to similar rule where grain is bought upon margin on the Board of Trade of Chicago, Corbett vs. Underwood, 83 Ill. 324; Moeller vs. McLagan, 60 id. 317. As to the difference between an unauthorized purchase by a Broker to cover a "short" sale, and of a purchase on a margin, see Campbell vs. Wright, 118 N. Y. 594. See also Perin vs. Parker, 126 Ill. 201. As to the legality of a usage on the Exchange to sell without demand for margin, see post, p. 418 et seq. And upon the New Orleans Cotton Exchange when, under its rules, contracts are "closed out" at stated times by the payment of differences, and a contract is "closed out" by a cotton factor although the opposite party does not demand more margins. Lehman vs. Feld, 37 Fed. Rep. 852.

[3] Supra, p. 170 et seq., and cases there cited.

the latter notice that his margin is diminished, and that further margin is required.[1]

An injunction, however, will not be granted to restrain a Stock-broker from selling stocks deposited with him as a margin in a speculative transaction, upon a mere general averment of irreparable injury, without showing in what respect this injury will be entailed. . Where there is no averment or proof of the Stock-broker's insolvency, the fact of a "low" market is not enough to justify the issuing of an injunction. The plaintiff in such a case has a perfect remedy at law in damages for the conversion of his stocks, if they are improperly sold.[2] Nor can a pledgor resist the sale of the stock on the ground that it can only be made at a great sacrifice.[3]

So where there is a written contract for the delivery of certain merchandise at a given price, to be delivered within a named time at the option of the seller, evidence offered by the purchaser of a usage existing, by which a "reasonable" margin should be put up to meet the fluctuations of the market, is rightfully excluded, because it is too indefinite and uncertain to establish a usage. Moreover, where there is no doubt or ambiguity on the face of the contract, evidence of the usage is inadmissible.[4]

(b.) Form of Notice; Upon whom Served; Reasonable Time.

There is no set form which the Broker is obliged to use in making this demand for more margin. Any language

---

[1] Baker vs. Drake, 66 N. Y. 518; Gruman vs. Smith, 81 id. 25; Ritter vs. Cushman, 35 How. Pr. (N. Y.) 284; s. c. 7 Robt. 294; Hanks vs. Drake, 49 Barb. 186; Stenton vs. Jerome, 54 N. Y. 480. .

[2] Park vs. Musgrave, 2 T. & C. (N. Y.) 571.

[3] Rasch vs. His Creditors, 1 La. Ann. 31.

[4] Oelricks vs. Ford, 23 How. (U. S.) 49.

is sufficient which brings clearly home to the Client a notice that additional margin is required.[1]

In one case[2] the demand for more margins was made orally, and this, no doubt, is equally as effective as a written demand, if it can be clearly proved.

But it seems that a demand for margins should specify the sum required; yet the Client may use such language as "I have no money," which will obviate the necessity of the sum being mentioned.[3] A notice without date or signature, left in the pledgor's office, stating that if a specified amount of the loan was not paid the stock would be "used," does not constitute a demand sufficient to authorize a sale.[4]

Respecting the person upon whom the demand should be made, the general rule is that it should be served upon or made to the Client in person, although there are cir-

---

[1] Milliken vs. Dehon, 27 N. Y. 364; Cameron vs. Durkheim, 55 id. 425; Corbett vs. Underwood, 83 Ill. 324; Moeller vs. McLagan, 60 id. 317. An examination of a Client before trial as to his receipt of notices for margin was allowed in Hardy vs. Peters, 30 Hun, 79.

[2] Cameron vs. Durkheim, 55 N. Y. 425.

[3] Cameron vs. Durkheim, supra; Stenton vs. Jerome, 54 N. Y. 480, at 486. See also Burkett vs. Taylor, N. Y. Ct. of Appeals, 86 N. Y. 618; sub nom., Burkitt vs. Taylor, 13 Weekly Dig. 75; Covell vs. Loud, 135 Mass. 41.

[4] Genet vs. Howland, 45 Barb. 560. A notice by a pledgee that he will sell unless an excessive sum is paid, renders the sale invalid. Pigot vs. Cubley, 15 C. B. N. S. 701.

The Client is precluded from objecting that the demand for margin was excessive if at the time of the demand, he did not make this objection, but refused to pay on another ground. Perin vs. Parker, 126 Ill. 201.

A verbal notice personally given by the Broker to the customer thus: "Let me close you out; let us buy that boat load, and we will take what ready money you can give us, and your note for the balance," which proposition the customer declined, is not; as matter of law, sufficient to enable the Broker to close the customer out, without further direction. McGinnis vs. Smythe, 18 J. & S. 103; aff'd 23 W. D. 203; 101 N. Y. 646; more fully 1 Sil. 23.

22

cumstances which would justify the service of the same upon an agent or representative of the latter.[1]

It may be made upon the clerk of the Client employed by him in that particular transaction, or upon a confidential clerk of the Client, where the latter is absent from the city.[2]

So a notice left at the dwelling or place of business of the Client would seem to be sufficient. Shaw, Ch. J., lays down the rule [3] that " all notices at one's domicile, and all notices respecting transactions of a commercial nature at one's known place of business, are deemed in law to be good constructive notice, and to have the legal effect of actual notice." [4]

In Burkett vs. Taylor [5] the Court of Appeals of the State of New York intimated that where a Client had given a place to the Brokers where all notices should be delivered, a notice sent to a different address would not be sufficient.

In the case of Milliken vs. Dehon [6] the facts showed that the transaction had been negotiated through one D., a clerk of the plaintiff, who sometimes did outdoor business for him, and that he acted as plaintiff's agent in the

---

[1] Cameron vs. Durkheim, and cases supra.

[2] Milliken vs. Dehon, 27 N. Y. 364; Cameron vs. Durkheim, supra, and cases heretofore cited.

[3] Granite Bank vs. Ayers, 33 Mass. 392.

[4] See also, to same effect, Bryan vs. Baldwin, 7 Lans. (N. Y.) 174; and cases cited under sub. (c.), post, p. 347; Burkett or Burkitt vs. Taylor, supra.

[5] 86 N. Y. 618; *sub nom.*, Burkitt vs. Taylor, 13 W. D. 75. Where it is agreed that if more margin is required no sale will be made, but the Broker will draw on the Client for the amount needed, the Broker has no right to sell without so drawing, even if the Client is without the State and to the Broker's knowledge has made no provision for the payment of the draft. Foote vs. Smith, 136 Mass. 92.

[6] 27 N. Y. 364.

transaction in question. On this evidence the question
was left to the jury, whether D. was authorized by the
plaintiff to receive the notice, and that this would depend
upon whether D. acted as plaintiff's agent or not. The jury
having found that he did act as agent, the instruction
was upheld by the appellate court. In delivering the
opinion, Marvin, J., said : " It is also insisted that the
defendant was bound to make a demand of payment of
the margin personally of the pledgor, and that notice to
redeem should have been given personally, and so as to
the time and place of sale. . . . It seems to me that a
demand upon an authorized agent, or notice given to
him, is, in law, equivalent to a notice to the principal, and no reasons occur to me why such demand
or notice should not bind the principal. It is not a
proceeding by which a personal judgment is to be recovered. A different rule would often be very inconvenient." [1]

[1] To same effect, Bank of U. S. vs.
Davis, 2 Hill (N. Y.), 451; Wade on
Law of Notice (2d ed.), § 672 et
seq., and cases cited; Potter vs.
Thompson, 10 R. I. 1. The agency
of a Stock-broker on margin transactions being one coupled with an
interest, his authority to act as
agent is not revoked by the death
of his customer, and he may, acting
in good faith, maintain the existing
deals, until a representative of the
estate shall be appointed. But as
to whether circumstances might not
exist which would justify the Broker in closing the transactions without awaiting the qualification of the
representative, quære. Hess vs.

Rau, 95 N. Y. 359. And after
executors have qualified, they, under a direction in the will to convert
stock into money, without limit as
to time, have a discretion to wait a
reasonable time for the performance
of the duty and there is no rigid and
arbitrary standard by which to
measure such time. The statutory
period allowed to close an estate
may sometimes mark the limit of
discretion; while always a circumstance to be considered, it is not necessarily conclusive. In re Weston,
91 N. Y. 502.

As to custom in England to close
transactions of deceased customer,
see cases cited, post, p. 1001.

And where several are jointly bound to do an act upon notice to them, notice to one is sufficient.[1]

Another very important inquiry is as to the length of time which the Broker should give the Client to respond; this cannot be definitely stated, but the Client should be allowed a reasonable time[2] within which to comply with the demand; and what constitutes a reasonable time depends upon the peculiar circumstances of each case. It may be an hour, a day, or a week, depending in each case upon the situation of the parties, the character of the market, or the nature of the stock.[3]

In Burkett vs. Taylor[4] the court intimated that a notice to a Client demanding additional margins before twelve o'clock of the day on which it is dated would not be a sufficient notice in point of time; also that a notice such as above should specify the time and place of sale in case of default to supply additional margins.

So where the Broker and his Client lived in the same city,

[1] Mandeville vs. Reed, 13 Ab. Pr. (N. Y.) 173.

[2] Markham vs. Jaudon, 41 N. Y. 235, at p. 243.

[3] Cameron vs. Durkheim, 55 N. Y. 425; Milliken vs. Debon, 27 id. 364; Stewart vs. Drake, 46 id. 449; Maryland Fire Ins. Co. vs. Dalrymple, 25 Md. 242; Willoughby vs. Comstock, 3 Hill (N. Y.), 389; Bryan vs. Baldwin, 7 Lans. (N. Y.) 174; Burkett or Burkitt vs. Taylor, supra; Perin vs. Parker, 126 Ill. 201; 17 Bradw. 169.

[4] Supra. In the case cited in the text the Client had requested the Broker to send him notice to the office of S. a friend, at 99 Maiden Lane, and the decision of the court was doubtless based upon the improbability of the notice reaching the Client in sufficient time, if his friend were obliged, in the Client's absence, to forward the notice to another address. See also Genet vs. Howland, 45 Barb. 560.

A letter, by the Broker, written on the 18th of the month, enclosing an account showing differences against the Client, and requesting instructions as to closing the account by 11 o'clock of the next day, was held to be an unreasonably short notice. Ellis vs. Pond, L. R. 1 Q. B. (1898) 428, 445.

a notice for margins, or in default thereof that the stock would be sold in two days from the date of the demand, was held timely and reasonable.[1] In that case defendants, Stockbrokers in the city of New York, purchased for plaintiff certain stocks under an agreement that they were to advance the money for the purchases, and he was to keep with them a satisfactory margin or security. A portion of the stock was sold by defendants without giving plaintiff notice of the time and place of sale. Plaintiff repudiated and disavowed the sale. Defendants acceded to such disavowal, and notified plaintiff they would not consider the sale as made on his account, but on their own; and by both parties it was subsequently treated as a nullity as between them. After that defendants notified plaintiff to furnish additional margin, and upon his failure so to do, in the afternoon of the 28th of April, served upon him personally a notice that unless a satisfactory margin was furnished, or the balance of his account paid, his stocks would be sold at public auction upon the 30th of April, at 12:30 P. M., at a place designated; and the stocks were sold in accordance with the notice. The plaintiff was held to have waived his right to recover as for a conversion of the stocks sold at the first sale. His default in furnishing a satisfactory margin, or paying the balance of the account, entitled the defendants to enforce their lien by the sale of the stock; and, the parties living in the same city, the notice of the sale was a timely and reasonable one, and the sale legal. It was held, further, that in an action brought to recover damages for the alleged unauthorized sale of the stock, the answer setting up a counterclaim, it was proper for the referee to state an account

---

[1] Stewart vs. Drake, 46 N. Y. 449.

between the parties, and to give judgment in favor of defendants for any balance found due them.

In the case of Gruman vs. Smith [1] the court said : " Upon failure to do so (furnish margins), the stock may be sold upon reasonable and *customary* notice."

It thus seems that, in respect to the time given by the notice to comply with the demand, the usages of Brokers may be well introduced to establish a limit, as this is one of the elements which may be assumed as understood in the inception of the relation of Broker and Client. [2]

In Milliken vs. Dehon, [3] which arose out of a transaction in cotton, similar in substance to a stock speculation, the pledgee, as he may be termed, gave the pledgor notice that, if the latter did not make his margins good the next day, he would sell the cotton, which was done, and there

[1] 81 N. Y. 25.

[2] See chapter on "Usages." If the usage of the Exchange justifies it, there may be a sale for failure to put up margins without any notice. Van Horn vs. Gilbough, 21 Am. Law Reg. (n. s.) 171. If the parties make no agreement as to notice, the Board of Trade rules apply. If the latter require notice, such must be given. If there is neither agreement, nor rule, then the common law requires reasonable notice. Denton vs. Jackson, 15 Chic. Leg. News, 309.

[3] 27 N. Y. 364. And in another case, it appearing that Brokers in Philadelphia had notified their Client in New York that as they had made an exception in his case to their usual requirement of five per cent margin, he should himself watch his account without waiting for notice from them, and further that if one per cent margin were not sent in by next morning's mail, stop orders to the best of their ability would be entered, it was held that the jury was warranted in finding that this notice of one day was reasonable, and that it had not been waived by the Brokers, on receipt next morning, of a letter from the Client directing stop orders at one point from the market, having telegraphed that they had entered stop orders at one half point. This showed that the Brokers had not accepted their customer's proposition, but acting in compliance with their notice had entered stop orders to the best of their ability. Harris vs. Pryor, 18 N. Y. Supp. 128. See also Johnston vs. Miller, 53 S. W. Rep. (Ark.) 1052.

was no point raised in the case that the notice was too short.

But a case[1] which arose out of a speculation in gold most strongly illustrates the question of what is a reasonable time in this respect. There the Brokers had made oral demands for more margins, to which the Client stated, in effect, that he had no money and was ruined, and that the Brokers must take care of themselves, whereupon the latter closed the account by a settlement. This the Court of Appeals held not only to be a waiver on the part of the Client of any more formal demand, but that it also authorized the Brokers to close the account in the manner in which they did. Church, Ch. J., in delivering the opinion of the court, said: " The defendants had sold $404,000 of gold short for the plaintiff, and, according to the usual custom in transacting that business, had borrowed the gold to deliver. They had received from the avails of the gold sold, and from the plaintiff, payment for the gold at 140. On the morning of the 23d gold was quoted at 140½, and at night it reached 143. On that day the defendants called upon the plaintiff for an additional margin of $7481.05, which would secure the gold at 141½. The plaintiff was absent from the city on that day, and his clerk delivered some collaterals to the defendants, accompanied by a promise to give a check the

---

[1] Cameron vs. Durkheim, 55 id. 425. In Massachusetts it was held that as the relation of Broker, carrying stocks on a margin, to a Client, was a contractual one, and not that of pledgor and pledgee, the Broker might sell without notice, when the Client failed to perform his part of the contract by making the necessary advances upon demand, and that even if the latter relation existed, the Client, by telling the Brokers he could pay no more, and requesting them to do the best they could for him, authorized a sale, without notice, if made in good faith. The question of a usage of the Boston Stock-brokers to sell without notice was not considered. Covell vs. Loud, 135 Mass. 41.

next morning, which was not done. On the morning of
the 24th, at ten o'clock, gold opened at 150, and rose rapidly
until, at about half-past eleven o'clock, it reached 162½, and
at a quarter-past twelve the market broke and went as low
as 136, and soon after dropped to 133. The effect of the
sudden and unprecedented rise in gold, as the evidence
shows, was to produce the most intense excitement and con-
sternation among those concerned in such transactions. At
one time the plaintiff was deficient in margin more than
$80,000, while within an hour afterwards he might have
closed the transaction with a balance in his favor of something over $25,000. The interviews between the parties
took place during the height of the excitement, when everything was uncertain. Whether gold would depreciate or go
to a much higher figure, whether the rise would continue
during the day or for several days, and whether it would remain permanent or not, were questions of doubt and appre-
hension. When the defendants called for additional margins, as they had a right to, if the plaintiff did say to them
in earnest and seriously, as claimed, 'I have no money ; I
cannot put up any more margin. This ruins me ; I hope it
won't ruin you ; you must take care of yourselves,'—it was
pregnant with authority and consent that the defendants
might take any course to save themselves from loss which
would be deemed prudent and judicious under the circumstances in which they were placed. It could scarcely have
been more significant if the language had been, ' The sudden
rise in gold ruins me, and I now authorize you to adopt any
course which will be most likely to save yourselves from loss
on my account.' This is the natural import of the language."[1]

[1] But compare Burkett vs. Tay- 45 Barb. 560. Where the Client's
lor, supra, and Genet vs. Howland, agent, when the Broker took his

In another case[1] the plaintiff employed the defendants, Stock-brokers, to buy certain stocks on time, making and agreeing to keep good, in the defendants' hands, a deposit, to indemnify them against depreciation in the market value. The stocks having fallen after their purchase, the defendants called on the plaintiff for a further deposit, and he replied that it was not convenient that day, but that he would make it the next day. At the same interview he gave them written authority to sell in these terms : "Please sell for my account 200 Ill. Central R. R. at 51." After receiving this written authority, the defendants sold the stocks the same day at 52. In an action against the defendants for making the sale, evidence was adjudged competent, on the part of the plaintiff, that it was agreed at the same interview, and before giving the authority to sell, that the defendants should wait until the next day for a further deposit, and that if the stock went down to 51 meanwhile (at which point the existing deposit would be exhausted), the defendants might sell the stock. This evidence does not contradict the written power. And such an agreement to delay is not void as being without consideration.

order for a "short" sale, had agreed to stay in the office and watch the market, and in case it went against his principal, would direct the Broker at once to cover it, and it appeared that two demands for margins were made on the day of closing, the Broker was justified in closing without further notice. Ware vs. Raven, 6 N. Y. St. Rep. 259. It has been made a question how far repeated demands for margin operated as a waiver of former demands. A waiver is the intentional relinquishment of a known right; and there must be both knowledge of the relinquishment of the right and an intention to relinquish it. A subsequent demand is not necessarily a waiver of a prior one, even if, because of changes in the market, the amount demanded in the subsequent notice should be different from that demanded in the former. Perin vs. Parker, 126 Ill. 201.

[1] Clarke vs. Meigs, 10 Bosw. (N. Y.) 337, 338. Where after margin has been demanded, the Client gives

The reasonableness of the notice may also depend upon previous dealings between the parties.[1]

So where the question was whether reasonable notice to make a deposit had been given by Brokers to their principal, and all the evidence on the subject was that furnished by a former transaction between the same parties, in which the same notice was given—the Brokers waited until the next morning, when the deposit was made and it was satisfactory—the court held that the principal had a right to suppose that the same course of dealing which had occurred in the former transaction, and was satisfactory to the Brokers, was expected in the present case; and that if the Brokers required compliance in any shorter time, they should have given notice accordingly.[2]

his time note, but it is not received by the Broker under any agreement that such shall be its effect, it does not operate as a deposit of margins nor does it extend the time for such deposit until the maturity of the note. Gould vs. Trask, 10 N. Y. Supp. 619. And it was also held that as the Client's action was for conversion, and not for a balance due on an account, he could not place in issue the question of excessive interest charged by the Broker, when the interest would not equal the deficiency in margins. Id. But if the note is accepted as cash, the account cannot be closed before its maturity. Donald vs. Gardner, 44 App. Div. 235.

[1] A Broker may close out without notice when memorandums sent their client in prior transactions so stipulated, and there were many previous transactions in running account. Robinson vs. Crawford, 52 N. Y. Supp. 560.

[2] Hanks vs. Drake, 49 Barb. (N. Y.) 186. As to whether this case is overruled on this point, see Markham vs. Jaudon, 41 N. Y. 243, per Hunt, Ch. J. See also cases cited under succeeding paragraph. So a pledgee cannot sell or dispose of the securities until payment of the note is demanded and refused (Lewis vs. Varnum, 12 Ab. [N. Y.] Pr. 305).

(c.) Notice of Sale for Failure to Comply with Demand for Margins.

But the mere failure of the Client to furnish margins, after notice of decline or advance in the market, as the case may be, and a demand for margins, is not sufficient to authorize a Broker to sell the stock or close the transaction. He must also give notice of the time and place of sale to the Client.[1]

In respect to the form or contents of the notice to the Client, no uniform rule can be laid down. No peculiar terms or words need be used. It may be oral or in writing; and it will be sufficient, if it conveys, by plain and

[1] Cases cited under preceding subdivisions, Gruman vs. Smith, 81 N. Y. 25; Stewart vs. Drake, 46 id. 449, 450 and 453; Wheeler vs. Newbould, 16 id. 392; Read vs. Lambert, 10 Ab. (N. Y.) Pr. n. s. 428; McGinnis vs. Smythe, 1 Sil. 23; 23 W. D. 203; and see, generally, Cortelyou vs. Lansing, 2 Caines (N. Y.) Cas. 200; Fletcher vs. Dickinson, 89 Mass. 23; Morris Canal and Banking Co. vs. Lewis, 12 N. J. Eq. 323; Eldridge vs. Metrop. Bk. N. Y. *Daily Reg.* Jan. 31, 1887. As to when the Broker is not liable in damages although the notice may have been insufficient, see Quinlan vs. Raymond, N. Y. *Daily Reg.* July 29, 1886; aff'd on other grounds, 3 St. Rep. 573. The question of want of notice of the time and place of sale cannot be raised for the first time on appeal. Knickerbocker vs. Gould, 115 N. Y. 533. See also cases cited under succeeding paragraph. Also Schouler on Bailm. (2d ed.) § 229. When usage justifies Broker in selling without notice, see Corbett vs. Underwood, 83 Ill. 324. In this case it was held that where a commission merchant contracts for the purchase of grain for another, to be delivered at a future time, the principal making an advance on the purchase, which is in the merchant's name, and agrees to keep the margin good up to the time of delivery, the relation of pledgor and pledgee will not be created, so as to require a notice of the time and place of a sale on failure to keep up the margins.

So, in England, Stock-brokers who have with their own money purchased stock for a principal are authorized to close a transaction without notice when it is apparent that their Client will be unable to respond to any loss, by reason of bankruptcy, death, or insolvency of the latter (Lacey vs. Hill [Scrimgeour's Claim], L. R. 8 Ch. App. 921; see also Colket vs. Ellis, 10 Phila. 375; s. c. 32 Leg. Int. 82).

simple language, the nature of the property to be sold, and the time and place of such sale. The notice should state the *time* and *place* of sale.[1] In respect to the *time* of sale, the general principle is that it should be *reasonable*. What constitutes a reasonable time depends upon the peculiar circumstances of each case, and no uniform rule can be laid down. The nature of the stock, the residence of the parties, and all the other elements and characteristics of the particular transaction control the question.[2] It is not necessary that this notice of sale should be made separately from, or subsequently to, the demand for more margins. They may both be embraced in one notice.[3]

In respect to the person upon whom this notice should be served, it has been decided several times that, in case of a

---

[1] Burkett vs. Taylor, 86 N. Y. 618, *sub nom.* Burkitt vs. Taylor, 13 W. D. 75; Lewis vs. Graham, 4 Ab. (N. Y.) Pr. 106; Castello vs. City Bank, 1 N. Y. Leg. Obs. 25; Markham vs. Jaudon, 41 N. Y. 235, at 243; Edwards on Bailm. (3d ed.) § 286 and notes 3, 4 and 5; Diller vs. Brubaker, 52 Pa. St. 498; Conyngham's App., 57 id. 474; Gay vs. Moss, 34 Cal. 125; Robinson vs. Hurley, 11 Iowa, 410.

[2] See this question considered in the preceding subdivision (*b*.). Morris Canal Co. vs. Lewis, 12 N. J. Eq. 323; Diller vs. Brubaker, supra; Conyngham's App., supra; Gay vs. Moss, supra; Little vs. Barker, Hoffm. Ch. 487; Genet vs. Howland, 45 Barb. (N. Y.) 560; s. c. 30 How. Pr. 360; Lewis vs. Graham, 4 Ab. (N. Y.) Pr. 106; Ogden vs. Lathrop, 3 J. & S. (N. Y.) 73; rev'd 65 N. Y. 158.

[3] Stewart vs. Drake, 46 N. Y. 449; Gruman vs. Smith, 81 id. 25; Cameron vs. Durkheim, 55 id. 425; Stenton vs. Jerome, 54 id. 480, at 486. It was intimated in a recent case that a notice sent by special messenger on the evening of the day previous to the sale, and after the closing of the Exchange, from the Broker's office at 44 Broadway to the Reform Club (the address given by the Client) would have been sufficient as a notification to the Client that his margins were exhausted, and his stock would be sold unless margin was kept up, if the inference could fairly be drawn that the Client actually received the notice, the latter having sworn that he did not receive it. Wolff vs. Lockwood, 75 N. Y. Supp. 605, 608.

pledge, there must be *personal* notice of the sale to the pledgor, or a notice left at his residence; and that if the pledgor cannot be found, so as to be served in this manner, resort must be had to judicial proceedings to foreclose the rights of the latter.[1] But notice to an authorized agent is sufficient.[2] And where it is impossible to give notice by reason of the acts of the pledgor, a sale may be made without notice.[3] And in some instances a sale may be made after publication of notice thereof in a newspaper.[4]

The case of Wheeler vs. Newbould,[5] although not one arising out of any stock transaction, is frequently met with in stock cases upon the question of the manner in which the pledgee should proceed to sell the pledge.

The defendant, in that case, purposely withheld from the plaintiff all knowledge of the time, the place, and manner of sale, and the sale, when effected, was made privately for about three fourths of the actual and nominal value of the securities. The court held that this was illegal.

It was said by Brown, J., that, "if we assume that the defendant had authority to sell the subject of the pledge in satisfaction of his debt, it was nevertheless his duty to give to the plaintiff personal notice of the time and place of the sale. . . . 'And personal notice to the pledgor to redeem and of the intended sale must be given as well in the one case

---

[1] Stearns vs. Marsh, 4 Denio, 227; Garlick vs. James, 12 Johns. 146; Story's Eq. Jur. (13th ed.) § 1008; Strong vs. Nat'l Bank'g Ass'n, 45 N. Y. 718; Bryan vs. Baldwin, 7 Lans. (N. Y.) 171; Donohoe vs. Gamble, 38 Cal. 340; Pigot vs. Cubley, 15 C. B. (n. s.) 701; City Bank of Racine vs. Babcock, 1 Holmes (C. C. U. S.), 180.

[2] Potter vs. Thompson, 10 R. I. 1.
[3] City Bank of Racine vs. Babcock, supra.
[4] Stokes vs. Frazier, 72 Ill. 428. See also cases cited under preceding subdivision (b). As to how far this rule may be affected by waiver, see post, pp. 353-6.
[5] 16 N Y. 392.

as in the other (whether the debt be payable presently or on time), in order to authorize a sale by the act of the party ;[1] and if the pledgor cannot be found, and notice cannot be given him, judicial proceedings to authorize the sale must be resorted to. Before giving notice, the pledgee has no right to sell the pledge ; and if he do, the pledgor may recover the value of it from him without tendering the debt.' " After a pledgee, however, has called upon the pledgor to pay the debt, and has given legal notice of sale, he is not bound to proceed and sell the same.

And this doctrine has been directly applied to the case of a transaction between a Stock-broker and his Client by the Supreme Court of Pennsylvania,[2] where it was decided that, upon the failure of the Client to respond to a proper demand, a Broker who is carrying stock for him, and who notifies the latter by letter to increase his margin or take up the stock, is not bound to sell in default of receiving an answer.

The rule is, that a pledgee of stocks or securities is under no obligation to sell the security after default in payment of the debt.[3] In the Granite Bank vs. Richardson,[4] a creditor holding as collateral security certain bank shares requested the debtor to pay the debt, and notified him that

---

[1] Sterns vs. Marsh, 4 Denio (N. Y.), 227.

[2] Esser vs. Linderman, 71 Pa. St. 76. It was intimated in the case of a sale upon margin of grain for future delivery that where additional margin is peremptorily refused, it is the duty of the Broker upon settled principles of law to buy in the grain with due diligence so as to limit the loss to himself and his customer. Perin vs. Parker, 25 Ill. App. 465; aff'd 126 Ill. 201.

[3] O'Neill vs. Whigham, 87 Pa. St. 394; s. c. 7 Reporter, 245; Robinson vs. Hurley, 11 Iowa, 410; Granite Bank vs. Richardson, 47 Mass. 407; Howard vs. Brigham, 98 id. 133; Williamson vs. McClure, 37 Pa. St. 402; Schouler on Bailm. §§ 244, 245.

[4] Supra.

if the request were not complied with immediately the
shares would be sold. The debt was not paid, and the
pledgee did not sell. The bank subsequently failed, and the
shares became worthless. The creditor then began an action to recover the money due him, and it was held that his
failure to sell the shares constituted no defence. There
was no duty on the part of the pledgee to sell the shares;
he simply held them as security, with perhaps the power
to sell attached. The debtor's remedy was to pay the debt
and redeem the shares. But where the pledgee or Broker
neglects to sell after request or demand so to do from his
pledgor or Client, it may be that the former would be liable
for any loss which might occur in consequence of his omission to sell.[1] Where a pledgee, however, has acquired the
right to sell for his own protection, either by a demand or
notice, or by waiver of such demand and notice, "all he
need do is to act in good faith."[2]

But in a grain transaction, where the seller, before the
time expires for the delivery of grain sold, notifies the purchaser that unless he places in his hands a deposit to cover
a decline in the price of the grain he will sell it, and afterwards does sell it, and notifies the buyer of the fact, he thereby rescinds the contract, and cannot subsequently renew it
without the concurrence of the purchaser.[3]

Where a pledgor of securities becomes a bankrupt after
a pledge and before the redemption thereof, it has been held
that such fact does not in anywise affect the rights of the
pledgee to sell and transfer the securities upon the bankrupt's default. The Bankrupt Act does not take away any

---

[1] Howard vs. Brigham, supra;   [2] Marfield vs. Goodhue, 3 Com-
O'Neill vs. Whigham, supra.   stock (N. Y.), 62-73.

[3] Lassen vs. Mitchell, 41 Ill. 101.

right secured to the pledgee by his contract,[1] nor is leave of the bankruptcy court necessary to sell the stock pledged.[2] But the mere fact that the Broker sells, without due notice to the Client of the time and place of sale, and by such act commits a conversion, does not preclude him from bringing an action against his Client to recover the debt arising out of the advance made by the Broker to purchase the stock.

And where a minor has employed a Stock-broker to buy stock for him, and, on coming of age, has repudiated the transaction, and retracted the authority given to the Broker, a sale of the stock bought by the latter, without notice or demand of payment on the Client, is a tortious conversion of the stock; and in an action by the Broker for the loss on the stock, under such circumstances the Client is entitled to recover, under a counterclaim, the amount deposited by him with the Broker to cover margins.[3] If a colorable sale has been made by the Broker, and subsequently rescinded, and he regains possession of the securities, he cannot make a second sale without notifying his Client.[4]

[1] Jerome vs. McCarter, 94 U. S. 734.

[2] In re Grinnell, 9 Nat'l Bankr. Reg. 137.

If a Broker makes a general assignment or becomes bankrupt, a demand by a customer, followed by tender, is not necessary. And the same rule applies to bankruptcy followed by a general assignment. In re Swift, 112 Fed. Rep. 315.

[3] Heath vs. Mahoney, 24 Hun (N. Y.), 341; s. c. reported more fully, 12 N. Y. Weekly Dig. 404. A Broker commissioned to buy corn did so, but, finding the price rapidly going down, sold it for his own protection; and, on the refusal of his principal to ratify the sale, replaced it, and tendered the elevator receipts. The principal refused to receive them, and the Broker sold the corn. Both sales were made at a loss, and the Broker sued his principal for damages. Held, that in estimating damages the first sale was immaterial (Gregory vs. Wendell, 40 Mich. 432).

[4] Leahy vs. Lobdell, 90 Fed. Rep. 665.

This right to notice of sale, however, may be waived, either expressly[1] or by implication; or, where there has been no notice, or an insufficient notice, the proceedings thereunder may be confirmed or ratified by the acts of the pledgor.[2]

[1] A bona fide sub-pledgee for value may sell the securities at public or private sale without notice, when the contract of sub-pledge expressly so provides, and this right is not affected by notice from the original pledgor, unless the latter pays or tenders the amount of the sub-pledge. Thompson vs. Bank, 113 N. Y. 328. See also Williams vs. Trust Co., 133 N. Y. 660. But if there is no such special agreement to sell without notice, the sub-pledgee is guilty of conversion when he sells without demand of the sub-pledgor of payment, and without notice. Smith vs. Savin, 141 N. Y. 328. If the contract of pledge authorizes a private sale "without advertisement or notice, which are hereby expressly waived," notice of the sale need not be given either to the pledgor or the public. A mere authorization of a private sale is an implied waiver of the notice. Dullnig vs. Weekes, 40 S. W. Rep. (Tex.) 178.

Although notice is dispensed with, Stock-brokers must however make the sale in good faith and in the exercise of a sound judgment when they consider the state of the market warrants. Wicks vs. Hatch, 62 N. Y. 535.

[2] Sparhawk vs. Drexel, 12 Nat'l Bankr. Reg. 450; Gruman vs. Smith, 81 N. Y. 25; rev'g 12 J. & S.

389; Stenton vs. Jerome, 54 N. Y. 480; Milliken vs. Dehon, 27 id. 364; Child vs. Hugg, 41 Cal. 519; Bryson vs. Rayner, 25 Md. 424; Hyatt vs. Argenti, 3 Cal. 151; Loomis vs. Stave, 72 Ill. 623; Md. Fire Ins. Co. vs. Dalrymple, 25 Md. 242-264; Colket vs. Ellis, 10 Phila. 375; s. c. 32 Leg. Int. 82; Baltimore Marine Ins. Co. vs. Dalrymple, 25 Md. 269; Hamilton vs. State Bank, 22 Ia. 306; Clark vs. Bouvain, 20 La. Ann. 70; Searing vs. Butler, 69 Ill. 575. But see Kenfield vs. Latham, 2 Cal. Leg. Rec. 235. Where it appears from the Client's own admission that he never intended to pay for and take up the stock, he is estopped from complaining of want of notice of sale, or any other informality in connection with it. The object of the notice is to enable a party to come forward, pay up and prevent the sacrifice of the pledge, but when he says he would not have availed himself of such a notice, nor have interfered to protect the stock by paying the amount owed upon it, what advantage would it have been to him to have notice, or what harm could come from the lack of it. Vanhorn vs. Gilbough, 21 Am. L. Reg. (n. s.) 171; 10 W. N. C. 317.

A sale of pledged securities may be made without notice or demand when (1) the parties have so expressly agreed, or (2) where the debt

In Stenton vs. Jerome [1] the question arose as to how far a conversion of the Client's stocks may be waived by a subsequent payment of an apparent balance of account to the Brokers.   There the Brokers had committed a conversion by an unauthorized sale of stocks, without a previous demand of margin.   This wrongful sale was made on the 11th of January, 1866, and a notification of it sent to the Client.   On the 14th of January the Brokers made up the account, showing a small balance due them, and leaving in their hands as security for such balance certain United States bonds.   Subsequently the Client called and complained of the manner in which she had been treated.   The Brokers having written several letters stating that unless the balance was paid they would sell her bonds, she finally, being in ill-health, and her husband having met with a serious accident needing her attention, and having pressing need for her bonds, wrote to her Brokers informing them of these facts, and sent therewith the balance of account ; thereupon the Brokers delivered the United States bonds to her messenger.   She subsequently brought an action to recover damages for the unlawful conversion of her stocks.   The court of ultimate resort, affirming the judgments of the lower tribunals, held that the action of the Client in accepting the account did not constitute an account stated between the parties ; and that her subsequent payment of the balance for the purpose of obtaining her bonds was not voluntary, but compulsory, con-

is to be paid on a specified day. Chouteau vs. Allen, 70 Mo. 290. In which case it was also held that when a note (the payment of which is secured by a pledge of bonds) is sub-pledged to secure acceptances, a sale of the bonds may be made at the maturity of the note. Id. If a pledgee assigns a security which is not negotiable, his assignee takes no greater title than he himself possesses. Id.

[1] 54 N. Y. 480.

stituting a duress of goods. One of the learned judges held that an action could have been sustained to recover back the balance paid to the Brokers; and that inasmuch as the present action was one of conversion, it, having once vested, could only be discharged by release under seal or the receipt of something in satisfaction.[1]

But where a sale of mining stocks was made without notifying the pledgor to make his margin good, and without sufficient notice of time and place of sale, still, if the pledgor knew of the time and place and made no objection, and, after the sale, he was presented with an account in which he was credited the amount received at the sale, and he admits the correctness of the same, approves of the sale, and promises to pay the balance claimed—these facts are sufficient to show a ratification of the illegal sale, and the court will not disturb the same.[2]

And where the notice of sale was dispensed with, but demand for payment of the debt was not, it was held that the Broker who sold his Client's stock without notice and

[1] To same effect, see Clarke vs. Meigs, 10 Bosw. (N. Y.) 337; s. c. 22 How. Pr. 340. As to the effect of tender, see Talmage vs. Third National Bk., 91 N. Y. 531 at 535.

[2] Child vs. Hugg, 41 Cal. 519; Gould vs. Trask, 10 N. Y. Supp. 619. Even if after a wrongful sale, the Broker presents an account to the Client showing such sale and a resultant loss, and the Client without objection to the manner of sale promises to settle the account, this promise is conclusive upon him, and the Broker may recover the loss. The promise may be considered either as a waiver of the right to notice of sale, or as a ratification of the method of sale adopted, and so does not require that the proof should reach to the conclusiveness of an account stated. Without an actual agreement upon a precise balance and a promise to pay it, there may still be such a promise on the part of the Client as necessarily recognizes and ratifies the sales made and the method which the Broker has pursued. Gillett vs. Whiting, 141 N. Y. 71, 73; s. c. 120 N. Y. 402, 406. See also upon this point, p. 212.

without demand was guilty of a conversion of the stock, and was liable in damages.[1]

Where, however, there has been a waiver of demand, or of notice of time and place of sale, there is still an obligation resting upon the pledgee to act with entire good faith, and to sell the securities for the highest price that he can obtain.[2]

(d.) *Place of Sale.*

The preliminary steps having been properly taken, the next inquiry is as to the *place* where the sale should be made. In the case of an ordinary dealing in stocks, where a Client orders his Broker to buy or sell, the place where the purchases or sales are to be made is at the Stock Exchange, unless the Broker is otherwise directed. That is the place where transactions of this description are customarily made, and, by employing a Stock-broker, the Client impliedly authorizes him to perform the business in the manner and at the place established by local usage.[3] And, on the other hand, the Broker, in his dealings for his Client, is likewise restricted by usage, and he violates his instructions by buying or selling in any other manner or place than that which usage justifies.[4]

But what is more particularly intended in this connection is to ascertain the proper place for buying or selling the

---

[1] Kenfield vs. Latham, supra.

[2] Sparhawk vs. Drexel, 12 Nat'l Bankr. Reg. 450, at 471 and 472; Genet vs. Howland, 45 Barb. (N. Y.) 560; Covell vs. Loud, 135 Mass. 41. See also Rogers vs. Wiley, 131 N. Y. 527; Fitzgerald vs. Blocher, 32 Ark. 742; and cases just cited, ante, p. 355. Even though there is failure, after notice, to put up margin, reasonable notice of the time and place of sale must nevertheless be given. Rothschild vs. Allen, 86 N. Y. Supp. 42.

[3] Rosenstock vs. Tormey, 32 Md. 169.

[4] Id.; see also title "Usages."

stocks where the Client is in default of margins after proper demand and notice, or where the Broker desires to close the transaction and the Client refuses to " buy in " or receive the stocks which are being " carried" for his account, or to authorize the Broker to do so.

In the first place, where the Client is " short" of stocks, and by a rise in the price his margin is exhausted, it would seem to be reasonable that the Broker, after due demand and notice, should be at liberty to " buy in" the stocks and close the transaction at the Stock Exchange. The very nature of a " short" sale requires that the Broker should make the purchase at the Exchange, which is always open, and where stocks may be bought at any time during the regular hours of business. It would be absurdly incongruous to hold that where, on a short sale, the Client was in default, the Broker should be required to make the purchase of the stock at public auction. The Broker would have no power to compel a public auction to be held, or to force any one to put up the kind and amount of stocks which he desired to buy. There would therefore seem to be no room for doubt that the Broker, in such a case, could make the purchase at the Exchange.[1]

But a different and more difficult question arises in a case where a Client is "long" of stocks and the Broker is carrying them for his account. In this event, as has been observed, the Broker occupies the relation of a pledgee to his Client, and upon failure of the latter to supply proper margins to meet the fluctuations of the market he may, after proper notice to the Client, as we have seen, sell the same. Where? Is the answer to be determined in precisely

[1] See authorities cited ante, under especially Knowlton vs. Fitch, 52 § VII., appertaining to a short sale, N. Y. 288.

the same manner as if the case were one of pure pledge, as, for instance, where money is advanced upon the security of personal property and the pledgor refuses to redeem it? Or, will the courts take into consideration the important element of usage, and hold that a sale made at the Exchange is binding upon the Client? The general principle is, that the pledgee of stocks must sell the same at public auction.[1]

The rule confining the place of sale to a public auction is very old and uniform. The theory of the law is, that the sale should be made at some place where all the parties interested may have an opportunity to attend and see that it is fairly conducted; that the pledgor may exert himself in procuring buyers, and thus enhance the price, and give him the right to redeem the pledge at any moment before the sale should be actually made.[2] And, in the absence of express agreement authorizing a different mode, there are cases that undoubtedly hold that mere local usage to sell at private sale cannot be allowed to modify this right of the pledgor.[3] In furtherance of this general rule, the courts have repeatedly held that a sale of pledged stocks cannot be made at the Board of Brokers in New York city, unless there was a stipulation to that effect, for the reason that by the regulations of the Board the sales are essentially private, no one being allowed to enter the room but members.[4]

[1] Milliken vs. Dehon, 27 N. Y. 392; 364; Wheeler vs. Newbould, 16 id. 392; Edwards on Bailm. (3d ed.) § 283; Schouler on Bailm. (2d ed.) § 230; Tyler on Usury, etc., 585 et seq.

[2] Id.

[3] Brown vs. Ward, 3 Duer, 660; Wheeler vs. Newbould, 16 N. Y.

Story on Bailm. (9th ed.) § 310, note 3; but compare Dykers vs. Allen, 7 Hill, 497; Castello vs. City Bank, 1 N. Y. Leg. Obs. 25, and other cases cited. Edwards on Bailm. (3d ed.) § 283, and cases cited in notes 2 and 3.

[4] Id.; Wood vs. Hamilton, cited in Castello vs. City Bank, supra; Ran-

It will be observed that in all of the cases just cited, the relation of pledgor and pledgee existed between the parties, *but that such relation did not grow out of speculations in stocks upon margins,* save in the case of Brass vs. Worth, In that case, however, the Brokers had sold the Client's stock without any notice to him that his margins had become exhausted, and the court said, "The defendants claim the right to sell the property pledged without notice to or knowledge of the pledgor the moment prices sank so that collaterals deposited are no longer equal to the margin of the five per cent stipulated in the contract;" and that this fact, coupled with the sale being made at the Board of Brokers, a place that the court held was private, rendered the transaction nugatory.

But the grounds upon which these decisions are based, holding that a sale at the Stock Exchange, in the absence of

---

kin vs. McCullough, 12 Barb. (N. Y.) 103; Brass vs. Worth, 40 id. 648. But where the limit of a stop order has been reached, the Broker may sell the stocks carried in any usual and ordinary way whether at the Stock Exchange or at private sale. Porter vs. Wormser, 94 N. Y. 431.

The difference between the case of a compulsory sale by a Broker on default of his Client to furnish margin, where the sale must be by public auction, and cases such as Porter vs. Wormser, is this: In the first case, as stated in the text (p. 358), "the theory of the law is that the sale should be made at some place where all the parties interested may have an opportunity to attend and see that it is fairly conducted; that the pledgor may exert himself in procuring buyers of his stock, enhance the price and give him the right to redeem the pledge at any moment before the sale should be actually made," while in the second case, there is no necessity for notice of place of sale to the Client, nor for him to be present in order to get an adequate price for his stock. He has himself fixed the price of sale in his stop order, and the Broker is at liberty to follow any usual and ordinary method of selling so long as he obtains that price.

There is in effect a waiver by the Client of notice of place of sale, and an authority to the Broker to obtain a certain price. This price being obtained it is immaterial by what method of sale it was done.

express agreement, is invalid, will, we think, when carefully examined, be found faulty and untenable at the present day. In the first place, a sale at the Stock Exchange is not in any broad sense made *privately ;* it is in almost every respect a public sale.   While it is true that the Stock Exchange is, to a certain extent, a private organization, from which all persons are sedulously excluded who are not members, yet it is the great mart for disposing of and establishing the prices of stocks; and in no public exchange could they be sold to better advantage.   And although strangers are not allowed to attend and bid, they can always be represented by Brokers of their own choosing, who will carry out the wishes of their principals.

In Sparhawk vs. Drexel[1] Cadwalader, J., in overruling an objection to a sale made at the Stock Exchange, says: " As to the mode, I am not aware of any reason that the sales should have been by auction.   On the contrary, I think that, considering the nature of the securities, this would not have been an advantageous mode of disposing of them, if there was a fair market for them at the Stock Exchange, or Brokers' Board, where the ruling prices ordinarily fix the standard value, from time to time, of such securities.   If the times of sale were proper, this mode was unobjectionable."   In that case, however, there was an express authority to sell at public or private sale. ·

It seems almost absurd to call a great mart like the Stock Exchange a private place, in face of the patent fact that all prices are established there; yet, as has been seen, the above cases hold that, in the absence of an agreement giving the pledgee a right to sell privately, a sale at the Board of

---

[1] 12 Nat'l Bankr. Reg. 450, at 470.

Brokers does not answer the requirements of the general law of pledges, requiring a sale of the pledge to be at public auction.

In the second place, the closing of a speculative transaction in stocks is different from that of an ordinary pledge. The parties to a stock speculation intend that the transaction shall be carried on and consummated at the Stock Exchange; indeed, there is no other place where such a speculation can be engaged in. It is, therefore, but reasonable that the Broker should be allowed, after giving all necessary preliminary notices, to close the transaction by a sale of the stocks at the Stock Exchange, and the introduction of the usages of Stock-brokers might go very far towards effecting this result.

This was the view adopted by the Court of Appeals of Maryland as early as 1866,[1] after a review of the New York cases holding to the contrary. The court said : " . . . Considering the requirements of the law, and the reason and nature of the transaction, we are of the opinion that the most proper and suitable place for a sale of stock is at the Board of Brokers. There is the Stock Market—the mart to which vendors and purchasers resort, by their agents, to buy and sell stock, where competition among bidders is most apt to be found. Such sales are public ; and unless there be, in the particular case, some ground for impeaching their fairness, we are of opinion they are reasonable and ought to be supported." And this doctrine was afterwards expressly confirmed by the same court.[2]

---

[1] Md. Fire Ins. Co. vs. Dalrymple, 25 Md. 242–265.

[2] Rosenstock vs. Tormey, 32 Md. 169. Similar language was used by

Andrews, J., in Sistare vs. Best, 88 N. Y. 534, in respect to a sale at the New York Stock Exchange. And the New York Court of Appeals in

And it has been held [1] that where a pledgor is notified that a sale of his stocks will be made at the Board of Brokers, if he is dissatisfied with the place of sale, he must promptly dissent, or his silence will be understood as an acquiescence. In Dykers vs. Allen,[2] however, the Supreme Court of New York held that where authority was given to sell stock at the Board of Brokers, the sale must be openly made. The court, upon this point, said : " The authority to sell the stock in question at the Board of Brokers for the payment of the debt, if such debt was not paid when it became due, did not authorize the pledgees, even if they had retained the stock in their own hands, to put *the same up secretly.*

---

holding that, in ascertaining the "actual" value of stock, for the purposes of taxation, the commissioners of assessment might probably have done injustice to the relator, in taking the book value instead of the market value of the stock, said (People vs. Coleman, 107 N. Y. 544): "So the market value of the shares of capital stock may sometimes be above and sometimes below the actual value. Such value may be greatly enhanced or depressed for speculative purposes without any change in the actual value. But the market value of any stock which is listed at the Stock Exchange in New York, and largely dealt in from day to day for a series of months will usually furnish the best measure of value for all purposes. The competition of sellers and buyers, most of them careful and vigilant to take account of everything affecting value of stock in which they deal, and each mindful of his own interests, and seeking for some personal gain and advantage, will almost universally, if time sufficient be taken, furnish the true measure of the actual value of the stock." The court, however, added: "But there is no law which compels assessors to resort to market value to find the actual value of capital stock. That standard is sometimes illusory and untrustworthy. The buyers or sellers may be too few, and the transactions not sufficiently numerous to furnish a real test of value." See Walter vs. King, supra, p. 380, cited in Brodhurst on "Stock Exchange Law" p. 215; see also in this connection Schepeler vs. Eisner, 3 Daly (N. Y.), 11, which, however, is in effect overruled by Markham vs. Jaudon, 41 N. Y. 235; and the question was raised, but not decided, in Child vs. Hugg, 41 Cal. 519; Laws of N. Y. of 1891, c. 34.

[1] Willoughby vs. Comstock, 3 Hill (N. Y.), 389.

[2] 7 Hill (N. Y.), 497.

But they should have put up the stock openly, and offered it for sale to the highest bidder at the Board of Brokers, stating that it was stock which had been pledged for the security of this debt, and with authority to sell it at the Board of Brokers if the debt was not paid. In this way only the stock would be likely to bring its fair market value at the time it was offered for sale. And in this way alone could it be known that it was honestly and fairly sold, and that it was not purchased in for the benefit of the pledgees by some secret understanding between them and the purchasers."

Altogether, the law upon this subject is in a very unsatisfactory condition; and if the remarks just quoted are accepted as correct, it is rendered even more uncertain. But we believe that the rule is otherwise, and that an authority to sell at the Board of Brokers includes the power to sell in accordance with the ways and manner in which sales are ordinarily conducted at that place.

A statement preceding the sale, that the stocks were being sold to close a transaction, as indicated above, would not enhance the price of the same, and would be of no conceivable benefit to the pledgor.[1] Upon the whole, we are inclined to think that, taking into consideration the character of a speculative transaction in securities on margin, the courts would uphold a sale at the Stock Exchange for the reasons heretofore advanced. Where several different kinds of stock are pledged as security for different loans, a judgment directing a sale in gross of all the stocks is erroneous. Unless the several stocks are pledged as security for

---

[1] See, as generally sustaining the above views, Wicks vs. Hatch, 62 N. Y. 535; Ogden vs. Lathrop, 65 id. 158; Quincey vs. White, 63 id. 370.

the same debt, it is not proper to apply the proceeds to the payment of the entire indebtedness.[1]

The doctrine of waiver may exercise a very important influence on all the questions heretofore discussed; because it has been held, in a number of cases, that the pledgor may waive his right not only to a notice of sale, but as to the manner and place where the sale should be made. This waiver, moreover, need not be expressly entered into by the pledgor, but it may be inferred by the court from the nature of the transaction, or the surrounding circumstances thereof.[2] And the pledgor may waive his rights to object to the informality of the proceedings of the sale of the pledged article by conduct on his part amounting to a ratification.[3] So acquiescence by a principal in the wrongful acts of his agents, to amount to a ratification, must have been continued for some length of time, and the principal must have been cognizant of his rights.[4] A principal, however, is not necessarily to be deemed to have ratified a wrongful act of his agent so as to exempt the agent from liability to him, merely because he does not notify to the agent his dissent at the earliest possible opportunity after being informed of the wrongful act.[5] But the ratification may be inferred from circumstances, as where the agent exceeds his authority a subsequent assent may be inferred,

---

[1] Mahoney vs. Caperton, 15 Cal. 313.

[2] See cases heretofore cited, p. 353. Bryson vs. Rayner, 25 Md. 424; Hyatt vs. Argenti, 3 Cal. 151; Loomis vs. Stave, 72 Ill. 623; Md. Fire Ins. Co. vs. Dalrymple, 25 Md. 242, 264; Baltimore Marine Ins. Co. vs. Dalrymple, id. 269; Colket vs. Ellis, 10 Phila. 375; s. c. 32 Leg. Int. 82.

[3] Hamilton vs. State Bank, 22 Iowa, 306; Child vs. Hugg, 41 Cal. 519; Clark vs. Bouvain, 20 La. Ann. 70.

[4] Brass vs. Worth, 40 Barb. (N. Y.) 648.

[5] Clarke vs. Meigs, 10 Bosw. (N. Y.) 338.

and the law will consider it as equivalent to an express ratification.[1]

(e.) *Broker Cannot Sell or Purchase.*

The general rule of law which governs the relation of principal and agent is applicable to that existing between a Stock-broker and his Client; and it is well settled that an agent cannot, without the knowledge and consent of his principal, either sell to or buy from the latter.

The principle is based upon the obvious reason, that the position of an agent being one of trust and confidence, many frauds and undue advantages would creep in if the law sanctioned his dealing with his principal in his own behalf. Such a transaction is therefore considered a breach of the agent's duty, and the contract is subject to rescission, irre-

---

[1] Searing vs. Butler, 69 Ill. 575. As to what will constitute an admission and ratification of the acts of a Stock-broker in a series of stock speculations, see Saltus vs. Genin, 3 Bosw. (N. Y.) 250. The failure to object to the sale for nearly a month after prompt notice that the stock had been sold, amounted to a ratification. Vanhorn vs. Gilbough, 21 Am. Law Reg. N. S. 171; 10 W. N. C. 347. See supra, p. 354, on this question of waiver. Although Brokers have been guilty of conversion by a sale, without notice, of securities carried on margin, the fact that the Client subsequently promises that the Brokers shall not lose anything, and deposits stocks with them to secure his indebtedness, is a substantial ratification of the sale, and such ratification cannot be afterwards repudiated. Peters vs. Edwards, 95 N. Y. 659 (no opinion), aff'g judgment of the General Term of the court of Common Pleas in the same case, *sub nom.*, Bayard vs. Edwards, on report of a referee, not reported. The report of the referee, and the opinion of Van Brunt and Van Hoesen, JJ., at General Term will be found in "Cases in the Court of Appeals," July, 1883, to July, 1884, vol. 703. As to what acts of the customer will constitute a waiver of any defect in the notice, see Quinlan vs. Raymond, N. Y. *Daily Reg.* July 29, 1886, in which case it was also held that although the notice was defective, the Brokers might recover, unless their claims might be offset by any damage the customer may have suffered. Aff'd on other grounds, 3 St. Rep. 573. But actual knowledge of

spective of any question of intentional fraud or actual injury.[1]

The law rejects indiscriminately all transactions, whether purchases from or sales to the agent, and whether there is any evidence or intention of fraud or not.[2] The mere fact

principal must be shown to establish ratification. Harris vs. Tumbridge, 83 N. Y. 92.

[1] Conkey vs. Bond, 36 N. Y. 427; Taussig vs. Hart, 49 id. 301; also s. c. 58 id. 425; Marvin vs. Weeks, 62 Barb. 468; Smith vs. N. Y. Stock and P. Clearing House, 25 N. Y. Supp. 261; Porter vs. Woodruff, 36 N. J. Eq. 174; Porter vs. Wormser, 94 N. Y. 431, 447; Day vs. Jameson, 33 N. Y. St. Rep. 375; Manville vs. Lawton, 19 N. Y. Supp. 587; Prout vs. Chisolm, 21 App. Div. 57; Pickering vs. Demeritt, 100 Mass. 416; Day vs. Holmes, 103 id. 306; Quincey vs. White, 63 N. Y. 370; Robinson vs. Mollett, L. R. 7 H. L. Eng. & I. App. Cas. 802; Brookman vs. Rothschild, 3 Sim. 153, 224; s. c. H. L. 5 Bligh (n. s.), 165; 2 Dow. & Cl. 188; Crull vs. Dodson, Macn. Sel. Cas. 114; Marye vs. Strouse, 5 Fed. Rep. 483; Gillett vs. Peppercorne, 3 Beav. 78; Kimber vs. Barber, L. R. 8 Ch. App. 56; Bentley vs. Craven, 18 Beav. 76; Trevelyan vs. Charter, 9 id. 140; Dunne vs. English, L. R. 18 Eq. 524; Maturin vs. Tredennick, 9 L. T. 82; s. c. 10 L. T. 331; Commonw. vs. Cooper, 15 Am. Law Rep. 360. Nor can the Broker sell to a firm of which he is a member (Martin vs. Moulton, 8 N. H. 504); 4th Kent's Comm. (7th ed.) 475. See also id. 14th ed. Nor may a Broker buy

from his partner to sell to his Client. Connor vs. Black, 119 Mo. 126; 24 S. W. Rep. 184. And authority to sell to any person whatsoever does not authorize the Broker to become the purchaser himself. Hamilton vs. Schaack, 16 W. D. (N. Y.) 423. See also Butcher vs. Krauth, 14 Bush (Ky.), 713; Worn vs. Fry, 84 Cal. 256. But a corporation which does brokerage business, may legally sell to another corporation, some of the officers of which are officers of the former corporation, in the absence of evidence that the customer was prejudiced. Van Dusen-Harrington Co. vs. Jungeblat, 77 N. W. 270. If, however, an agent is given an interest in a contract which he is authorized to make, such a contract is voidable at the election of the principal. Smith vs. Seattle, L. S. & E. Ry. Co., 72 Hun, 202.

[2] The rule is intended to be preventive of the possibility of wrong, as well as remedial of actual wrong done, and is rigidly enforced. It involves a question of public policy and is applied, although perfect good faith was intended and no loss has been sustained. Mayo vs. Knowlton, 16 Daly, 245. But if Stock-brokers deal in securities on their own account they may sell such bonds as vendors to their Clients as vendees. The relations between them is then

of a purchase by an agent from his principal, without the knowledge of the latter, *ipso facto* vitiates the transaction. Hence it would seem that although the agent paid the full market value for the article in question, and that no higher price could be obtained, yet there is no answer in the mouth of the agent to an action to set the transaction aside.

But how far should this rule be followed in a case where the stocks are sold or purchased by the Broker at the Exchange? Suppose A., who has 100 shares of stock in the office of a Broker, directs the latter to sell the same; can the Broker himself purchase the stock at the Board of Brokers at the market price? Or suppose the Broker is directed to sell the stock, and by another Client is directed to buy the same kind of stock; can the Broker legally execute both of the orders by a simple transfer through his books at the market price? We should answer both these questions negatively; for, while the Broker might show that his principal was just as much benefited as if a third person had bought the stock, yet the opportunity for fraud would be obviously too great to establish any other rule. The Broker, knowing the temper of the market, might sell his Client's stock when the prices were lowest, so as to buy cheaply for himself. Or he might sell the stocks when the market would not take so many shares without a great sacrifice of the real price. Altogether, the reasons seem to be too

that of vendor and vendee, not that of principal and agent. Porter vs. Wormser, 91 N. Y. 431, 442. A Stock-broker may, if he acts as a principal, buy and resell at a profit, and even if his agent makes a fraudulent representation, viz., that the price at which the Stock-broker would purchase was the best price obtainable, whereas he had previously arranged to sell the same stocks at 15 per cent advance, he will not be chargeable with such advance, when the plaintiff vendor did not rely on the fraudulent representation. Taylor vs. Guest, 58 N. Y. 262.

strong to authorize a departure from the general rule, even where the sale or purchase takes place at the Open Board.[1]

In the State of New York these views have received confirmation in the case of Taussig vs. Hart,[2] where Brokers trading in stocks on a margin for a Client had made, among other transactions, a purchase for the latter of 100 shares of Pacific Mail, which they had subsequently transferred from defendant to themselves, reporting to him the existing market price and crediting him therefor. The court held that

[1] This state of facts occurred in Terry vs. Birmingham Savings Bank (Ala.), 13 So. 149; 99 Ala. 566; but the Broker instead of attempting to execute the orders in the way suggested in the text, employed another Broker to openly bid on the Exchange, the price limited in his purchasing customer's order and made the sale at that price, which was not below the fair market value of the stock. It was held that the principle of law that the same person cannot be both buyer and seller did not apply, because here the sale was made by the Broker at the instance of a pledgee of the stock, and the objection to the mode of sale was made by the pledgor in defence to an action against him for the balance of his debt. Thus the objection was to the mode of sale which had been adopted by the pledgor, and as it appeared that neither the pledgee nor the purchaser of the stock had any knowledge of the Broker's co-existent order to sell and purchase, the above principle was held to be inapplicable. This is not a conclusive authority. Suppose a Broker receives orders from different Clients —one to sell a certain stock, the other to buy the same stock. As Broker for the seller it is obvious that it is his duty to sell at the highest figure, and as Broker for the buyer his duty is to purchase at the lowest figure and he cannot properly serve the two masters. It is therefore his duty to inform the Clients of his dual employment so that they may withdraw or continue as they choose. McDevitt vs. Connolly, 15 L. R. (Ireland) 500. If, however, he does not so inform them, but executes both orders by making an entry on his books and sending bought and sold notices respectively to his Clients, and thereupon receives payment, having authority to do so, for the selling Client, the latter is bound thereby, and the purchasing Client is entitled to the stocks, though the Broker in whose possession they remain, by subsequent bankruptcy is unable to pay the purchase money to the selling client. McDevitt vs. Connolly, supra, where, however, it was held that the Broker had no authority to receive payment for the vendor and therefore the latter was still entitled to retain the stocks.

[2] 49 N. Y. 301.

the Client had the right to treat the sale of this stock by the Brokers to themselves as void, and to demand an actual sale of the stock, in which event he would incur the risk of any loss arising from its depreciation, and be entitled to the benefit of any rise, or he could elect to affirm the sale and hold the Brokers to the price which they had reported; but he could not do both. If the Brokers, after taking the stock to their own account, sold it at an advance, the Client could charge them with any profit realized by them from the transaction, or he might treat them as having converted the stock to their own use, and charge them with damages for the conversion; but he could not charge the Brokers with the price or value of the stock, either as purchasers or as having converted it, and at the same time claim that the stock is undisposed of, and the account for that reason not closed.[1]

The rule we are considering was likewise most impressively laid down by the House of Lords in the year 1829 in the case of Brookman vs. Rothschild.[2] This case arose out of a transaction with the well-known banking house of Rothschild. It appeared that the plaintiff was a holder of 20,000 French rentes. The defendant resided in London, and dealt

---

[1] And a usage of the Stock Exchange authorizing Brokers who are entitled to sell stock or shares of a customer for the realization and payment of money due to them by such customer, to take over to themselves, at the price of the day, stock or shares of the customer, for which there is an inadequate demand, where a forced sale would lower them in selling, is not binding upon a customer unacquainted with the same. Hamilton vs. Young, 7 L. R. (Ireland) 289. If a Stockbroker illegally acts for the purchaser after having been employed by the seller, the purchaser although entitled to rescind the contract, cannot recover profits made by the Broker. Illingworth vs. DeMott, 45 Atl. Rep. (N. J.) 272.

[2] 3 Sim. 153, aff'd in H. L. 5 Bligh, 165.

largely in foreign securities, and had contracted for the
Prussian loan ; he was also a partner with his brothers in the
Paris firm.   The plaintiff employed the defendant to sell his
rentes.   The defendant, without the plaintiff's knowledge,
purchased them for himself and his partners, but gave the
plaintiff the market price.   The plaintiff then purchased
Prussian bonds of the defendant, and agreed that they
should remain in his hands as a security for the purchase-
money, which remained unpaid, but no bonds were appropriated or set apart for the plaintiff.   The defendant, however, had always in his hands bonds to a greater amount.
Subsequently defendant was directed to sell the bonds ; and
he informed the plaintiff that he had sold them accordingly,
and gave the plaintiff credit for the alleged price.   The
plaintiff then purchased 115,000 rentes of the defendant,
which he was to pay for on a future day, and the rentes
were then to be transferred to him ; but no rentes were
set apart for the plaintiff or identified as belonging to him.
Before the day of payment arrived, the defendant, by the
plaintiff's desire, sent an order to his partners to sell the
rentes ; and they subsequently informed the plaintiff that
they had sold them accordingly, and gave the plaintiff
credit for the alleged proceeds.   The accounts between the
plaintiff and defendant were afterwards settled, and the
plaintiff paid the balance which appeared due from him to
the defendant.   Four years afterwards, the plaintiff having
discovered that the 20,000 rentes had been purchased by the
defendant and his partners, and that there was no appropriation on the two after-purchases, filed his bill to have all
the transactions set aside.   The vice-chancellor, in an elaborate opinion, sustained the plaintiff's claim, and set the
transaction aside.   Upon appeal to the House of Lords,

this decree was unanimously sustained without hearing the respondents. Lord Wynford, who delivered an opinion of great force, but which is extraordinary in its opening, said: " . . . I am very sorry to say that, with respect to one of the parties in this case, it is perfectly clear that he is a most desperate gambler in the funds, and he has met with that fate which most of those meet with who become such gamblers; for I believe, whenever a man puts his foot into the Stock Exchange, not being a member of that Stock Exchange, his ruin is certain, and the only question is a question of time." He then proceeds with his opinion, some extracts from which vividly illustrate the subject upon which we are treating. " It has been said at the bar, that if a man in the country sends to his Broker in London, and desires him to sell stock for him, the Broker in London may take that stock for himself, and charge him with the day's price on it. If Brokers in London do this, I have no doubt they do it fairly; but I will take leave to say that Brokers in London are not to be trusted in these things any more than any other description of agents. If I live in Dorsetshire, and I write to my Broker in London to sell my stock, I fancy that I have the advantage of that Broker's assistance as to the day on which it is proper to sell. I fancy that, living in London, he has a knowledge of the facts which will act on the market. If the Broker in London, instead of going to the Stock Market, or instead of exercising a discretion as to the period when he should sell any stock, is to take that stock to himself, he deprives me of the security I have and the confidence I repose in his skill and intelligence; and if there is a loss to me, he is the person who takes advantage of that loss. I take it to be a general principle of law and equity that a man cannot

be a seller for me and a buyer of that property himself."[1]
This principle is also forcibly illustrated by the case of
Gillett vs. Peppercorne.[2]   There the defendant, a Stock-
broker, was largely interested in the shares of a water-works
company, of which he was also an active director.   Having
recommended the plaintiff to make investments therein, the
plaintiff in May, 1826, December, 1830, and January, 1831,
respectively, purchased through the defendant twenty-five
shares in the company, which shares were transferred to
the plaintiff by certain persons who held them as trustees
for the defendant, and who so held them simply to enable
the defendant to make a transfer of the shares through
third parties.   Some of the shares had, after their purchase,
been transferred by the plaintiff to his sons by way of ad-
vancement; but they were retransferred the day previous
to the institution of the suit.   The plaintiff made the discovery of the real nature of the transaction in 1837; and
in 1838 he filed his bill to set aside the transaction on the
ground that it was not competent for a Stock-broker, or
agent employed to purchase, to sell his own shares to his
principal in the name of another party.   The court so held.
The court found that in one of the transactions the defendant acted as a gratuitous agent of the plaintiff, but held

---

[1] Brookman vs. Rothschild was
followed in Bischofscheim vs. Baltzer, 20 Fed. Rep. 890, and a transaction in which the Broker undertook to deliver his own bonds to his
Client was set aside, and the bonds
having subsequently become worthless, it was held that the loss should
be borne by the Broker, and the
purchase price of the bonds be
stricken from his account.   See also
Crull vs. Dodson, Macn. Sel. Cas.
114; Hamilton vs. Young, 7 L. R.
(Ireland) 289.

[2] 3 Beav. 78.   See also Skelton vs.
Wood, 71 L. T. 616, in which case it
was held that the Broker could not
recover if he bought stocks, and resold them without his Client's
knowledge and then bought them
back again, charging his Client with
the differences.

that this made no difference, and that the same principle would apply ; and it refused to countenance such a transaction because it was said to be an every-day practice among Brokers. The court, in its opinion, said that the plaintiff might say, " Put me in the situation in which I was before. Whether these shares were of greater value or not, I do not choose to be at the risk of selling the shares which now stand in my name. They have been transferred to me in a manner which the law does not warrant, and I desire to be placed in the situation in which I should have been if the transaction had not taken place." The court directed that the defendant should take back the shares, with all the dividends which had been paid upon them ; and he ought to pay to the plaintiff the purchase-money, with interest, and the costs of the suit. In regard to the question of laches in discovering the fraud and bringing the suit, the court said : " It is not sufficient to say that the plaintiff, being a proprietor, might have gone to the books and made a search, and found out all these matters, or that the son, being a director and having the books before him, might have made the search ; the knowledge, in my opinion, ought to have been brought home to the plaintiff—and this has not been done." The court also held that the transfer of the shares made previous to the suit did not affect the plaintiff's right of action.

When the case of Taussig vs. Hart,[1] before referred to, came before the Court of Appeals of New York for a second time, the court reiterated the doctrine that, upon an order by a Client to buy stock, the Broker could not deliver his own, " for the reason that the law does not permit an agent

[1] 58 N. Y. 425.

employed to purchase to buy of himself. It is no reason
that the intention was honest, and that the Brokers did
better for their principal by selling him their own stock
than they could have done by going into the open market.
The rule is inflexible, and although its violation in the
particular case caused no damage to the principal, he cannot be compelled to adopt the purchase."

And the case of Robinson vs. Mollett[1] carries the principle
still further, by establishing the rule that not even a local
custom of Brokers will sanction a Broker in selling his own
goods to his principal, without the knowledge and consent
of the latter.

In that case plaintiff, a merchant in Liverpool, gave orders to a tallow Broker in London to buy certain quantities
of tallow for him. The Broker did not buy the specified
quantities from any person, though he sent bought notes
in the usual form—" Bought of A. on your account ;" but,
both before and after the order, he bought from various
persons in his own name larger quantities of tallow, proposing to allot to plaintiff the quantities he had desired to be
bought. On plaintiff's refusal to accept, the Broker sold
the tallow and brought an action for the difference. This
case was very elaborately argued by counsel and decided
upon several different opinions, the judges being unanimous,
except one, that the suit could not be maintained, although
the evidence showed such a mode of dealing to be the usage
in the London tallow market, it appearing that the principal had no knowledge of it. And it was further held that
the mere fact of employing a Broker to execute a commis-

[1] L. R. 7 H. L. Eng. & I. App.   Kimber vs. Barber, L. R. 8 Ch. 56;
Cas. 802. See also Bank of Bengal   Wilson vs. Short, 6 Hare, 366.
vs. McLeod, 7 Moo. P. C. C. 35;

sion as a Broker in a market where such usage prevails would not make the principal liable; and that mere usage, without express knowledge and assent, could not be admitted to convert a Broker employed to buy for his employer into a principal to sell for him. Quoting the language of Willes, J., below, Mr. Justice Mellor said that " it is an axiom of the law of principal and agent that a Broker employed to sell cannot himself become the buyer, nor can a Broker employed to buy become himself the seller, without distinct notice to the principal, so that the latter may object if he think proper; a different rule would give the Broker an interest against his duty."

So in Massachusetts it has been held[1] that an order of the Client to a Broker, to buy stock deliverable at the buyer's option in 60 days, does not authorize the Broker to buy the stock himself at 30 days, and deliver it to his Client at the end of 60 days at an increased price and interest, besides the usual commission, and a usage of Brokers to do so is bad; nor is the exchange of bought and sold notes between Broker and his Client, nor the giving of his note to his Broker in payment for the stock, in ignorance of the Broker's conduct, a ratification of his acts.[2]

When a person gives an order to a Stock-broker " to buy stocks on margin," he employs the Broker to act for him and in his interest; accordingly the Broker has no right to put himself in a position antagonistic to the interests of his employer; he cannot make himself both buyer and seller, and any custom to this effect, unknown to the employer, is against public policy and illegal.[3]

[1] Day vs. Holmes, 103 Mass. 306.

[2] To same effect, Pickering vs. Demeritt, 100 id. 416; Todd vs. Bishop, 136 Mass. 386.

[3] Commonw. vs. Cooper, 15 Am.

And in the case of Marye vs. Strouse the same rule was laid down by the Circuit Court of the United States in Nevada.[1] There mining-stock Brokers were ordered by their Client to purchase 500 shares of a certain mining stock at the San Francisco Mining-stock Board. They purchased 125 shares at the latter place ; and at the same time F., one of the members of the firm of Brokers, turned over to his firm 375 shares for the purpose of filling the Client's order. The Client never received the stock into his possession, never assented to this mode of filling his order, and had no knowledge of it until the time of bringing a suit against him to recover the amount thereof.

The court held that he was not chargeable with the amount of the 375 shares. The court said : "It is not claimed that there was any fraud in fact here, but evidence establishing the transfer of the stock to have been *bona fide* and for a fair price is unavailing. The inquiry does not reach the question whether there was or was not fraud in fact." The court cited among other cases the decision of the Supreme Court of the United States in Michoud vs.

Law Rev. 360; s. c. 15 Mass. Law Rep. No. 24, May 4, 1881. And the burden of proof lies on the agent to show that he has made a full disclosure to his principal; but his simple, uncorroborated evidence to that effect will not avail where it is contradicted by his principal (Dunne vs. English, L. R. 18 Eq. 524). A Broker does not meet the burden of proof which is upon him to show that he has executed his Client's orders to purchase, by showing that he has transferred his own stocks to the Client. Lonergan vs. Peck, 136 Mass. 361.

Although an agent employed to sell stock is guilty of bad faith in acting both for buyer and seller, and if the transaction were completed without his principal's knowledge, would forfeit his commissions, yet if before fulfilment, the principal, with knowledge of the real state of facts, does not repudiate the sale, but closes with the purchaser, he cannot decline to pay the agent's commission. Hafner vs. Herron, 46 N. E. Rep. (Ill.) 211.

[1] 5 Fed. Rep. 483.

Girod,[1] and further decided that the mere fact that there was an account stated between the parties subsequent to the transaction did not alter the rule, in the absence of knowledge on the part of the Client. Finally, where a Client has dealt with his Broker several times as a principal in stock transactions, it does not annul his character as Broker, or deprive the Client of the protection which the law extends to him by reason of the relation which exists between him as principal and the Broker as such.[2]

The question as to what evidence is sufficient to warrant the submission to the jury of an instruction that if a pledgee became, through a third person, a purchaser at his own sale there was no sale sufficient to bind the Client, came up in a recent case.[3] It was there held that when the Brokers furnished the purchase money, and that one of them was alleged to have stated that they still carried the stock for the Client on their books, the instruction should have been submitted to the jury, although an employee of the Brokers testified that the purchase was made for the wife of an outside Broker who had deskroom in plaintiff Broker's office, and was so entered on their books, when neither the outside Broker, nor his wife, was called as a witness to show that she was the purchaser.

If there is any principle of law that is well settled, it seems to be the one which we are considering, and we do not deem it within the purpose of this work to refer to any cases upon the subject other than those in which Stock and Produce Brokers have been involved; although the principle is framed so comprehensively as to embrace every

[1] 4 How. (U. S.) 503. [3] Cummann vs. Huntington, 85
[2] Bragg vs. Meyer, 1 McAll. (C. N. Y. S. 434.
C.) 408, 417.

relation in which the slightest element of trust or confidence exists.[1]

The solicitude with which the law of England has watched over the rights of Clients to protect them from any misplaced confidence or frauds on the part of Brokers is very apparent from a perusal of the acts passed in the reigns of William III.[2] and Queen Anne,[3] and the subsequent acts amendatory of the latter act, passed in the reigns of George III., and Victoria,[4] as also of the acts referred to in chapter I. pp. 2-4.

By the first of these acts (8 and 9 William III.), Brokers were compelled to become licensed, and the jurisdiction over them was placed in the hands of the court of the Mayor and Aldermen of London, and they were required to enter into a bond and take an oath of office. The act also prohibited the Broker from dealing on his own account. By the act passed in the reign of Queen Anne, all persons were to be admitted as Brokers in the city of London, under regulations to be made by the mayor and aldermen. Regulations in pursuance of this act were made by the mayor and aldermen and a form of bond and oath prescribed. The form of this bond and oath is fully

[1] Nor can a Broker who is directed to purchase bonds sell them to his Client at a higher price. Levy vs. Loeb, 85 N. Y. 365, aff'd on new trial, 89 N. Y. 386.

[2] 8 & 9 Wm. III. ch. 32.

[3] 6 Anne, ch. 16.

[4] 57 Geo. III. ch. 60; and 33 & 34 Vict. ch. 607. But by a statute of 1884 (47 Vict. ch. 3) the jurisdiction of the city over Stock-brokers and jobbers was terminated, and at present the only control exercised over them is that by the committee of the Stock Exchange. The acts of William and Anne have been also repealed by the Stat. L. Rev. Acts 1867 and 1887. But the repeal of these statutes did not, however, in any way weaken or modify the principle mentioned in the text as to the illegality of a Broker acting in the dual capacity of principal and agent at the same time, except in so far as it has been relaxed in recent years. See p. 380.

given in the case of Green vs. Weaver[1] and from a perusal of the bond it appears that one of its conditions is similar to the provision contained in the act of William III., i. e. that a Broker shall not deal on his own account.

But although by the provisions of those acts, and of the regulations passed by the city, a Broker was prohibited from trading on his own account, the consequences of his so trading were merely confined to the penalty of the bond, dismissal from office, and to his liability to be prosecuted criminally for a violation of his oath, and they did not extend to create a disability to sustain an action in respect of these prohibited dealings. Therefore if he traded on his own account openly and in public he might recover on account of such transactions, but if he acted ostensibly as Broker whilst actually a principal in the same dealing, he was guilty of a gross fraud, and could not recover.[2]

And in Proctor vs. Brain[3] Best, C. J., used the following significant language: "A man who is a sworn Broker cannot be a principal (in the same transactions), and this is for the wisest reasons. . .. I am satisfied that no body of men will rejoice more in seeing the regulations enforced than the Brokers themselves. If I employ a Broker, I pay him for his assistance, and I suppose that I have the benefit of his judgment; I suppose that he is acting honestly; but what security have I if a man is to shift his character at pleasure from that of Broker to principal?"[4]

---

[1] 1 Sim. 401, 424; s. c. 6 L. J. Ch. 1. See form of bond and oath given, post p. 944. Kemble vs. Atkins, 1 Holt, 427, 431, note; Clark vs. Powell, 1 Nev. & Man. 492, 501.

[3] Ex parte Dyster, 1 Mer. 155.

[2] 2 Moo. & P. 284; 3 C. & P. 536.

[4] See also remarks of Lord Ellenborough in London, etc., vs. Brandon, Holt, 438, note; see also cases cited under the next subdivision (/), and report of Royal Stock Exchange Commission, July, 1878.

Of late years, however, in England the courts have relaxed something of the stringency of the rule which forbade
a Broker to deal with his principal whilst acting as a
Broker in any other capacity than that of agent. It seems
that although a Broker is on all occasions bound to use his
best endeavors in his employer's interests, yet, if in doing
so, he is compelled to abandon the position of an agent and
take up that of a principal, he will not be held to have
acted wrongfully[1] and, as he is, under the rules of the
Exchange, personally liable on contracts, he may, to mini-
mize his loss, sell and repurchase from a jobber at a fair
price fixed by the jobber,[2] but if the sale and repurchase is
one and the same transaction, he must account to the Client
for any profit made.[3]

There seems to be an exception to the principle above
stated, which was made for the first time by the Court of
Appeals of the State of New York in the case of Quincey
vs. White.[4] It was there held that where stocks were
sold at the Board of Brokers "under the rule"[5] by a Broker
who had loaned money on them to a fellow-Broker, the
proceeding was in the nature of a foreclosure, and the
creditor might himself become the purchaser. The court
said: " It must be assumed that a person selling stock
under the rule (as it is called) has a right to purchase himself. The object is to foreclose the claim of the mortgagor
or pledgor, and, in analogy to other similar cases, the
pledgee or mortgagee may become the purchaser." And

---

[1] Petre vs. Sutherland, 3 T. L. R.
422; Sachs vs. Spielman, 5 T. L. R.
487.

[2] Walter vs. King, 13 T. L. R.
270; Macoun vs. Erskine, L. R. 2 K.
B. (1901) 493.

[3] Erskine vs. Sachs, L. R. 2 K. B.
(1901) 594.

[4] 63 N. Y. 370–376.

[5] Art. XXVIII. Constitution N.
Y. Stock Exchange.

the rule seems to be settled, that a Broker or pledgee may become the purchaser of the pledged security at a judicial sale held under a decree to foreclose the pledge.[1]

And the parties may expressly agree that the pledgees may become purchasers at their own sale.[2] The court said: "Such a sale is not absolutely void, but only voidable, for it may be sanctioned or ratified by consent, and this is shown by numerous authorities." And further: "If voidable, then capable of ratification; if thus capable, then also of a prior authorization."

[1] Quincey vs. White, 63 N. Y. 370–376; Jones on Mort. (4th ed.) § 1636; Newport, etc., Bridge Co. vs. Douglass, 12 Bush (Ky.), 673, 720.

In the case of Lacombe and others vs. Forstell's Sons, 123 U. S. 562 (1887), the United States Supreme Court, without passing on the question, suggest a well founded doubt as to whether the pledgee of securities can cut off the pledgor's right by putting them into the hands of a Broker to be sold on the market in the usual way, and instructing another Broker to see that they are not sacrificed, authorizing him to say that they would pay more for them to the purchaser than they would sell for. Defendants claimed that in this way the securities were returned to them, and that this was done without fraudulent purpose, but to secure the highest market price for the bonds at the sale.

The court say that although the question of intentional fraud was repelled, "the transaction is one which it might be difficult to sustain in a court of equity."

Quære, whether Brokers not members of the Stock Exchange who borrow money from Brokers, members of the Exchange, on a pledge of securities, are bound by the rules of the Exchange as to the sale of collaterals, even though the loan was effected on the floor of the Exchange by a Broker employed by the borrowers. Morris vs. Grant, 34 Hun, 377. In that case it was also held that a buyer who had purchased at such a sale, and had received the securities, but declined to pay the purchase money, could be compelled to complete the purchase, notwithstanding a decision of the committee on securities to the contrary, because the latter had no jurisdiction of the matter, there was no question as to the legal rights of the parties to be adjudicated, and the borrowers had no notice of, and did not attend, the committee meeting. Morris vs. Grant, 34 Hun, 377.

[2] Chouteau vs. Allen, 70 Mo. 290, 335.

Courts of equity do not, however, go so far as to prevent an agent dealing with his principal in all cases. They only require that he shall deal with him at "arm's length," and after a full disclosure of all he knows with respect to the property.[1]

And where the Broker buys or sells his own stock on his Client's account, and thereby makes a profit, his principal may either repudiate the transaction altogether, or he may adopt it, and claim for himself the benefit made by his agent.[2]

If a Broker purchases bonds from a Broker apparently for an undisclosed principal, but in reality for himself, and shields himself from all liability as agent, he is estopped from suing for a breach of the contract either as principal or agent.[3]

(f.) Effect of Sale or Purchase by Broker.

The effect of a purchase by a Broker or pledgee of the stocks of the Client or pledgor, as we have seen, is to render

[1] Evans on Ag. (2d ed.) 324; Trevelyan vs. Charles, 9 Beav. 140; Dunne vs. English, L. R. 18 Eq. 524; Robinson vs. Mollett, L. R. 7 H. L. 815, 816.

[2] Evans on Ag. (2d ed.) 324; Kimbar vs. Barber, L. R. 8 Ch. App. 56. See also notes to Fox vs. Macreth, 1 L. C. Eq. (6th ed.) 141. A Broker is not precluded by the form of his notices of purchase or sale, from showing that the transactions were made with third parties. Porter vs. Wormser, 94 N. Y. 431, 447. The sale by a pledgee to himself is not absolutely void, but voidable only at the election of the pledgor. He may ratify the sale, and if he elects to do so, then the sale becomes perfectly valid and effectual. Roach vs. Duckworth, 95 N. Y. 391, 402, confirming Bryan vs. Baldwin, 52 N. Y. 232.

And where a Broker mixes his own with his principal's bonds in selling, and refuses to disclose the time of the sale, and the amount realized, the jury are at liberty to find that all of the bonds sold are the principal's. Bate vs. McDowell, 49 Super. Ct. Rep. (17 J. & S.) 106.

The rule that all advantages gained by an agent in unauthorized dealings or speculations with his principal's property, enure to the principal, is declared and the cases cited and examined in Keiran vs. Hoyt, 33 Hun, 145, s. c. more fully, N. Y. Daily Reg. Oct. 4, 1884.

[3] Paine vs. Loeb, 96 Fed. Rep. 164.

the transaction void, and the cases hold that such a purchase does not change the creditor's relation to his debtor, but that the securities are still held by the creditor under the original titles as security for the original debt. The transaction is treated precisely as if no sale had been made; and the debtor, in order to obtain another sale of the securities, or to redeem them, is not required to prove that the Broker or pledgee made a fraudulent sale or one disadvantageous to himself, but only that he became the purchaser. The Broker or pledgee in selling the securities is in the position of trustee for the Client or pledgor, and the law will not allow of the temptation to fraud or the possibility of the same through the trustee becoming purchaser at his own sale. But the pledgor has the option to treat the sale as valid, and to accept the benefits thereof.[1]

In Brookman vs. Rothschild,[2] where the 20,000 rentes were purchased by the Brokers themselves, the decree of the court was that they should deliver the same to the Client, together with all of the dividends thereon, upon being repaid

---

[1] Brookman vs. Rothschild, 3 Sim. 224; aff'd H. L., 5 Bligh (n. s.), 165; Pigot vs. Cubley, 15 C. B. (n. s.) 702; Stokes vs. Frazier, 72 Ill. 428; Chicago Artesian-well Co. vs. Corey, 60 id. 73; Bank vs. Dubuque & Pacific R. R., 8 Iowa, 277; Hamilton vs. State Bank, 22 id. 306; Md. Fire Ins. Co. vs. Dalrymple, 25 Md. 242; Baltimore Marine Ins. Co. vs. Dalrymple, id. 269; Bryson vs. Rayner, id. 421; Star Fire Ins. Co. vs. Palmer, 9 J. & S. (N. Y.) 267; Richardson vs. Mann, 30 La. Ann. 1060; Wright vs. Ross, 36 Cal. 411; Bryan vs. Baldwin, 7 Laus. 174, aff'd 52 N. Y. 232; Duncomb vs. N. Y. & N. H.

R. Co., 84 N. Y. 204; Hope vs. Lawrence, 1 Hun, 317; Duden vs. Waitzfelder, 16 id. 337; Hamilton vs. Schaack, 16 N. Y. W. D. 423; Middlessex Bank vs. Minot, 45 Mass. 325; Ainsworth vs. Bowen, 9 Wis. 318; Hestonville R. Co. vs. Shields, 3 Brews. (Pa.) 257. See also First National Bank vs. Hall, 22 App. Div. 356; Glidden vs. Bank, 13 L. R. A. 737. Consult also the following notes in L. R. A., "Purchase by pledgee," 13 L. R. A. 755; "Who may purchase," 53 L. R. A. 861.

[2] Supra.

the sum with interest which the Client had originally received for them ; or that the Client should receive an amount equal to the present value of the rentes.

And the other cases cited above hold that the Client, if the Broker has sold the stocks, may elect to affirm the sale and recover the proceeds ; or that he may treat the illegal disposition as a conversion and recover damages for the same.[1] And where a Broker sold shares in a Water Company to his Client, through third parties, the court directed that the defendant Broker should take back the shares with all the dividends which had been paid upon them, and that he should pay to the plaintiff, his Client, the purchase-money, with interest at the rate of five per cent, and the costs of the suit.[2] So, where a Broker purchases shares from a third party with the view of selling them himself to his Client, in the execution of an order to purchase, and does sell the same to his principal at a price higher than that at which he himself purchased, the Client may recover the difference between the price at which the Broker bought and that at which he sold the shares ; and this, although the Client has parted with a portion of the shares, so that he might not be in a position to rescind the transaction.[3]

[1] See, in addition to the authorities just cited, Taussig vs. Hart, 49 N. Y. 301; id. 58 N. Y. 425; Pickering vs. Demeritt, 100 Mass. 416; Day vs. Holmes, 103 id. 306. But the Client cannot follow both of these courses. Mayo vs. Knowlton, 16 Daly, 245.

[2] Gillett vs. Peppercorne, 3 Beav. 78.

[3] Kimber vs. Barber, L. R. 8 Ch. App. 56. In Levy vs. Loeb, 89 N. Y. 386, it appeared that instead of performing their contract of agency to purchase bonds, the defendants purchased the bonds in their own name at prices stated and then charged them to plaintiffs at higher prices, and reported the purchases as made for them at those enhanced prices. Relying upon this false statement and in consideration of an agreement to carry the bonds for a certain time on part payment of the purchase price, plaintiffs paid the sum called for. Held that upon

One B., a Broker, knowing that one K. was desirous of obtaining shares in a certain company, called upon K. and told him that he knew where the shares could be purchased at £3 per share, and was authorized to make the purchase at that price. B. then went to a person who had the shares for sale and bought them for £2 per share, and made the sale and transfer of the shares to K. through a third person. K. subsequently discovering that B. was, in fact, the owner of the shares, brought an action against B., in which he prayed for alternative relief, either that B. might be decreed to pay K. the difference between the prices paid, or otherwise that the sale of the shares might be set aside, and the purchase-money repaid upon a retransfer of the shares. Previous to bringing the suit, K. had transferred part of the shares; and the Master of the Rolls, on this ground, held that the transaction could not be set aside. And he refused to give the plaintiff the difference between the prices paid, for the reason that it would be making a new contract between the parties. On appeal, the decree of the Master of the Rolls was reversed, and the plaintiff, K., was allowed to recover the difference in the prices paid. But the court did not undertake to decide whether the transaction could be set aside, K. having parted with a portion of the shares.[1]

IX. When Broker can Close Transaction.

In the absence of express agreement, the Broker may, at his option, upon reasonable notice, require the Client to take

the discovery of the facts, plaintiffs were authorized and justified in repudiating the fictitious transaction reported, and could recover back the sum paid.

[1] Kimber vs. Barber, L. R. 8 Ch. App. 56.

the stocks which he may be carrying for him, and thus close the transaction.[1] As the Client may at any time require the delivery of the stocks to him or the transaction closed upon paying the amount advanced for their purchase, with commissions and interest, so the Broker, in the absence of agreement, has the reciprocal right to require the Client at any time to "take up" the stocks or close the transaction, and to repay him the amount due thereon. Although the Client's margin may not be exhausted, the Broker is not bound to continue the transaction for an indefinite period. He earns his commission by making the transaction, and in the absence of agreement it would seem but reasonable to assume that he should be able to discontinue the relation after a reasonble time at least. But there is no express adjudication upon this point, and much can be said on both sides of the question.[2]

So there is another instance where the Broker seems to be entitled to sell the Client's stocks, viz., where the latter becomes a bankrupt;[3] and it has been decided[4] that where a Broker holds stock for a Client on a margin, and the latter becomes a bankrupt, it is the duty of the Broker to take notice of this fact; and that where the Broker continued to hold the stocks after such bankruptcy for an unreasonable time, and then sold them without any application or consent of the assignee or bankruptcy court, and without no-

---

[1] Stenton vs. Jerome, 54 N. Y. 480, 482; White vs. Smith, id. 522; Sterling vs. Jaudon, 48 Barb. (N. Y.) 459; Merwin vs. Hamilton, 6 Duer (N. Y.), 244; Esser vs. Linderman, 71 Pa. St. 76. As to when Broker may close transaction on the death of his Client, see Lacey vs. Hill, post, 387.

[2] Id.

[3] The authority of an agent is determined by notice of the bankruptcy of his principal. Markwick vs. Hardington, 15 Ch. D. 339.

[4] In re Daniels, 13 Nat'l Bankr. Reg. 46; s. c. 1 N. Y. W. D. 271.

tice to any one, the bankrupt's estate was not properly chargeable with the loss.

So also a Stock-broker is justified in immediately closing the account on the death of his Client.[1] The authority given by the deceased Client becomes determined at his death.[2] But the Broker cannot, on the plea that he had a continuing authority from the deceased to carry over from settling day to settling day, carry over the account for a considerable period after notice of his Client's death.[3] And if he has a continuation account with a Client, and on notice of the latter's death, does not close the account immediately, but makes a further continuation, and ultimately sells at a loss, he cannot recover the amount of the loss from the Client's estate.[4]

But it has been held in the State of New York that when a Broker acts in good faith, he may continue the account until the appointment of a legal representative, as, the agency being coupled with an interest, the case presents an exception to the rule that the death of the principal terminated the agent's authority.[5] But circumstances might justify him in closing the account immediately.[6] And in case of a stock option where the one liable to deliver the stock dies before the option expires, the holder of the option must make a demand of the stock from the legal representative when appointed. A demand made at the bank where the stock was made payable, immediately after the death, is insufficient.[7]

[1] Lacey vs. Hill, L. R. 8 Ch. App. 921.

[2] Phillips vs. Jones, 4 T. L. R. 401.

[3] Id.

[4] In re Overweg, L. R. (1900) 1 Ch. D. 209.

[5] Hess vs. Rau, 95 N. Y. 359.

[6] Id.; see Demery vs. Burtenshaw's Est., 91 N. W. Rep. 617.

[7] Prince vs. Robinson's Admrs., 14 Fed. Rep. 631.

If the transaction be a " long one "—viz., a purchase of stocks for the Client—the better practice would be for the Broker to make up a statement of the account and tender the securities to the Client with a blank power of attorney to transfer, and offer to deliver the same upon payment of the amount due.[1]

If, on the other hand, the transaction consists of a short sale, the Broker should give the Client a notice, informing him that he desired the transaction closed either by a purchase of the stock or a transfer of the operation to some other person or office, as has been indicated above under the head of " short sale."

When a Stock-broker fills an order for the purchase of stock, and his principal makes default, and he thereupon resells the stock at a loss, it is necessary for him, in order that he may recover the amount of such loss from his principal, to show that the stock was actually purchased by himself or by an agent under his direction, at its fair market price on the day of purchase, and that he actually paid the purchase-money therefor ; that he notified his principal of the purchase, and requested him to receive the stock and pay the price paid for it with reasonable commissions ; that at the time of this notice he was in condition to deliver the stock, by having it or other proper *indicia* of title actually in hand or in the hands of his agent ; that on the failure of the principal to receive the stock he, after reasonable time and notice to that effect to the principal, directed it to be sold; and that it was sold by his agent either at public sale in market overt, or at a sale publicly and fairly made at the

[1] Merwin vs. Hamilton, 6 Duer 32 Md. 169; Genin vs. Isaacson, 6 (N. Y.), 244; Wynkoop vs. Seal, 64   N. Y. *Leg. Obs.* 213. Pa. St. 361; Rosenstock vs. Tormey,

Stock Exchange, or a Stock Board or a Board of Brokers, where such stocks are usually sold at a fair market value on the day of sale.[1]

So it has been held[2] that where Brokers purchased in their own names, and without disclosing the name of the Client, certain stocks for the latter, before they could maintain an action against the latter for a depreciation in the price of the stocks, they were bound to tender the stocks to the Client; and that where it appeared that this was not done, and that the Brokers sold the stock without any notice of the sale, they could not recover from their principal.[3]

But where the Brokers have not sold the stocks purchased for their Client, in an action against him to recover the advances made by the Brokers and their commissions on such purchase, it is not necessary for them to produce the certificates of stock on the trial or account for their non-production, where they give testimony that they bought and have the same in their possession. It is not until the Client has paid or tendered the sum laid out that he can demand its delivery.[4] And where plaintiffs' Brokers and copartners brought an action to recover an amount claimed to be due

[1] Rosenstock vs. Tormey, 32 Md. 169.

[2] Merwin vs. Hamilton, 6 Duer (N. Y.), 244.

[3] Upon a contract to deliver stocks to another for cash on delivery, the acts of delivery and payment are simultaneous and neither can maintain an action against the other without showing on his part an actual performance or a legal offer to perform; Kelley vs. Upton, 5 Duer, 336; Genin vs. Tompkins, 12 Barb. 265. But see cases cited in next note.

[4] Id. And where upon a contract to deliver certain shares of stock "at seller's option, sixty days," the purchaser makes his demand for the stock at the proper time and in the proper form, is then ready to pay the price, and is refused the delivery on the ground that the seller was not able to make it, it is not necessary to the former's right of action for the breach that

upon an alleged agreement as to the sale and purchase of stocks on defendants' joint account, it appeared that plaintiffs purchased for defendant T. 56,650 shares of a certain stock. The referee, in stating the account between the parties, credited plaintiffs with 24,200 shares sold by them, and excluded from such account 32,450 shares, although he found that plaintiffs had bought and paid for the latter on account of the defendant T. As to them he also found that on April 20, 1874, they were not in the possession of plaintiffs, but prior to that time had been pledged by them for a loan of money for their use, and had never been tendered to T. and the amount due thereon demanded. He found, as conclusions of law, that plaintiffs could not recover for the purchase of said 32,450 shares, unless they showed performance of a contract on their part. He also found that the pledge of the stocks and suffering them to be sold by the pledgee was not such a performance, and that defendants were not bound to redeem the stock so pledged, and plaintiffs could not recover for the purchase of such stock. Plaintiffs claimed that their pledge of the stock was not a failure to perform a condition precedent, but a breach of a condition subsequent, which is to be compensated in this action by a recoupment or counterclaim of the damages.

Held, that the finding of the referee was erroneous; that the purchase of the stock was upon T.'s account, and was a

he should have made an actual offer or tender of the money (Wheeler vs. Garcia, 40 N. Y. 584). Munn vs. Barnum, 24 Barb. 283. A tender may be made by Brokers acting for principals in another state although the former were the owners of the stock at the time of tender. Clews vs. Jamieson, 182 U. S. 461, 496.

Bankruptcy of the Broker dispenses with the necessity of demand and tender. In re Swifte, 172 Fed. Rep. 315, 321. See also Mayo vs. Knowlton, 134 N. Y. 250. As to when tender before action is unnecessary, see Maguire vs. Halstead, 45 N. Y. Supp. 783. See also Speyer vs. Colgate, 67 Barb. 192.

proper charge against him; and the sale of the stock was a failure to perform a subsequent duty, and no condition precedent was broken which prevented plaintiffs from charging T. for the purchase of the stock.[1]

If after a Broker has closed out a transaction owing to the failure of his Client to furnish sufficient margin, the rendering of an account to the customer may, under circumstances, and when not objected to by the latter, constitute an account stated. Thus if several accounts have been rendered each showing a balance brought forward from the previous account, and suit is commenced three weeks after the rendition of the final account, all of the accounts having been retained by the Client without objection, the Client will be deemed to have assented to their accuracy,[2] and such facts when alleged in the complaint will entitle the plaintiff to recover for moneys advanced, and for commissions and expenses, and also upon an account stated.[3]

X. When Broker can Act by Substitute.

The general rule of law is, that a Broker, like an attorney, is selected as a specialist on account of his presumed skill and discretion, and of the confidence consequently bestowed on him by the principal. He cannot, therefore, depute his duties, so far as they are discretionary, to another, except in cases of necessity, *or in cases in which such deputation is sustained by usage, of which it may be implied that the*

---

[1] Capron vs. Thompson, 13 N. Y. Weekly Dig. 199; s. c. Ct. of App., 86 N. Y. 418. See also Cahill vs. Hirschman, 6 Nev. 57.

[2] Knickerbocker vs. Could, 115 N. Y. 533; Beach vs. Kidder, 8 N. Y. Supp. 587. See also McKay vs.

McKay, 35 N. Y. Supp. 415; 89 Hun, 612; Gillett vs. Whiting, 111 N. Y. 71; Donald vs. Gardner, 41 App. Div. 238; Coit vs. Goodhart, 5 App. Div. 444.

[3] Knickerbocker vs. Gould, supra.

principal is cognizant.[1] The rule being that, if a principal constitute an agent to do a business which obviously, and from its very nature, cannot be done by the agent otherwise than through a substitute, or if there exist in relation to that business a known and established usage of substitution, in either case the principal would be held to have expected and have authorized such substitution.[2] Applying these general principles to the business of Wall Street, it will be very easy to sustain the usage, so universally prevalent there, of transacting business through one or more subordinate Brokers who are necessarily employed, either for secrecy or despatch, in the execution of the Client's business or orders. And where an order to purchase stocks is given by a Client to his Broker in Baltimore, and the order is general in its terms—not directing the purchase to be made in any particular place or mode, and not containing any restrictions as to price—the Broker has the right to make the purchase in New York through correspondents—Brokers or sub-agents residing and doing business in that city.[3]

---

[1] Wharton on Ag. §§ 709, 711; Mechem on Agency, §§ 195, 197. Cockran vs. Irlam, 2 Maule & S. 301. Of course if the discretion has ceased, the Broker may act through a sub-agent. If a discretion is vested in a Broker as to whether a sale should be made of stocks or not, and if he determines upon a sale, then the discretion is exercised, and he may employ a sub-agent to make the actual sale. Sims vs. May, 16 St. Rep. 780.

[2] Moon vs. Guardians of Whitney, Union, 3 Bing. (N. C.) 814; Ledoux vs. Goza, 4 La. Ann. 160; White vs. Fuller, 4 Hun (N. Y.), 631; Commercial Bank vs. Norton, 1 Hill (N. Y.), 501, 505; Elwell vs. Chamberlain, 2 Bosw. id. 230.

[3] Rosenstock vs. Tormey, 32 Md. 169; Skiff vs. Stoddard, 63 Conn. 198. In the latter case see the nature of the business done through New York correspondents described in full detail, p. 205 et seq.

The sub-agent has no right of action against the Client, where the first Broker in employing the sub-agent acts only as an independent contractor, that is, employs a sub-agent to execute an order intrusted

But it has been held that when a Broker, not being in London, employs a second Broker to make a bargain for him on the Stock Exchange, there is no privity between the principal and such second Broker; and therefore, if the principal seek to make the latter a defendant in a suit for specific performance, the bill will be demurrable.[1]

Defendants, who were bankers and Brokers, gave to plaintiff a letter to their correspondent G., a Stock-broker in Philadelphia, stating, "This will introduce to you J. Any orders he may give you please execute on our account and advise us." G. took his orders from plaintiff in the purchase and sale of stocks, but reported to defendants and made his calls upon them for the necessary margins. In their accounts, defendants also treated plaintiff as dealing

for execution to himself. This he may do, but he cannot appoint an additional co-ordinate agent. The sub-agent is the agent merely of the first Broker and not of the Client, and there is no such privity of contract between him and the Client as would enable him to sue the Client for any balance due. Hill vs. Morris, 15 Mo. App. 322. But the first Broker may recover from his principal the amount of his indebtedness to the sub-agent. Id.; 21 id. 258; Mechem on Agency, § 197, and cases there cited.

The fact that one employing a Broker to sell property, is himself acting as Broker for another, does not discharge him from liability for the second Broker's commissions, if the agency of the first Broker were not disclosed Jarvis vs. Schaefer, 105 N. Y. 289.

Where a trustee makes an ordi-nary purchase on the Stock Exchange, he is not liable for any loss which may arise to the trust estate in consequence of the default of the Broker employed by him, if he has selected him with care, and no circumstances of suspicion have been brought to his knowledge which should have induced him to distrust the Broker. Speight vs. Gaunt, 48 L. T. R. (n. s.) 279; s. c. 28 Alb. Law J. 59; aff'd by House of Lords, 32 Week. Rep. 435. (Compare Franklin vs. Osgood, 14 Johns. 527, aff'g 2 Johns. Ch. 1; Suarez vs. Rumpelly, 2 Sandf. Ch. 336; Roosevelt vs. Roosevelt, 6 Abb. N. C. 417; Merrill vs. Farmers' Loan & Trust Co., 24 Hun, 297; Newton vs. Bronson, 13 N. Y. 587; Lewis vs Ingersoll, 3 Abb. Ct. App Dec. 557.)

[1] Booth vs. Fielding, 1 Week. Notes, 245. But see Gregory vs. Wendell, 40 Mich. 432.

directly with them ; and he was charged on their books with the stocks, commissions, and interest, and credited with the proceeds of sales. Held, that defendants were the agents of plaintiff, and they could not ignore G.'s agency, and cast the responsibility of a loss upon plaintiff, simply because his orders were taken and obeyed in the purchase and sale of the stocks.[1]

XI. Commission of Broker.

In respect to the commissions or compensation which a Stock-Broker is entitled to receive for transacting the business of the Client, the amount thereof rests either upon an express or an implied agreement. Of course, whenever there is an express agreement by which the amount of the commissions is definitely fixed, all greater or other rates are excluded.[2] But frequently, in employing a Stock-

[1] Gheen vs. Johnson, 90 Pa. St. 38. To same effect, see Smith vs. N. Y. S. & P. C. Co., 25 N. Y. Supp. 261. See also Ryman vs. Gerlach, 153 Pa. St. 197. Where orders are given by various persons to a Broker in one place, and by him executed through a second Broker in another place, the second Broker being given the name of the principal in each transaction, he cannot apply the gains on one of such principal's trades, to the losses resulting from those of another such principal. Baxter vs. Allen, 46 Ill. App. 464.

Although a New York Broker who has been instructed to sell mining stock employs a San Francisco Broker to sell it, there being no market in New York, he is liable as a trustee for the proceeds of the sale when received from his correspondent in San Francisco. Waters vs. Marrin, 12 Daly, 445. As to the effect of the bankruptcy of an agent employing a correspondent, see Le Marchant vs. Moore, 150 N. Y. 209.

[2] Wharton on Ag. § 323; Bowers vs. Jones, 8 Bing. 65; Ware vs. Hayward Rubber Co., 85 Mass. 84. An express agreement as to commission and its construction appears in Blakeslee vs. Ervin (58 N. W. Rep. 850), where a Broker contracted to sell certain stocks for the owner, retaining as compensation whatever they sold for above par, and he made a sale at par and an unaccrued dividend. This was held to be a sale at a price above par by the amount of such dividend and the Broker was entitled to that amount.

broker, nothing is said as to the amount of his commissions, in which case they must be ascertained by other means. There is a uniform rate fixed by the New York Stock Exchange which is generally observed by the Brokers in dealings with their Clients.[1] And the law seems to be that where a Broker is employed, and no special compensation is agreed upon, the rate of brokerage customarily charged for the same services is the proper measure of damages. The parties are then presumed to have contracted in reference to the usage.[2]

As has been shown in the chapter on "Usages," the law

[1] Art. XXXIV. Const. New York Stock Exchange. By sec. 2 all commissions shall be calculated on the par value of securities, and the rates shall be as follows: (a) On business for non-members, including joint account transactions in which a non-member is interested, transactions for partners not members of the Exchange, and for firms of which the Exchange member or members are special partners only, the commission shall not be less than one eighth of one per cent; (b) On business for members of the Exchange, the commission shall not be less than one thirty-second of one per cent, except where a principal is given up, in which case the commission shall not be less than one fiftieth of one per cent; (c) On mining shares and subscription rights such rates, to members and non-members, as may be determined from time to time, by the committee on commissions, with the approval of the governing committee; (d) Government and municipal securities are exempted from the provisions of the article. By § 4 a proposition to accept less rates shall constitute a violation of the article, the penalty for which is suspension for a first offence, and expulsion for a second offence (§ 6).

These rules, like any other rules and regulations in the contemplation of the parties when contracting, would be admissible in evidence in an action by the Broker for his commissions. Bibb vs. Allen, 149 U. S. 481. If the contract is denied, evidence of the New York rates of commission is admissible. Rubino vs. Scott, 118 N. Y. 662.

[2] Morgan vs. Mason, 4 E. D. Smith (N. Y.), 636; Miller vs. Ins. Co. of North America, 1 Ab. New Cas. id. 470, and note, which contains a collection of cases on the extent to which usage is admissible to establish a rate of compensation; see also Erben vs. Lorillard, 2 Keyes (N. Y.), 567; Adams vs. Capron, 21 Md. 186; Deshler vs. Beers, 32 Ill. 368; Potts vs. Aechternacht, 93 Pa. St. 138; Bibb vs. Allen, 149 U. S. 481.

is that where there is a general usage in any particular
trade or branch of business, parties. having knowledge of
the usage are presumed to contract in reference to it; and,
if the usage does not conflict with the terms of the contract,
it will be deemed to enter into and constitute a part of it.
Knowledge of the usage may be established by presumptive
as well as by direct evidence. It may be presumed from
surrounding facts, as the uniformity, long continuance, and
notoriety of the same.[1]

And it is held[2] that an agreement between Brokers to share
commissions earned by one on information given by the
other is legal.

But it seems that a Broker or Agent is not always entitled to a commission, although he may have performed
the work or transacted the business for which he was employed.

Mr. Parsons lays down a proposition[3] which seems to be
very generally accepted by the courts, that "neither a factor nor a Broker can have any valid claim for his commissions or other compensation if he has not discharged all the
duties of the employment which he has undertaken with
proper care and skill and entire fidelity." This necessarily
embraces all acts of bad faith on the part of the Broker;
and it even applies where a Broker, without fraudulent intent, receives commissions from a conflicting interest.[4]

In the State of New York, however, it has been held

---

[1] See chap. on "Usages" and
cases cited above. See also Easterly vs. Cole, 3 N. Y. 502.

[2] McLaughlin vs. Barnard, 2 E.
D. Smith (N. Y.), 372. See also
Hart vs. Garrett, 87 A. D. 536.

[3] Pars. on Con. (7th ed.) *100, and
authorities cited.

[4] Wharton on Ag. § 336; Story on
Ag. (9th ed.) § 331; Levy vs. Loeb,
85 N. Y. 365, aff'd on new trial, 89
N. Y. 386; Hafner vs. Herron, 165
Ill. 242.

that where a trustee wrongfully invested trust funds in securities not authorized by law, such act did not deprive him of his right to commissions; and Mr. Justice Woodruff doubted whether even misconduct or gross negligence would operate to debar trustees of their authorized compensation, where no imputation of fraud rests upon them.[1]

A Broker is never entitled to commissions for unsuccessful efforts, even though, after his failure and the termination of his agency, his labor proves of use and benefit to his principal. He does not, however, lose his commissions where his efforts are rendered a failure by the fault of his principal, or where the purchaser declines to complete because of a defect which is the fault of the principal.[2]

[1] King vs. Talbot, 40 N. Y. 76; Vanderheyden vs. Vanderheyden, 2 Paige (N. Y.), 288; Rapalje vs. Norsworthy, 1 Sand. Ch. (id.) 406; Meacham vs. Stearns, 9 Paige (id.), 405.

[2] Sibbald vs. Bethlehem Iron Co. (N. Y. Ct. App.), 11 N. Y. *Week. Dig* 445; Berg vs. San Antonio, 42 S. W. Rep. 647. When the Broker, employed to effect a sale or purchase, has found a party ready and willing to sell or purchase upon the terms offered and of sufficient responsibility, he has performed his contract and is entitled to his commissions. Thompson vs. Mayor, 58 N. Y. Supp. 203; Owl Canon Gypsum Co. vs. Ferguson, 30 Pac. Rep. 255; 2 Colo. App. 219; Duclos vs. Cunningham, 102 N. Y. 678; Mattingly vs. Roach, 84 Cal. 207; Mechem on Agency, § 966. Therefore, if the Client repudiates the Broker's contract, it is not necessary for the latter to take any further steps to ward sending or tendering the money to him, in order to maintain an action for commissions. Mattingly vs. Roach, 84 Cal. 207; see supra, s. c. *sub nom.* Mattingly vs. Pennie. The readiness of the prospective purchaser or vendor, procured by the Broker to buy or sell, can only be made to appear by showing that the Broker had procured from him a valid contract of purchase or sale. A verbal agreement only with a Broker to do something which by the terms of the Statute of Frauds should have been agreed to be done in writing, does not entitle the Broker to commissions. Mattingly vs. Pennie, 105 Cal. 514.

And if the party found by the Broker procures another person (without being authorized so to do by the Broker) to purchase the stock which the Broker was employed to sell, the Broker is not entitled to commissions. Jones vs.

What constitutes a faithful performance of the Broker's duties depends greatly upon the nature of the business committed to his hands. It has been held, for instance, that he is obliged to keep and render a correct account of the business transacted.[1] And, although he may not absolutely forfeit his commission by a failure to do this, it may be construed as a failure of duty on his part, or as a suppression of evidence.[2]

The case of Hoffman vs. Livingston[3] peculiarly illustrates the question of a right of a Stock-broker to recover his commissions. The plaintiff there sued to recover his commissions on transactions in stocks made for account of defendant. The transactions were conducted by the plaintiff under an arrangement by which the latter speculated for the defendant under a discretionary order, buying and selling whenever he deemed it advisable. Under this arrangement plaintiff made numerous transactions, resulting in a

Frost, 53 N. Y. Supp. 575, aff'd 62 N. Y. Supp. 1102. If the right to recover commissions is, under the contract of employment to sell bonds, made to depend upon the fact of the bonds being sold and their proceeds received, the Broker is not entitled to commissions on bonds which he contracts to sell at a price which the vendor refuses to accept. Coffin vs. Coke, 6 T. & C. (N. Y.) 71.

The Broker, however, need not personally introduce the purchaser to the principal, Hafner vs. Herron. 165 Ill. 242, and it is immaterial if the principal effects a sale on other terms with the party introduced. Id. As to when the allega-tions in an answer will not suffice to defeat a Broker's claim for commissions and advances, see Myers vs. Paine, 13 App. Div. 332; aff'd 57 N. E. Rep. 1118.

[1] Clark vs. Moody, 17 Mass. 145. If the Broker reports fictitious dealings he is not entitled to commissions. Prout vs. Chisolm, 21 App. Div. 58. As to evidence on which the Broker may go to the jury, see Armstrong vs. Village, 159 N. Y. 315. See also Burns vs. Campbell, 71 Ala. 271.

[2] Lupton vs. White, 15 Vesey, 432. 640; Hart vs. Ten Eyck, 2 Johns. Ch. 42, 108.

[3] 14 J. & S. (N. Y.) 552.

loss to the defendant of a large sum, more than one half of which was for commissions. Notice of each transaction was not given to the defendant in accordance with the custom of Brokers.

The action was contested on the ground that the circumstances showed that the operations were made with a view of merely yielding commissions for the benefit of the Broker, and it was held that the failure of the latter to give notice to his Client of each transaction was a neglect of duty which was a sufficient bar to the recovery of commission. The rule of law is that if the Broker's services are wholly abortive, or executed in such a manner that no benefit results from them, he is not entitled to recover either his commissions or even a compensation for his trouble. That the question is one of due diligence and ordinary skill, and the want of this may be the result of inattention or incapacity. It is not necessary in such case for defendant to show actual fraud.[1]

It has also been held that a Broker employed to purchase government bonds for a Client cannot act in the same transaction as agent for the seller, and receive commissions from

---

[1] For cases where Stock-brokers have sued for commissions earned in illegal transactions, and for money laid out, etc., in the same, see chapter "Stock-jobbing."

It cannot be interposed as a valid defence or answer to the Broker's demand for commissions that his contracts, in the making and execution of which his right to commissions arose, were not enforceable under the Statute of Frauds, or for want of other form, if, in fact, they have been fully executed and com- pleted. Bibb vs. Allen, 149 U. S. 497; Quinlan vs. Raymond, *Daily Reg.* July 29, 1886, aff'd 3 N. Y. St. Rep. 573, which also held that the statute should be specially pleaded as a defence. If a statute or ordinance prescribes that Stock-brokers shall be licensed, an unlicensed Broker, in selling stocks, does an unlawful act, and cannot maintain an action for commissions on such sale. Hustis vs. Pickands, 27 Ill. App. 270.

both sides,[1] although this may be done where the Client expressly assents to the same.[2]

Neither is a grain Broker entitled to commissions when his principal's intention is to "corner" the market, and such intent is known to the Broker.[3] Nor can a Broker, employed to sell bonds, recover commissions, although he procures a purchaser able and willing to buy, when, by the agreement between the principal and the Broker, the payment of the commissions depended upon the payment of an instalment of the purchase money, which by reason of a prior sale of the bonds to the vendors, having been declared illegal, and the delivery thereof perpetually enjoined, was not made.[4]

XII. Communications between Broker and Client not Privileged.

A wise public policy dictates that certain kinds of evidence should not be received in legal controversies, either

[1] Levy vs. Loeb, 85 N. Y. 365, aff'd on new trial, 89 N. Y. 386; Rice vs. Davis, 136 Pa. St. 439; Platt vs. Baldwin, 2 City Ct. 281; Hafner vs. Herron, 165 Ill. 242.

[2] Levy vs. Loeb, 85 N. Y. 365; s. c. 89 N. Y. 386. A Broker may recover commissions from both parties, if it was promised with full knowledge that the Broker held the same relation to the other party. Rice vs. Davis, 136 Pa. St. 439; Jarvis vs. Schaefer, 105 N. Y. 289; Rowe vs. Stevens, 53 N. Y. 621. The fact that a Broker for the sale of stock receives a compensation from the purchaser for his services, with the knowledge of the vendor, and without any objection from him, will not constitute a waiver of the rule that a Broker

cannot act for both sides, and so preserve the Broker's claim for compensation from the vendee. Nothing short of an express agreement to waive that rule would be sufficient for that purpose. Rice vs. Davis, 136 Pa. St. 439.

[3] Samuels vs. Oliver, 130 Ill. 73.

[4] Owen vs. Ramsey, 23 Ind. App. 285. As to when a Broker will be considered as employed yearly, and as to recovery in such a case, see Dean vs. Woodward, 52 Hun, 421. Evidence that the principal had, in a prior brokerage transaction, by sharp practice, deprived the Broker of his commissions, inadmissible. Brown vs. Barse, 3 App. Div. (N. Y.) 257.

because of the confidential relations existing between the parties, as in the case of husband and wife, or because of the subject-matter of the evidence itself. Under this last head are included secrets of State and papers and communications confided by a Client to his legal adviser. In the latter case the attorney's mouth is not sealed because of the confidential relations existing between him and his Client, for the privilege was not extended to other professions by the common-law, but because the interests of justice demand that the Client should be able to lay before his counsel the full facts of his case without fear of future disclosure; and this not only for his own assurance, but also to enable the attorney to exercise properly the duties of his profession.[1]

It may be added that in some of the States the same protecting policy has been extended to confessions made to a clergyman, in the course of the discipline enjoined by the rules of his denomination, and to knowledge gained by a physician in attending a patient, which knowledge was necessary to enable him to prescribe for the disease.[2] And in England[3] Best, C. J., said that he for one would never compel a clergyman to disclose a communication made to him by a prisoner.

It seems, however, that the privilege may be waived.[4] The principle which underlies the exclusion of this evi-

---

[1] The earliest reported case on the subject is Berd vs. Lovelace, Cary (anno 19 Eliz), 88; see also Greenough vs. Gaskell, 1 Myl. & K. 101; 1 Greenleaf on Ev. (16th ed.) § 236 et seq., and cases cited.

[2] Wis Rev Stat. 1898, §§ 4074-4075; Iowa Code, 1897, § 4608; Supp of 1902, § 4608, and cases cited; N Y. Code of Civil Proc.

§§ 833, 834; Rev. Stat. of Mo. 1899, § 4659; Rev. Stat. of Mich. 1897, §§ 10,180-10,181.

[3] Broad vs. Pitt, 3 Car. & P. 518.

[4] 1 Greenleaf on Ev. (16th ed.) § 236. In New York it must be an express waiver, upon the trial or examination, by the person confessing, the patient, or the Client. N. Y. Code Civ. Proc § 836

26

dence is that of public policy: the public benefit arising
from its suppression, in the great majority of cases, over-
weighs the occasional hardship of the rule when applied to
particular instances.[1]

Although, in practice, the communications and transactions
between a Broker and his Client are regarded and observed
as sacredly confidential, yet they are not considered as being
in anywise embraced within the rules to which we have
alluded. In a case in England[2] a Stock-broker was held
bound to discover the names of the persons for whom he
had purchased shares in a joint-stock company which had
neither been incorporated, chartered, nor registered, and
which was regulated by no deed of settlement, and whose
shares passed by delivery. The case is valuable in demon-
strating that the liability of a Broker to answer, in ordinary
transactions between himself and Client, is unquestioned;
that only in cases presenting special features can he refuse to
answer, and his refusal in such cases would be grounded on
no peculiar privilege extended to Brokers, but on a protection
common to all classes; as, for instance, where the Broker
relies on the rule of law exempting persons from testifying
where their answers would expose them to a fine, penalty,
or criminal prosecution.[3]

The case of The Mercantile Credit Association[4] also
strongly illustrates this point. In winding up this association the name of one D. appeared on the list of shareholders

[1] Greenleaf on Ev. § 236.
[2] Re Mex. and So. Am. Co., re
Aston, 27 Beav. 474; aff'd 18 L. T.
596.
[3] Thus a Stock-broker may refuse
to answer questions as to stock
transactions on the ground that his
answer might subject him to the
penalties of the stock-jobbing act.
Short vs. Mercier, 3 M. & G. 205.
And see Cloyes vs. Thayer, 3 Hill,
564; Poindexter vs. Davis, 6 Gratt.
481.
[4] 37 L. J. (n. s.) pt. 1, 295.

as a holder of certain shares. "Calls" had been made by the official liquidator on these shares, no part of which had been paid. The liquidator having caused inquiries to be made with respect to the ability of D. to pay the calls, it was discovered that he had no property whatever; and that, at the time the shares were transferred to him, he was an infant living with his father, receiving wages as clerk to a law stationer, but with no other source of income. The transfer had been made to him with his consent, and, although he had come of age, he had not repudiated it. One C., a Broker, had proposed to act on his behalf in the matter of the transfer, and it was through C.'s agency that D.'s name was placed upon the register. The official liquidator applied to the Broker for information as to the circumstances attending the transfer, in the hope of being able to make the transferor liable for the amount due on the shares, but the Broker refused to give any such information. The liquidator accordingly moved for an order to summon him before the court for the purpose of being examined as a person whom the court might deem capable of giving information concerning the trade, dealings, estate, or effects of the company.

Wood, V. C., in giving his opinion, said that he "was surprised that such applications should always be strenuously opposed on behalf of the proposed witness;" and he accordingly ordered that C. should be summoned to attend the judge in chambers at such times as the judge might designate, to be examined as the judge might direct touching the estate and effects of the association.[1]

[1] To same effect, Contract Corporation, 40 L. J. Ch. 15. See also Rawlings vs. Hall, 1 Car. & P. 11; Green vs. Weaver, 1 Sim. 401; Williams vs. Tyre, 18 Beav. 366; Mathew's Est., 4 Am. L. J. (n. s.) 350;

The few adjudicated cases show that the courts, recognizing no public policy sufficiently urgent to demand the secrecy of such transactions, have uniformly checked the effort of the Broker to place himself in the category of those protected by the law of privileged communications.

It by no means follows, however, because such transactions are not privileged, that they are public; that a resort to a Broker's books can be had *ad libitum*, to satisfy an idle curiosity,[1] or entries thrown open to what the courts have termed a "fishing excursion." On the contrary, the the courts scan with jealous eyes all attempts of that nature; and it is only where the party shows a clear legal right to the remedy, and in cases where the interests of justice demand a discovery, that a Broker's books or a Broker's testimony as to dealings with his Client is evidence at the instance of an adverse suitor.

XIII. Puts, Calls, Straddles and Pools Considered Apart from their Wagering Aspect.

It is proposed to consider these dealings apart from any aspect they might have as wagering transactions, as to which see Chapter V., "Stockjobbing."

When a "put" is purchased outside of the Stock Exchange through a Broker not a member of the Stock Exchange, a rule of the Exchange that dividends declared prior to the closing of the transfer books shall, as to transactions other than for cash, be "dividend off" (i. e. shall not be payable to the owner of the stock), is not applica-

---

In re Finan. Ins. Co. (Lim.), 36 L. J. (n. s.) 687.

[1] A Broker examined to prove the market value of a stock cannot be compelled to state the names of the person with whom he has dealt in such stock. Jonau vs. Ferrand, 3 Rob. (La.) 366.

ble where a dividend has been declared on the stock prior
to the contract, but is not payable till after the closing of
the transfer books, and after the day when the option to
deliver the stock expires. In such a case the dividend belongs to the owner of the stock at the time it was declared,
and therefore, in the case under consideration, it was held
to belong to the seller of the stock.[1]

A "call" is an agreement to sell, and as such it required
a stamp under the War Revenue Act of 1899, since repealed,
although a "put," or an agreement to buy, did not require
such a stamp.[2]

If a Broker sells a "straddle" it is his duty to close
the contract thereby created by exercising the option at the
most favorable time in the purchaser's interests within the
period during which the option may be exercised, and if he
sells "short" the day after the making of the contract, and
the stock subsequently goes up, he will be liable to pay the
purchaser what the latter lost by his neglect.[3]

If one of the parties to a "pool" formed to speculate in
certain stock, should withdraw from the pool, and take up
and pay for his interest therein, notice should be given by the

---

[1] Hopper vs. Sage, 112 N. Y. 530, and cases cited.

[2] Treat vs. White, 181 U. S. 264.

[3] Harris vs. Tumbridge, 8 Abb. N. C. 291, aff'd 83 N. Y. 92. The par-
ties to a "straddle" may, of course, by special agreement, vary its effect, and settle their rights under it before the period of its expiration, by giving and receiving a fixed sum therefor, or otherwise. Van Norden vs. Keene, 55 N. Y. Super. Ct. 67.

The term "bearer" used in a "straddle" means not simply a
person having the paper in his indi-
vidual custody, but one apparently exercising an individual dominion thereof as owner, and the party ob-
ligated by the "straddle" is still bound to the true owner, though he may have settled with one presenting it to him, if it was presented un-
der circumstances that charged him with the risk of the one presenting it not being the transferee thereof. Id.

Brokers to the other parties thereto, but the failure to give such notice is not material if the other parties in interest are not prejudiced.[1]   And in an action by the Brokers to recover commissions and outlay, an answer alleging the pool combination, and that one of the parties withdrew from the pool, but which does not allege that the Brokers failed to notify defendants of such withdrawal, or that injury resulted to defendants, and which merely asks for a dismissal of the complaint, does not raise sufficient matter of defence.[2]   In that case defendant on the trial claimed that the failure to give notice was a breach of contract, and that defendant was therefore entitled to the market price of his stock as of the day of the breach, and not as of the day of the closing, some months later, when the stock had fallen considerably, but the court, as already stated, found against this contention, as the issue was not properly raised by the pleadings and prayer for relief in the answer.[3]

When a pool was formed between certain persons and a firm of Brokers to purchase and sell land, the profits and losses to be divided in certain proportions, and the Brokers to receive a certain commission and to buy and sell as principals, it was held that they could not be sued as Brokers without recourse to the agreement, and as the latter was for an illegal purpose, viz., to " corner " land, the action could not be maintained.[4]

XIV. The Clearing House.

The Stock Exchange Clearing House was established in New York City in May, 1892 (in extension of the system of

[1] Myers vs. Paine, 13 App. Div. 332; aff'd 57 N. E. Rep. 1118.
[2] Id.
[3] Id
[4] Leonard vs. Poole, 55 N. Y. Super. Ct. 213; aff'd 114 N. Y. 371.

clearings established by the banks of that city in October, 1853) to prevent the necessity of numerous transfers of stock from hand to hand. Matters are settled by a combination of stock balances and cash balances, both being very small in proportion to the aggregate of business done,[1] and similar institutions have been established in some of the principal cities of the United States.

The London Stock Exchange had adopted the clearing principle in 1874. Vide Chapter X., p. 991, note 1. See also Brodhurst on the Law of the Stock Exchange (pp. 70–72), in which the method of settlement of large transactions, through the aid of the Clearing House, is shown in full detail.

Notwithstanding the great advantage of the Clearing House from a business point of view, in rendering unnecessary the manual delivery of a great number of stock and share certificates, and of the actual payment and receipt of large sums of money representing the price of securities bought and sold, the Supreme Court of Pennsylvania has held that a delivery made on the Clearing House sheet was a mere settlement of differences, and void at common law ;[2] but that this view is erroneous is thus ably pointed out by the Messrs. Biddle in their excellent work on the Law of Stock-brokers, at p. 61 : " The Clearing House is the agent of both of the parties, and where a selling Broker sends to it his account of sold shares, the Clearing House in such a case is authorized by the buying Broker to accept such shares, and if such an account were to contain nothing

[1] Johnson's Universal Cyclopædia, vol. 2, p. 323, title "Clearing House"; Biddle on Stock-brokers, p. 55 et seq.; Bisbee & Simond's Law of the Produce Exchange, § 38. See also Watson's Clearing House Law; Arts. XXVI. and XXVII. Const. of the N. Y. Stock Exchange.

[2] Dickson's Executor vs. Thomas, 10 W. N. C. 112. See also Kuchizky vs. De Haven, 10 W. N. C. 109.

but sold shares, the Clearing House, as the agent of a buying Broker, would simply direct the selling Broker to deliver the shares to his (the Clearing House's) principal; but
where the account contains bought as well as sold shares,
the Clearing House then, acting as the agent of both the
Brokers, sets off one transaction as against the other. This
the principals themselves might perfectly legally do, and
consequently it is obvious that their agents may do the
same. In fact the sheets sent to the Clearing House by
the different Brokers are substantially nothing but bills of
sale made by them, and made to them, and sent to their
common agent, the Clearing House."

And that transactions closed in accordance with the
Clearing House Rules of the Chicago Stock Exchange are
not gaming contracts, where there is no evidence of an intention merely to settle differences, has been decided by the
Supreme Court of the United States in Clews vs. Jamieson,[1]
in the report of which case the rules of the Chicago Clearing House as to buying and selling "for the account" are
set forth at length. And settlements of differences through
the Clearing House have been also held valid in Van Dusen-
Harrington Co. vs. Jungeblut,[2] by the Supreme Court of
Minnesota.

That the Clearing House system cannot be used as a cover
for fictitious transactions, but that, on the contrary, its
records can (in the absence of proof by the Broker's books,
showing the names of parties from whom they bought or
to whom they sold stock, that the transactions were real)
be used in evidence for the purpose of showing that, as the
majority of the alleged transactions were never cleared,

---

[1] 182 U. S. 461.   [2] 77 N. W. Rep. 970.

they never in fact occurred, is the result of the decision in Prout vs. Chisolm.[1]

In that case, in which a Client sought to recover moneys and securities deposited with his Broker as margins, on the ground that numerous transactions of buying and selling reported by the Broker were all fictitious, it was held that, as it appeared that the Clearing House sheets transmitted to the Clearing House daily by the Brokers who had bought and sold on the Exchange were destroyed at the end of thirty days, the Clearing House ledgers were competent evidence of the facts stated therein, when the clerk who made the entries testified to their accuracy, and that he made them from the Clearing House sheets themselves, and it was also held that where a failure to clear or report the transaction was continuous, the conclusion was justified that the transactions did not occur, although such a presumption might not arise if only a few transactions were not reported or cleared.

In some localities a custom similar to the Clearing House system, and known as "ringing up," prevails amongst Brokers and commission merchants, by which, when a series of contracts have been made for the sale of the same kind of grain for future delivery, the Brokers acting for buyers and sellers settle by what they call a "ring," that is, by which they reciprocally surrender, or cancel, contracts and adjust differences.[2] This custom, when not adopted to promote a gambling contract, is not illegal.[3]

---

[1] 21 App. Div. 51.

[2] See Williar vs. Irwin, 11 Biss. 60, for a detailed description of this custom.

[3] Clarke vs. Foss, 7 Biss. 518; Ward vs. Vosburgh, 31 Fed. Rep. 12. See also Home Co. vs. Favorite, 46 Ill. 263; Lonergan vs. Stewart, 55 Ill. 44; Doane vs. Dunham, 79 Ill. 131; Bailey vs. Bensley, 87 Ill. 556; Lyon vs. Culbertson, 83 Ill. 33; Oldershaw vs. Knowles, 4 Brad. 63.

CHAPTER IV.

USAGES OF STOCK-BROKERS.

I. General Rules relative to Usages.
II. Cases in which Usages of Stock-brokers held Binding.
　(*a.*) *In the United States.*
　(*b.*) *In England.*
III. Cases in which Usages have been Rejected.
　(*a.*) *In the United States.*
　(*b.*) *In England.*

I. General Rules relative to Usages.

A rule of law laid down in the elementary works as being well settled is, that a contract should be interpreted in accordance with the intention of the parties thereto, and that the "usage" or "custom" of any particular trade, occupation, business, or place, when it is reasonable, uniform, well settled, and not in opposition to fixed rules of law or in contravention to the express terms of a contract, is deemed to form a part of the contract and to enter into the intention of the parties.[1]

---

[1] Evidence of a custom of the London Stock Exchange that a Broker, not disclosing the name of his principal, is personally liable, being conflicting, the jury was unable to agree as to its existence. The court charged that the custom to be binding should be a universal usage of the Stock Exchange, reasonable, certain and known to its members. Wildy vs. Stephenson, 1 C. & E. 3.

See Title "Custom" in Ency. of the Laws of England, vol. 4; Robinson vs. N. Y. and Texas S. S. Co., 75 App. Div. (N. Y.) 431; Blakemore vs. Heyman, 6 Fed. Rep. 581.

There are different kinds of customs, such as the custom of merchants, *lex mercatoria*, which is recognized by the law of the land ; but the "usages" of which we treat in this chapter must be proved as any other facts, and, when proved, may be used as presumptive evidence to establish the contract.[1] Mr. Justice Brett, in a case[2] which powerfully illustrates the connection between the usages of trade and the law, said : "Customs of trade, as distinguished

---

[1] Starkie on Ev. 455; Maxted vs. Paine, L. R. 4 Ex. 81; id. (2d case) 205; 2 Phillips on Ev. (Cowen's, Hill's, and Edward's notes, 4th Am. ed.) 726; 2 Pars. on Cont. (8th ed.) 535; 1 Greenleaf on Ev. § 292, 294; Starkie on Ev. 637, 710; Broom's Leg Max. 7th ed. 705 et seq.; Walls vs. Bailey, 49 N. Y. 464. See also Lawson on Usages, 287, 288, where the law on this subject is exhaustively discussed.

It has been recently decided in England that a usage as to the negotiability of bearer bonds, has been so often proved, that it must be now noticed by the courts judicially and this although the usage has been of recent origin. Edelstein vs. Schuler, 71 L. J. K. B. 572. And see observations of the court as to judicially noticing the custom of calling of "margins." Hill vs. Morris, 21 Mo. App. 256.

See also Cole vs. Skrainka, 37 Mo. App. 427; Thomas vs. Hooker Colville Steam Pump Co., 28 Mo App. 563 (trade usages need not be ancient, if sufficiently known). As to evidence which was held insufficient to support an alleged trade usage of the New York coffee market to sell one kind of coffee as another, see

O'Donoghoe vs. Leggett, 134 N. Y. 40. A custom of mining Stockbrokers to charge an arbitrary sum for telegrams was not shown to be well established, certain and uniform and known to both parties. Marye vs. Strouse, 5 Fed. Rep. 487.

Particular trade usages or customs, however extensive they may be, must be proven. And therefore an alleged usage of Brokers to require a lender of stock, borrowed to cover a short sale, to put up margins to secure the seller against the decline of the stock, is not proved by the mere opinion of the seller, and of his secretary, that such a usage existed. Morris vs. Jamieson, 68 N. E. Rep. 747. See also Waugh vs. Seaboard Bank, 54 N. Y. Super. Ct. (22 Jones & S.) 283; Weld vs. Barker, 153 Pa. St. 465; 26 Atl. Rep. 239; The Innocenta, 10 Ben. (U. S.) 410; Blake vs. Stump, 73 Md. 160; Overman vs. Hoboken City Bank, 30 N. J. L. 61; Greeley vs. Doran-Wright Co., 148 Mass. 116; Kershaw vs. Wright, 15 Mass. 361.

[2] Robinson vs. Mollett, L. R. 7 H. L. Eng. & I. App. Cas. 802, 816.

from other customs, are generally courses of business invented or relied upon in order to modify or evade some application which has been laid down by the courts of some rule of law to business, and which application has seemed irksome to some merchants. And, when some such course of business is proved to exist in fact, and the binding effect of it is disputed, the question of law seems to be whether it is in accordance with fundamental principles of right and wrong. The mercantile custom is hardly ever invoked but when one of the parties to the dispute has not, in fact, had his attention called to the course of business to be enforced by it; for if his attention had, in fact, been called to such course of business, his contract would be specifically made in accordance with it, and no proof of it as a custom would be necessary. A stranger to a locality or trade or market is not held to be bound by the custom of such locality, trade, or market because he knows the custom, but because he has elected to enter into transactions in a locality, trade, or market wherein all who are not strangers do know and act upon such custom. Where considerable numbers of men of business carry on one side of a particular business, they are apt to set up a custom which acts very much in favor of their side of the business. So long as they do not infringe some fundamental principle of right and wrong, they may establish such a custom; but if, on dispute before a legal forum, it is found that they are endeavoring to enforce some rule of conduct which is so entirely in favor of their side that it is fundamentally unjust to the other side, the courts have always determined that such a custom, if sought to be enforced against a person in fact ignorant of it, is unreasonable, contrary to law, and void."[1]

[1] See Hamilton vs. Young, 7 L. R. I. 289, in which the court after

It will be the object of the present chapter to ascertain how far these general views and the principles hereafter set forth have been introduced into cases arising out of trausactions between Stock-brokers and their Clients ; and it will be seen, in the application of these general principles to the facts, that the courts have exercised a very wide range of discretion, and that their conclusions have not by any means been uniform or harmonious.

The importance of allowing the introduction of usages of Stock-brokers in all cases arising out of transactions on the Stock Exchange cannot be overestimated. The business of buying and selling stocks, although of modern origin, has grown to be one of gigantic magnitude, employing yearly more capital, perhaps, than any other commercial pursuit.

As the system of conducting a transaction in stocks is *sui generis*, the usages of the business have generally arisen out of its necessities, and to fail to give effect to them in a litigation is practically to determine it upon principles and facts which have no existence in the original transaction. In truth, it is entirely impossible to make out or understand intelligently an ordinary transaction, either of the London or the New York Stock Exchange, without the aid of these usages. The time required to make a sale of securities at either of these places is but momentary. It often happens that barely a half-dozen words are spoken in a transaction : a nod, the raising of a hand, or other signs and ejaculations, are frequently used to bind a buyer or seller to a contract embracing thousands of shares of securities. One transaction is the representative of thousands. Very often the Brokers make no memorandum of the business, or, when

quoting the last two sentences of with "this lucid exposition of the the above extract, concurs entirely law."

one is made, it is apt to be of the scantiest character and utterly decipherless without the explanation of persons acquainted with the course of dealing on the Exchange. What actually transpires between the buying and selling Brokers constitutes, it may be, but the framework of the transaction, and an intelligible, full, living agreement can only be made out by a resort to other evidence, involving, perhaps, not only a consideration of the rules of the Stock Exchange, but of the unwritten usages, so to speak, of the Brokers.

With these preliminary observations, we shall proceed to state certain general rules which have been established by the courts upon the doctrine of usage, together with such criticisms upon them as seem reasonable and appropriate.

First. It may be laid down as a proposition well settled in the law that the usage of a business is never permitted to make an *entire* or *new* contract for the parties. What usage does is to take a contract which is deficient and incomplete in its terms or expressions, and supply the omissions; and, unless some contract is shown, evidence of usage or custom is immaterial.[1]

When therefore a proposed amended complaint sought to base a contract liability wholly upon an alleged usage amongst London bond-dealers to protect their customer's interests, and to expend money in their behalf, which money was refunded by the customers, a motion to serve the complaint as so amended was denied.[2]

---

[1] Tilley vs. County of Cook, 103 U. S. Rep. 155; Lombardo vs. Case, 30 How. Pr. (N. Y) 117; Parsons vs. Martin, 77 Mass 111; Smith vs. Barringer, 37 Minn. 94; 33 N. W. Rep. 116; Dobson vs. Kuhula, 66 Hun, 627; 20 N. Y. Supp. 771. Usages of Brokers may explain, but not prove, a contract. Goddard vs. Garner, 109 Ala. 98.

[2] Municipal Inv. Co. vs. Industrial & Gen. Trust Co., 89 Fed Rep. 254.

Second. So the usage of a business plays an important part in the interpretation of technical words and phrases in a contract, because, if language is employed which is only known in a certain business, the law, to enlighten itself as to what is meant by the contract between the parties, invites individuals skilled in that business to explain or unlock the meaning of the terms used. This branch of the law is also comparatively uniform and clear.[1]

Third. Another rule is also well settled—viz., that a written and express contract cannot be contradicted or varied by usage, i. e., where the terms of a contract are full and complete and can be deciphered by the courts without resort to extrinsic evidence; as where A, of New York, agrees to sell B, of the same place, ten barrels of flour, each barrel to weigh one hundred pounds: here an offer to show that the ordinary barrels of flour known among the flour trade of

---

[1] When a customer buys bonds and does not pay for them, and the holders of the bonds "continue" them, it was held that "continue" was a technical term of the London Stock Exchange and meant a sale and an agreement to repurchase. Bongiovanni vs. Société Générale, 54 L. T. 320. This decision was followed in In re Overweg; Haas vs. Durant, 69 L. J. Ch. 255, where a Broker who, on his Client's death, has "continued" instead of selling, was held liable to his client as if there had been an immediate sale at the price on the carrying over day. See also Bentinck vs. London Joint-Stock Bank (1893), 2 Ch. 120, and the early English cases of In re Dennison, 3 Ves. 552; Andre vs. Crawford, 1 Br. P. C. 366.

A "certification" of a transfer means that if the seller's certificate includes more shares than he sells, he does not deliver it to the buyer, but an officer of the company, whose shares are being sold, or an officer of the Stock Exchange, writes on the transfer "Certificate produced" and buyers and Brokers act on this as if the original certificate were produced. Bishop vs. Balkis Co., 25 Q B. D. 512. This "certification" does not warrant title, and does not estop a company from denying plaintiff's title when the transfer to his vendor was invalid. Ib.

A "friendly loan" is a loan of money or stocks for business purposes. Sheppard vs. Barrett, 42 Leg. Int. (Pa.) 140.

New York weigh only ninety pounds could not be received. So that evidence of usage is generally receivable only in cases where the contract, whether written or oral, is doubtful, incomplete, or deficient, or where technical terms or phrases are to be translated.[1]

Fourth. A statement is frequently met with in the elementary treatises and in adjudicated cases, that usage, when it is not in opposition to·" fixed rules of law," and is not unreasonable, is deemed to form a part of the contract, and to enter into the intentions of the parties thereto.[2]   What

[1] When a Stock-broker sold certain shares of stock to his customer, representing that he would deliver the same, evidence of a custom amongst Stock-brokers to purchase stock in their own name and to become personally liable on the contract is inadmissible, when the Broker in fact had no such shares. Wolf vs. Campbell, 110 Mo. 114, and cases cited. See also Municipal Investment Co. vs. Industrial & General Trust Co., Ltd., 89 Fed. Rep. 254.

A contract by a Broker to sell bonds and "past due" interest, means, so ·far as regards interest, such interest as has matured, and is collectible on demand, and does not include current interest, to the date of sale, not yet due, and evidence of a custom of Brokers and bankers in St. Louis that "past due" interest included current interest to the time of sale, was properly excluded, as the meaning of the contract was clear. Coquard vs. Bank of Kansas City, 12 Mo. App. 261. See Cook on Corporations, 5th ed. § 453, and cases cited. See also Transconti-

nental Go. vs. Hilmers, 20 Fed. Rep. 717; German Savings Bank vs. Renshaw, 28 Atl. 281; Gilbert vs. McGinnis, 114 Ill. 28; O'Donohue vs. Leggett, 134 N. Y. 40; Hecht vs. Ratcheller, 147 Mass. 335; Silberman vs. Clark, 96 N. Y. 522; Bigelow vs. Legg, 102 N. Y. 652; Connell vs. Averill, 8 App. Div. (N. Y.) 528; Gibney vs. Curtis, 61 Md. 192.   And the cases cited in Danforth's Index-Digest to New York Supreme Court cases under title, "Custom and Usage," p. 565.   See also Hopper vs. Sage, 112 N. Y. 535, and cases cited.

[2] Starkie on Ev. 637, 710; Williams vs. Gulinan, 3 Greenl. 276; Walls vs. Bailey, 49 N. Y. 464. Hopper vs. Sage, 112 N. Y. 535 (seller of stock entitled to dividend declared at sale but payable thereafter, although by the usage of the Stock Exchange the buyer would be entitled).   See also Ashner vs. Abenheim, 19 App. Div. (N. Y.) 287, and cases cited; Britton vs. Ferrin, 171 N. Y. 235; Municipal Inv. Co. vs. Industrial & Gen. Trust Co., 89 Fed. Rep. 254; Gilbert vs. McGinnis,

is the meaning, in this connection, of the phrase "fixed rules of law?" If by such expression it is meant that all usages of business contrary to the express prohibitions of statutes are void, the proposition can perhaps be easily sustained; for no usage can, or should, have the force and effect of a legislative enactment. And for the same reason contracts, either express or implied, are void if they conflict with similar statutes. But there are a great many contracts contrary to the "fixed rules of law" which are valid, and which are made for the express purpose of evading or avoiding the rules of the law. For instance, it seems to be well settled in the State of New York that where A pledges stock or securities for the payment of a loan, so that a pledge is created, B, before he can sell the same, must demand payment, and, upon default, give A reasonable notice of time and place of sale.[1] This principle seems to be a "fixed rule of law;" in fact, all the principles of law are "fixed rules." The fundamental essence of a law is its fixity. Law is a rule, to distinguish it from *advice* or *counsel*, which one is at liberty to follow or not as he sees proper; it is also a rule, to distinguish it from a *compact* or *agreement*, the latter being nothing but a promise proceeding from us, whereas the law is a command directed to us: its language is, "Thou shalt or shalt not do this."[2] But this rule, in relation to a pledge, may be waived by the pledgor, so that the pledgee may sell without notice. The former can make a contract by which he agrees to allow B, in default of payment, to sell the stocks without notice of

114 Ill. 28; Geyser-Marion Gold Mining Co. vs. Stark, 53 L. R. A. 684.

[1] Markham vs. Jaudon, 41 N. Y. 235.

[2] Blackstone's Com. (Sharswood's ed.) * 45.

27

any kind, at any place, and such a waiver is entirely legal.[1]
Here we find a " fixed rule of law " set aside at the option
of the parties to an agreement. Can A, by an implied contract, do that which he can do by an express contract ? It
is just here that the difficulty arises in the application of
the doctrine of usage to contracts. For if a usage exist in
a certain locality, or among a certain class of merchants or
traders, which does not conflict with the prohibitions of a
statute, or which is not *contra bonos mores*, or contrary to
public policy, but which merely extends or limits a principle
of commercial law, or a "fixed rule of law," and parties
contract with a knowledge of the usage, why should it not
be presumed that it entered into their intentions, and that
they have made it a part of their contract to the same
extent as if they had specifically embodied it in the instrument ?

In Markham vs. Jaudon [2] evidence was offered to prove
the existence of a usage in the city of New York by which
Brokers have the right to sell out the Client's stock on the
exhaustion of the margin, without notice to the latter. The
appellate court held that such evidence was legally rejected
upon the ground *that it was in hostility of the terms of the
contract.*[3] If it were so, unquestionably the usage should

---

[1] Markham vs. Jaudon, supra.

[2] 41 N. Y. 245.

[3] In Covell vs. Loud, 135 Mass. 41,
this usage was held illegal by the
trial court, and the Client held entitled to recover the value of the
stock from the Broker, but on appeal this decision was reversed on
the ground that the contract relation was not that of pledgor and
pledgee but merely an executory

agreement entitling the Broker to
sell without notice.

It was held by the New York
Court of Appeals in 1886 that evidence could not be admitted of a
custom of Brokers and dealers in
wool, to consider a sales note of
wool a mere memorandum, amounting to a proposition which might be
accepted or rejected by either side,
and, until rejected or accepted by

have succumbed to the plain agreement of the parties. But there was no written contract in the case, and the conclusion was based upon the general principles of the law relating to the subject of pledges.

Ordinarily, of course, where persons do not specifically agree upon the terms of a contract, the presumption is that they contract with reference to the existing law, and the contract will be enforced according to prevailing principles ; but where a usage exists with reference to which parties are assumed to contract, why should not this usage be imported into the contract, with the result of varying the " fixed rules of law," to the same extent as if an express understanding had been entered into ?

In the case in question it was not disputed but that the Client could have waived his right to demand notice. Did he not, by entering into a transaction with a Stock-broker, adopt as part of the business the usages which prevail among Brokers, respecting the sale of securities held under the circumstances there disclosed ? There were two dissenting opinions in that case,[1] which held that such evidence was admissible, on the ground that it explained a doubtful contract. And it has been directly decided in England that

---

both, might be left open, when the contract contained in the sales note was a binding one. When it was of such a character, no usage could control the rule of law applicable to its construction. Bigelow vs. Legg, 102 N. Y. 652; 6 N. E. Rep. 107. A custom of commission merchants in New Orleans to charge more than the legal rate of interest, being contrary to law, parol evidence thereof is inadmissible. Cooper vs. Sandford, 4 Yer. 455.

And a custom of Produce Exchange Brokers to cancel contracts, without their principals being in some effective way substituted, being contrary to established legal principles, is not binding on the principal, even with his assent. Kent vs. Woodhull, 55 N. Y. Super. Ct. 311.

[1] Grover and Woodruff, JJ.

a usage of the Stock Exchange to close an account before the account-day, where the Client becomes insolvent, should be upheld as a reasonable and just usage;[1] although it must be confessed that this case is weakened by the intimations of the court that, if the account is summarily closed before the account-day, the Broker is liable to indemnify the Client if the market changes in favor of the latter on the last-named day.[2] As we have said, a fixed principle or rule of law may be expressly waived. So, even in cases where the legislature has regulated the law of a certain subject by statute, parties may contract to avoid its effect, and such contracts are perfectly legal. Many statutory provisions are merely declaratory of the common law, and are made to govern cases where parties have not entered into any agreement in reference thereto.

For instance, if an act of the legislature of a state specifically allows three days' grace on negotiable instruments (and we use this illustration because it is made in the case in Markham vs. Jaudon[3] by the learned judge who delivered the opinion of the court), a promissory note which should, on its face, state that it was to be without days of grace would be perfectly valid, because the party had chosen to waive the benefits of the existing law. And if there exist a known usage among the merchants of a certain place to allow no days of grace, would not such a usage bind a person who executed a note and made it payable at such place ? Would he not be presumed to have made the in-

---

[1] Lacey vs. Hill (Scrimgeour's Claim), L. R. 8 Ch. App. 921. See Ellis vs. Pond, 67 L. J. Q. B. 345; Michael vs. Hart, 70 L. J. K. B. 1000.

[2] But see Colket vs. Ellis, 10 Phila. (Pa.) 375; s. c. 32 Leg. Int. (Pa.) 82; Corbett vs. Underwood, 83 Ill. 324.

[3] 41 N. Y. 235.

strument with express reference to such usage? The courts of Pennsylvania and California say that he would.[1]

So a custom on the part of all the banks of a particular place to demand payment and give notice to endorsers of negotiable paper on the *fourth* day of grace is binding on an endorser if known to him.[2] And the reasoning of the Supreme Court of the United States shows the fallacy of the argument used in the case of Markham vs. Jaudon to reject the usage there sought to be upheld. And the general principles of law relating to the time and place of demand and notice in the case of notes and bills may be overruled by usage.[3]

The Supreme Court of the United States, in Barnard vs. Kellogg,[4] decided a question which strongly illustrates the general subject. There it was held that the well-known rule of *caveat emptor* could not be affected by a local custom by which the seller was made to warrant the quality of the goods; but the learned judge who delivered the judgment of the court, in concluding his opinion, laid great stress upon the fact that it appeared the parties had *no knowledge* of the custom invoked.

A still further and more ambiguous limitation of the doctrine of usages, in their influence upon contracts, was made by Mr. Justice Brett, in the case of Robinson vs. Mollett,[5] where he said: "So long as they do not infringe some

---

[1] Lawson vs. Richards, 6 Phila. (Pa.) 179; Champion vs. Gordon, 70 Pa. St. 476; Minturn vs. Fisher, 4 Cal. 35.

[2] Renner vs. Bank of Columbia, 9 Wheat. 582.

[3] See article "The Power of Usage and Custom," by John D. Lawson, Esq., 7 South. L. Rev. 43; see also Bowen vs. Newell, 4 Seld. 190; 3 Kern. 290, where the usage of the banks of Connecticut, to regard checks payable after date as not entitled to days of grace, was held admissible.

[4] 10 Wall. 383.

[5] L. R. 7 H. L. Eng. & I. App. Cas. 802, 816; see also Tilley vs. County

fundamental principle of right and wrong, they may establish such a custom," but that "customs fundamently unjust, if sought to be enforced against persons ignorant of them, are void."

In that case a usage was attempted to be introduced which allowed a Broker, commissioned to purchase certain merchandise for his principal, to become himself the purchaser. The order to purchase was given by a Liverpool merchant to a London tallow-broker, and the usage pertained to the London tallow market ; but the principal was not shown to have had any knowledge of the usage ; and upon the ground of the principal's ignorance of the same it was rejected. The learned judges who delivered opinions in the case did not pass upon the question as to the influence of such a usage upon a contract made by persons having knowledge thereof ; but it is not difficult to perceive that, if such knowledge had been shown, the case would have been differently determined.[1]

Without pursuing the subject further, it seems to us that harmony can only be reached in this branch of the law by keeping in constant view the distinction between contracts void in law and those which are valid.

In the former class, whether the contracts are void because made so by statute, or are against public policy, the law will not enforce them. In the latter class, embracing

---

of Cook, 103 U. S. Rep. 161, where the court say that *absurd* and *unreasonable* customs are not binding.

[1] The case of Robinson vs. Mollet, supra, was followed in Irwin vs. Williar, 110 U. S. 499, where proof of a similar custom amongst Baltimore commission merchants was rejected, on the ground that it worked a complete change in the nature of the principal's rights and obligations, and such change could not be made without his assent, which could be only implied from knowledge of the custom. See also Hamilton vs. Young, L. R. 7 Ir. 289.

all contracts not included in the former, agreements will be enforced, although they contravene fixed rules of the law merchant, or common law, and frequently statutory provisions.

As usage is considered a portion of the contract between the parties, it would seem to follow logically that it should be sustained in every instance where an express contract is upheld, providing, of course, the evidence is sufficient to show that the parties had knowledge of such usage.

In fine, whenever an express contract is valid, a known usage, which is but another way of proving what the parties intended and agreed upon, should be declared equally so.[1] There is one answer which may be made to this conclusion —viz., that "public policy" requires, where parties assume obligations which the law does not impose, or release obligations which it does impose, it should be done by *express* contract.

This view was advanced by Chapman, J., in a case where a usage was set up that certain goods were always sold with a warranty, where the law implied none.[2] The learned judge said: " . . . If the parties agree that there shall be a warranty where the law implies none, they can insert the warranty in the bill of sale; or if the manufacturer sells without warranty, he can so express it. But if such usages were to prevail, they would be productive of misunderstanding, litigation, and frequent injustice, and would be deeply injurious to the interests of trade and commerce. They would make it necessary to prove the law of the case by witnesses

---

[1] These views, since they were written, have received a powerful endorsement from two elaborate and able articles on the "Power of Usage and Custom," by John D.

Lawson, Esq., of the Missouri Bar, 7 South. L. Rev. (n. s.) 1; 6 id. 845; see also Colket vs. Ellis, 10 Phila. (Pa.) 375; s. c. 32 Leg. Int. (Pa.) 82.

[2] Dickinson vs. Gray, 89 Mass. 29.

on the stand, and it would be settled by the jury in each particular case ; " and he concludes that " public policy " requires that such usages should be expressly incorporated in contracts.

The exclusion of usage on the ground of " public policy " invokes an argument which we have not discovered in many cases ; and, if it were well-founded, it would require the rejection of all usages, because it would apply to all with the same force that it did to the one set up in the case in question. And this mere statement would seem to be all the answer which such an argument requires. There is another complete answer, however—viz., that a large number of the many contracts which come before the courts are proved by parol ; and there is no more practical difficulty in proving usages, which are but portions of contracts, than there is in proving any other terms or stipulations expressly agreed upon by the verbal utterances of parties.

Fifth. The rule has been established, in a large number of cases, that where one employs a Broker he is presumed to authorize him to deal with reference to the custom of Brokers ; and that a Stock-broker, in the execution of his orders, has an implied authority to follow the rules and usages of the Stock Exchange.[1]

[1] Sutton vs. Tatham, 10 Ad. & E. 27; Pollock vs. Stables, 12 Q.B. 765; Mitchell vs. Newhall, 15 M. & W. 308; Smith vs. Lindo, 5 C. B. (n. s.) 587; Mortimer vs. McCallan, 6 M. & W. 58–61; Magee vs. Atkinson, 2 id. 440; Lloyd vs. Gilbert, 25 L. J. Q. B. 74; Nickalls vs. Merry, L. R. 7 Eng. & I. App. Cas. 530: Bayliffe vs. Butterworth, 1 Ex. 425; Higgins vs. Senior, 8 M. & W. 834; Stray vs. Russell, 29 L. J. Q. B. 279; Lacey vs. Hill, L. R. 8 Ch. App. 921; Coles vs. Bristowe, L. R. 4 C. P. 36; Cruse vs. Paine, L. R. 4 Ch. App. 441; Johnson vs. Osborne, 11 A. & E. 549; Maxted vs. Paine, L. R. 4 Ex. 81; id. (2d action) 205; notes to Wigglesworth vs. Dallison, 1 Sm. L. C. 843–857 (6th ed.); Stewart vs. Cauty, 8 M. & W. 160; Robinson vs. Mollett. L. R. 7 H. L. Eng. & I.

In England this rule was first clearly laid down in the case of Sutton vs. Tatham,[1] where Lord Denman said: " I think a person employing one who is notoriously a Broker must be taken to authorize his acting in accordance with the rules of the Stock Exchange."

This rule was recently reiterated in the House of Lords by Mr. Justice Cleasby in Robinson vs. Mollett,[2] and lim-

App. Cas. 802–826; Westropp vs. Solomon, 8 C. B. 345; Hodgkinson vs. Kelly, L. R. 6 Eq. 501; Adams vs. Peters, 2 C. & K. 723; Marten vs. Gibbon, 33 L. T. (n. s.) 561; Nourse vs. Prime, 4 Johns. Ch. 490; s. c. 7 id. 69; Horton vs. Morgan, 19 N. Y. 170; Lawrence vs. Maxwell, 53 id. 19; Whitehouse vs. Moore, 13 Ab. Pr. 142; overruled on other points, White vs. Baxter, 9 J. & S. (N. Y.) 358; aff'd 71 N. Y. 254; Kingsbury vs. Kirwin, 11 J. & S. (N. Y.) 451; aff'd 77 N. Y. 612; Walls v. Bailey, 49 id. 464, 473; Rosenstock vs. Tormey, 32 Md. 169; Sumner vs. Stewart, 69 Pa. St. 321; Durant vs. Burt, 98 Mass. 161. See also cases cited in Chapter X., where the question as to liability for calls is discussed.

[1] 10 Ad. & E. 27.

[2] L. R. 7 H. L. Eng. & I. App. Cas. 802-806.

When an outside principal employs a member of the Stock Exchange to sell shares subject to its rules, he is bound by these rules unless they are illegal or unreasonable or not known to him, Harker vs. Edwards, 57 L. J. Q. B. 117, and even if the rule be unreasonable, he is bound by it, if it is known to him. Smith vs. Reynolds, 66 L. T. 808

(per Denman, J.), in which case the principal was a dealer in stocks, although not a member of the Stock Exchange, and he knew well the rule, and that it would be relied on by the broker with whom the principal dealt. But it was held in Blackburn vs. Mason, 68 L. T. 510, that the customer is not bound by an unreasonable custom unless known to him, and he agreed to be bound by it.

It was held by the Privy Council in Forget vs. Baxter, 69 L. J. P. C. 101, that when one employs a Broker to do business on the Stock Exchange, he should, in the absence of contrary evidence, be taken to have employed the Broker on the terms of the Stock Exchange. And if in accordance with the practice of the Stock Exchange, the Broker receives a check for the price of shares payable to himself which he deposits in his own bank, the latter is not liable to repay the amount thereof on the Broker's insolvency, unless it has knowledge of the fraudulent conduct of the Broker whose account at the time was overdrawn to an amount larger than the deposit, and who absconded a few days subsequently. Thomson vs. Bank (1893), App. Cas. 282.

ited in certain particulars which are important to notice : "I quite agree that by employing the Broker, who acts upon a particular market, you authorize him to make contracts upon all such terms as are usual upon the market, otherwise his hands would be tied, and he might not be able to contract at all. *Therefore, as regards all such matters as the time and mode of payment, the time and mode of delivery, the various allowances to be made, the mode of adjusting disputes as to quality, and all such matters as arise upon the contract made in the market,* the principal would be bound by the usage ; but not, I apprehend, because he must be supposed to have made inquiries and to have known them, but for the reason given by Mr. Justice Willes—because they were within the authority conferred upon his agent."

The rule has also received judicial sanction in Davis &

When the customers knew that their Connecticut Brokers would deal with New York Brokers, they authorized a course of dealing in accordance with the usage of both stock markets, viz., that their Brokers might repledge securities which they carried on a margin. Skiff vs. Stoddard, 63 Conn. 198; 21 L. R. A. 102. When one employs another to deal in a particular market, he will be held as intending that the mode of performance should be in accordance with the usages of the market. Id. See also Smith vs. Pryor, 7 N. Y. Supp. 662; Bailey vs. Bensley, 87 Ill. 556; Van Dusen vs. Jungeblut, 75 Minn. 298. But the Broker cannot so pledge securities deposited with him that they cannot be restored to the owner on repayment of latter's indebtedness, Oregon & Transcontinental Co. vs. Hilmers, 20 Fed. Rep. 717, as such a use would be inconsistent with the contract of pledge, and no evidence of usage is admissible which would destroy the contract. See also. Perin vs. Parker, 126 Ill. 207 (as to usages of Chicago Board of Trade); Denton vs. Jackson, 106 Ill. 433.

When a principal sends an order to a Broker doing business in an established market or trade, for a transaction in that trade, he thereby confers upon the Broker authority to deal according to any well-settled usage in such trade or market. Bibb vs. Allen, 149 U. S. 489; see also Clews vs. Jamieson, 182 U. S. 461, where the rules and usages of the Chicago Stock Exchange are fully considered. In that case the plaintiff, acting through a firm of Chicago Stock-brokers and the de-

Co. vs. Howard,[1] where it was held that a usage of the London Stock Exchange that all contracts for carrying over are made subject to the differences being paid on pay-day, and failing payment on pay-day, a Broker has a right, in the absence of cover and collateral security, to close his principal's account, provided he has sent the account showing the balance due by the customer, to the latter, at least on the evening before pay-day, was reasonable. The court said "that although this specific usage had not been decided to be valid, the principle upon which it rested had been recognized in decided cases, and that principle was the right of the Broker to protect himself in consequence of the peculiar position in which he is placed owing to the nature of the business which he transacts for his principal."

In the United States this rule seems to have been first

fendants, also Chicago Stock-brokers, admitted that the transactions were under the rules of the Chicago Stock Exchange, and it was held that although such rules provided a remedy for their violation, they did not assume to provide a remedy to the exclusion of the jurisdiction of the courts. If they did, they could not be enforced. The statute organizing the New York Cotton Exchange, and its rules, are admissible in evidence when the principal knew that his Broker would act in accordance therewith. Bibb vs. Allen, 149 U. S. 481.

In Taylor vs. Bailey, 48 N. E. Rep. 200, it was held that where a customer employed Brokers to purchase stock for him, and they bought on the New York Stock Exchange, he is bound by the usages of that market, whether known to him or not, even although he did not instruct his Brokers to buy in the New York market, when he subsequently agreed to pay for the shares.

Evidence of the custom of bankers and Brokers in St. Louis is not admissible, when there is no offer to show that the principal, who lived in Kansas City, knew of the custom, and contracted in St. Louis with reference to it. If the contract was made in Kansas City, evidence of the St. Louis custom would be incompetent. Coquard vs. Bank of Kansas City, 12 Mo. App. 261.

The rules of the Chicago Board of Trade are admissible in evidence when known to the customer. Hansen vs. Boyd, 161 U. S. 397.

[1] 21 Q. B. Div. 691.

applied in the case of Nourse vs. Prime,[1] decided by the Court of Chancery of the State of New York, in the year 1820, where it was held that Stock-brokers purchasing stocks for their Clients, and holding them as collateral security for the repayment of the purchase-money, need not keep on hand the identical shares purchased, but that the usages of Brokers, which impliedly become a part of the contract, authorize them to use such stocks in their business, keeping on hand an equal number of similar shares ready for delivery to their Clients.

But although a Client may be presumed to have consented that a transaction be conducted according to the custom of Brokers, the Client is entitled also to presume that the Broker or his agent will not act contrary to the custom, and therefore if a Broker's agent receives an order forbidden by the rules of the Exchanges, the Broker cannot repudiate his agent's act.[2]

Sixth. And the general rule last stated does not relate solely to dealings between Brokers and their Clients; but it applies to dealings between themselves, and they are presumed to know the usages of their own business.[3]

---

[1] 4 Johns. Ch. 490; 7 id. 69

[2] Newman vs. Lee, 84 N. Y. Supp. 106. See also Caswell vs. Putnam, 120 N. Y. 153; Douglas vs. Carpenter, 17 A. D. (N. Y.) 329; Whitlock vs. Seaboard National Bank, 29 Misc. 84; Harding vs. Field, 1 App. Div. (N. Y.) 391; Hubbell vs. Drexel, 11 Fed. Rep. 115.

[3] Durant vs. Burt, 98 Mass. 161; Colket vs. Ellis, 10 Phila. 375, s. c. 32 Leg. Int. (Pa.) 82; Hoffman vs. Livingston, 14 J. & S. (N. Y.) 552. So the rules of the New York Gold Exchange are binding upon its members, and its constitution and by-laws become part of their contracts with each other (Peabody vs. Speyers, 56 N. Y. 230).

The rules of the New York Stock Exchange are also binding upon its members, when not in conflict with the law of the land. White vs. Brownell, 2 Daly, 329, followed in Hutchinson vs. Lawrence, 67 How. Prac. 38, and Haight vs. Dickerman, 18 N. Y. Supp. 559, 63 Hun, 632. But a seat cannot be sold to

From the cases cited under the two general rules last mentioned, it appears that the Client is bound, whether he knows the usage or not; and here we find a decided exception to the general rule, which requires that one can only be bound by a usage of which he is shown to have knowledge.[1] By employing a member of the Stock Exchange to transact business, one must necessarily give him the means to carry it through, which can only be done by making the transaction in accordance with the course of business there prevailing, founded upon the rules and usages of the Exchange; and hence such a person cannot avail himself of his supposed ignorance of the mode of dealing there prevailing.[2]

pay debts not coming within the scope of the rules. Cochran vs. Adams, 180 Pa. 289. A rule as to notice must be obeyed strictly. Williamson vs. Ellis, 12 Phila. 338. But a usage of the New York Petroleum Exchange to settle all transactions between members at 2: 15 P. M. the next day, does not apply to a principal, a non-member, who instructed a member to buy oil for him on margin. Greeley vs. Doran-Wright Co., 18 N. E. Rep. 878.

[1] See also Scott vs. Godfrey, 70 L. J. K. B. 954. When one deals in a particular market, he will be presumed to deal in accordance with its usages, whether he knows of them or not. Samuels vs. Oliver, 130 Ill. 73. So also one who employs a board of trade Broker is bound by a custom of the board although ignorant of it. Curtis vs. Wright, 40 Ill. App. 491.

But it was held in Marye vs.

Strouse, 5 Fed. Rep. 483, that a custom of mining stock Brokers to charge the full cost of a telegram to each customer, although a dozen customers' orders might be included in the one telegram, was unreasonable, and did not bind the customer unless he had knowledge of it.

[2] See particularly, on this point, remarks of Pollock, C. B., in Mitchell vs. Newhall, 15 M & W. 308; Pollock vs. Stables, 12 Q. B. 765; Bayliffe vs. Butterworth, 1 Ex. 425; and see also Maxted vs. Paine, L. R. 4 Ex. (2d action) id. 203. As to its being unnecessary to set up in a pleading against a client that he had knowledge of the existence of the usages of Brokers, see Whitehouse vs. Moore, 13 Ab. (N. Y.) Pr. 142. The general doctrine, however, of this case, while perhaps overruled by Stenton vs. Jerome, 54 N. Y. 480, is not affected in the above respect. See also Miller vs. Insurance Co, 1 Ab. New Cas. 470.

There may arise cases in which the courts will not apply the two general rules which we have just laid down, without some evidence that the party sought to be affected by the usages had knowledge of them; but they may confine their application to the cases embraced in the remarks of Mr. Justice Brett in Robinson vs. Mollett, heretofore cited.

Seventh. The proof that a party to a contract had knowledge of a usage need not be direct. It may be proved, like any other fact of this description, by presumptive evidence; by the circumstances surrounding the transaction.[1] In Stewart vs. Cauty[2] the rules of the Liverpool Stock Exchange were admitted in evidence as the best means of showing what was the understanding of the parties in the contract in question by "reasonable time" for its completion.

Eighth. The usages of a particular Broker, firm, or business may also be introduced to interpret or govern a contract when they are known to the party sought to be charged with the same.[3] In Baker vs. Drake[4] the plaintiff employed defendants to purchase stocks for him upon margin, he

---

The fact that a special settling day (under a rule of the London Stock Exchange) was fraudulently obtained, will not affect a sale of shares of a new company, so far as regards members not concerned in the fraud. Ex parte Ward, 51 L. J. Ch. 752. The rules of the London Stock Exchange are imported into all contracts made by its members. Ex parte Ward, 52 L. J. Ch. 73. See Loring vs. Davis, 32 Ch. Div. 625.

Board of trade usages are binding whether known to the customer or not. Pardridge vs. Cutler, 68 Ill. App 569.

[1] Stewart vs. Cauty, 8 M. & W. 160. To charge any person, however, with a custom confined to any particular house in any particular trade, it must be shown that he had express knowledge of the same (Moore vs. Voughton, 1 Stark. 487; Scott vs. Irving, 1 B. & Ad. 605; Stewart vs. Aberdein, 4 M. & W. 211).

[2] Supra.

[3] Baker vs. Drake, 66 N. Y. 518; Loring vs. Gurney, 22 Mass. 15; see also cases cited under Rule VII. in note.

[4] 66 N. Y. 518.

agreeing, in writing, that all the transactions should be in every way subject to the usages of defendant's office. In an action for a conversion by an alleged sale without notice of stocks purchased, defendants offered to prove that it was the custom of their office to sell on account of failure to furnish sufficient margin at the Stock Exchange without giving notice to the Client of the time and place of sale. This offer was rejected, and the appellate court held that such rejection was error. The court, in the prevailing opinion (there being three out of the seven judges who dissented), expressly adhered to the decision in Markham vs. Jaudon,[1] that oral proof of the usage of Brokers in such cases is not admissible to add to or make part of the contract; but held that inasmuch as the paper had been admitted in the case without objection, by which the Client agreed that all transactions in stocks should be in every way subject to the usages of the defendant's office, such paper must be construed, and that parol proof was admissible to explain what those usages were; and that if parol proof should show that it was a usage of the defendant's office for want of a margin to sell stocks in pledge at the public Board of Brokers, without notice to the pledgor of the time or place of sale, such proof tended to establish an agreement to that effect, and that such an agreement would not contravene any statute nor infringe upon public policy.[2]

---

[1] 41 N. Y. 235.

[2] See also, in this connection, Colket vs. Ellis, 10 Phila. (Pa.) 375; s. c. 32 Leg. Int. 82. The habitual course of dealings between the parties may be shown as justifying a cotton Broker to make a sale without notice. Robinson vs. Crawford, 31 App. Div. (N. Y.) 228. And a Stock-broker is liable to a corporation when he witnesses a power of attorney to transfer its bonds, under a custom of railway transfer offices in New York City to accept such witnessing as a guaranty of identity. Jennie Clarkson

Ninth. On the other hand, a Broker cannot bind his Client without his express agreement by transacting business, committed to him, in any other than the ordinary and customary method.[1]

Tenth. Although it is in general the province of a court to construe a *written* instrument, the construction of a particular mercantile expression therein is for the jury.[2]

Eleventh. In respect to proving a commercial usage, it has been held that one witness is sufficient to establish the same, if his means of knowledge are abundant and his testimony full and satisfactory.[3] With this preliminary state-

Home vs. Chesapeake R. R. Co., 83 N. Y. Supp. 913.

A custom of Stock-brokers of Salt Lake City to carry in their names, as trustees, the stock of third parties, and to transfer it without the consent of their cestuis que trust, is inoperative unless assented to both by the customer and Broker. Geyser-Marion Gold Mining Co. vs. Stark, 53 L. R. A. 64.

[1] Wiltshire vs. Sims, 1 Gampb. 258; Brown vs. Boorman, 11 Cl. & Fin. 1; Maxted vs. Paine, L. R. 4 Ex. 81; Maxted vs. Morris, 21 L. T. (n. s.) 535; Fletcher vs. Marshall, 15 M. & W. 755; Hoffman vs. Livingston, 14 J. & S. (N. Y.) 552. See also Chap. III.

[2] Chitty on Cont. 82; Smith vs. Blandy, Ry. & M. 260; Hutchinson vs. Bowker, 5 M. & W. 540; Smith vs. Bouvier, 70 Pa. St. 325; Dawson vs. Kittle, 4 Hill, 107; Goodyear vs. Ogden, id. 104.

Whether a custom exists is for the jury (Sullivan vs. Jernigan, 21 Fla. 264), although its reasonableness and validity are for the court. (Id.)

See also Milroy vs. Chicago, M. & St. P. Ry. Co., 67 N. W. 276; Scott vs. Brown, 60 N. Y. Supp. 511; 29 Misc. 320. When there is sufficient evidence of a custom as to the calling of "margins," the question of its existence will be submitted to the jury, the court saying that the custom is so general among American Exchanges in regard to the sale of grain, provisions, cotton, stock, and bonds for future delivery, that it might be doubted whether it might not be noticed judicially. Hill vs. Morris, 21 Mo. App. 256. See also Scollans vs. Rollins, 60 N. E Rep. 983.

[3] Vail vs. Rice, 5 N. Y. 155; Thomas vs. Graves, 1 Mill (S. C.), Const. Rep. 150; Parrot vs. Thatcher, 26 Mass. 426; Patridge vs. Forsyth, 29 Ala. 200. Some cases, however, hold that one witness is not sufficient to prove a custom. Bissell vs. Ryan, 23 Ill. 566; Wood vs. Hickok, 2 Wend. (N. Y.) 501; Halwerson vs. Cole, 1 Spears (S. C.), 321. But an isolated instance is not sufficient to prove a custom, nor

ment of some of the leading general principles governing usages, we shall now proceed to set forth the most prominent cases in both countries relating to Stock-brokers in which their usages have been sustained and rejected, with such comments as the circumstances seem to call for in the light of these general rules.

II. Cases in which Usages of Stock-brokers held Binding.

(a.) *In the United States.*

In the State of New York the first case in which the usage of Stock-brokers was sustained is Nourse vs. Prime, to which we have already referred.[1] That case was followed in Horton vs. Morgan,[2] where the plaintiff had ordered the defendant, a Stock-broker, to purchase stock for him at the New York Stock Exchange, advancing part of the money as margin to pay for the same, the Broker making up the balance from his own funds. It appeared that defendant did not keep the identical stock on hand which he had purchased, but, upon demand of his Client, sent to him certificates in the name of his clerk, with blank powers of attorney signed by the latter. It was proved by Brokers that purchases of stock at the Board of Brokers were always made in the name of the Broker without disclosing

---

will evidence of the custom of one person be sufficient to establish a general course of trade (Burr vs. Sickles, 17 Ark. 428; Cope vs. Dodd, 13 Pa. St. 33; Adams vs. Otterback, 15 How. [U. S] 539).

It is not necessary that all the witnesses should agree to prove the custom It is then a question for the jury. Dickinson vs. Poughkeepsie, 75 N. Y. 77. If the testimony as to a custom of cotton factors is denied by another witness, it is not proved. Wootters vs. Kauffman, 67 Tex. 488.

[1] Ante, pp. 253, 427.
[2] 19 N. Y. 170.

28

his principal's name, and that his liability to his principal was limited to transferring to him the required number of shares when called upon, without regard to the particular or identical shares bought.

The court, on appeal, held that this practice, by which Brokers only, and not their Clients, are known in their dealings with each other, was not unreasonable ; and the plaintiff, by directing the purchase to be made, must be understood as consenting that it should be done in the usual manner ; and that the plaintiff had no interest in having his shares kept separately from the mass of defendant's stock, one share being precisely equal in value to every other share.[1] Although the court in this case expressly refrained from passing upon the question whether a usage of Stock-brokers to use or hypothecate stocks held by them on margin for their Clients was valid, there is abundance of reason and authority for sustaining such usage.[2] And it has also

[1] The principle of these cases has been several times reaffirmed in New York. See Ch. III. p. 253. See also Caswell vs. Putnam, 120 N. Y. 153; Harding vs. Field, 1 App. Div. (N. Y.) 391.

[2] Lawrence vs. Maxwell, 53 N. Y. 19, and also cases collected in Ch. III. at p. 253. As to how far evidence is admissible to show that a Client may be bound, when he refuses to put up additional margins, by a usage of Wall Street authorizing a settlement of his account at private instead of public sale, see Cameron vs. Durkheim, 55 N. Y. 425. See also Skiff vs. Stoddard, 63 Conn. 198; 21 L. R. A. 102, and cases cited, where the relation between Brokers and Clients as to margin carried stocks is very fully considered.

Reasonable notice must be given to furnish more margin, Lazare vs. Allen, 20 App. Div. 616, in which case, although a judgment for defendant Stock-broker, upon a directed verdict, was affirmed, the court expressed an opinion that a notice of a little over an hour, was unreasonable. See also Hess vs. Rau, 95 N. Y. 362; Gillett vs. Whiting, 120 id. 402; Rogers vs. Wiley, 131 id. 527; Swan vs. Baxter, 36 Misc. (N. Y.) 233.

See Douglas vs. Carpenter, 17 A. D. 329, as to liability of Broker for conversion if he pledges his Client's securities with others, for a larger amount than his Client owes him.

been held in New York that the rules of the Board of Brokers are binding upon third persons who employ members thereof to make transactions with other Brokers relative to stocks. And, accordingly, where W. and C., being members of the Open Board of Brokers, and W. as Broker of B., but in his own name, entered into a contract with C. for the sale of certain stocks, according to the rules of the Exchange, of which B. had knowledge, and thereafter, under the rules, C. called on W. for further margin ; whereupon W. notified B., and reminded him that he would be liable to suspension if he did not comply ; and B. then agreed that if W. would not put up the margins he would protect him against all loss which should ensue from such refusal, and if he was suspended, would pay him during the time of his suspension from the board at a rate equal to the average business of W. for the previous year, with ten per cent added thereto : and W. did refuse to put up the margin, and was suspended—held, that he could recover from B. under this agreement ; that there was sufficient mutuality and consideration, and the same was perfectly valid.[1]

After all advances have been paid, the Broker is not entitled to pledge the stock, and is liable as for a conversion. Van Voorhis vs. Rea Bros. & Co., 153 Pa. 19. See also Transcontinental Co. vs. Hilmers, 20 Fed. Rep. 717; Whitlock vs. Seaboard National Bank, 29 Misc. (N. Y.) 84.

In the case of De Cordova vs. Barnum, 130 N. Y. 615, it was held that a Stock-broker is not obliged to sell collateral security before suing his customer for the balance of his account, when there is no agreement to that effect and evidence of a custom of Stock-holders to sell such collateral and credit the customer with the proceeds, was properly excluded, as whatever the custom of Brokers may be while a speculation is pending, it cannot apply to the broker's right to recover what is due him after he has carried his customer's stocks as long as requested, and finally sold them pursuant to his express order.

[1] White vs. Baxter, 9 J. & S. (N. Y.) 358; aff'd 71 N. Y. 251. See also, for other cases in which usages of Brokers have been upheld, Whitehouse vs. Moore, 13 Ab. (N. Y.) Pr. 142, which in the main,

Baker vs. Drake,[1] which has been fully noticed under the *eighth* general rule,[2] should here be alluded to as further extending the law of usage, and laying down the precedent that parties may also be bound by the usages of a particular Broker's office.[3]

So a Client engaged in speculative purchases and sales of cotton was held to be presumed to know the usages in respect to Cotton-brokers and the Cotton Exchange ; and it being shown that he had had previous dealings in the business, he was not permitted to set up ignorance of the meaning of the term " closing-out," and the mode in which it was done.[4]

Pennsylvania also furnishes a very strong precedent for upholding the usages of Brokers in the case of Colket vs. Ellis.[5] There, the parties being members of the Philadelphia Stock Exchange, the plaintiffs borrowed on " call " a sum of money from defendants, depositing as collateral security certain stocks. It was shown that there was an established general usage among Brokers, when a " call " loan is not paid on the day it is demanded, to sell out the

however, is overruled by Baker vs. Drake, 66 N. Y. 518, 522; Corbett vs. Underwood, 83 Ill. 324; Hill vs. Morris, 21 Mo. App. 256; 3 West. 409; also cases cited under Ch. III. p. 253.

[1] 66 N. Y. 518.

[2] Ante, p. 430.

[3] The above cases in New York, the case of Colket vs. Ellis, 32 Leg. Int. 82, s. c. 10 Phila. (Pa.) 375, and the English case of Lacey vs. Hill (Scrimgeour's Claim), L. R. 8 Ch. App. 921, would seem to be irreconcilable with the case of Markham vs. Jaudon, 41 N. Y. 235.

[4] Kingsbury vs. Kirwin, 11 J. & S. (N. Y.) 451; aff'd 77 N. Y. 612. A usage of the New York Stock Exchange not to make any distinction, in distributing the proceeds of the transfer of a membership, between debts due individual members, and debts due partnerships, one of whose members was a member of the Exchange, was held established in In re Hayes, 75 N. Y. Supp. 312, so as to give effect to an ambiguous rule of the Exchange.

[5] 32 Leg. Int. (Pa.) 82; s. c. 10 Phila. (Pa.) 375.

collateral securities at the Board of Brokers without further notice to the borrower. The trial court found that both parties were familiar with the usage, and both acted throughout on the basis of its validity. The money not having been paid upon call made in the regular way, the defendants sold the stock on the same day at the Stock Exchange, first notifying the plaintiffs of their intention, and rendered the former accounts of the sale. The plaintiffs subsequently tendered the amount of the loan, and demanded the return of the stocks pledged as collateral; and, upon refusal, brought an action of trover to recover for the conversion of the same upon the ground that the usage under which the sale was made was in contravention of the rule of law requiring a sale of collaterals to be public after due notice. But the trial judge, Mitchell, J., overruled this defence, holding, in a well-considered opinion, that where no statute or principle of public policy intervenes but a rule of law, which is a mere privilege, and may be waived, there is no reason why the waiver may not be as well established by a custom known to and acquiesced in by the parties as by an express contract; and, without intimating what would be the effect if such a usage were set up against an outside party, he was of the opinion that, as between the parties before him, both members of the Board of Brokers, and familiar with and dealing on the basis of such usage, it was valid and lawful, and controlled the rights of the parties.

This case confirms the views heretofore expressed under the *fourth* general rule laid down in this chapter,[1] and we confess that we can perceive no legal or substantial reason

---

[1] P. 416.

for not applying the rule as well to third persons who have full and complete knowledge of the usage as to members of the Stock Exchange—the whole basis of the doctrine of usage resting upon the knowledge of the parties—and why evidence of a similar usage should not have been received in the case of Markham vs. Jaudon.[1] In Massachusetts evidence has also been held admissible to show that by the custom of Brokers in Boston, " when they receive an order to buy stocks on margin, it means that the Broker makes a contract, verbal or written, with any person whatever, that within sixty days from said date, if the stock goes up the seller shall pay in cash the difference, and if the stock goes down the buyer shall pay in cash the difference ; and that the money, or margin, put up by the buyer is for security

[1] 41 N. Y. 245; see also, in this connection, Lacey vs. Hill (Scrimgeour's Claim), L. R. 8 Ch. App. 921.

In Van Horn vs. Gilbough, 21 Am. L. R. (n. s.) 171; 10 W. N. 347; 13 Lan. Bar 61, where a Stockbroker bought railroad stock for his Client, and, according to a Broker's usage, pledged it as collateral for payment of a balance of the purchase price, it was held that, under a custom of Brokers, he was justified in pledging and the pledgee in subsequently selling the stock, on the fall of the market price, without notice to his Client, to whom both customs were known, and was entitled to recover what was owing to him by his Client on the transaction. See note as to the effect of Stock Exchange usages on non-members appended to the report of last cited case in 21 Am. L. N. (n. s.) 171. See Covell vs. Loud, 135 Mass. 41.

It has been also held in Pennsylvania that when a Broker is employed to sell stock, the fact that the Broker transferred the stock to his own name was in accordance with the legitimate, if not the usual, course of business, and when he sold only a small part of it, and the rest remained on his hands because he could not dispose of it without a heavy sacrifice, a jury was not warranted in charging him with the whole value of the stock, unless he refused to account, or return it. Leddy vs. Flanigan, 3 Phila. 355.

Likewise it was held in Sheppard vs. Barrett, 42 Leg. Int. (Pa.) 140, that the term "friendly loan" by the custom of Brokers is universally understood to be a loan of money or stocks, between Brokers for business purposes, and under the rules of the Philadelphia Stock Exchange such are entitled to a preference out of

that he shall perform his contract."[1]   And it is not error
on the part of a judge to instruct a jury that the fact that
both parties were Brokers, and might be presumed to know
the usages of their business, was entitled to great weight.[2]

The most important recent decision as to the relation of
Stock-brokers and their customers so far as regards the
carrying of margins is furnished by the State of Connecticut where it was held in Skiff vs. Stoddard [3] (per Prentice,
J.), that when a Client in Connecticut employed a Broker
in New Hartford to effect transactions for him on the New
York Stock Exchange, he would be bound by the usages of
that market, provided they were not unreasonable, and that
a custom to repledge a customer's stock held on margin was
not unreasonable.

In Ohio the evidence showed the existence in New York
and Cincinnati of a usage of Stock-brokers to look to each
other personally when the principals are not brought into
the transaction.   This evidence was uncontradicted, but the

the proceeds of a member's seat.
See also Thompson vs. Adams, 93
Pa. 55.

[1] Commonwealth vs. Cooper, 4
Mass. L. R. (May 4, 1881) No. 24;
s. c. Am. L. Rev. 360 (May, 1881).

The custom of "ringing up"
amongst grain Brokers in Baltimore
is valid. Ward vs. Vosburgh, 31
Fed. 12.   A custom of the board of
trade by which a buyer of grain
with warranty must within a given
time object to the quality, is reasonable as between its members.
Everringham vs. Lord, 19 Ill. App.
565.   See also Riebe vs. Hellman,
69 Ill. App. 19, and Kinney's Ill.
Dig., title "Board of Trade." The

rules of the New Orleans Cotton Exchange as to substitution of contracts are binding upon principals
who are acquainted with them.
Conner vs. Robertson, 37 La. Ann.
815; Lehman vs. Feld, 37 Fed. 852;
Irwin vs. Williar, 110 U. S. 499;
Barnett vs. Warren, 82 Ala. 557 (2
So. 457) (usage of cotton Factors to
acquire lien on cotton stored for
sale for moneys advanced, binding);
Burbridge vs. Gumbel, 72 Miss. 371
(evidence of a usage to apply instructions as to insuring cotton only
to the season in which the instructions were given, is admissible).

[2] Durant vs. Burt, 98 Mass. 162.

[3] 63 Conn. 198; 21 L. R. A. 102.

jury ignored it, and gave a defendant Broker, who was sued for the sum paid for forged bonds, and whose defence was that he was acting for a principal, and that he, as agent was not liable, a verdict in his favor, and the court on motion of plaintiff granted a new trial, saying the trial court had fully instructed the jury upon this question, and the effect of it.[1]

In the same State a custom of the pork trade to close the year on October 31st, and to charge extra commissions on stock carried over, has been held reasonable.[2]

It has also been lately held in Massachusetts that a usage of Bankers and Brokers and others engaged in dealing in securities, to treat certificates endorsed in blank as negotiable, and as enabling the bearer to give a good title to a *bona fide* purchaser, is binding.[3]

A usage obtaining in Baltimore, on the Stock Exchange, and amongst Bankers and Brokers, requiring registered consols to be transferred in writing, and to be accompanied by a power of attorney acknowledged before a notary public, has been held in Taliferro vs. Bank[4] to be binding, and to put an intended pledgee on inquiry as to ownership, but the usage must be itself proved, and not the rules of the Stock Exchange, the existence of which is not evidence of the usage.

A usage of the Stock Exchange that when a Stockbroker is employed to sell stock, and he is subsequently employed by another person to purchase the same kind of

---

[1] Souther vs. Stoeckle, 7 Ohio Dec. Rep. 511. See Bailey vs. Galbraith, 100 Tenn. 599.

[2] Mathews vs. Briggs, 7 Ohio Dec. Rep. 23.

[3] Scollans vs. Rollins, 60 N. E. Rep. 983.

[4] 17 Atl. 1036.

stock, at a limited price, he may secure the services of another Broker to bid the prices fixed by the intending purchaser, has been held valid in Alabama in Terry vs. Birmingham National Bank,[1] when neither the buyer nor seller had any knowledge of each other's intentions, or of their instructions to the Broker.

Although the usages of the London and New York Stock Exchanges are similar as to requiring the execution of transfers of shares in blank to be authenticated by the proper officer, yet it was held in Colonial Bank vs. Cady,[2] that such a transfer, by executors, in England, of shares in an American corporation, did not estop the executors from claiming them from defendant bank to whom they had been pledged by a Stock-broker for value without notice, although if the case were decided by American law such a transferee would take title even if the executors' signatures to the transfer were not verified by the consul.

(b.) In England.

In England the question of the effect of usage upon contracts has been carefully and thoroughly considered by the courts.

There are two classes of cases in which the usages of Stock-brokers have been sustained which have already been referred to at length, and they need not be here set forth.[3] The first class comprises those cases in which a principal or Client directed his Broker to buy or sell securities or to make contracts upon the Stock Exchange; and where the Broker has sought indemnity at the hands of his Client for acts per-

---

[1] 13 So. 140. [3] See Ch. X.
[2] 15 App. Cas. 267; L. R. 38 Ch. Div. 399.

formed by him in pursuance of directions of his Client. The principle applied was, that parties who make or direct a bargain or transaction to be made in connection with a particular trade are taken to have contracted subject, or with reference, to the known usages of that trade. Sutton vs. Tatham and Pollock vs. Stables[1] are illustrations of this class, as are the other cases cited under the *fifth* general rule.[2] As the most important of these cases have been set forth in Chapter III.,[3] a reference to them is all that is necessary in this connection.

The second class comprises those cases in which the principal question involved was upon whom the liability for "calls" rested where stocks were sold on the Stock Exchange. In these cases the courts fully investigated the various steps of a purchase and sale upon the Stock Exchange, and rigorously and uniformly applied the usages and rules of Stock-brokers to explain the contracts there entered into, and to fix the ultimate responsibility for "calls" made where the capital stock was not fully paid up to the limit fixed by the charter or articles of incorporation. As these cases have been fully described in Chapter X., it is only necessary, in this connection, to refer to that portion of the work ;[4] but their perusal will forcibly illustrate the extent to which the English courts have gone in applying this doctrine of usage. In considering the soundness of the cases

---

[1] Ante, p. 424. The following usages have been held binding: the customer, when the Broker becomes a defaulter, has no option to close at "hammer" prices, and a Broker who is instructed to buy a specific number of shares may buy from more than one jobber. Levitt vs. Hamblet, 6 Com. Cas. 79; 5 ib. 326, which also held that a Broker might, in carrying over, transfer two parcels of shares bought from two jobbers for two customers, from one jobber to another.

[2] P. 424.

[3] P. 218 et seq.

[4] At p. 981 et seq.

in which usage has been rejected, these English adjudications should be prominently kept in view.

There are some cases in England that do not fall within either of these classes, and to them a more special reference should be made. Thus,[1] it has been decided that evidence of the course of business and custom of London Brokers should be admitted to explain the authority meant to be given to a London banker by a power of attorney to sell stock sent through a country banker.

So in an action for the non-acceptance of railway shares, which by the contract (made at Liverpool through Brokers) were to be delivered in a reasonable time, a written rule of the Liverpool Stock Exchange, stated to be acted upon by all the Liverpool Brokers, "that the seller of shares was in all cases entitled to seven days to complete his contract by delivery, the time to be computed from the day on which he was acquainted with the name of his transferee," was held admissible upon an issue whether the plaintiff, within a reasonable time, was ready and willing and offered to transfer the shares; although it was not proved that either of the parties or their Brokers were members of the Liverpool Exchange.[2] And, in avoidance of a sale made by a Broker, the defendant may prove that by the custom of the trade the authority to sell expires with the day on which it was given.[3]

It has also been held that parol evidence is competent to show that a person acted as a Broker for the plaintiff; and that parol evidence as to the usage of trade in making Bro-

---

[1] Adams vs. Peters, 2 C. & K. 309. Also Field vs. Lelean, 6 H. & N. 617.

[2] Stewart vs. Cauty, 8 M. & W. 723.

[3] Dickenson vs. Tilwall, 1 Stark. 128 ; 4 Gumpb. 279.

kers liable where their principals are not disclosed is also admissible, on the ground that such evidence does not vary the terms of a written contract, but merely annexes a particular or incident thereto which, though not mentioned in the contract, was connected with it, or with the relations growing out of it. Such evidence is admitted with a view of giving effect, as far as possible, to the presumed intentions of the parties.[1]

It has been likewise held that under a practice of the London Stock Exchange (where a loan is made by one Broker to another on a deposit of stock) that the lender send back the securities on the morning of the day of payment, the borrower to send a good check, or return the same, or similar, securities later in the day, the lender did not lose his right to the securities by returning them to the borrower, when he did not receive a check or other securities to replace them.[2]

So also where shares have been sold and the purchase money paid at the transfer under the usages of the Stock Exchange, the seller is not liable although the company subsequently declines to register the transfer.[3]

This decision was followed in Casey vs. Bentley,[4] where, in a similar state of facts, specific performance, or a rescission of the contract, was sought by the vendor. The authorities are fully discussed, and the court (Fitzgibbon, L. J., dissentiente) held that as the sale took place subject to the usages of the Dublin Stock Exchange, which were

[1] Humfrey vs. Dale, 7 El. & Bl. 266; Thomson vs. Davenport, 9 B. & C. 78; Pennell vs. Alexander, 3 El. & Bl. 77, 288.

[2] Burba vs. Ricardo, 1 C. & E. 478.

[3] London Founders Association vs. Clarke, 57 L. J. Q. B. 291; following Stray vs. Russell, 1 E. & E. 888.

[4] (1902) 1 Ir. R. 376.

similar to those of the London Exchange, the plaintiff was entitled to neither, although if the sale took place outside the Exchange, she should have judgment for rescission, as the company refused to register the vendee. The result of the decision was that the plaintiff became a trustee for the purchaser, with right of indemnity to the vendor by the defendant against calls.

In Ward in re [1] it was decided that the amount due by a defaulter to a Stock Exchange creditor under its rules is a liquidated sum within the meaning of the Bankruptcy Act, and will support a bankruptcy petition by the creditor, and in Ratcliffe vs. Mendelsohn,[2] a defaulting Broker, was held liable to stock jobbers for the difference between " hammer " and contract prices, as the jobbers under the rules were bound to hand the official assignee the amounts received by them on completion of the contracts.[3]

A rule of the London Stock Exchange which provided that the seller of shares of stock is responsible for the genuineness of all documents delivered, and for such dividends as may be received until reasonable time has been allowed to the transferee to execute and lodge the same for verification and registration, and that when an official certificate of registration has been issued, the committee will not (unless bad faith is imputed to the seller) take cognizance of any subsequent dispute as to title until the legal issue has been decided, was held to be reasonable in Smith vs. Reynolds,[4] in which case a principal was held bound to indemnify his Broker who, under a resolution of the committee, was obliged to make good a loss arising from a forged transfer. So

[1] 52 L. J. Ch. 73.
[2] (1902) 2 K. B. 653.
[3] See King vs. Hutton (1900), 2 Q. B. 505.
[4] 66 L. T. 808.

also in Harker vs. Edwards,[1] rule 57 providing that the Stock Exchange in all dealings will only recognize its own members, and Rule 11, that the decision of the committee (as to questions arising out of the contract) was to be final, were held to be reasonable and binding.

A commercial and Stock Exchange usage to treat bearer bonds as negotiable has been held binding, although of recent origin.[2]

When a Broker becomes a defaulter, and the Client, for whom the Broker has sold shares, elects to complete the transaction on his own account, the Client is not entitled to nominate a person to transfer the shares to the jobber to whom sold, the usage of the Stock Exchange not permitting such nomination, as the effect would be to substitute the nominee as principal.[3]

In Scott vs. Godfrey [4] a custom of the Stock Exchange by which Brokers lump together the orders of their Clients and execute them by means of one contract with the jobber, was established to the satisfaction of the jury, and in the opinion of the court was a reasonable one. In that case the jury also found that the Client gave his order on the terms that it might be so executed. The court said that as to the latter finding it doubted whether there was evi-

---

[1] 57 L. J. Q. B. 147.

[2] Bechuanaland Exportation Co. vs. London Trading Bank (1898), 2 Q. B. 658; Rumball vs. Metropolitan Bank, 2 Q. B. D. 194; London Joint Stock Bank vs. Simmons (1892), App. Cas. 201; Venables vs. Baring Bros. (1892), 3 Ch. 527; Bentinck vs. Bank (1893), 2 Ch. 120; Edelstein vs. Schuler, 71 L. J. K. B. 572 (in which case the court said the custom was now so universal that it should be judicially noticed). See Picker vs. London and County Banking Co., 18 Q. B. D. 515; Colonial Bank vs. Cady, 15 App. Cas. 267 (the usage must be an English one).

[3] Currie vs. Booth, 7 Com. Cas. 77; rev'g s. c. 6 Com. Cas. 74.

[4] 70 L. J. K. B. 954.

dence to support it, but it was immaterial, as the Client gave his order to be executed according to the usages of the Stock Exchange.[1] The jury also found that there was a custom by which a jobber and each Client of the Broker became bound to each other to carry out the contract applicable to the particular Client's order. The court, however, did not think the evidence established the latter custom, nor was it necessary in the particular instance, as the facts themselves established privity.

It was held in Stoneham vs. Wyman[2] that, having reference to Rule 155 of the London Stock Exchange rules, if a jobber who has been paid in full his differences up to the date of the default of a Broker with whom he had dealt, subsequently recovers from the Broker's customer a larger sum, he is bound to account to the official assignees for an amount equal to that which he has already received, and the rule was held to be a reasonable one. See also Davis vs. Howard, supra.[3]

A usage of the Toronto Stock Exchange that all transactions must be "settled" on the following day, or, if Saturday intervenes, on the following Monday, has, in Boultbee vs. Growski,[4] been held reasonable, in which case it was also held that the word "settled" meant the completion of the transaction, and if the purchasing Broker does not disclose his principal on the day of settlement, he incurs a personal responsibility.

[1] See p. 429.

[2] 6 Com. Cas. 174.

[3] L. R. 24 Q. B. D. 691.

[4] 29 Can. S. C. 54; 24 Ont. App. 502.

III. Cases in which Usages have been Rejected.

(a.) *In the United States.*

There are in the United States a number of cases arising out of transactions in stocks in which the usages of Brokers have been rejected. A close examination of some of these decisions, however, shows that in many instances they are utterly irreconcilable with the rules which we have laid down, as well as with the theory upon which usage is admitted in evidence.

Beginning with the cases in the State of New York, we find the well-known case of Allen vs. Dykers.[1] In that case it appeared that A. borrowed of D., a Stock-broker, a certain sum of money, for which he placed in his hands as collateral security certain bank stock, at the same time giving to the Broker a promissory note agreeing to pay the loan at a time stated, and, in default, empowering the Broker to sell the same at the Board of Brokers. The Broker immediately transferred the stock into his own name, and, before the maturity of the note, pledged or parted with the same.

In defence of an action against the Broker, brought to recover the difference between the value of the stock and the money loaned, he offered to prove that, when Brokers took assignments of stocks as collateral security for the money loaned, it was not the custom to retain the stocks in specie, but to transfer it by hypothecation or otherwise, if they thought proper; and, on payment or tender of the principal debt, to return to the debtor an equal quantity of the same kind of stock, and that this custom was known to the plaintiff when the transaction was made. The court held

[1] 3 Hill, 593; aff'd 7 id. 497

that this evidence was illegal and properly ruled out. The
Brokers proved that from the date of the note until after
it fell due they had a larger quantity of stock than that
mentioned in the note; but it appeared that all of this
stock, except seventy-two shares, stood in the names of persons to whom it had been pledged as collateral security for
various loans made to defendants, the Brokers. The court
said : " The defendants being Stock-brokers and dealers in
stock, their counsel offered to prove on the trial that it was
the usage, when stock was transferred to such dealers by
way of collateral security, not to hold it specifically, but to
transfer it by hypothecation or otherwise, at pleasure, and,
on payment or tender of the money advanced, to return an
equal quantity of the same kind of stock; also that this
usage was general, and known to the agent who made the
loan in question. The object of the offer was to lay the
foundation for insisting that the usage should be regarded
as incorporated in and forming part and parcel of the agreement, thus making the latter import a consent on the part
of the plaintiff that the defendants might use the stock
during the running of the loan, the same as if they were
the absolute owners. *It is not necessary to determine what
effect would be due to such proof in the case of a simple
pledge, as collateral security without any further agreement.*
Possibly the known usage in like cases might be considered
as attaching itself to the transaction, and constituting a
part of it. But where the parties have chosen to prescribe
for themselves the terms and conditions of the loan, they
must be held to abide by them, and we are especially
bound to refuse effect to any general or particular usage
when in direct contravention of the fair and legal import of
a written contract."

29

The ground upon which the court rested its judgment in this case—viz., that the usage in question conflicted with the terms of the contract—is perfectly sound. But did the usage conflict with the written contract? There was nothing said in the contract as to what disposition might be made of the stock during the pendency of the loan ; but the argument of the learned judge delivering the opinion was that it was to be inferred, from the language contained in it, that no disposition could be made of the same by the pledgee, upon the maxim *Expressio unius est exclusio alterius.* With the utmost deference for the opinions of Chief-justice Nelson, it seems to us that, in the absence of express provision to the contrary, the usage mentioned should have been held operative. The knowledge of the usage made it a part of the contract, and there is no room for the application of the maxim. The court sought to distinguish the case from Nourse vs. Prime,[1] on the ground that in the latter case the Stock-brokers proved that they had always on hand a number of shares equal to the amount pledged with them, whereas in the present case there was no such proof. It is very difficult, however, when the facts of both cases are carefully analyzed, to reconcile them ; for it did appear in Allen vs. Dykers that the Brokers were, during the existence of the pledge, the owners of more than the number of shares pledged with them. The fact that the Stock-brokers had pledged, for the purposes of their business, nearly all of the particular stock held by them does not affect the question, because the Brokers could have repossessed themselves of it by paying off the loan.

The doctrine of Allen vs. Dykers does not seem to have

[1] 4 Johns. Ch. 490; 7 id. 69.

been very heartily accepted by the Court of Appeals in the subsequent case of Horton vs. Morgan ;[1] for although it was quoted by counsel in the argument,[2] it was not mentioned in the opinion ; and the court seems to have regarded the question, which was apparently settled in Allen vs. Dykers, as still open, by saying, " It is unnecessary to pass upon the ruling by which evidence was admitted to show the custom of Brokers to sell and hypothecate stock held by them as security on advances, and we do not give any judgment upon that question." Yet the case has never been directly overruled.

It seems to us that there can be no substantial reason to charge a pledgee with a conversion of securities for parting with or repledging the same, where he can establish that the usages of Stock-brokers, and the peculiar nature of their business, known to the pledgor, permits and makes such a practice necessary ; and where, upon the expiration of the loan, or upon demand, as the case may be, the pledgee is ready to deliver to the pledgor shares of the identical character deposited with him.[3]

[1] 19 N. Y. 170.

[2] See Brief of Counsel, N. Y. Ct. of App. Dec., on file in N. Y. Law Inst.

[3] See, as sustaining these views, Horton vs. Morgan, 19 N. Y. 170; Lawrence vs. Maxwell, 53 id. 19; see also Ch. III. p. 250. On the other hand, as sustaining Allen vs. Dykers, see Taylor vs. Ketchum, 35 How. (N. Y.) Pr. 289; also Currie vs. Smith, 4 N. Y. Leg Obs. 313; Wheeler vs. Newbould, 16 N. Y 393, where the court held that evidence was inadmissible of a local usage in the city of New York to sell commercial paper pledged as security for a loan, at private sale, and for the best price that could be obtained, after demand of payment and notice that such sale would be made in case of default The court said that such a custom, if it existed, would be illegal and void. See also Transcontinental Co. vs. Hilmers, 20 Fed. Rep. 717; Jones on Pledges, 2d ed. p. 538 et seq., and cases cited. In Allen vs. Dubois, 117 Mich. 115, it was held that in the case of collateral, pledged to secure a loan, the pledgor is entitled to a return of the identical shares

The next case which we shall notice is the familiar one of Markham vs. Jaudon.[1] We have already criticised this case in this chapter in connection with the question of usage,[2] and it is unnecessary to devote much space to it here. In that case the defendants, in answer to an action for the conversion of certain stocks which they were "carrying" for the plaintiff on margin, offered to prove the existence of a custom in the city of New York between Brokers and their Clients by which Brokers have the right to sell out the Clients' stocks on the exhaustion of the margin. The court, in commenting upon such evidence, said: "This was an offer not to explain the meaning of particular terms, or to prove attending circumstances to enable the court to construe the agreement, but to change the rights of the parties to a contract. By the law, as I have interpreted it, the customer did not lose the title to his stock by any process less than a sale upon reasonable notice, or by judicial proceedings. The Broker has no right to sell without such a notice. A practice or custom to do otherwise would have no more force than a custom to protest notes on the first day of grace, *or a custom of Brokers not to purchase* the shares at all, in a case like the present, but to content themselves with a memorandum or entry in their books of the contract made with their customer. Such practice, in each case, would be in hostility to the terms of the contract, an attempt to change its obligations, and would be void. The proof could not therefore be legally given."

pledged if he can identify them, although if a Broker buys stock and holds it as security for moneys advanced, a sufficient number of the same kind of shares need only be returned. See Stuart vs. Bigler, 98 Pa. St. 80; Hubbell vs. Drexel, 11 Fed. Rep. 115.

[1] 41 N. Y. 245. For history of this case, see Ch. III. p. 191, and Ch. on "Measure of Damages."

[2] Ante, p. 418.

The objections to the conclusions reached in this case, as above set forth, may be thus summarized.

I. There is no doubt but that the "notice" alluded to could have been waived by express agreement.[1] A knowledge of the existence of a usage to sell without notice would have the same effect, and should be regarded as incorporated in the contract.[2]

II. Under the circumstances disclosed, this usage was a perfectly reasonable one, and it is erroneous to consider the case as if it were one of pure bailment arising between pledgor and pledgee.

III. The question has been settled differently in England.[3]

There are but two other cases in the State of New York upon this question of usage, to which we deem it necessary to call special attention—viz., Spear vs. Hart,[4] and Lombardo vs. Case.[5] In Spear vs. Hart, the court held, in accordance with the general rule upon the subject, that on a sale of stock deliverable at a future day at the option of the seller, a dividend declared before the sale, but not payable until after the day fixed for the delivery of the stock, belongs to the seller, and does not pass to the buyer under the contract. The effect of this rule was sought to be changed by the introduction of a usage of Wall Street. This evidence was ruled out.

The defendant had agreed to deliver certain railway stock, seller's option, in ten days from March 28, 1865. This matured on the 7th of April. On the 23d of March the railroad company declared a dividend of five per cent, pay-

---

[1] Baker vs. Drake, 66 N. Y. 518.

[2] See also ante, p. 424.

[3] Lacey vs. Hill (Scrimgeour's Claim), L. R. 8 Ch. App. 921, and practically in Pennsylvania. Col-

ket vs. Ellis, 32 Leg. Int. 82; s. c. 10 Phila. (Pa.) 375; see also Corbett vs. Underwood, 83 Ill. 324.

[4] 3 Rob. 420.

[5] 30 How. (N. Y.) Pr. 117.

able on the 10th of April, and closed their transfer-books on
the 31st of March. The court, through Monell, J., said :
" I do not think such a custom could alter well-settled principles applicable to the law of contracts. . . . But under a
contract to sell 100 shares of stock, a custom that something
more passes to the purchaser cannot be allowed. It varies
the agreement by adding to it, and it would not be merely
an explanation or interpretation of it."

The facts of this case are very meagrely reported, and it
does not appear whether the sale was made on the Stock
Exchange. The invariable rule or usage of Stock-brokers is
to sell stock with the " dividend on," until the books are
closed, after which event the stock sells " ex dividend." [1]

Under ordinary circumstances, therefore, the purchaser
in the above case would have been entitled to all dividends
on the stock at the time of the closing of the books on the
31st of March, the sale having been made before that time,
that fact actually entering into and affecting the market price
of the stock. And, according to the views which we have
already expressed, such a usage is perfectly valid, because it
becomes a part of the contract of the parties. Persons entering into agreements through Brokers understand that sales
of stock made at the Board of Brokers at any time before
the day fixed for the closing of the transfer-books of the
company, declaring a dividend payable at a future day,
carry with them the dividend so declared, and the price is
regulated accordingly. After the books are closed, the sales
are understood to be " ex dividend," and the price is accordingly affected by the fact that the seller retains and is to
collect the dividend.[2]

[1] See Art. XXXII., Sec. 1, Const.
N. Y. Stock Exchange.

[2] These usages were recognized in
the case of Hill vs. Newichawanick

So, in Lombardo vs. Case, the contract made by a Stock-broker was as follows: "New York, October 8, 1863. For value received, the bearer may call on me for one thousand shares of the stock of the Cleveland and Pittsburgh Railroad Company, at one hundred and seventeen (117) per cent, any time in six months from date, without interest. The bearer is entitled to all dividends declared during the time to half-past one P. M. each day." It was held, on demurrer to the complaint for a dividend declared prior to the making of the contract, that an alleged custom among Brokers and dealers in stocks, that the words "dividends or surplus dividends" in the contract were intended to mean dividends declared on the stock without regard to whether they had been announced *before or after the date of the contract, provided* that on the day the contract was made the stock was selling in the market "*dividend on*," and not "ex dividend," would not be allowed to be proved on the trial, for the reason that effect could not be given to the custom without making a new contract between the parties, as six months from date could not mean or include "a day or two before date." Consequently, a dividend of four per cent, which had been declared and announced at the time of the making of the contract, could not be recovered by the purchaser, although the stock was then selling "dividend on."[1]

In Harris vs. Tumbridge,[2] it was held proper to exclude proof that it was common for parties purchasing "straddles"

Co., 8 Hun (N. Y.), 459, aff'd 71 N. Y. 593. But see Jones vs. R. Co., 57 N. Y. 196.

[1] Lombardo vs. Case, 30 How. (N. Y.) Pr. 117; Hopper vs. Sage, 12 N. Y. *Weekly Dig.* 78; s. c. on new trial, 112 N. Y. 530. Evidence of the usage was also held properly rejected when the contract was made outside of the Stock Exchange, and the Broker was not a member thereof. Id.

[2] 83 N. Y. 92.

to operate in stocks, holding the straddle as security ; but no custom or usage such as to modify the contract, or become interwoven with its terms, was in any manner shown in that case. The court said that "a custom or usage which binds the parties to a contract does so only upon the principle either that they have knowledge of its existence, or that it is so general that they must be supposed to have contracted with reference to it."

In closing this criticism of the New York cases, in which the usages of Stock-brokers have been rejected, we are compelled to say that they are far from being satisfactory.

The usages of Brokers, bankers, and others cannot be set up to defeat the well-settled and universally applied principle of the commercial law that the purchaser of negotiable paper past due takes it subject to the equities of other parties, and can acquire no better title than his transferror.[1] In the last cited case a number of United States Treasury notes had been stolen from an express company and purchased by a firm of bankers, after the date at which they were payable or convertible into bonds. Evidence was introduced to show that securities of the kind in question continued to be bought and sold by bankers and Brokers after they had become due. The court held that this fact did not avail to alter the law. " Bankers, Brokers, and others," said the court, "cannot, as was attempted in this case, establish by proof a usage or custom, in dealing in such paper, which in their own interest contravenes the established commercial law. If they have been in the habit of disregarding that law, this does not relieve them from the consequences, nor establish a different law."

---

[1] Vermilye vs. Adams Exp. Co., 21 Wall. 139.

A close examination of this case will show, however, that the evidence offered did not amount to a proof of a general usage of Bankers and Brokers to deal in negotiable paper after it was due, and to treat it as not due, and the case should be confined to the peculiar facts there stated. Moreover, there seems to be an insuperable objection to such a usage, as it would operate to defeat the rights of third persons not parties to it. Usage is only admissible as forming a part of a contract. In the case in question the dispute was between adverse claimants for the possession of certain personal property, the Treasury notes, and it is not very clear how such a usage as that invoked could avail in such a controversy.[1]

The subject of usages was considered in the case of Evans vs. Waln,[2] by the Supreme Court of Pennsylvania. There the plaintiffs employed M. & Bro., Brokers, in Philadelphia, to sell certain stock for them. M. & Bro. in turn employed one W., another Broker in Philadelphia, to sell the stock, and the sale was eventually made through the defendants, Stock-brokers in New York. W. being in debt to the defendants, and becoming insolvent, the latter deducted the amount of such indebtedness from the proceeds of the sale of plaintiffs' stock, and remitted the balance. In an action

---

[1] As certificates of stock are not negotiable, a custom of Stock-brokers to the contrary cannot be proved. East Birmingham Land Co. vs. Dennis, 2 L. R. A. 836, and cases cited. A custom of the Petroleum Exchange that all deliveries of oil should be of oil that had storage charges paid thereon, does not, in the absence of contract, bind one not a member. Waugh vs. Seaboard Bank, 54 N. Y. Super. Ct. 283.

A custom of the New York Cotton Exchange that a Broker may sell before the contract matures, when the principal does not advance margins, does not bind the latter unless known to him. Blakemore vs. Heyman, 23 Fed. Rep. 618. See also Higgins vs. McCrea, 23 Fed. Rep. 782; 116 U. S. 671; Dillard vs. Paton, 19 Fed. Rep. 619.

[2] 71 Pa. St. 69.

by the plaintiffs to recover the full purchase-money, it was shown that the defendants knew that the stock belonged to the plaintiffs, and that W. was acting as Stock-broker for them. The defendants offered to prove a custom by which Brokers keep transactions with one party all in one account, and remit the balance. This was ruled out. The appellate court held that the ruling was correct, and that such a custom, if proved, would have constituted no defence, as the defendants had no right to credit W.'s account with the proceeds of the stock: he was not the owner of it, and had no title or claim to its proceeds; the defendants had not received the stock from W., and they were not bound to account to him for the price at which it was sold.

As it was not shown that the account of W. was credited with the proceeds, the court held that it was clear the case was not within the operation of the custom, if any such existed. The court, in conclusion, based its reason for rejecting such evidence upon the following ground: "If there is a custom among Stock-brokers, when dealing with others, to appropriate money belonging to the principal to the payment of his Broker's indebtedness, the sooner it is abolished the better—*Malus usus est abolendus.* A custom so iniquitous can never obtain the force or sanction of law, and the marvel is that it should be set up as a defence in this action." It will be observed that not even the express agreement of W. could have produced the result claimed for by defendants.[1]

[1] To same effect, Fisher vs. Brown, 104 Mass. 259; Pearson vs. Scott, 38 L. T. (n. s.) 747; see also Sweeting vs. Pearce, 7 C. B. (n. s.) 449; and no usage will authorize a factor or agent to depart from positive instructions (Barksdale vs. Brown, 1 Nott. & M. [S. C.] 517). In Blackburn vs. Mason, 68 Law T. 510, this custom was held unreasonable, and not binding on the client unless he agreed to be bound

In another Pennsylvania case [1] the custom averred was rejected, but not on its merits. Plaintiff bought from defendants (bankers and Brokers in Philadelphia) certain stocks and bonds, with an option to plaintiff at the end of a year from the date of the contract, April 21, 1890, to resell them at cost to defendants, who subsequently made an assignment. Plaintiff exercised his option on April 22, 1891, and it was held that the general rule that "one year from the date of the contract" was to be computed by excluding the day of the date, could not be modified by an averment by defendants on information and belief of a good general custom in New York, Boston and Philadelphia, known to dealers in bonds and stocks, that an option to sell at the end of a given period expired on the last day of such period, and that therefore plaintiff was one day late, as the defendants were bankers and Brokers, who presumably knew the customs of such business, but they did not allege such custom of their own knowledge, nor their ability to prove it, and moreover the custom was alleged to be known to dealers in bonds and stocks, without saying that plaintiff was such a dealer. But, waiving these defects, the custom alleged was as to an option to sell at the end of any given period, whereas the contract provided for an option to demand a rescission

by it, and in Crossley vs. Magniac, (1893) 1 Ch. 594, the evidence failed to prove this custom, and the court said that, even if it were proved, it could not bind a foreign principal from whom the London Broker received, through the country Broker, a power of attorney to sell his shares. See also Anderson vs. Sutherland, 13 Times L. R. 163. In Ryman vs. Gerlach, 153 Pa. St. 197, in a state of facts similar to

Evans vs. Waln, supra, the court held defendant Brokers liable for a conversion, inasmuch as they were aware that their correspondent's client was the owner, although, if they had not such knowledge, and as a blank assignment was attached to the certificate, they would not be liable.

[1] Weld vs. Barker, 153 Pa. St. 465; 26 Atl. 239.

of a sale after a year of obligatory retention by the purchaser of the stocks sold.

Proof of a local custom in the oil trade, to regard future sales of oil, at an advance of the market price at the time of the contract, as merely to be settled by payment of differences, cannot be allowed, when its effect will be to vary the terms of a written contract.[1]

It was held in Commonwealth vs. Barrett,[2] that no custom of Brokers can legalize fraud.

Massachusetts furnishes several instances where the usages of Brokers have been rejected.   In Parsons vs. Martin,[3] which appears to be the earliest reported case in that State upon the subject, it was held that a Broker to whom a certificate of shares in a corporation were intrusted by their owner, with written directions to sell under circumstances specified, had no right to transfer the shares for any other purpose, to the name of another person or his own name, and that evidence was inadmissible of a custom among Brokers so to do; and the owner may treat such transfer as a sale, and recover of the Broker the market price of the shares on the day of the transfer, although the Broker afterwards tenders him another certificate of an equal number of such shares, which he refuses to receive and does not retransfer to the Broker.

The court further held that a custom among Stock-brokers in Boston, permitting a Broker to make a sale of stock, not on account of plaintiff, but for some other person, using plaintiff's shares for that purpose, and replacing them with other shares of a like kind, was bad.   No usage or custom such as that which defendant attempted to show could affect the legal rights of the parties; nor, if fully proved, would the law

---

[1] Scofield vs. Blackman, 17 W.   [2] 40 Leg. Int. (Pa.) 474.
N. C. (Pa.) 518.   [3] 77 Mass. 111.

sustain or tolerate it. Proof of usage is admissible to interpret the meaning of the language of the contract, or, where
its meaning is equivocal and obscure, to ascertain its nature
and extent, but not to vary its terms or introduce new conditions, or authorize *the doing of acts which are in direct contravention of its provisions.*

"From these considerations," said the court, "it is obvious, and, indeed, it seems to be a necessary consequence
from them, that the general proposition stated by the court,
'that if the defendant caused the shares of stock belonging
to the plaintiff to be transferred to himself, in such a way
and under such circumstances that they were not afterwards
to be traced or distinguished from other shares held by
the defendant, such a transfer, if made without the plaintiff's authority, could not be justified by any usage to that
effect among Brokers,' was correct. And, having thus
violated his duty by making a disposition of the stock which
was unauthorized and unjustifiable, he became immediately
responsible for the value of the property with which he had
been intrusted. It was, in effect, a conversion of it to his own
use. It is no defence to a claim arising under an unlawful conversion of property by such an unauthorized proceeding as
this, that the defendant was, at all times afterwards, either
actually possessed of, or had the means of immediately obtaining, other shares of stock in the same company of equal value
with those disposed of, which he was ready and intended,
whenever called upon, to substitute for those belonging to
the plaintiff which he had disposed of. The misappropriation had already taken place, the wrong had been done, and
the right to an adequate remedy had already accrued. The
shares which the plaintiff had owned could no longer be
identified, and there was no pretense, therefore, that they

could ever be restored to him.   He was not bound to take others in their stead, but was entitled to recompense for those which had been unlawfully taken from him."

We have set out thus fully the views of the court in this case because, although the general result reached in the case may be correct, this reasoning directly conflicts with the New York cases, in which it is held that a Broker purchasing shares on margin, or speculatively, is not bound to keep on hand the identical stock purchased, but that he fulfils his duty to his Client by having ready to deliver, upon demand, similar shares of stock—there being no difference between them, one share being equal in value to the other.[1]

In Pickering vs. Demeritt[2] the court intimated that it would be very difficult to support a usage by which a Broker employed to purchase stock might, without the knowledge of his principal, buy the stock of himself.   In another case[3] it was held that a certificate of stock expressing on its face to be " transferable only on the books of the company by the holder thereof in person, or by a conveyance in writing recorded on said books, and surrender of this certificate," and transferred in blank upon its back, is not a negotiable instrument.   The certificate was in the name of " E. Carter, Trustee."   In this case it was attempted to be shown that it was usual with dealers in the stock market to deliver, by way of sale or pledge, certificates of stock with a blank transfer upon the back ; that it is usual for holders of certificates of stock transferred in blank to fill them up by inserting the name of some person as transferee or purchaser ; that it is a matter of common occurrence for certificates of stock to be

[1] See this subject discussed in Ch. III. p. 252.
[2] 100 Mass. 416.
[3] Shaw vs. Spencer, 100 Mass. 382; cited and approved in Fisher vs. Brown, 104 id. 261.

issued in the name of some other person as trustee ; that certificates of stock issued to a designated person as trustee are constantly bought and sold in the stock market by a simple endorsement of the certificate by the person named as the holder, without inquiry as to the authority by which, or to the use or purpose for which, the transfer was made. But the judge, at the trial, ruled that the propositions were immaterial and inadmissible, and the ruling was sustained on appeal.[1] The court said : " A usage to disregard one's legal duty, to be ignorant of a rule of law, and to act as if it did not exist, can have no standing in the courts."

Again, it was held in the same State[2] that the order of a Client to a Broker to buy stock deliverable at any time, at buyer's option, in sixty days, does not authorize the Broker to buy the stock himself at thirty days, and deliver it to his customer at the end of sixty days at an increased price and interest, besides the usual commissions, and that a usage of Brokers so to do is bad ; and that an exchange of bought and sold notes between the Broker and the Client, and the giving of his note by the latter in payment for the stock, in

---

[1] An offer to prove a similar custom was ruled out in Pennsylvania in the case of Aull vs. Colket, 2 W. N. C. 322; 33 Leg. Int. 44; compare with these authorities the English case of Goodwin vs. Robarts, L. R. 10 Ex. 76, where it is held that negotiability may be established by usage. And see also Denny vs. Lyon, 38 Pa. St. 98, where the custom was held vicious. See, however, contra, Pratt vs. Tilt, 28 N. J. Eq. 479; Jones on Pledges, 2d ed. p. 487, and cases cited. And see also Ryman vs. Gerlach, 153 Pa. St. 197. But it has been recently held in Bank vs. Taliaferro, 72 Md. 169, that evidence of such a custom was properly excluded, as no such usage could change the legal character of a power of attorney merely to sell, and authorize the attorney to pledge the securities for his own debt, a result not contemplated by the party who executed the power. And in Allen vs. St. Louis National Bank, 120 U. S. 20, a similar usage between banks and cotton Brokers in St. Louis was also rejected. And see Bank vs. Bank, L. R. 20 Q. B. D. 232.

[2] Day vs. Holmes, 103 Mass. 306.

ignorance of the Broker's conduct, was not a ratification of his acts.

The court said : " The usage alleged by the plaintiffs to ex-ist among Stock-brokers in Boston cannot avail them.   There are many forcible objections to its validity ; but a conclusive one is, that it is against *sound policy and good morals*.   It authorizes the Broker, in his discretion, to disregard his in-structions, and, instead of acting solely in the interests of his principal, to speculate upon the transaction for his own benefit.   It creates in an agent an interest adverse to his principal, and is inconsistent with his duty and the obliga-tions which the law imposes upon him when he enters into the contract of agency.   Such a usage, *unknown to the prin-cipal*, cannot be supported."   The court cited the earlier case of Pickering vs. Demeritt.[1]   While the *result* reached in this case may be correct,[2] the ground upon which it is put does not seem to be tenable, for the court intimates that if the usage had been known to the principal it might have been supported ; yet the ground of its rejection is, that it is against sound policy and good morals.   If the usage be against pub-lic policy, or *contra bonos mores*, the courts would reject it, whether known to the principal or not, just as they would reject an express agreement under the same circumstances. The result of such a usage would be to convert a Broker into a principal, and to make him a seller instead of an interme-diary.   And if parties agree, and all the circumstances are fair and free from fraud, there would seem to be no element of morals or public policy to prevent such a transaction. Agents or Brokers may deal directly with their principals the same as third persons, and it is only where the Broker

[1] 100 Mass. 416.   [2] It is fully sustained in Robinson vs. Mollett, infra, p. 471.

acts in a dual character that the law is shocked and his transactions vitiated.

So a custom of Stock-brokers, when they receive an order from a Client to purchase securities, to assume it themselves, instead of making contracts with third persons, is inadmissible.[1]

In the case of Oelricks vs. Ford [2] it was held that where there was a written contract for the delivery of a certain number of barrels of flour, at a given price, to be delivered within a named time, at the seller's option, and evidence was offered by the purchaser of a usage existing that a margin should be put up, the court below was right in refusing to allow this evidence to go to the jury, because it was too indefinite and uncertain to establish a usage.

And in Clews vs. Jamieson [3] a rule of the Chicago Stock Exchange by which, when sales of the same kind of securities are made by different Brokers, and the latter's accounts are balanced by other transactions, a substitution of buyer and seller is made, and that the principals are to conform to such rule, was held not to bind a principal in so far as to compel him to sell at a lower figure than that at which he authorized his Broker to sell, nor to compel the purchaser to buy, although the Brokers would be bound by the rule. In Municipal Investment Co. vs. Industrial & Gen. Trust Co. [4] it was held that a usage of London bond dealers which empowered them, after an absolute sale of securities, to control litigation which might affect their validity, and charge the costs thereof to their customers,

[1] Commonwealth vs. Cooper, 4 Mass. L. R. (May 4, 1881) No. 21; s. c. 15 Am. Law Rev. 360 (May, 1881).

[2] 23 How. (U. S.) 49; see also Curtis vs. Gibney, 59 Md. 155.

[3] 89 Fed. 63. See Kent vs. Woodhull, 55 N. Y. Super. Ct. 311.

[4] 89 Fed. Rep. 254.

30

would, without the consent of the customers, be unreasonable.

Evidence of a custom of St. Louis Bankers and Brokers that a sale of bonds with "past due" interest included interest accruing and not yet due, to date of sale, is inadmissible, unless the principal, living in Kansas city, know of it, and contracted in St. Louis in reference to it.[1]

A custom of mining Stock-brokers to charge an arbitrary sum for telegrams has been held to be unreasonable.[2]

(b.) In England.

Although formerly the courts in England were more liberal in sustaining the usages of Stock-brokers, the tendency for the past nearly quarter of a century has been the other way, and the number of such usages rejected by the English courts nearly double those which have not been sustained by the American decisions.

Stock transferred to secure advances, and which stock was, by the pledgee, transferred to third persons by way of loan, was in In re Dennison[3] held a sale as of the date of the latter transfer, so as to charge the pledgee with the then price, although the contention of the pledgee was that such loans of stock were never considered sales.

In the case of Pearson vs. Scott[4] the plaintiffs, as executors, instructed S., a solicitor, to have some stock and shares sold, and authorized him to receive the proceeds of such sale. S. employed in the business the defendant, a Stock-broker, with whom he had at the time a current account

---

[1] Coquard vs. Bank of Kansas City, 12 Mo. App. 261.

[2] Marye vs. Strouse, 5 Fed. Rep. 483.

[3] 3 Ves. 552. See Andre vs. Crawford, 1 Br. P. C. 366.

[4] 38 L. T. (n. s.) 747.

for differences, upon private speculative transactions on the Stock Exchange. The defendant, having sold the property, paid a portion of the proceeds to S., and by his directions placed the balance to the credit of S. in the current account. S. never paid the balance to the plaintiffs, but subsequently absconded, and was declared a bankrupt. The court found that the defendant had notice of the agency of S. in the business, and it was held that the defendant was liable for the balance; and that a usage of the London Stock Exchange to the contrary would be unreasonable, and could not be upheld in the absence of knowledge of it on the part of the principal.[1]

In the case of Duncan vs. Hill [2] the plaintiffs, Brokers on the London Stock Exchange, bought for the defendant (who was not a member of the Stock Exchange) certain shares for the account of the 15th of July, 1870, and on that day, by his instruction, carried them over to the account of the 29th of July, and paid differences amounting to £1688. The defendant, and various others, principals of the plaintiff, not having paid the amount due from them in respect of contracts for the 15th of July, the plaintiffs became defaulters; and on the 18th, in conformity with the rules of the Stock Exchange, they were so declared, and their transactions were closed, and accounts were made up at the prices current on that day. On the closing of the accounts, a further sum became due from them in respect of differences upon the contracts carried over by them for the defendant. In an action to recover this sum and the £1688, held (reversing the decision of the court below) that the defendant was not liable

---

[1] To same effect are the American cases of Fisher vs. Brown, 104 Mass. 259; Evans vs. Waln, 71 Pa. St. 469.

[2] L. R. 8 Ex. 242. See Ellis vs. Pond, (1898) 1 Q. B. D. 426.

for anything beyond the £1688, there being no implied promise by a principal to his agent to indemnify him for loss
caused, not by reason of his having entered into the contracts,
which he was authorized to enter into by the principal, but
by reason of his own insolvency; although the transaction
had been carried out in accordance with the customs and
rules of the Stock Exchange, which, however, were not
proven to have been known to the defendant.   The court,
through Mr. Justice Blackburn, upon the subject of usage,
said : "It must be admitted that for any loss incurred by
the agent by reason of his having entered into such contracts,
according to such rules, unless they be wholly unreasonable,
and where the default is without any personal fault of his
own, he is entitled to be indemnified by his principal upon
an implied contract to that effect.   But it is argued that
where the agent, as in this case, is subjected to loss, not by
reason of his having entered into the contracts into which he
was authorized to enter by his principal, but by reason of a
default of his own—that is to say, as in this case, by reason
of his insolvency, brought on by want of means to meet his
other primary obligations—it cannot be said that he has
suffered loss by reason of his having entered into the contracts made by him on behalf of his principal, and couse-
quently there is no promise which can be implied on the part
of his principal to indemnify him, and in the present case
there certainly was no express promise to this effect. . . .
The plaintiffs' insolvency was, so far as regards the defendant, entirely the result of their own default." [1]

[1] But if the client chooses to accept the assignee's closing, he is
bound to indemnify the defaulting
Broker in respect of the difference
found by the assignee to be against
the Broker (Hartas vs. Ribbons,
58 L. J. Q. B. 187, distinguishing
Duncan vs. Hill, supra), and if there

In Tompkins vs. Saffery [1] it appeared that C. was a member of the Stock Exchange ; he notified the secretary that he was unable to meet his engagements on the Exchange. In such a case the rules of the Exchange prescribe the course to be followed : the defaulter ceases to be a member of the body ; two members of the Exchange act as official assignees of the defaulter ; a meeting of the creditors is called ; the defaulter (as he is required to do) makes his statement ; and the assembled creditors having decided what is to be done, the official assignees carry the decision into execution.   C. made his statement that he had no debts outside of the Exchange.   The creditors of C., members of the Stock Exchange, then consented to accept a composition ; and, to provide for a part of it, he, at the demand of the official assignees, gave them a check for £5000, then standing to

was privity of contract between the client and a jobber from whom the Broker bought or sold, the jobber might sue the client for completion, or vice versa. Beckhusen vs. Hamblet, 69 L. J. Q. B 431 ; 70 L. J. K. B. 600, in which case a jobber failed to recover by reason of the want of privity between him and the client occasioned by the Broker lumping several orders besides his client's in the one contract, and a usage of the Stock Exchange to the contrary, was held not proved, but in Scott vs. Godfrey, 70 L. J. K. B. 954, such a usage was held established and it was also held that it was reasonable.   See also May vs. Angeli, 13 Times L. R. 568, reversed on other grounds, 14 T. L. R. 551.   In Anderson vs. Beard, 69 L. J. Q. B. 610, it was held that the customer had an option to close with the jobber at the "hammer price," but in Levitt vs. Hamblet, 5 Com. Cas. 326 ; 6 ib. 79, it was held that no such option existed.
[1] L. R. 3 App. Cas. 213.   Tompkins vs. Saffery was considered in Richardson vs. Storment, Todd & Co., 69 L. J. Q. B. 369, in which it was held that the "assets" (Stock Exchange Rule 176) to be collected by the official assignee meant the defaulter's entire assets, and not merely the Stock Exchange assets, and that the transfer of a part thereof, with the intention to transfer all, was a cessio bonorum empowering the assignee to sue for recovery of the entire, without setting off a debt of the defaulter to defendants, who had been Stockbrokers and were well acquainted with the rules.

his credit in the Bank of England.   It afterwards appeared
that C. owed debts to a number of outside creditors and was
declared a bankrupt.   The trustee in bankruptcy, on behalf
of these creditors, claimed this sum from the official assignee
of the Stock Exchange, and the court decided that the
trustee was entitled to claim it, for the action of C. in paying
it to the official assignees amounted to a *cessio bonorum*, and
constituted an act of bankruptcy ; and that the rules of the
Stock Exchange as to defaulting members of the body, are
the rules of a domestic forum, which have no influence on
the rights of those who are not amenable to the jurisdiction
of that body.   They cannot, therefore, govern the rights of
the general creditors of a defaulting member.[1]

[1] See also Ex parte Neilson, 3 De
G. M. & W. 560, note, where Skir-
row, Com., said: "The rules of the
Stock Exchange are inoperative
that interfere with the law of the
land." It has been also held that
the rules of the Stock Exchange as
to defaulting members, do not prevent a creditor, a member of the
Exchange, who has received a dividend from the official assignee, from
suing for the balance of his debt
(Ex parte Ward, 51 L. J. Ch. 752;
Ratcliffe vs. Mendelsohn, 71 L. J.
K. B. 984), or from instituting bankruptcy proceedings.   In re Mendelsohn, (1903) 1 K B. 216.   In Ex
parte Ward, just cited, also it appeared that there was a rule (54)
which prevented a Stock Exchange
creditor from suing at law without
the consent of the other Stock Exchange creditors, which consent had
been obtained.   Jessel, M. R. said:
"If they (the creditors) had not assented, it does not appear to me

that that would destroy the debt."
Cotton, L. J., said the rule was applicable, but no question arose, as
the assent had been obtained. · The
question was not raised in the second
case just cited.

In Levitt vs. Hamblet, 6 Com.
Cas. 79; 5 ib. 326, it was held that
Rules 53, 54 and 177 of the London
Stock Exchange, although binding
upon its members, did not bind outsiders.   Rule 53 provided that the
Exchange in its dealings would only
recognize members.   Rule 54 contained certain inhibitions as to enforcing claims, and Rule 177 had
reference to a defaulting member.
A usage amongst Brokers to settle
in account was held not to bind
outsiders.   Anderson vs. Sutherland, 13 Times L. Rep. 163.   See
also Crossley vs. Magniac, (1903) 1
Ch. 594 (supra, p. 459) in which the
court said that a custom of London
Stock Exchange. Brokers to debit
country Broker's accounts with the

But the case in which the extent of usages in controlling contracts was most thoroughly considered was that of Robinson vs. Mollett,[1] which we have before referred to. There R., a merchant of Liverpool, gave orders to a tallow-broker in London to buy certain quantities of tallow for him. The Broker did not buy the specified quantity from any person, though he sent bought notes in the usual form —"Bought of A. on your account;" but both before and after the order he bought from various persons, in his own name, large quantities of tallow, proposing to allot to R. the quantities R. had desired to be bought. On R.'s refusal to accept, the Broker sold the tallow, and brought an action for the differences.   Held, that though the evidence showed such a mode of dealing to be the usage in the London tallow market, the action was not maintainable against a principal who did not appear to have had knowledge of its existence. A custom in a particular market, that a Broker who has purchased and is purchasing goods of a particular kind, in his own name, may take portions of those goods and supply

proceeds of stock of the latter's clients was not proved, and, even if proved, was unreasonable, in so far as it would relieve an agent from his obligation to his principal, who, in this case, had given a power of attorney to the London Brokers. The latter might be justified in paying the country Broker, if he were so authorized by the client, in cash or by check, but not in debiting his account in running account, and mixing it up with other transactions. In Blackburn vs. Mason, 68 Law T. 510, such a custom was also held unreasonable.

A usage of the London Stock Ex-change to treat share certificates, with transfer executed in blank, as negotiable instruments, was held not binding, as they were intended to pass by transfer only.   London and County Bank vs. London and River Plate Bank, L. R. 20 Q. B. D. 232; 21 ib. 535.   See Bank vs. Hepworth, 30 Ch. D. 36; France vs. Clark, 26 Ch. Div. 257; Williams vs. Colonial Bank, 38 Ch. Div. 388; aff'd 15 App. Cas. 267; Lindley on Companies, 6th ed. 656, et seq.

[1] L. R. 7 H. L. Eng. & I. App. Cas. 802.   See also Johnston vs. Usborne 11 A. & E. 549.

them to principals who have employed him in his character
of Broker to buy such goods for them, is one of a peculiar
nature, and cannot be supported as against a principal not
proved to have been acquainted with it when he gave the
order.[1]

The principle of the decision in Robinson vs. Mollet was
followed in Hamilton vs. Young,[2] in which case a usage
of the Dublin Stock Exchange by which a Stock-broker, entitled to dispose of stock or shares of a customer for non-
payment of money due to him by the customer, might, instead of selling the stock or shares, take over to himself, at
the market price of the day, such portion of the stock, as
would be necessary to meet the demand, or a forced sale
whereof would prejudice the price to the disadvantage of
the customer, was held to be more unreasonable even than
the usage in Mollet vs. Robinson.   Although no improper or
unfair dealing was imputed to defendant Broker, the court
said : " The case requires to be disposed of on higher and
more general grounds than either actual fraud committed
or unfair profit made, and on those rules of equity, which
it would be dangerous to disturb or infringe."

In the case of Neilson vs. James [3] a Stock-broker was employed by the registered owner of certain shares to sell them,
which he subsequently did to a jobber, but the bought and
sold notes did not, in accordance with a custom of the
Bristol Stock Exchange, give the name of the registered
owner as required by statute, thus rendering the contract of
sale void.   The bank stopped before name day, and the
purchaser, named by the jobber, repudiated the purchase.
The court held that the custom was both unreasonable and

[1] See also Langton vs. Waite, L.
R. 6 Eq. 165.

[2] L. R. 7 Ir. 269.
[3] 9 Q. B. Div. 546.

illegal, and for the breach of duty committed by the Broker, awarded the owner, as damages, the price for which the
shares were sold. It did not appear in that case that the
plaintiff knew of the custom, and the judgment of the court
is on the assumption that he was ignorant of it, for Brett,
L. J., says, "the plaintiff is only bound by such a custom as
is both reasonable and legal, for to that extent only can a
person who is ignorant of a custom be assumed to acquiesce
in, and be bound by, it." This decision was followed in
Perry vs. Barnett,[1] in which case in was shown that the
Client was ignorant of the custom, but in a similar state
of facts it was held in Seymour vs. Bridge,[2] that, as the
Client had many prior transactions on the Stock Exchange,
and was acquainted with the custom, he was bound by it.
In Coates vs. Pacey[3] the contract note did not give the number of the shares as required by statute, and there was a
verdict for the defendant Client, but in that case no evidence
of the custom was given. The Court of Appeals affirmed
the decision[4] on the ground that the Brokers had not acted
in accordance with the authority given to them, which was
to make a valid contract.

In conclusion we think that an examination of the American cases will show that the effect of the usages of Stock-
brokers upon contracts made upon the Exchange have not
been sufficiently considered or applied.

The system of business transacted between Stock-brokers
and their Clients is so novel when contrasted with the
ordinary relation of principal and agent, the business is
generally despatched with such marvellous promptness, and

[1] 14 Q. B. Div. 467; 15 Q. B. Div.
388.
[2] 14 Q. B. Div. 460.
[3] 8 T. L. R. 351.
[4] 8 T. L. R. 474.

its results very often involve sums of such great magnitude, that, in a contest where either the Broker or the Client seeks to be relieved from the responsibilities of his position, the usages of the Exchange, when fully proved, should play an important part, especially in the absence of an express agreement; and even if these usages seem at times to intrench upon abstract principles of law, it should be remembered that the business of dealing in shares upon speculation is a comparatively new one, full of legal anomalies, and that it should not be too strongly governed by rules that were made for a different and simpler condition of business in times long since passed.

CHAPTER V.

STOCK-JOBBING.

I. Dealings in Stocks at Common-law.

At common-law there is nothing illegal in the sale of the shares or scrip of a corporation.[1] They are treated the

---

[1] Barklay's Case, 26 Beav. 177; Aston's Case, 4 De G. & J. 320; Harrison vs. Heathorn, 6 Man. & G. 81; Tempest vs. Kilner, 2 C. B. 300, 308; Bagge's Case, 13 Beav. 162; Noyes vs. Spaulding, 27 Vt. 429; Chitty on Cont. (11th ed.) 1011, 1012, note (*d*). But in England, by statute 7 & 8 Vict. c. 110, the sale of shares of certain named companies was prohibited until the company had obtained a certificate of complete registration. Even then sales made by any subscriber not registered as a shareholder were made illegal, § 26; see also Ex parte Neilson, 3 De G.

same as any other kind of property, and are subject to no
restrictions or limitations except such as are imposed from
time to time by acts of the legislature, as will be hereafter
noticed.

II. Stock-jobbing Acts.

Early in the reign of George the Second the speculation
in public stocks or securities became so prevalent, and as-

M. & G. 556; Morris vs. Cannan, 4
De G. F. & J. 582. This statute
was repealed, and the prohibitions
never extended to companies the
formation of which was commenced
before the 1st of November, 1844 (in
reference to which see Baker vs.
Plaskitt, 5 C. B. 262; Aston's Case,
27 Beav. 474), nor to railway or
other companies requiring the authority of Parliament (Young vs.
Smith, 15 M. & W. 121; Bousfield
vs. Wilson, 16 id. 185; Lawton vs.
Hickman, 9 Q. B. 563). Companies
formed since 1862 are now regulated
by the Companies Acts of 1862 and
1867, and their amending acts.

Some of the American decisions
holding that shares of stock are alien-
able at common law, are Sergeant
vs. Franklin Insurance Co., 25 Mass.
90; Heart vs. State Bank, 2 Dev.
Eq. (S. C.) 111; Brightwell vs. Mal-
lory, 10 Yerg. (Tenn.) 196; Allen
vs. Montgomery R. R., 11 Ala. 437,
451; Choteau Spring Co. vs. Harris,
20 Mo. 382; Cole vs. Ryan, 52
Barb 168; Mobile Mutual Insurance
Co. vs. Cullom, 40 Ala. 558; Boston
Music Hall Association vs. Cory,
129 Mass. 435.

It has also been held that if a
company, or a prospected company,
is itself illegal, the sale of its shares
or scrip is also illegal (Joseph vs.
Pebrer, 3 B. & C. 639; Buck vs.
Buck, 1 Gampb. 547). When the
business of a company is carried on
in the colonies, the fact that it is
registered in England does not
make it illegal. Hunt vs. Chamberlain (1896), 12 L. T. R. 186.
But there is nothing illegal in the
sale of shares in companies which
are being wound up. Rudge vs.
Bowman, L. R. 3 Q. B. 689. See
Emmerson's Case, 1 Ch. 433 (as to
enforcing a contract for the sale of
shares in a company in liquidation).

By the statute of 14 Geo. III.
c. 48, no insurance shall be made on
the life of any person, *or on any
other event* wherein the person for
whose use or benefit, or on whose
account, such policy shall be made
shall have an interest by way of
gaming or wagering. Under this
enactment it was decided, in Paterson vs. Powell (2 Moo. & S. 399; 9
Bing. 320), that an engagement, in
consideration of forty guineas, to
pay one hundred pounds in case
Brazilian should be at a certain
price on a certain day, subscribed
by several persons each for himself,
is a void wagering policy.

sumed so many different forms of gambling, that the whole business community became infected and demoralized by it. Accordingly, in 1734, a statute was enacted,[1] which by a subsequent statute in 1737[2] was made perpetual, entitled "An Act to Prevent the Infamous Practice of Stock-jobbing." This statute will hereafter be stated in full. It was enacted for the purpose of preventing gambling in the funds, by parties who never intended to buy or sell, but merely to speculate upon the future price of stock, by making what are called "time bargains," and compounding for differences. It was never intended to affect the *bona fide* sale of stock, where the stock was actually transferred, although the seller was not possessed of it at the time of making the contract.[3]

This act was called "Sir John Barnard's Act," after the name of the individual who was instrumental in procuring its passage. The preamble, which briefly summarizes the effects of stock-jobbing, was as follows: "Whereas, great inconveniences have arisen, and do daily arise, by the wicked, pernicious, and destructive practice of stock-jobbing, whereby many of his Majesty's good subjects have

[1] 7 Geo. II. c. 8.

[2] 10 Geo. II. c. 8.

[3] Addison on Cont. (2d Am. ed.) *122. In Chitty on Bills (11th Am. ed.), *92, note (e), a stock-jobbing transaction is defined as follows: "Neither buyer nor seller have any stock, but the buyer agrees nominally to buy of the seller stock (say £1,000) on a certain day. When that day arrives, if the stock is at a lower price than when the bargain was made, the buyer pays the seller as much *per cent.* on the £1,000 as the stock has fallen; but, if the stock has risen, the seller pays the buyer in a similar way. The sums so paid are called differences. In fact, a time bargain is a mere wager, the seller betting that the stock will fall, the buyer that it will rise." See Rawlings vs. Hall, 1 G. & P. 13, note (a). Whether a legal contract, giving a right of action, can arise out of illegal transactions, or by payments made on account of another in settling differences upon transactions within the Stock-jobbing Act, *quære.* Ex parte Daniels, 14 Ves. 191

been and are diverted from pursuing and exercising their lawful trades and vocations, to the utter ruin of themselves and families, to the great discouragement of industry, and to the manifest detriment of trade and commerce." The statute then enacts that all contracts and agreements upon which any premium shall be given or paid for liberty to put upon, or deliver, receive, accept or refuse any public or joint-stock or other public securities whatsoever, or any part, share, or interest therein, and also all wagers and contracts in the nature of wagers, and all contracts in the nature of puts and refusals, relating to the then present or future price or value of any such stocks or securities as aforesaid, shall be void; and all premiums or sums of money given, received, paid, or delivered upon any such contracts or agreements, or upon any such wagers, or contracts in the nature of wagers, shall be restored or repaid to the person who shall give, pay, or deliver the same, who shall be at liberty, within six months after the agreement, or laying the wager, to sue for and recover the same from the person receiving the same, etc." [1]

[1] The following is an interesting history of "time bargains," from Beawes, Lex. Mer. 482 (5th ed. 1792):

"Time Bargains.

"But if the business of Stock-Brokers was confined solely to buying and selling the real Property of their Employers in the Funds, there would not be Half the number that now follow this Profession; it is therefore necessary to take notice, that the interest which Foreigners have in our funds, particularly the Dutch, gave rise to Time Bargains —that is to say, to contracts for purchasing and selling any Quantity of Stock to be delivered or adjusted at a future time. The usual Times for which Bargains, founded on real Property, and intended to be settled *bona fide*, were made, were from three months to three months, four times within the year; viz. in February, May, August, and November; and those Periods of settling the accounts of such Time Bargains was called the Rescounters, from a Dutch mercantile term for adjusting Accounts Current between merchant and merchant. The Impossibility of ascertaining whether the

There were numerous decisions under "Sir John Barnard's Act," the most important of which have been classified under the following heads:

1. *Nature of Stock embraced in the Act.*—The act only applied to " public stocks," and not to railway and joint-stock shares.[1] It did not apply to time bargains in foreign funds;[2] nor were such agreements illegal at common

Commissions from abroad given by letters from Foreigners, or by their Correspondence here, to Brokers to buy and sell Stocks for Time were founded upon real Property or not, gave Birth to Stock-Jobbing, or Dealing in the Funds upon Speculation, and the Persons that play at this Game, for Gaming it is of the first Magnitude, whether Principals or Brokers, are called Stock Jobbers. They purchase or sell for a given time, frequently without being possessed of any property in the Funds they bargain for, merely upon speculation. For instance, A imagines that a Peace, or some other advantageous national Event, will raise the Price of any given Fund within the space of three months considerably above the price of the Day on which he makes his Time Bargain: On this Principle he gives his Broker Orders to buy a large Quantity to be taken and paid for three months from that date; when the time expires, if the Stock has risen according to his expectation, instead of taking it, for probably it has been bought of a person, who had it not to sell even, he receives from the Broker the Difference in money between the price on the day the Bargain was made, and the price at the expiration of the three months, and this is his Profit. If, on the Contrary, the Stock has fallen below the price of the day on which he purchased for three months, he must pay the Difference, and this will be a losing Account. It is computed that the Bargains on Stock Jobbing Accounts made in the course of a year exceed by many millions the transfers made at the Books of real Property, and the Conclusion is apparent that great Fortunes are made and lost by Stock Jobbing. It is to be observed likewise, that the Brokers job for their own account, which occasions frequently Failures at the Stock Exchange."

[1] Williams vs. Tyre, 18 Beav. 366; Hewitt vs. Price, 5 Sco. N. R. 229, and 4 Man. & G. 355; 3 Railw. Cas. 175; Ex parte Turner, 3 De G. & J. 46, and cases cited; Thacker vs. Hardy, L. R. 4 Q. B. Div. 685, 689; Noyes vs. Spaulding, 27 Vt. 429.

[2] Ellsworth vs. Cole, 2 M. & W. 31; 2 Gale, 220; Henderson vs. Bise, 3 Stark. 158; Wells vs. Porter, 3 Sco. 141; s. c. 2 Bing. N. C. 722; 2 Hodg. 78; Oakley vs. Rigby, 3 Sco. 194; s. c. 2 Bing. N. C. 732; 2 Hodg. 42; Robson vs. Fallows, 4 Sco. 43; s. c. 3 Bing. N. C. 392;

law.[1] The act was confined to the stocks of England, and not of other countries;[2] and time bargains in India funds were held valid upon appeal to the Privy Council.[3] But jobbing in *omnium* was within the statute.[4]

2. *Transactions under the Statute.*—The act did not apply where the seller was really possessed of the stocks intended to be transferred;[5] and it was sufficient if at the time of the sale, through the medium of a Broker, the principal was possessed of the stock, although his name was not disclosed by the Broker.[6] A person who had *omnium* was considered as potentially in possession of stock, and could legally contract to sell out *omnium* to be replaced by stock.[7]

So where C., being indebted to G. in £1,000, agreed to transfer within a given time £100 per annum, long annuity, at the then price, and in the meantime pay G. the dividends, and that the debt of £1,000 should constitute part of the purchase-money, but the stock was not purchased at the time, and there was a rise in the price of the same— held, that the agreement was not usurious or within the Stock-jobbing Act,[8] and there was nothing in the statute to prevent a loan of stock—i. e., a transfer of stock from A. to B. on the strength of an understanding by B. that the

3 Hodg. 41; Morgan vs. Pebrer, 4 Sco. 230; 3 Bing. N. C. 457; 3 Hodg. 3; Paterson vs. Powell, 9 Bing. 329; 2 Moo. & S. 399. See Bryan vs. Lewis, Ry. & M. 386; Lorymer vs. Smith, 1 B. & Cr. 3.

[1] Id.

[2] Id.

[3] Ramloll Thackoorseydass vs. Soojumnull Dhondmull, 12 Jur. 315.

[4] Brown vs. Turner, 7 T. R. 630; 2 Esp. 631; s. p., Olivierson vs. Coles, 1 Stark. 496.

[5] Saunders vs. Kentish, 8 T. R. 162; Tate vs. Wellings, 3 id. 531.

[6] Child vs. Morley, 8 id. 610.

[7] Olivierson vs. Coles, 1 Stark. 496.

[8] Clark vs. Giraud, 1 Madd. 511.

same stock, or a like amount of stock, should be transferred to A. at a future day.[1]

An executory contract to transfer stock of which the party was not possessed was, however, regarded as void and illegal, although the transaction did not fall within the mischief, as it certainly did not within the express prohibition, of the act, inasmuch as an actual transfer of the stock was intended.[2] So a contract to pay the difference which may become due on the settling-day on the sale of consols is void.[3]

In respect to the procedure under the act, the court held, in Windale vs. Fall,[4] that the six months in the first section meant lunar months, and no discovery lay where the cause of action arose prior to the expiration of six lunar months; and a plea of the Stock-jobbing Act to a bill for discovery of stock transactions was overruled, the second section of the act requiring parties to make a discovery whereon to found an action.[5]

The second section of the act—which enacted as follows: " That for the better discovery of the moneys or premiums which shall be given, paid, or delivered, etc., every person liable to be sued shall be obliged, etc., to answer under oath, etc., any bill of discovery in equity," etc.—only applied to discoveries as to moneys recoverable back, and not to the recovery of penalties under the fifth and eighth sections.[6]

In an action to recover damages against one who had re-

[1] Saunders vs. Kentish, 8 T. R. 162.

[2] Mortimer vs. McCallan, 9 M. & W. 636; 6 id. 70; 7 id. 20.

[3] Sawyer vs. Langford, 2 C. & K. 697.

[4] 3 Bro. C. C. 11.

[5] Bancroft vs. Wentworth, 3 Bro. C. C. 9, note.

[6] Bullock vs. Richardson, 11 Ves. 373.

fused to accept and pay for stock agreed to be sold to him, it was necessary to prove an actual transfer of the stock to some other person before the action brought; and the proof alone of a contract to sell to such other person before the action brought, though followed up by an actual transfer afterwards, was not sufficient to sustain the action.[1] But it seemed not to have been necessary for the plaintiff to show that he made such transfer on the next possible day after default made by the original contractor, though delay affected the damages.[2] The act did not compel a party in a court of law to give evidence criminating himself; and therefore, in an action on a bill at the suit of an endorser against the acceptor, it was held that the drawer, a Stock-broker, might refuse to give evidence that the consideration for it was Stock-jobbing differences, though such Broker was bound to produce his books.[3] A Stock-broker was held bound, however, to discover the names of the persons for whom he had purchased shares in a company which had not been incorporated, chartered, or registered.[4] Nor could such a Broker resist a discovery under 7 Geo. II. c. 8, by alleging the illegality of the transaction, no penalty being imposed by the act.[5]

But in Pritchett vs. Smart[6] the court refused to entertain an application by a defendant, in an action on a bill of exchange, to compel the plaintiff, as Stock-broker, to pro-

---

[1] Heckscher vs. Gregory, 4 East, 607. A different rule was, however, laid down in New York in the case of Vaupell vs. Woodward, 2 Sandf. Ch. 145, 146.

[2] Bordenave vs. Gregory, 5 East, 105; Dorriens vs. Hutchinson, 1 Smith, 420. Whether an action of assumpsit can be supported on stat-

ute 7 Geo. II. c. 8, see Billings vs. Flight, 2 Marsh. 124; 6 Taunt. 419; Billings vs. Polley, 2 id. 125 n.; 6 Tuant. 422.

[3] Rawling vs. Hall, 1 C. & P. 11; Thomas vs. Newton, 2 id. 606.

[4] Aston's Case, 27 Beav. 474.

[5] Williams vs. Trye, 18 Beav. 366.

[6] 7 C. B. 625.

duce his books kept pursuant to this section,[1] in order to enable the defendant to plead the statute.

3. *Actions for Money Used, etc., and Commissions in Stock-jobbing Transactions.*—Where, to an action of debt upon a bond, the defendant pleaded the act of 7 Geo. II. c. 8, that the plaintiff and one R. were jointly concerned in certain contracts contrary to that statute; that the plaintiff voluntarily paid the differences; and that the bond was given by the defendants for securing to the plaintiff R.'s proportion of that loss—on demurrer, the court was clearly of opinion that the plaintiff was entitled to recover the amount which he had paid under the special authority of R., though for an illegal purpose.[2]

Upon the authority of the last-named case, the court, in Petrie vs. Hanney,[3] held, against the opinion of Lord Kenyon, that where two persons engaged jointly in an illegal stock-jobbing transaction, and incurred losses, and employed a Broker to pay the differences, and one of them, with the privity and consent of the other, repaid the whole sum to the Broker, he might recover a moiety from the other as money paid to his use, notwithstanding the statute 7 Geo. II. c. 8, on the ground that the defendant had expressly authorized the plaintiff to make the payment for him.

But these cases were afterwards departed from, and are no longer regarded as authority in England.[4]

---

[1] § 9 of act.

[2] Faikney vs. Reynous, 4 Burr. 2069; 1 W. Black. 633, and cases cited note (*n*), where this case is considered as overruled.

[3] 3 T. R. 418.

[4] See 2 Chitty on Cont. (11th Am. ed.) 896 and 897, citing McBlair vs. Gibbs, 17 How. (U S.) 232, 236;

Armstrong vs. Toler, 11 Wheat. 258; also Ex parte Mather, 3 Ves. Jun. 373; Aubert vs. Maze, 2 B. & P. 371; Brown vs. Turner, 7 T. R. 630; Booth vs. Hodgson, 6 T. R. 405; Steers vs. Lashley, id. 61; Mitchell vs. Cockburn, 2 H. Bl. 379, and other cases cited in Cannan vs. Bryce, 3 B. & Ald. 181. And see

Thus in Thwaite vs. Warner,[1] where parties were engaged in stock-jobbing transactions, in violation of the statute, the court held that one of them would not be permitted to maintain an action against the other to recover money paid to a Broker under such transactions.

And the direct question was at issue in Cannan vs. Bryce,[2] where it was decided that money lent, and applied by the borrower for the express purpose of paying or compounding differences on illegal stock-jobbing transactions to which the lender was no party, cannot be recovered back by him in an action for money had and received.[3]

So, there are several cases in which the results of stock-jobbing transactions were represented by bills, checks, or other written instruments, and the courts have concurred in the above rule of law.

In Ex parte Bulmer[4] promissory notes were given by a Stock-broker for the balance of an account of money advanced to him to be employed in stock-jobbing transactions, contrary to the statute. Part of the consideration consisted of the profits of these transactions. Proof under his bankruptcy was restrained to the residue—viz., the money received which he had applied to his own use. So a bill given for the amount of stock-jobbing differences was held void in the hands of an endorsee with notice,[5] and where it had been endorsed for value after it became due.[6] And a bond given to an endorsee

---

also opinion of Abbott, C. J., id. 183, and cases cited and commented upon in Paley on Agc. by Lloyd, 119 n. (*t*). See also remarks of Church, C. J., in Woodworth vs. Bennett, 43 N. Y. 278.

[1] Esp. N. P. Dig. 88.

[2] 3 B. & Ald. 179.

[3] See also McKinnel vs. Robinson, 3 M. & W. 434.

[4] 13 Ves. Jun. 313.

[5] Steers vs. Lashley, 6 T. R. 61; 1 Esp. 166.

[6] Brown vs. Turner, 7 T. R. 630; 2 Esp. 631.

in lieu of a promissory note orginally given for an illegal stock-jobbing transaction, of which the endorsee had notice before he took the bond, was held void.[1] But a bill of exchange or promissory note given upon a stock-jobbing transaction is valid in the hands of a party who afterwards took it, before it was due, for value, and without notice of the illegal consideration.[2]

To a declaration for work done, commissions, and for money paid, a plea that the plaintiff was a stock and share Broker, and as such made contracts with persons for the defendant by way of wagering, contrary to 8 and 9 Vict. c. 109, under the semblance of pretended sales, respecting the future market price of public and other stock, shares, and scrip, whereby the defendant was to receive or pay the difference between the price of the said public stock on the days on which the contracts were made and the price on certain future days, according as the price had become lower or higher; and that the work was done, and the commission claimed in respect of the making such contracts, and the money paid in discharging the differences which had become payable—held, first, that this was no defence under the statute of Vict.; secondly, that the plea disclosed no defence under the Stock-jobbing Act, as it was not alleged that each contract related to *public stock*.[3]

In an action by the assignees of a bankrupt, for money

---

[1] Amory vs. Meryweather, 4 D. & Ry. 86; 2 B. & Cr. 573.

[2] Day vs. Stuart, 6 Bing. 109; 3 M. & P. 334; Greenland vs. Dyer, 2 M. & Ryl. 422; Amory vs. Meryweather, 2 B. & C. 573; 4 D. & R. 86. See Rawlings vs. Hall, 1 C. & P. 11, as to evidence, etc.

[3] *Query*, whether the defence under the latter act was open on the plea, reference being expressly made to the other act (Knight vs. Fitch, 15 C. B. 566; 1 Jur. [n. s.] 526; 21 L. J. C. P. 122).

received by the defendant for their use, it appeared that the defendant was official assignee of the Stock Exchange for the management of the estates of those members who, being unable to fulfil their engagements on the Stock Exchange, became defaulters. Before the receipt of the money, the bankrupt, a Stock-broker and member of the Stock Exchange, was declared a defaulter, having at the time contracts open with the members of the Stock Exchange, which had the form of legal contracts, for the sale and delivery of stock; but there was no intention that stock should be delivered, and the contracts were to be settled by the payment of differences. Under the rule of the Stock Exchange, the defendant collected the differences upon the contracts upon which the bankrupt was a gainer, and, before notice of an act of bankruptcy, distributed among members to whom he was indebted for differences all said money except a small amount, which was paid over after he was adjudged a bankrupt to the treasurer of a fund for decayed members, according to the rules of the Stock Exchange. Held, that the action could not be maintained. As to the money paid over before the adjudication of the bankruptcy, it was not money had and received by the defendant to the use of assignees of the bankrupt; and as to the money paid over after the adjudication of bankruptcy, the contracts, as well as the payment and receipt of the differences, being illegal by 7 Geo. II. c. 8, neither the bankrupt nor his assignees could maintain an action to enforce the contracts or recover the sums paid; and that the differences were not paid to the defendant as the agent of the bankrupt, but for the purpose of being distributed among his Stock Exchange creditors.[1]

[1] Nicholson vs. Gooch, 5 El. & Bl. 137. For actions by Brokers for 999; 2 Jur. (n. s.) 303; 25 L. J. C. P. commissions and money laid out in

In June, 1860, the act of George II. was totally repealed, the text of the repealing act clearly indicating that, after a trial of one hundred and twenty-five years, the English people were satisfied that dealings in the public securities should be left untrammeled, even at the cost of having business men speculate in them. The preamble to the act is as follows: "Whereas an act was passed, in the seventh year of the reign of King George the Second, chapter eight, to prevent the practice of stock-jobbing, and by another act, passed in the Tenth year of the said King's reign, chapter eight, the said first-mentioned act was made perpetual. And whereas the said acts impose unnecessary restrictions on the making of contracts for the sale and transfer of public stocks and securities, and it is therefore expedient to repeal the same: Be it enacted by the Queen's Most Excellent Majesty, by and with the advice and consent of the Lords Spiritual and Temporal, and Commons, in the present Parliament assembled, and by the authority of the same, as follows: I. From and after the passage of this act, the said two several acts before mentioned shall be, and the same are hereby repealed."[1]

The repeal of the act of George II. of course immediately swept away all restrictions upon dealings in the public stocks, and placed persons in reference thereto in the same condition as if they were dealing in shares of private or other corporations. But it should be stated in this connection that there is an existing English statute relative to the sale or transfer of shares in any joint-stock banking

transactions contrary to act relating to wagers, see post, p. 551.

[1] 23 & 24 Vict. c. 28. See also

Thacker vs. Hardy, L. R. 4 Q. B. D. 685, 688; Lathavo vs. Barber, 6 T. R. 70.

company, the substance of which is given below.[1] The object of this enactment is to prevent runs on banks, which might be occasioned by a fall in the price of their shares resulting from "short" sales or gambling transactions.

And by the Bankruptcy Act, 1890, section 8 (extending the principle of the Bankruptcy Act, 1849, section 201), the discharge of a bankrupt may be refused or suspended, if he has brought on his bankruptcy by rash and hazardous speculations.[2]

In the State of New York an act against stock-jobbing is found among the Revised Laws passed in 1812, the text of which is:

"That all contracts, written or verbal, hereafter to be made, for the sale or transfer, and all wagers concerning the prices present or future, of any certificate or evidence of debt due by or from the United States or any separate

---

[1] By 30 Vict. c. 29, § 1, it is enacted that all contracts made after the 1st day of July, 1867, for the sale or transfer of any shares, stock, or interest in any joint-stock banking company in England or Ireland, constituted under or regulated by any act of Parliament, royal charter, or letters-patent, issuing shares or stock, transferable by any written instrument, shall be void unless such contract sets forth in writing the distinguishing numbers of such shares, stock, or interest on the register; or, if there is no register, the person in whose name such shares, stock, or interest shall at the time of making such contract stand in the books of the company. Although a custom of the Stock Exchange not to give names or numbers in the contract note as required by this act has been declared illegal (see chapter on Usages) the contract itself is merely void. A Broker who disregarded the act was held liable in damages to his client (Neilson vs. James, 9 Q. B. D. 546), and a purchaser, to whom shares were transferred, was held bound to indemnify the vendor as to calls (Loring vs. Davis, 32 Ch. D. 625). See also Perry vs. Barnett, 15 Q. B. D. 388; 14 Q. B. D. 467; Seymour vs. Bridge, 14 Q. B. D. 460; Coates vs. Pacey, 8 T. L. R. 351, 474; Mitchell vs. City of Glasgow Bank, 4 App. Cas. 624; Casey vs. Bentley, 1 Ir. Rep. 376.

[2] Ex parte Rogers, 13 Q. B. D. 438.

state, or any share or shares of the stock of any bank, or any share or shares of the stock of any company established, or to be established, by any law of the United States, or any individual state, shall be, and all such contracts are hereby declared to be absolutely void; and both parties are hereby discharged from the lien and obligation of such contract or wager; unless the party contracting to sell and transfer the same shall at the time of making such contract be in the actual possession of the certificate, or other evidence of such debt or debts, share or shares, or to be otherwise entitled in his own right or duly authorized or empowered by some person so entitled to transfer the said certificate, evidence, debt or debts, share or shares, so to be contracted for. And the party or parties who may have paid any premium, differences, or sums of money in pursuance of any contract, hereby declared to be void, shall and may recover all such sums of money, together with damages and costs, by action on the case, in assumpsit for money had and received to the use of the plaintiff, to be brought in any court of record." [1]

This statute was re-enacted by the Revised Statutes of 1830 in the language given in the notes.[2] There were a number of decisions under these New York statutes, a reference to the principal of which will be found pertinent in this connection.

The act did not apply to sales of distributive shares of the

---

[1] 2 R. L. 187, § 18; Frost vs. Clarkson, 7 Cow. (N. Y.) 26.

[2] "All contracts for the sale of stocks are void unless the party contracting to sell the same shall at the time of making such contracts be in the actual possession of the certifi- cates of such shares, or to be other- wise entitled thereto, in his own right, or to be duly authorized, by some person so entitled, to sell the certificates or shares so contracted for" (1 Rev. Stat. 710, § 6).

effects of a dissolved corporation, such shares not being stock, but were non-negotiable things in action.[1] It was likewise held not to apply to any other kind of property than stocks.[2]

In the case of Frost vs. Clarkson,[3] where a vendor, by contract in writing, agreed to transfer one hundred shares of stock in sixty days, and it appeared that he owned that number at the time of making the contract, but in the interval between the contract and time of transfer sold sixty shares, leaving him the owner of only forty shares, it was decided that the statute[4] did not avoid such a contract, and that it only applied where the vendor did not own the stock at the time the agreement was made ; that the sale was not of any particular one hundred shares, but any one hundred shares in the company ; and if the vendor is ready to receive a transfer and pay, any other one hundred shares may be procured in the market. Subsequently[5] the Court of Appeals held that where a Broker sold for his principal shares of a certain stock which neither owned at the time of the sale, deliverable at the option of the principal in thirty days —the transaction being illegal—the principal, under the maxim *in pari delicto potior est conditio defendentis*, could not recover from the Broker any differences to which he might otherwise be justly entitled ; and that section 8,[6] giving an action to recover back money paid or property delivered did not aid the plaintiff, as that section only applied to the parties who actually paid or delivered the money and to those

---

[1] James vs. Woodruff, 10 Paige, 541; aff'd 2 Den. 574, but opinion not reported.

[2] Cassard vs. Hinman, 1 Bosw. (N. Y.) 207.

[3] 7 Cow. (N. Y.) 26.

[4] 2 R. L. 187, § 18.

[5] Staples vs. Gould, 9 N. Y. 520.

[6] 1 Rev. Stat. 710.

who actually received it—viz., the Broker defendant, and the third person to whom the Broker had made the sale of the stocks. So it was further held that to avoid a contract as against the Stock-jobbing Act the burden of proof is upon the party alleging a violation to show that when the contracts were made the other party did not own, and was not authorized to sell, the stock contracted for;[1] that where a contract is valid on its face all the plaintiff has to do to entitle him to recover is to show a readiness and offer on his part and a refusal by the defendant; and that such a contract at common law and in the absence of statute being clearly valid, the courts will not presume that the party contracting to sell stocks was not the owner thereof for the purpose of rendering the contract void. The court refused to recognize a contrary doctrine laid down by the Supreme Court of Massachusetts in Stebbins vs. Leowolf,[2] which arose out of a contract made in the State of New York.[3]

But where one placed money in the hands of a Broker to indemnify him for any losses which might accrue upon the sale of stock, which the Broker was to make for him on time, in violation of the above statute, he can recover it back if the Broker has not paid it over, without notice of the illegality or not to pay.[4]

In Vaupell vs. Woodward[5] the question arose as to whether, in an action by a Broker against a purchaser for not accepting stock sold on time, it was not incumbent on the Broker to prove a resale before bringing his action.

[1] Dykers vs. Townsend, 24 N. Y. 57.

[2] 67 Mass. 143.

[3] See also Staples vs. Gould (decision below), 5 Sandf. (N. Y.) 411;

McIlvaine vs. Egerton, 2 Rob. (id.) 422.

[4] Cram vs. Stebbins, 6 Paige Ch. 124.

[5] 2 Sandf. Ch. 145, 146.

The argument in favor of this view was, that a Broker with 100 shares of a particular stock could make a dozen or more sales of 100 shares of that stock to as many different persons on time ; and on their failure to perform, might sustain a suit against them all, upon proof of his having owned the 100 shares; and that, if all the buyers should fulfil and demand their stocks, his 100 shares would not go far towards completing the contracts on his part. The English Stock-jobbing Act, it appeared, contained a provision requiring such a resale on time contracts. While the court admitted the cogency of this argument, it nevertheless overruled the same, and held that the statute contained no provision requiring a resale, and that the apparent defect could only be remedied by further legislation. In another case[1] it was further held, that a Broker who purchased for another by the express direction of the latter, and did not himself agree to sell, was not within the act. In this case there was no evidence that the sellers were not possessed of the stock when they agreed to sell it.[2]

It seems, however, that the statute of New York was not very efficacious in preventing " short sales" of stock,[3] and in the year 1858 it was repealed by an act which is herewith given in full :

" No contract, written or verbal, hereafter made for the purchase, sale, transfer, or delivery of any certificate, or other evidence of debt, due by or from the United States, or any separate state, or of any share or interest in the stock

---

[1] Genin vs. Isaacson, 6 N. Y. Leg. Obs. 213.

[2] See also Cassard vs. Hinman, 14 How. (N. Y.) Pr. 84; aff'd 1 Bosw. 207; Thompson vs. Alger, 53 Mass. 428, where the New York statute is construed.

[3] See remarks of Hoffman, J. in Cassard vs. Hinman, supra.

of any bank, or of any company incorporated under any law of the United States, or of any individual State, shall be void, or voidable, for any want of consideration, or because of the non-payment of any consideration, or because the vendor at the time of making such contract is not the owner or possessor of the certificate or certificates, or other evidence of such debt, share, or interest."[1]

By this act the selling of securities "short" is legalized, and the doctrine of the common law re-established.[2] The courts of New York have held that the effect of the repeal of the statute relating to stock-jobbing takes away the defence of illegality as to contracts made during its existence, precisely as if such statute had never been passed ; the theory of the law being that the repeal of a statute which makes contracts illegal on the ground of public policy, legalizes those entered into during its continuance, in violation of the same.[3] Nor is it necessary, in an action to recover damages for the non-performance of a contract for the purchase of stock, for the plaintiff to allege in his complaint that he was the owner of the stock at the time of making the contract, or that the contract was in writing.[4]

The effect of the repeal of the Stock-jobbing statute, however, was not to avoid the necessity of having a contract for the sale of shares of stock reduced to writing, within the Statute of Frauds. The latter statute is still in force, and

[1] Ch. 134, Laws, 1858, repealed by the Personal Property Law, and re-enacted in amended form therein (§ 22).

[2] Except in so far as it was abrogated, as to officers and directors of railroad corporations, by L. 1881, ch. 223, which made it a criminal offence for such officials to sell "short," but this law was repealed by the General Corporation Law, as amended in 1892.

[3] Washburn vs. Franklin, 35 Barb. (N. Y.) 599; s. c. 13 Ab. Pr. 140; rev'd 24 How. Pr. 515; 11 Ab. Pr. 93.

[4] Id.

unaffected to the extent, at least, of requiring such a contract to be in writing properly subscribed.[1]

In the State of Massachusetts[2] there is a law which declares that a contract for the sale or transfer of a certificate, or other evidence of debt due from the United States, or a State, or of any stocks, or any share or interest in the stock, of a bank, company, city, or village incorporated under a law of the United States, or a State, is void, unless the party contracting to sell or transfer the same is, at the time of making the contract, the owner or assignee thereof, or is authorized by the owner or assignee, or his agent, to make the sale or transfer. This statute has been before the courts for construction in several cases.[3]

In Durant vs. Burt[4] the court held that where a Client gave his Broker an order to purchase stock for him, and the Broker does so, in accordance with the instructions and the usages of the Stock Exchange, and the Client subsequently refuses to take the stock, should the Broker, after notice, sell it, the latter is entitled to recover the loss sustained, together with his commissions. The court further decided that the plea that the contract was illegal, because made by the Broker with another member of the Stock Exchange, in violation of the above statute, was no defence

---

[1] Johnson vs. Mulry, 4 Robt. (N. Y.) 401.

[2] Laws, 1836, ch. 279; Gen. Stat. Mass. ch. 105, § 6. Now re-enacted in Rev. Laws of 1901, Title XIII. ch. 74, § 7.

[3] Barrett vs. Mead, 92 Mass. 337; Barrett vs. Hyde, 73 Mass. 160; Durant vs. Burt, 98 id. 161; Price vs. Minot, 107 Mass. 49; Brown vs. Phelps, 103 id. 313, 314; Brigham vs. Mead, 92 Mass. 245. See also Stebbins vs. Leowolf, 57 Mass. 137; Thompson vs. Alger, 53 Mass. 428; opinion of Parker, C. J., in Howe vs. Starkweather, 17 Mass. 243; Sargent vs. Franklin Ins. Co. 25 Mass. 98. See also United States vs. Vaughan, 3 Binn. 394. See also, for other cases interpreting the Massachusetts statute, Rock vs. Nicholls, 85 Mass. 342; Colt vs. Clapp, 127 Mass. 476; and cases cited post.

[4] Supra.

to the action; especially where the purchasing Broker is not shown to have been aware of this fact, or to have been aware that the contract was illegal under the Statute of Frauds. The case of Brown vs. Phelps[1] also arose under the Stock-jobbing Statute of Massachusetts. There a Broker, employed to purchase stock, contracted for it in his own name with J. S., who owned it at the time, but had made a prior contract for its sale. The employer, for groundless reasons, repudiated the contract; but the Broker, having no knowledge of, or reason to suspect, the prior sale by J. S., paid for the stock when tendered to him. Held, that the statute[2] making void contracts for the sale of stocks not owned by the seller did not debar the Broker from recovering from his employer the amount so paid.

" The defendant," said the court, " contends that the case of Stebbins vs. Leowolf is a decisive authority against the plaintiff's claim in respect to these shares. That case related to a statute of the State of New York, but our own statute is substantially like it, and must receive the same construction. In that case the plaintiff had contracted to purchase the stocks as agent of the defendant; but he was conversant with all the facts and of the objections to the validity of the contract entered into by him, and volunteered to pay the claims of the vendors of the stock without any legal liability on his part. Under these circumstances, the court say that he must be taken to have paid the money in his own wrong, if the contract he entered into was in fact illegal. And they held that the burden of proof was on him to show a legal contract, in order to make a *prima facie* case. The decision was in conformity with the elementary law of agency, ac-

---

[1] 103 Mass. 313.   re-enacted in Rev. Laws of 1901,
[2] Gen. Stat. ch. 105, § 6, now tit. XIII. c. 74, § 7.

cording to which, if an agent knowingly pays money on an illegal contract, after it has been repudiated by his principal, he cannot thereby bind his principal. But in the present case no such knowledge of facts appears in the agreed statement. The plaintiffs contracted to purchase the shares of one who actually owned them. They were not bound to presume that he had previously contracted to sell them ; and there was nothing to put them on inquiry ; nor does it appear that they had any means of ascertaining, by the use of reasonable diligence, what private contracts Spencer had made with other persons."

Nor is an agreement to purchase stocks for another, and sell them again within a certain time, and share the profits, but bear alone any loss, within the statute.[1] And a contract for the sale of railroad stock by one who had originally pledged it, and of which the pawnee held the certificate, but which the pawnor had authorized the pawnee to sell whenever he had an opportunity, is not within the New York statute concerning stock-jobbing.[2]

A promissory note given in consideration of money paid by request of the maker to a Broker, for losses sustained in stock-jobbing, negotiated by the latter for the former, in violation of the statute, is valid ; but money paid for losses in stock-jobbing cannot be recovered back.[3] Nor can the payee of a check received in payment for shares, which were not owned by him at the time when he undertook to sell them, maintain an action thereon against the drawer.[4]

A promise by the holder of more than 300 shares in the stock of a corporation, to transfer 300 shares whenever he

---

[1] Barrett vs. Hyde, 73 Mass. 160.
[2] Thompson vs. Alger, 53 Mass. 428.
[3] Wyman vs. Fiske, 85 Mass. 238.
[4] Rock vs. Nichols, id. 342.

shall acquire enough shares to enable him to do so, and still retain a majority of all the shares in the corporation, is not within the statute.[1]

An interesting case arose in the Supreme Court of Massachusetts, in which the validity of speculations in selling certain stock "short" in New York was reviewed under the statute of that State. The case had been referred to an auditor. The facts showed that the plaintiffs in 1872 were partners as Brokers in New York. Prior to that time the defendants' testator, D., had employed and made sales and purchases of stock through them. On the 25th of October, 1872, the plaintiffs received and executed an order from D. to sell "short" 100 shares of the "common" stock of the Chicago and Northwestern Railway, and on the 26th they received and executed an order to sell another 100 shares. The first was sold at $76\frac{3}{8}$ per share and the latter at $82\frac{5}{8}$.

The auditor found that in "short" sales the seller is required neither to own nor part with the stock sold. The seller's Broker borrows the stock and pays the agreed price, generally in a certified check. The borrower or lender may at any time close the transaction, the one by tendering and the other by demanding the stock. If called for and not returned, the lender has a right to buy in the stock at the market price, and, in case of an advance, to charge the borrower with the difference. With this course D. was familiar. On November 23, 1872, O. & Co., of whom the plaintiffs had borrowed the stock, called for its return. Since November 20 the stock had been rapidly rising, and on the 21st, 22d, and 23d the plaintiffs "addressed" numerous letters and telegrams to D., asking him to come and settle or cover

---

[1] Price vs. Minot, 107 Mass. 49.

his margins. The plaintiffs received no reply, and they proceeded to act on D.'s previous general instructions—to use their discretion in the protection of his interests. On November 23, therefore, they bought 100 shares at $150, and, on November 25, 100 more at $175 per share, and with these 200 replaced the stock borrowed from O. & Co. The loss on the transaction was $16,625. The plaintiffs had a previous balance of $1,924.28 to the credit of D. The balance due them was, therefore, $14,700.72, and this sum, with interest, was sought to be recovered against D.'s estate. The defendants set up several defences. The first was that the sales were illegal ; if not illegal, that the plaintiffs failed to give due notice to D. to make his margin good (there being no evidence that the letters and telegrams were delivered), or that in default thereof the plaintiffs would buy in stock to replace that borrowed ; that if there was notice the plaintiffs were only bound to furnish "preferred" stock, which sold at $87.25 on November 23 and 25, instead of "common;" and that the plaintiffs bought stock for a less price in transactions of their own on the same day. There was also a declaration in set-off for the $1,924.28 had and received by the plaintiffs to the defendants' use. The auditor found that the plaintiffs were entitled to recover in the sum of $18,829.09, but the case was recommitted to him to report the evidence, which he did. Coming before the Supreme Court, the case was opened to a jury and the report of the auditor submitted. The defendants' counsel contended and argued that although such a transaction, if proved, was authorized by the statute of New York which permitted stock-jobbing and such "short" sales, still a court of Massachusetts was not bound by comity to enforce the contract here, there being an express statute of the State prohibiting such transactions, and, apart from such statute, that the transaction was contrary to public policy and good morals. It was contended and argued at length by the counsel for the plaintiffs that such a contract was not illegal, and that it could be enforced by the Massachusetts courts; that being valid in New York, where the contract was made, it could be enforced here, where the remedy is sought. In the New York case of Knowlton vs. Fitch,[1] the court held that, so long as these transactions are not prohibited by law, there is no reason for relieving either party from the responsibilities which he incurs by engaging in them. The court ruled that the action could not be maintained, and directed a verdict for the defendants.[2]

---

[1] 52 N. Y. 288.

[2] Leonard vs. Hart, N. Y. *Herald*, Oct. 2, 1877. Although a contract is void under the Massachusetts statute, a Stock-broker may recover moneys paid under such contract from his principal. Jones vs. Ames, 135 Mass. 431. The sale of shares before the date of delivery does not make the contract illegal, when the vendor had possession at the date of the contract. Pratt vs. American Bell Telephone Co., 141 Mass. 225. See Duchemin vs. Kendall, 149 Mass. 171; Meehan vs. Sharp, 151 Mass. 561. When a Stock-broker, a member of the Boston Stock Exchange bought stocks on a Saturday, and sold a portion of them the same day to another member, and on Monday, according to the custom of the Exchange, he received the certificates, and written memoranda of the sale and purchase were delivered, it was held that he had not violated the statute, and that the transaction was not gambling. Mann vs. Bishop, 136 Mass. 495.

An agreement between two persons to share equally in the profits and losses on stock then owned by one of them, is not within the statute, nor does the fact that it was bought by agents of the Brokers of the owner, who had not put up any margin, make it a wagering transaction, when by reason of other transactions, his credit with the Brokers was good. Bullard vs. Smith, 139 Mass. 492. .

When the Stock-broker had in his possession certificates for the number of shares of stock sold by him, and which he was duly authorized by his principal to sell, the case is not within the statute. Frazier vs. Simmons, 139 Mass. 531.

A similar statute also existed in Pennsylvania,[1] but it has been repealed.[2]

By the Revised Statutes of Illinois,[3] it is enacted that " whoever contracts to have or give to himself or another the option to sell or buy at a future time any grain or other commodity, stock of any railroad or other company, or gold, or forestalls the market by spreading false rumors to influence the price of commodities therein, or corners the market, or attempts to do so, in relation to any such commodities, shall be fined not less than $10 or more than $1,000, or confined in the county jail not exceeding one year, or both ; and all contracts made in violation of this section shall be considered gambling contracts, and void." [4]

[1] Act of May 22, 1841 (L. 1841, p. 398), § 6.

[2] For decisions under this statute, see Chillas vs. Snyder, 1 Phila. (Pa.) 289; Krause vs. Setley, 2 id. 32.

[3] Ch. 38, § 130 (Cothran's ed. 1881). See also Hurd's edition, (1901) p. 614, c. 38, § 130.

[4] See the able and interesting charge of Mr. Justice Jamieson to a grand jury of the criminal court of Chicago, October 12, 1881, given in full at p. 635, in which this statute is interpreted and discussed. The decisions under this act have been very numerous, and nearly all relate to dealings in grain, pork, and other like commodities.

In the following cases, such transactions have been held to be within the statute: Pickering vs. Cease, 79 Ill. 328; Webster vs. Sturges, 7 Ill. App. 560; Beveridge vs. Hewitt, 8 id. 467; Commercial Bank vs. Spaids, id. 493; Doxey vs. Spaids, id. 549; Ex parte Young, 6 Biss. 53; Colderwood vs. McCrea, 11 Ill. App. 543; Kreigh vs. Sherman, 105 Ill. 49; Brand vs. Henderson, 107 Ill. 141; Pearce vs. Foote, 113 Ill. 228; Osgood vs. Bauder, 75 Iowa, 550; McCormick vs. Nicholls, 19 Ill. App. 334; Coffman vs. Young, 20 Ill. App. 76; Higgins vs. McCrea, 116 U. S. 671; Carroll vs. Holmes, 24 Ill. App. 453; Griswold vs. Gregg, 24 Ill. App. 384; New York & Chicago Grain & Stock Exchange vs. Mellen, 27 Ill. App. 556; Wheeler vs. McDermid, 36 Ill. App. 179; Foss vs. Cummings, 149 Ill. 353; Samuels vs. Oliver, 130 Ill. 73; Pope vs. Hanke, 155 Ill. 629; Miles vs. Andrews, 40 Ill. App. 155; Watte vs. Costello, 40 Ill. App. 307; Powell vs. McCord, 121 Ill. 330; International Bank vs. Vankirk, 39 Ill. App. 23; Kennedy vs. Stout, 26 Ill. 133;

Statutes have also been enacted in several other states, prohibiting option contracts, dealings in futures or "on margin" or "bucket shop" transactions in stocks or commodities, where no delivery is intended.

Wright vs. Cudahy, 168 Ill. 86; Treat vs. Snydecker, 92 Ill. App. 458; Butler vs. Nohe, 98 Ill. App. 625; Pardridge vs. Cutler, 168 Ill. 504; Gardiner vs. Meeker, 169 Ill. 40; Kruse vs. Kennett, 181 Ill. 199; Walker vs. Johnson, 59 Ill. App. 448; Calumet Co. vs. Williams, 97 Ill. App. 365; Illinois Trust & Savings Bank vs. La Toushe, 101 Ill. App. 341; Brown vs. Alexander, 29 Ill. App. 626; Central Grain & Stock Ex. of Chicago vs. Bendinger, 48 C. C. A. 726.

Decisions in which dealings in grain and produce have been held not to be gambling within the statute are: Pixley vs. Boynton, 79 Ill. 351; Sanborn vs. Benedict, 78 Ill. 309; Walcott vs. Heath, id. 433; Cole vs. Milmaine, 88 id. 349; Gilbert vs. Gauger, 8 Biss. 214; Jackson vs. Foote, 11 Biss. 223; Miller vs. Bensley, 20 Ill. App. 528; White vs. Barber, 123 U. S. 392; Roche vs. Day, 20 Ill. App. 417; King vs. Luckey, 21 Ill. App. 132; Benson vs Morgan, 26 Ill. App. 22; Grubey vs. National Bank of Illinois, 35 Ill. App. 354; Ward vs. Vosburgh, 31 Fed. 12; Curtis vs. Wright, 40 Ill. App. 491; Hitchcock vs. Corn Exchange Bank, 40 Ill. App. 414; Brand vs. Lock, 48 Ill. App. 390; Fox vs. Steever, 55 Ill. App. 255; Minnesota &c. Co. vs. Whitebreast &c. Co., 160 Ill. 97; Lamson vs. Boyden, 160 Ill. 613; Hall vs. Barrett, 93 Ill. App. 642; Cothran vs. Ellis, 125 Ill. 496; Pearce vs. Rice, 142 U. S. 28; Warren vs. Scanlon, 59 Ill. App. 138; Dillon vs. McCrea, 59 Ill. App. 505; Barnett vs. Baxter, 64 Ill. App. 544; Bryan vs. Lamson, 88 Ill. App. 261; Clews vs. Jamieson, 182 U. S. 461; Riebe vs. Hellman, 69 Ill. 19; Scanlon vs. Warren, 169 Ill. 142; Schlee vs. Guckenheimer, 179 Ill. 593; West vs. Marquart, 78 Ill. 61; Munns vs. Donovan Commission Co., 91 N. W. 789; Prentiss vs. Press, 63 Ill. App. 430; Morris vs. Dixon National Bank, 55 Ill. App. 298; Marvel vs. Marvel, 96 Ill. App. 609; Bank vs. Edman, 99 Ill. App. 235.

Transactions in stocks have been held to be within the statute in the following cases: Schneider vs. Turner, 130 Ill. 28; Locke vs. Fowler, 41 Ill. App. 66; Wolsey vs. Neeley, 62 Ill. App. 141; Peterson vs. Currier, 62 Ill. App. 163; aff'd 163 Ill. 528.

And in the following cases stock and bond transactions were held not to come within its purview: Clews vs. Jamieson, 182 U. S. 461; Grubey vs. National Bank of Illinois, 35 Ill. App. 354; Wolf vs. National Bank of Illinois, 178 Ill. 85; Ubben vs. Binnian, 182 Ill. 508; Taylor vs. Bailey, 169 Ill. 181; Skinner vs. Osgood, 83 Ill. App 454.

There is a distinction made between a contract for future delivery,

By Laws of 1887, in force July 1, 1887 (Starr & Curtis's Ann. St., vol. 1, p. 1304), keeping a bucket shop in Illinois, to deal in stocks, grain, etc., on margins, is declared unlawful, and penalties of fine and imprisonment are inflicted. A conviction under this act for keeping a bucket shop and dealing in grain on margins therein was sustained, although defendant was only agent for a Chicago firm of Brokers.[1] The intention of the person keeping the bucket shop need not be proved.[2]

A statute as to options resembling that of Illinois was passed in Ohio in 1882.[3] Under this statute, an option contract in stocks or commodities, where both parties

where the time of delivery, within fixed and reasonable limits, is optional with either party, and a contract whereby either party is given an option to buy or sell, at a future time, grain or other commodity. The former is binding, but the latter, as being a gambling contract, is not. Webster vs. Sturges, 7 Ill. App. 560. In Schneider vs. Turner, 130 Ill. 28, it was held that, prior to the passage of the act, it was lawful to have or give an option to sell or buy grain or stocks, and such contracts were not void or voidable at common law, but the statute made all such contracts void whether it was intended to settle by differences or not. In Booth vs. People, 186 Ill. 43, aff'd 184 U. S. 425; the statute was held to be constitutional.

Option contracts in coffee, where delivery was intended, were held valid by the common law of New York, where the contracts were to be executed. Postal Telegraph Cable Co. vs. Lathrop, 33 Ill. App. 400.

[1] Soby vs. The People, 134 Ill. 66.

[2] Caldwell vs. People, 67 Ill. App. 368. The object of the statute is to prevent gambling. Board of Trade vs. Central Stock & Grain Exchange, 98 Ill. App. 218; aff'd 196 Ill. 396. As to what transactions will sustain an allegation that a bucket shop was kept, see Christie vs. Board of Trade, 96 Ill. App. 235.

Even although the maker of a note might have a good defence in an action to recover the amount, on the ground that it was given in bucket shop transactions, the fact that he surrendered it and gave another in lieu thereof, estops him from making such a defence. Fosdick vs. Myers, 81 Ill. App. 544. Ninety per cent of the transactions on the Chicago Board of Trade are violative of this statute. See cases cited ante, p. 24.

[3] Bates Annotated Stats. of Ohio, § 6934a.

understood that differences only were to be settled, is a
wager, and moneys paid on such a contract are recoverable
under section 4270, and the defendant cannot avoid payment on the assumption that he acted as a commission
merchant only.[1] If one gives money to another as his
agent to invest in illegal option contracts in wheat, and
the latter places the money with Brokers, the owner may
recover it, and resulting profits, from the agent.[2]

By §§ 6934 a 1–5 of the Ohio statutes bucket shops are
prohibited, and a penalty for gambling in stocks, bonds, petroleum, cotton, grain, and other produce is imposed. By
§ 4270, moneys paid by the loser to the winner may be
recovered, and, by § 4271, the loser may also recover from
other persons interested.[3]

Under the Code of Georgia a contract to do an immoral

---

[1] Lester vs. Buel, 49 Ohio St.
240.

[2] Norton vs. Blinn, 39 Ohio St.
145. But if the money has been
actually invested by the agent, and
the illegal transactions in wheat are
not yet closed, it cannot be recovered
by the one advancing it. Rogers
vs. Corre, 10 Ohio Cir. Ct. R.
346.

Option dealings in oil with no intention to deliver are within the
statute. Morris vs. Norton, 75
Fed. 912.

[3] A telegraph company cannot be
enjoined from removing its "tick-
ers" from bucket shop rooms.
Bradley vs. Western Union Telegraph Co., 8 Ohio Dec. Rep. 707;
Griffith vs. Same, 8 id. 571. See
Kahn vs. Walton, 46 Ohio St.
195.

As to evidence which was deemed
insufficient to prove a transaction
in grain, on the Chicago Board of
Trade, a gambling one, see Preston
vs. Cincinnati, C. & H. V. R. Co., 36
Fed. Rep. 54.

If there is an intent to deliver
and receive stocks and bonds, the
transaction is not a gambling one,
although the sales and purchases
are for speculation. Goodhart vs.
Rostert, 10 Ohio Dec. 40. And
both parties must intend to gamble,
to make the transaction of a wagering character. Id. Persons who
merely back gambling transactions
in grain and pork futures by furnishing telegraphic wires and market
quotations, and have a share in
the commissions, are nevertheless
liable under sec 4271. Rogers vs.
Edmund, 21 Ohio. Cir. Ct. Rep. 675.

or illegal thing (§ 3666), or a wagering contract (§ 3668), is void. Short sales are also void (§ 3537).[1]

Dealing in options in corporation stocks and grain, in bucket shops, was also declared unlawful in 1891 by the Code of Iowa (§ 4967), and the keeper is subject to fine and imprisonment (§ 4968).[2]

---

[1] A contract for the future delivery of cotton was held void under this statute, § 3537. Branch vs. Palmer, 65 Ga. 210; Thompson vs. Cummings, 68 Ga. 124; and of wheat, Porter vs. Massengale, 68 Ga. 296. Damages cannot be recovered from a telegraph company for failure to deliver a message in such transactions in coffee. Cothran vs. Western Union Telegraph Co., 83 Ga. 25, overruling Tel. Co. vs. Blanchard, 68 Ga. 299, nor can a bank be compelled to perform its agreement to advance money on cotton "futures." Moss vs. Exchange Bank, 102 Ga. 808, but if a bank advances money through one of its officers on such transactions, it cannot recover. Singleton vs. Bank, 113 Ga. 527. Such transactions are not protected by the interstate commerce clause of the United States Constitution. Alexander vs. State, 86 Ga. 246.

[2] Prior to this statute there should have been an intent to deliver. Lowe vs. Young, 59 Iowa, 364; Gregory vs. Wattower, 58 Iowa, 711; Bank vs. Packing Co., 66 Iowa, 41; Douglas vs. Smith, 74 Iowa, 408. An intention by one of the parties was sufficient. Merry vs. Ochiltree, 59 Iowa, 435, but there might be a bona fide intent, with possibility of paying differences only. Tomblin vs. Callen, 69 Iowa, 229.

The mere fact of putting up margins does not make option contracts in futures void. The question is did the parties intend delivery. Union Bank vs. Carr, 13 Chicago L. News, 197; 4 Ky. L. R. 635; Hocker vs. Western Union Tel. Co., 34 So. (Fla.) 901.

The intention of both parties to an optional contract in grain on the Chicago Board of Trade as to whether there shall be delivery is to be determined, not only from the contract, but from the conduct of the parties. Where the evidence is conflicting the verdict of the court, sitting as a jury, will not be disturbed. Press vs. Duncan, 69 S. W. Rep. 543.

An option for future delivery to be performed in Chicago was held void under the law of that State. Osgood vs. Bauder, 75 Iowa, 550. A note in settlement of a gambling deal in futures is void in the hands of an innocent holder. Bank vs. Carroll, 80 Iowa, 11.

Under the statute, the intention to make the transaction a gambling one must be mutual, and if the commission merchant does not disclose from whom he made the purchases, the jury may find the con-

Contracts in " futures " in stocks and certain commodities, without intent to deliver, are declared void in North Carolina by Laws of 1889, c. 221, and persons engaging therein are guilty of misdemeanor. Money lent to pay losses in such transactions may, however, be recovered, if the lender was not connected therewith.[1] When a commission Broker testified that certain contracts in " futures " in meat were speculative contracts, and that either party might demand delivery, there was a question for the jury as to whether the contracts were within the statute.[2]

By the Civil Code of South Carolina, § 2310 (§ 1859, Rev. Stat. of 1883), it is provided that future sales of bonds, stocks, cotton, grain, or certain other products, shall be void unless the vendor is the owner, or unless it is the intention of the parties to have actual delivery.[3]

And by § 2311 in actions to enforce such contracts, the

tract a wagering one. Counselman vs. Reichart, 103 Iowa, 430. A note given in settlement of a bucket shop transaction is void both under the statute, and independent of it. People's Savings Bank vs. Gifford, 108 Iowa, 277.

[1] Ballard vs. Green, 118 N. C. 390.

[2] Cantwell vs. Boykin, 127 N. C. 64.

[3] A contract for the future sale of cotton in New York, although valid in the latter state, was held void under the above statute. Gist vs. Telegraph Co., 45 S. C. 344. Brokers in cotton and grain cannot recover for advances, where contracts made by them are void under this statute. Riordan vs. Doty, 50 S. C. 542; Harvey vs. Doty, 51 S. C. 382. If it is the bona fide intention of the parties to have delivery, the contract is valid under the statute, and such contract may be made by a cotton mill. Sampson vs. Camperdown Cotton Mills, 82 Fed. Rep. 833.

When the contract is void under the statute, a principal may recover margin deposited with cotton Brokers. Saunders vs. Phelps Co., 53 S. C. 173. And cotton Brokers are not precluded, under the statute, from recovering margins advanced by them, where they make purchases in good faith, although the principal secretly intended to speculate. Parker vs. Moore, 115 Fed. Rep. 799.

If the contract is valid in New York, where made, it will nevertheless not be enforced in South Carolina, if contrary to the statute, or public policy of that State. Id.

burden of proof is on plaintiff to show that both parties intended delivery.[1]

Dealing in futures was declared gambling and made a misdemeanor in Arkansas by act of March, 1883 (Sandels & Hills' Dig. §§ 1634–5).

Under this statute a conviction for gambling in grain futures against a Broker who kept a " bucket shop " was sustained as being *particeps criminis*,[2] and in a civil action he cannot recover losses on such dealings in cotton.[3]

But when it plainly appears that the plaintiffs, New York cotton Brokers, bought cotton for the defendant, at his order, strictly under the rules of the Exchange, which made them personally liable for any losses by reason of the decline of the market, and that it was not possible for defendant to cease to perform his part of the contract at any time, neither the letter nor the spirit of the law is violated, although plaintiffs might have been aware that defendant could not pay for the cotton (500 bales) ordered, as defendant would have the cotton itself to pay its value at the time, or its purchase price, and he would therefore be only personally responsible for the difference in market prices at the closing. The fact that plaintiffs informed defendant that he would make some money out of the transaction did not indicate an intention to gamble, as the mere making of money is not evidence that the method of making it is unlawful.[4]

---

[1] The Brokers may recover for moneys advanced, when the rules of the New York Cotton Exchange provide for actual delivery, and the purchases were reported as made subject thereto, even though defendant did not intend delivery, when such intention was not known to the Brokers. Parker vs. Moore, 125 Fed. Rep. 807.

[2] Fortenbury vs. State, 47 Ark. 188.

[3] Phelps vs. Holderness, 56 Ark. 300.

[4] Johnston vs. Miller, 67 Ark. 172.

When a contract for the future delivery of cotton is valid, and the seller intended to, and did, deliver the cotton, it must be shown by the principal that he intended, with the knowledge of the Broker, to gamble in differences.[1]

By the constitution of California (Treadwell's Ann. Const. p. 112, Art. IV. section 26) all contracts for the sale of the shares of the capital stock of any corporation or association on margin to be delivered at a future day are declared void, and moneys paid thereon recoverable. This provision was adopted just after a period of remarkable stock speculation which resulted in disaster to many persons,[2] and the court will take judicial notice that it was intended to put an end to the particular kind of gambling specified.[3]

By the Code of Tennessee, § 3166 (Laws, 1883, ch. 251, §§ 1–3), dealing in bonds, stocks, grain, cotton, or other produce for future delivery, on margin only, without intention of either party to have actual delivery, is declared gaming and made a misdemeanor, but by acts of 1883, chs. 105 and 106, and 1885, ch. 1, such dealing becomes legal if the Broker takes out a license. It is not necessary that the customer should be licensed.[4] Prior to the passage of the Act of 1883, ch. 251, dealing in futures, without an intention of *both* parties to have delivery was void under the Gaming Acts (Code, § 2440). The act made it gaming, if either party did not intend delivery,[5] and a note given by the principal to his agent is void in the hands of an innocent holder for value before maturity.[6] When the under-

---

[1] Ponder vs. Jerome Hill Cotton Co., 100 Fed. Rep. 373.

[2] Cushman vs. Root, 89 Cal. 382.

[3] Ib. See also Parker vs. Otis, 130 Cal. 322; Rued vs. Cooper, 119 Cal. 463; Kullman vs. Simmens,

101 Cal. 595; Sheehy vs. Shinn, 89 Cal. 373.

[4] State vs Duncan, 84 Tenn 79

[5] McGrew vs. City Produce Exchange, 85 Tenn 572

[6] Snoddy vs. Bank, 88 Tenn 573.

standing of both parties was that there was to be no delivery of cotton in dealings therein for future delivery, the Broker cannot recover, even though he is a mere agent.[1] The wife of one who has lost margins deposited in grain "futures" may recover the amount thereof, under § 2441.[2]

In Allen vs. Dunham[3] it was held that margins deposited with a firm of Stock-brokers might be recovered, when it was the intention of both parties that there should be no delivery of stocks bought or sold. In that case the transactions were large, and it would be quite beyond the financial ability of the customer, a bank teller, to actually pay for the stocks purchased, and the transactions were held gambling, both under, and without the aid of, the statute. A principal cannot recover the amount of a note given by Stock-brokers in respect of dealings in stocks, void by this act.[4]

By ch. 81 of L. of Wisconsin of 1883 (Wisconsin Statutes of 1898, § 2319a) it is provided that contracts in "futures" as to personal property shall not be void, when either party intends performance, and extrinsic evidence shall not be allowed to vary such contracts.[5]

The rule laid down in Barnard vs. Backhaus,[6] that

---

[1] Beadles vs. Ownby, 84 Tenn. 424.

[2] Dunn vs. Bell, 85 Tenn. 581.

[3] 92 Tenn. 257.

[4] Mechanics Bank vs. Duncan, 36 S. W. Rep. 887.

[5] It was held in Kerkhoff vs. Atlas Paper Co., 68 Wis. 674, that this statute referred only to written contracts and was doubtless passed to obviate the decisions in Barnard vs. Backhaus, 52 Wis. 593, and Everingham vs. Meehan, 55 Wis.

354, in which the court held that although the contracts were in form for future delivery, they were invalid when no delivery was intended.

When the transactions were enormous, and were carried on with disproportionate capital, transactions in grain, pork and lard were held to be gambling. Atwater vs. Manville, 81 S. W. Rep. 985.

[6] 52 Wis. 593.

to uphold a grain contract in "futures" upon a board of trade, it must affirmatively appear that there was to be actual receipt and delivery of the goods, was not changed by § 2319a.[1] And where the contract is to be partly performed in Wisconsin and partly in Illinois, the statute of the former State governs in an action by Brokers to recover for advances and commissions.[2]

By the Rev. Stats. of Missouri of 1899, c. 15, § 2337, option dealing in stocks and produce without intention to deliver is made a criminal offence. Intention by one of the parties is sufficient (§ 2338). Keeping places for such deals is forbidden (§ 2339). Commission merchants must furnish names of purchasers or buyers (§ 340). "Bucket shops" are also prohibited (§§ 2221-27).

In State vs. Logan[3] the keeper of a place where unlawful dealings in "futures" in stocks, grain, etc., were carried on, was found guilty of violating § 2339 (being § 3933 of the Revision of 1889), as the transactions actually took place

---

[1] Bartlett vs. Collins, 109 Wis. 477.

[2] Id.

[3] 84 Mo. App. 584. The statute against option dealing was held in State vs. Critzer, 134 Mo. 512, not to be unconstitutional, and not to have an extra-territorial effect. In that case the evidence was held insufficient to convict a grain dealer for alleged option dealings with a Chicago firm. And although a transaction in grain is gambling within the statute, an agent may be convicted of embezzling moneys given to him by the principal. State vs. Cunningham, 154 Mo. 176. It was held in Connor vs. Black, 119

Mo. 126, that the provision as to "bucket shops" did not apply to commission merchants.

A demand note given to secure continuing option gambling transactions, may be recovered by the holder, although he purchased it 23 days after date, and suspected that the note had been given for such purposes. Mitchell vs. Catchings, 23 Fed. Rep. 710. As to a New York contract, see Edwards vs. Stevenson, 160 Mo. 516.

An information in the language of § 2339, charging defendant with keeping a bucket shop, was held sufficient in State vs. Kentner, 77 S. W. Rep. 522.

within the State in the place kept by defendant, whose alleged agency to make the deals in Chicago was a subterfuge.

By Laws of Mississippi of 1882, p. 140, Annotated Code of 1892, § 2117, future contracts for the purchase or sale of commodities are not enforceable unless the parties intend delivery, and §§ 1120 and 1121 inflict penalties for dealing in futures.[1]

In Western Union Telegraph Co. vs. Littlejohn[2] it was held that the act did not apply to the buying and selling of stocks for present and not for future delivery, although such purchases and sales might follow each other hourly in rapid succession, and a principal was entitled to recover from a telegraph company the amount of damages sustained by him owing to delay in the transmissions of telegrams between him and his Broker, and resultant losses on deals in stocks. The Act of 1882, §§ 1 and 2, did not repeal § 990 of the Code of 1880 (§ 2114 of the Code of 1882), voiding all wagering contracts.[3]

By Laws of 1899, c. 77, §§ 1 and 2 (Dassler's Gen. Stat. of 1901, §§ 2247, 2450), dealings in futures in, and the keep-

---

[1] It was held in Lemonius vs. Mayer, 71 Miss. 514, that contracts for future delivery of cotton could not, under the second section of the act of 1882, be enforced in Mississippi, although they might, as between the firms of Mississippi and Liverpool Brokers between whom they were made, be enforced in England, in which country the contracts were effected. To same effect, White vs. Eason, 15 So. 66. And in Violett vs. Mangold, 27 So. 875, it was held that the amount of a note given to a Broker in such transactions in wheat could not be recovered by the Broker, but as the statute does not cover the case of one loaning money to pay gambling debts in futures, it was held in Searles vs. Lum, 89 Mo. 235, that such may be recovered at common law, where the lender is not a participant. See also Dillard vs. Brenner, 73 Miss. 130.

[2] 72 Miss. 1025.

[3] Campbell vs. New Orleans Bank, 23 So. Rep. 25.

ing of "bucket shops" for dealing in, stocks and commodities in Kansas, are made misdemeanors punishable by fine and imprisonment.

Prior to the enactment of this statute dealing in options in grain in the Chicago Board of Trade were held, on the evidence submitted to the jury, to be illegal, and the Chicago Brokers were held not entitled to recover the amount of a note given to them by the customer in such transactions.[1]

In Michigan, § 11373 of the Compiled Laws of 1897 prohibits the purchase and sale of stocks or produce on margins for future or optional delivery without any intention of receiving or paying for the property so bought or sold.[2]

Dealings in futures in stocks, etc., without intent to deliver, and bucket shops, are prohibited by the Revised Penal Code of Texas of 1895, Art. 377. (Act of March 1, 1877.) Prior to the enactment of this statute such transactions were held void as against public policy.[3]

Moneys paid to Brokers in gambling transactions in

---

[1] Washer vs. Bond, 40 Kan. 84.

[2] In an action against a telegraph company for damages for failure to deliver a telegram ordering wheat for future delivery, it was held in Carland vs. Western Union Telegraph Co., 76 S. W. Rep. 762, that as the claim of defendant that the transaction was a gambling one, under the statute, was disputed, the verdict of the jury in favor of plaintiff would not be disturbed. In Donovan vs. Daiber, 82 N. W. Rep. 843, a Broker was held entitled to recover for losses on wheat as the case did not come within the statute.

A telegraph company, although under contract to furnish reports of the market prices of stocks, etc., to a "bucket shop," is not bound to observe such a contract, Smith vs. Western Union Tel. Co., 84 Ky. 664. Even though the keepers are members of the Chicago Board of Trade. Bryant vs. Western Union Tel. Co., 17 Fed. Rep. 825.

[3] Henson vs. Flannigan, 1 White & W.'s Civ. Cas. Ct. App § 566; Seeligson vs. Lewis, 65 Tex. 219; Floyd vs. Patterson, 72 Tex. 202; Oliphant vs. Markham, 79 Tex. 543.

cotton futures cannot be recovered, when they were paid to the Brokers as principals and not as agents of the plaintiff.[1]

And if one lends money to be used in such transactions, he cannot recover if he becomes interested therein or acts as the borrower's agent, although, if he merely knew that the money was to be so used, he might maintain an action for recovery.[2]

And mere intention to speculate in a future dealing in bacon is not illegal, unless there is an intention not to deliver.[3] An indictment under the statute is bad, which fails to allege that certain dealings in futures were with reference to future contracts in cotton, about which the contracts were made.[4]

But the indictment need not allege specific dealings if it charges the defendant with dealing in futures.[5]

When from the testimony of one of the parties to a contract for the future sale of bacon, and the correspondence between them, it might be gathered that actual delivery was intended, it was held error not to submit the question as to whether the contract was void, as being a dealing in "futures," to the jury.[6]

By Act 16 of 1898, p. 20, gambling in futures on agricultural products or articles of necessity, without intent to deliver, is made a misdemeanor in Louisiana. The Constitution of 1898 had directed the legislature to enact such a statute. When money is advanced to invest in cot-

[1] Floyd vs. Patterson, 72 Tex. 196; 202.

[2] Oliphant vs. Markham, 79 Tex. 543.

[3] Burr vs. Davis, 27 S. W. Rep. 589.

[4] Cothran vs. State, 36 Tex. Cr.

R. 196; 36 S. W. Rep. 273; Goldstein vs. State, 36 Tex. Cr. R. 193.

[5] Fullerton vs. State, 75 S. W. Rep. 534.

[6] Heidenheimer vs. Cleveland, 17 S. W. Rep. 524.

ton futures, and there is no evidence that purchases of cotton were not made with a view to future delivery, the defence of illegality cannot be sustained.[1]

Dealing in futures in cotton, grain, or anything whatsoever, is made a misdemeanor by Indian Territory Stats., §§ 1191–2.

In this connection it should also be stated that contracts for the purchase or sale of gold are legal.[2] The theory of these cases is, that where a contract is made for the sale or purchase of gold, the latter is regarded as a commodity, and subject to all the rules of law relating to agreements for the purchase or sale thereof—as, for instance, the Statute of Frauds, requiring in certain cases a memorandum in writing.[3] So, in the case of Appleman vs. Fisher,[4] a contract to sell gold " short " was upheld as legal.

By an act of the Congress of the United States passed in March, 1863,[5] " all contracts for the purchase or sale of gold or silver coin or bullion, and all contracts for the loan of money or currency secured by pledge or deposit, or other disposition of gold or silver coin of the United States, if to be performed after a period exceeding three days, shall be in writing or printed, and signed by the parties, their agents, or attorneys, and shall have one or more adhesive stamps, as provided in the act to which this is an amendment, equal in amount to one half of one per centum, and interest at the

[1] Allen vs. Whitstone, 35 La. Ann. 850.

[2] Peabody vs. Speyers, 56 N. Y. 230; Bigelow vs. Benedict, 9 Hun (N. Y.), 429, aff'd 70 N. Y. 202; Fowler vs. Gold Exchange Bank. 67 id. 138–140; Chatterton vs. Fisk, 1 Ab. New Cas. 88; Mills vs. Gould, id. 93.

[3] Id.

[4] 31 Md. 540. For construction of certain contracts relating to the purchasing or selling of gold, see Kinne vs. Ford, 43 N. Y. 587; Meyer vs. Clark, 45 id. 285

[5] March 3, 1863, 2 Bright. Stat. at Large, 144; 12 U. S. Stat. 719.

rate of six per centum per annum on the amount so loaned, pledged or deposited. And if any such loan, pledge, or deposit, made for a period not exceeding three days, shall be renewed or in any way extended for any time whatever, said loan, pledge, or deposit shall be subject to the duty imposed on loans exceeding three days. And no loan of currency or money on the security of gold or silver coin of the United States, as aforesaid, or of any certificate or other evidence of deposit payable in gold or silver coin, shall be made exceeding in amount the par value of the coin pledged or deposited as security; and any such loan so made, or attempted to be made, shall be utterly void. *Provided*, that if gold or silver coin be loaned at its par value, it shall be subject only to the duty imposed on other loans. *Provided*, however, that nothing herein contained shall apply to any transaction by or with the government of the United States; and all contracts, loans, or sales of gold and silver coin and bullion, not made in accordance with this act, shall be wholly and absolutely void; and, in addition to the penalties provided in the act to which this is an amendment, any party to said contract may, at any time within one year from the date of the contract, bring suit before any court of competent jurisdiction, to recover back, for his own use and benefit, the money paid on any contract not in accordance with this act." This act was repealed in 1864.[1]

The history of these Acts seems to prove conclusively that they have not been effective in preventing illegal speculation in stocks and produce. In England, and the

[1] See 13 U. S. Stat. p. 303; Laws, U. S. 1864, ch. 173, § 173; see also Revision of Statutes of U. S. 1874, 2d ed. (1878), p. 1085. An ab- stract of the act is, however, given in 1 Ab. Nat. Dig. 553, as late as 1871.

States of New York and Pennsylvania, after lingering for years on the books, scorned and violated by "the unbridled and defiant spirit of speculation,"[1] despite the earnest efforts of the courts to enforce them, they have finally been repealed. In a recent case,[2] transactions in produce in boards of trade are alluded to by the court as "board of trade" transactions, having no reference to actual receipt or delivery of grain, and in another case[3] the court found that 95 per cent of the transactions of the Chicago Board of Trade were simply gambling dealings, closed immediately by a settlement of differences, and for that reason refused to restrain the defendants from using the board's quotations.

It is perhaps better to allow the evil to correct itself, as it surely does, than to bring the administration of justice into contempt by filling the books with useless laws, which are at all times openly violated and laughed at, and which seem hardly more effective to prevent the practices at which they are aimed, than legislation directed against the laws of nature.[4]

III. Wagers.

(a.) At Common-law.

According to the definition of Bouvier, which has been substantially sustained by the courts, as appears from the de-

---

[1] As Mr. Justice Hoffman puts it in Cassard vs. Hinmann, 14 How. Pr. (N. Y.) 84, 90.

[2] Merrill vs. Garver, 96 N. W. Rep. (Neb.) 619.

[3] Board of Trade vs. Kinsey, 125 Fed. Rep. (Ind.) 72.

[4] See a very ably written article entitled "The Functions of the Stock and Produce Exchanges," by Mr. Charles A. Conant in the Atlantic Monthly for April, 1903, in which he distinguishes between transactions in bucket shops, or associations established purely to gamble in the price of stocks or commodities, and dealings in the Stock and Produce Exchanges, which he stoutly defends, although differences only may be settled.

cisions hereafter referred to, "a wager is a bet; a contract by which two parties or more agree that a certain sum of money or other thing shall be paid or delivered to one of them on the happening or not happening of an uncertain event."[1] And a contract upon a contingency, by which one may lose, although he cannot gain, or the other may gain, but cannot lose, is a wager, as where property was sold at its real value to be paid for if a third person be elected.[2] Yet in Quarles vs. The State[3] it was decided that to constitute a wager there must be a risk by both parties.[4] And in Cassard vs. Hinman[5] the court said : "A wager is something hazarded on the issue of some uncertain event ; a bet is a wager, though a wager is not necessarily a bet."

Wagers, at common-law, were not *per se* void, unless they were calculated to injure third persons, and thereby disturb the peace and comfort of society, or lead to indecent evidence, or when they militated against the morality or public policy of the country.

[1] Bouvier's Law Dict. tit. "Wagers." See the definition of a wagering contract in Gaw vs. Bennett, 153 Pa. St. 247.

[2] Shumate's Case, 15 Gratt. (Va.) 653.

[3] 5 Humph. (Tenn.) 561.

[4] See also Marean vs. Longley, 21 Me. 26; Trammel vs. Gordon, 11 Ala. 656; Fisher vs. Waltham, 4 Q. B. 889. If either of the parties may lose, but cannot win, it is not a wagering contract. Cahill vs. Carbolic Smoke Ball Co. (1892), 2 Q. B. 484; aff'd (1893) 1 Q. B. 256. The chance of gain or loss must be contemplated by either party. Ib., and see "Law of Gambling,"

Coldridge & Hawksford (London), 1895, pp. 4 and 26.

[5] 1 Bosw. (N. Y.) 207, on appeal. There may be an element of risk, and yet the contract may not be a gambling one. So held in Plumb vs. Campbell, 129 Ill. 101, where it appeared that stocks and bonds were sold at a fixed sum, the Broker to pay any deficiency under the market price, or to keep any surplus thereover by way of commission. And also so held in Phillips vs. Gifford, 104 Iowa, 458, which was an action in reference to a saloon, the sale of which was to be void if the purchaser were obliged to discontinue the liquor business by reason of legislative enactment.

Some of the cases will fully illustrate this proposition. A wager on the future price of foreign funds was held legal;[1] so was one whether S. T. had or had not before a certain day bought a wagon belonging to D. C.;[2] also a wager on the age of plaintiff and defendant;[3] and likewise a wager on the result of an appeal from the Court of Chancery to the House of Lords has been held good, no fraud being intended, and the parties having no power to bias the decision.[4] On the other hand, a wager as to the conviction or acquittal of a prisoner on trial on a criminal charge is illegal as being against public policy;[5] likewise a wager as to the event of a cock-fight[6] or a dog-fight,[7] or whether a horse can trot eighteen miles within an hour.[8] Wagers such as the above were held to be illegal as tending to create disturbances and to encourage cruelty.[9] Those upon the result of any election are held to be void, both in England and this country, upon the ground that they are contrary to public policy and tend to impair the purity of election.[10] But notwithstanding the rule upholding certain wagers, the English courts frequently reprehended such contracts and expressed their regret that they had ever been sanctioned.[11] Thus Ashhurst, J.,[12] questioned whether it would not have been better for the public welfare if the courts

---

[1] Morgan vs. Pebrer, 4 Sco. 230.

[2] Good vs. Elliott, 3 T. R. 693.

[3] Hussey vs. Crickitt, 3 Campb. 168.

[4] Jones vs. Randal, Cowp. 37; and see generally, upon this subject, Lord Campbell in Thackoorseydass vs. Dhondmull, 6 Moo. P. C. 300; Doolubdass vs. Ramloll, 3 Eng. L. & Eq. 39.

[5] Evans vs. Jones, 5 M. & W. 77.

[6] Squires vs. Whisken, 3 Campb. 140.

[7] Egerton vs. Furzeman, 1 C. & P. 613.

[8] Brogden vs. Marriott, 3 Bing. (N. C.) 88.

[9] Id.

[10] Pars. on Cont. (8th ed.) 755 n., and cases there collected.

[11] Robinson vs. Mearns, 16 E. C. L. R. 253; Walpole vs. Saunders, id. 276; Gilbert vs. Sykes, 16 East. 150; Fisher vs. Waltham, 4 Q. B. 889.

[12] Atherford vs. Beard, 2 T. R. 610.

had originally determined against all actions to enforce the payment of wagers; and Buller, J., in the same case, did not consider it to have ever been established as a position of law, that a wager between two persons not interested in the subject-matter was legal.   This, however, was *obiter dictum*, and he proceeded to determine the wager by distinctions taken in former cases.   And Lord Ellenborough [1] leans to the view of Buller, J.; [2] and Le Blanc, J., in the same case, uses the following language: " It has often been lamented that actions upon idle wagers should ever have been entertained in courts of justice.   The practice seems to have prevailed before that full consideration of the subject which has been had in modern times."

The principle of the common-law upholding wagers was adopted in this country by the States of California,[3] Texas,[4] Illinois,[5] New Jersey,[6] Alabama,[7] Iowa,[8] Kentucky,[9] Missouri,[10] North Carolina,[11] and Delaware; [12] and the United States court in Grant vs. Hamilton [13] held that a wager fairly made was recoverable at common-law.   And the early tendency of the New York courts was to sustain wagers as valid within the rules of the common-law.[14]

[1] Gilbert vs. Sykes, 16 East, 159.

[2] Atherford vs. Beard, 2 T. R. 610.

[3] Johnston vs. Russell, 37 Cal. 670.

[4] As to horse racing only, but not as to other kinds of wagers. Wheeler vs. Friend, 22 Tex. 683; Monroe vs. Smelly, 25 Tex. 586.

[5] Smith vs. Smith, 21 Ill. 244.

[6] Trenton, etc., Ins. Co. v. Johnson, 4 Zabr. (N. J.) 576.

[7] Tindall vs. Childress, 2 Stew. & P. (Ala.) 250.

[8] Sipe vs. Finarty, 6 Iowa, 394.

[9] Greathouse vs. Throckmorton, 7 J. J. Marsh. (Ky.) 17.

[10] Waddle vs. Lober, 1 Mo. 635.

[11] Shepherd vs. Sawyer, 6 N. Car. 26.

[12] Dewees vs. Miller, 5 Harr. 347.

[13] 3 McLean (7th Circ. Mich.), 100.

[14] Bunn vs. Riker, 4 Johns. 426; Campbell vs. Richardson, 10 id. 406, And see the later case of Zeltner vs. Irwin, 25 App. Div. 228, holding that wagering contracts were not

(b.) Wagers under Existing Laws.

In England the strictures of the courts upon wagers led to the passage of a statute[1] in the year 1845, by § 18 of which it is provided that "all contracts or agreements, whether by parole or in writing, by way of gaming or wagering, shall be null and void; and no suit shall be brought or maintained in any court of law or equity for recovering any sum of money or valuable thing alleged to be won upon any wager, or which shall have been deposited in the hands of any person to abide the event on which such wager shall be made."[2]

By the Revised Statutes of New York,[3] "All wagers,

invalid at common-law unless they were against public policy, and, in the absence of proof to the contrary, that the same rule prevailed in another State.

[1] 8 & 9 Vict. c. 109.

[2] For decisions under statute of Vict. consult Higginson vs. Simpson, L. R. 2 C. P. D. 76; Beeston vs. Beeston, L. R. 1 Ex. D. 13; Inchbald vs. Cockerill, 4 Jur. (n. s.) 693. See also Grizewood vs. Blane, 11 C. B. 539; Rees vs. Fernie, 4 N. R. 539; Hibblewhite vs. McMorine, 5 M. & W. 462; Barry vs. Croskey, 2 J. & H. 1; Ex parte Phillips, and Ex parte Marnham, 2 De G. F. & J. 634; Loughton vs. Griffin, (1895) A. C. 104.

[3] 1 Rev. Stat. 661, § 8. Transactions in futures in wheat without intent to deliver are void under this statute. Copley vs. Doran & Wright Co., 17 N. Y. St. Rep. 601, aff'd 49 Hun, 610. But an action for recovery of moneys paid to a Broker in such transactions is not

on contract, but for recovery of moneys to which defendant has no title. Willard vs. Doran & Wright Co., 48 Hun, 402. Chapter IX of title X of the Penal Code also contains provisions against gaming. It was held in People vs. Todd, 58 Hun, 446, that although contracts made by one who kept a room with a stock quotation ticker in it, indicating the fluctuation of prices on the New York Stock Exchange, were wagering ones, there being no intention to deliver stocks, they did not violate sec. 343 of the Penal Code, making it a misdemeanor to keep a room for gambling.

Thereupon that section was amended by L. 1889, c. 428, which in effect made the keeping of a bucket shop a misdemeanor. Under this section as so amended, a conviction against the keeper of a "bucket shop" was sustained People vs. Wade, 59 Sup. 846.

The constitution of the State of New York, as amended in 1894, also

bets, or stakes made to depend upon any race, or upon any gaming by lot or chance, casualty or unknown or contingent event whatever, shall be unlawful. All contracts for or on account of any money or property or thing in action so wagered, bet, or staked shall be void."

It is provided by statute in Massachusetts (L. 1890, c. 437, L. 1901, c. 459, now embodied in the Revised Laws of Massachusetts, Revision of 1901, c. 99, § 4) that a recovery may be had by any one contracting, upon credit or margin, to buy or sell securities, when no actual sale is intended, and such intention is known to the other party, whether principal or agent, unless an actual sale or purchase has been made. Section 5 protects the rights of third parties. By § 6, the fact that the seller did not own the securities, and that settlements were made without the completion of the sale, shall be *prima facie* evidence that there should be no sale. And § 7 defines securities. This statute was held to be constitutional as intended to suppress gambling.[1] The statute of 1890, was amended and not repealed by the statute of 1901.[2] And a declaration following the language of the amendment, as to transactions prior to its enactment, is not demurrable.[3] And after a cause of action under the statute had accrued it might be released under seal.[4] But to recover collateral, a plaintiff must prove that he had no intention to sell, and that such was known to the defend-

---

prohibits all kinds of gambling, and directs the legislature to pass appropriate laws in respect thereto. Art. I. § 9. Money deposited upon the event of a wager may be recovered. 3 R. S. (8th ed.) p. 2218.

[1] Crandell vs. White, 164 Mass. 54.

[2] Wilson vs. Head, 69 N. E. Rep. 317.

[3] Loughlin vs. Parkinson, 69 N. E. Rep. 319.

[4] Wall vs. Metropolitan Stock Exchange, 168 Mass. 282; Shea vs. Same, ib. 284.

ant,[1] and that the defendant acted as plaintiff's agent or employee, and that defendant performed the service for an agreed compensation ;[2] and a set-off cannot be allowed defendant Stock-brokers for the amount of profits previously paid plaintiff.[3] When a Broker actually buys securities, and the principal so understands, and that the Broker will sell them when the customer requests, the transaction is not within the statute, although the principal intended to gamble in differences.[4]

And although the statute (§ 2) only gives the loser a right to recover, in an action on contract, any money paid, or the value of anything delivered, equity will enable him to enjoin the foreclosure of a mortgage, and the surrender of a note, given to a Stock-broker to secure losses.[5] The maintenance of an "exchange" telephonic communication between "living rooms" in which was a "ticker," and a Stock-broker's office, and the general course of the dealings between the parties, were held to tend to show that the Brokers had reasonable cause to believe that a Client would not carry out her contracts.[6] When money is lent, with the lender's knowledge, to speculate in stocks in " bucket shop" transactions, and the lender is to receive a moiety of the profits, a bill of sale to secure the loan is void.[7] As the statute was intended to suppress gambling in stocks, it cannot be nullified by an agreement by the Client to save the Broker harmless from the consequence of its violation,

[1] Davy vs. Bangs, 174 Mass. 238.

[2] Bingham vs. Scott, 177 Mass. 366. 208.

[3] Lyons vs. Coe, 177 Mass. 382.

[4] Rice vs. Winslow, 62 N. E. Rep. 1057; Post vs. Leland, 69 N. E. Rep. 361.

[5] Rice vs. Winslow, 65 N. E. Rep.

[6] Ballou vs. Willet, 62 N. E. Rep 1064.

[7] Marden vs. Phillips, 103 Fed. Rep. 196.

and equity will not restrain an action by the Client to recover advances by reason of such agreement.[1]   When no
stock was delivered under a contract, which was terminated
by the decline in the market value of the securities to the
amount of the deposit, which thereupon became the Broker's
property, it was held in Marks vs. Metropolitan Stock Exchange[2] that this was a "settlement" within the meaning
of § 6, importing that the principal had no intention to perform the contract, and that the Broker had reasonable cause
to so believe.   A Stock-broker sued for recovery of margins
deposited in breach of the statute, is not entitled to a general verdict, because some of the securities may not have
been securities within its meaning, when other securities
dealt in came within its purview, nor can he claim that the
transactions were through an agent, without proof of such
agency, when the evidence proved the agency, and the
wagering character of the contracts in violation of the statute is shown by the cross-examination of plaintiff, in which
he testified that speculation in the rise and fall of prices
only was intended, although such evidence, if offered by
plaintiff, would be incompetent.[3]   When the testimony
clearly shows that there was no intention to receive or
deliver stocks, the transaction is within the statute and the
words in § 6, "the fact that settlements had been made"
refer to settlements in the transaction in suit, and not to
previous settlements.[4]   In Winward vs. Lincoln[5] § 6 was
held, in stock transactions which originated in Rhode Island, to have no extra-territorial effect and therefore not

---

[1] Corey vs. Griffin, 181 Mass. 229;
63 N. E. Rep. 420.

[2] 181 Mass. 251; 63 N. E. Rep.
410.

[3] Allen vs. Fuller, 65 N. W. Rep.
31.

[4] Thompson vs. Brady, 65 N. E.
Rep. 419.

[5] 51 Atl. Rep. 106.

applicable to an action in the Rhode Island courts respecting such transactions.

In the Massachusetts statute (c. 99, Rev. Laws of 1901, *supra*) it is also provided (§§ 1–3), that money lost at gaming may be recovered, but these sections only relate to gaming as that term is ordinarily used, as is evidenced by §§ 4–7, *supra*, as to stock dealings.

In Ohio it is enacted (Bates' Annotated Stats. 2d ed. § 6938), that " whoever plays at any game whatsoever for any sum of money or other property of any value, or makes any bet or wager for any sum of money or other property of any value, shall be fined not more than $100, or imprisoned not more than six months, nor less than ten days, or both." And by § 4270, money lost in wagering may be recovered.[1]   And Iowa (Code of 1897, § 4964), Indiana (Revision of 1881, with amendments to 1902, § 2081, Horner's edition), West Virginia (Warth's Code of 1899, cs. 97, 151) and Wisconsin (Statutes of 1898, § 4535) have similar statutes.

The Revised Statutes of Indiana (§ 4950, Horner's edition, § 6675, Burn's edition) also provide that notes and securities given in wagering transactions shall be void. This section was held not applicable to moneys loaned to gamble in grain options at sometime in the future. The statute is confined to a case where money is loaned at the time of the wager.[2] In Pearce vs. Dill[3] it was held that option dealings in grain in Illinois without intention to deliver were void as against public policy, and that a wife was entitled to recover from the keeper of a bucket shop, and from a bank, moneys of

---

[1] See Lucas vs. Harper, 24 Ohio St. 328; Roulstone vs. Moore, 10 Ohio Dec. Rep. 275.

[2] Plank vs. Jackson, 128 Ind. 424.
[3] 149 Ind. 436.

hers deposited in the bank, paid by her husband as her trustee, in such dealings. Section 4951 of the Indiana Statutes, Horner's edition (§ 6676, Burn's edition), also provides that money lost by betting on any *game* may be recovered by suing therefor within six months. It was held in Boyce vs. O'Dell Commission Co.[1] that money lost by plaintiff in "bucket shop" transactions could not be recovered under this section, as such transactions were not "betting on any game" within the meaning of this section.

In Pennsylvania gaming contracts are void, and money lost at a game or play of address or hazard may be recovered (Act of April 22, 1794).[2] In Merriam vs. Stock Exchange[3] it was held that the act did not cover stock, grain, and oil transactions on margins, where differences only were settled, such being entirely unknown at the passage of the act, and money paid by the customer to the Broker could not be recovered under the 9th section of the act, the transaction being a gambling one, and against the policy of the law, and therefore void, although if the customer had not paid it, he could not be compelled to do so. To the same effect is Hirst vs. Maag.[4] An innocent holder for value of a negotiable note given in a stock gambling transaction may recover the same before maturity.[5] Equity will not compel the return of notes (in the hands of a *bona fide* purchaser for value without notice) given by a customer to his Broker to cover losses in stock gambling transactions.[6]

Election bets are punishable by fine in Kansas (Dassler's

---

[1] 109 Fed. Rep. 758.

[2] See Edgell vs. McLoughlin, 6 Whart. 176, overruling Morgan vs. Richards, 1 Bro. 171.

[3] 1 Pa. Co. Ct. R. 478.

[4] 13 Pa. Sup. Ct. Rep. 4.

[5] Northern National Bank vs. Arnold, 187 Pa. St. 356.

[6] Albertson vs. Loughlin, 173 Pa. St. 525.

Gen. Stats. of 1901, § 2252) and gambling is prohibited by §§ 2228 and 2233.

In Missouri (Rev. Stats. of 1899, c. 32, §§ 3424, 3432) money lost on wagers may be recovered, if sued for within three months after the cause of action has accrued. This statute does not apply to gambling transactions in grain, as money lost therein is not lost "at any game or gambling device."[1] Even if it does, the action must be brought within the three months' limitation.[2] A note in grain gambling transactions in the hands of an innocent holder for value, is enforceable.[3]

In New Hampshire (Public Stats. c. 270, § 16) wagers are declared void. And an agreement in which the parties have no interest, except that created by such agreement, shall be deemed a wager (§ 18), and money received thereunder may be recovered (§ 17).[4]

In Maine all wagers are held to be void.[5] By the statute of that State gambling is punishable by fine (Rev. Stat. of Maine, c. 125, § 2), and securities given for gambling debts (except in the hands of innocent holders) are void (Ib. § 10). In O'Brien vs. Luques[6] it was held that a customer could

---

[1] Crawford vs. Spencer, 92 Mo. 498; Connor vs. Black, 132 Mo. 150.

[2] Connor vs. Black, 132 Mo. 150. See also Bank vs. Harrison, 10 Fed. Rep. 213, deciding that the statute does not apply to "options."

[3] Third National Bank vs. Tinsley, 11 Mo. App. 498; Third National Bank vs. Harrison, 10 Fed. Rep. 243; Sondheim vs. Gilbert, 117 Ind. 71; 10 Am. St. Rep. 23, and note. Neither the statutes of New York nor Indiana invalidate such a note, Id.; Crawford vs. Spencer, 92 Mo. 498; 1 Am. St. Rep. 745, and note, but the Illinois statute does, even in the hands of an innocent holder. Root vs. Merriam, 27 Fed. Rep. 909, and cases cited in appended note.

[4] Margins in stock transactions where there is to be no delivery, may be recovered under these sections. Wheeler vs. Exchange, 56 Atl. Rep. 751.

[5] Lewis vs. Littlefield, 15 Me. 233.

[6] 81 Me. 46.

not recover deposits made with a Broker to gamble in grain, even though the latter represented that the purchases were to be made of a firm of Chicago Brokers, when they were not in fact so made. But in Nolan vs. Clarke[1] it was held that a principal might, under § 8, recover from a Broker, payments made in "futures" in corn, when delivery was not intended, even though the forms of sale and purchase were observed, and although the Broker was agent for a Boston company, when he did not disclose such fact to his principal. It was held in Morris vs. Telegraph Co.[2] that as dealings in stocks between Broker and customer although in form valid, were gambling transactions, there being no intent to make delivery, the customer could not recover damages from a telegraph company for non-delivery of a telegram by which loss resulted to him in such transactions.

In Vermont money paid to the winner of a wager cannot be recovered.[3] The statutes as to wagering and gambling (§§ 5133-9), permitting recovery from the winner, only apply to sports or games.[4] It was held in Soules vs. Welden National Bank[5] that a Commission Broker, acting for a New York stock-broking company, could not recover deposits made by him in a bank, as the company's agent, pursuant to an arrangement between him and the New York company, on the ground that the transactions were wagering ones. The keeping of a "bucket shop" to deal in stocks and commodities, is made a criminal offence in Vermont by L. 1888, No. 147, § 1 (Vermont Stats. §§ 5128-32). A conviction under this statute was not sustained, when

[1] 91 Me. 33.
[2] 94 Me. 423.
[3] West vs. Holmes, 26 Vt. 530.
[4] Id.
[5] 61 Vt. 375.

the indictment did not sufficiently connect the defendant with the illegal offence charged.[1] In State vs. Corcoran[2] it was held that an indictment which alleged that the respondent kept a "bucket shop," in which, following the language of the statute, he conducted the business thereby prohibited, was good.

By the General Statutes of Connecticut, § 4531, wagering contracts are declared void, and by § 1920, municipalities may prohibit bucket shops and dealings in margins. A speculative contract in stocks is not necessarily illegal as a gambling contract.[3]

Although the gambling statute of Rhode Island (General Statutes, ch. 92) does not forbid gambling in stocks, such transactions are void as against public policy when there is to be no delivery, even though the transactions have the appearance of a sale, or of a sale and resale.[4] If transactions in stocks are void as against public policy in Rhode Island, they cannot be enforced in that State, although valid under L. 1890, ch. 437, of Massachusetts, in which State the contract was executed.[5]

By the General Statutes of New Jersey, p. 1606, § 1, all wagering is declared unlawful. Speculations in stock on margins, are within this statute.[6]

---

[1] State vs. McMillan, 37 Atl. Rep. 278.

[2] 73 Ver. 401.

[3] Hatch vs. Douglas, 48 Conn. 116; Ingraham vs. Taylor, 58 id. 503; Skiff vs. Stoddard, 63 id. 211.

[4] Flagg vs. Gilpin, 17 R. I. 10.

[5] Winward vs. Lincoln, 51 Atl. Rep. 106. In that case, however, it was held that a Broker might recover moneys due from a customer in such transactions, by the law of both States, as there was an intent to have actual delivery, although there was in fact no actual purchase or delivery, and although the principal did not intend to receive stocks purchased, or pay therefor, where he intended that the Broker should receive and pay for them, or the Broker had reason to believe he had such intention. Id.

[6] Tantum vs. Arnold, 15 Stew. 62; Flagg vs. Baldwin, 11 Stew. Eq. 219.

Gaming on any contingency is also declared unlawful in the State of Maryland. Poe's Supp. to Public Gen. Laws, Art. 27, § 124a.

By General Statutes of Minnesota, ch. 99, § 13 (now General Statutes, 1894, § 6593), money lost at play or gambling may be recovered. It was held in Dows vs. Glaspel[1] that this statute did not relate to "option deals," and that money paid, as margins, in such transactions in grain, could not be recovered, in a counterclaim by defendant customer who relied on the statute. It was also held that when no proof of the statute was offered by plaintiff Broker, the latter was not entitled at common-law to recover advances or commissions, when the purpose of the principal was to gamble. A "stock" clock was held in State vs. Grimes,[2] to be a gambling device within the meaning of the charter of the city of Minneapolis.

Gambling is made punishable as a criminal offence by the Code of Mississippi, § 1122, and by § 2114, contracts, judgments, etc., on any wager, are declared void. It was held in Campbell vs. National Bank[3] that contracts for future delivery are void, when the intent of the parties is merely to speculate on the rise and fall of prices, when differences only are to be settled, and there is to be no delivery, and as such a contract was one of wagering, a judgment on a note given by a principal to a Broker in payment of moneys due on such transactions, and by the Broker endorsed to the plaintiff bank, could not, under § 990 of the Code of 1880 (§ 2114 of the Code of 1882), be enforced. And in Virden vs. Murphy[4] it was held that a note given to secure money loaned by plaintiff to defendant

[1] 4 N. D. 251.   [3] 74 Miss. 526.
[2] 49 Minn. 443.   [4] 78 Miss. 515.

to be used in a "bucket shop" business carried on by defendant in Philadelphia, could not be recovered, the business being a gambling one under § 2114 of the Code. And Lum vs. Fauntleroy[1] decided that in a suit on a judgment of another State, the defendant was not precluded from setting up the gambling nature of the transactions (viz., dealing in futures), upon which the judgment was based, and which, as they took place in the State of Mississippi, were illegal by the statutes of that State.

The Delaware statute against gaming (Laws of Delaware, ch. 454, vol. II.), would seem to be directed against gaming tables, etc., and would not therefore include gambling in "futures."

In Virginia by the Code of 1887, § 2836, all gaming contracts are declared void. In Krake vs. Alexander[2] it was held that when one lends money which is used by the borrower in paying off a judgment obtained against him on a note given by him as surety in respect of alleged gambling transactions in pork and grain options, and of which transactions the lender had no knowledge, the latter is not debarred from recovering the money lent by reason of the alleged gambling nature of the transactions.

In North Carolina, gaming or betting contracts are void. Code, c. 22.

Gaming is forbidden by the Civil Code of South Carolina (§§ 2305-9).[3]

Under the Code of Georgia (§§ 2753, now 3671), all wagering contracts are void, and evidences of debt executed upon a gaming consideration, are void in the hands of any person. Under this section, a bank cannot recover on a prom-

---

[1] 80 Miss. 757. [3] See Rice vs. Gist, 1 Strob. (S. C.)
[2] 86 Va. 206. 82.

issory note given in a transaction in cotton futures, even though a *bona fide* purchaser for value before maturity without notice.[1] A principal may recover from a telegraph company, damages occasioned by a mistake in transmitting a message as to such deals,[2] but this doctrine was subsequently overruled, and it was held that a telegraph company was not, under such circumstances, obliged to respond in damages,[3] nor should a bank, with whom collateral had been deposited, under an agreement to honor a draft given by the depositor in payment of margins in "cotton" futures, be compelled to observe such agreement.[4]

The constitution of Louisiana of 1898 directs the legislature to pass laws to suppress gambling. Arts. 188 and 2983 of the Revised Civil Code prohibit gaming, except games of skill. An optional contract to purchase flour in St. Louis, which expressed that, if the vendee did not want the flour, differences might be settled at the prices quoted by the St. Louis Merchants Exchange, was held to be a gaming contract under the statute.[5]

By the Rev. Stats. of Illinois, § 131, wagering contracts are declared void, and by § 132 moneys paid to the "winner" in such transactions may be recovered. It was held in Pearce vs. Foote[6] that moneys paid to a Broker in grain option contracts may by recovered from the Broker as a winner under § 132.[7]

---

[1] Cunningham vs. Bank, 71 Ga. 405.

[2] Telegraph Co. vs. Blanchard, 68 Ga. 299.

[3] Cothran vs. Telegraph Co., 83 Ga. 25; 9 S. E. Rep. 836.

[4] Moss vs. Exchange Bank, 30 S. E. Rep. 267.

[5] E. O. Stannard Milling Co. vs. Flower, 46 La. Ann. 315; 15 So. Rep. 16.

[6] 113 Ill. 228.

[7] This decision was followed in Elder vs. Talcott, 43 Ill. App. 439, in a like contract, notwithstanding contra decisions in Higgins vs. McCrea, 116 U. S. 671 (option contracts in pork and lard), and White

By the Code of Tennessee (§ 2438), gaming and wagering contracts are declared void, and by § 2440, money lost thereon may be recovered. Moneys paid in wagering contracts in produce "futures," may be recovered under the latter section.[1]

By the General Statutes of Kentucky (art. 1, ch. 47, § 1, now ch. 58, § 1955, of the Kentucky Statutes), all gaming or wagering contracts are declared void. It was held in Lyons vs. Hodgen[2] that gambling in futures was within this statute, although not practised at its enactment.

By the Code of Alabama of 1897, § 2163, all contracts founded on a gambling consideration are void.[3]

vs. Barber, 123 U. S. 392 (like contracts in grain). See also Kennedy vs. Stout, 26 Ill. App. 133; Jamieson vs. Wallace, 167 Ill. 388; Walker vs. Johnson, 59 Ill. App. 448; N. Y. &c. Stock Ex. vs. Mellen, 27 id. 556, to same effect. Treble the amount paid may be recovered. Kruse vs. Kennett, 181 Ill. 199. But not in the Federal court. Sticktenoth vs. Central Ex. of Chicago, 99 Fed. Rep. 1.

[1] McGrew vs. City Produce Exchange, 85 Tenn. 572. And a note given in such transactions is void even in the hands of a bona fide holder before due. Snoddy vs. Bank, 88 Tenn. 575.

[2] 90 Ky. 280. See also to the same effect, Sawyer vs. Taggert, 77 Ky. 727; Smith vs. Western Union, 84 Ky. 664; Beadles vs. McElrath, 85 Ky. 230; Farmers Bank vs. Unser, 13 Ky. L. R. 565.

Transactions in grain "futures" are illegal and against public policy when there is no intention to de-liver (Bryant vs. Telegraph Co., 17 Fed. Rep. 825), and a telegraph company may not be enjoined from refusing to supply a "bucket shop" keeper with the market quotations. Smith vs. Western Union Telegraph Co., 84 Ky. 664. When it clearly appeared that stocks were never bought or sold, differences only being settled, the transactions are gambling ones within this section, and moneys paid to a company engaged therein may be recovered. Boyd vs. Coates, 24 Ky. L. Rep. 730; 69 S. W. Rep. 1090.

[3] It was held in Hawley vs. Bibb, 69 Ala. 52, that dealing in "cotton" futures, without intent to deliver, was gambling within this statute, and that the amount of a note given in such a transaction in Alabama could not be recovered even by an innocent holder for value, but when it took place in New York, it might be recovered at common-law, in the absence of proof of a New York statute to the contrary.

Money lost on wagers may be recovered in Arkansas (Sandels & Hill's Dig. of Statutes, § 3501), and judgments, etc., given in respect thereof are void (§ 3504).

The keeping of gaming tables is forbidden in the District of Columbia (Laws of January 31, 1883 ; Code of 1902, § 864).[1]

In Colorado gaming contracts are declared void (Mills' Anno. Stats. § 1344). When one gave a note on transactions alleged in his defence to be gambling in "futures" in grain on the Chicago market, but which, he testified on the trial, was given as accommodation paper, a verdict against him was properly directed in an action brought by a *bona fide* holder of the note for value without notice.[2]

Gaming is also prohibited in Michigan (Comp. L. §§ 5929–38). Section 5933 (formerly § 1996 of the Comp. L. of

When no proof is offered that there was not to be delivery, a plea by a telegraph company that a "cotton future" was a gambling transaction, will not be considered, Western Union Tel. Co. vs. Way, 83 Ala. 561; Same vs. Chamblee, 25 So. Rep. 232, and where the contract was to be performed in Germany, it cannot be held a gambling transaction in the absence of proof of the law of Germany. Id. See also Lee vs. Boyd, 86 Ala. 283; Peet vs. Hatcher, 112 Ala. 514 (as to cotton futures). In Perryman vs. Wolffe, 93 Ala. 290; 9 So. Rep. 148, it was held that a contract for the sale of stock to be delivered at the end of twelve months, with an option to the seller to deliver during the time, was valid, even though the seller had not the stock at the time, as it appeared he intended delivery.

[1] A note given in transactions in "futures" in stocks is void, even as against innocent holders without notice. Lully vs. Morgan, 21 D. C. 88. This case was decided under the English statute of 9 Anne, c. 14, § 1, which was held to be in force in the district, following Justh vs. Holliday, 2 Mack. 346, where the transactions were similar, but it has been recently decided in Wirt vs. Stubblefield, 17 App. D. C. 283, that 9 Anne, c. 14, § 1, and 16 Car. 2, ch. 7, were repealed by the "Negotiable Instruments Law" (Act of Congress of January 12, 1899), so far as inconsistent therewith, and that a note in gambling stock transactions might be recovered by a bona fide holder.

[2] Pendleton vs. Smissaert, 1 Col. App. 508; 29 Pac. Rep. 521.

1871), voiding notes given in gaming transactions, was held in Shaw vs. Clark[1] not to apply to "option dealings" in wheat.

In Texas cities may suppress gambling houses and fraudulent devices (Sayle's Texas Civ. Stats. art. 431, Act, March 15, 1875, § 44). And gaming is prohibited by ch. 3 of the Texas Penal Code.

In North Dakota it is provided that losses incurred by betting on any game may be recovered (Rev. Stats. of 1895, § 7235).

In Oregon gambling contracts are void (Codes and Statutes of Oregon of 1902, § 1945).

The keeping of any gambling apparatus is declared unlawful by § 7852 of the South Dakota Statutes of 1899. The following circumstances warranted a finding that transactions in grain and other commodities were mere gambling on the market prices: The fact that the Brokers knew that the customer could not financially make the large purchases which had been made; that he was not in the business of dealing in such commodities; that notwithstanding formal orders to buy and sell, differences only were settled; the customer's own testimony to that effect, and similar testimony of other customers of plaintiffs.[2]

In Arizona gaming by unlicensed persons is punishable by fine or imprisonment (Rev. Stats. of 1901, ch. IX).

Gaming is also made a criminal offence by the Indian Territory Statutes, ch. 38; by the Montana Stats. (Sander's edition), ch. 9; and by the Comp. Stats. of Nebraska of 1901, § 6877.

Gambling is punishable by fine or imprisonment in Flor-

---

[1] 49 Mich. 384.   [2] Waite vs. Frank, 86 N. W. Rep. 645.

ida (Rev. Stats. § 2651, as amended by L. 1895, p. 364);
and in Idaho, by Penal Code, § 4846.

In Nevada gambling, except by licensed persons, is forbidden (Comp. Laws, § 1263).

In New Mexico securities given for gambling debts are void (Comp. Laws, § 3202).

Gambling is made a criminal offence by the Statutes of Oklahoma, ch. 56.

In Utah gaming is a misdemeanor (Rev. Stats. of 1898, § 4261). Also in Washington (Codes and Stats. of 1897, § 7260). And in Wyoming all gambling contracts are void (Rev. Stats. of 1899, § 2187).

Gambling is also prohibited by the Penal Code of California (§ 350), but this statute apparently would not include transactions in "futures." See the constitutional provision, *supra*. The same observation applies to the Indian Territory Stats. (§ 1170–90). See *supra* as to dealing in "futures." And the Penal Code of Montana, § 600, and § 214 of the Criminal Code of Nebraska also prohibit gaming at faro, etc., and do not cover transactions in "futures."

In Metropolitan Bank vs. Jansen[1] it was held that gambling in grain "futures" without intent to deliver, is now void in the United States, even in the absence of a prohibitory statute, and a bank cannot recover the amount of a note given in such transactions.

In conclusion it may be said that the general tendency of the courts of the various States is to consider all gaming and wagering contracts as utterly void; to look upon them as insidious enemies to our modern public policy and standard of morality, fostering unhealthy desires for sud-

[1] 47 C. C. A. 497.

den gain, destroying the spirit of patient labor, and presenting easy avenues to demoralizing habits of speculation
—often to positive crime.[1]

We shall now proceed to examine the cases under the
statutes and principles governing "wagers" which have
arisen out of transactions in securities and in "petroleum,"
"cotton"[2] and "grain"—operations in the three last-
mentioned kinds of merchandise being very similar to
dealings in stocks—first setting forth those adjudications
in which the defence of "wager" has been sustained;
secondly, those in which it has been overruled; and,
thirdly, deducing the results of the cases into general principles.

In the outset, the general proposition upon the subject of
wagers may be stated as follows: If the agreement between
the parties is a *bona fide* contract to buy and sell, the law
will sustain it; but where it appears from the evidence
that there is no real contract of sale, and that the whole
arrangement is to be settled by the payment of "differences," it will be set aside.[3] This statement is conceded in

[1] See Irwin vs. Williar, 110 U. S.
499, and cases cited.

[2] See "Ray on Contractual Limitations," p. 38 et seq., and valuable
note on "Cotton Futures" by Mr.
Alfred B. Shepperson, contained in
the appendix to that work, as also
"Protest of the New York Cotton
Exchange" against the passage of
bills in Congress to prevent dealing
in options and futures.

[3] And not only will the original
contract be set aside, but certain
classes of collateral contracts arising therefrom. Thus when a contract for the sale of rye in Chicago

was illegal, there being no intention
to deliver, or to hand over warehouse receipts, but merely to settle
differences, damages cannot be recovered from a telegraph company
for a loss on sales occasioned by
delay in the delivery of a telegram.
Melchert vs. American U. Tel. Co.,
3 McCrary, 521. See valuable note
on option sales by Mr. Francis
Wharton appended to the report of
this case.

It was held in Bryant vs. Western
Union Telegraph Co., 17 Fed. Rep.
825, that a dealer in grain and pork,
who kept a "bucket shop" could

all of the cases; and whatever inconsistency or want of
harmony there may be in the decisions will be found to
arise from the different interpretations the courts have
placed upon the facts, and which can only be ascertained
by a review of the adjudications.

(c.) *Wagers between Principals.*

There is a marked distinction in those cases which have
arisen between the *direct* parties to a contract—as, for instance, a vendor and a vendee—and those in which a
Broker, acting for a principal, has entered into agreements
with third persons in behalf of his principal, and then
seeks indemnity from the latter for money laid out, etc.,
and commissions in such transactions. In the former class,
if the intention of the parties is not to deliver or receive
property, but to settle by the mere payment of differences,
the contract is a wager. But a Broker may be ignorant of
the unlawful intention of his principals, and may then recover for money paid out, commissions, etc., although the
principals would be unable to enforce the contract as between themselves.[1]

This important distinction will be found to be supported
in all of the well-considered cases. Under this head, therefore, we shall set forth the cases arising between *principals*
in stock transactions, remarking in the beginning that the
cases seem to be few in which the defence of wager has
been sustained.

not compel a telegraph company to
furnish him with "ticker" quotations from the Chicago Board of
Trade, although he was a member
of that board, and although there is
no statute in Kentucky making
such gambling criminal.

[1] Warren vs. Hewitt, 45 Ga. 201,
and cases cited under subd. (d),
p. 551.

The first case which arose under the act of Victoria was that of Grizewood vs. Blane.[1] The plaintiff, who was a Stock-jobber in London, brought an action of assumpsit against the defendant, who had, through his Broker, contracted to sell certain shares of stock, which he did not own, to the plaintiff, deliverable at a future time. The market in the meantime having advanced, the defendant could not deliver the stocks at the price the plaintiff had bargained to pay for them, whereupon it was agreed between the parties that, instead of delivering the stocks, the defendant should pay the differences between the contract and the market price on the day they were to be delivered. The action was upon this last agreement to recover the "differences." The defendant interposed the defence that the contract was illegal, as a wager on the price of the shares, setting forth in his plea the very language of the act. The court, upon special demurrer, gave judgment for the plaintiff, holding that the plea was bad, and that the defendant was bound to show the circumstances which made the contract set forth in the declaration a gaming one. The case subsequently came to trial on the issues of fact. The court left it to the jury to say what was the intention of the parties at the time of making the contract, whether either party really meant to purchase or sell the shares in question; that, if they did not, the contract was a gambling transaction and void. The jury found for the defendant. Upon appeal, this ruling was sustained, and the rule thus established of leaving the intention of the parties to be determined by the jury has, it seems, been substantially ad-

[1] 20 Eng. L. & Eq. 290; for declaration in the case, see 8 id. 415; s. c. 11 C. B. 538.

hered to, except by the courts of Pennsylvania, to which allusion will hereafter be made.[1]

In Whitlark vs. Davis[2] it was held that an outside Broker (who acted as a principal) was entitled to recover differences when he was ready to deliver the securities at any time if called upon by defendant to do so, and that the contract was a real one, and not within the statute.

In The Universal Stock Exchange vs. Strachan[3] it was decided however by the House of Lords that when the intention was that "differences" only should be accounted for, and that no stocks or shares should be delivered, an option to demand delivery or acceptance thereof did not take the case out of the statute, but securities deposited by one party with the other to secure the payment of "differences" might be recovered, as they were not deposited "to abide the event," but it was held in Strachan vs. Universal Stock Exchange, Ld. (No. 2),[4] that if money so deposited had been appropriated by the depositee as against losses, to the knowledge of the depositor, the latter could not recover.

The decision of the House of Lords in Universal Stock Exchange vs. Strachan, *supra*, as to the effect of an option, was followed in Re Gieve[5] and it was held in Ex parte Waud[6] that as such a contract was illegal, a promise by a Broker, acting as a principal, to deliver stock in payment of differences, was without consideration, and damages could not be recovered for the non-delivery.

In the United States, beginning with the State of New

---

[1] See also s. c. 11 C. B. 526; Marshall vs. Thurston, 3 Lea (Tenn.), 743.
[2] 10 Times L. R. 425.

[3] (1896) App. Cas. 166.
[4] (1895) 2 Q. B. D. 697.
[5] (1899) 1 Q. B. 794.
[6] (1898) 2 Q. B. 383.

York, we find a case [1] somewhat analogous to Grizewood vs. Blane, where a demurrer was interposed to the complaint, but with a different result from that reached in the English case. In that case the Superior Court of New York interpreted the statute upon the subject of wagers, and held that an answer to a complaint for damages for non-delivery of certain pork, which set up " that it was not the intention of the defendant to make any actual sale or delivery of pork to the plaintiff, nor was it the intention of the plaintiff actually to buy or receive any pork from the defendant; that it was the mutual design of both the plaintiff and defendant, at the making of the said supposed contracts, that the same should not be specifically performed in whole or in part; but, on the contrary, that at the maturity of said supposed contracts, the differences between the then market value of the pork therein mentioned and the price of the same fixed in said supposed contracts should be paid by the one party to the other, as performance or satisfaction of said supposed contracts," was good. The court distinguished the case from Grizewood vs. Blane on the ground that the language of the New York statute was broader than the English act, but fully concurred in the result of that case. There are other cases where the defence of wager has been sustained, especially in the State of Pennsylvania, but they more appropriately belong to the other subdivisions of this chapter. [2]

Beginning with England, we find that the decided tendency of the courts of that country has been to reject the defence of wager where it has been introduced to defeat a

---

[1] Cassar l vs. Hinman. 1 Posw 207; aff'g 14 How. (N Y) Pr 81. [2] See post, p. 556.

recovery in actions growing out of Stock Exchange transactions.

To illustrate this tendency, it is necessary to set forth
but a few of the leading modern cases. In the following
cases, the court, under a defence of wager, examined dealings of members of the London Stock Exchange *inter se*,
and pronounced them invulnerable under the statute of Victoria before cited. A, B, and C were members of the Stock
Exchange, according to the rules and customs of which
there are two days appointed in a month for settling transactions relating to foreign securities; and, in case of a loan
upon or a sale of such securities, the lender or seller has the
right, in case of non-payment of the loan or non-completion
of the purchase, either to sell or take them at their market
value—the deficiency, if any, in the price being paid to the
borrower or purchaser, and the surplus, if any, beyond the
loan or purchase-money being paid by him to the lender or
seller, who, if the borrower or purchaser is declared a defaulter, is bound to take the securities at a price fixed by
the official assignees of the association. According to these
rules and customs, A lent to C money on the security of
foreign railway shares, which were of the full value of the
loan, and on each succeeding settling-day the amount of depreciation or increase in the value of the shares was paid by C
or A respectively to the other, till C was declared a defaulter,
when A took the shares at the price fixed by the official
assignee. C was afterwards adjudged a bankrupt, and A
tendered a proof for the balance due him in respect of the
transaction, after deducting the price at which he had taken
the shares.

According to the same rules and customs, B agreed with
C to sell him one hundred foreign railway shares for a cer-

tain sum. The transaction was not completed, but on each succeeding settling-day the differences were paid by B or C, as in A's case; and, on C being declared a defaulter, B likewise took the shares at their value, and, on C's bankruptcy, tendered a proof for the balance due to him in respect of the said shares. The proofs were both rejected on the ground that the transactions were illegal as wagers. On appeal, the Court of Appeals reversed this ruling, and held that the transactions were regular and legal. The court, in the opinion, laid stress upon the facts proved in each case—that the transactions had been conducted in accordance with the rules of the Stock Exchange; that there was an actual advance of money and a deposit of shares in the one case, and that in the other case the dividends on the shares alleged to have been sold were accounted for to the bankrupt.[1]

In the case of Shaw vs. Caledonian Railway Co.[2] the court held that transactions between a principal and an outside stock dealer were not gambling ones, although plaintiff, who was the only witness examined, swore that he had no contract except for the payment of differences, the court holding that if either one, or both, of the parties, could demand or give delivery of the stocks, the transaction was a real one, and not for the payment of differences.

The principle of this decision was followed in Lowenfeld vs. Howat,[3] the court holding that where there was a clear contract disclosed by the bought and sold notes, the transactions were not gambling ones, unless it could be shown by

---

[1] In re Morgan, Ex parte Phillips and Ex parte Marnham, 6 Jur. (n. s.) 1273; 9 W. R. 131; 2 De G. F. & J. 634; 30 L. J. Bank. 1; 3 L. T. (n. s.) 510.

[2] (1890) 17 Court Ses. Cas. (4th Series) 466.

[3] 19 Court Ses. Cas. (4th Series) 128.

some other written or oral contract, that the original contract was not intended to be a real one, and the evidence did not disclose such a subsidiary agreement.

To the same effect is Universal Stock Exchange vs. Stevens,[1] where it was held that plaintiff stock-jobbers were entitled to recover the balance due them, as, although the parties contemplated that actual deliveries of stock should not take place except under special circumstances, the contracts were in fact sales and purchases of stock, and not wagering, although the parties thought that the contracts would in the long run result in the mere payment of differences.

In the State of New York the leading case upon the subject of wagers is Bigelow vs. Benedict,[2] where the instrument sued on was as follows :

" ATTICA, *Jan.* 23, 1865.

" Know all men by these presents, that I, C. B. Benedict, for and in consideration of the sum of $250, do agree to receive from M. C. Bigelow, at any time within six months from date he may choose to deliver the same, $2,500 in gold coin of the United States, for which I agree to pay to the said B. 95 per cent. premium on the dollar, or at the rate of $195 in good current funds for each and every $100 of coin. The said B. does not contract to deliver the coin, but pays the $250 for the privilege of delivering or not, at his option.

Signed,   " C. B. B."

The plaintiff Bigelow tendered the gold before the time mentioned in the contract had expired, brought suit and recovered judgment for the difference between the market value in current funds of gold at the time of tender and the price specified in the contract, with interest. The validity of the contract was assailed on the ground that it was a

---

[1] 66 L. T. R. 612.   [2] 70 N. Y. 202.

wager. The appellate court held that there was nothing illegal on the face of the contract; and as no evidence had been given showing former dealings between the parties, or any vicious intent, the judgment below was sustained. The court was of opinion that the circumstances relied on to show that the contract was a wager—viz., first, that it was a contract for the sale of gold; and, second, that it was optional on the part of the seller—did not authorize the inference that it was illegal. While the court admitted that, if the contract in question was a mere device to evade the statute, it would be illegal, the question was, did the contract on its face disclose an illegal transaction? The court concluded that it did not, and that the defence of illegality was not established, the burden of proof resting upon the defendant to establish the same.[1]

But in a later case in the Supreme Court of Wisconsin,[2] it was decided that to " uphold a contract in writing for the sale and delivery of grain at a future day for a price certain, it must affirmatively and satisfactorily appear that it was made with an actual view to the delivery and receipt of the grain, and not as a cover for a gambling transaction." The law upon this subject is clearly and well stated in Kirkpat-

---

[1] See also Peabody vs. Speyers, 56 N. Y. 230; Cameron vs. Durkheim, 55 id. 425; Cook vs. Davis, 53 id. 318; 43 id. 209; Trebilcock vs. Wilson, 12 Wall. (U. S.) 687; McIlvaine vs. Egerton, 2 Robt. (N. Y.) 422; Stanton vs. Small, 3 Sandf. 230; Tyler vs. Barrows, 6 Robt. 101. The fact that only a part of the price of gold (i. e., a margin) is furnished, does not make the contract illegal. Wheeless vs. Fisk, 28 La. Ann. 732.

[2] Barnard vs. Backhaus, 52 Wis. 593. This decision was followed in Lowry vs. Dillman, 59 Wis. 197, where it was held that the question whether a note given by the customer to the commission merchant was 'for losses on "future" dealings in barley without intent to deliver, was for the jury. Where one of the parties intends delivery it is not gambling. Wall vs. Schneider, 59 Wis. 352.

rick vs. Bonsall,[1] and the views there expressed accord with
common-sense and the ordinary course of business transactions. As was remarked by Agnew, J., in this case:
" We must not confound gambling, whether it be in corporation stock or merchandise, with what is commonly called
speculation. Merchants speculate upon the future prices of
that in which they deal, and buy and sell accordingly. In
other words, they think of and weigh—that is, speculate upon
—the probabilities of the coming market, and act upon this
lookout into the future in their business transactions; and
in this they often exhibit high mental grasp and great
knowledge of business and of the affairs of the world.
Their speculations display talent and forecast, but they act
upon their conclusions, and buy or sell in a *bona fide* way."
And the law does not condemn such transactions, providing
the intention really is that the commodity shall be actually
delivered and received when the time for delivery arrives.
Consequently no legal objection exists to such time contracts,
which are to be performed in the future by the actual delivery of the property by the vendor, and the receipt and
payment of the price by the vendee, if the contract is in
writing; and it is also true that a contract for the sale of
goods to be delivered at a future day is not invalidated by
the circumstance that at the time the contract was made the
vendor has neither the goods in his possession nor has
entered into an agreement to buy them. A party may go
into the market and buy the goods which he has agreed to
sell and deliver.[2]

It has also been decided that a purchase of grain at a cer-

---

[1] 72 Pa. St. 155; Rumsey vs.   [2] Barnard vs. Backhaus, supra.
Berry, 65 Me. 570; Gregory vs.
Wendell, 39 Mich. 337.

tain price per bushel, made in good faith, to be delivered in the next month, giving the seller until the last day of the month, at his option, in which to deliver, is not an illegal or gambling contract, and that the purchaser would be entitled to its benefit, no matter what may have been the secret intention of the seller.[1]

An interesting question arising on contracts for the sale of grain, settled by payment of differences, was passed on by Judge Gresham in the United States Circuit Court for Indiana. It had already been well settled in previous cases that a contract, which on its face does not show an intention not to deliver, is presumed to have been an actual purchase or sale, and, though optional, is valid until the party impeaching the contract shows an illegal intent. The question as to what evidence will show the intent, and particularly whether the fact that the contract was actually settled by adjustment of differences, or that there was a usage to do so, necessarily shows it to have been illegal, or suffices to raise a legal presumption that the intent to make such a settlement existed in the inception of the contract, arose in the case before Judge Gresham, and he ruled that such a usage did not necessarily make the contract void.

The testimony tended to show that a general custom obtained among grain commission-merchants in Baltimore to the following effect: When one commission-merchant, upon the order of a Client, sells to another commission-merchant a quantity of grain for future delivery, and where it occurs that at some other time before the maturity of the contract the same commission-merchant receives an order from another Client to purchase the same or a larger quantity of

---

[1] Pixley vs. Boynton, 79 Ill. 351.

the same kind of grain, for the same future delivery, and he executes this second order by making the purchase from the same commission-merchant to whom he had made the sale in the other case—then in such case the two commission-merchants meet together and exchange or cancel the contracts as between themselves, adjusting the difference in the prices between the two contracts, and restoring any margins that may have been put up ; and from that time forth the first commission-merchant holds, for the benefit of the Client for whom he sold, the order or contract of the purchaser for whom he bought, so that the wheat of the selling Client may, when delivered, be turned in on the order or contract of the purchasing Client, and the commission-merchant is held responsible as guaranty to his Client. The evidence also tended to show a custom obtaining among commission-merchants in Baltimore to the further effect that though the second transaction may have been had with a different commission-merchant from the one with whom the first transaction was had, yet where it can be found that a series of contracts are in existence for the sale of like grain for like delivery, so that the seller owes the wheat to the buyer to whom he sold, and he to another who owes like wheat for like delivery to the first commission-merchant, then in such case they settle by what they call " a ring "—that is, they all reciprocally surrender or cancel their contracts, adjust the price differences between themselves, and surrender all margins that had been put up ; that in all such cases the commission-merchant substitutes the contract of another Client in place of that with the commission-merchant whose contract has been cancelled or surrendered, and that he guarantees to his Client the performance of the contract originally made on his behalf.

The judge instructed the jury that these customs were founded in commercial convenience; that they are not in contravention of the law; and that they were valid. He also charged them that the burden of showing that the parties were carrying on a wagering business, and were not engaged in legitimate trade or speculation, rests upon the defendant. On their face these transactions are legal, and the law does not, in the absence of proof, presume that parties are gambling. A transaction which on its face is legitimate cannot be held void as a wagering contract by showing that one party only so understood and meant it to be. The proof must go further, and show that this misunderstanding was mutual—that both parties so understood the transaction.[1]

In Pennsylvania the following contract was sustained: "November 10, 1870. In consideration of $1,000 we agree to deliver B., should he call for it during the first six months

---

[1] Williar vs. Irwin, 12 Chic. Leg. News, 241, aff'd as to the definition of a wagering contract, 110 U. S. 507. See also, in this connection, Gregory vs. Wendell, 40 Mich. 432.

If two persons have a deal in grain "futures" with the keeper of a "bucket shop," and one advances half the sum required for margin, for which he takes the borrower's note, he cannot recover the amount of such note. Davis vs. Davis, 119 Ind. 511.

If, however, delivery was intended, and warehouse receipts are actually delivered by the Brokers to the principals, one of the latter may recover the amount of a note given by the other, being his moiety of a loss on sale. Fisher vs. Fisher, 8 Ind. App. 665.

If a note is given by grain Brokers for profits made by their customer in gambling transactions in futures, the latter cannot recover on the plea that the relation of principal and agent exists. Nave vs. Wilson, 12 Ind. App. 38.

Mere knowledge on the part of one loaning money that the borrower intends to gamble in grain futures in Chicago, when the lender is not a party to such transactions, will not defeat a recovery, Jackson vs Bank, 125 Ind. 347, but it is otherwise if he is interested in such transactions. Plank vs. Jackson, 128 Ind. 424.

of 1871, 5,000 barrels of oil. If said oil is called for, this call becomes a contract; ten days' notice shall be given; and B. agrees to receive and pay for the same, cash on delivery, at 10½ cents a gallon." This contract was attacked as a gambling transaction; but the court, upon reasoning similar to that used by the courts of New York in Bigelow vs. Benedict,[1] held that this did not appear from the face of the instrument; but that it was for the jury to say whether, in view of all the facts, it was a mere scheme to gamble upon the chance of prices.[2] In fine, in the language of Lord Coke : " It is a general rule that whensoever the words of a deed, or of the parties without deed, may leave a double intendment, and the one standeth with law and right, and

---

[1] Ante, p. 542.

[2] Kirkpatrick vs. Bonsall, 72 Pa. St. 155.

A note given by one partner to another in dealings in oil, on margins, where no delivery was had, is not recoverable. Hall vs. Law, 1 Pa. C. C. R. 477; McGrew vs. McGregor, 4 Penny. 100. If one of two principals should die, a claim by the other arising out of a stock gambling transaction is not enforceable against the former's estate. Thompson's Est., 11 W. N. C. 371. When, however, one actually buys, through a Broker, stock for another, at the latter's request, and holds it till the purchase money is paid by his co-principal, he can recover from the latter the loss occasioned by a sale of the stock when it is not taken up by the borrower. Potts vs. Dunlop, 110 Pa. St. 177. If the stocks are delivered, the transaction is not a gambling one. Stewart vs. Parnell, 147 Pa. St. 323.

When the parties are sui juris, money given to invest in stock gambling is not recoverable. Ib. When the transactions in stocks are large, but the amount of money advanced, small, the inference is that the dealings were upon a wager, and one principal cannot recover from another, even though there was an account started, and a promise to pay. Patterson's Appeal, 13 W. N. C. 154. A judgment given by one principal to another, to cover his share of the losses in dealing in stocks on margin, is not recoverable. Collings vs. Nevin, 30 P. L. J. 238.

See Waugh vs. Beck, 114 Pa. St. 422; 6 Atl. Rep. 923 (one who lends money and takes a note therefor to further a wagering transaction may recover, even although he has knowledge that it is to be so used, provided he does not confederate with the borrower as to the use of the money advanced).

the other is wrongful and against law, the intendment that
standeth with the law shall be taken." [1]

In Wakefield vs. Farnum [2] it was held that there was
evidence that defendants, Brokers in Boston, dealt with
their customer residing in Massachusetts as principal, in
wheat transactions which were held by the court below to
be gambling ones by the common-law of Massachusetts, although they carried out their contracts through Chicago
Brokers, and therefore the contract was made in Boston between the customer and the Boston Brokers and not between
the Chicago Brokers and the unknown persons with whom
they dealt, and it was not necessary to show that the contract was a wagering one in Chicago. In this case the Boston Brokers had furnished an account showing a balance
due their Client, and it was held that the latter could not
recover such balance. And in Northrup vs. Buffington [3] it
was held that a customer could not recover margins and
profits on stock transactions from Boston Stock-brokers,
although the latter were doing a commission business for
New York Brokers, through whom the transactions were
effected, the contracts having been found to be gambling
ones. When one employs a Stock-broker to sell shares, and
the shares are sold by the Broker, the contract is not a wagering one unless both seller and buyer understood that
there was to be no delivery of the shares. [4]

A contract for the delivery of cotton, not then in existence, to be received in payment of fertilizers and supplies, is illegal in Georgia. [5] One who deals in cotton " fu-

[1] Co. Lit. 42, 188; but compare
Matter of Chandler, 13 Am. Law
Reg. (n. s) 310.
[2] 170 Mass. 422.
[3] 171 Mass. 468.
[4] Barnes vs. Smith, 159 Mass.
541.
[5] Inman vs. Swifte, 89 Ga. 376.

tures " during the day, and buys or sells during the night to cover himself, is a principal and not an agent, and cannot recover.[1]

A note given by customers to Brokers, to cover margins in futures, cannot be recovered by an endorsee, when the transactions are gambling ones.[2]

When two principals jointly made purchases of wheat through commission merchants, one is entitled to recover from the other, a moiety of the losses on the transactions, and commissions paid to the Broker, when, although there might be a suspicion that the parties through whom the plaintiff principal dealt, through his Brokers, were dealers in " options," yet it was not so pleaded or proved, and the court would not presume the contract to be illegal.[3] But where the intention of both parties clearly was to settle by differences only, and not to deliver the commodities (hogs), although actually in possession of one of the parties at the time, the transaction is a pure wagering one.[4] When in a contract for the sale of corn, the plaintiff vendee contemplated actual delivery to him, but the defendant merely intended to speculate on differences without delivery, the contract is not a wagering one, and the fact that plaintiff knew that defendant intended to gamble, does not make such intention, the intention of both parties, so as to render the contract one of a gambling character.[5] If the buyer of corn for future delivery intends actual delivery, and the seller intends to deliver the corn if he can obtain it at a profit,

---

[1] Thompson vs. Cummings, 68 Ga. 124.

[2] First National Bank vs. Oskaloosa Packing Co., 66 Iowa, 41.

[3] Cockrell vs. Thompson, 85 Mo. 510.

[4] Johnson vs. Kaune, 21 Mo. App. 22.

[5] Jones vs. Shale, 34 Mo. 302.

otherwise to pay the difference in money, the contract is not a gambling one under the statute as to "futures."[1]

It was held in Texas, in the case of Cleveland vs. Heidenheimer,[2] that where a contract for future delivery of bacon was doubtful, a request by the vendee to have the goods delivered on delivery day, and an attempt by the vendor to deliver them, validates it.

(d.) *Actions by Brokers for Money Laid Out, etc., and Commissions in Stock Transactions.*

We propose to consider separately those cases in which the defence of " wager " has been set up in actions brought by Stock-brokers to recover for money laid out in stock transactions at the request and for the use of the Client, together with commissions due him for services in such dealings, again calling attention to the distinction drawn by the decisions between this class of cases and those in which the contest is between the direct parties to the contract.

In the outset it will be noticed that the statute of Victoria does not render wagering contracts themselves " illegal," but declares that they shall be " null and void," and that no suit shall be maintained upon them. In this respect it differs from the Stock-jobbing Act of Sir John Barnard, by which similar contracts were prohibited under a penalty. Accordingly, no claim arising out of such contracts could be enforced at law because of its illegality. The distinction between the two acts is forcibly illustrated in actions by Brokers for commissions. As we have seen

---

[1] Deierling vs. Sloop, 69 Mo. App. 416.　　[2] 44 S. W. Rep. 551.

under "Sir John Barnard's Act," a Broker could not recover as against his principal for commissions, or for money
laid out for him, in transactions in the nature of gaming,
because the Broker could not establish his rights except
by showing that he had done something forbidden under a
penalty, and consequently illegal.[1] Yet, under the act of
8 and 9 Victoria, the contracts being voidable only,[2] a
Broker could recover,[3] even if he knew that the contract
entered into was void under the statute;[4] for if one person requests another to pay any loss that may occur in
such a transaction, there is a continuing request to pay until revoked.[5] In fine, the law as to gaming contracts is,
that all such contracts are simply null and void. They
are not, therefore, illegal, and the parties making them are
not liable to any actions or penalties.

These distinctions were very forcibly noticed in Rosewarne vs. Billing, where all of the decisions were referred
to. In that case, Erle, C. J., said : " I am clearly of opin-

---

[1] Ante, p. 483; see also Wells vs. Porter, 2 Bing. (N. C.) 722.

[2] Higginson vs. Simpson, L. R. 2 C. P. D. 76.

[3] See cases ante, p. 483; also Jessopp vs. Lutwyche, 10 Ex. 614; Knight vs. Chambers, 15 C. B. 562; Knight vs. Fitch, id. 566; 3 C. L. R. 567; I Jur. (n. s.) 526; 24 L. J. C. P. 122; Bubb vs. Yelverton, 24 L. T. (n. s.) 822.

[4] Rosewarne vs. Billing, 15 C. B. (n. s.) 316; Ex parte Rogers, 15 Ch. Div. 207; Read vs Anderson, 13 Q. B. D. 779 (as to betting agents); Forget vs. Ostigney, (1895) A. C. 318 (as to Canadian Stock-brokers,

the Canadian Civil Code being similar to the English statute).

[5] Id. See also Oldham vs. Rams-
den, 44 L. J. C. P. 309; Bubb vs.
Yelverton, 24 L. T. 822; Higginson
vs. Simpson, L. R. 2 C. P. D. 76;
Beeston vs. Beeston, L. R. 1 Ex.
Div. 13; Ex parte Pyke, In re Lus-
ter, L. R. 8 Ch. Div. 754. A jobber
may recover on notes given by one
to an outside Broker employed by
him to conduct dealings in stocks
and shares, which were known by
the jobber to be gambling transactions, and which were endorsed
over by the Broker to the jobber for
valuable consideration. Lilly vs.
Rankin, 56 L. J. Q. B. 248.

ion that if a man loses a wager, and gets another to pay
the money for him, an action lies for the recovery of the
money so paid."[1] And the court held that the fact that
the Broker made the contracts for the payment of differences in his own name, according to the usage of Brokers,
but for the account of his principal, made no difference in
the result. Of course, these views are subject to modification and change where the language of a statute is not in
substantial accord with that of Victoria, heretofore cited;
for such terms may undoubtedly be used by the legislature
as would prevent any recovery upon wagering contracts
either directly or indirectly.[2]

In the case of Cooper vs. Neil[3] it appeared that the defendant employed one B., a Broker, to enter into contracts
upon the Stock Exchange for the purchase of shares. B.
knew the defendant did not intend to accept the shares,
but only to receive or pay "differences" according to the
rise or fall in the market price of the shares. B. entered
into contracts with Jobbers for the purchase of shares, in
pursuance of the defendant's instructions, and, according to
the rules of the Stock Exchange, became personally liable
on the contracts. He was afterwards declared insolvent,
and the plaintiff, as his trustee, sued upon an implied contract of indemnity against the claims of the Jobbers. At
the trial the jury found that the contracts with the Jobbers were mere time bargains, and judgment was given
for the defendant. The court, upon appeal, however, held
that the verdict was unsatisfactory, and a new trial was directed; and, in giving its opinion, the court foreshadowed

---

[1] But see Hare, P. J., contra, in Fareira vs. Gabell, 89 Pa. St. 89.

[2] See as to the effect of the Gam-ing Act, 1892, post, p. 555.

[3] 13 Week. Notes, 128.

the result reached in Thacker vs. Hardy[1] by laying down the proposition that if the defendant employed B. to make contracts upon the Stock Exchange with the Jobbers, according to the rules of the latter body, and therefore contracts that were real so far as the Jobbers were concerned, but that B. undertook with the defendant that he would so manage, or endeavor to manage, the contracts with the Jobbers that the defendant would never be called upon to pay or receive more than differences if B. succeeded, the implication was that there was an implied contract that if B. incurred liabilities without his own fault the defendant would indemnify him.[2]

But where the agreement was that the Broker should, at the Client's direction, buy shares and sell them, the profits to belong to the Client—the Broker being *personally liable to him for these profits*—and the losses to be borne by the Client, the Broker personally, and not by way of indemnity, receiving those losses—held, a wagering contract within the statute.[3] The fact that the Brokers are in either case to receive their commissions and charges does not alter the result.[4]

The court, however, laid stress upon the want of averment by the Brokers that the latter, in making for the defendant a contract of purchase and sale, contracted any liabilities themselves to the vendor and vendee, or that they paid any money to the vendor or received any money from the vendee.

[1] Post.

[2] See also, as explaining and distinguishing this case, Thacker vs. Hardy, L. R. 4 Q. B. D. 685; and see also Lyne vs. Siesfield, 1 H. & N. 278.

[3] Byers vs. Beattie, 16 W. R. 279; 2 Ir. R. C. L. 220.

[4] Id. It was also held that this invalidity might be taken advantage of by demurrer without any special plea.

In Reggio vs. Stevens & Co.,[1] which was an action by a principal to recover winnings, and a sum deposited as cover, the defendant, an outside Broker, pleaded that the transactions were gambling ones under the act of 1845, and the court upheld this plea so far as regarded the winnings, on the ground that neither party intended to take up the stock, but held plaintiff entitled to the "cover." The evidence indicated that the plaintiff might have the right to call for delivery, but this question was not considered by the court, as it appeared that he had no intention of taking up the stock.

So in Re Green [2] it was held that "contracts of sale which do not contemplate the actual *bona fide* delivery of the property by the seller, nor payment by the buyer, but are intended to be settled by paying the difference in price at some future time, are void under the Wisconsin statute against gaming contracts." And this rule was applied to a Broker who had advanced the differences on such a contract for a bankrupt. It was decided he could not prove his claim for the amount so advanced. In that case the court, in rendering its opinion, said: " But, plain as it appears, the case of Rosewarne vs. Billing, cited by the claimant's counsel, seems to sanction a different doctrine. But I do not think that case can be regarded as the law upon this point in England. There are cases in conflict with it, so I think it may be safely asserted that the weight of English authorities is with Steers vs. Lashley." [3]

But, as we shall see, the case of Rosewarne vs. Billing has been directly endorsed by the English courts.

In 1892 the gaming act [4] was passed as a result of the de-

---

[1] 4 T. L. R. 326.　　　　　　　[3] 6 Term R. 61.
[2] 15 Nat. Bank. Reg. 198.　　　[4] 55 & 56 Vict. c. 9.

cision in the betting case of Read vs. Anderson[1] which held that a betting agent might recover from his principal the amount of a bet paid by him on behalf of his principal, although if the bet had not been paid, the winner could not, under the provisions of the act of 1845, recover it. It provided that promises to repay sums paid under contracts void by 8 and 9 Vict. c. 109, should be null and void. There have been no decisions under this statute, as to transactions on the Stock Exchange, or between Stock-brokers and their principals, although there have been several decisions as to betting and wagering generally, from which it would seem that a Broker cannot now recover unless he was ignorant of the fact that the transactions were gambling ones, or unless the law of estoppel aids him.[2]

Mr. G. Herbert Stutfield, in his works on " Betting, Time-Bargains and Gaming," and " Rules and Usages of the Stock Exchange," is of opinion that the act of 1892 does not affect the relations between Stock-broker and Client, as transactions in the Stock Exchange are never "difference bargains" or wager contracts, although "bucket shop" transactions might be otherwise. In a footnote to Chitty's English Statutes, vol. 4, p. 57, the editor, Mr. Lely, is also of opinion that this statute does not make Stock Exchange speculative transactions void even as between Broker and principal, as ordinarily conducted. Although an agent cannot, under the act, recover, a principal may recover bets paid to the agent.[3]

Pennsylvania presents a number of decisions in which the

[1] 13 Q. B. D. 779.

[2] Tatem vs. Reeve, (1893) 1 Q. B. 44; Carney vs. Plimmer, (1897) 1 Q. B. 635; Saffrey vs. Mayer, (1901) 1 K. B. 11; O'Sullivan vs. Thomas, (1895) 1 Q. B. D. 698; Burge vs. Ashley, (1900) 1 Q. B. 754.

[3] De Mattos vs. Benjamin, 70 L. T. 560. See also Coldridge "Law of Gambling," chapters IX and X

defence of "wager" was interposed to actions by Stock-brokers, and the highest tribunal in that State has laid down the doctrine in favor of sustaining the defence, with such manifest rigidity and so inconsistently with the leading decisions of England and the States of the Union as to draw forth sharp criticisms both from the bench and the bar of its own State.[1]

The first case which we deem it necessary to notice is Brua's Appeal.[2] In that case one K. made a contract in writing with one II., as follows: "I have this day sold and agreed to deliver to J. S. II., or to his order, twenty-five days from this date, two hundred shares Harlem Railroad common stock, at the rate of sixty dollars per share;" and at the same time delivered his promissory note for $1,000, as margin on the contract, it being a "short sale;" and subsequently, as the stock rose in price, delivered to II. other notes as additional margin. K. having made an assignment, these notes were proved as claims against his estate, and were allowed by the auditors. Upon appeal the Supreme Court reversed this judgment, upon the ground that as the auditors had found as a fact that " the notes were a component part of a stock-gambling transaction, in which K., in effect, betted that in twenty-five days Harlem stock would sell at less than $60," such finding was conclusive upon the court, and it necessarily followed that, being a " gambling contract, it could not be enforced; and that the holder of the promissory notes, having known this, and having taken them after they were due, it was established that

<hr>

[1] See article of Mr. Justice Briggs, 38 Leg. Int. (Pa.) 116; Lewis on Stocks, etc., 109, where it is said, "The law of Pennsylvania upon this question is unique, and opposed to all authorities." See also Biddle on Stock brokers, 115.

[2] 55 Pa. St. 294.

there was no legal consideration for them, and that the holder was not in a position to escape the taint that renders them worthless." This is the whole of that case, and it will be observed that it was not one which occurred through the instrumentality of Stock-brokers, but was a transaction between *the parties themselves;* and the appellate court found, in addition to the facts stated, that "the actual transfer of stock between these parties was not contemplated by them."

The court did not decide that "short sales" were illegal, but it used this language: "It is said the form in which this contract appears enters largely into the business of stock-brokerage. *This is a mistake;* the *bona fide* purchase of stocks, no doubt, can be conducted in a legitimate way, and is so, generally, without trenching in the least on the gambler's province."

In fact, in the next case upon the subject which is reported in that State, Smith vs. Bouvier,[1] a "short sale" was distinctly upheld. In that case one K., not owning stock, employed Brokers to sell stock for him at a named price, to be delivered on a particular day. The Brokers sold as ordered, and, as is customary, borrowed the stocks for delivery; the stock appreciating in price, the Brokers bought the same "in," and commenced an action for money laid out and expended. The main contention in the case was whether or not the transaction was a gambling one, and would for that reason prevent the Brokers recovering money advanced and commissions earned. The court below submitted to the jury the question, whether the transaction was one in which the parties agreed that mere differences

[1] 70 Pa. St. 325.

were to be paid, or a real transaction; and the jury found for the plaintiff.

Upon appeal, the defendant contended " that the jury should have been instructed that all purchases of stocks, with a view to resell and make profit on their rise, or contracts to furnish stocks on time, should be declared gambling transactions and illegal, not only between buyer and seller, but as to Brokers and agents through whom the sales or purchases had been made." Commenting upon this argument, the learned court said : " This would make a great inroad into what has, for an indefinite period, been regarded as a legitimate business, and would either destroy it altogether, or, if continued, put the Brokers at the mercy of those for whom they transact such business. Let it be understood that a Broker has no power to recover either for advances or commissions, however honestly he may have dealt, and there will be found enough persons whose easy consciences would throw their losses upon the shoulders of those who advanced the money and earned commissions in their service. It would be a very palpable wrong to the Brokers, who are licensed to do such business, if such were held to be the law. To this extent Brua's Appeal[1] never was intended to go." In conclusion, the court said : " Whether the transactions embraced in this case were *bona fide*, or were merely in a form to cover gambling transactions, after a full explanation, was left to the jury."

It will be observed that the above was a clear case of speculating on " margins," which the courts, in the opinions hereafter referred to, regarded as so obnoxious ; and that

[1] Ante, p. 557.

upon a "margin" capital of $10,000 the Client sold 2,000 shares of stock "short," of the market value of $334,000.

Then follows the case of Maxton vs. Gheen.[1] That was an action of assumpsit, brought by Stock-brokers against their Client to recover a balance of account arising from transactions in stocks. The defence was that the indebtedness arose out of gambling in stocks. It appeared that the transactions were "short" sales of stock; but the Brokers, in the first instance, had no knowledge that the defendant did not have the stock, although after the second sale they knew he was selling "short." It also distinctly appeared that the stocks were sold for account of defendant on "margin;" the Brokers testifying "that when they sold stock short they required from two to ten dollars per share on margin, unless the party left the stock with them." The plaintiffs had a verdict, which was affirmed by the appellate court, Agnew, C. J., delivering the opinion, and holding that the facts did not disclose "a transaction in stocks by way of margin, settlement of differences and payment of the gain or loss, without any intention to deliver the stocks."

The next case to which we will refer is Fareira vs. Gabell.[2] That was an action on certain promissory notes made to plaintiff, a Stock-broker, some of the notes being given as "margins on stock contracts," and the others for an indebtedness arising out of losses in stock transactions. The defence was that the transactions were "wagers." The facts of this case are very meagrely reported; but it seems that the defendant proved that the contracts made through the agency of plaintiff were simply wagering con-

---

[1] 75 Pa. St. 166.   [2] 89 Pa. St. 89.

tracts. The learned trial judge very fairly submitted the question to the jury whether the transactions were gambling ones; but he illustrated the general rule of the law by stating a suppositious case between *two persons dealing directly together in wheat,* without any intention, on the one hand, to deliver, or, on the other hand, to receive. But that illustration is entirely ineffective in presenting a contract in which a Stock-broker, *acting for a commission,* makes transactions for his Client upon a Stock Exchange with *third persons,* actually advancing money, and actually receiving, in some form, the securities. However, the question of wager or no wager was submitted to the jury, and a verdict was found for the defendant. Upon appeal to the Supreme Court this conclusion was affirmed without any opinion, the court merely referring to Brua's Appeal and Smith vs. Bouvier as entirely sustaining the judge's charge.

As we have said, the facts of this case are reported so sparsely as to deprive us of the power of criticising the results reached by the jury; but as the case stands, in view of the fact that the question was fairly submitted to the jury, their decision would seem to be conclusive. But the next case—North vs. Philipps[1]—which is reported in the same book as the preceding case and was decided at the same term, is utterly irreconcilable with the previous decisions of the courts of that State. In that case the defendants, Stock-brokers, purchased certain stock for account of the plaintiff on "margin," the contract being that plaintiff should constantly keep with the Brokers ten per cent of the par value of the stock. The stock declining, defendants requested

---

[1] 89 Pa. St. 250.

additional margins, and upon failure to accede to the demand, the stocks were sold. The plaintiff thereupon brought an action of assumpsit against the Brokers to recover damages, upon the erroneous theory that there had been a purchase and sale of the stock between the *plaintiff and defendants;* and recovered a verdict based upon the difference between the value of the stock on the day it was sold, and the highest value it had reached down to the day of the trial. Upon appeal to the Supreme Court, the doctrine of the court below upon the question of damage was repudiated; and the appellate court did not notice the *form of the action*, but (through Mr. Justice Gordon) mainly occupied itself in examining the character of the contract between the parties, and adjudged it to be a mere gambling transaction. The court held that the stock, although *purchased* by the Brokers at the request and for the account of the Client, was not his property, but that it belonged to the Brokers; and in face of the fact that the plaintiff had testified that he expected to pay for the same and take it up, and ignoring the powerful circumstance that the jury had passed upon the transaction and decided in favor of its validity—the reasoning of the learned court being that the disparity between the Client's wealth and the amount of the purchase-money required to purchase the stock proved conclusively that the contract was a mere gambling devise. The learned court paid no attention whatever to the finding of the jury. We shall reserve our criticism upon this case until we have examined the other cases, merely observing that the form of the action would have more properly been *ex delicto* in trover for the conversion of the Client's stocks by an untimely and illegal sale of the same by the Broker.

In Gheen vs. Johnson[1] the court, through the same learned judge, went out of its way to assert the same doctrine as that contained in the preceding case, and was only prevented from applying it by the fact that the record did not raise the legality of the contracts. But the principle established in Fareira vs. Gabell was most vigorously upturned in the subsequent cases of Ruchizky vs. De Haven[2] and Smith vs. Thomas.[3] In Ruchizky vs. De Haven the court held that money received by a Stock-broker from a minor to carry on transactions in stocks may be recovered back from the Broker, such a contract being void *ab initio*. In reversing the opinion of the court below,[4] Mr. Justice Gordon said: "When, under the case stated, the court below assumed that the defendant must be regarded as the agents of R. [the infant], . .. it committed an error. The parties were not dealing in stocks, but in margins, and R. knew no principals but De H. and T. [the Brokers]." The court concluded that the contracts fell under the ban of a gambling transaction; and that the Client, being an infant, could recover the money and securities deposited with the Brokers as margin, although the Brokers had no knowledge that he was not *sui juris*. The court, in its opinion, animadverted most severely, but without the slightest foundation in fact, upon the conduct of the Brokers. In speaking of their want of knowledge of the infancy of their Client, the following language was used: "Moreover, they did not know because

---

[1] 90 Pa. St. 38.

[2] 38 Leg. Int. 115; 97 Pa. St. 202.

[3] Id , s. c. *sub nom*. Dickson's Exr. vs. Thomas, 97 Pa. St. 278.

[4] Per Mitchell, J., 36 Leg. Int. (Pa.) 174. When the parties are

sui juris, money paid to the Broker in settlement of differences in stock transactions cannot be recovered back. Merriam vs. Public Grain & Stock Exchange, 1 Pa. Co. Ct. Rep. 478, distinguishing Ruchizky vs. De Haven, supra.

they did not choose to inquire. They were getting his money; and like all other persons engaged in unlawful callings, they cared not whether that money came from man, woman, or child—whether their victim was young or old, sane or insane. . . . We repeat, therefore, there is nothing to be returned to the defendant. They lost nothing in this transaction, and hence can the more easily return to the plaintiff's estate that which belongs to it."

Then follows the case of Smith vs. Thomas,[1] in which the court took occasion to review the subject anew and to reiterate most emphatically its former decisions. In that case the action was assumpsit, and was brought by a Stockbroker against his Client to recover a balance due on certain stock transactions. Upon the trial the plaintiff had judgment; but on appeal this was reversed, the opinion being again delivered by Mr. Justice Gordon. That learned judge's statement of the facts is as follows: " Thomas [the Broker] swears that he sold for Dickson 500 shares of Pennsylvania Railroad stock short; and so Thomas further on explains by saying that at the time he professed to sell this stock he had no such stock in his hands to sell. Nevertheless, he says, when he sold these 500 shares he delivered them. This anomalous kind of testimony he explains by saying that this delivery was made on the clearing-house sheet, which means a mere settlement of differences. It appears also from this same testimony that, in order properly to keep up appearances when the time came for delivery, he had to borrow 500 shares of stock from somebody, whose name does not appear, and of those there was no actual delivery, but, as the witness says, it came through the clearing-

---

[1] 38 Leg. Int. 115; *sub nom.* Dickson's Exr. vs. Thomas, 97 Pa. St. 278.

house sheet. All this means, in common parlance, that Thomas sold for Dickson 500 shares of stock, which Dickson at that time neither had nor intended to have, and that, under the pretence of meeting this contract when it fell due, Thomas pretended to borrow 500 shares, which were not delivered to him ; that this altogether fictitious transaction was accomplished through the agency of the clearing-house, and was one in which no other parties were known but Thomas and Dickson, who were to account to each other for differences only." And upon this remarkably erroneous statement the learned judge predicated the result reached, that " confessedly, then, this was a dealing in differences or margins—a wagering contract—and therefore utterly void ;" and that there was no question as to a *bona fide* contract upon which the jury was to pass.

The above represent some of the leading decisions of the Supreme Court of Pennsylvania upon this subject of wager in respect to stock transactions; and it is difficult to conceive how a court whose decisions are received with such universal homage could have gone so far astray upon a subject which vitally affects one of the most important moneyed interests of that State.

First. The decisions of the court are in hostility to each other. In Smith vs. Bouvier[1] the facts were precisely similar to those of Smith vs. Thomas. They both represented " short " transactions in stocks upon a margin. In Smith vs. Bouvier the jury found for the Broker and the verdict was sustained ; but in Smith vs. Thomas a similar verdict was reversed, the court arbitrarily setting aside the conclusion of the jury. The element of the clearing-house which

[1] 70 Pa. St. 325.

appeared in Smith vs. Thomas can make no difference between the cases, because that system, as all familiar with its
workings know, was created to facilitate the business; and,
indeed, the fact of stocks being " cleared," if it shows anything, proves that the transactions were real. It is utterly
impossible to reconcile the two cases, and yet Smith vs.
Bouvier was cited with approval in Smith vs. Thomas. It is
equally impossible to harmonize the last-named adjudication
with the case of Maxton vs. Gheen,[1] where the Client was
selling stock " short " on margins, and where a verdict for
the Broker was sustained. Although the Broker swore
that at first he did not know that his Client was selling
" short," yet he admitted that after the second transaction
he acquired that knowledge; and it is perfectly manifest,
from reading the case, that it was an everyday speculation
on margin. North vs. Philipps[2] and Ruchizky vs. De
Haven[3] are illustrations of " long " transactions—that is,
purchases of stocks for Clients on margin. The facts involved were in no sense different from those presented in
the case of Wyncoop vs. Seal,[4] where stocks were purchased
on a margin; and it did not occur either to the counsel or
court, in the last-mentioned case, to suggest that the transaction was void as a " wager."

Second. The fundamental error into which the Pennsylvania court has fallen arises from the fact that the decisions
have proceeded upon the assumption that the dealings were
merely between the *Broker* and *his Client*, without the in-
tervention of any third persons; in fine, of treating a
transaction in stocks conducted through the medium of the

[1] 75 Pa. St. 166.   [3] 38 Leg. Int. 115. See ante, P.
[2] 89 Pa. St. 250.   See ante, p. 563.
561.   [4] 64 Pa. St. 361.

Stock Exchange as one in effect between a vendor and vendee, bargaining for mere differences. This is very far from the fact. In the third chapter of this book, the details of a speculative transaction in stocks is fully set forth, and it is not necessary to repeat the same here;[1] but the court does a manifest injustice to the Stock-broker when it treats him as one *deriving benefit from his Client's losses.* This, with great respect, is as absurd as it is unfair. The Broker has no interest in the business except to the extent of his commissions, when he makes actual sales or purchases with third persons on account of his Client, which was clearly shown in the cases in question. The version of the transaction given by Mr. Justice Gordon is that of a sharper fleecing his innocent victim; and in that case, upon such erroneous premises, the Broker was compelled to lose a considerable sum of money, which he proved he had actually paid out for his Clients.

The character of the business is shown by a simple illustration. A orders B, a Stock-broker, to purchase 100 shares of a certain stock at par, and deposits with him $1,000. The Broker, in consideration of the commission and of receiving interest for his money, or for such other consideration as may enter into the arrangement, thereupon purchases at the Stock Exchange from C, a fellow-Broker, the stock, which is duly delivered to B, and the sum of $10,000 paid to C. B advances the difference between the amount he receives from his Client and the purchase-money from his own funds, and holds the stock as security. Thereupon the stock becomes the property of the Client; he receives the dividends; pays the calls; it

[1] Ch. III. p. 181.

passes to his assignee in bankruptcy, should he become bankrupt; and, in fine, all of the attributes of ownership attach to the Client.[1] We find here, then, an actual purchase and delivery of stock. This is the view of the transaction presented in Wynkoop vs. Seal.[2] Hare, P. J., in Fareira vs. Gabell,[3] defines a wager to be "a contract in which the parties stipulate that they shall gain or lose upon the happening of an uncertain event, in which they have no interest except that arising from the possibility of such gain or loss." But it is perfectly apparent that the transaction which we have set forth is not embraced within this definition. It might apply as between A, the vendor, and C, the vendee; but as between A, the vendor, and B, his Broker, there is clearly no bet or wager, B's interest in the transaction being merely to the extent of his commissions. Nor does the Broker act as the Client's agent in gambling sales and purchases of stocks. The Broker, in pursuance of his Client's directions, makes *actual* bargains enforceable in the courts and in the forum of the Stock Exchange, and whose non-fulfilment renders him liable to heavy damages. In fine, the doctrine of wager must be confined to the actual parties concerned, and cannot reasonably be extended to defeat the right of a Broker to recover moneys paid out for his Client in *real* transactions with *third* persons. These views are forcibly illustrated in the case of Thacker vs. Hardy,[4] which should be consulted in this connection.

Third. But, in any event, the question as to whether a particular transaction constitutes a wager is one for the jury; and this well-settled rule, although laid down in

---

[1] See also Ch. III. p. 182, where the transaction is further illustrated.

[2] 64 Pa. St. 361.

[3] 89 Pa. St. 89.

[4] 27 W. R. 158.

Smith **vs.** Bouvier,[1] has been ruthlessly violated by the Pennsylvania courts in the cases referred to.[2]

The case in which the dealings of the Stock Exchange

[1] 70 Pa. St. 325.

[2] See also Kirkpatrick vs. Bonsall, 72 Pa. St. 155; Bigelow vs. Benedict, 70 N. Y. 202. A summary of the decisions of the courts of Pennsylvania subsequent to those mentioned in the text is here appended, and it only remains to add that, as late as 1896, the District Court, in Taft vs. Riesenman, 7 Pa. Dist. R. 496, quoted with approval the decition in Ruchizky vs. De Haven, supra, that "When a person enters into stock gambling transactions through the medium of a Broker, he will be deemed to be dealing with such Broker, as a principal, and not as an agent."

In Griffith's Appeal, 16 W. N. C. 249; 42 L. I. 277, it was held that as contracts in stocks on margins are not enforceable, a judgment on a bond given by a Client to his Broker to secure the margins cannot be enforced by an assignee, unless the doctrine of estoppel applies. Such a bond is invalid for want of consideration. Griffiths vs. Sears, 112 Pa. St. 523.

It was held in Peters vs. Grim, 149 Pa. St. 163, that when there is an intention to deliver stocks there is no gambling, even though the delivery is postponed, and the stock carried on margins in the interval. And even if the transactions were gambling ones, money deposited can be recovered from the Broker when the transactions are closed. Ib.; Repplier vs. Jacobs,

149 Pa. St. 167; McNaughton vs. Haldeman, 160 Pa. St. 144. The fact that the customer's means were inadequate to enable him to carry out a stock contract, may be considered by the jury. Myers vs. Tobias, 24 W. N. C. 432.

In an action by a Broker to recover for loss on an oil transaction, the question whether there was a bona fide intention to deliver the oil was for the jury. Thompson vs. Rieber, 123 Pa. St. 457. When stock transactions amounted within three years to about $70,000, and it was shown that the Client had only about $8,000 invested in business, from which he derived a yearly income of $5,000, and that there was no intention to deliver or receive stocks, a note given to the Broker for losses was held irrecoverable. Gaw vs. Bennett, 153 Pa. 247.

When a customer paid 25 per cent upon each purchase of stock, and, when only a small portion thereof was bought, he deposited half the amount of such latter purchase with the Broker in bonds as collateral, and paid the balance due upon the entire purchase, which was large, within eighteen months, the transaction was not a gambling one to be settled by payment of differences. Com. vs. Barrett, 40 Leg. Int. (Pa.) 474.

When stocks were purchased by a Broker and paid for by the Client, and were then sold by the Broker, who retained the proceeds, out of

were examined most thoroughly in its relation to the act concerning wagers is the one of Thacker vs. Hardy.[1] This action was brought by a Broker against his principal for

which he bought other stocks for the Client, and a number of similar transactions followed in which the stocks bought were received by the Broker for the customer, and those sold were delivered by him to the purchaser, the transactions were not of a wagering character, and the Broker was held entitled to recover a balance due to him on the transactions. Hopkins vs. O'Kane, 169 Pa. St. 478. And although stock transactions are gambling ones, yet if the Client finally demands the stock, and the Broker tenders it, the latter may recover the value when the Client refuses to receive it. Anthony vs. Unangst, 174 Pa. St. 10.

One who has given notes and judgments in gambling transactions in futures in wheat and pork in Illinois cannot enjoin their collection, Smith vs. Kammerer, 152 Pa. St. 98. Nor compel the return of a promissory note given to a Broker to secure a balance due in stock gambling transactions. Albertson vs. Laughlin, 173 Pa. St. 525.

One to whom a Broker has transferred a non-negotiable instrument given to secure gambling transactions in oil, cannot recover thereon, although he paid a valuable consideration. Dempsey vs. Harm, 20 W. N. C. 266. Margins deposited with a banker as security for gambling transactions in stocks and grain, may be recovered from the bank as a stakeholder, when not paid over by the bank to the Broker.

Dauler vs. Hartley, 178 Pa. St. 22. When the intention is that there is to be no delivery of stocks, and the transactions, during fifteen months, involve purchases amounting to over $300,000, the transactions are merely wagers, and the Broker cannot recover. Wagner vs. Hildebrand, 187 Pa. St. 136. Nor can the customer, in such gambling transactions in oil, compel an accounting by the Broker. Taft vs. Riesenman, 7 Pa. Dist. Rep. 496. If the Broker actually buys and sells stocks, he does not gamble, even although his principal intended to gamble, and the Broker does not deliver the stocks to the customer in person. A delivery by sale, as ordered, is a sufficient delivery. Young vs. Glendinning, 8 Pa. Dist. Rep. 57, aff'd 194 Pa. St. 550. If the last transaction is an actual purchase, and a settlement is made, and the account closed, it validates all prior transactions, although the latter might be held gambling ones. Id. 194 Pa. St. 550. When there was a bona fide intent to receive and deliver, the transactions are not illegal, although delivery may be postponed. Dealing in stocks on margins is not necessarily gambling, and, if even the transactions were wagering, the agreement of the parties to make the sales actual, will validate them. Taylor's Assigned Estate, 192 Pa. St. 304, 309, 313.

[1] L. R. 4 Q. B. D. 685.

indemnity against liabilities incurred by the former in buying and selling stocks and shares upon the London Stock
Exchange by his authority. It appeared that the defendant was a speculator, and known as such to plaintiff; and
that he (defendant) knew that, in order to carry out the
transactions which he had employed plaintiff to make, the
latter would have to enter into contracts to sell or buy respectively, and that there was no other way in which to
speculate for defendant; that the plaintiff did buy and sell
as per order; and defendant never expected, nor intended
to accept, actual delivery of what plaintiff might buy for
him, nor actually deliver what he might sell. For losses
incurred by such speculations and commissions the suit
was instituted by the Broker. The main defence was that
the claim was founded upon gaming and wagering transactions.[1] The court, per Lindley, J., in delivering the opinion, said : " The agreement between the plaintiff and the
defendant rendered it necessary that the plaintiff should
himself, as principal, enter into real contracts of purchase
and sale with Jobbers, and the plaintiff accordingly did so;
and in respect of these contracts he incurred obligations,
for the non-performance of which actions could, and can
now, be brought against him. . . . What the plaintiff was
employed to do was to buy and sell on the Stock Exchange,
and this he did ; and everything he did was perfectly legal,
unless it was rendered illegal as between the defendant and
himself by reason of the illegality of the object they had
in view, or of the transactions in which they were engaged.
. . . . In answer to the argument that a contract which is
void and unenforceable cannot be made the foundation of

----

[1] 8 & 9 Vict. c. 109, § 18.

an implied promise to indemnify, it appears to me sufficient to say that an obligation to indemnify is created whenever one person employs another to do a lawful act which
exposes him to liability ; and that, in my view of the evidence, the defendant did authorize the plaintiff to incur liability by buying and selling as above described." Upon
appeal these views were fully endorsed by the judges composing the Court of Appeals, and a judgment for the plaintiff affirmed.[1]

The case of Thacker vs. Hardy was subsequently used
by the court to sustain its decision in the later case of Ex
parte Rogers,[2] where it was held that where a person has
instructed a Broker to speculate for him at the Stock Exchange, by buying and selling stocks for him, with the intention that he should only receive or pay " differences,"
and authorized the Broker to pay any losses for him, the
Broker is entitled to recover any sums which he has so paid
for the Client, even though he has not entered into separate
contracts on his behalf, but has appropriated to him parts
of larger amounts of stock which the Broker has bought
as a principal with the view of dividing them among different Clients, for whom he has been instructed to buy. So
where the petitioner, a Stock-broker, applied under the
Bankruptcy Act to have respondent, who was not a member of the Stock Exchange, adjudicated a bankrupt—the
debt arising from transactions which the respondent had
authorized the petitioner to make upon the Stock Exchange
—and the petition was resisted on the ground that the debt
was a gaming one under the statute of Victoria, it was held

---

[1] See also Rosewarne vs. Billing,   bers, 15 C. B. 562; Knight vs. Fitch,
15 C. B. (n. s.) 316; Knight vs. Cham-   id. 566.
[2] L. R. 15 Ch. D. 207.

that the petitioner was merely an agent; and since the respondent must be taken to have known that by the rules of the Stock Exchange the petitioner was bound to pay to members of the Stock Exchange any sums of money which might be due from the respondent to them in regard to the transactions, a request to pay such sums must be implied.[1]

Although the soundness of the decision in Thacker vs. Hardy has been extrajudicially questioned upon the ground that all of the ordinary transactions between Client and Broker fall within the Gambling Act,[2] it is submitted that an analysis of such transactions shows that they are perfectly legal.

First. There is no agreement that mere differences shall be paid *per se* without anything further being done; but the transaction is begun by an order from the Client to buy or sell shares of stock, at a fixed or market price.

Second. The Broker is employed *as such.* He is not a party to the arrangement; neither the profit nor the loss of the transaction is his. The Broker's only interest in the matter is to the extent of his commission.

Third. That the transaction thus made is in law a real one fully appears from the note of the contract given by

---

[1] Ex parte Godefroi, In re Hart, Week. Notes, 95 (1870). So in the case of Marten vs. Gibbon, 33 L. T. (n. s.) 561, the court held that sales of prospective dividends are not contrary to law. There is no ground known to the law of England against a person possessed of property in railway shares selling the dividends to arise therefrom, even though the amount be unascertained. Such a transaction is not contrary to the statute in rela-tion to "wagers," any more than a contract to pay for all the oil in a whaling-ship, although it is impossible to tell how many whales the ship may bring back (per Blackburn, J.). See also two spirited articles on Option Contracts, 10 Cent. L. J. 221, 211.

[2] See 5 *Law Mag. and Rev.* (4th Series), 401, entitled "The Legal Relations between a Stock-broker and his Customer," by Messrs. Piggott & Whinney, Barristers.

the Broker to his Client. This may contain the name of the purchasing or selling Jobber—sometimes it does, generally it does not; but it conclusively shows that the Broker has made an operation for the principal with a *third* person. From this contract so made by the Broker with the Jobber there are evolved legal liabilities. We may mention two of them : 1st. If the Jobber should refuse to execute the contract and to deliver the securities, the Client would have a cause of action against him.[1] 2d. But the Client would not have any cause of action against his own Broker for any neglect or refusal of the Jobber. Why? Because the Broker, having transacted the business of his employment in accordance with his instructions, is, upon familiar principles, not liable.[2]

Fourth. The fact that the Broker may enter into a contract or contracts for more than the specific amount of stock ordered to be bought or sold by one Client does not alter the legal status of the parties. If the Broker act in good faith to his Client, he is not debarred from transacting similar business for other Clients. Nor does the fact of the establishment of a clearing-house, and the system of tickets, enabling him to balance his business at one time, militate against the legality of these stock transactions. All of these things are mere auxiliaries to the Broker's business, calculated to enlarge its volume, and to enable him to despatch it with greater ease and promptness.

Although it was found as a fact, in Thacker vs. Hardy, that the Client never expected nor intended to accept actual delivery of what the Broker might buy for him, nor actually deliver what he might sell for him, and that the Broker

---

[1] See cases cited in Ch. X.   [2] Ch. III. p. 220 et seq.

knew this, yet it was also found that the Client, nevertheless, knew he incurred the risk of having to accept or deliver, but was content to run that risk in the expectation
and hope that the Broker would be able so to arrange
matters as to render nothing but differences actually payable
to or by him, as the case might be. Nor is the fact that
the Broker may himself speculate of any relevancy, so long
as he is not the actual party who makes a contract with his
Client for the payment of the differences, in which case he
ceases to be a Broker, and becomes a principal. This risk
of being obliged to accept or deliver takes speculative transactions on the London Stock Exchange out of the operation
of the gambling statute, although it remains to be seen what
effect the Gaming Act of 1892 will have upon such transactions.

The principle of the decision in Thacker vs. Hurdy, *supra*,
was followed by the Privy Council in Forget vs. Ostigny,[1]
where the facts were similar. The case was decided under
the Canadian statute, which was substantially equivalent to
the English statute of 1845, and it was held that as the
Broker was employed to make actual contracts on the
Stock Exchange, they were not within the statute, although
the principal intended to speculate, and delivery of the
shares purchased was never asked for or tendered.

Most of the American decisions follow the rule laid down
by the English courts as to the intermediate character of
the Broker, with this substantial difference, however, that
if the Broker is privy to the illegality, he cannot recover
commissions or advances.

In the case of Lehman vs. Strassberger[2] the question

---

[1] (1895) A. C. 318.   [2] 2 Wood, C. C. 554. This de-

was fully discussed in the Circuit Court of the United States. In that case the plaintiffs, who were cotton-factors in New York, bought and sold as such for the defendant cotton for future delivery ; it being the understanding between them that, in all sales and purchases of cotton by them for him, there was to be no delivery, but that differences should be paid, except when special instructions were given to receive or deliver cotton. These contracts were entered into by plaintiff according to the rules of the Cotton Exchange of New York. By these rules, which were given in evidence, an actual delivery of cotton is provided for and required in every contract, unless waived in some mode by the subsequent assent or conduct of both parties ; or unless the party having the option to make or require an actual delivery fails or declines to exercise his option or to insist upon delivery. The action was based upon a note given by defendant to the plaintiffs, the consideration arising out of the transactions of defendant in such contracts, and included losses on contracts paid by plaintiffs for defendant, and their commissions for buying and selling. It did not appear that the names of the parties with whom plaintiffs made the transactions were disclosed to the latter. The defence was that the note was void under the statute of New York in relation to gaming. There was a verdict below for the defendant, and the case was reviewed on exceptions to the charge of the judge, upon the subject of wager contracts.

The Circuit Court held that, while it might be conceded that contracts for the future delivery of cotton, when it is agreed that there shall be no delivery, but that differ-

cision was followed in Hentz vs. Jewell, 20 Fed. Rep. 592, in a similar state of facts.

ences shall be paid, are wagering contracts, and void as
between the parties, it was not the case disclosed in the
record ; the parties here were not *parties* to any contract
for the sale or delivery of cotton. The plaintiffs never
sold to or bought from the defendant any cotton. The
parties with whom the defendant contracted were persons
other than plaintiffs, whose names were not disclosed, and
plaintiffs were only factors of defendant to make contracts
with other parties, the plaintiffs being mere agents for the
defendant in the transaction. "This is the case," said the
court, " to put it in its strongest light for the defendant,
of an agent who advances money to his principal to pay
losses incurred in an illegal transaction, and takes his note
for the money so advanced. In such a case the contract
between a principal and agent, made after the illegal
transactions are closed, although it may spring from them
and be the result of them, is a binding contract." [1]

The question has also been discussed in several cases in the
Supreme Court of the United States. In Roundtree vs.
Smith,[2] Brokers in Chicago recovered judgment for commissions and advances in the purchase of grain, pork, and lard
for defendant, and the court, in affirming the judgment, held
that there was no evidence that the contracts were wagering ones. The defendant testified that he had no understanding as to whether there was to be actual delivery, and
plaintiffs testified that there was no such understanding,
and nothing was proved of the intention of the parties with
whom plaintiffs contracted, and, as the contracts were al-

---

[1] Citing Durant vs. Burt, 98 Mass. See also Tenant vs. Elliot, 1 Bos.
167; Petrie vs. Hannev, 3 T. R. 418; & P. 3; Farmer vs. Russell, id.
Owen vs. Davis, 1 Bailey, 315; Arm- 296.
strong vs Toler, 11 Wheat. 271.   [2] 108 U S. 260.

ways in writing, it was further held that evidence that a large majority of similar transactions at the Board of Trade in Chicago were merely difference contracts, was not sufficient to prove a violation of the law in the transactions in question. The court said that plaintiffs were not suing on the contracts, but for services performed and money advanced for defendant, and although they might, under some circumstances, be so connected with the immorality of the contract as to be affected by it, if proved, they were certainly not in the same position as a party sued for the enforcement of the original agreement. In Irwin vs. Williar[1] the court reversed a judgment of the Circuit Court in favor of Brokers in Baltimore for a balance due to them on sales of wheat for future delivery on grounds foreign to the subject of this chapter, but, as the question of wagering had been raised, the court disposed of it by accepting the charge of the court below that, to void the contract, the proof should show that the intention was merely to settle for differences and both parties so understood it, but said: " In England, it is held that the contracts, although wagers, were not void at common law, and that the statute has not made them illegal, but only non-enforceable. Thacker vs. Hardy, *ubi supra*. While generally, in this country, all wagering contracts are held to be illegal and void as against public policy," and further " a Broker might negotiate such a contract (i. e. a wagering one) without being privy to the illegal intent of the principal parties to it which renders it void, and in such a case, being innocent of any violation of law, and not suing to enforce an unlawful contract, has a meritorious ground for the recovery of compensation for services and advances.

[1] 110 U. S. 509.

But we are also of the opinion that when the Broker is privy to the design of the parties, and brings them together for the very purpose of entering into an illegal agreement, he is *particeps criminis*, and cannot recover for services rendered or losses incurred by himself on behalf of either in forwarding the transaction."

This certainly narrows the liberality of the doctrine enunciated in Thacker vs. Hardy, where it was held that the Client should indemnify the Broker, although both parties knew that differences merely were to be settled, but it is submitted this decision will not generally affect transactions on the Stock Exchange where, as already stated, there is a delivery of the securities sold, although the principle of this decision was followed in Stewart vs. Garrett,[1] where, although the plaintiff stock and grain Brokers assumed that as they sued, not on the contracts themselves but for services performed and money advanced, they did not stand in the same position as if seeking to enforce the original agreement, the court held that, as they were *particeps criminis* to a gambling transaction, they could not recover. In Embrey vs. Jemison[2] it was held that as Brokers employed to buy cotton in New York for future delivery were *particeps criminis* to the illegal contract entered into on behalf of the customer, they could not recover.

In Bibb vs. Allen[3] it was held that as the Brokers made future sales of cotton, understanding that there would be actual delivery, the customer was liable for advances and commissions, although he meant to gamble and nothing more.

[1] 4 Atl. Rep. 399.
[2] 131 U. S. 345.
[3] 149 U. S. 492. To the same

effect is Lehman vs. Feld, 37 Fed. Rep. 852; Boyd vs. Hanson, 41 Fed. Rep. 171.

The United States Circuit Court held in Jackson vs. Foote[1] that the Illinois statute prohibiting dealing in options to buy or sell at a future time, was not violated by a time contract to deal wholly in grain, pork or lard, for differences, although such a contract might be a wager at common law, and that notes given by the customer to his Broker in payment of the latter's advances and commissions might be recovered by a third party who was a *bona fide* holder for value.[2]

And it was held by the United States Supreme Court, in Higgins vs. McCrea,[3] that when grain Brokers testified that their contracts with their principal were not made with intent to wager, but the principal testified that he intended to gamble merely, and that the contract was violative of the Chicago statute, the former may recover advances and commissions, but the latter cannot counterclaim for margins. In that case the plaintiff was held not entitled to judgment on another ground, viz., that he had canceled the contracts made by him without substituting other principals as required by the rules, but, if he had not done so, he could have had judgment both on his cause of action and on the counterclaim.[4]

---

[1] 11 Biss. 223.

[2] See also Gilbert vs. Guager, 8 Biss. 214; Union Nat. Bank vs. Carr, 15 Fed. Rep. 438.

[3] 116 U. S. 671.

[4] See Kirkpatrick vs. Adams, 20 Fed. Rep. 287; Bartlett vs. Smith, 13 Fed. Rep. 263; Bangs vs. Hornick, 30 Fed. Rep. 97; Edwards vs. Hoeffinghoff, 38 Fed. Rep. 635. See also the following cases: Bennett vs. Covington, 22 Fed. Rep. 816 (the burden of proof is on defendant principal to show that the transaction was a gambling one); Tomblin vs. Callan, 23 N. W. Rep. 573 (where the intent is to deliver, a grain Broker was held in Iowa entitled to recover, although most of the transactions were settled by differences).

The Circuit Court of the United States for the District of Kansas held in Cobb vs. Prell, 22 Am. Law Reg. 609, that when the parties did not intend actual delivery of corn

And where the Client gives his Broker an order to purchase stock for him, and the latter does so in accordance with the instruction and the usages of the Stock Exchange, but the Client subsequently refusing to take the Stock, the Broker, after notice, sells it, the latter is entitled to recover the loss made, together with commissions, etc. ; and it is no defence to the action that the contract made by the Broker with another member of the Stock Exchange is illegal, as being contrary to the statute of Massachusetts (declaring sales of stock void when the seller has no stock at the time of the alleged sale), especially where the purchasing Broker is not shown to have known this fact, or that the same was not legal under the Statute of Frauds.[1]

When it appeared, however, that contracts made in the Chicago Board of Trade were clearly gambling contracts as being intended to be settled by payment of differences only,

contracted for, but did intend to speculate on the future market, a commission merchant could not recover from his principal the differences the former was obliged to pay owing to his having contracted to sell in his own name. See note appended to this case discussing the subject, and collecting many cases. It was also held in that case, and in Justh vs. Holliday, 11 Wash. L. Rep. 418, in a transaction in stocks, that a Broker in a case of the kind, was to be considered a principal, and not an agent.

In Illinois an option as to the time of delivery, and the settlement of differences on such a contract, does not make it a wagering one under the Illinois statute, and an Illinois Broker may recover advances and commissions from a Wisconsin citizen, although if the transaction took place in that State he could not recover. Ward vs. Vosburgh, 31 Fed. Rep. 12.

Under the Georgia statute voiding gaming contracts (Code, Ga. § 3671) a "cotton future" contract where the intention is merely to settle differences, is void. Waldron vs. Johnson, 86 Fed. Rep. 757. When the customer's order (by telegraph) on its face shows that an actual sale of stock "short" was intended, he must, to prove that a transaction thereunder was a gambling one, show that there was no intent both of himself and the Broker to have an actual sale and delivery. Boyle vs. Henning, 121 Fed. Rep. 376.

[1] Durant vs. Burt, 98 Mass. 161.

it was held that such contracts were not only void but illegal by the common law of Massachusetts (which was the law applicable to the case, there being no evidence of the common law of Illinois), and that Brokers who knowingly made such contracts could not recover for advances or commissions.[1]

Nor can a principal recover from a Stock-broker the amount of margins deposited, nor the proceeds of sales received by the latter,[2] when no actual transactions were intended.

In Barnes vs. Smith [3] the rule of law was thus stated. If there was an understanding between customer and Broker that no shares should be actually delivered, but that the Broker should either make bargains to that effect with the purchaser or buyer, or that he should protect the customer from making or accepting actual delivery, then the contract was illegal, and the Broker could not recover. But a mere expectation on the part of Client and Broker that the purchaser would settle by paying or receiving differences when there was no understanding to that effect, or that the Broker should protect the Client from making or receiving actual delivery, would not make the contract illegal, and the Broker would be entitled to his commissions and advances.

In a case in Kentucky [4] the Court of Appeals examined

---

[1] Harvey vs. Merrill, 150 Mass. 1.

[2] Northrup vs. Buffington, 171 Mass. 468.

[3] 159 Mass. 344.

[4] Sawyer vs. Taggart, 14 Bush (Ky.), 727. To same affect, Warren vs. Hewitt, 45 Ga. 201. But when from the character of the transactions, and from the state-ments of the Brokers it appeared there was a tacit agreement that no cotton was to be delivered, and from the testimony of the defence (the principals being persons of limited means who would be quite unable to pay for the large purchases made for them) the contracts were held to be wagering ones, and

the subject in a very able and exhaustive opinion, in which they reviewed the entire method of transacting business upon the Cotton and Produce Exchanges of New York in a case where a Broker was directed to make operations for a Client, and fully sustained their validity. In that case H. & Co., commission-merchants, at various times directed S. & Co., commission-merchants and members of the New York Cotton and Produce Exchanges, to buy for their account, for future delivery, certain specified quantities of cotton, pork, and lard. These purchases, II. & Co. knew, were made on the Exchanges, subject to the rules and regulations of the trade. As the time approached when, according to the terms of the contracts of purchase, the goods were deliverable, II. &. Co. directed the purchases to be "transferred" to subsequent months. This was understood and intended to be a direction to sell the goods, and purchase a like quantity for delivery in the months designated. The rules of the Exchanges required that all contracts should be made in the names of members; and, H. & Co. not being members, their contracts were made in the name of S. & Co., who became liable on the contracts as principals, and advanced the money necessary to cover the loss. II. & Co. failed, and for the advances so made for them, and brokerage and other expenses, S. & Co. made claim against their assignee. Payment was resisted on the ground that the transactions were mere illegal wagers, to be settled by the payment of "differences." In each instance it was shown that S. & Co. entered into agreements with third persons, and the

the Brokers not entitled to recover. Although the contract was in writing, parol evidence was admitted to show the real nature of the transactions. Bradley vs. McElrath, 3 S W. Rep 152; 85 Ky. 230.

transactions were carried on in a manner similar to the method of doing business on the Stock Exchange.

S. & Co. having thus shown that they entered into contracts valid on their face for the purchase of the goods they were directed by H. & Co. to buy; that, pursuant to directions, they resold the same, and delivered to the purchasers delivery orders which they had received; and that on such resales there were losses, which they paid—the court held that they made out a clear *prima facie* right to recover; that the fact that some of the persons with whom S. & Co. made contracts for purchases had not the goods contracted for on hand at the times of entering into the contracts, and that they had no reasonable expectation of acquiring them except by purchasing in the market, did not render the contracts unenforceable, much less vicious. The court also held that the fact that the purchaser for future delivery did not intend to receive and pay for the goods, but to resell them before the date of the delivery, furnished no ground for holding that it was tacitly understood the contract was not to be performed, and was to be settled by the payment of differences.

The court cited, to sustain this last proposition, the case of Ashton vs. Dakin.[1] In that case the plaintiff, a Stock-broker, was directed by the defendant to buy for him certain stock for future delivery, which was done through another Broker, who made the contract in his own name, and became liable for its performance. Before the day of delivery the defendant ordered the stock to be sold, and it was sold at a loss, which the Broker paid. The plaintiff repaid the Broker, and brought his action for the amount. The defendant

[1] 4 Hurl. & Norm. 867.

pleaded that the transaction was a mere wager on the market price of the stock. The arbitrators found that the defendant never, in fact, intended to take a transfer of the stock, and that the plaintiff was fully aware of this when the orders were given, and that they were given and accepted on the implied terms and understanding that the plaintiff should not be called on by the defendant to deliver the stock or any part thereof, and that he should not be called on to receive or pay for it; but that it should be resold by the plaintiff before the time of payment arrived, and the defendant should, on the resale, either pay or receive the difference, after debiting him with the plaintiff's charges on the purchase and resale. The court held that this was not a gaming transaction.[1]

In the case of Marshall vs. Thurston[2] a suit was brought by a bank upon notes given for money advanced by it. The defence interposed was, that the defendant having been engaged in speculating in the future prices of Tennessee State

---

[1] In the following cases the defence of wager was sustained: Pickering vs. Cease, 79 Ill. 328; Lyon vs. Culbertson, 83 id. 33; Waterman vs. Buckland, 1 Mo. App. 45; Rourke vs. Short, 34 Eng. L. & Eq. 219. On examination, however, these cases will be found to be "optional contracts" in an illegal sense. i. e. speculations in the differences of market values, the seller having the privilege of delivering or not delivering, and the buyer the privilege of calling or not calling for the subject-matter of the contract, as they saw fit. In the following case, in dealings in cotton, the defence of wager was also sustained. Mutual Life Ins. Co. vs. Watson, 30 Fed. Rep. 653. Cases in grain dealings in which the defence of wager was not sustained, are, Powell vs. McCord, 121 Ill. 330; Ware vs. Jordan, 25 Ill. App. 534; Champlain vs. Smith, 164 Pa. St. 481. Although the Broker has a verdict in his favor, the judgment thereon will be reversed, and the case remanded by reason of erroneous instructions. Pardridge vs Cutler, 168 Ill 504; Riebe vs. Hellman, 69 Ill. App 22.

[2] Supreme Ct. of Tenn ; reported in 10 Cent. L. J. 212. See also Vanderpoel vs. Kearns, 12 E. D. Smith, 170.

bonds, the notes in suit were given for the differences due on settlement; and the question arose whether the bank's furnishing the money to the defendant had any necessary connection with the speculative transactions in bonds. The court, at the trial, instructed the jury that if defendant, in his gaming transactions, had sustained losses, "and the bank, at his request, paid the amount of such losses, or if the bank paid such losses without being requested, and defendant afterwards ratified its action, and gave his notes for the amount so paid, such amount can be recovered of him in this action;" but "if the bank furnished defendant with money for the purpose of enabling him to engage in an unlawful undertaking, it could not recover of him the amount so furnished." Both these instructions were sustained as unexceptionable by the appellate court. In response to the suggestion that mere knowledge on the part of the bank of the intended use of the money by defendant would make it an aider and abettor in the gambling, Cooper, J., explained that the test in such cases is whether the plaintiff requires any aid from the illegal transaction in order to establish his claim, or whether he was in fact a participant in the illegal transaction. And a recovery by the bank was allowed in that case, because no such participation appeared.[1]

Since the enactment in Tennessee of L. 1883, ch. 251, *supra*, such a note is void even in the hands of an innocent holder for value before maturity.[2] It was held in the same State that dealing in cotton futures, where the intention of the parties was that there should be no delivery, was wagering, and that cotton factors could not recover advances, although they only acted as agents.[3]

[1] See also Hatch vs. Douglas, 16 Am. Law. Rev. 181.

[2] Snoddy vs. Bank, 88 Tenn. 573.
[3] Beadles vs. Ownby, 84 Tenn. 424.

This decision was followed in Dunn vs. Bell[1] where it was held, however, that any winnings paid to the customer may be set off as against the margin deposits. In Mechanics' Bank vs. Duncan[2] it was held, in the same State, that notes given by Stock-brokers to plaintiff for profits on stock dealings and margins deposited, could not be recovered, the dealings being clearly gambling ones without any intention to deliver, and the consideration being therefore in part illegal.

In a well considered case in Indiana[3] where the authorities are fully reviewed, it was held that commission merchants in grain were entitled to recover advances and commissions, when they intended in good faith to make delivery, although the customer only intended to gamble.

And in Fisher vs. Fisher[4] it was held that an allegation in an answer that a note given by defendant to plaintiff Brokers was given for an illegal consideration, viz., the payment of margins on wheat that had never been delivered to defendant, was bad, as the mere payment of margins did not vitiate the contract.

In the State of New York it was held in Earl vs. Howell[5] that, notwithstanding the statute against wagering, a Stock-broker was entitled to recover the balance of his account with his Client, even though he arranged to settle for "differences" only, as he was not a principal, notwithstanding that he did not ask for the usual margin, and therefore the wagering act did not apply.

[1] 85 Tenn. 581.
[2] 36 S. W. Rep. 887.
[3] Whitesides vs. Hunt, 97 Ind. 191-210.
[4] 113 Ind. 474. See also

Schmueckle vs. Waters, 125 Ind. 265, where a speculative transaction in "Bohemian oats" was held to be of a gambling nature.
[5] 11 Abb. N. C. 171.

And when it appeared that the Client intended that stocks should be actually bought by her Brokers, and held by them subject to her order for sale, and after they had been sold that differences might be settled, it was held in Cunningham vs. Stevenson[1] that such a transaction was not a gaming contract, and that plaintiff's action for conversion of stock by the Brokers was maintainable.

In Vischer vs. Bagg[2] it was held that an agreement between Client and Broker to buy stock on joint account, the defendant Broker to carry it until a sale was agreed on between them, was not a wagering contract. Expectation of a "rise" in the price did not make it an unlawful one, as most people buy stock with a view to selling it at a better price.

In Dwight vs. Badgley[3] it was held that when a customer positively testified that it was understood between him and his Brokers that they were to buy and sell wheat on options and settle by differences, and there was no evidence that plaintiff Brokers owned any grain or purchased any for delivery to the customer, it was error to direct a verdict for plaintiff as there was a question of fact for the jury presented by the evidence. When a complaint avers that there was no intent to deliver wheat in contracts for future sale thereof, but that differences only were to be settled, it sufficiently states a cause of action by a customer to recover moneys paid to defendant Brokers in such transactions.[4]

In Nichols vs. Lumpkin[5] it appeared that defendant car-

---

[1] 20 N. Y. *Weekly Digest*, 82.
[2] 21 N. Y. *Week. Dig.* 399, aff'd 106 N. Y. 674.
[3] 75 Hun, 174; see s. c. 60 Hun, 144.
[4] Copley vs. Doran & Wright Co., 17 N. Y. St. Rep. 601.
[5] 19 N. Y. Super. Ct. Rep. 88.

ried on a " bucket shop " business in Boston, and bought and sold stocks for plaintiff on margins without any actual delivery, and the transactions were held gambling ones, under the authority of Irwin vs. Williar, *supra*,[1] but that plaintiff could not recover the amount of notes given to him by defendant, as he should have disaffirmed the contracts, and sued directly under the statute.

In Jemison vs. Citizens' Savings Bank[2] it was held that cotton Brokers could not recover for advances and commissions on future dealings in cotton, from a bank, as they were bound to know that its charter did not authorize such dealings.

It was held in Peck vs. Doran & Wright Co.,[3] that the evidence showed that the contracts made by plaintiff, as principal, with defendant grain Brokers, were wagering ones within the statute, as plaintiff's evidence clearly showed that the understanding was to settle differences merely, and that no deliveries were to be made, and this although the written contracts were against plaintiff, who was held entitled to recover the money lost by him upon the contracts. But in Amsden vs. Jacobs[4] it was held that such a contract is not rendered invalid by a secret intention of the principal to evade it, unknown to the Broker.

The cases of Kenyon vs. Luther[5] and Dwight vs. Badgley,[6] however, decided that evidence of such intention should be permitted to be given, as it might aid the jury in discovering what was the intention of the parties ; and in West vs. Wright[7] parol evidence was held to be admissible to show

[1] 110 U S. 499.
[2] 44 Hun, 412.
[3] 57 Hun, 343.
[4] 75 Hun, 311.
[5] 1 Supp. 498.
[6] 60 Hun, 111.
[7] 86 Hun, 436.

that the understanding between the parties was that differ-
euces only should be settled.[1]

When, under a custom of the New York Produce Exchange and the Chicago Board of Trade, the plaintiff
Brokers canceled their customers' contracts and substituted
themselves in place of the released parties, it was held in
Kent vs. Woodhull[2] that the contract was reduced to a
mere wagering one, although valid in its inception. So
also when it was the understanding of the parties that there
was to be no actual delivery of coffee, the contract is a
wagering one, although made under the Coffee Exchange
rules, which required actual delivery.[3] And transactions
in grain and coffee are not illegal because the customers
secretly intended to gamble, when the Brokers intended
delivery.[4]

When, however, defendant Stock-brokers charged their ·
customers, who ordered stocks bought, with the market
price on their books, and in like manner credited the market
price to customers who ordered stocks sold, and bought or
sold shares to equalize the contracts, the contracts were
gambling ones, and margins deposited by the customer
might be recovered.[5]

When although in the inception of stock transactions

[1] See also Cyrus vs. Portman, 1
City Ct. Rep. (Supp.) 1 (contract for
the future delivery of cotton valid,
when made in good faith). The
illegality of such a contract should
be pleaded (Ib.) and the intention
of the parties is for the jury (Ib.
and Ball vs. Davis, 1 St. Rep. 517),
otherwise if, on the admission of the
parties, the transactions in stocks
are gambling ones (Fleet vs. Wern-
berg, 2 City Ct. 421). In oil transactions, the burden is on the customer, in an action by the Broker
for losses, to show that no delivery
was intended (La Gar vs. Carey, 12
St. Rep. 171, aff'd 120 N. Y. 647).

[2] 23 J. & S. 311.

[3] Mackey vs. Rausch, 15 N. Y.
Supp. 4.

[4] Hentz vs. Miner, 18 Supp. 880.

[5] Smith vs. New York Stock and
Produce Clearing House Co., Ltd.,
25 N. Y. Supp. 261.

only differences were to be settled, yet when the Brokers subsequently at the customer's request actually bought and sold stocks, they are not wagering ones.[1]

If the Broker is privy to a gambling contract in oil, he is a stakeholder within the New York statute against gambling, and margins may be recovered from him by the customer, but to do so the latter must repudiate the contract and sue for the stake.[2]

When defendant Stock-broker purchased stocks on the written order of his customer who, not being able to pay therefor, left them with the Broker as security, and directed the latter to sell them if they reached a certain figure, which they never did, but declined to a figure below the purchasing price, it was held, that the customer was not entitled to a return of a deposit left with the Broker, on the ground that the transaction was a gambling one, when the Broker was willing to deliver the stocks on being paid the balance of the purchase money.[3]

When, however, the understanding was that differences only were to be settled, money deposited with the Broker may be recovered under the statute, and parol evidence is admissible to show what the understanding was.[4]

An allegation in a defence that plaintiff Brokers were dealing in stocks upon margin deposited by divers persons who engaged themselves and plaintiffs in the risk and chance of a rise or fall in the stock market, is bad, as not stating that plaintiffs dealt with defendant in such trans-

[1] Whittmore vs. Malcomson, 16 Abb. N. C. 303.

[2] Rockwood vs. Oakfield, 2 St. Rep. (N. Y.) 331.

[3] Eggleston vs. Rumble, 20 N. Y. Supp. 819.

[4] West vs. Wright, 86 Hun, 136.

actions, and it was held in the same case that such transactions were not unlawful.[1]

In the State of Maine it was held in Dillaway vs. Alden[2] that when a Stock-broker always keeps on hand a sufficient quantity of stock to make delivery at any time his customer demands, and a number of dealings is closed, by actual delivery of the stocks representing the balance, the transactions are not gambling within the statutes of Massachusetts or Maine, when it is not shown that actual delivery was never intended.

In New Jersey it was held in Flagg vs. Baldwin[3] that when it appeared that in margin transactions between defendant Broker and plaintiffs, it was never intended that the stocks purchased or sold should become or be treated as the stocks of plaintiffs, the transactions were wagers within the meaning of the first section of the act to prevent gaming,[4] and a mortgage given to secure the Broker was, under the third section of the act, void. In that case it appeared the transactions were enormous, and that plaintiffs, who speculated their entire fortune, would be utterly unable to pay for the stocks purchased. Although the transactions took place in New York, it was held that the common law, which in the absence of other proof was the law of that State, could not apply, as it would violate the public policy of the State of New Jersey as to wagering.[5]

---

[1] Ennis vs. Ross, 37 Misc. Rep. 160; 74 N. Y. Supp. 860.
[2] 88 Me. 230.
[3] 38 N. J. Eq. 219.
[4] General Stat. vol. 2, p. 1606.
[5] See Zeitner vs. Irwin, 25 App. Div. 228, where it was held that a contract made in Pennsylvania, although invalid in New York, was valid by the common law in the absence of evidence of the Pennsylvania statute.

In Pratt vs. Boody [1] it was held that large transactions in stocks on the New York Stock Exchange by Brokers as agents for complainant's intestate were valid, where deliveries were actually made as to some of the transactions, and no proof was offered to show an agreement to settle by differences merely.

When the plaintiff Broker's testimony showed that they intended actual purchases and deliveries, the contract was held, in Missouri, in the case of Williams vs. Tiedemann, [2] not to be a wagering one, although the plaintiff intended merely to settle differences, and in Kent vs. Miltenberger, [3] in a similar state of facts, viz., the purchase of grain by plaintiff Brokers for future delivery, as there was no evidence

---

[1] 35 Atl. Rep. 1113; and see also In re Hunt, 26 Fed. Rep. 739. A wife who assigned to a Stock-broker two mortgages on her separate property, and also gave him her promissory note secured by bond and mortgage on her property to enable her husband to gamble in stocks, may sue to have them transferred to her by the Broker's assignee. Tantum vs. Arnold, 15 Stew. (N. J.) 60.

And where the transactions are clearly gambling in futures on the New York Cotton Exchange, from the fact that the margins furnished were entirely disproportionate to the large amount of the dealings, and the fact that deliveries were not to be made till several months had elapsed, so that each transaction could be covered by a counter transaction, the New Jersey courts will not aid New York Brokers who had obtained a judgment against their principal, to recover

their judgment, although the contracts were valid in New York where made, and although the defendants were not residents of New Jersey, and had not alleged the gambling nature of the transactions. Minnesheimer vs. Doolittle, 45 Atl. Rep. 611. And transactions in stocks, by New York Brokers, are gambling ones, when in a long series of such dealings there is no actual delivery to, or receipts of stocks by, the customer, although the Brokers actually bought and sold the stocks, in the former case there being actual delivery thereof to them, and in the latter case there being an actual delivery (either of stock in their possession, or of stock borrowed for the purpose) by them. When, however, in one transaction there was an actual delivery to the customer, such a dealing was valid. Sharp vs Stalker, 52 Atl Rep 1120.

[2] 6 Mo App Rep 269

[3] 13 Mo. App. Rep. 503.

38

of an agreement to settle differences merely, the contract was held valid, although defendant testified he only intended to settle by payment of differences, and that this intention was known to plaintiffs. It was also held that the burden was on defendant of proving the invalidity of the contract, which was valid on its face. The court, however, reversed a judgment for plaintiffs and remanded the case on the ground that they had given no evidence of the average market value of wheat on the day of settlement in accordance with a rule of the Exchange, and that the burden was on them to do so.

It was held in Third National Bank vs. Tinsley[1] that, although a wagering contract in grain to settle for differences only, was void as *contra bona mores*, it did not come within the gaming statute of Missouri, and notes given to the Broker were recoverable in the hands of a *bona fide* holder for value without notice, and this decision was followed in Third National Bank vs. Harrison, *supra*.[2]

When the intention of the parties is that grain dealings are to be settled by differences only, the transactions are void,[3] and the Broker cannot enforce recovery on the ground that he was merely an agent, when it was shown that he was *particeps criminis*, and was the instigating cause of the wagering transactions.[4]

When the answer to a complaint by a Broker against his principal avers that the contracts to purchase grain made by the Broker with the unknown vendor were wagering ones,

[1] See the decision cited in Third National Bank vs. Harrison, 10 Fed. Rep. 249, aff'd 11 Mo. App. 498.

[2] 10 Fed. Rep. 243.

[3] McClean vs. Stuve, 15 Mo. App. 317; Ream vs. Hamilton, id. 577; Van Blarcom vs. Donovan, 16 Mo. 535.

[4] Ream vs. Hamilton, McClean vs. Stuve, supra.

it is sufficient, and it is not necessary to allege that the principal intended the transactions to be gambling ones, and the Broker cannot recover on a note given by his principal.[1]

When there is no evidence of intention not to deliver, the question as to whether transactions in grain for future delivery were wagering ones, should not have been submitted to the jury.[2]

When it is the understanding not only between the principal and his Brokers, but also between the latter and those with whom they dealt that grain transactions were merely to be settled by differences only, the Brokers cannot recover, distinguishing Cockrell vs. Thompson,[3] but a note given by the principal to the Broker may be recovered by an innocent holder for value before maturity, as such a note is not within the gambling statute rendering notes void which are given for money or property won at games.[4]

But the principal, in order to defeat the Broker's right to recover, must not only show that he intended an option deal in grain, but that the Broker, and those with whom he dealt, also so intended.[5]

[1] Buckingham vs. Fitch, 18 Mo. App. 91.

[2] Cummiskey vs. Williams, 20 Mo. App. 606.

[3] 85 Mo. 713.

[4] Crawford vs. Spencer, 92 Mo. 498.

[5] Teasdale vs. McPike, 25 Mo. App. 341. A Broker in wheat for future delivery is entitled to his advances and commissions, although he knows that his principal intended gambling, unless the party with whom the Broker contracted understood the transaction to be a wager.

Taylor vs. Penquite, 35 Mo. App. 389.

It was held in Wright vs. Fonda, 44 Mo. App. 644, that whether a transaction in grain was a wager or not, was for the jury.

When principal and Broker both *intend* that cotton is not to be purchased or sold, the latter cannot recover for advances or commissions. Hill vs. Johnston, 38 Mo. App. 383 In the last cited case the court adverted to the fact that the decision in Crawford vs Spencer, supra, had taken a step in advance of previous

In the State of Minnesota it has been held in Mohr vs. Miesen,[1] that grain Brokers who know that their customer intends gambling in "futures," cannot recover for advances and commissions, and the court may consider all the circumstances surrounding the transactions for the purpose of ascertaining such knowledge on the Broker's part.

In the last cited case the contract was made in Wisconsin, and the decision was made in accordance with the principles

decisions in making the *understanding* or *intent* of the parties the circumstance which vitiated the contract, and not merely their unlawful agreement. It was held in Connor vs. Heman, 44 Mo. App. 346, that an instruction by the court that if the parties mutually agreed and *understood* that there was to be no delivery of wheat, the Broker could not recover, was not erroneous, as the word "*understood*" was tantamount to the word "*intended.*"

When a Broker sold oats in September, to be delivered in the following May, but, on the death of his principal, closed out the transaction in October at a loss, instead of waiting till May, when the oats were to be delivered, it was held in Scott vs. Brown, 54 Mo. 606, that this circumstance, coupled with the previous dealings of the parties, stamped the transaction as a wagering one.

To make a contract for the sale of stocks and commodities invalid under the statute (Rev. Stat. § 3931), one of the parties must not have intended delivery, and such intention must be known to the other party. Mulford vs. Caesar, 53 Mo. App.

263; Schreiner vs. Orr, 55 Mo. App. 406.

But these decisions must be considered as overruled by the decision in Connor vs. Black, 119 Mo. 126; 132 Mo. 150, where it was held that grain Brokers could not recover, when the principal did not intend delivery, whether the Broker, or the purchaser of the grain sold by them, knew of the vendor's intention or not.

When Stock-brokers bought stocks for their customer through Brokers in New York city, the contract was held a New York one, and the presumption being, in the absence of contrary proof, that the common law prevailed in New York, the Brokers were held entitled to recover, in the absence of proof that they knew that the customer intended to gamble. Edwards Brokerage Co. vs. Stevenson, 160 Mo. 516. Where the evidence is conflicting as to whether the Broker had such knowledge, its weight is for the jury, or the court, when acting as a jury. Id. To the same effect is Gaylord vs. Duryea, 69 S. W. Rep. 607.

[1] 47 Minn. 228.

of the common law, in the absence of proof of any Wisconsin statute.

And in McCarthy vs. Weare Commission Co.,[1] affirming a verdict for plaintiff customers for the amount of profits on stock transactions alleged to be due to them by defendant Brokers, it was alleged that the burden was upon the party alleging that the transactions were gambling ones of proving such allegation, and if the plaintiffs acted in good faith, they might enforce the contracts.

In Mississippi it was held in Clay vs. Allen[2] that where either party intended delivery of cotton in the future, he was entitled to the benefit of the contract whatever might be the intention of the other party, and when the principal alleged that the contract was a wagering one, he should prove it. As the transaction in this case occurred prior to the passage of the act of 1882, prohibiting dealing in "futures," the construction of the act was not involved in the case.

In California it was held that an agreement between Brokers by which one purchased and sold stocks for account of the other, advanced money for the purpose, and paid assessments on the stock purchased, did not violate the constitutional provision as to purchase of stocks on margins,[3] but when the customer simply receives or pays differences, and the Broker holds the stock bought as security for advances, the transactions were within the constitutional provision, and the Broker could not recover advances or commissions, but the customer might recover moneys paid to the Broker,[4] but not interest thereon.[5] The question

[1] 91 N. W. Rep. 33.

[2] 63 Miss. 426.

[3] Kutz vs. Fleisher, 67 Cal. 93.

[4] Wetmore vs. Barrett, 103 Cal. 246.

[5] Baldwin vs. Zadig, 101 Cal. 594.

as to whether the constitution has been infringed is one of fact.[1] The constitutional provision does not violate the Federal Constitution, as although it does not distinguish between legitimate and gambling contracts, it is none the less a proper police regulation, and the court, in construing it, will protect lawful transactions.[2]

When the principal becomes insolvent and dies, his right to recover margins paid to Stock-brokers under the constitutional provision, survives to his assignee.[3]

There have been several decisions in the State of Georgia as to speculations in cotton "futures." Such dealings have been held gaming contracts and void.[4] A principal may recover deposits with a Broker in illegal grain transactions, but not profits.[5] But a demand for deposits made in gambling stock and produce transactions, must first be made.[6] Losses sustained in buying or selling "futures" cannot be recovered.[7] A note given in illegal transactions in cotton futures is void and cannot be recovered.[8]

In Maryland the principle of the decision in Irwin vs. Williar[9] was followed, and it was held that Brokers in stocks and grain could not recover for commissions and advances in gambling contracts, as they were *particeps criminis*, and it was competent for the plaintiff to give evi-

[1] Kullmen vs. Simmens, 104 Cal. 595.

[2] Parker vs. Otis, 130 Cal. 322, aff'd 187 U. S. 606.

[3] Rued vs. Cooper, 109 Cal. 682. See Maurer vs. King, 127 Cal. 114, where the constitutional provision was held not to apply to a conditional delivery of stock on purchasing land.

[4] Cunningham vs. Bank, 71 Ga. 400; 75 Ga. 366; Walters vs. Comer, 79 Ga. 796; 5 S. E. Rep. 292.

[5] Clarke vs. Brown, 77 Ga. 606.

[6] Daney vs. Phelan, 82 Ga. 243.

[7] Lawton vs. Blitch, 83 Ga. 663.

[8] Benson vs. Warehouse Co., 99 Ga. 303.

[9] 110 U. S. 499.

dence showing the real nature of the transaction.[1] It was also held in Billingslea vs. Smith[2] that a Stock-broker could not recover advances when it was intended that there was to be no delivery of stocks. But when the Broker actually contracts for the purchase of stocks, and at the Client's request makes advances to the purchaser, such advances may be recovered.[3]

It has been held in Ohio in Kahn vs. Walton[4] that speculations in wheat and pork for future delivery, being mere speculative transactions without any intention to actually deliver the property and therefore gambling transactions, are illegal and void. Whether prohibited by statute or not, the customer could not recover from his Broker the amount paid by him for margins.

In Alabama it was held in Hubbard vs. Sayre[5] that at common law (in the absence of proof of any New York statute to the contrary) New York Cotton-Brokers could recover for advances and commissions on cotton futures, when the principal promised to pay them, or allowed the transactions to proceed. Nor is it gambling when a Cotton-Broker merely, to oblige his customers, deals, in their name, in cotton futures for them, with a New York firm.[6]

In Louisiana Cotton-Brokers were held entitled in Connor vs. Robertson[7] to recover for advances and commissions in dealings in cotton for " future " delivery, when they proceeded according to the rules of the New Orleans Cotton Exchange, which required actual delivery, and the fact that plaintiffs, when defendant did not perform his contract by

---

[1] Stewart vs. Schall, 65 Md. 289.
[2] 77 Md. 501.
[3] Gover vs. Smith, 82 Md. 586.
[4] 46 Ohio, 195.
[5] 105 Ala. 410.
[6] Thompson vs. Maddox, 117 Ala. 468.
[7] 37 La. Ann. 814.

actual delivery, purchased transferable orders from responsible parties for the same amount and quality of cotton, and delivered same to their vendees, did not make the transaction a wagering one. This decision was followed in Grüner vs. Stucken,[1] where it was held that New York Cotton-Brokers, who had dealt under the rules of the New York Cotton Exchange, were entitled to recover advances and commissions, although, in previous transactions, the parties had settled differences only, the evidence in the present case showing no such intention.

In Texas it was held in Drouilhet vs. Pinckard[2] that dealings in cotton futures were not gambling transactions when the evidence showed that there was an intention to deliver, although no delivery was made, but sales were made by the Broker to prevent loss, and it was also held that an agreement to pay margins, did not necessarily make the transaction a gambling one.

It was held in Beer vs. Landman[3] that a note given by a principal to Cotton-Brokers in payment of moneys alleged to be due in dealings in cotton futures, was void, the evidence showing that there was no intent to receive or deliver, or that the principal knew the other parties to the contracts.

And in Cunningham vs. Fairchild[4] it was also held that moneys paid by a principal to persons engaged in the business of procuring contracts in cotton " futures," and by the latter paid to Cotton-Brokers to deal in such " futures," without intent to deliver, could not be recovered.

When a contract for the purchase of grain, for future de-

---

[1] 39 La. Ann. 1076.　　　　　[3] 30 S. W. Rep. 64, 726.
[2] 42 S. W. Rep. 135.　　　　　[4] 43 S. W. Rep. 32.

livery, is on its face valid, and the evidence shows that delivery was intended, it was held in Nebraska, in Morrissey vs. Bromal,[1] that such a contract was not a gambling one. But if the principal intends to gamble in wheat futures, and such intent is known to the Brokers, they cannot recover for advances and commissions.[2]

In Mendel vs. Boyd[3] it was also held that where transactions in grain were of a gambling character, the Broker should repay to a surety on a bank cashier's bond, moneys advanced as margins by the cashier out of the bank's funds, even though he was unaware of the fact that the money belonged to the bank, but he was entitled to credit for any sums repaid to the cashier, which could be traced as having been received by the bank.

It was decided in the District of Columbia in the case of Justh vs. Holliday[4] that when neither party contemplated the delivery of stocks sold for future delivery, the contract was a wagering one and void, although on its face it purported actual delivery.

(*e.*) " *Options*," " *Puts*," " *Calls*," " *Straddles*," *or* " *Spread Eagles*."

Both in England and the United States a large number of transactions in stocks are made through the instrumentality of what are termed " option " contracts, and we have consequently separated that class of cases from the bulk of

[1] 37 Neb. 766.
[2] Rogers vs. Marriott, 59 Neb. 759; 82 N. W. Rep. 21. See also Sprague vs. Warren, 26 Neb. 326; Watte vs. Wickersham, 27 Neb. 457. It is not necessary that the defendant repudiate the contract. Merrell vs. Garver, 96 N. W. Rep. 619.
[3] 91 N. W. Rep. 860.
[4] 2 Mackey's Rep. 346.

decisions in which the defence of wager has been interposed, although, as we shall see, these "options" are not treated differently from other wagering contracts by the courts, where it appears that they are mere covers for gambling operations, and the parties to them contemplate and intend that mere "differences" shall be paid.

An "option," in the sense of the present work, may be explained as a contract by which A, in consideration of the payment of a certain sum to B, acquires the right or privilege of buying from or selling to B specified securities at a fixed price within a certain time.[1]

These options are of three kinds—viz., "calls," "puts," and "straddles," or "spread-eagles."[2] A "call" gives A the option of calling or buying from B, or not, certain securities. A "put" gives A the option of selling or delivering to B, or not, certain shares of said securities. A "straddle," or "spread-eagle," is a combination of a "put" and a "call," and secures to A the right to buy of or sell to B, or not, a certain number of shares of specified securities.[3]

These optional contracts are recognized both in the rules of the London[4] and of the New York Stock Exchange.[5]

Option contracts, or "putting or receiving stock" (to use the words of the statute), that is, contracts to pay or receive a certain sum of money for the liberty to deliver, or not to deliver, or to accept or refuse, a certain quantity of stock on a given day, were prohibited in England by the

[1] Story vs. Salomon, 71 N. Y. 420; see also opinion of Van Hoesen, J., in court below, 6 Daly (N. Y.), 531; Yerkes vs. Salomon, 11 Hun (N. Y.), 471; Harris vs. Tumbridge, 83 N. Y. 93.

[2] Id.
[3] Id.
[4] Rule 76, London Stock Exch.
[5] Arts. XXIII. XXXI. XXXII. Const. N. Y. Stock Exch.

first section of the Stock-jobbing Act (7 Geo. II. c. 8).[1] Such a contract was declared void, the money paid was recoverable, and both parties were subject to a penalty unless the money were refunded. But this statute was, as has been stated, repealed in 1860 by the 23d and 24th Vict. c. 28. The Stock-jobbing Act did not apply to shares, or to foreign stocks, so that "option" contracts in such securities were not illegal under the Stock-jobbing Act, and, since its repeal, option contracts in stocks are valid. Such contracts have been held not to be of a gambling nature, but see the observation of Lord Esher cited in footnote.[2]

It is perfectly plain that in England, as in the United States, these options frequently represent real transactions,

[1] London Stock Exchange Commission Report, 1878, pp. 20–22; Cavanagh's Law of Money Securities, 2nd ed. p. 532; Stutfield's "Law of Betting, Time Bargains and Gaming," 3d ed.

[2] In Sadd vs. Foster, 13 T. L. R. 207, where Stock-brokers sued their principal for a balance due out of a "put and call option," and the defence was that plaintiffs had bought the shares as principals and not as agents, it was held (per Lord Esher, M. R.) that plaintiffs were entitled to recover, as it was a modified transaction of principal and agent, and that plaintiffs had exercised the option which had been given them. Lord Esher added, however, that "For some reason which he did not understand it had been held that such a transaction did not amount to gambling." Lopes and Chitty, L. JJ., concurred in affirming the judgment for plaintiffs, but on the ground that they were entitled to recover the agreed sum, and that it was immaterial whether plaintiffs should be deemed principals or agents.

Mr. Stutfield in his work on "Betting, Time Bargains and Gaming," gives his reasons for the view that options are not in the nature of wager contracts.

If the intention of the parties is to settle "differences," the contract will not be rendered valid by the fact that the parties have the option to demand acceptance or delivery of the shares. Universal Stock Exchange vs. Strachan, (1896) A. C. 166; In re Gieve, (1899) 1 Q. B. 794. See also In re South African Trust & Finance Co., 74 L. T. 769 (as to damages for breach of an option contract, in which case the question of gambling was not raised); Stutfield on "Rules of the Stock Exchange," 52. And see Hargreaves vs. Parsons, 13 M. & W. 561.

and that there may be a *bona fide* intention of delivering or receiving stocks when they are issued. As it has been well said,[1] " Let us suppose a person who is possessed of certain securities to be desirous of selling if he could get a bid, say one per cent higher than the present price, and to be at the same time desirous of doubling his holding if he could buy at a price - one per cent lower. If he gives his instructions in this form to his Broker, it may well happen that the price does not fluctuate sufficiently to make it possible to carry out either transaction. But the same practical result may be attained with certainty by the owner of the securities taking a one per cent price for the put and call of them, for the money thus received would be, as it were, a reduction of one per cent in the purchase price if the security is put upon him, and would equally, as it were, go to increase the selling price if it is called from him. There is, of course, this difference, that if the security is at precisely the same price on the option day as on the day the bargain was made, it may happen that the security is neither put nor called, and in that case the owner will have secured his one per cent without further liability, and be in a position to repeat the process. Under such circumstances, the option could not be said to be void as a wager."

And these observations are equally forcible when applied to dealings in stock options in the United States, many, if not most of them, being issued under the circumstances above disclosed.

In Story vs. Salomon[2] the cause of action was based upon what is known as a "straddle"—i. e., a double privi-

[1] Law and Customs of Stock Exchange, by Melsheimer and Laurence (London, 1879), 24.

[2] 71 N. Y. 420.

lege, a "put" and "call" combined, in the following form :

" NEW YORK, May 15, 1875.

" For value received the bearer may call on the undersigned for one hundred shares of the capital stock of the Western Union Telegraph Company at seventy-seven and one half per cent any time in thirty days from date.

" Or the bearer may, at his option, deliver the same to the undersigned at seventy-seven and one half per cent at any time within the period named, one day's notice required.

" All dividends or extra dividends declared during the time are to go with the stock in either case, and this instrument is to be surrendered upon the stock being either called or delivered.

" S. N. S."

The defendant Salomon, having suspended payment, subsequently agreed with the plaintiff to settle with him, and thereupon endorsed upon the contract " Settled at market, seventy-two and three quarters," which was the price of the stock on that day. The defence was that the contract was in violation of the statute against gaming ; but the court held, in the absence of parol proof to the contrary, that there was nothing illegal on the face of the contract.

One may pay for an option to take at a future day, at a certain price, a farm, or article of personal property, and most contracts for the purchase or sale of merchandise at a future day are made with a view to the market price on the day of performance. There is always an element of speculation and uncertainty as to that ; but it has never been supposed that there is any betting by such contracts. The court in such a case will not infer an illegal intent unless obliged to ; and the transaction, unless intended as a mere cover for a bet or wager on the future price of the stock, is legitimate. If it had been shown that neither party intended to deliver or accept the shares, but merely to pay differences according to the rise or fall of the market, the contract would have been illegal. But, in the absence of such evidence, upon the above reasoning the contract was sustained.

The later case of Harris vs. Tumbridge[1] reiterates the law concerning stock options. In that case the plaintiff entered into a speculation in stock, purchasing through her Broker a straddle contract on 100 shares of Lake Shore at 62¾. The Broker on the day after the purchase sold short against the straddle. The result was a loss to the plaintiff. This short sale was assailed by the plaintiff as unauthorized, negligent, and unskilful, and defended by the Broker as prudent and customary, and ratified by his principal. The questions of want of skill, negligence, and authorization having been decided against the Broker, the court, per Finch, J., next attacked the further argument of the defendant—viz., that the transaction was a gambling one, and as such prohibited by statute : " The contract was not of necessity a wager contract. That it might have been, does not at all dispense with the necessity of proving that it was. The evidence now relied on is contained in a description of a 'straddle' given by the witness L. He describes it first, and then adds, ' In other words, it is a bet that the stock will fluctuate so much.' He speaks of a straddle generally. He does not speak of the actual transaction between these parties at all. As to that, there is no proof of its character as a mere wager. We cannot supply it by suspicion, or infer it from the making of a contract not necessarily within the prohibition."

[1] 83 N. Y. 92.

The form of the contract, however, is not binding, and does not decide the question, because it would not be difficult to make the contract relating to a bet apparently lawful, while the intent with which it was entered into would be to avoid or evade the statute; accordingly, parol evidence is always admissible to show the intent of the parties. And where the question was asked, " Was it your intention, at the time those contracts, or either of them, were made, to tender or call for the stock, or merely to settle upon the difference ?" the Supreme Court of New York held that the evidence should have been admitted, and reversed a judgment on the ground of its exclusion.[1]

It was held in Lewis vs. Wilson [2] that to render optional contracts for the future delivery of stock void, it should appear affirmatively that they were entered into as gaming contracts, and not as real transactions for the purchase and sale of property.

But such a wager, although void as a contract, did not constitute a crime under § 343 of the New York Penal Code, prior to its amendment in 1889,[3] but under that section, as so amended, a conviction against the keeper of a " bucket shop " was sustained.[4]

The courts of Illinois, in several cases arising out of transactions in grain, have very strongly condemned " puts " and " calls," when it appeared that mere differences were to be settled by them, without any real delivery or acceptance of the grain being contemplated or intended.

---

[1] Yerkes vs. Salomon, 11 Hun (N. Y.), 471. But see Porter vs. Viets, 1 Biss. 177.

[2] 50 Hun, 166, aff'd 121 N. Y. 284.

[3] People vs. Todd, 58 Hun, 446.

[4] People vs. Wade, 59 N. Y. Supp. 846.

In Wolcott vs. Heath,[1] in distinguishing such contracts from *bona fide* time bargains, the court said : " What the law prohibits, and what is deemed detrimental to the public interests, is, speculations in differences in market values, called, perhaps, in the peculiar language of the dealers, ' puts ' and ' calls,' which simply means a privilege to deliver or receive the grain or not, at the seller's option. It is against such fictitious gambling transactions, we apprehend, the penalties of the law are levelled."

And in the subsequent case of Pickering vs. Cease[2] the court declared that optional contracts, where the seller had the privilege of delivering or not delivering, and the buyer the privilege of calling or not calling for the grain just as they chose, and which on the maturity of the contracts were to be filled by adjusting the differences in the market values, were in the nature of gambling transactions, and would not be tolerated by the law.

And upon the authority of these cases, the same court[3] held that a contract for the sale of wheat in store, to be delivered at a future time, which required the parties to put up margins as security, and provided that if either party fails on notice to put up further margins, according to the market price, the other might treat the contract as filled immediately, and recover the difference between the contract and market price, without offering to perform on his part, or showing an ability to perform, is illegal and void, as having a pernicious tendency.[4]

---

[1] 78 Ill. 433.

[2] 79 Ill. 328.

[3] Lyon vs. Culbertson, 83 Ill. 33.

[4] See also Rudolf vs. Winters, 7 Neb. 125, where the court holds that a contract to operate in grain options, to be adjusted according to the differences in the market value thereof, is a contract for a gambling transaction, which the law will not tolerate; but, upon the facts reported, it would seem very difficult to

The same question came before the United States District Court in Illinois, in the interesting case of In re Chandler.[1] In that case C. conceived the idea of making a corner in oats for the month of June then ensuing, and with that view he purchased all the "cash oats" as they arrived in the market, and took all the "options" offered him for June delivery—his purpose being to own all the oats in the market, and compel those who had sold "options" for June to pay his price, or, in other words, to settle with him by paying such differences as should exist between the prices at which he purchased the options and the price he should establish for cash oats on the last day of June, when the options matured. In pursuance of this plan, he purchased between the 15th of May and the 18th of June 2,500,000 bushels of cash oats—being all, or substantially all, the cash oats in the market—and also bought June "options" to the amount of 2,939,400 bushels. The total amount of oats in store in Chicago on the 18th of June was only 2,700,000 bushels, and the total amount received during the remainder of the month was only 800,000 bushels. As part of the machinery of this corner, C. also sold "puts," or privileges of delivering to him oats during the month of June, in the following form, duly signed:

"Received of E. F. $50, in consideration of which we give him, or the holder of this contract, the privilege of delivering to us or not, prior to 3 o'clock P. M. of June 30, 1872, by notification or delivery, 10,000 bushels No. 2 oats, regular receipts, at 41 cents per bushel, in store; and if delivered, we agree to receive and pay for the same at the above price."

The amount paid by the purchaser of these "puts" was one

sustain the conclusion of the court   [1] 13 Am. Law Reg. (n. s.) 310.
in that case.

half cent per bushel. " Puts " of this description were issued
to the extent of 3,700,000 bushels. The market having heav-
ily declined, C. failed, and before the time of the maturity
of the "puts" the holders of the same claimed to have
made tender to the bankrupt of the quantity of oats called
for by their contracts, and, the oats not having been accepted and paid for, they sold them upon the market under
the rules of the Board of Trade, and proved their claims
for the differences. These claims they sought to charge
against the estate of C., and his assignee moved to expunge
them from the record on the ground that they constituted
mere gambling transactions. The court found that all of
the claimants knew that C. was engaged in manipulating
the market with express reference to a "corner;" that C.
was endeavoring to keep the price up, while the sellers of
"options" and holders of "puts" were endeavoring to break
down the price; and that the "contracts in question par-
take of all the characteristics of a wager," and "that it was
as manifestly a bet upon the future price of the grain in
question, as any which could be made upon the speed of a
horse or the turn of a card;" that it conclusively appeared
that no delivery of the grain was intended by these holders
of puts, because they knew that C. controlled all the oats
in the market and fixed the price, and that their only expectation of success depended on their being able to break
the market before their time for delivery had expired. The
court held that the test was—" Did the parties intend to
sell on one side and buy on the other the oats which purported to be the subject-matter of the transaction? or did
they only intend to adjust the differences ? " and that the
evidence was overwhelmingly against the claimants on this
point. The court further held that, although the above

transaction might not be contrary to any statutory law of the State of Illinois, the wagers were, nevertheless, void at common law, as contrary to public policy. The idea was disaffirmed that it was intended to be understood that every "option" contract or "put" for the delivery of grain or stock was void; but upon the evidence in the present case it was established that the transactions were bets upon the price of oats, and that as it was obvious that the effect of them was to beget wild speculations, to derange prices, to make prices artificially high or low, thereby tending to destroy healthy business and unsettle legitimate commerce, there can be no doubt of their injurious tendency, and they should be held void as against public policy.[1]

Upon a close examination, these cases will be found not to conflict with the cases of Bigelow vs. Benedict[2] and Kirkpatrick vs. Bonsall,[3] heretofore referred to, where, in the absence of extrinsic evidence to show that they were intended as wagers, the court sustained option contracts as legal.

In a later case[4] in Illinois, however, it was held that an option contract was void under the statute, whether it was intended to settle merely for differences or not, and Bigelow vs. Benedict[5] is distinguished. An option contract to settle by differences only, was void at common law as being a gambling transaction, but where delivery was intended, such a contract was valid at common law. The statute, however, now voids such contracts, whether it is intended to settle by paying differences or not.[6]

---

[1] See also Waterman vs. Buckland, 1 Mo. App. 45.

[2] 70 N. Y. 202.

[3] 72 Pa. St. 155.

[4] Schneider vs. Turner, 130 Ill. 38.

[5] 70 N. Y. 202.

[6] 130 Ill. 38, supra.

It is well settled that, in the absence of statutory prohibitions, a *bona fide* contract or time bargain for the
future delivery of stocks, gold, or any commodity—as
grain, for instance—is legal, although at the time the vendor has not the stocks, gold, or commodity which he
has agreed to deliver. The vendor may reasonably expect
to produce or acquire them in time for future delivery;
and, while wishing to make a market for them, is unwilling
to enter into an absolute obligation to deliver, and therefore
bargains for an option which, while it relieves him from
liability, assures him of a sale in case he is able to deliver.
And the purchaser may, in the same way, guard himself
against loss beyond the consideration paid for the option
in case of his inability to take the goods.[1]

We select from the large bulk of cases that sustain this
proposition two of the leading ones which fully illustrate it.

In England the question was considered in Hibblewhite
vs. McMorine.[2] In that case the plaintiff brought an action

[1] Hibblewhite vs. McMorine, 5 M.
& W. 462 (overruling a contrary
doctrine laid down by Lord Tenterden in Bryan vs. Lewis, Ry. & M.
386; see also Lorymer vs. Smith, 1
B. & C. 1; 2 D. & R. 23); Mortimer vs. McCallan, 6 M. & W. 58,
and 9 id. 636; Thacker vs. Hardy,
L. R. 4 Q. B. D. 685, 688; Ex parte
Phillips and Ex parte Marnham, 2
De G. F. & J. 634; Currie vs. White,
45 N. Y. 822; Bigelow vs. Benedict,
70 id. 202; Kingsbury vs. Kirwin,
11 J. & S. (N. Y.) 451, aff'd 77 id.
612; Wolcott vs. Heath, 78 Ill. 433;
Sanborn vs. Benedict, id. 309; Pixley vs. Boynton, 79 id. 351; Pickering vs. Cease, id. 328; Logan vs.
Musick, 81 id. 415; Cole vs. Milmine,
88 id. 349; Corbett vs. Underwood,
83 id. 324; Lyon vs. Culbertson, id.
33; Porter vs. Viets, 1 Biss. 177;
Clarke vs. Foss, 7 id. 540; Brua's
Appeal, 55 Pa. St. 294; Smith vs.
Bouvier, 70 id. 325; Noyes vs.
Spaulding, 27 Vt. 420; Brown vs.
Hall, 5 Lans. (N. Y.) 180; Rumsey
vs. Berry, 65 Me. 570; Cassard vs.
Hinman, 14 How. (N. Y.) Pr. 84,
aff'd 1 Bosw. 207; Stanton vs. Small,
3 Sandf. 230; McIlvaine vs. Eger-
ton, 2 Robt. (N. Y.) 422; Brown vs.
Speyer, 20 Gratt. 309; Bartlett vs.
Smith, 13 Fed. Rep. 265.

[2] 5 M. & W. 462.

of assumpsit to recover damages for the breach of a contract with defendant, by which the latter agreed to purchase from plaintiff certain shares of a railroad company, " to be transferred, delivered, and paid for on or before the 1st day of March, 1839, or at any intermediate date that defendant might require them." The declaration averred a readiness and offer on the part of the plaintiff and a refusal of defendant to accept the shares. The defence pleaded was that the plaintiff never possessed or owned the shares in question, and had no reasonable expectation of becoming possessed of the same within the time provided for the fulfilment of the contract otherwise than by purchasing the same after the making of the contract. To this plea a demurrer was interposed, which was unanimously sustained and judgment ordered for the plaintiff. Parke, B., said: " I cannot see what principle of law is at all affected by a man's being allowed to contract for the sale of goods of which he has not possession at the time of the bargain, and has no reasonable expectation of receiving." All the judges repudiated the contrary doctrine of Lord Tenterden.[1]

In New York the Court of Appeals[2] has held that a contract whereby A, for a valuable consideration, agrees to purchase of B gold coin at a specified price within a specified time, B having the option to deliver or not, was not invalid on its face. By the contract the defendant bound himself to take the gold if delivered within the time specified at the price named, and he ran the hazard of loss in case the market price of gold should be more than ten per cent less, at the time specified for the delivery, than the price he agreed to

---

[1] In Bryan vs. Lewis and Lorymer vs. Smith, supra.

[2] Bigelow vs. Benedict, 70 N. Y. 202.

pay. That there was an element of hazard in the contract is plain ; but the same hazard is incurred in every optional contract for the sale of any marketable commodity, when for a consideration paid one of the parties binds himself to sell or receive the property at a future time at a specified price, at the election of the other. The contract in the case in question was attacked on the ground that it was a wager within the statute of New York, and in that respect it differs from Hibblewhite vs. McMorine.

The principle of these cases is fully sustained in all of the other States, and particular allusion has been made under the foregoing subdivisions to such of them as were deemed important.

In fine, " options " stand on the same footing as any other species of contract. Where it appears that the intention of the parties is to contract for the payment of " differences " merely, and not to deliver or accept stock, the law pronounces it a wager, irrespective of the form used to cover the transaction ; but, on the other hand, where there is a *bona fide* intention to deliver or receive property, the agreement will be sustained.

In Illinois, however, as we have seen (Schneider vs. Turner, *supra*), these contracts have, under the statute of that state, been declared void, whether it is intended to have delivery or not. And in Nebraska, such option contracts have been declared gambling transactions (Rudolf vs. Winters, *supra*). Whether the sweeping provision of the Californian constitution, *supra*, includes such contracts, has not been decided.[1]

---

[1] In a recent case in Missouri the sale of a "put" was illegal, (Lane vs. Logan Grain Co., 79 S. W. under the statute, the evidence 722), the court, whilst holding that showing that no delivery was in-

(f.) " *Conspiracy* " *to Affect Stocks, etc.; " Pools," " Corners,"*
" *Rigging the Market.*"

1. *Conspiracies.*—At common law there were three criminal offences against public trade, which were distinctly
known as " forestalling," " regrating," and " engrossing."

" Forestalling " was defined by statute 5 and 6 Edw. VI.
c. 14, to be the buying or contracting for any merchandise
or victual coming in the way to market, or dissuading persons from bringing their goods or provisions there, or per-
suading them to enhance the price when there—any of
which practices makes the market dearer to the fair trader.[1]

" Regrating," by the same statute, was described to be
the buying of corn or other dead victual in any market, and
selling it again in the same market, or within four miles of
the place. This also enhances the price of the provisions,
as every successive seller must have a successive profit.[2]

" Engrossing " was the getting into one's possession or
buying up large quantities of corn or other dead victual,
with intent to sell them again. This was considered to be
injurious to the public by putting it in the power of one or
two rich men to raise the price of provisions at their own
discretion. And the total engrossing of any other commodity, with an intent to sell it at an unreasonable price,
is an offence indictable and finable at common law.[3] The
penalty for these misdemeanors by the common law was
discretionary fine and imprisonment.

Under the head of " Monopolies," in a subsequent chapter
of the same statute, combinations among victuallers or ar-

tended, would also seem to hold   [1] 4 Black. Com. (Sharsw. ed.)
that such a contract is void *ab initio,*   158.
as " there could be no intention to   [2] Id.
deliver, when there is an option of   [3] Id.
this sort."

tificers to raise the price of provisions or any other commodities, or the rate of labor, were punishable as misdemeanors.

The statutes concerning the above offences were repealed
by 12 Geo. III. c. 71, and by 7 and 8 Vict. c. 24, the law of
engrossing or regrating was abolished.[1]

The effect of the repeal of these statutes was not, however, to render transactions such as above defined legal.
On the contrary, many of the acts embraced in these statutes were, and still are, illegal and criminal at common law.[2]
But it is a question, not free from difficulty, as to the ex-

---

[1] Mr. Wharton, in his excellent treatise on Criminal Law (10th ed. vol. ii. § 1849), gives the following history of these misdemeanors: "These offences are taken from the Roman law. The Roman title is 'Dardanariatus,' and consists in the artificial production of dearness and scarcity in any market staple (*ne dardanarii ullius mercis sint*), but especially of grain. Popular feeling was then, as it has been often since, aroused against the monopolizers or hoarders of food. The Ædiles were vested with jurisdiction to repress such offences; and Plautus illustrates the process of prosecution before them in a passage where the Parasite calls for proceedings against those *qui consilium iniere* [something like our own conspiracies to raise prices] *quo nos victu et vita prohibeant.* So Livy tells us of a fine imposed upon *frumentarii ob annonam compressum.* The proceedings allowed in such cases took definite shape in the famous *Lex Julia de Annona*, which declared the usurious hoarding of grain to be a public crime. In the exposition of the law we are told that *lege Jul. de ann. pœna statuitur adversus eum qui contra annonam fecerit societatemve coierit, quo annona carior fiat;* and by the first section a penalty is imposed on interference with transportation, or in any way preventing the free carriage of grain: *Eadem lege continetur, ne quis navem nautamve retineat aut dolo ne faciat, quo magis detineatur.* Still sharper edicts followed, of which Ulpian mentions one: *Ne aut ab his: qui coemtas merces supprimunt* [purchasers] *aut a locupletioribus* [hoarders of their own produce] *annona oneratus.* Zeno issued a special statute against monopolizers who, to create an artificial scarcity, buy up all a necessary staple, in order subsequently to sell at their own price. Such offenders, on conviction, were to be sentenced to confiscation of goods and to banishment."

[2] Raymond vs. Leavitt, Sup. Ct. of Mich. 13 Cent. L. J. 110.

tent the old common-law principles in this respect should be applied to the present methods of transacting business. A most cursory perusal of the definitions of "forestalling," "regrating," and "engrossing" will show that if they were enforced at the present day the commercial interests of the world would be seriously curtailed and impeded ; and there is no doubt that many of the old doctrines have been practically abrogated.[1]

In England it was held that the common-law offence of engrossing applied only with respect to the necessaries of life ;[2] and it is very evident that these statutes did not embrace, and were not intended to apply to, dealings in securities or stocks, for the very obvious reason that the latter description of property did not come into existence in England until many years after they were passed ; but, as we shall see, the comprehensive and elastic principles of the common law upon the subject of illegal conspiracies have practically kept alive the spirit of these old statutes, and furnished remedies sufficiently adequate to prevent combinations in this new species of property when they threatened the public property, trade, or commerce.

The modern rule, then, would seem to be this: that the offences of " regrating," " forestalling," and " engrossing," as they were defined under the statutes of Edward, no longer exist (unless revived by express legislation) either in England or in this country, so far as *individual* action or prop-

---

[1] Raymond vs. Leavitt, supra; Story on Sales, 647; Benjamin on Personal Property, 414 (1873); 2 Whart. Cr. Law (10th ed.), § 1850 and note (3).

The writer of an article in 3 Political Sci. Quart. 592, 598, doubts whether the offence of regrating ever existed at common law. See also 4 Harv. L. Rev. 128.

[2] Pettamberdass vs. Thackoorseydass, 5 Moo. Ind. App. 109; 7 Moo. P. C. C. 239; 15 Jur. 257.

erty is concerned; but in place thereof the common law declares that combinations or conspiracies by *several* persons to engross or absorb any particular necessary staple of life, to the detriment of the public, are illegal and the subject of indictment.[1]

The case of Rex vs. Waddington[2] illustrates this proposition, it being there held that the spreading of rumors with intent to enhance the price of hops, in the hearing of hop-planters, dealers, and others, that the stock of hops was nearly exhausted, and that there would be a scarcity of hops, with intent to induce them not to bring their hops to market for a long time, and thereby greatly to enhance the price, constituted the offence of "ingrossing" (engrossing), at common law, notwithstanding the repeal of 5 & 6 Edw. VI. c. 14 by 12 Geo. III. c. 71. Although this case has been severely criticized, it has not, it seems, been directly overruled.[3] And, as we have intimated, the general rule has been extended to embrace combinations or conspiracies to affect the price or market for stocks and government securities.

[1] See authorities heretofore cited under this subdivision, and consult also, in this connection, the interesting case of In re Chandler, 13 Am. Law Reg. (n. s.) 310; s. c. 6 Biss. C. C. 53, *sub nom.* Ex parte Young. See also Ray on "Contractual Limitations" and cases therein cited; Eddy on "Combinations" and cases cited. And see United States vs. Knight Co., 156 U. S. 1 (purchase of sugar refineries not in restraint of commerce); Ertz vs. Produce Exchange, 51 L. R. A. 825 (Produce Exchange of Minneapolis held to be a combination in restraint of trade); Hawarden vs. Coal Co., 55 L. R. A. 828 (coal combination illegal); People vs. Milk Exchange, 27 L. R. A. 437.

It has been decided by the English Privy Council that the law of the Colony of Natal does not make it illegal for any person or any body of persons to buy shares with a view to selling them at a profit. Laughton vs. Griffin, (1895) App. Cas. 104.

[2] 1 East, 143–160.

[3] See 1 Bish. Cr. Law, §§ 527, 528, and notes to 7th ed.; Raymond vs. Leavitt, Sup. Ct. Mich. 13 Cent. L. J. 110.

This was held in the celebrated case of the King vs. De Berenger and others.[1] In that case De Berenger and seven others were tried and convicted of conspiracy in disseminating false reports and rumors that a peace would soon be made between England and France, and that Napoleon Bonaparte was dead, thereby attempting to occasion, without any just or true cause, a great increase and rise of the public government funds and securities, to the injury and damage of the subjects of the king, who should, on a certain day, purchase and buy such securities. The defendants moved an arrest of judgment upon several grounds: *inter alia*, that no crime known to the law had been committed; that no adjudged case of conspiracy had gone as far as this; and that, if it were not a crime in itself to raise the price of government funds, a conspiracy to do so would not be illegal unless some collateral object were stated to give it a criminal character. Lord Ellenborough, C. J., in an opinion, the doctrine of which was endorsed by all of the judges, overruled all of the grounds relied on, holding that the conspiracy was by false rumors to raise the public funds and securities. The crime lay in the act of conspiracy and combination to effect that purpose, and it would have been complete although it had not been pursued to its consequences, or the parties had not been able to carry it into effect. The purpose of such a conspiracy is itself mischievous, as it strikes at the price of a vendible commodity in the market, and, if it gives it a fictitious price by means of false rumors, it is a fraud levelled against all the public, being against all such as may possibly have anything to do with the funds on that particular day. While the raising or lowering of the public funds is not *per se* a

[1] 3 Mau. & S. 67.

crime—for a man may have occasion to sell out a large sum, which may have the effect of depressing the price of stocks, or may buy in a large sum and thereby raise the price on a particular day—yet the conspiracy by a number of persons to raise the funds on a particular day is an offence prejudicial to a certain class of subjects.[1]

This case was directly approved by the English courts in 1876 in Reg. vs. Aspinall,[2] where it was held that a conspiracy to procure, by fraud and falsehood, the shares of a company to be quoted in the official list, and thus give a fictitious value to the shares beyond what they would otherwise bring in the market, is a fraud upon the public, and an indictable offence. In that case the indictment alleged that the defendants were promoters of the E. Company, Limited, and that application had been made, on behalf of the company, to the Committee for General Purposes of the Stock Exchange to order the quotation of the company in the official list of the Stock Exchange, under the 129th Rule, to the effect that the committee would order the quotation of a new company in the official list, provided that the company was of *bona fide* character, etc.; that the requirements of Rule 128 had been complied with, requiring the production of documents, etc., and list of allottees, etc.; that two thirds of the whole nominal capital proposed to be issued had been applied for and unconditionally allotted to the public; and that a member of the Stock Exchange was authorized by the company to give full information as to the formation of the undertaking, and able to

---

[1] See also Rex vs. Gurney, 11 Cox C. C. 414. So a combination to fix the price of salt is unlawful (Rex vs. Norris, 2 Ld. Ken. 300).

[2] L. R. 1 Q. B. D. 730; aff'd 2 id. 48. See also Rex vs. Mott, 2 Cas. & P. 521.

satisfy the committee as to all particulars they should require. It was also averred that defendants requested a firm of Stock-brokers to give the information before mentioned and to apply to the committee to order the quotation of the shares of the company in the official list, and employed the Brokers to sell 5000 shares of the company on behalf of alleged vendors of patents; and that defendants unlawfully conspired and agreed, by divers false pretences, to injure and deceive the committee, and to induce them, contrary to the true intent and meaning of the rules of the Exchange, to order a quotation of the shares of the company in the official list of the Stock Exchange, to induce persons who should buy and sell the shares to believe that the company was duly formed and constituted, and had, in all respects, complied with the rules of the Stock Exchange, so as to entitle the company to have their shares quoted in the official list; and that defendants in pursuance of the conspiracy, falsely pretended to Z. and other members of the committee that the number of shares applied for by the public was 34,365, and that the amount received thereon, at 10s. per share, was £17,282, and that 15,000 had been allotted to the patentee, and that no shares had been conditionally allotted, and thereby induced the committee to order the shares to be quoted in the official list.

Upon a motion in arrest of judgment, after conviction, the Court of Queen's Bench held that this count was sufficient, and the case had been fully made out against the defendants. The Court of Appeals affirmed this judgment. The court held that, as the rules of a public body of such celebrity as the London Stock Exchange must be widely known to Brokers and others dealing in shares, it was plain that to obtain a quotation of their shares in the official list must be advantageous to companies and enhance their value. Purchasers, on seeing the shares so quoted, would have a right to believe that the requirements of the Stock Exchange had been complied with, and that the company whose shares they proposed to purchase had therefore satisfied an independent body like the committee, of its respectability and solvency, and it could not be doubted that they would be willing to give a higher price for the shares in consequence. It was further held that the crime of conspiracy is completely committed the moment two or more have agreed that they will do at once, or at some future time, certain things; but that it was not necessary, in order to complete the offence, that any one thing should be done beyond the agreement; and that an agreement made with a fraudulent mind to do that which, if done, would give to the prosecutor a right of suit founded on fraud, is a criminal conspiracy.

Another phase of an indictable conspiracy was presented in Reg. vs. Esdaile.[1] There the information charged that the defendants, intending to deceive, defraud, and prejudice such of the shareholders of the Royal British Bank as were not aware of the true state of the affairs of the bank, and to induce others to become customers and creditors of the bank, and to purchase and hold shares therein, did conspire falsely and fraudulently to publish and represent that the bank and its affairs had been during the year 1855, and then were, in a sound condition, and producing profits; and that defendants published and distributed a balance-sheet apparently showing such a condition, and also paid a dividend, knowing that such dividend had

[1] 1 F. & F. 213.

not been earned, and also fraudulently issued new shares while the bank was in an unsound state. Upon the trial thereof, Lord Campbell, C. J., charged the jury that if, at the time mentioned, the bank was insolvent, which fact was known to the defendants, and that they nevertheless entered into the design to represent that the bank was in a prosperous state, with a view to deceive the shareholders or to delude the public into becoming shareholders, a conspiracy would be made out. And the defendants were all convicted.[1]

[1] The rule of law in civil cases is even more stringent than that of the criminal law, and the general principle may be stated that, in every case of fraud for which an indictment can be sustained, an action for damages or relief in law or equity will lie at the instance of the grieved party. The general principles upon which a civil liability for fraud rests were stated by the vice-chancellor in Barry vs. Croskey, 2 J. & H. 1, as follows: "First, every man must be held responsible for the consequences of a false representation made by him to another, upon which that other acts, and, so acting, is injured or damnified. Secondly, every man must be held responsible for the consequences of a false representation made by him to another, upon which a third person acts, and, so acting, is injured or damnified; provided it appear that such false representation was made with the intent that it should be acted upon by such third person in the manner that occasions the injury or loss. And, thirdly, but to bring it within the principle, the injury must be the immediate and not the remote consequences of the representations thus made."

These principles have been applied to an infinite number of transactions in which the directors, promoters, organizers, or originators of companies or schemes, either through the instrumentality of Stock Exchanges or otherwise, have been guilty of fraud or deceit in inducing persons to become purchasers of shares or interests in the company. The following are some of the leading cases: Peek vs. Gurney, L. R. 6 H. L. Cas. 377; Pasley vs. Freeman, 3 T. R. 51; Bevan vs. Adams, 19 W. R. 76; 22 L. T. (n. s.) 795; Beattie vs. Ebury, L. R. 7 H. L. Cas. 102; Pontifex vs. Bignold, 3 Scott N. R. 390; Shrewsbury vs. Blount, 2 id. 588; Clarke vs. Dickson, 6 C. B. (n. s.) 453; Moore vs. Burke, 4 F. & F. 258; Gray vs. Collins, id. 302; Smith vs. Clem'h, id. 578; Cross vs. Sacket, 6 Ab. (N. Y.) Pr. 247; Wakeman vs. Dalley, 11 Barb. (N. Y.) 498; Cazeaux vs. Mali, 25 id. 578; s. c. 15 How. Pr. 317; Morse vs. Swits, 19 id. 275;

By the law of New York (Penal Code, §§ 168–170), no conspiracies are punishable criminally except those there stated, and, among others, the conspiring of two or more persons " *to commit any act injurious* to the public health, to public morals, or *to trade or commerce*, or for the perversion or obstruction of justice or the due administration of the laws," shall constitute a misdemeanor. Under this broad and comprehensive language, which is practically the rule in all of the States, either by adoption of the common law or express statute, infamous conspiracies or combinations are punishable, whether their object be to

Newbery vs. Garland, 31 Barb. 121. And see the following: Davidson vs. Tulloch, 3 Macq. (H. L.) 783; Derry vs. Peek, 14 A. C. 337; Fenn vs. Curtis, 23 Hun, 384; Perry vs. Hale, 143 Mass. 540; Prosser vs. First National Bank, 106 N. Y. 677; Compton vs. Chelsea, 128 N. Y. 537; Trumble vs. Ward, 97 Ky. 748; Merchants National Bank vs. Armstrong, 65 Fed. Rep. 932; Foley vs. Holtrey, 43 Neb. 133; Exchange Bank vs. Gatskill, 37 S. W. Rep. 100; Investment Co. vs. Eldridge, 2 Pa. Dist. Rep. 394; Parker vs. McQuesten, 32 Q. B. R. (Can.) 273; Bellairs vs. Tucker, L. R. 13 Q. B. D. 163; Morgan vs. Skiddy, 62 N. Y. 319; Kountze vs. Kennedy, 147 N. Y. 124; Andrews vs. Mockford, 73 Law Times R. 726; Brackett vs. Griswold, 112 N. Y. 454; s. c. 13 N. Y. Supp. 192, aff'd 128 N. Y. 644; People vs. Garrahan, 19 App. Div. (N. Y.) 347; Shattuck vs. Robins, 68 N. H. 565. See also Cook on Corporations, 5th ed., chs. IX. and XX., and numerous cases cited in the notes thereto.

And where the directors of a joint-stock bank, knowing it to be in a state of insolvency, issued a balance-sheet showing a profit, and thereupon declared a dividend of 6 per cent, and issued advertisements inviting the public to take shares upon the faith of their representations that the bank was in a flourishing condition, on an *ex officio* information filed by the attorney-general they were found guilty of a conspiracy to defraud. Reg. vs. Brown, 7 Cox C. C. 442; Same vs. Esdaile, 1 F. & F. 213.

It was held, however, in Salaman vs. Warner, 65 L. T. R. 132, in which a Stock-broker brought an action for deceit and conspiracy against the promoters of a company, alleging that he had, owing to their having fraudulently obtained control of the majority of the shares, been obliged to purchase same at an exorbitant price in fulfilment of his contracts, that plaintiff failed to make out a case of deceit, within the meaning of the three general principles already stated, and that

affect the " necessaries " of life, or securities, or other property in which the public have an interest.

A conspiracy to depress the stock of the Brooklyn Rapid Transit Company, dealt in on the Stock Exchange, is a conspiracy to injure trade or commerce within the meaning of this section.[1]

In 1874 the Legislature of the State of New York (Laws, 1874, ch. 440) passed a very stringent law against persons circulating rumors to affect the stock market, as follows :

" Sec. I. Every person who shall knowingly circulate false intelligence with intent of depreciating or advancing the market price of the public funds of the United States, or of any State or Territory thereof, or of any foreign country or government, or the stocks, bonds, or evidence

an action for conspiracy was not known to the law. If the defendants had agreed to do an unlawful act, they might be indicted, although their agreement did not result in any act. An action might be brought against several defendants who had agreed to do an act which resulted in an infringement of plaintiff's legal rights, but the cause of action was not the agreement, but the infringement of plaintiffs legal rights, which in this case had not been shown.

In Scott vs. Brown, (1892) 2 Q. B. D. 724, it was held that principals could not obtain a rescission of a contract made by them with Stock-brokers to purchase shares, and recover the money paid for them, on the ground that the Brokers had delivered their own shares to them, instead of buying them for plaintiffs on the Stock Exchange,

when it appeared that plaintiffs and defendants had agreed that the purchase was to be made on the Stock Exchange with the view of inducing the public to believe there was a market for them, although, as the parties knew, there was not such a market, and the court further held that such an agreement was a conspiracy for which the parties might be indicted. The court itself raised the question of illegality, which was not advanced by the parties. And see Secor vs. Goslin, N. Y. L. J. March 26, 1901, p. 2310, where motions to vacate orders of arrest were denied on the ground that plaintiff Stock-brokers had been induced by the fraud and conspiracy of defendants to purchase worthless stock.

[1] People vs. Goslin, 73 N. Y. Supp. 520, aff'd 171 N. Y. 627. See in this connection, People vs. Putnam, 90 A. D. 125.

40

of debt of any corporation or association, or the market price of any merchandise or commodity whatever, shall be deemed guilty of a misdemeanor, and shall be punished, upon conviction thereof, by a fine of not exceeding five thousand dollars, and imprisonment for a period not exceeding three years, or either.

" Sec. II. Every person who shall forge the name of any person, or the officer of any corporation, to any letter, message, or paper whatever with intent to advance or depreciate the market price of the public funds of the United States, or of any State or Territory thereof, or of any foreign country or government, or the market price of bonds or stock, or other evidence of debt issued by any corporation or association, or the market price of gold or silver coin or bullion, or of any merchandise or commodity whatever, shall, upon conviction, be adjudged guilty of forgery in the third degree, and shall be punished by imprisonment in a state prison for a term not exceeding five years."

This statute was repealed by L. 1886, ch. 593, § 1, subd. 49. Its provisions have been substantially re-enacted in the Penal Code, § 435.   An indictment under this section charged the defendants with conspiring to occasion a fall in the market price of the stock of a corporation by " contriving, propagating, and spreading " false rumors concerning its financial condition, well knowing the same to be false—held that the indictment was sufficient, as the words " contriving, propagating and spreading " were the full equivalent of the statutory word " circulating," and motive, intent and guilty knowledge were also sufficiently charged. The defendants had published advertisements in New York newspapers to the effect that the stock of the corporation would fall, that it would be obliged, under a decision of the court, to pay a heavy tax under the Ford act, and that it was going into the hands of a receiver, and it was held that the evidence was sufficient to sustain a conviction for having violated the provisions of this section, subd. 3.[1]

It is provided by Laws of New York of 1899, c. 690, that combinations to create a monopoly in the manufacture or sale of any article in common use are illegal, and punishable. It was held in Rourke vs. Elk Drug Co.[2] that any person suffering special injury on account of such acts had a right of action, and plaintiff druggists might maintain an action against defendants for conspiring to injure their business. The act of 1899 was held constitutional in Matter of Davies,[3] and in Kellogg vs. Lehigh Valley R. Co.[4] it was held that averments in a complaint as to an alleged unlawful combination against plaintiff grain elevator firm, were good. A joint stock company may unite with a rival corporation, where no restriction is placed upon anyone from engaging in the business carried on.[5] Combinations of corporations in restraint of trade are prohibited by the Stock Corporation Law, § 7. A combination of gas companies was held not to violate this section.[6] An examination under the Monopoly act is not extrajudicial.[7]

In Illinois it was held that the Board of Trade could be compelled to continue to supply the plaintiff corporation (the New York Grain and Stock Exchange) with their market quotations as it could not create a monopoly therein, although the Board of Trade was a private corporation,

[1] People vs. Goslin, 73 N. Y. Supp. 520, aff'd 171 N. Y. 627.

[2] 77 N. Y. Supp. 373.

[3] 168 N. Y. 89.

[4] 70 N. Y. Supp. 237.

[5] Francis vs. Taylor, 65 N. Y. Supp. 28.

[6] Rafferty vs. Buffalo City Gas Co., 56 N. Y. Supp. 288.

[7] Re Attorney General, 47 N. Y. Supp. 883.

when its property was devoted to a public use and became affected with a public interest.[1]

2. *"Corners," "Rigging the market," " Pools."*—Closely akin to the foregoing is the subject of "Corners," "Rigging the market" and " Pools."

A " corner " is a scheme or combination of one or more " bulls" who are " long" of certain stocks or securities, to compel the " bears," or persons " short" of the stock, to pay a certain price for the same. Or it may be a combination to force a fictitious and unnatural rise in a market for the purpose of obtaining the advantage of dealers and purchasers, and all persons whose necessities or contracts compel them to use or obtain the thing " cornered." [2]

" Rigging the market " is described as a process by which " an artificial value is given to securities by means of dealings upon the market which are not genuine dealings on behalf of the public." See Brodhurst's Law and Practice of the Stock Exchange, p. 26.[3]

A " pool " is defined as a combination of persons contributing money to be used for the purpose of increasing or depressing the market price of stocks, grain, or other commodities; also the aggregate of the sums so contributed.[4] A " pool " is also defined as a joint adventure by several owners of a specified stock or other security temporarily subjecting all their holdings to the same control for the

---

[1] Stock Exchange vs. Board of Trade, 127 Ill. 153.

[2] Raymond vs. Leavitt, 13 Cent. L. J. 110. As to when it is not libelous per se to say of a Cotton-Broker that he cornered the market, see Labouisse vs. Evening Post, 41 N. Y. Supp. 688.

[3] Scott vs. Brown, (1892) 2 Q. B. 724; Begbie vs. Phosphate Sewage Co., 35 L. T. 350; Marzetti's Case, 42 L. T. 206; Twycross vs. Grant, 2 C. P. D. 469; Gray vs. Lewis, L. R. 8 Ch. App. 1035.

[4] Webster.

purpose of a speculative operation, in which any sacrifice of the shares contributed by one, and any profit on the shares contributed by another, shall be shared by all alike.[1]

A "corner" is manifestly much more obnoxious to reason and to the law when it has for its object the artificial enhancement of the market value of any kind of property which purchasers are compelled to buy, than when the scheme is formed to "squeeze" the "bears," or persons who have sold property which they did not possess, hoping to buy it when it reached the level of their expectations. Yet it is doubtful whether the "corner" is not equally illegal in the one case as in the other.

But, in any case, a combination or scheme which has for its object the fraudulent inducing of persons to sell property for future delivery, with the intention or purpose of compelling such persons to buy in or purchase the same at a price fixed by the combination, destroying a chance or opportunity of a fair purchase, is void.[2]

These "corners" are carried out in forms varying as they relate to different kinds of property, or as they are managed in one or more places, where the course of dealing is not the same. A "corner" in stocks may be illustrated in this manner: The "bears" in the market are those persons who, from a variety of reasons, believe or hope that the price of a certain security will decline, and without having any of it, they sell the same, borrowing the security for delivery from some third person, expecting to buy it at a lower price and

---

[1] Century Dictionary. It was held in Green vs. Higham, 161 Mo. 333, that where three persons, owning between them 600 shares of the stock of a company, agreed to "pool" said shares for their mutual benefit, the word "pool" had no technical meaning, and that the word should be read in the light of the whole contract.

[2] Barry vs. Croskey, 2 Johns. & H. 1, and cases hereafter cited.

return it to the lender. The difference between the price at which they sell the security and the price which they are compelled to pay for the same constitutes the profit or loss of the transaction. If the security decline, there is a profit; if it advance, there is a loss. "The bulls," on the other hand, discovering that there is a "short" representation in the security, sufficiently large to justify the movement, combine together to buy all, or as much of the security as will enable them to accomplish their object; and when they have succeeded they become masters of the situation. The "bears" are then compelled to buy; but, as all the security is in possession or under the control of the "bulls," they are forced to pay any price which the cornering party chooses to ask for it. The "corner" is then complete.

The validity of the combinations which we have here briefly described has been passed on by the courts on several occasions, and in many instances they have been declared illegal.

In the interesting case of Barry vs. Croskey,[1] which arose out of certain dealings on the London Stock Exchange, a state of facts was revealed which showed that the defendants, having first put themselves in control of all the shares and allotments of a certain company, induced a Stock-jobber to sell a number of shares for future delivery—i. e., the next settling-day—and then compelled him to settle his contracts at figures satisfactory to them, before he knew of the whole truth of the transaction. He subsequently brought a bill in Chancery, in which he averred that defendants, the directors and secretary of a projected rail-

[1] 2 Johns. & H. 1. See also British and American Telegraph Co. vs. The Albion Bank, L. R. 7 Ex. 119; Gray vs. Lewis, L. R. 8 Ch. App. 1035; Salaman vs. Warner, 65 L. T. N. S. 132.

way company, having, partly by allotments to fictitious persons and partly by purchase, obtained possession of all the shares of a given class in the company, though their Broker induced plaintiff, a Stock-jobber, to contract to sell them certain of such shares, to be delivered upon the settling-day to be appointed by the committee of the Stock Exchange ; and that they then, by false and fraudulent representations made by them in their official character to the committee of the Stock Exchange, procured the appointment of a settling-day ; upon the arrival of which plaintiff, being by reason of the scheme thus contrived by defendants unable to procure the shares he had contracted to deliver, except at a ruinous premium, was compelled to pay defendants a sum specified in the bill to release him from his contract ; and the bill prayed for a declaration that such a contract was fraudulent and void, or inoperative, and for repayment to plaintiff of the amount he had paid in respect thereof. The company having been joined as defendants to the bill, upon the ground that they had adopted the fraudulent representations made by their directors and secretary to the committee of the Stock Exchange, the court held, on demurrer by the company, that although the company might have benefited by the fraudulent representations—e. g., by obtaining a quotation and an increased price for their shares—and although they might be answerable for that increased price, or for any other direct advantage derived from such fraudulent representations, yet it not being shown that the company knew such representations were made by their directors with intent to defraud the plaintiff, by compelling him to perform his contract, or even that they knew of the existence of such a contract, the company were not responsible for the loss plaintiff had thus incidentally sustained, and the company's demurrer was allowed; but it was further held that the bill was not open to demurrer on the part of the other defendants on any ground, it having averred that the several defendants had combined to practise jointly this "scheme of deceit," as the court termed it.[1]

The case of Salamon vs. Warner, *supra*, affords an example of the difficulty of successfully maintaining a civil action against a cornering combination, although, upon the facts as stated, the defendants might have been indicted.

Sampson vs. Shaw [2] presents an action between members of the cornering combination. In that case it appeared that the plaintiff, the firm of T. & Co., and one R., entered into an agreement to operate in the stock of a certain railway company for the purpose of getting a "corner," T. & Co. taking one half, and the plaintiff and R. each a quarter interest in the operation, the plan of operation being as follows: T. & Co. were to be the managers, and were to buy up a large quantity of the stock and control it in such a manner as to make a large demand for it, so that parties selling on time would be compelled to pay large differences; T. & Co. were then to receive and make proposals and agreements thereon for the purchase of stock to be delivered at a future day, the parties agreeing to sell not then having the stock in possession or owning it, and then the sellers, when the day for delivery should arrive, would be compelled to pay such prices or differences as the parties to the combination might ask; the money to carry on the

---

[1] As the result of an inquiry by the Stock Exchange Committee the company attempted to be promoted in the case mentioned in the text (Barry vs. Croskey, 2 Johns. & H. 1) was subsequently ordered to be stricken from the official list.

[2] 101 Mass. 145.

operation was to be furnished, and the profits or losses shared or borne by the parties in proportion to their respective interests; that said stock at the time was of little, if any, intrinsic value, and was selling in the market for about five dollars per share; that R. paid in money from time to time as called for under the agreement for carrying on the operations. T. & Co. did proceed to make purchases, and in so doing expended a large sum of money. The operation in the stock was not successful, and the money invested therein was substantially lost. The plaintiff brought an action against the representatives of T. & Co. for money had and received. The defendant, in answer, showed that the amount had been actually appropriated or expended in carrying out the above-described agreement.

The auditor to whom the cause was referred ruled that the agreement for operating in the above manner was illegal and void; and this ruling was sustained, on appeal, by the Supreme Court, which held that neither party as against the other could enforce what remained to be done, or correct what had been done, under a conspiracy of that description, and that such an agreement did not make the parties partners.

In a case in Michigan[1] the Supreme Court examined the subject of a "corner" in grain. In that case the plaintiff advanced certain money to the defendants for the purpose of controlling the wheat market, with a view of forcing up prices and producing a "corner," and compelling parties who had contracts to fill to pay a higher price for wheat to fill them. The action was to recover the money advanced to the defendant for this purpose, and the court, through

---

[1] Raymond vs. Leavitt, 13 Cent. L. J. 110.

Campbell, J., in a very able and thorough opinion, held that the plaintiff was not entitled to recover. The court said that "the object of the arrangement between these parties was to force a fictitious and unnatural rise in the wheat market, for the express purpose of getting the advantage of dealers and purchasers whose necessities compelled them to buy, and necessarily to create a similar difficulty as to all persons who had to obtain or use that commodity, which is an article indispensable to every family in the country. That such transactions are hazardous to the comfort of the community is universally recognized. This alone may not be enough to make them illegal, but it is enough to make them so questionable that very little further is required to bring them within distinct prohibition."

The cases of The Morris Run Coal Co. vs. Barclay Coal Co.[1] and Arnott vs. Pittston, etc., Coal Co.[2] held contracts involving similar dealings in coal to be against public policy. "And," said the court, in Raymond vs. Leavitt, *supra*, "we think the reasoning of these cases is based on familiar common-law principles, which apply more strongly to provisions than to any other articles. . . . At common law there is no doubt such transactions as were here contemplated, although confined to a single person, were indictable misdemeanors under the law applicable to forestalling and engrossing. Some of our States have abolished the old statutes which were adopted on this subject, and which were sometimes regarded as embodying the whole law in such cases. . . . But, so long as the early statutes only were repealed, it was considered that enough remained of the common law to punish combinations to enhance the

[1] 68 Pa. St. 173.   [2] 68 N. Y. 558.

value of commodities. And when this doctrine became narrowed, it seems to have been considered that such combinations to enhance the price of provisions remained under the ban. . . . We do not feel called upon to regard so much of the common law to be obsolete as treats these combinations as unlawful, whether they should now be held punishable as crimes or not. The statute of New York, which is universally conceded to be a limitation of common-law offences, is referred to in the case in 68 N. Y. 558, as rendering such conspiracies unlawful. . . . There may be difficulties in determining conduct as in violation of public policy, where it has not before been covered by statutes as precedents. But in the case before us the conduct of the parties comes within the undisputed censure of the law, and we cannot sustain the transaction without doing so on the ground that such dealings are so manifestly sanctioned by usage and public approval that it would be absurd to suppose the legislature, if attention were called to them, would not legalize them. We do not think public opinion has become so thoroughly demoralized ; and until the law is changed, we shall decline enforcing such contracts. If parties see fit to invest money in such ventures, they must get it back by other than legal means."

There are other American cases which sustain the doctrine laid down in Raymond vs. Leavitt.[1]

---

[1] The following charge of Mr. Justice Jamieson to a grand-jury of the Criminal Court of Chicago, Oct. 12, 1881, illustrates the condition of the law of Illinois upon the subject of which we are treating, so forcibly and thoroughly that we give it in full:

"GENTLEMEN OF THE GRAND-JURY.—Besides the statutes against gambling, selling liquor to minors, and acts of violence to person or property, which form the subject of your ordinary deliberations, I wish to call your attention to one which I will now read: 'Whoever con-

In the State of New York the Supreme Court has decided that the law will not aid either party to enforce an agreement entered into for the purpose of advancing the

tracts to have or give to himself the option to sell or buy at a future time any grain or other commodity, stock of any railroad or other corporation, or gold, or forestalls the market by spreading false rumors to influence the price of commodities therein, or corners the market, or tries to do so, in relation to any of such commodities, shall be fined not less than $10 nor more than $1000, or confined in the County Jail not exceeding one year, or both' (Revised Statutes, Illinois, ch. 38, § 130). By this section are denounced three separate misdemeanors—the sale of options, forestalling the market, and cornering the market. All these have, either in name or in spirit, been always interdicted by the common law, and that of forestalling was, at a very early day, made punishable in England by statute. Over a century ago a movement arose in England for abolishing the restrictions upon the freedom of trade, and these statutes were, or a part of them, repealed; but the common law has remained, both there and in this country, unchanged, though fallen into disuse. The exigencies of the times induced our legislature a few years since to re-enact the statute against forestalling, and to add to it those touching 'options' and 'corners,' which I have read— offences to which the criminal ingenuity of our ancestors seems not to have been equal. The first offence is the illegal sale of options

for future delivery of grain and other commodities. The fact that property is sold to be delivered at a future day does not make the contract illegal, although it is not at the time possessed or owned by the seller, or that the time of its delivery is left within fixed limits, optional with the buyer or seller, though in one sense any such sale is a sale of an option apparently within the statute. What makes it a gambling contract is the intent of the parties that there shall not be a delivery of the commodity sold, but a payment of differences by the party losing upon the rise or fall of the market. Of this intent the jury are to be the judges, and it may be inferred directly from the terms of the contract or indirectly from the course of dealing of the parties (Pickering vs. Cease, 79 Ill. 328; Walcott vs. Heath, 78 id. 433; Pixley vs. Boynton, 79 id. 351). By this legislation the General Assembly had no purpose to interdict *bona fide* sales of commodities, but only such as are colorable or fraudulent, contrived by both parties as a cover merely for gambling transactions. The offence of forestalling originally consisted in the buying or contracting for merchandise or victuals coming to market, or dissuading persons from bringing their goods or provisions there, or inducing them to raise their prices (2 Whart. Crim. Law, 1849). Our statute has narrowed the offence so that it covers

selling price of stocks by means of fictitious dealings designed to produce a false impression on the minds of observ-
ers concerning their real value, and in that way to induce

only forestalling the market by spreading false rumors to influence the price of commodities therein. The obvious purpose of the legislature in making this provision was to protect the people—the consumers as well as innocent traders—from the damage resulting from unnatural and fictitious fluctuations of prices, brought about by the false suggestions of interested persons. The offence of cornering the market is not, so far as I am aware, mentioned in the books, but it is one of a numerous family of frauds, of which the various members in their fight with society assume an infinitude of shapes and colors.

"To detect and punish these, notwithstanding the novelty and apparent innocence of their disguises, is the first business of courts of justice. The thing which we know as a 'corner' in the market might be briefly described as a process of driving unsuspecting dealers in grain, stock, and the like into a corral, and relieving them of their purses. The essence of the offence consists in the party securing a contract for the future delivery of some commodity at his option, and then, by engrossing the stock of such commodity in the market, making it impossible for the other party to complete his contract save by purchasing of his adversary at his own price, or paying in cash the difference fixed by such adversary. As was said of another great wrong, if this is not wrong then nothing is wrong. Public rumor on the street and in the press justifies me in saying that these offences are rife among us; and in asking you, if evidence to that effect should reach you, to make them the subject of inquiry, your duty and mine is plain. However powerful the combination to defy the laws, and however difficult to detect and punish the crimes, we rank ourselves with the criminal if we fail to bring the terrors of the law to bear upon him. For one, I refuse not to hear what fills the ears of all to the discredit of the business men and methods of this city. The crimes indicated are being committed. It imports much that the validity of our statute and its sufficiency to reach the guilty parties should be early tested. If the spread of gambling has infected our business men, the consequences cannot but be disastrous. The course of business, instead of proceeding quietly and healthily, will become broken by fits of fever and panic; unlawful gains will be preferred to the slow profits of legitimate trade; our farmers, partaking of the prevalent spirit, will hold back their crops in expectation of corner processes, borrowing money on mortgage to carry on their operations, instead of realizing by the sales of farm products. It is said that these phenomena are already apparent, and they are charged to be the effects of violations of the law. I will only

them to invest their money in such stocks. Such an agreement is void and against public policy.[1] But, as the facts are not given in the last-mentioned case, it is impossible to determine its value as a precedent.

And a contract entered into by the grain-dealers of a town which, on its face, indicates that they have formed a partnership for the purpose of dealing in grain, but the true object of which is to form a secret combination which would stifle all competition, and enable the parties, by secret and fraudulent means, to control the price of grain, costs of storage, and expense of shipment at such town, is in restraint of trade, and consequently void on the ground of public policy.[2]

It was also held in Wright vs. Cudahy,[3] that a contract of partnership between two persons under which large quantities of pork were purchased, with a view to getting the market "short," and thus advancing the market price of

add that it is not your duty to seek inquisitorially for evidence that crimes have been committed. Should evidence come to you through the regular channels, your duty will be to consider it, and act fearlessly and promptly to vindicate the laws. I think I may promise, on the part of the judiciary of the county, that if you present men for crime it will not go unpunished, so far as the enforcement of the laws depends on them."

[1] Livermore vs. Bushnell, 5 Hun, 285. The court cited Thompson vs. Davies, 13 Johns. 112; Brisbane vs. Adams, 3 Comst. 129; Hooker vs. Vandewater, 4 Denio, 349; Stanton vs. Allen, 5 id. 434; Marsh vs. Russell, 2 Lans. 340; 2 Kent (7th ed.),

699-703; Morris Run Coal Co. vs. Barclay Coal Co., 68 Pa. 173; Commonwealth vs. Carlisle, Brightly, 36; King vs. De Berenger, 3 Mau. & S. 67, 72; 3 Rev. Stat. (5th ed.) 973, sub. 6 of § 8.

[2] Craft vs. McConoughy, 79 Ill. 346; s. c. 22 Am. Rep. 171. Combinations to corner the market in grain are illegal, Wright vs. Crabb, 78 Ind. 487, but a Broker who is unaware of his principal's intention, may recover the amount of a note given to him by the principal in settlement of his account. Id. See also Wells vs. McGeoch, 71 Wis. 196, holding a combination to corner grain illegal.

[3] 48 N. E. Rep. 39.

pork, was within the Illinois statute, § 130, and therefore void, although the deal eventually proved unsuccessful.

So, an agreement entered into by several commercial firms, by which they bound themselves for the term of three months not to sell any Indian cotton-bagging except with the consent of the majority of them, was held to be a combination to enhance the price of the article, which was in restraint of trade and contrary to public order, and that the agreement could not be enforced in a court of justice.[1] So of a combination to control the sale and price of coal.[2]

In Arnot vs. Pittston Co.[3] the Court of Appeals of New York said, in speaking of a combination to enhance the price of coal by keeping the latter out of the market, "that a combination to effect such a purpose is inimical to the interest of the public, and that all contracts designed to effect such an end are contrary to public policy, and therefore illegal, is too well settled by adjudicated cases to be questioned at this day. Every producer or vendor of coal or other commodity has the right to use all legitimate efforts to obtain the best price for the article in which he deals; but when he endeavors to artfully enhance prices by suppressing or keeping out of the market the product of others, and to accomplish that purpose by means of contracts binding them to withhold their supply, such agreements are even more mischievous than combinations not to sell under an agreed price. Combinations of that character have been held to be against public policy and illegal. If they should be sustained, the prices of articles of mere necessity, such

---

[1] India Association vs. Kock, 14 La. Ann. 168.

[2] Arnot vs. Pittston Canal Co., 68 N. Y. 558; 23 Am. Rep. 190; Morris Run Coal Co. vs. Barclay Coal Co., 68 Pa. St. 173.

[3] Supra.

as coal, flour, and other indispensable commodities, might be artificially raised to a ruinous extent far exceeding any naturally resulting from the proportion between supply and demand."

But an agreement to combine stock for the purpose of terminating mismanagement by a change in the direction, through the instrumentality of a majority of votes at a regular election, is not in conflict with the requirements of the law, and in no wise derogates from its policy.[1] Nor is an agreement made between a like number of stockholders, in regard to holding their stock and selling the same together, invalid and in contravention of public policy and law.[2] So an agreement to form a "pool" for speculating in a particular stock is not necessarily void as against public policy.[3]

By L. 1887, c. 175, L. 1889, c. 257, and L. 1891, c. 158, Dassler's Gen. Stats. §§ 2427-46, pooling in grain and stock or other unlawful specified combinations to control prices and in restraint of trade, are made misdemeanors in Kansas, and similar statutes have been enacted in Nebraska. Comp. Stats. 1901, §§ 6959-64, and Kentucky, Ky. St. § 3915. Other like statutes prohibiting trusts, and unlawful combinations in restraint of trade have been passed in several other States and by Congress, and many decisions interpreting them have been rendered by the courts.[4] A pool of a num-

---

[1] Havemeyer vs. Havemeyer, 11 J. & S. (N. Y.) 513.

[2] Id. 507.

[3] Quincey vs. White, 63 N. Y. 370, 383.

[4] See the following article: "Anti-monopoly legislation from the days of Elizabeth to the Anti-Trust Act of 1890," in 55 Cent. Law Jour. 144,

and "Excessive Combination and its Remedy," in 6 Law Notes, 101. Under the Anti-Trust Act of 1890, a combination of stock-holders of two competing railroads by which a majority of its stock is transferred to a corporation organized to vote same, and thus prevent competition, is illegal. U. S. vs. Northern

ber of persons to advance the price of lard, being unlawful under the New York statutes, an accounting cannot be had against Brokers who acted as agents for the pool in carrying out the scheme.[1]

In concluding our review of these miscellaneous authorities in reference to combinations or corners, it is very important, as bearing upon their validity, to keep in mind that by the statute of New York "short" sales of securities are legalized.[2] This statute would seem to show most emphatically that the "public policy" of the State of New York sustains the practice of selling "short," which, as we have seen, is reprobated by the statutes of Massachusetts, Georgia and South Carolina; and the legislature, having encouraged and legalized these "short" contracts, it becomes a question of very grave doubt whether the judicial powers should be used to relieve persons selling "short" from these "corners," which are, after all, but the logical consequences of their own acts.

Where the parties organizing a corner are guilty of fraud, as in Barry vs. Croskey,[3] or where other circumstances intervene which render it manifestly unjust to enforce the result of the combination against the sellers of stocks, the courts may interfere. But, in the ordinary case of a "short" sale of stocks, it is very doubtful whether the courts should be used to protect persons from the consequences of their own folly in selling that which they do not own, in the hope and expectation that by such sales the property of others

Securities Co., 120 Fed. 721, aff'd by the Supreme Court, March, 1904.

[1] Leonard vs. Poole, 111 N. Y. 371. See also as to sugar, People

vs. Sugar Refining Co., 54 Hun, 354.

[2] Laws, 1858, ch. 134, now § 22 of the Personal Property Law.

[3] 2 John. & H. 1.

will be so much affected as to make their undertaking a success. And, if their expectations should fail, there would seem to be neither reason nor justice, especially in those States where "short" sales are sanctioned by statute, in the courts aiding them to get relief from their contracts.

In England "corners" sometimes arise out of the peculiar system which there prevails of dealing in shares before allotment, and they were the subject of investigation by the Royal Commission to which we have before alluded.[1] The operation is there explained as follows:

There is yet another aspect of the dealings in shares before allotment. It may be called the "stock-jobbing" aspect. Quite independently of the object of floating the company by getting its share capital subscribed, the promoters of worthless companies have the immediate object of receiving larger profits to themselves by traffic in these new shares. Dealings before allotment give them the requisite facilities for so doing.

There is another way in which this dealing before allotment operates on the Stock Exchange. The promoters of a new company send into the market and buy at a premium a large quantity of their own shares—a quantity so large, perhaps, relatively to the entire share capital, that when the settling-day comes after the allotment, and the sellers have to procure the shares to deliver, they find themselves in a difficulty; for the promoters—who, it must be remembered, have the allotment entirely in their own hands—have allotted so many shares to themselves or their friends, or to other persons, with an understanding that they must keep the shares allotted to them and not sell them, or have kept

[1] Rep. of Stock Exch. Com. 1878.

back so large a quantity of shares and not allotted them at all, that they have practically obtained the entire control of the market; and the dealers who have sold, in the expectation of having a free market of the entire share capital to buy in for the purpose of delivery, find themselves, as it is called, "cornered," and obliged to pay such prices as the sellers choose to ask, to enable them to complete their contracts.

This practice of buying shares or other securities—the buyer having already possessed himself, or in some other manner procured the control, of so large a quantity of the thing which the seller has contracted on a future day to deliver, that the seller is "cornered," and virtually placed at the mercy of the buyer—is not confined to the dealings before allotment in the shares of a new company or loan; but it is obvious that the allotment of the shares of a new company, being entirely in the hands of the promoters, gives them, if they choose to purchase their own shares before the allotment, unusual facilities for carry out such an operation. Accordingly, the rules of the Stock Exchange, as administered by the committee, provide methods of defeating such combinations.

In the case of new companies, all bargains before allotment are made for some future day, which is not fixed at the time the bargains are made, but it is to be fixed at a future day by the committee of the Stock Exchange; and if the committee refuse to fix a day of special settlement, all bargains that have been previously made are void. This system enables the committee to defeat operations of the character we have been just describing in cases where they can arrive at the necessary facts. They bear and entertain any objection that any member may make to the settlement

being granted; and if it is shown to them that the promoters
have by their dealings, coupled with the allotment, practically
obtained the command of the market, and placed the dealers
or sellers in an unfair position, the settlement is refused.

If false statements are made to the committee in order to
induce them to grant quotation or settlement, the guilty parties may at law be made criminally or civilly liable. Thus
in the Eupion Gas case, before referred to,[1] the promoters
of the company were convicted on a charge of agreeing together by false pretences to deceive the members of the
committee, and to induce them, contrary to the true intent
and meaning of the rules, to order a quotation of the shares
of the company in the official list; and thereby to induce
and persuade all persons who should thereafter buy and
sell the shares of the said company to believe that the latter
was duly formed and constituted, and had in all respects
complied with the rules so as to entitle them to have their
shares quoted.

But it was held in Ex parte Ward, that if the settling day
has been obtained from the committee by a fraud to which
the contracting parties were not privy, the contract does
not become void.[2]

---

[1] Reg. vs. Aspinall, 1 Q. B. D.
730; 2 id. 48. In Rees vs. Fernie, 4
N. R. 539, 13 W. R. 6, it was held
that where a person owning only
thirty shares in a company, contracted for the purchase of between
700 and 800 shares for future delivery but was unable to deliver
them in consequence of his intended
vendees being in control of the company's shares, the court will not set
aside the contracts, which were in
the nature of gambling contracts,
although the defendants did not
deny the fraud practiced by them
on plaintiff.

[2] 20 Ch. Div. 356.

The Penal Code of California,
§ 395 (Pomeroy's Annotated Codes,
p. 175), makes it a misdemeanor for
any person to employ any fraudulent means to affect the market
price of property, and under the
Illinois statute, supra, cornering the
market is punishable by fine and
imprisonment. An attempt to cor-

(g.) General Principles Deducible from the Cases.

The general result of the decisions, heretofore commented upon, or cited in this connection in the notes, upon the subject of wagering contracts, may be summed up as follows:

1. Where a contract is made for the delivery or acceptance of securities at a future day at a price named, and neither party, at the time of the making of the contract, intends to deliver or accept the shares, but merely to pay differences according to the rise or fall of the market, the contract is void either by virtue of statute or as contrary to public policy.[1]

2. That in each transaction the law looks primarily at the intention of the parties, which intention is a matter of fact for the jury to determine.[2]

3. That the form of the transaction is not conclusive; and oral evidence may be given of the surrounding circumstances and condition of the parties to show their intention, and that a contract purporting on its face to be a contract of sale is a

---

ner the market in corn is within the latter statute. Foss vs. Cummings, 149 Ill. 353. Neither Broker nor principal can enforce contracts arising out of "cornering" the wheat market. Samuels vs. Oliver, 130 Ill. 73. In an action against defendants to recover an excess of price paid for grain by reason of a "corner" by defendants, latter cannot be compelled to testify that they "cornered" the market. Lamson vs. Boyden, 160 Ill. 613. A certificate of deposit given in connection with a "cornering" transaction in wheat in violation of the Illinois statute, may be sued on by a bank ignorant of the use to which such deposit was put. Armstrong vs. American Exchange Nat. Bank, 133 U. S. 433.

[1] Grizewood vs. Blane, 11 C. B. 538, and all of the other authorities agree upon this proposition. The intention of the parties, however, formed after the making of the contract, does not affect its validity (Sawyer vs. Taggart, 14 Bush (Ky.), 727). If stock transactions are illegal in their inception, they become valid by subsequent actual receipt and delivery. Smith vs. New York Stock &c. Exchange, 25 N. Y. Supp. 261.

[2] All of the authorities agree upon this proposition.

mere gambling device, although the contract is in writing under seal.[1]

4. That option contracts — viz., " puts," " calls," and " straddles"—are not *prima facie* gambling contracts.[2]

5. To make a contract a gambling transaction, both parties must concur in the illegal intent.[3]

6. The defence of wager must be affirmatively pleaded, and the burden of proof is upon the party asserting the same.[4]

7. In construing a contract, that construction is to be preferred which will support it, rather than one which will avoid it.[5]

8. A Broker who makes real contracts with third persons in behalf of his Client, with the understanding between the Client and Broker that the former shall never be called upon to pay or receive more than differences, can recover the amount paid out for his Client in the transactions, together with his commissions.[6]

[1] Yerkes vs. Salomon, 11 Hun (N. Y.), 471; Story vs. Salomon, 71 N. Y. 420; Hibblewhite vs. McMorine, 5 M. & W. 466; North vs. Phillips, 89 Pa. St. 250; Smith vs. Thomas, 10 Weekly Notes (Pa.), 112; Gresham, J., in Williar vs. Irwin, 12 Chic. Law News, 241; Waite vs. Frank, 86 N. W. Rep. 105. Porter vs. Viets, 1 Biss. 177, if contrary to this, is against all the authorities. See, however, Universal Stock Exchange vs. Stevens, 66 L. T. R. 612.

[2] Story vs. Salomon; Yerkes vs. Salomon, supra. But see Wolcott vs. Heath, 78 Ill. 43; Pickering vs. Cease, 79 id. 328; Lyon vs. Culbertson, 83 id. 33; Schneider vs. Turner, 130 Ill. 38.

[3] Lehman vs. Strassberger, 2 Wood C. C. 554; Hibblewhite vs. McMorine, 5 M. & W. 462; Gresham, J., in Williar vs. Irwin, 12 Chic. Law News, 241. But see Connor vs. Black, 119 Mo. 126; 132 Mo. 150.

[4] Dykers vs. Townsend, 24 N. Y. 57; Bigelow vs. Benedict, 70 id. 206; Story vs. Salomon, 71 id. 420; Sprague vs. Warren, 26 Neb. 326. But see Rudolf vs. Winters, 7 Neb. 127; Bernard vs. Backhaus, 3 Wis. L. N. 338.

[5] Bigelow vs. Benedict, 70 N. Y. 202; Story vs. Salomon, supra.

[6] Thacker vs. Hardy, 27 W. R 158.

9. A Broker who advances money to his principal to pay losses incurred in a stock-wagering transaction can recover the same either on a note or otherwise.[1]

10. A bill of exchange or promissory note given upon a stock-jobbing transaction is valid in the hands of a party who took it before it was due, for value, and without notice of the illegal consideration.[2]

11. But such a bill is void in the hands of the original parties, or in the hands of a person who takes it after it is due or with notice of the facts.[3]

---

[1] Id.; Lehman vs. Strassberger, 2 Wood C. C. 554; Woodworth vs. Bennett, 43 N. Y. 273–277; compare Sampson vs. Shaw, 101 Mass. 145; Wyman vs. Fiske, 85 id. 238; Cannan vs. Bryce, 3 B. & A. 179; Amory vs. Meryweather, 2 B. & C. 573; Gregory vs. Wendell, 39 Mich. 337. See, however, the decisions in Illinois under the gaming statutes of that State, contra.

[2] Day vs. Stuart, 6 Bing. 109; 3 Moo. & P. 334, Chit. Jr. 1448; Greenland vs. Dyer, 2 M. & Ryl. 422; Faikney vs. Reynous, 4 Burr. 2069; Amory vs. Meryweather, 2 B. & C. 573; s. c. Chit. Jr. 120; Rawlings vs. Hull, 1 C. & P. 11; Woodworth vs. Bennett, 43 N. Y. 273–277; Wyman vs. Fiske, 85 Mass. 238. But see Tenney vs. Foote, 4 Brad. (Ill.) 594; Hawley vs. Jones, 69 Ala. 52; Cunningham vs. Bank, 71 Ga. 405; Campbell vs. Bank, 74 Miss. 526; Snoddy vs. Bank, 88 Tenn. 575. It was held in the District of Columbia that such a note could not be recovered, Lully vs. Morgan, 21 D. C. 88, but this case has been overruled owing to statutory enactment. Wirst vs. Stubblefield, 17 App. D. C. 283.

[3] Danforth vs. Evans, 16 Vt. 538; Brown vs. Turner, 7 T. R. 630; 2 Esp. 631; Aubert vs. Maze, 2 Bos. & P. 374; Steers vs. Lashley, 6 T. R. 61; Chit. Jr. 533; Amory vs. Meryweather, 2 B. & C. 573. As to relieving parties from wagering transactions, see "Remedies," Ch. VII.

Chapter VI.

STOCK EXCHANGE SECURITIES ; NEGOTIABILITY AND NON-
NEGOTIABILITY ; DEALING WITH APPARENT OWNERS ;
FRAUD ; ILLEGALITY.

I. *Stock Exchange Securities.*
    (*a.*) *Negotiable Securities.*
    (*b.*) *Non-Negotiable Securities.*
II. *Negotiability.*
    (*a.*) *Origin and Nature of Negotiability.*
    (*b.*) *How Negotiability may be Established.*
    (*c.*) *Requisite Elements of Negotiability.*
    (*d.*) *Results of Negotiability; Bona Fide Holders.*
III. *Non-Negotiability.*
    (*a.*) *Doctrine of Non-Negotiability.*
    (*b.*) *Negotiability as Applied to Stock Certificates.*
    (*c.*) *Forged Transfers.*
IV. *Dealing with Apparent Owners ; Fraud ; Illegality.*

I. Stock Exchange Securities.

In this subdivision of this chapter we propose to discuss
the different kinds and general character of the property in
which Stock-brokers deal, and which is comprehended under
the general name of "securities."

Securities may be divided into two classes—first, those
which are negotiable and, secondly, those which are not
negotiable, and, as it is of the utmost importance to ascertain

whether an instrument is negotiable or not, it being obvious that, if it has the former character, its value is greatly enhanced, we have in the second and third subdivisions of this chapter entered more fully into a discussion of the subject of negotiability and non-negotiability than perhaps the scope of this work might warrant, confined as it is to the transactions of Stock-brokers, and the securities in which they deal.

It will be seen hereafter that many of the securities classed as negotiable, may, for various reasons, be, or become non-negotiable, whilst on the other hand, non-negotiable instruments, may, under circumstances, become negotiable, and the decided tendency of the courts is to uphold the usage of Brokers giving them that quality when accompanied by blank transfers and powers of attorney in blank.

(a.) *Negotiable Securities.*

The negotiable securities usually dealt in on the Stock Exchange are:

1. *United States bonds.* These bonds are issued by the Secretary of the Treasury under authority of acts of Congress, and are negotiable.[1] There is no doubt that genuine Treasury notes form part of the negotiable commercial paper of the country;[2] and that when the United States become parties to commercial paper they incur just the same responsibilities as private persons under the same circumstances.[3]

In Seybel vs. National Currency Bank[4] United States

[1] Cooke vs. United States, 12 Blatchf. 43, rev'd 91 U. S. 389.

[2] Vermilye vs. Express Co., 21 Wall. 138; Dinsmore vs Duncan, 57 N. Y. 573; Frazer vs. D'Invilliers, 2 Pa. St. 200.

[3] United States vs. Bank of Metropolis, 15 Pet. 377; The Floyd Acceptances, 7 Wall. 666.

[4] 54 N. Y. 288.

bonds were held to be negotiable, so that a dealer in them was not bound to ask any questions whatever from one offering them for sale, and that omission to examine notices affecting them left at his office was not enough to prove bad faith.

2. *United States gold certificates* are also negotiable instruments.[1]

3. *Certificates of deposit of silver bullion* were admitted to regular trading on the New York Stock Exchange about the year 1885.[2]   In an early case in Pennsylvania these certificates were held not negotiable, as they were not for the payment of a certain sum of money, and did not contain a fixed time of payment.[3]   *Quære*, however, whether these certificates may not be negotiable under the Negotiable Instruments Law, and the usages of the exchange.

4. *Bonds of foreign governments or companies*, also may be negotiable.   It is so held of Prussian bonds in England.[4]

[1] Kulb vs. United States, 18 C. Cls. 560.

[2] Johnson's Encyclopædia, title, "Stock Exchange."

[3] Hegeman vs. McCall, 1 Phila. 529.

[4] Gorgier vs. Milville, 3 B. & C. 45. The following have been also held to be negotiable: Spanish bonds (Haseltine vs. Siggers, 1 Ex. 856); fully paid Russian and Hungarian scrip (Goodwin vs. Robarts, 1 App. Cas. 476); unified Egyptian bonds, Egyptian Preference Government bonds, and New South Wales bonds (London vs. London, 21 Q. B. D. 535); French bonds (Symons vs. Mulkern, 30 W. R. 875); Russian bonds (Attorney General vs. Bouwens, 4 M. & W. 171); mortgage bonds of the Buenos Ayres Land Mortgage Bank (London Joint-Stock Bank vs. Simmons, [1892] A. C. 201); American Railroad bonds (Venables vs. Baring, [1892] 3 Ch. 527; Bentinck vs. London Joint-Stock Bank, [1893] 2 Ch. 120; Edelstein vs. Schuler, [1902] 2 K. B. 144).

But foreign bonds to which the coupon sheets are not attached are not negotiable.   Picker vs. London and County Banking Co., 18 Q. B. D. 515.

And from Lang vs. Smith, 7 Bing. 284, it may be inferred that foreign instruments are not negotiable, unless negotiable where made. See Smith's Leading Cases, 11th ed. (note to Miller vs. Race) vol. 1, p. 479.

Bonds are generally so distinctive and invariable that it can be said of them, as a class, that they are negotiable.[1] But they are not negotiable unless they possess the elements of negotiability, *e. g.*, East India bonds;[2] but these were made so by a statute passed in the reign of George the Third.[3]

5. *Scrip of foreign governments* is also negotiable because treated as such in the stock markets.[4]

6. *Municipal bonds* are usually in negotiable form like promissory notes.[5]

7. *State bonds.*[6]

8. *County bonds.*[7]

9. *City bonds.*[8]

---

[1] See Odell vs. Gray, 15 Mo. 337.

[2] Glyn vs. Baker, 13 East, 509.

[3] 51 Geo. III. c. 64, § 4.

English Exchequer Bills are negotiable. Wookey vs. Pole, 4 B. & A. 1; Brandao vs. Barnett, 1 M. & Gr. 909.

[4] Goodwin vs. Robarts, L. R. 1 App. Cas. 467, followed in Rumball vs. Metropolitan Bank, L. R. 2 Q. B. Div. 194; 46 L. J. Q. B. 346; Sheffield vs. Bank, L. R. 13 A. C. 342.

But if "*Bordereaux*" and "*Coupons*" entitling the bearer to portions of the public debt of the kingdom of Naples, do not pass in England like money, they are not negotiable. Lang vs. Smith, 7 Bing. 284.

[5] See Am. & Eng. Ency. of Law (2d ed.), vol. 21, p. 54, and cases cited.

[6] State of Ill. vs. Delafield, 8 Paige, 527, aff'd 2 Hill, 159; Railroad Cos. vs. Schutte, 103 U. S. 118;

Finnegan vs. Lee, 18 How. Pr. 186; State vs. Cobb, 64 Ala. 127.

[7] Colson vs. Arnot, 57 N. Y. 253.

[8] Dutchess, etc., Ins. Co. vs. Hachfield, 73 N. Y. 226; Elizabeth City vs. Force, 29 N. J. L. 587; Bloomington vs. Smith, 123 Ind. 51. If the name of the payee is left blank, they are still negotiable, although they state on their face that they were intended to be issued as registered, as the requirement of registration was for the purpose of a record. Manhattan Savings Inst. vs. N. Y. &c. Bank, 170 N. Y. 58.

When, however, city bonds bear upon their face a statement that they are transferable only at the office of the city treasurer, and are made payable to a named payee, they are not negotiable, even although assigned by endorsement in blank. Scollans vs. Rollans, 173 Mass. 275. But see S. C., 179 Mass. 346.

10. *Village bonds.*[1]

11. *Railroad bonds.*[2] And the purchaser of such bonds in open market in the ordinary course of business is not bound to a close and critical examination of them to escape the imputation of bad faith.[3] In the State of New York a railroad bond payable to bearer may be made non-negotiable by endorsing thereon and subscribing a statement that the same is the property of the owner.[4]

12. *Coupons.* It was a disputed point at first whether coupons were negotiable; and in the case of Jackson vs. Y. & C. Railroad Co.,[5] it was held, against the dissenting opinion of Goodenow, J., that an action could not be maintained by an assignee upon interest coupons not containing negotiable words. But the Supreme Court of the United States, in the case of Comrs. of Knox Co. vs. Aspinwall,[6] fully sustained their negotiability, as did the Supreme Court of Pennsylvania,[7] though in both of these cases the coupons were in negotiable terms. Since which time the courts have universally declared them negotiable, if negotiable in form and not matured.[8]

---

[1] Bank of Rome vs. Village of Rome, 19 N. Y. 20.

[2] Welch vs. Sage, 47 N. Y. 143; Brainard vs. N. Y., etc., R. R. Co., 25 N. Y. 496; Murray vs. Lardner, 2 Wall. 110; Fisher vs. Morris, 3 Am. Law Reg. 423.

But if there is uncertainty as to the time of payment, they are non-negotiable. Allen vs. Choteau, 70 Mo. 290. And if the payee's name is inserted, there should be an assignment to enable the purchaser to sue in his own name. Bunting vs. Camden R. Co., 81 Pa. St. 254. See Am. & Eng. Ency. of Law (2d ed.),

vol. 23, pp. 837–840, and cases cited.

[3] Birdsall vs. Russell, 29 N. Y. 220.

[4] L. 1871, ch. 84, § 1, repealed by the Negotiable Instruments Law (L. 1897, c. 712), § 66 of which provides that an endorsement of a negotiable instrument may be restrictive, thus (subd. 1) prohibiting the further negotiation of the instrument.

[5] 48 Me. 147.

[6] 21 How. U. S. 539.

[7] Beaver vs. Armstrong, 44 Pa. St. 63.

[8] Evertson vs. Nat. Bank, 66 N.

Coupons are in form and terms nothing else than promissory notes, and their negotiability is a question of law to be determined from the instruments themselves, by the same fixed and well-settled rules which apply to promissory notes;[1] and they are entitled to days of grace, the same as promissory notes, so that a purchaser of them before the expiration of the days of grace is a purchaser before maturity.[2] Their negotiability is not affected by detaching them from the bonds, and the holder may recover upon them without producing the bonds;[3] and yet a coupon in the ordinary form is but a repetition of the contract which the bond itself makes for the payment of interest, and simply a device for the convenience of the holder; and is therefore so far aided and protected by the bond that it was at one time understood not to be barred by limitation unless the bond also was so barred.[4]

But in the case of Clark vs. Iowa City[5] the court held that when dissevered from the bond coupons were subject

Y. 14; Murray vs. Lardner, 2 Wall. 110; Gelpcke vs. Dubuque, 1 id. 175; Meyer vs. Muscatine, 1 id. 385; Gilbough vs. Norfolk & Petersburg R. R. Co., 1 Hughes (U. S.), 410; Morris Canal & Bank Co. vs. Lewis, 12 N. J. Eq. 323; Same vs. Fisher, 9 id. 667; and see Green's Brice's Ultra Vires (2d ed.), 270, where authorities are collected. See also Kerr vs. City of Corry, 105 Pa. St. 282; Copper vs. Mayer, 44 N. J. L. 634; Gilman vs. New Orleans &c. R. Co., 72 Ala. 566. And see Am. & Eng. Ency. of Law (2d ed.), vol. 8, p. 3, and cases cited.

[1] Jackson vs. Y. & C. R. Co., 48 Me. 147; Spooner vs. Holmes, 210 Mass. 503; Evertson vs. Nat. Bank, 66 N. Y. 14. Contra, Arents vs. Commonwealth, 18 Grattan, 773; Chaffee vs. R. R. Co., 146 Mass. 233.

[2] Id.

[3] Knox County vs. Aspinwall, 21 How. (U. S.) 539; Beaver County vs. Armstrong, 44 Pa. 63; Thompson vs. Lee County, 3 Wall. 327; Daniel on Neg. Insts. vol. 2, p. 492, and cases cited.

[4] The City vs. Lamson, 9 Wall. 477; Lexington vs. Butler, 14 id. 282; Reading vs. Porter, 2 Pac. Rep. (Cal.) 888; Meyer vs. Porter, 65 Cal. 67.

[5] 20 Wall. 583; Amy vs. Dubuque, 98 U. S. 470.

to the Statute of Limitations, and that it began to run from their dates. The court said : " Coupons for the different instalments of interest are usually attached to these bonds in the expectation that they will be paid as they mature, however distant the period fixed for the payment of the principal. These coupons, when severed from the bonds, are negotiable and pass by delivery. They then cease to be incidents of the bonds, and become in fact independent claims. They do not lose their validity if for any cause the bonds are cancelled or paid before maturity, nor their negotiable character, nor their ability to support separate actions ; and the amount for which they are issued draws interest from their maturity. Every consideration, therefore, which gives efficacy to the Statute of Limitations should be applied to actions upon the coupons after their maturity. . . . All statutes of limitation begin to run when the right of action is complete ; and it would be exceptional and illogical to hold that the statute sleeps with respect to claims upon detached coupons, while a complete right of action upon such claims exists in the holder. But, if coupons not negotiable in form are detached from the bonds, the negotiability of the latter is not communicated to them."[1]

It has been held that where bonds and coupons issued to *bona fide* holders for value are valid by the judicial decisions of a State when issued, their validity in such hands should not be allowed to be impaired by a change of decision ;[2] and any such judicial oscillation was censured by

[1] Evertson vs. Nat. Bank, 66 N. Y. 14. See also to same effect, Koshkonong vs. Burton, 104 U. S. 668.

[2] The City vs. Lamson, 9 Wall. 477.

the Supreme Court of the United States in Gelpcke vs. Dubuque.[1]

In England these coupons and interest warrants are held to be promissory notes and negotiable according to the same rules.[2]

Interest runs on coupons from their maturity;[3] and although detached from the bonds, they are still liens under the mortgage given to secure the same, whether the holders are entitled to a *pro rata* distribution or are entitled to payment in the order in which the coupons fall due.[4]

The purchaser in good faith for value of overdue coupons from negotiable bonds that have been stolen, acquires no title against the owner of the bonds, although the bonds were stolen before the coupons were due.[5]

13. *Debenture bonds payable to bearer.* These have been held to be negotiable, if a custom to that effect is proved, although the custom is of recent origin.[6] And a recent

---

[1] 1 Wall. 175, 206. See also 2 Edwards on Bills and Notes (3d ed.), ch. XI. p. 655; Burroughs on Public Securities, ch. XII, p. 570; 1 Southern Law Rev. (Old Ser.) 189; 8 id. (New Ser.) 354; Eaton & Gilbert's Commercial Paper, § 29, and cases cited. If the coupons refer, as to the interest, to the bonds and mortgage securing same, they are not negotiable. McLelland vs. Norfolk, 110 N. Y. 469.

[2] Ex parte Colborne, L. R. 11 Eq. 478; Ex parte City Bank, L. R. 3 Ch. App. 758.

[3] See cases collected in Green's Brice's Ultra Vires, 270, and also cases collected in Am. & Eng. Ency. of Law (2d ed.), vol. 8, p. 10. See

also Daniel Neg. Insts. § 1513, et seq.

[4] Green's Brice's Ultra Vires, 271. Am. & Eng. Ency. of Law (2d ed.), vol. 8, p. 13.

[5] Hinckler vs. Merchants' Nat. Bank, Mass. S. J. C. (April, 1881), 24 Alb. L. J. 436; 131 Mass. 147; Daniel Neg. Insts §§ 1461, 1470, and cases cited.

[6] Bechuanaland Exploration Co. vs. London Trading Bank, (1898) 2 Q. B. 658. In a prior case such bonds were held not negotiable, especially when conditions were attached. Crouch vs. Credit Bank, L. R. 8 Q. B. 374. But the former case held that the last cited case was overruled by Goodwin vs. Robarts, 1 App. Cases, 476.

English case[1] held that it is not now necessary to tender evidence that such bonds are negotiable, that being a fact of which the courts will take judicial notice.

14. *Share warrants to bearer.* Shares in a company transferable by share warrants to bearer are negotiable.[2]

(b.) Non-negotiable Securities.

1. *Certificates of stock.* Certificates of stock are the customary and convenient evidence of the holder's interest in the corporation issuing it.[3]

They are not regarded as negotiable instruments[4] although, in certain circumstances, they may practically become so.[5]

2. *Dividend warrants.* It has been held in England that dividend warrants (i. e. Bank of England checks drawn upon its cashier, and payable to a named payee, but without negotiable words) are not negotiable.[6]

II. Negotiability.

(a.) Origin and Nature of Negotiability.

At common law choses in action were not assignable, so that the assignee could bring an action in his own name.[7] Blackstone's views of a chose in action,[8] "that all property

[1] Edelstein vs. Schuler, (1902) 2 K. B. 144.

[2] Brodhurst's Law of the Stock Exchange, p. 81. Share warrants for fully paid up shares are negotiable by statute. 30 & 31 Vict. c. 131, § 28.

[3] Daniel, Neg. Inst. (5th ed.) p. 728.

[4] Id., p. 726, and cases cited in note 1.

[5] Id., and cases cited in notes 2 and 3.

[6] Partridge vs. Bank of England, 9 Q. B. 396.

[7] Co. Litt. 214a, 266a; Greenby vs. Kellogg, 2 Johns. 1; Pitt vs. Holmes, 10 Cush. 92, 96; Tiernan vs. Jackson, 5 Pet. 580; Edwards on Bills, 55; Chitty on Bills (*7), 9; Eaton & Gilbert on Commercial Paper, 10; Daniel on Negotiable Instruments (5th ed.), 1.

[8] 2 Bl. Comm. 397.

in action depends entirely upon contract, either express or implied, which are the only regular means of acquiring a chose in action," is now regarded as too limited. A better definition is given by Bronson, C. J.,[1] who, adopting the distinction made by Blackstone between a chose in possession and a chose in action, proceeds to define the latter as including "all rights to personal property not in possession which may be enforced by action, and it makes no difference whether the owner has been deprived of his property by the tortious act of another, or by his breach of contract, express or implied. In both cases the debt or damage of the owner is a thing in action."

Under the term "chose in action" were included all instruments acknowledging an indebtedness or promising to pay money. The inconvenience of this doctrine of non-assignability, in a country whose great aim was to foster and encourage commerce, was sufficient to condemn it; and we find the courts very early recognizing a custom of merchants by which bills of exchange were made "negotiable" —that is, they could be transferred, and the holder, endorsee, or assignee might enforce payment of the same in his own name.[2]

---

[1] Gillet vs. Fairchild, 4 Den. 80.

[2] In Thompson vs. Dominy, 14 M. & W. 403, 407, Parke, B., said: "I never heard it argued that a contract was transferable except by the law merchant." And, speaking of a bill of lading, he added: "It transfers no more than the property in the goods; it does not transfer the contract."

The assignee of a chose in action could maintain an action at law in the name of the assignor (Grover vs. Grover, 24 Pick. 261; Pitt vs. Holmes, 10 Cush. 92, 97; Amherst Academy vs. Cowls, 6 Pick. 427); and the assignor acting in collusion with the debtor could not withdraw such a suit so as to bar a similar subsequent suit by the assignee (Welch vs. Mandeville, 1 Wheat. 233, aff'd 5 id. 277). The right of the assignee to use the assignor's name is incidental to the assignment, as Morton, J., said, in Eastman vs. Wright, 6 Pick. 316, 322:

A negotiable instrument is a chose in action even before maturity, and may be transferred by assignment in the same manner as an ordinary chose in action ; and if payable

"The assignor, by the assignment, gives authority to the assignee to use his name in any legal proceedings which may become necessary to give full effect to the assignment. The assignor becomes the trustee of the assignee, and a release made by him after notice of the assignment would be a fraud upon the assignee, and would not defeat an action brought for the benefit of the latter in the name of the former."

In a court of equity the assignee of a chose in action could always sue in his own name, irrespective of any promise by the debtor to pay him if he had no remedy at law (Lett vs. Morris, 4 Sim. 607; Row vs. Dawson, 1 Ves. Sen. 331). In the case last cited the Lord Chancellor said: "And though the law does not admit an assignment of a chose in action, this court does, and any words will do." See also Ensign vs. Kellogg, 4 Pick. 1. If the assignee could enforce his legal demand, he was left to his action at law in the name of the assignor; but if the latter refused to allow him to use his name, or otherwise acted in collusion with the debtor, then, upon sufficient facts shown, equity would allow the assignee to sue in his own name (Ontario Bank vs. Mumford, 2 Barb. Ch. 596; Carter vs. United Ins. Co., 1 Johns. Ch. 463; Hammond vs. Messenger, 9 Sim. 327).

It is provided by the English Judicature Act (1873, § 25, subd. 6)

that a debt or other legal chose in action may be assigned so that the assignee shall have the same remedies thereon as the assignor, but subject also to all equities, at least to the extent of the assigned obligation (Young vs. Kitchin, L. R. 3 Ex. D. 127).

In the State of New York an action may be maintained by the transferee of a claim (Code Civ. Proc. § 1909) but certain claims are not assignable (§ 1910). See cases cited in notes appended to these sections in Stover's Anno. Code (5th ed.), and Bliss's Anno. Code (5th ed.). And, no doubt, in most of the States, an assignee of a chose in action may sue in his own name, either by force of statute or of established usage. Cox vs. Sprigg, 6 Md. 274; Smith vs. Schibel, 19 Mo. 140; Long vs. Constant, id. 320; Cobb's Dig. (Ga.) 519; Prioleau vs. South W. R. Bank, 16 Ga. 582; Worthington vs. Curd, 15 Ark. 491. In Allen vs. Brown (44 N. Y. 228), Hunt, C., referring to §§ 111 and 113 of N. Y. C. of P., from which sections 1909–10 of the present Code are derived, says: "These provisions are intended to abolish the common-law rule which prohibited an action at law otherwise than in the name of the original obligee or covenantee, although he had transferred all his interest in the bond or covenant to another." See Eaton & Gilbert's Commercial Paper, § 8.

to order and transferred without endorsement by parol and manual delivery only, the transferee acquires only the rights he would have had had the instrument been originally non-negotiable—i. e., the rights of the payee at the time of the transfer.[1]

In Freund vs. Importers, etc., Bank[2] the payee of a check payable to order transferred it to B without endorsement, and it was held that he thereby became the lawful assignee and owner of it, and entitled to have and enforce payment from the bank which had certified it, but that he had no greater right than he would have had if it had been originally non-negotiable.[3]

It would not be profitable to enter into an abstract inquiry as to the meaning of the word *negotiable*, based either upon its etymology or history. It has no specially interesting or valuable history apart from its somewhat technical use as a word of commerce. The meaning of the original Latin word *negotium* is *business*,[4] and indicates that a negotiable instrument should relate to and facilitate business affairs; the past and present use of the word *negotiable* is therefore quite in harmony with its literal import,[5] and we

[1] Negotiable Instruments Law, § 60 et seq.

[2] 76 N. Y. 352.

[3] Whistler vs. Forster, 14 C. B. (n. s.) 248. Therefore, if the holder of a bill payable to bearer assigns it by deed to D., and afterwards transfers it by delivery to E., who takes it for value and without notice, E.'s title prevails over D.'s (Aulton vs. Atkins, 18 C. B. 249); but if E. had notice of the prior assignment, it would be sustained (Sheldon vs. Parker, 3 Hun, 498). See Eaton & Gilbert's Com. Paper, § 69.

[4] Andrew's Freund's Latin Dict.

[5] Primarily the word negotiability means the capability of being negotiated—that is, transferred by endorsement and delivery so as to give the endorsee a right of action on the negotiated instrument, in his own name—and is nothing more; therefore, an instrument, e. g., a bill of lading, may be made negotiable by a statute or declared to be so by a court, and yet its negotiation may not be attended with all the consequences and effects which generally, but not always, result from the ne-

may at once proceed to state the accepted definition of a negotiable instrument as a *written promise, order, or request for the payment of a certain sum of money to A, or order, or bearer,*[1] a definition which was (as to promissory notes) substantially adopted by and implied in the New York Revised Statutes,[2] which enacted that "all notes in writing made and signed by any person whereby he shall promise to pay to any other person or his order, or bearer, any sum of money therein mentioned, shall, etc., and shall have the same effect and be negotiable in like manner as inland bills of exchange, according to the custom of merchants."

This provision was taken without material change from 3 and 4 Anne, c. 9, the preamble of which recites that it had been held that promissory notes were not endorsable over like bills of exchange.[3]   This act contains several items of internal English history pertinent to the subject now un-

gotiation of bills and notes (Shaw vs. Railroad Co., 11 Otto, 557, 563).

[1] The definition of a negotiable instrument in the text has been adopted in California (Code, § 3087) as to six kinds of negotiable instruments, viz., bills, notes, bank notes, checks, bonds and certificates of deposit.

The following definition of negotiable instruments is given in Black's Law Dictionary, title "Negotiable Instruments:" "Any written securities which may be transferred by indorsement and delivery, or by delivery merely, so as to vest in the indorsee (or holder) the legal title, and thus enable him to sue thereon in his own name."

In Daniel on Negotiable Instruments (5th ed.), § 1, it is stated that an instrument "is called negotiable when the legal title to the instrument itself, and to the whole amount of money expressed upon its face, may be transferred from one to another by indorsement and delivery by the holder, or by delivery only."

The Negotiable Instruments Law (§ 20), sets forth the requirements necessary to make an instrument negotiable.

[2] 1 Rev. Stat. 768, § 1; R. S. pt. II. ch. 4, tit. II. § 1.   Repealed by the Negotiable Instruments Law (L. 1897, c. 612), § 20 of which makes provision as to the form of a negotiable instrument.

[3] Referring, it is supposed, to Clerke vs. Martin, 2 Ld. Raym. 757.

der examination: 1. That prior to it (1704) promissory notes were not negotiable; 2. That bills of exchange were; 3. That such negotiability had its origin in the custom of merchants.[1]

When this custom was established is not precisely known. Daniel says[2] (citing Anderson's History of Commerce, vol. 1, c. 361), "There is reason to believe that bills of exchange were known in England as early as 1307, since in that year King Edward I. ordered certain money collected in England for the Pope, not to be remitted to him in coin or bullion, but by way of exchange (per viam Cambii)." And Chitty[3] says that the statutes show that bills of exchange (foreign) were in use by English merchants as early as the middle of the fourteenth century, but that there is no mention of them in the law reports until the time of James I.[4]

Inland bills of exchange came into use somewhat later, it is said, and did not come before the courts until the case of Chat vs. Edgar,[5] which was within the memory of Lord Holt.[6] They were at first regarded with great disfavor by the courts and their use restricted to merchants;[7] but, by the statutes of Anne[8] and William III.,[9] they were placed substantially on the same footing as foreign bills.

Promissory notes were not introduced into England until about the middle of the seventeenth century, or perhaps

---

[1] See Richards vs. Warring, 39 Barb. 42, 46.

[2] Neg. Ins. (5th ed.) p. 4.

[3] Bills of Ex. (*11) 16.

[4] Martin vs. Bowie, 2 Croke's Rep. 6 (10 Jac. 1).

[5] 1 Keb. 636, in 1636.

[6] Buller vs. Crips 6 Mod. 29.

[7] Bromwick vs. Loyd, 2 Lut. 1582 –85.

[8] 3 & 4 Anne, c. 9.

[9] 9 & 10 William III. c. 17.

somewhat later. They had been previously in use upon the
continent of Europe.[1]

(b.) *How Negotiability may be Established.*

As the doctrine of the negotiability of bills of exchange
was first established by the custom of merchants, some passing observations upon these customs, and their force and
effect in the law, will not be out of place.

The law-merchant consists of those general customs of
merchants which have received the sanction of judicial decisions, and are thereby recognized as binding and authorita-
tive. Thus Lord Campbell says[2] that, " when a general
usage has been judicially ascertained and established, it becomes part of the law-merchant which courts of justice are
bound to know and recognize." Quite in harmony with this
authority is the judicial exposition of Foster, J.,[3] where he
says: " But the custom of merchants, or law of merchants,
is the law of the kingdom, and is part of the common-law ;"
and, again (referring to two cited cases), "therefore these
judicial determinations of the point are the *lex mercatoria*
as to this question, which is part of the law of the land.
But this finding of the jury in the present case is directly
contrary to the *lex mercatoria* so fully settled and established by legal adjudications."

Thus the law-merchant, being made up of venerable and
solemnized customs, according to some authorities, prevails
over any modern usage, and to a large extent over the express stipulation of parties. As Blackburn, J., says in

[1] Daniel on Neg. Ins. (5th ed.)
p. 5; Strong on Notes, § 6; Buller
vs. Crips, 6 Mod. 29.

[2] Brandao vs. Barnett, 3 C. B.
519, 530.

[3] Edie vs. East India Co., 2 Burr.
1216, 1226, 1228.

Crouch vs. Crédit Foncier,[1] "There is no decision or authority that it is competent to a party to create by his own act a transferable right of action on a contract;" and again, "Where the incident is of such a nature that the parties are not themselves competent to introduce it by express stipulation, no such incident can be annexed by the trial stipulation arising from usage. *It may be so annexed by the ancient law-merchant*, which forms part of the law, and of which the courts take notice. Nor if the *ancient law-merchant* annexes the incident can any modern usage take it away." But it is very doubtful whether the courts at the present day will carry the *lex mercatoria* to such an extent as this language seems to contemplate.[2] And we find the definition of the law-merchant which we have given above adopted almost verbatim by Cockburn, C. J., in a case where the doctrine of negotiability was established by the custom of Banker and Brokers.[3] "It is neither more nor less than the usages of merchants of trade, ratified by the decisons of courts of law, which, upon such usages being proved before them, have adopted them as settled law with a view to the interests of trade and the public conven-

---

[1] L. R. 8 Q. B. 374, 386.

[2] See chapter on "Usages." Since the text was written it has been held that the doctrine enunciated in Crouch vs. Crédit Foncier, supra, was overruled by the decisions in Goodwin vs. Robarts, supra, and Rumball vs. Metropolitan Bank, 2 Q. B. D. 194, and that, as there was sufficient proof of a mercantile usage to treat debenture bonds payable to bearer as negotiable, the latter decisions should be followed. Bechuanaland Trans-portation Co. vs. London Trading Bank, 2 Q. B. D. 658. In that case the plaintiff's secretary fraudulently abstracted certain bearer debenture bonds from plaintiff's safe and pledged them with defendant bank, who in good faith, advanced money thereon, and it was held that the defendants were entitled to hold the bonds as they were negotiable instruments passing by delivery. Id.

[3] Goodwin vs. Robarts, L. R. 10 Ex. 337, 346.

ience. . . . By this process, what before was usage only, unsanctioned by legal decision, has become engrafted upon or incorporated into the common-law, and may thus be said to form part of it." And in Williams vs. Williams[1] the endorsee of a promissory note having declared on the *custom of merchants*, it was objected that, the note having been made in London, the custom, if any, should have been laid as the custom of London; but the courts answered "that this custom of merchants was part of the common-law, and the courts would take notice of it *ex officio*, and therefore it was sufficient to say that such a person, *secundum usum et consuetudinem mercatorum*, drew the bill."

So, in a case in the State of New York, the Court of Appeals held that the courts will take judicial notice of the general course of business in a community, including the universal practice of banks.[2]

It is interesting to notice with what jealousy this custom of merchants was regarded by the courts, and even Lord Holt was provoked by its aggressive influence to exclaim " that it amounted to the setting-up of a new sort of specialty unknown to the common-law, and invented in Lombard Street, which attempted in these matters of bills of exchange to give laws to Westminster Hall."[3] There is no doubt that the judges were at that time intent in restraining the attempted aggressions of the merchants; for Lord Mansfield, in Grant vs. Vaughan,[4] speaks of the "first struggle of the merchants which made Holt so angry with them."

In more modern times we also find striking examples of

[1] Carth. 269.
[2] Merchants' Nat. Bank vs. Hall, 83 N. Y. 338.
[3] Clerke vs. Martin, 2 Ld. Raym. 757.
[4] 1 W. Bl. 485, 487.

the disposition of courts to act as conservators of legal principles when they are imperilled by encroaching customs and innovations.   Thus in Donnell vs. Columbian Ins. Co.,[1] Story, J., says: "I am among those judges who think usages among merchants should be very sparingly adopted as rules of court, . . . as they are often founded in mere mistake, and still more often in the want of enlarged and comprehensive views of the full bearing of principles," and in The Reeside[2] he "rejoices to find that of late years the courts of law, both in England and America, have been disposed to narrow the limits of the operation of such usages, and to discontinue any further extension of them;"[3] and Stone, J., another American judge, uttered the warning that "it became us to feel our way cautiously, lest there grow up in our midst some third estate (of customs and usages) which shall in time usurp the government."[4]

In Dykers vs. Allen[5] Senator Wright remarks, with some asperity, that "to allow the usages of Wall Street to control the general law in relation to any matter might result in the establishment of principles not always in accordance with sound morals.   I prefer that legal principles should have a universal application, and that contracts should receive the same interpretation in the thronged and busy mart of a commercial metropolis that they do elsewhere." Whatever may have been the spirit in which these ani-

---

[1] 2 Sumn. 367.

[2] Id. 567.

[3] Similarly plain and pertinent expressions of judicial criticism were made by Gibson, C. J., in Bolton vs. Colder, 1 Watts, 360; by Tilghman, C. J., in Stoever vs. Whitman, 6 Binn. 416; by Stuart, J., in Harper vs. Pound, 10 Ind. 32; by Perkins, J., in Cox vs. O'Riley, 4 id. 368; and by Miller J., in Partridge vs. Ins. Co., 15 Wall. 573, 579.

[4] Barlow vs. Lambert, 28 Ala. 704.

[5] 7 Hill, 497.

madversions were made, it should be observed that they were, for the most part, directed against local customs and limited usages. But the power of the judges has been futile in arresting the usages or customs of trade, even when confined to certain localities and to particular occupations; and, as appears by the leading case of Goodwin vs. Robarts,[1] the usages of Stock-brokers and Bankers have been successfully invoked, even to confer upon instruments the powers of negotiability.[2]

If the original law-merchant had been a fixed and stereotyped system incapable of expansion, the negotiability of commercial paper would have ended where it began, with bills of exchange, or, more accurately, with foreign bills of exchange. Such, however, was not its character, and could not, and cannot be, in the very nature of things, because regulations for public convenience which are sufficient for the wants of one generation are not fully adapted and adequate to the changed and multiplied wants of another. Lord Holt, indeed, attempted to stop the growth of the law-merchant and to exclude promissory notes from its operation;[3] but the British Parliament took sides with the merchants and passed 3 and 4 Anne, ch. 9, and admitted notes to a substantial equality with bills. Later on in English history, a similar attempt ended with a similar result; the decision in Glyn vs. Baker,[4] that East India bonds were not negotiable, was followed by the immediate passing of 51 Geo. III. ch. 64, by which such bonds became transferable by delivery.

[1] L. R. 10 Ex. 337.
[2] See this question further discussed in chapter on "Usages," p. 411.
[3] Clerke vs. Martin, 2 Ld. Raym. 757.
[4] 13 East, 509.

So also, when the circulating qualities of bank-notes came to be judicially examined in Miller vs. Race,[1] Lord Mansfield said, "They are treated as money in the *ordinary course* and transactions of business by the general consent of mankind," which was clearly a case of a universal usage receiving judicial sanction.

And in Goodwin vs. Robarts, already cited, Cockburn, C. J., after showing by abundant illustration to what a broad scope it has expanded in the present day, asks, with great force, " Why is the door to be now shut to the admission and adoption of usage in a matter altogether of cognate character, as though the law had been finally stereotyped and settled by some positive and peremptory enactment ?" Whenever, and as fast as, new instruments are required, it is safe to predict that they will come into use ; custom will adopt them, and then, in its turn and in the fulness of time, the custom will receive the sanction of the law. In this very case we have a most instructive example of the manner in, and the conditions upon, which custom adds to the number of negotiable instruments. The subject of litigation was scrip of the Russian government issued in England, by which that government promised not to pay money, but to give certain bonds. This scrip was unlawfully pledged by one not the owner, and then sold by the pledgee to a *bona fide* purchaser. The contention on behalf of the owner was that scrip of this description not coming under the category of any of the securities for money which by the law-merchant are capable of being transferred by endorsement and delivery, and not being a security for money at all, but only for the future delivery of a bond, the

---

[1] 1 Burr. 452, 457.

rights of the true owner could not be divested by the fraudulent transfer of the chattel by a person who had no title as against the owner. Cockburn, C. J., in rendering judgment, said: "The ninth paragraph of the special case contains the following statement, upon which, as it appears to us, the decision of the case turns: The scrip of loans to foreign government, entitling the bearer to bonds for the same amount when issued by the government, has been well known to, and largely dealt in by, bankers, money dealers, and the members of the English and foreign Stock Exchanges, and through them by the public, for fifty years. It is and has been the usage of such bankers, money-dealers, and Stock Exchanges, during all that time, to buy and sell such scrip, and to advance loans of money upon the security of it before the bonds were issued, and to pass the scrip upon such dealing by mere delivery as a negotiable instrument transferable by delivery; and this usage has always been recognized by the foreign government, or their agent, delivering the bonds when issued to the bearers of the scrip."

The very serious point made by the plaintiff, that the scrip was not negotiable because it was not a *promise to pay money*, but to deliver a bond, was disposed of as follows: "We think that substantially, and in effect, *it is a security for money*, which till the bond shall be delivered stands in the place of that document, which, when delivered, will be beyond doubt the representative of the sum it is intended to secure. . . . The usage of the money market has solved the question whether scrip should be considered security for, and the representative of, money, by treating it as such."

In Crouch vs. Crédit Foncier,[1] which is in contrast with the last case, but not inconsistent with it in its main feature, we find an example of the judicial rejection of a usage because, if admitted to exist, it was recent, and because an incident or attribute of negotiability could not be annexed to an instrument by the tacit stipulation of such a usage which could not be introduced into it by the express stipulation of the parties.

But in Venables vs. Baring,[2] decided in · the year 1892, it was held that American railroad bonds, payable to bearer, were negotiable according to the law merchant.   And in the later case of Bechuanaland Exploration Co. vs. London Trading Bank[3] it was held that English debenture bearer bonds were negotiable, if a custom to that effect, although of recent origin, was proved.

The recent case of Edelstein vs. Schuler[4] went further and held that the time had passed when the negotiability of bearer bonds could be called in question ; the existence of the usage to treat them as negotiable had been so often proved, and its convenience was so obvious, that it must be now taken to be part of the law-merchant ; and accordingly it was not now necessary to tender evidence to prove that such bonds were negotiable instruments, that being a fact of which the court will take judicial notice.   In that case the bonds consisted of South African Railroad and Mining bonds, and American Railroad Bonds.

There may be also negotiability by estoppel. · The effect

---

[1] L. R. 8 Q. B. 374, overruled by Goodwin vs. Robarts, supra; Bechuanaland Exploration Co. vs. London Trading Bank, id. (1898) 2 Q. B. D. 658.

[2] (1892) 3 Ch. 527.

[3] (1898) 2 Q. B. 658.

[4] (1902) 2 K. B. 144. See articles in 15 London Quarterly Review, 130, 245.

of the decisions in Goodwin vs. Robarts and Rumball vs. Metropolitan Bank, *supra*, seems to be, that if one deposits with an agent a security on the face of it, payable to bearer, he cannot recover it from a *bona fide* holder for value, in case the agent fraudulently puts it into circulation, whether the instrument is negotiable or not.[1]

But usage cannot make instruments *on the face of which* the right to sue is limited, negotiable.

Thus in Glyn vs. Baker[2] (decided before the passing of the Act of 51 Geo. 3, c. 64, § 4, making India bonds negotiable), it would appear from the judgment of the court that even if the jury had found the India bond to be negotiable, it could not have been made so in contemplation of law, as it appeared on its face to be payable to the original obligee, thus limiting the right to recover its amount to the latter or his representatives.

This was accepted as a correct statement of the law in Partridge vs. Bank of England.[3]   In that case the plea was that dividend warrants, payable to a specific person, without negotiable words, were, by a sixty years' custom of the bankers and merchants of London, transferable by delivery only, without endorsement.   The Queen's Bench sustained the plea ; but the Court of Exchequer rejected the custom, because it appeared by the instrument that it was payable to a particular person, and that usage could not make an instrument so limited negotiable.

And although an instrument may be negotiable, the trans-

---

[1] See also as to estoppel, Crouch vs. Crédit Foncier, supra; Colonial Bank vs. Cady, 38 Ch. D. 388; 15 App. Cas. 267; Fine Art Soc. vs. Union Bank, 17 Q. B. D. 705; Bentinck vs. London Joint Stock Bank, (1893) 2 Ch. 120.
[2] 13 East, 509.
[3] 15 L. J. Q. B. 395.

feree must take *bona fide* and for value.[1] Gross negligence was formerly held evidence of *mala fides*.[2] But in Goodman vs. Harvey[3] it was held that there must be actual *mala fides*.

Mere negligence on the part of the transferee, to detect his transferor's bad title, cannot be pleaded as a defence to an action by the transferee.[4]

But if an agent pledges negotiable instruments for an amount beyond the limits of his authority, and the pledgee has notice of the limit, he can only retain the securities in pledge to secure the amount authorized.[5]

Although if the pledgee has not such notice he may recover the full amount due to him.[6] Mere knowledge that the pledgor is a Broker is not sufficient notice.[7]

And it has been held that the owner of a negotiable instrument, which has been stolen, has no title to it as against a *bona fide* holder for value, although he prosecutes the thief to conviction.[8]

There are English cases in which the usage of a particular trade has been held to be binding on the persons engaged in the trade.

Thus in Merchant Banking Co. vs. Phœnix Bes. Steel Co.,[9] a usage of the iron trade that warrants for goods " deliverable to A. B., or assigns, by endorsement hereon," were considered to pass to the holders for value, free from

---

[1] London Joint Stock Bank vs. Simmons, supra.

[2] Gill vs. Cubitt, 3 B. & C. 466.

[3] 4 A. & E. 870.

[4] Venables vs. Baring, (1892) 3 Ch. 527.

[5] London Joint Stock Bank vs. Simmons, supra; Sheffield vs. London Joint Stock Bank, 13 App. Cas. 333.

[6] Bentinck vs. London Joint Stock Bank, supra.

[7] Baker vs. Nottingham Bank, 60 L. J. Q. B. 542. See also in this connection, cases cited in Smith's Leading Cas. vol. I. p. 489.

[8] Chichester vs. Hill & Son, 52 L. J. Q. B. 160.

[9] L. R. 5 Ch. D. 205.

any vendor's lien, was held to be binding on the steel company, which was the vendor. This usage was shown to have been quite general in the iron trade for nearly forty years, and Jessel, M. R., found that the steel company knew of it and gave the iron-warrant for the purpose of having it dealt with in accordance with the usage ; and that having given such a document to a person knowing that he could use it, and intending that he should use it by obtaining money on it, it could not afterwards be allowed to set up against persons from whom he had obtained money, that they should not have the benefit thereof ; that the company was estopped from so doing on the most elementary principles of equity.[1]

Without discussing the question further, it is sufficient for our purposes to show that by the English authorities, the custom of Bankers and Stock-brokers, such as was presented in the case of Goodwin vs. Robarts, is sufficient to confer upon instruments the important attributes of negotiability ;[2] and it will be important hereafter to consider this doctrine in connection with the subject of certificates of stock, which are technically non-negotiable.

The precise question how far usage will be allowed to operate in extending negotiability has not been much discussed in our courts, but the general rules imposing limitations upon usage are strictly applied in the State of New

[1] Consult also, in this connection, Talty vs. Freedman's Trust Co., 1 MacArth. 522; Matter of Leland, 6 Ben. (U. S.) 175; Humboldt Township vs. Long, 92 U. S. 642; Gaar vs. Louisville Co., 11 Bush (Ky.), 180; Dinsmore vs. Duncan, 57 N. Y. 573, rev'g 4 Daly, 199; Pardee vs. Fish, 60 N. Y. 265.

[2] This case was followed and endorsed by Rumball vs. Metropolitan Bank, L. R. 2 Q. B. Div. 194; 46 L. J. Q. B. Div. 346; 36 L. T. N. S. 240; 25 W. R. 366. See, however, Colonial Bank vs. Cady, 15 App. Cas. 267.

York. Thus, in Security Bank vs. National Bank,[1] an attempt was made, by proof of usage among Bankers, to give the word "certification" a larger scope than it had received by settled legal construction, and such proof was excluded.

But in Massachusetts it has been held[2] that a custom in Boston to treat certificates endorsed in blank as negotiable, was, on being proved, sufficient to enable a *bona fide* holder for value to assert his title as against the true owner, if the latter entrusted the instrument to another who pledged it for his own debt.

And in a case in Iowa, it was shown that there was a usage among the merchants of the city of Burlington to regard certain paper—a note—payable "in currency" as negotiable. This usage was resisted on the ground that by the constitution of that State all laws were required to be uniform, and therefore a note could not be negotiable in one city and not so in another, nor could a custom be recognized which would result in the same thing. In passing upon this question, the court said : "It must be remembered, however, that we have no statute prohibiting such custom. A custom in a particular locality, when not in violation of law, becomes a law to parties contracting with a knowledge of it. The same general rule as to what makes custom, and its application in the construction of contracts, obtains uniformly over the State. It might as well be claimed that all parties must make the same kind of contracts, as that they may not contract in reference to different customs." And the usage was sustained.[3]

---

[1] 67 N. Y. 458.

[2] Scollans vs. Rollins, 179 Mass. 346.

[3] Rindskoff vs. Barrett, 11 Iowa, 101. See also Vermilye vs. Adams Express Co., 21 Wall. 138.

But the effect of a custom of the Stock Exchange and of Bankers and Brokers in Baltimore, requiring Virginia registered consols to be transferred in writing, and to be accompanied by a power of attorney acknowledged before a notary public, is to restrict negotiability, as, in the absence of such a custom, they would, as strongly resembling promissory notes, be transferable by endorsement merely.[1]

In some of the United States attributes of negotiability have been conferred upon certain instrument by statute, which are not recognizable as negotiable by the law-merchant.

In Iowa[2] bonds and other instruments, without words of negotiability are made assignable by indorsement, and the assignee shall have a right of action in his own name, subject to all defences which the assignor might have had prior to endorsement.

In Illinois bonds or other instruments payable in money or "personal property," may be assigned by indorsement in the same manner as bills of exchange.[3]

A similar statute was passed in Georgia in 1799,[4] and the *bona fide* purchaser of negotiable paper not dishonored is protected, though the seller had no title.[5]

In Kansas[6] all receipts for grain issued by any warehouse shall be negotiable by endorsement in blank, or by special endorsement, in the same manner as bills of exchange and promissory notes.

---

[1] Taliaferro vs. Baltimore &c. Bank, 17 Atl. Rep. (Md.) 1036. See also cases cited, ante, p. 462 et seq.

[2] Rev. Stats. of 1897, § 3045.

[3] Rev. Stats. Ill. ch. 98 (4). They need not contain the words "or order" in connection with payee's name. Russell vs. Bosworth, 106 Ill. App. 314.

[4] Code, § 3682.

[5] Id. § 3538.

[6] Dassler's Stats. of 1901, § 1441.

(c.) Requisite Elements of Negotiability.

The Negotiable Instruments Law contains the following provision (Art. II., § 20) as to form:

" Form of Negotiable Instrument.—An instrument to be negotiable must conform to the following requirements:

1. It must be in writing and signed by the maker or drawer.

2. Must contain an unconditional promise or order to pay a sum certain in money.[1]

3. Must be payable on demand, or at a fixed or determinable future time.

4. Must be payable to order or to bearer; and

5. Where the instrument is addressed to a drawee, he must be named, or otherwise indicated therein with reasonable certainty."

And other sections of Art. II. contain provisions interpreting these various requirements as to form.

The statutory provision is merely declaratory of the law as it existed prior to its enactment.

The Negotiable Instruments Law (codifying the law as to negotiable instruments) has now been adopted in twenty-two States of the Union, and also in the District of Columbia,[2] and as it will doubtless be enacted in the remaining

---

[1] A particular kind of current money may be designated (Neg. Insts. Law, § 25, subd. 5). And by statute, in some of the States, the instrument may be payable in property or labor. Sec ante, p 671, and Neg. Insts. Law, § 25 (last sentence).

[2] In New York, Colorado, Connecticut and Florida in 1897. In Maryland, Massachusetts and Virginia in 1898. In the District of Columbia, North Carolina, North Dakota, Oregon, Rhode Island, Tennessee, Utah, Washington and Wisconsin in 1899. In Pennsylvania and Arizona in 1901. In Ohio, Iowa and New Jersey, in 1902. In Idaho and Montana in 1903

It should be borne in mind that

States and Territories within the next few years, it has been deemed sufficient to set forth a few of its principal provisions, and to give a digest of the decisions affecting the negotiable instruments usually dealt in by Stock-brokers or dealers, and in which they may have been directly or indirectly concerned, and a few of the leading cases as to negotiable instruments in general, without encumbering this work with a digest of the great mass of decisions (chiefly relating to bills and notes, or to transactions outside of the Exchanges, or between persons other than Brokers) as to such instruments.[1]

A negotiable instrument must be a complete and perfect instrument when it is issued, or there must be authority reposed in some one to supply anything needed to make it perfect.[2]

Independent of statute, the rule is well established that there must have been delivery to render an incomplete instrument, filled up without authority, negotiable. Therefore, when railroad bonds and coupons payable to bearer, were made payable either in British currency in London, or in United States currency in New York or New Orleans, and the president was authorized to endorse on the bonds the place of payment, but the bonds were never issued, or

the English codification statute (Bills of Exchange Act, 1882) is confined to bills and notes, whereas the Negotiable Instruments Law includes the instruments (enumerated at p. 649 et seq.) usually dealt in by Stock-brokers, provided such instruments comply with the requirements of its 20th section. Therefore the law as to the negotiability of such instruments must in England be sought in the de-cisions of the courts, whereas in the United States i is practically now contained in the Negotiable Instruments Law (supplemented by the rules of the law merchant, Neg. Inst. Law, § 7), as interpreted by the courts.

[1] For the law as to negotiable instruments in general, see Daniel on Neg. Inst. (5th ed.), and Eaton & Gilbert on Commercial Paper.

[2] See Neg. Insts. Law, §§ 32–5.

the endorsement made by the president, and the bonds were stolen from the company while still in its possession, a *bona fide* holder for value was not authorized to fill the blank for the place of payment, and could convey no title to the bonds.[1]

And the 34th section of the Negotiable Instruments Law is now declaratory of the general rule, as follows : " Where an incomplete instrument has not been delivered, it will not, if completed and negotiated without authority, be a valid contract in the hands of any holder, as against any person whose signature was placed thereon, before delivery."

But if the incomplete instruments (e. g., city bonds) have been delivered, with authority to negotiate them, the holder may fill up the blanks.[2]   And this rule is now incorporated in the 33d section of the Negotiable Instruments Law.

Delivery may sometimes be presumed until the contrary is proved.[3]

In Cooke vs. The United States[4] certain Treasury notes had been printed, stamped, and sealed by the proper agents of the government, but they had not been issued ; but an innocent purchaser of them was held to be protected.   There is no doubt that genuine Treasury notes form part of the negotiable commercial paper of the country.[5]

But if state coupon bonds have been redeemed, and other bonds issued in their stead, and the former have been sub-

---

[1] Ledwich vs. McKim, 53 N. Y. 307.

[2] Manhattan Savings Inst. vs. Bank, 170 N. Y. 58. This case, although not one in which Stock-brokers were concerned, is here cited, as being a leading recent New York case upon the subject of negotiability.

[3] Neg. Inst. Law, § 35.

[4] 91 U. S. 389, reversing 12 Blatchf. 43.

[5] Vermilye vs. Express Co., 21 Wall. 138.

sequently stolen from the State, and purchased by the plaintiffs in good faith from a New York Stock-broker, the plaintiffs are not entitled to have other bonds issued to them, as the redemption of the bonds was equivalent to a return of the bonds to the maker (the State), and the subsequent theft was not a delivery of the bonds making them negotiable.[1]   •

A negotiable instrument (a United States gold certificate) made payable by special indorsement to the order of the holder, can be only transferred by the indorsement of such holder.[2] If such indorsement is erased, an innocent purchaser for value does not acquire title, although the erasure is so skilfully made that it cannot be detected by the most careful scrutiny.[3] Such is the general rule.[4] The purchase of such a certificate by a share dealer in London at £30 below its market price, although such certificates can always be sold at their market value, and the not calling the seller as a witness, made the transaction suspicious, and deprived the purchaser of the benefit of any exceptions to the general rule.[5]

(d.) Results of Negotiability; Bona Fide Holders.

1. *Results of Negotiability.*—The change in the law which we have indicated, making choses in actions assignable, so that the assignee might sue and enforce the same in his own name, if it had stopped there would have accomplished much. What the commercial necessities of England required was that negotiable securities should pass from

---

[1] Branch vs. Commissioners, 80 Fed. Rep. 427.

[2] Kulb vs. United States, 18 Ct. Cls. 560; Neg. Inst. Law, § 64.

[3] Id. Neg. Inst. Law, § 205.

[4] Id.

[5] Id.

hand to hand, free from all restrictions and conditions; that they should become representatives of money; and that every person accepting or receiving them should be entitled to collect them, without being subject to impediment or hindrance on the part of the maker, except his financial ability. And, growing out of this necessity of commerce, we have now firmly established in law the main and principal result of negotiability, and which is often erroneously confounded with the doctrine of negotiability itself[1]—viz., that a purchaser or transferee in good faith, for value, and before maturity of a negotiable instrument, is not affected by any latent equities between the original parties, or in favor of third persons, unless they are brought to his notice. And in law this extensive privilege is commouly designated as "the rights of a *bona fide* holder or purchaser."[2] But, to bring one within the protection of this broad rule, it is necessary that certain conditions should exist in his favor, the nature of which we shall now proceed to examine briefly.

He must be a purchaser, 1st, in good faith without notice; 2d, before maturity; 3d, for value.[3]

1st. *He must be a purchaser in good faith without notice.* For if he have notice that there are defects in the title of his assignor, or the party from whom he receives the negotiable paper, it follows that he is not entitled to avail him-

---

[1] See distinctions set forth in Shaw vs. R. R. Co., 101 U. S. 557.

The rule does no extend to persons not *bona fide* purchasers or holders, nor to their agents. Kimball vs. Billings, 55 Me. 147; Swim vs. Wilson, 5 Bank. L. J. 286. But see Zulick vs. Markham, 6 Daly, 129, where a Stock-broker who in-

nocently sold securities for another Broker was held not liable to the principal of the latter.

[2] Brown vs. Spofford, 95 U. S. 474. The rule of law set forth in the text is now embodied in the 96th section of the Negotiable Instruments Law.

[3] See Neg. Inst. Law, § 91.

self of the protection afforded by the rule in question, and no commercial necessity would seem to require that he should receive such protection. Express or actual notice would bar his rights as a *bona fide* holder,[1] and leave the maker to assert any defence to the paper which existed in his favor. But the numerous cases on this extensive subject have mainly arisen in attempts to fix upon the holder *constructive* notice of defects, and the courts have experienced no small difficulty in applying the familiar doctrine to the facts. The form and condition of a negotiable instrument are of themselves constructive notice to the purchaser. Constructive notice to a person is the imparting to him of sufficient information to put him upon inquiry; and the true rule as to the meaning of " put upon inquiry " is declared[2] to be, that the rights of a purchaser of negotiable paper are not affected by constructive notice of a defect of title, unless it clearly appears that the inquiry suggested by the fact disclosed at the time of the purchase would, if fairly pursued, result in the discovery of the defect. In that case it was held that, the number of a bond not being an integral part of it, an erasion and alteration of the number was not constructive notice that the bond had been stolen; and for the further reason, also, that the line of inquiry suggested by the fact of alteration would not, if pursued, lead to the detection of the larceny. Such a notice as will put a prudent man on his guard is not enough, e. g., the absence of certificates referred to in the bond.[3] In

[1] Cass County vs. Green, 66 Mo. 498.

[2] Birdsall vs. Russell, 29 N. Y. 220.

[3] Welch vs. Sage, 47 id. 143. If Stock-brokers pledge railroad bearer bonds, placed in their hands for sale, with a bank, which receives them in the ordinary course of business in good faith, and for a valuable consideration, and without notice of the own-

fact, clear knowledge of fraud must be proved on the part of the holder, and is not to be presumed on slight evidence; and, if the evidence is but slight, the court may withdraw it from the jury.[1]

If no actual notice of incipient fraud is given to the intending purchaser of a note, he is not affected by notice that the payee promised not to negotiate it, and by an indefinite notice that he is buying a lawsuit, and he is not thereby put upon inquiry for a fraud which actually entered into the incipiency of the note; that is, no complicity in fraud is ever to be presumed as against a holder for value of negotiable paper.[2] Even though he does not pay full value and there may be enough to excite suspicion, his title is not thereby impaired.[3]

It is a general rule that persons dealing with property are bound to take notice of any suit pending with respect to its title,[4] even though not themselves parties to it;[5] but it seems that it is the *pendency* of the suit which creates the notice, so that after the cause is ended the decree is not notice.[6]

Negotiable paper not due is, however, excepted from the

ers title, the bank acquires a good title to such securities as against the owner, a customer of the Stockbrokers. Thompson vs. St. Nicholas Nat. Bank, 113 N. Y. 325; id. 9 N. Y. St. Rep. 363.

But where the bonds of a railroad, signed by a trustee, are placed by him upon the market, and they are sold for a trifling sum, the purchaser should have made inquiry as to the regularity of the issue. Riggs vs. Pennsylvania &c. R. R. Co., 16 Fed. Rep. 804.

[1] Battles vs. Laudenslager, 84 Pa. St. 446.

[2] Heist vs. Hart, 73 Pa. St. 286.

[3] Cromwell vs. County of Sac, 96 U. S. 51.

[4] Murray vs. Balou, 1 Johns. Ch. 566; Garth vs. Ward, 2 Atk. 174.

[5] Bishop of Winchester vs. Paine, 11 Ves. 194.

[6] Worsley vs. Scarborough, 3 Atk. 391.

general rule, because of the high favor in which it is held as a circulating medium, unless there is actual notice of the suit.[1]

The question arose in the case of Leitch vs. Wells[2] whether a purchaser of certificates of stock was affected by the pendency of a suit, and the court held in conformity with the above views, Earl., C., saying: " Since the decision of the case of McNeil vs. Tenth National Bank, above cited, certificates of stock, with blank assignments and powers of attorney attached, must be nearly as negotiable as commercial paper. The doctrine of constructive notice by *lis pendens* has never yet been applied to such property. This doctrine must have its limitations. It could not be applied to ordinary commercial paper, nor to bills of lading, nor to government or corporate bonds payable to bearer. Indeed, I do not find that it has ever been applied, and I do not think it ought to be applied, to any of the articles of ordinary commerce. Public policy does not require that it should be thus applied. On the contrary, its application to such property would work great mischief and lead to great embarrassments."

If a first endorsee for value takes without notice of any prior equities, a second endorsee for value takes a good title, although he had notice of such equities. As was declared by Field, J.,[3] " the rule has been too long settled to be ques-

---

[1] Orleans vs. Platt, 99 U. S. 676, 683; County of Warren vs. Marcy, 97 id. 96; Winston vs. Westfeldt, 22 Ala. 760; Stone vs. Elliott, 11 Ohio St. 252; Mims vs. West, 38 Ga. 18; and see Leitch vs. Wells, 48 N. Y. 585.

In Ohio it has been held that the doctrine of *lis pendens* does not apply to negotiable paper (railroad bonds) purchased before due. Pittsburgh &c. Co. vs. Lynde, 55 Ohio St. 23.

[2] Supra.

[3] Cromwell vs. County of Sac, 96 U. S. 51.

tioned now, that whenever negotiable paper has passed into the hands of a party unaffected by previous infirmities, its character as an available security is established, and its holder can transfer it to others with the like immunity." In such case the second endorsee takes a new title from the first endorsee, and therefore knowledge of any infirmities in the old title does not affect him.[1]

The rights of a holder of a negotiable instrument are to be determined by the simple test of honesty and good faith; he is not bound to be on the alert for circumstances which might excite suspicion.[2]

The possession of an instrument, endorsed in blank or made payable to bearer, is *prima facie* evidence that the holder is the owner and lawful possessor of the same; and no degree of negligence, and nothing short of fraud on his part, is sufficient to overcome the effect of that evidence and invalidate his title.[3]

But if a negotiable instrument (a United States gold certificate) is made payable by special endorsement to the holder's order, it is only transferable by the latter's endorsement, and if it is stolen, and the special endorsement be erased, London stock-dealers, who purchased the same for a

---

[1] Commissioners, etc., vs. Clark, 94 U. S. 278, 286; Riley vs. Schawacker, 50 Ind. 592; Mornyer vs. Cooper, 35 Iowa, 257; Simon vs. Merritt, 33 id. 537; Woodman vs. Churchill, 52 Me. 58; Roberts vs. Lane, 64 id. 108; Woodworth vs. Huntoon, 40 Ill. 131; May vs. Chapman, 16 M. & W. 355; Masters vs. Ibberson, 8 C. B. 100; Central & Banking Co. vs. Farmers' Loan & Trust Co., 116 Fed. Rep. 700; Simmons vs. Taylor, 38 Fed. Rep. 682; Porter vs. Pittsburgh Steel Co., 122 U. S. 267. Neg. Inst. Law, § 97.

[2] Magee vs. Badger, 34 N. Y. 247. Bad faith on the part of the holder must be shown. Neg. Inst. Law, § 95. And see Eaton & Gilbert's' Com. Paper, p. 372, and cases cited.

[3] Goodman vs. Harvey, 4 Ad. & El. 870. Neg. Inst. Law, §§ 91, 98.

valuable consideration, and without notice of the fraud, acquire no title.[1]

In Dutchess Co. Ins. Co. vs. Hatchfield,[2] New York Brokers bought Poughkeepsie bonds which had been stolen. The circumstances which were charged against them, indicating bad faith, were—1st, that they had bought a bond before from the same party which had turned out to be stolen; and, 2d, that, instead of offering the bonds in New York city, they took them to Poughkeepsie and Albany. The Brokers having proved that they had received an explanation of the first transaction of the stolen bond, and having offered to prove a usage of Brokers consistent with their own course in offering the bonds for sale, they were sustained in their possession of and title to the bonds, and Church, C. J., laid down the rule applicable to such cases as follows: "It is not sufficient that a prudent man would be put upon inquiry, nor that the purchaser was negligent, nor that he did not exercise a proper degree of caution. A purchaser of such securities will be protected if he is honest and believes that the seller has a good title."[3]

Seybel vs. Nat. Cur. Bank[4] was a case, to say the least, of gross negligence and reckless disregard of others' rights. Bonds were stolen from the plaintiff in the evening; the next morning he served printed notices of the theft, with description of the property, at defendant's office, on their

---

[1] Kulb vs. United States, 18 C. Cls. Rep. 560. See Neg. Insts. Law, § 64.

[2] 73 N. Y. 226. But in East Birmingham Land Co. vs. Dennis, 39 Alb. L. J. (March 23, 1889) 223, it was held in Alabama that an innocent purchaser for value of a stolen certificate endorsed in blank, acquired no title, the usages of Stock-brokers to the contrary notwithstanding.

[3] See also Brown vs. State, 1 Atl. Rep. (Md.) 54.

[4] 54 N. Y. 288.

cashier, who said they did not care for notice; the same day defendants bought the stolen bonds; and on their testimony that they did not examine the notice, and had no time to examine such notices, the court sustained them, and adopted the rule laid down in the leading case of Goodman vs. Simonds,[1] to wit: "Suspicion of defect of title, or the knowledge of circumstances which would excite such suspicion in the mind of a prudent man, or gross negligence on the part of the taker at the time of the transfer, will not defeat his title. That result can be produced only by bad faith on his part."

In Goodman vs. Simonds[2] this subject is fully considered, English and American cases examined, and Goodman vs. Harvey[3] referred to as the leading case in England. In the case last cited, Lord Denman said: "We are all of opinion that gross negligence only would not be a sufficient answer where a party has given consideration for the bill."

The case of Gill vs. Cubitt,[4] laying down the doctrine that the purchaser of negotiable paper must exercise ordinary care and prudence, is overruled both in England and in this country. It stands alone.[5]

The title and rights of a *bona fide* purchaser of negotiable paper are not affected by the fact that the person from whom he received it before maturity had possession of it

---

[1] 20 How. (U. S.) 343.

[2] Supra.

[3] 4 Ad. & El. 870. The purchaser is not effected by constructive notice unless there is a natural or logical connection between the facts appearing, and the fact of a defective title in the vendor. Manhattan Sav. Inst. vs. New York &c. Bank, 170 N. Y. 58.

[4] 3 B. & C. 466.

[5] Belmont Branch Bank vs. Hoge, 35 N. Y. 65; Goodman vs. Harvey, supra; Uther vs. Rich, 10 Ad. & El. 784; Arbouin vs. Anderson, 1 Q. B. 498, 504.

for a specific purpose and misappropriated it,[1] nor by the fact that the apparent owner from whom he bought it was an agent who sold it in breach of his duty to his principal.[2]

The presumption is that the holder of negotiable paper has paid value for it in the usual course of business.[3] So that, in bringing suit on it, all he has to do in opening is to prove the signature and introduce it in evidence.[4]

Ordinarily, it is no defence against a *bona fide* holder of a note that the maker was induced to sign it by fraud;[5] and a thief of negotiable paper can give a good title to it to a *bona fide* purchaser;[6] but it is otherwise as to non-negotiable paper.[7] But if a negotiable note is stolen before delivery by the maker, it has no inception, and the thief can give no title.[8]

Negotiable paper in the hands of an innocent holder is

[1] Collins vs. Gilbert, 94 U. S. 753; Park Bank vs. Watson, 42 N. Y. 490.

[2] Belmont Branch Bank vs. Hoge, supra.

But if a Stock-broker knows that railroad bonds pledged with him by a bank cashier were not the latter's property he cannot hold them as against the true owner, although he had not express notice of the particular individual who was the real owner. Perth Amboy Mut. Loan Assn. vs. Chapman, 80 A. D. 556. See Pittsburgh &c. Co. vs. Lynde, 55 Ohio St. 59.

[3] Goodman vs. Simonds, 20 How. 343; Pittsburgh Bank vs. Neal, 22 id. 96; Murray vs. Lardner, 2 Wall. 110; Manhattan Sav. Institution vs. N. Y. &c. Bank, 170 N. Y. 58. Neg. Inst. Law, § 98.

[4] Pettee vs. Prout, 69 Mass. 502;

Agra, etc., Bank vs. Leighton, L. R. 2 Ex. 61.

[5] Fenton vs. Robinson, 4 Hun, 252.

[6] Welch vs. Sage, 47 N. Y. 143; Seybel vs. Nat. Cur. Bank, 54 id. 288; Birdsall vs. Russell, 29 id. 220; Colson vs. Arnot, 57 id. 253; Peacock vs. Rhodes, 2 Doug. 633; Miller vs. Race, 1 Burr. 452.

If the payee's name is left blank in a city bond, and is stolen, a *bona fide* purchaser from the thief may fill in the blank in his own name and acquire title thereto as if he had purchased it from the lawful holder. Manhattan Sav. Inst. vs. N. Y. &c. Bank, 170 N. Y. 58.

[7] Ledwich vs. McKim, 53 N. Y. 307.

[8] Hall vs. Wilson, 16 Barb. 548.

not invalidated by an illegal consideration unless expressly declared void by statute.[1]

If a person buys from a pretended owner, who is not in possession, he is not a *bona fide* purchaser, and takes no better title or greater rights than the vendor;[2] nor is he if he buys from a known agent who endorses it without authority;[3] nor will he be made so by the principal's ratification of the endorsement after maturity.[4]

2. *He must be a purchaser before maturity.*

The fact that a bill or other instrument is overdue is equivalent to notice of all facts relating to it; thus, where a note was endorsed after maturity, the maker, being sued, was allowed to defend himself by showing that he had paid it to the original payee.[5] If there is any fact relating to a bill, notice of which would disentitle a holder who took the bill before maturity, the existence of such a fact disentitles a holder who takes the bill after maturity irrespective of notice.[6] In other words, if a note is negotiated when overdue, the maker, when sued by the endorsee, may set up any equitable defence which he had against the payee.[7]

The taker of an overdue note is but the assignee of a chose in action, and takes only such title as his assignor had.[8]

Instruments not payable on demand mature with the last

---

[1] Grimes vs. Hillenbrand, 4 Hun, 354.

[2] Muller vs. Pondir, 55 N. Y. 325.

[3] Gilbert vs. Sharp, 2 Lans. 412.

[4] Id.

[5] Brown vs. Davies, 3 T. R. 80. See Cripps vs. Davis, 12 M. & W. 159.

[6] Lloyd vs. Howard, 15 Q. B. 995.

[7] Merrick vs. Butler, 2 Lans. 103;

Nellis vs. Clark, 4 Hill, 424; O'Callaghan vs. Sawyer, 5 Johns. 118; Van Valkenburgh vs. Stupplebeen, 49 Barb. 99. See Eaton & Gilbert's Com. Paper, p. 361, and cases cited.

[8] Farrington vs. Park Bank, 39 Barb. 645; De Mott vs. Starkey, 3 Barb. Ch. 403.

day of grace.[1] An accommodation note transferred on the last day of grace by the payee to plaintiff, during banking hours, as collateral security for an indebtedness of the payee and to be applied thereon, makes the plaintiff a *bona fide* holder before maturity.[2] An instrument payable in instalments is deemed wholly overdue when any instalment is overdue;[3] but not from the mere fact that interest is overdue,[4] though it is held in New York[5] that a note is dishonored by overdue interest.

In Vermilye vs. Express Company[6] the Supreme Court of the United States held that bonds and Treasury notes of the United States payable to holder or bearer at a future

---

[1] Evertson vs. Nat. City Bank, 66 N. Y. 14. But under the Neg. Inst. Law, § 103, a negotiable instrument is payable at the time fixed therein, without grace. In some of the States adopting that law, days of grace have been retained, and in several of the States which have not enacted it, days of grace have been abolished. Eaton & Gilbert's Com. Paper, p. 476.

[2] Continental Nat. Bank vs. Townsend, 13 N. Y. *Week. Dig.* 295; N. Y. Ct. App. Nov. 22, 1881.

[3] Vinton vs. King, 86 Mass. 562; Field vs. Tibbetts, 57 Me. 358.

[4] Nat. Bank vs. Kirby, 108 Mass. 497; Cromwell vs. County of Sac, 96 U. S. 51; Kelley vs. Whitney, 45 Wis. 110; Boss vs. Hewitt, 15 id. 260; Brooks vs. Mitchell, 9 M. & W. 15.

If the president of a railroad company (which had intrusted its negotiable bonds to him for sale or exchange) pledges them with Brokers to secure his own debt, and they subsequently come, by sale in the open market, into the hands of a bona fide purchaser for value, the latter acquires a good title thereto, although two of the interest coupons were overdue at the time of purchase. Long Island Loan & Trust Co. vs. Columbus &c. R. R. Co., 65 Fed. Rep. 455, and cases cited. As to what circumstances will not constitute the holders of railroad bonds, bona fide holders for value before maturity, see Simmons vs. Taylor, 38 Fed. Rep. 682.

[5] Newell vs. Gregg, 51 Barb. 263.

[6] 21 Wall. 138. To the same effect is Cornell vs. District of Columbia, 20 Ct. Cls. Rep. 229, where it was held that a bona fide purchaser of District of Columbia coupon bonds stolen from the Board of Audit, after they had become due, could not recover, and that if he wished to avail of the rights of prior holders, he should prove that they purchased before maturity.

definite time were subject to this principle, and that a purchaser after they were overdue took subject to the rights of antecedent holders.

In an earlier case[1] it had been held that negotiable government securities redeemable at the pleasure of the government, after a specified day, but in which no date was fixed for final payment, ceased to be negotiable, as overdue, after the day when they first became redeemable, but this ruling was subsequently[2] limited to cases where the purchaser acquired title with notice of the defect of title, or under circumstances discrediting the instrument, such as would affect the title of negotiable demand paper purchased after an unreasonable length of time from the date of the issue. Therefore when it appeared that United States 5–20 bonds (redeemable at the pleasure of the United States after the 1st day of July, 1870, and payable on the 1st day of July, 1885), were stolen from the owner, in October, 1878, and purchased in the year 1879, by the plaintiffs in London, in the usual course of business, from responsible parties, it was held that as the bonds in suit were called for redemption between October, 1878, and March, 1879, they became payable on demand without interest after the maturity of the call, until the date for absolute payment, and as the title of the purchasers of the bonds was acquired at a time when no unreasonable length of time had elapsed after the maturity of the call, the title of the purchasers should prevail against the owners.[3]

But if detached coupons of bonds of a State are intrusted by the owners to a firm for collection only, and by

---

[1] Texas vs. White, 7 Wall. 700.
[2] Morgan vs. United States, 113 U. S. 476.
[3] Morgan vs. United States, supra; Brown vs. United States, 20 C. Cls. Rep. 416.

44

the latter are, long after their maturity, pledged to a bank to secure a debt of the pledgors, the pledgee acquires no title as against the true owner.[1]

And the law of the State of New York must prevail over that of a foreign jurisdiction, when the plaintiff and one of the defendants are residents of New York, and the property, the subject of contention, has been voluntarily brought within that State. Therefore when detached coupons of Pacific Railroad bonds were purchased after maturity, in good faith, by Stock-brokers on the Stock Exchange at Frankfort-on-the-Main, and were by them sent to New York for collection, their title cannot prevail against the plaintiff, the true owner, although by the law of Frankfort they would acquire a good title whether the coupons were purchased before or after maturity.[2]

3. *He must be a holder for value.*

The rule in England seems to be that one who takes a negotiable instrument as a security for a pre-existing debt is a holder for value as well as one who parts with value at the time he takes it;[3] and yet, in De la Chaumette vs. Bank of England,[4] it was mentioned as a fact adverse to plaintiff that although the balance was in his favor at the time he received the stolen bank-note, he did not make any further advance or give any further credit on the strength of it; he was considered as an agent rather than a holder for value, and failed to recover against the bank.

---

[1] Stern Brothers vs. Bank, 34 La. Ann. 1119.

[2] Wylie vs. Speyer, 62 How. Pr. 107. It was also held in that case that as the relief asked for was equitable, the relief could be equitable only, and that plaintiff was not entitled to a money judgment for the proceeds of the coupons.

[3] Currie vs. Misa, L. R. 10 Ex. 153; see Whistler vs. Forster, 14 C. B. (n. s.) 248.

[4] 9 B. & C. 208, 216.

It was said in Currie vs. Misa,[1] by Lush, J., that he was not aware of any cases directly in point, and the only authority he cited was Story, Promissory Notes, § 186.

In England, as in this country, it is likely that an extension of time or the suspension of an existing demand by the taker of a negotiable instrument would make him a holder for value.[2]

The Supreme Court of the United States adopted a similar rule, as laid down in Swift vs. Tyson,[3] that one who takes commercial paper as security for any existing debt is a holder for value, but certainly such cases as are cited below[4] do not go so far, because in them there is an extension of time or other forbearance granted to the debtor, which constitutes a parting with present advantage on the part of the creditor. However, in the case of Brooklyn City, etc., R. R. Co. vs. Bank[5] the subject was exhaustively examined, and the doctrine of Swift vs. Tyson was affirmed.

Swift vs. Tyson has been followed to a great extent in this country;[6] though in some of the cases the important distinction between taking negotiable paper as absolute payment and taking it as a mere security of a pre-existing debt is not kept in view. The same rule is followed in Connec-

[1] Supra.

[2] Morton vs. Burn, 7 Ad. & El. 19; Baker vs. Walker, 14 M. & W. 465. And now by the English Bills of Exchange Act (1882) any antecedent debt or liability constitutes a valuable consideration for a bill or note.

[3] 16 Pet. 1.

[4] Oates vs. Nat. Bank, 100 U. S. 239; Goodman vs. Simonds, 20 How. U. S. 343 370; McCarty vs. Roots, 21 id. 430.

[5] 102 U. S. 150. See also Cummings vs. Mead, Fed. Cas. 3176.

[6] Fisher vs. Fisher, 98 Mass. 303; Stoddard vs. Kimball, 60 id. 469; Atkinson vs. Brooks, 26 Vt. 569; Holmes vs. Smith, 16 Me. 177; Manning vs. McClure, 36 Ill. 490; and see a very thorough discussion of this subject, endorsing the view laid down in Swift vs. Tyson, 1 Am. Law Rev. (n. s.) 479. See also Crawford's An. Neg. Inst. Law, 2d ed. p. 33, and cases cited.

ticut on the ground that the taking of negotiable paper as a collateral security is in the ordinary course of business.[1]

In New York a purchaser of negotiable paper *for value* is one who parts with some value, money, property, or existing security, or forbears the exercise of a valuable right at the time he receives it, and as the consideration of its acquisition, e. g., if he makes a loan on a note and at the same time takes the negotiable paper as collateral security,[2] or surrenders a security,[3] or takes negotiable paper in payment of a note already due which he surrenders or cancels,[4] or who receives negotiable paper as absolute payment of any existing indebtedness and not merely as security for its payment;[5] and the last case supposed is stronger if in connection with it he pays present money or value as part consideration;[6] but if a creditor receives negotiable paper from his debtor, it seems that no presumption arises from the mere fact of receiving it that it is taken in absolute payment of the debt.[7]

The rule laid down in Coddington vs. Bay,[8] that in order to be a purchaser for value there must be a parting with present value or with a present advantage, has been followed in this State up to a recent period without shadow of turning; and therefore in New York, prior to the passage of

[1] Roberts vs. Hall, 37 Conn. 205.
[2] Bank of New York vs. Vanderhorst, 32 N. Y. 553.
[3] Chrysler vs. Renois, 43 N. Y. 209.
[4] Pratt vs. Coman, 37 N. Y. 440; Brown vs. Leavitt, 31 id. 113; Meads vs. Mer. Bank, 25 id. 143, 149; Youngs vs. Lee, 12 id. 551; Bank of Salina vs. Babcock, 21 Wend. 499; Bank of St. Albans vs. Gilliland, 23 id. 311.
[5] Potts vs. Mayer, 74 N. Y. 594; Bank of Sandusky vs. Scoville, 24 Wend. 115.
[6] Mechanics' etc., Bank vs. Crow, 60 N. Y. 85.
[7] Bradford vs. Fox, 38 N. Y. 289.
[8] 20 Johns. 637.

the Negotiable Instruments Law in 1897, one who received negotiable paper merely as security for a debt already existing was not a purchaser or holder for value.[1]

This principle was rigidly applied to Stock-brokers. In the case in question defendants, Stock-brokers in New York, received from one Van A., residing at Lyons, orders by telegraph to buy Erie stock, he agreeing to send margin. On the day of sending and receipt of telegrams defendants contracted for the stock ordered, to be delivered three days thereafter, at which time they were delivered to and paid for by defendants. On the day of the sending of the telegrams, but whether before or after does not appear, Van A. stole $6,500 of United States coupon bonds belonging to plaintiff, which he forwarded to defendants as a " margin." The bonds were received by the defendants before the delivery of and payment for the stock. In an action for the conversion of the stock, it was decided that defendants gave credit to the promise of Van A. and not to the bonds; that the receipt of the bonds and the fulfilment of the contract for the purchase of the stock after such receipt did not make them *bona fide* holders, and that they were therefore liable; also, that if defendants, after receipt of the bonds, purchased upon the credit thereof any stocks for Van A., they were entitled to hold them as security for any loss arising in that transaction; but the sale of bonds beyond the amount necessary for such indemnity was a conversion for which an action would lie.[2]

But now by the Negotiable Instruments Law (§ 51) an

[1] Turner vs. Treadway, 53 N. Y. 650; Lawrence vs. Clark, 36 id. 128; Bright vs. Judson, 17 Barb. 29; Stalker vs. McDonald, 6 Hill, 93

[2] Taft vs. Chapman et al., 50 N. Y. 115; s. c. on new trial, Brownson vs. Chapman, 63 N. Y. 625.

antecedent debt constitutes value, thus overruling the doctrine of Coddington vs. Bay.[1]

In Pennsylvania the rule was the same as in New York.[2] The holder must have paid some present value or relinquished some present advantage.[3]

Referring to the conflict of opinion as to what constitutes a holder *for value*, Leonard, J., says [4] that "twenty years of judicial construction have not fully terminated the controversy in this State so ably discussed in the conflicting cases of Swift vs. Tyson [5] and Stalker vs. McDonald.[6] The case last mentioned was determined in the late Court of Errors; . . . it expressly endorses Coddington vs. Bay [7] and Rosa vs. Brotherson [8] as the law of this State, and condemns the case of Swift vs. Tyson."

Although the conflict still continues, yet, as the States of New York and North Carolina have overruled the doctrine of Coddington vs. Bay [9] and as at least four of the States which have followed that doctrine (viz., Pennsylvania, Iowa, Ohio and Wisconsin) have adopted the Negotiable Instruments Law, whilst of the States which have followed the ruling in Swift vs. Tyson, five (viz., Connecticut, Maryland, Massachusetts, New Jersey and Rhode Island) have also enacted that law, it will be seen that the day is fast

---

[1] Brewster vs. Schrader, 20 Misc. 480. Crawford's An. Neg. Inst. Law, 2d ed. p. 32.

[2] Petrie vs. Clark, 11 Serg. & R. 377; Lenheim vs. Wilmarding, 55 Pa. St. 73; Bronson vs. Silverman, 77 id. 94.

[3] Kirkpatrick vs. Muirhead, 16 Pa. St. 117.

[4] Cardwell vs. Hicks, 37 Barb. 458.

[5] 16 Pet. 1. See very able article in 30 Am. L. Reg. 689, upholding this decision.

[6] 6 Hill, 93.

[7] 20 Johns. 637.

[8] 10 Wend. 85.

[9] Brewster vs. Shrader, 20 Misc. 480; Brooks vs. Sullivan, 30 S. E. (N. C.) 822.

approaching when, with the universal acceptance of the codifying statute, it will come to an end.

It has been held that the *bona fide* holder of negotiable paper may recover what he paid therefor, when there was fraud in its origin. Thus in the case of Louisiana State bearer bonds which had been fraudulently reissued, and which had been sold by a Broker (without disclosing his principal), the Broker was held liable to refund the price paid therefor, although he had no suspicion that there was anything wrong in the bonds.[1] But whether there was fraud in the origin of such paper, or the maker had other equities, the holder can only recover what he paid.[2]

These decisions are based upon the idea that a holder of negotiable paper is only entitled to protection from loss, and should not be allowed to make a profit out of the maker if the latter has been wronged.[3] Thus in Stalker vs. McDonald,[4] Walworth, Ch., says: "This principle of protecting the *bona fide* holder of negotiable paper who has paid value for it, is derived from the doctrines of the courts of equity in other cases where the purchaser has obtained the legal title without notice of the equitable right of a third person to the property. . . . And if he has paid but a part of the consideration or value of the property, he is only

---

[1] Pugh vs. Moore, 10 So. Rep. (La.) 710. This decision was followed in Herwig vs. Richardson, 11 So. Rep. (La.) 135, where similar bonds were purchased by plaintiff from defendants through Stockbrokers. See also Meyer vs Richards, 163 U. S. 386; Rogers vs. Walsh, 12 Neb. 28. But see Otis vs. Cullum, 92 U. S. 428. See also

[1] Daniel Neg. Inst. (5th ed.) § 734a.

[2] Huff vs. Wagner, 63 Barb. 215; Cardwell vs. Hicks, 37 id. 458; Youngs vs. Lee, 18 id. 189, aff'd 12 N. Y. 551. Also Chicopee Bank vs Chapin, 49 Mass. 40; Stoddard vs Kimball, 60 Mass. 469.

[3] Todd vs. Shelbourne, 8 Hun, 510.
[4] 6 Hill, 93.

entitled to be considered as a *bona fide* purchaser *pro tanto.*" [1]

On the contrary, in Cromwell vs. County of Sac,[2] Field, J., expressed the opinion that a purchaser of a negotiable security before maturity, and not personally chargeable with fraud, is entitled to recover its full amount though he may have paid less than its par value, and whatever may have been its original infirmity. He admitted that there were many adverse decisions, but thought it a sound rule, "and in consonance with the common understanding and usage of commerce, that the purchaser, at whatever price, takes the benefit of the entire obligation of the maker."

And in the case of Railroad Companies vs. Schutte,[3] it was held that bonds of the State of Florida in the open market purported to be what they called for ; and that as the "Railroad Companies" had put them out, and in legal effect endorsed them, they must to a *bona fide* holder respond to their endorsement commercially—that is, by paying the bonds according to their face, regardless of what their maker or they themselves may have got for them.[4]

This seems to be the better rule, and certainly more consonant to the general dealings of Wall Street, where many securities are sold and bought under the par value, upon the expectation of the purchasers that they will eventually obtain their full face value. And the rule has now been incorporated into the Negotiable Instruments Law, § 96 of which provides that a holder in due course (i. e. a *bona fide* holder, for value, without notice, and be-

---

[1] This is the rule in England. Edwards vs. Jones, 7 Car. & P. 633. But see the English Bills of Exchange Act, § 38.

[2] 96 U. S. 51, 60.
[3] 103 U. S. 118, 145.
[4] Per Waite, C. J.

fore maturity) may enforce payment of the instrument for the full amount thereof.[1] In concluding this branch of the subject, it will be observed that the Supreme Court of the United States has been foremost in upholding and advancing doctrines which tend to make commercial securities almost unassailable in the hands of innocent purchasers.

III. Non-negotiability.

(a.) *Doctrine of Non-negotiability.*

The modern doctrine of non-negotiability is simply this: that while the assignee of a contract or chose in action, by statute or usage, can sue upon the same in law or equity, the action is subject to all of the defences and equities between the original parties, to the same extent and in the same manner as if they were themselves before the court.[2] The effect of this doctrine is, of course, to lower the commercial standing and value of non-negotiable instruments, for the obvious reason that a purchaser of them must beware of what he is buying, for he is chargeable with notice of all defects in the title of his assignor, and of all defences or equities which may exist in favor of the party or corporation against whom he proposes to enforce the same. The cases which we give in the notes fully illustrate the doctrine of non-negotiability.[3]

It is, perhaps, not finally settled whether the assignee of

---

[1] See Crawford's Ann. Neg. In. Law, pp. 96-8.

[2] Davis vs. Bechstein, 69 N. Y. 440; Wood vs. Travis, 24 Misc. 589. And see 2 Am. & Eng. Enc. Law, 2d ed. p. 1080, and cases cited.

[3] In Davis vs. Bechstein, 69 N. Y. 440, a bond and mortgage were intrusted to R. to enable him to get a note discounted by using them as collateral security. R. did not use them for that purpose; and it was held that, inasmuch as R. could not enforce them against the mortgagor, he could give no greater right to an assignee than he had himself. In Union College vs. Wheeler, 61 N. Y. 88, the mortgagee received his mort-

a chose in action takes it subject only to the original equities—that is, the equities between the assignor and the debtor—or subject also to the latent equities of third persons. There are most respectable authorities on both sides of this question,[1] but in the State of New York the weight of opinion at present is in favor of the latter doctrine, that the purchaser of a chose in action must abide the case of the person from whom he buys, for the reason that the holder of a chose in action cannot alienate anything but the beneficial interest he possesses. It is a question of power or capacity to transfer to another, and that capacity is to be exactly measured by his own rights.[2] But the doctrine is subject to the important modification that the real owner

gage knowing that the mortgagor had executed contracts of sale to various persons of portions of the mortgaged property. It was held that the mortgage was a chose in action, that the mortgagee took it subject to the rights and equities of the purchasers under the contracts, and that his assignee of the mortgage occupied simply his position and took subject to the same rights and equities. In Ingraham vs. Disborough, 47 N. Y. 421, the decision was precisely the same on a similar state of facts. See also Clute vs. Robinson, 2 Johns. (N. Y.) 612.

[1] See p. 1081, 2 Am. & Eng. Enc. Law, 2d ed., and cases cited.

[2] This doctrine is sustained by Union College vs. Wheeler, supra, where it was held that the assignee of the bond and mortgage took subject not only to original equities, but also to the rights and equities of the third persons to whom contracts of sale had been executed. In Bush vs. Lathrop, 22 N. Y. 535, the only thing in issue was a latent equity of a third person. Denio, J., cited and discussed all of the New York cases and many others, and repudiated any supposed distinction between latent equities and those existing between the original parties; he referred, with approval, to the declaration of Lord Thurlow in Davies vs. Austen, 1 Ves. 247, that "a purchaser of a chose in action must always abide by the case of the person from whom he buys." But this case was modified by Moore vs. Metropolitan Nat. Bank, 55 N. Y. 41. See cases cited in next note. Except as so modified its doctrine stands. Fairchild vs. Sergent, 104 N. Y. 108. Probably the most powerful advocate of the doctrine that the assignee of a chose in action is only subject to original equities was Kent, C. J. In Bebee vs. Bank of New York, 1 Johns. 529, he says (p. 573): "When it is said

will be estopped from asserting his title as against a *bona fide* purchaser from one upon whom he has conferred apparent ownership.[1]

It has been held, however, that where a chose in action is assigned as a security of a negotiable note which is itself transferred before maturity for value, it is taken by the assignee free from all equities, on the ground that the security partakes of the nature of the debt.[2] Thus, in Kenicott vs. Supervisors,[3] where, on a bill to foreclose a mortgage given to secure negotiable railroad bonds, it appeared that the bonds were transferred to a *bona fide* holder for value, no other or further defences were allowed as against the mortgage than would be allowed were the action brought in a court of law upon the bonds. And in another case in the same court,[4] Swayne, J., says: "Equity puts the principal and accessory on a footing of equality, and gives to the assignee of the evidence of the debt the same rights in regard to both. . . . This dependent and incidental relation takes the case out of the rule applied to choses in action, where no such relation of dependence exists."[5] So we shall here-

---

that an assignee of a chose in action takes it subject to all equity, it is meant only that the original debtor can make the same defence against the assignee that he could against the assignor." He was, however, outvoted by four judges to one, and Tompkins and Spencer, JJ., delivered decidedly contrary opinions. Kent's opinion was followed in James vs. Morey, 2 Cow. 246, and the doctrine which it advocates is supported by Mott vs. Clark, 9 Pa. St. 398; Bloomer vs. Henderson, 8 Mich. 395. But it has not prevailed in the State of New York.

See Merchants Bank vs. Weill, 163 N. Y. 486.

[1] Moore vs. Metropolitan Bank, 55 N. Y. 41; Merchants Bank vs. Weill, 163 N. Y. 486.

[2] Batesville Institute vs. Kauffman, 18 Wall. 151; Taylor vs. Page, 6 Allen, 86; Croft vs. Bunster, 9 Wis. 504, 510.

[3] 16 Wall. 452.

[4] Carpenter vs. Longan, 16 Wall. 271.

[5] And see Palmer vs. Yates, 3 Sandf. 137; Morgan vs. Smith Am. Organ Co., 73 Ind. 179; Cornell vs. Hichens, 11 Wis. 353; Fisher vs.

after see that the doctrine of non-negotiability has been
directly applied to certificates of stock, and the transferees
or assignees thereof have been made subject to all defences
existing between the original parties.[1]

(b.) *Negotiability as Applied to Stock Certificates.*

We come now to consider the doctrine of negotiability as
directly applied to stock certificates; and the importance of
this subject to Stock-brokers, banks, and capitalists cannot
be overstated, because dealings in these securities constitute
the bulk of their business, and hundreds of millions of dollars are employed in their purchase and sale each week in
the city of New York alone.   Stock certificates, as we have
seen, are not technically, negotiable instruments.   They are
not promises to pay money, and, in a word, lack almost
every element necessary to constitute negotiability.   They
are certificates showing that the individual named therein
is entitled to a share in the capital stock of a corporation,
to its profits and dividends when they are declared, to a
proportionate share of its property upon its being wound up
or dissolved.   The courts have everywhere with marked
unanimity placed them in the category of non-negotiable
instruments.[2]   And it has been held in the State of New
York that the Negotiable Instruments Law is not applicable
to stock certificates.[3]

The effect of non-negotiability we have already considered,
and it is very manifest that if that doctrine were to be ap-

Otis, 3 Chand. 83; Martineau vs.
McCollum, 4 id. 153. See this subject fully discussed, and many cases
cited, in 1 Daniel on Neg. Inst. 5th
ed. pp. 842-8.

[1] P. 700.
[2] See Church vs. Citizens R. R.
Co., 78 Fed. 526.
[3] Cowles vs. Kiebel, 65 N. Y. S.
349.

plied in its full force and rigor to stock certificates, the consequences to the financial world would be most alarming and serious. But we shall see that while the courts, on the one hand, treat them as non-negotiable, on the other hand, through the equitable doctrine of estoppel, stock certificates, with a power to transfer them endorsed in blank thereon, can be dealt in with almost the same immunity as bills, notes, and other negotiable instruments.[1] As a general rule, the company issuing a stock certificate does not recognize a transfer of the same until it has been registered on its books. This is ordinarily performed by an assignment of the stock in writing, made by the former owner of it, with a power of attorney to transfer it on the books of the corporation. Books of transfer are kept for that purpose; and on the production of the above papers the nominated attorney makes the formal transfer, the old certificate is cancelled, and a new certificate is issued to the new owner. And it seems the courts will take notice of this general mode of transfer.[2]

But despite the rules of the companies requiring transfers upon their books, these certificates with an assignment and irrevocable power of attorney executed in blank thereon pass from hand to hand in the same manner as other negotiable instruments. And when they possess a market value they are sold with the same, if not a greater, facility than bills

---

[1] In a recent leading New York case, the Court of Appeals (per Andrews, Ch. J.) said: "But the courts of this country, in view of the extensive dealings in certificates of shares in corporate enterprises, and the interest both of the public and the corporation, have given to them some of the elements of negotiability." Knox vs. Eden Musee Co., 148 N. Y. 454. And see American Press Assn. vs. Brantingham, 37 Misc. 426; aff'd 78 N. Y. Supp. 305.

[2] Burrall vs. Bushwick R. Co, 75 N. Y. 211; McNeil vs. The Tenth Nat. Bank, 46 N. Y. 325, 331.

or notes, and the transactions in the former are very much greater in volume and amount than in those of the latter kind. Indeed, it may be affirmed that stock certificates to-day constitute the chief commercial security of the age. And dealings in them are not confined to one market or locality ; they are bought and sold in every market in the world, and by universal usage pass from hand to hand.

In view of all of these considerations, it is a grave question whether the time has not arrived for a change in the legal character of these certificates, either by an alteration of the language of the latter so as to bring them within the rule of the law-merchant, or by the courts receiving evidence of the general usages of the commercial community, which usages, as we have seen, have been heretofore successfully invoked to raise non-negotiable securities to the full rank and dignity of negotiable instruments.[1] This last-

---

[1] See ante, p. 662 et seq. Since the text was written, the New York Court of Appeals has taken a more conservative view of this subject, for the court in Knox vs. Eden Musee Co., 148 N. Y. 456 (per Andrews, C. J.), said: "It is plain, we think, that the argument in support of the judgment in this case, based on the complete negotiability of stock certificates, is not supported by, but is contrary to the decisions. If public policy requires that a further advance should be made in more completely assimilating them to commercial paper in the qualities of negotiability, the legislature and not the courts should so declare. . . . It may, perhaps, be doubted, taking into consideration the interest of investors as well as dealers, whether it would be wise to remove the protection which the true owner of a stock certificate now has against theft, accident, or robbery. The system of registry of negotiable bonds, which prevails to a considerable extent, authorized by statutes of some of the states, and of the United States, seems to indicate a tendency to restrict rather than to extend the range of negotiable instruments." But see Masury vs. Bank, 93 Fed. Rep. at p. 607.

In view of the decision in German Savings Bank vs. Renshaw, 78 Md. 475, a change in the language of the transfer usually endorsed on the back of the certificate may help to enlarge the negotiability thereof. It was in that case held that as a

mentioned means has been attempted, but so far unsuccessfully. In the case of Aull vs. Colket [1] Stock-brokers in the ordinary course of their business received certain certificates from a clerk who had abstracted them from a box belonging to his employers, and they offered to show "that the general custom among banks and Brokers was to transfer title to stocks, especially non-dividend-paying stocks as these were, on certificates and powers signed in blank, and that this class of securities has assumed an important relation to trade and commerce; that thousands of such shares are circulated daily on the Stock Exchanges of New York and Philadelphia, and pass by mere delivery of certificates and powers; that by the general custom among Brokers and Bankers these certificates and powers pass by delivery the same as commercial paper or coupon bonds;" but the usage was rejected.

A somewhat similar case of the rejection of a Stock Exchange usage occurred in Taylor vs. Grant Ind. Penin. R. Co.,[2] where an owner of £2 and £20 shares desired to sell the former, and for that purpose gave his Broker transfers, which were blank as to name of transferee and as to value and distinctive numbers of the shares. The Broker, in fact, sold the £20 with fraudulent intent. For the purpose of giving validity to the transaction and compelling the owner to stand by the wrongful and unauthorized act of the

---

bank (a pledgee of stock) had notice from the transfer that the stock was for *sale* only, and not for *pledge*, it was not a bona fide holder. See, however, Gilbert vs. Erie Bldg. Assn., 39 Atl. (Pa.) 291 contra.

[1] 2 Week. Notes Cas. 322; 33 Leg. Int. 44. To same effect is East Birmingham Land Co. vs. Dennis, 85 Ala. 565. See also Sherwood vs. Meadow, 50 Cal. 412; Winter vs. Belmont, 53 Cal. 428; Barstow vs. Savage, 64 Cal. 388.

[2] 5 Jur. (n. s.) 1087.

Broker, it was claimed to be the universal practice of the Stock Exchange to execute such transfers in blank, at least as to the tranferee's name.   The court assumed the practice to exist, but refused to sanction it, and remarked: " It is clear that these shares were not transferred by him [the owner], for the law is settled upon this subject, and the safety of property depended upon it.   This case is, indeed, a remarkable instance of the value of the existing rule of law upon the subject.   To permit the practice of Stock-brokers and Stock-jobbers to prevail against such a rule was entirely out of the question.   Brokers must, like all other persons, be bound by the law and must observe its rules."

A similar usage was also condemned in Denny vs. Lyon,[1] where it was proved that the name of the transferee of stock was usually not inserted in the power of attorney, and that it was more convenient not to have it inserted, and the court remarked: "We know that this is the commercial usage.   It was probably orginated by the banks.   If not, they have countenanced it and thus brought people to practise it.   And yet it is a vicious usage, which no considera-tions of convenience are sufficient to justify.   *Malus usus abolendus est.*   A power of attorney signed, sealed, and delivered, what is it but a finished legal instrument?   Who may alter it to the prejudice of another without incurring liability to the charge of forgery?   If commerical usage permit the attorney to insert the names of P. & W. and then erase them, then insert the name of W. N. and next erase it, and then insert his own name as agent, what other legal instrument may not commercial usage tamper with in

[1] 38 Pa. St. 98.   But see Scollans vs. Rollins, 179 Mass. 346.

like manner?" The usage was not sanctioned, and the authority of the attorney was held to be exhausted by the insertion of the single name originally contemplated by the owner of the stock.

But, notwithstanding the refusal of the courts to receive such evidence and to invest these certificates with the attributes of negotiability, the modern decisions have, as we have said, practically placed them upon an equality with bills, notes, and other negotiable instruments; and we shall find that a *bona fide* purchaser for value of such certificates, with powers of sale endorsed in blank thereon, can, with two or three exceptions, to which we shall refer, hold them even against the true and rightful owner; and this proposition forms the principal exception to the rule that the assignee of a negotiable chose in action takes it subject to existing equities.[1]

[1] The principal. English authorities for this proposition are as follows: Ex parte Swan, 7 C. B. (n. s.) 400; Swan vs. North British Australasian Co., 7 H. & N. 603; same vs. same, 2 H. & C. 175; Taylor vs. Great Indian Peninsula Ry. Co., 5 Jur. (n. s.) 1087; 1 Story Eq. 375, § 390; Pearson vs. Scott, L. R. 9 Ch. Div. 198; 38 L. T. (n. s.) 747; 26 W. R. 796; Rumball vs. Metropolitan Bank, L. R. 2 Q. B. Div. 194; 46 L. J. Q. B. Div. 346; 36 L. T. (n. s.) 240; 25 W. R. 366; Goodwin vs. Robarts, 45 L. J. Ex. Div. 748; L. R. 1 App. Cas. 476; 35 L. T. (n. s.) 179 H. L; Easton vs. Bank, 34 Ch. D. 95. But see Colonial Bank vs. Cady, 15 App. Cas. 267.

The principal American authorities are as follows: Bank vs. Lanier, 11 Wall. 369; Budd vs. Monroe, 18 Hun, 316; McNeil vs. Tenth Nat. Bank, 46 N. Y. 325; Commercial Bank vs. Kortright, 22 Wend. 348; Moore vs. Metropolitan Nat. Bank, 55 N. Y. 41; N. Y. & New Haven R. R. Co. vs. Schuyler, 34 N. Y. 30; Weaver vs. Barden, 49 N. Y. 286; Leitch vs. Wells, 48 N. Y. 585; Zulick vs. Markham, 6 Daly, 129; Printing Co. vs. Washburn, 77 A. D. 280; Dickinson vs. Dudley, 17 Hun, 569; Matthews vs. Mass. Nat. Bank, 10 Alb. L. J. 199; Wood's Appeal, 8 Week. Notes Cas. 411; 92 Pa. St. 379; Burton's Appeal, id. 505; s. c. 93 Pa. St. 214; Ellis's Appeal, id. 538; Aull vs. Colket, 2 Week. Notes Cas. 322; 33 Leg. Int. 41; Moody vs. Bank, 3 Week. Notes Cas. 118; Thompson vs. Toland, 18 Cal 99; Winter vs Mining Co, 7 Rep. 332; Tome vs Parkersburgh R. R. Co,

45

The general rule applicable to property other than ne-gotiable instruments undoubtedly is, that the vendor or pled-gor can convey no greater right or title than he has. *Nemo dat quod non habet.* But this maxim is applicable to a sim-ple transfer from one party to another where no other ele-ment intervenes. It does not interfere with the well-es-tablished principle that where the true owner holds out an-other, or allows him to appear, as the owner of, or as having full power of disposition over, the property, and innocent third parties are thus led into dealing with such apparent owner, they will be protected. Their rights in such cases do not depend upon the actual title or authority of the party with whom they deal directly, but are derived from the act of the real owner, which precludes him from disputing as against them the existence of the title or power which, through neg-ligence or mistaken confidence, he caused or allowed to ap-pear to be vested in the party making the conveyance.[1]

It may therefore be stated as a well-settled proposition that where the owner of a certificate of stock with a power of attorney in blank endorsed thereon, attached thereto, or connected therewith, intrusts it to an agent, servant, or other person, so that by the recognized usages of business it will pass from hand to hand, or the owner is guilty of neg-ligence in respect thereto,[2] a *bona fide* purchaser or holder without notice will be protected in his possession, although

39 Md. 36, 17 Am. Rep. 540; Mount Holly Turnpike Co. vs. Terrel, 17 N. J. Eq. 117; Prall vs. Tilt, 28 N. J. Eq. 479; Bridgeport Bank vs. R. R. Co., 30 Conn. 231; Atkinson vs. At-kinson, 90 Mass. 15; Garvin vs. Wiswall, 83 Ill. 215. See also Cin-cinnati &c. R. Co. vs. Citizens' Bank, 43 L. R. A. 777, and many cases cited therein; Graves vs. Mining Co., 81 Cal. at p. 325; Real Estate Trust Co. vs. Bird, 90 Md. 229; Westinghouse vs. Bank, 46 Atl. 380.

[1] Per Rapallo, J., McNeil vs. Tenth Nat. Bank, 46 N. Y. 325.

[2] Aull vs. Colket, 2 Week. Notes Cas. 322; 33 Leg. Int. 44.

the agent or person to whom the certificate has been intrusted has diverted it from the purposes for which it was committed to him, or has been guilty of fraud or a breach of trust in relation thereto.[1]

The rights of a *bona fide* holder as against the true owner of the stock, to whom the apparent holder has either sold or pledged it, do not depend on the negotiable character of the certificates, but rest on a different principle—viz., that one who has conferred upon another, by a written transfer, all the *indicia* of ownership of property, is estopped to assert title to it as against a third person who has in good faith purchased it for value from the apparent owner. And this is a most just and reasonable rule, for when an owner of one of these certificates executes a blank assignment, with a power of attorney to transfer the stock on the books of a corporation, such as is ordinarily used, without any notice on the face of the same that it is intended to be restricted to a particular purpose, he commits a commercial act. If he then intrust it to a faithless agent, or if, by his own negligence, the certificate gets into circulation and into the hands of an innocent party, the owner should suffer.

---

[1] See authorities cited ante, p. 705. But where a Broker received, in the course of trade, a transfer in blank of stock which had in fact been stolen and sold, in a mining company organized under the laws of California, held, that he was liable to the true owner for its value and damages (Bercich vs. Marye, 9 Nev. 312; Swim vs. Wilson, 9 Bkg. & L. J. 286, and article on Stock-brokers' responsibilities in such cases, id. 273; and see Bangor &c. Co. vs. Robinson, 52 Fed. Rep. 520) On the same principle, where a trustee is clothed with full power to manage and control the trust estate, an assignment by him of a mortgage impressed with the trust to a *bona fide* purchaser cannot be impeached by the cestui que trust (Dillaye vs. Commercial Bank, 51 N. Y. 345); and Grover, J., states the reason of the exception in the following words (Moore vs. Metropolitan Nat. Bank, 55 N. Y. 41): "One reason why an owner of corporate shares or of goods and chat-

The whole question then resolves itself into one of *notice*, Had the purchaser or holder of the stock certificate notice of the rights of the true owner? Had he knowledge of the purpose for which the owner placed it in the hands of his agent? If he had no notice, the law protects him; if otherwise, it will not protect him.

We shall now proceed to consider what notice is sufficient to prevent the true owner from being deprived of his title; and the cases upon this subject resolve themselves into three classes: 1st, those in which the notice appears on the face of the certificate; 2d, where it is dehors the certificate, and is gathered from the circumstances surrounding the transaction; and, 3d, those cases in which the *bona fide* purchaser or holder acquires the right to hold the certificate by reason of the negligence or carelessness of the owner.

1. *Cases in which notice appears on the face of the certificate.*

It is a familiar and well-established rule, both in England and the United States, that persons who deal with or receive written instruments are chargeable with constructive notice of their contents and of their legal effect, and are bound thereby, whether they examine them or not.[1]

In Baring vs. Corrie[2] the defendants bought goods from

---

tels who has conferred upon another the apparent ownership, without transferring to him a valid title, was held precluded from asserting his title against a *bona fide* purchaser from such apparent owner is that such purchase was made upon the faith of the title which he had apparently given, and that it would be contrary to justice and good conscience to permit him to assert his real title against an innocent purchaser from one clothed by him with all the *indicia* of ownership and power of disposition."

[1] Farmers,' etc., Nat. Bank vs. Logan, 74 N. Y. 568, 580; City Bank vs. Rome, Watertown, etc., R. Co., 44 id. 136; Turner vs. Liverpool Docks, 6 Ex. 543.

[2] 2 B. & Ald. 137.

one whom they knew to be both a merchant and Broker, but at the time of the sale they received from him a sold note, exactly in proper form, supposing him to have sold in his character of Broker. It was held that this was sufficient notice to put them upon inquiry for the principal, and, having failed to make such inquiry, they were not permitted, in settlement for the goods, to offset a claim which they had against the Broker, but were obliged to pay the principal in full. In this case the owner had not intrusted the Broker with possession of the goods, and thereby enabled him to appear as owner, and therefore it was distinguished from the early English case of Hern vs. Nichols,[1] where the owner was held answerable for the deceit of his factor, and Holt, C. J., said that, "seeing somebody must be a loser by this deceit, it is more reasonable that he that employs and puts a trust and confidence in the deceiver should be a loser than a stranger."[2]

In Pannell vs. Hurley[3] one P conveyed in trust to C. B. & D, who opened a trust account with bankers, headed in their books "H. P.'s Estate." The bankers dissolved, and defendant continued the business, receiving the old books and carrying on the trust account. D, one of the trustees, drew out of the trust account and paid a deficit in his private account. Held, that defendant was chargeable with notice by the heading of the trust account, *inter alia*, and must settle with the Pannell estate, independently of any set-off he had against the trustee D.

Taylor vs. Great Ind. Penin. R. Co.[4] was a case of con-

[1] 1 Salk. 289.

[2] George vs. Clagett, 7 T. R. 359, and Rabone vs. Williams, id. 360,

turned on the same point as Hern vs. Nichols.

[3] 2 Coll. 211.

[4] 5 Jur. (n. s.) 1087.

flicting equities, where either the owner of stock or its purchaser must suffer loss through the fraud of a Broker employed by the former; and the purchaser contended that the owner ought to bear it because he had been negligent in executing the transfer of the stock in blank, and thereby made it possible for the Broker to effect the fraud; but it was held that inasmuch as the transfers, at the time they were delivered to the purchaser, were still in blank as to the value and distinctive numbers of the shares, and the name of the transferees, they carried on their face constructive notice of their invalidity to all concerned. The court, however, in this case, did reflect upon the plaintiff for the imprudent manner in which he had executed the transfers, and therefore allowed him no costs. This case would seem to teach that where equities are to be balanced between an owner and a purchaser of stock, both of whom have been negligent, and one of whom must suffer loss through the fraud of another, the scale will turn in favor of him who has been least negligent.

The registered proprietors of stock have the legal title to it; and therefore an instrument of transfer by them, or any other writing which suggests who are the registered proprietors, is sufficient to put a purchaser upon the inquiry whether they are not also the absolute and equitable owners. Accordingly,[1] a purchaser is not justified in dealing with the solicitor of executors as a principal, because he received notice from the form and terms of the transfer which was signed by the executors, and from the accompanying letter, that they, and not the solicitor, had the legal title.

In Shropshire Union R. & C. Co. vs. The Queen[2] certifi-

---

[1] Pearson vs. Scott, L. R. 9 Ch. D. 198.   [2] L. R. 7 H. L. Cas. 496.

cates of railway stock were intrusted to one of the directors, who was also the Banker of the company, and he also stood on the register of the company as the owner of the said stock. He borrowed money from R., and deposited the certificates with him as security, but R. died without having applied to be registered as owner. His widow and executrix made such application, and was refused, on the ground that if R. had made proper inquiries he would have found that his transferor was only a trustee; that negligence sufficient to affect their equitable title could not be imputed to the other directors and the company in thus allowing the apparent title to rest in the one director; and that consequently the equitable title of R. could not prevail against the earlier equitable title of the company. And Lord Cairns, it seems, was of the opinion that any one dealing in stock or corporate property was always bound to make inquiry as to the actual ownership and condition of the title; for he says,[1] " He ought to have known that although II.'s name appeared upon the register as the owner of these shares, and although II. could present to him the certificates of this ownership, still it was perfectly possible either that these shares were the beneficial property of II. himself, or that they were the property of some other person." In brief, that the only way he could perfect his title was to go to the company and have a transfer of those shares from II.'s name to his own in the register. But it is questionable whether the conclusion reached in this case is not in conflict with the best authorities both in England and in the United States.

So where the incomplete and non-negotiable bonds of a

----

[1] P. 505.

railroad corporation were conditioned for the payment of either of two specified kinds and amounts of national currency, to be determined by the place to be fixed for their payment, and contained a clause authorizing the president of the corporation to fix, by his endorsement, such place of payment, and the bonds were endorsed in blank by the president, without fixing the place of payment, the *bona fide* purchaser of such bonds was held chargeable with notice of their defects, and could neither acquire nor convey a title to the bonds.[1]

A certificate of stock containing the words " in trust," or other equivalent words, is constructive notice of a trust to all who deal with the certificate, and puts them upon inquiry as to the authority of the trustee to dispose of the stock.[2] If such a certificate is pledged by the trustee to secure his own debt, the pledgee is by the terms of the certificate put upon inquiry as to the character and limitations of the trust.[3]

[1] Ledwich vs. McKim, 53 N. Y. 308.

[2] Budd vs. Munroe, 18 Hun, 316; Sprague vs. Cocheco Mfg. Co., 10 Blatchf. 173; Gaston vs. Amer., etc., Bank, 29 N. J. 98.

If Stock-brokers at all times knew that securities placed with them for speculative purposes stood in the name of one of their customers as trustee for the other, they are chargeable with notice of the trust, and are bound to inquire into the ownership of the property. Leake vs. Watson, 58 Conn. 332.

It is actionable negligence for a corporation to cancel a certificate of its stock and transfer the stock on the signature of the trustee to the assignment without any inquiry for the cestui que trust, or for his assent to the transfer. Geyser-Marion Gold Mining Co. vs. Stark, 106 Fed. Rep. 558, and many cases cited.

[3] Shaw vs. Spencer, 100 Mass. 382; Duncan vs. Jaudon, 15 Wall. 165; Swan vs. Produce Bank, 24 Hun, 277; Atkinson vs. Atkinson, 90 Mass. 15, where same rule is applied to a guardian. Compare Ashton vs. Atlantic Bank, 85 Mass. 217; 2 Perry on Trusts, §§ 814, 815, and cases cited.

And see the recent case of Farmers' Bank vs. Diebold Safe & Lock Co., 58 L. R. A. 620, and note, and cases cited at id. 624.

The old rule seems to have been that ordinarily it was a breach of trust for a trustee of stock to transfer it, of which a purchaser was chargeable with notice; and therefore the *cestui que* trust was entitled to have the individual stock restored to him.[1]

Brewster vs. Sime[2] seems to be contrary to the general current of authority, for it holds that the addition of the word "trustee" after the name of a person to whom stock is transferred is not sufficient to put persons dealing with the trustee upon inquiry as to the trustee's title or as to the owner's equitable right. Crockett, J., in his opinion, assigns as a reason for his position that "considerations of public policy and common justice demand that when stock is placed in the name of a trustee under these circumstances, the secret owner shall be bound by the act of his trustee dealing with persons who have no actual notice of the relations between the parties."[3] And although, as we have said, this position is exceptional to the general run of the cases, many strong reasons may be urged in support of it. But this and the other decisions cited have not been followed "and the reason of the case, the later decisions of the courts, and the declarations of the text books have united to make the proposition we have announced the established law of the land."[4]

But an executor is not under the same disability as a trustee, and a purchase of stock from him is ordinarily valid, though affected with some peculiar trust or equity, because

---

[1] Harrison vs. Harrison, 2 Atk. 121.

[2] 42 Cal. 139. And see Stinson vs. Thornton, 56 Ga. 377.

[3] To same effect, Thompson vs Toland, 48 Cal. 99; Albert vs. Balti-more, 2 Md. 159, 171. But the latter case was overruled in Marbury vs. Ehlen, 72 Md. 206, 216.

[4] Marion Co. vs Stark, 106 Fed. Rep 558. See also Jones vs. Williams, 24 Beav. 62.

the purchaser cannot be presumed to know that the sale is not required in order to discharge the testator's debts,[1] it being the executor's primary duty to dispose of assets and settle the estate,[2] which differs in this respect from the duty of a trustee, which is that of custody, and not of administration or sale;[3] but if the purchaser from an executor has a reasonable ground for believing that he intends to misapply the proceeds, he will not be protected.[4]

In Pennsylvania the highest court of the State in two cases, almost simultaneously reported, has fully secured the rights of a *bona fide* holder or purchaser of stock certificates.

In Wood's Appeal,[5] G. R. W., one of several executors, abstracted from a fire-proof safe certificates of stock belonging to the estate without the knowledge of his co-executors. These certificates stood in the name of C. S. W., the testator, and were accompanied by a blank bill of sale and power of attorney to sell and transfer, signed "G. R. W., acting executor." G. R. W. was engaged in stock specula-

---

[1] Hutchins vs. State Bank, 53 Mass. 421.

[2] Leitch vs. Wells, 48 N. Y. 585; Wood's Appeal, 92 Pa. St. 379; Prall vs. Tilt, 28 N. J. Eq. 479.

So also Stock-brokers are not negligent if they sell bonds at the instance of a trustee, who misappropriates the proceeds, although the bonds stood in the name of a prior deceased trustee who was also executor of the will under which the trust was created, when it is not shown that they were aware of the latter's death, or of the then condition of the trust property. Cooper vs. Illinois &c. R. R. Co., 38 A. D. 22.

[3] Bayard vs. Farmers,' etc., Bank, 52 Pa. St. 232; Jaudon vs. Nat. City Bank, 8 Blatchf. 430.

[4] Lowry vs. Commercial, etc., Bank, Taney's Dec. 310.

And when Brokers have notice that an executor transfers stock to secure a personal loan, they cannot, on purchasing the stock, compel the corporation to transfer it to them, or recover damages for its refusal to do so. Davis vs. National Eagle Bank, 50 Atl. Rep. (R. I.) 530.

[5] Wood vs. Smith (s. c.), 92 Pa. St. 379; Burton's Appeal, 93 id. 214.

tions, and delivered these certificates, with the power, etc., to his Broker, who in turn pledged them with another Broker, the defendant, to secure certain transactions between them. In an action by the co-executors of G. R. W. against the defendant, it was decided that they could not recover from the defendant, he having purchased in good faith, and that there was nothing to put him upon an inquiry. The court held that, if the action had been against the first Broker, the plaintiffs could have recovered, "for they [the Brokers] participated in the wrongful act of G. R. W.; the transaction itself gave them notice of the misapplication; that the fact of the power of attorney being signed by an executor made the case no different than if it had been signed by the testator himself, an executor having an absolute power of disposal over personal effects, and the *bona fide* alienee being perfectly protected by such sale." The court distinguished the case from one had directly with trustees, where there is no presumption of a right to sell it,[1] or from a case where it appeared that the party dealing with an executor had notice of the transaction.[2]

This decision was followed in Clemens vs. Hecksher,[3] in which case it appeared that securities standing in the names of trustees were pledged by a firm of Stock-brokers (of which one of the trustees was a member) and the pledgees were held liable to the trust estate.

And if a corporation issue stock to a trustee, knowing the name of the beneficiary, it is chargeable with notice of the terms and limitations of the trust, and cannot, by any par-

---

[1] Duncan vs. Jaudon, 15 Wall. 165; Shaw vs. Spencer, 100 Mass. 382.

[2] Prall vs. Hamil, 28 N. J. Eq. 66.

[3] 185 Pa. St. 476.

ticipation with the trustee in a violation of the trust, defeat the rights of the beneficiary.[1]

The effect of notice to a purchaser, which is intrinsic to the muniment of title, is well exemplified in Atkinson vs. Atkinson.[2] In this case the corporation issued a certificate to a guardian for ten shares of stock in his capacity as such, and also two other shares to the same guardian without qualifying him as such. His assignment of the ten shares was set aside because of the notice to the transferee contained in the certificate, while the transferee of the two shares was protected because he had no notice or knowledge of the violation of the trust.

2. *Notice dehors the documents of title.*

If one who buys stock of an executor has notice that it belongs to the testator's estate, and actual knowledge that there are other executors who do not join, he is thereby put upon inquiry as to the propriety of the sale; and, if he omits such inquiry, will be decreed to return the stock to the estate discharged from the lien of his advances.[3]

If a person buys stock from one whom he knows to be acting in an official capacity, he is chargeable with notice of the legal duty imposed by law upon such official—e. g., he is bound to know that an administrator is required by law to sell at public sale.[4]

A purchaser of stock is not chargeable with notice of a by-law, however, which the corporation has no authority to make either by its act of incorporation or by general law;

[1] Loring vs. Salisbury Mills, 125 Mass. 138.
[2] 90 Mass. 15.
[3] Ellis's Appeal, 8 Week. Notes Cas. 538. And see Roots vs. Williamson, 38 Ch. D. 485; France vs.

Clark, 22 Ch. Div. 830; Simmons vs. Bank, (1891) 1 Ch. 270; Societé Générale vs. Walker, 11 App. Cas. 20.
[4] Nutting vs. Thomason, 46 Ga. 34.

and is not put upon inquiry for a lien declared by such law arising out of the indebtedness of the seller of the stock to the corporation.[1] But he is chargeable with notice of original articles of association, which have been adopted into the charter of the corporation, providing that a share-holder should not transfer his stock as long as he was in-debted to the corporation.[2] Where the owner of stock delivers the certificate to his pledgee with a power to trans-fer it, the fact that his name is in the certificate is not notice of his rights as against third persons, who take it for value from the pledgee.[3]

In Crocker vs. Crocker[4] the firm of L. & Co. advanced moneys to one of the partners, Stephen Crocker, and took as security certain shares of stock which they knew he held in trust for his brother, and not in his own right; there-fore, as against the *cestui que* trust, they took nothing by the fraudulent transfer.

In Jaudon vs. National City Bank[5] the transaction of loan indicated that the transferee of stock was not selling the same in the ordinary course of his business as trustee, but that he was borrowing money for his private use on a pledge of trust property; and therefore they were obliged to disgorge.

And Stock-brokers do not become the *bona fide* holders of certificates of stock belonging to a customer of a bank and pledged with them by the cashier of the bank (after trans-

---

[1] Driscoll vs. West Bradley, etc., Mfg. Co., 59 N. Y. 96.

[2] Leggett vs. Bank of Sing Sing, 21 N. Y. 283; McDowell vs. Bank of Wilmington, etc., 2 Del. 1; Union Bank vs. Laird, 2 Wheat. 390. And of by-laws passed in accordance with act of incorporation. Cum-mings vs. Webster, 43 Me. 192; Bar-rett vs. Union Mutual Ins. Co., 61 Mass 181.

[3] Felt vs. Heye, 23 How. Pr. 359.

[4] 31 N. Y. 507.

[5] 8 Blatchf. 130.

fer to his name) to secure a call loan (at exorbitant interest), which he alleged was for the bank, but which in reality he obtained for himself. The cashier had been buying and carrying stocks on margin through the Stock-brokers for several years, and this fact, coupled with the unusual circumstance that a bank would borrow a large sum at an usurious rate of interest, charged the Brokers with the duty of making inquiries, which they wholly neglected.[1]

In Merchants' Bank vs. Livingston[2] it appeared that defendant L. delivered to defendant B. a certificate of stock as collateral for a loan of $3,000. B. applied to W., plaintiff's agent, for a loan thereon of $8,000, stating that he wanted it for a Client. W. agreed to make the loan if B. would procure a proper power of attorney to be attached to the certificate. B., by representing that he ought to have the instrument to secure his loan, procured from L. a transfer and irrevocable power of attorney to make a transfer executed in blank. B. filled up the blanks save the name of transferee and attorney, and delivered it with the certificate to W., who thereupon made the loan. B. had no authority from L. to borrow or to pledge the stock. In an action to foreclose plaintiff's alleged lien upon the stock—held, that as B. did not claim to be the owner of the stock, but only to be acting as agent for the owner, and as he had, in fact, no authority or apparent authority so to act, L. was not estopped from asserting his title to the stock, and plaintiff could not assert a lien save at most for the amount for which the stock was pledged to B.; that while the transfer and power of attorney gave to B. an apparent ownership in case he had claimed title or an apparent authority to sell as

[1] Williamson vs. Mason, 12 Hun, 97, 105.   [2] 74 N. Y. 223.

agent, it did not hold him out as authorized to make a loan or to pledge the stock, or, at most, it only indicated that he could pledge the stock for an authorized loan. The court said: "If he [B.] had been authorized by L. to borrow the money, he could probably have pledged the stock in his possession to secure it. And he could have taken the certificate and power of attorney and gone into the market claiming to act as the agent of the plaintiff, and have sold the stock and given a good title. The possession of the certificate and full power of attorney would have given him the apparent authority to sell."[1]

3. *Cases in which the bona fide purchaser or holder acquires the right to hold the certificate by reason of the negligence or carelessness of the owner.*

The owner of stock certificates may also lose his title to the same by his own negligence or carelessness in respect thereto, the rule of law being that, where one of two innocent persons must suffer by the fraud or negligence of a third, whichever has accredited him must bear the loss.[2] And a question as to whether it was negligence in the plaintiffs to leave their certificates with their clerk or bookkeeper, so that the latter could fill in the blanks and transfer them to innocent purchasers, is one for the jury.[3] A few of the leading cases will fully illustrate the rule upon this subject.

In Davis vs. Bank of England[4] Best, C. J., says: "It has ever been an object of the legislature to give facility to the transfer of shares in the public funds. This facility

---

[1] See also Porter vs. Parks, 49 N. Y. 564, which is a case of actual notice.

[2] Aull vs. Colkel, 33 Leg. Int. 41;

[2] Week. Notes Cas. (Pa.) 322; Mundorff vs. Wickersham, 63 Pa. St. 87.

[3] Aull vs. Colket, supra.

[4] 2 Bing. 393, 408.

of transfer is one of the advantages belonging to this species
of property, and this advantage would be entirely destroyed
if a purchaser should be required to look to the regularity
of the transfers to all the various persons through whom
such stock had passed. Indeed, from the manner in which
stock passes from man to man, from the union of stocks
bought of different persons under the same name, and the
impossibility of distinguishing what was regularly transferred from what was not, it is impossible to trace the title
of stock as you can that of an estate." These views are
well illustrated by the history of the Bank of England
stock. There was a time when the Bank, in dealing with
executors or trustees under a will, had to take cognizance
of the will and of the limitations of the trust therein contained; but this became so onerous when almost every
man in the kingdom became the owner of its stock that a
relaxation of the rule became a necessity. As was remarked by the Lord Chancellor, in Hartga vs. Bank of England,[1] "All the former strictness of practice in the Bank
could not have prevented the stock from being put into the
name of Stonehouse [executor]; when once put into his
name, to which he was distinctly entitled, could the Bank
look farther and inquire whether the stock standing in his
name was trust stock? If so, the Bank would be charged
with all the trusts in the kingdom. It was enacted by 1
Geo. I. c. 19, that such portion of a will as related to the
disposition of stock should be registered in the office of the
chief accountant of the Bank of England; and in default
thereof the Bank need take no notice of it, but might allow
the executor full control as to the transfer and disposition

[1] 3 Ves. 55.

Lightning Source UK Ltd.
Milton Keynes UK
UKHW031956020219
336576UK00009BA/262/P